Alice in Action with Java

Joel Adams
Calvin College

Australia • Brazil • Japan • Korea • Mexico • Singapore • Spain • United Kingdom • United States

Alice in Action with Java
Joel Adams

Acquistions Editor: Amy Jollymore

Senior Product Manager: Alyssa Pratt

Production Editor: GEX Publishing Services

Marketing Manager: Penelope Crosby

Editorial Assistant: Erin Kennedy

Print Buyer: Julio Esperas

Art Director: Bruce Bond, Kathleen Fivel

Cover Designer: Suzanne Heiser

Compositor: GEX Publishing Services

ISBN-13: 978-1-4239-0096-2

ISBN-10: 1-4239-0096-0

Course Technology
25 Thomson Place
Boston, Massachusetts 02210
USA

Cengage Learning is a leading provider of customized learning solutions with office locations around the globe, including Singapore, the United Kingdom, Australia, Mexico, Brazil, and Japan. Locate your local office at: **international.cengage.com/region**

Cengage Learning products are represented in Canada by Nelson Education, Ltd.

For your lifelong learning solutions, visit **course.cengage.com**

Purchase any of our products at your local college store or at our preferred online store **www.ichapters.com**

Printed in China by China Translation & Printing Services Limited
4 5 6 7 8 9 14 13 12 11

Contents

Preface

I wrote this book to remedy some of the problems in today's introductory computer programming (CS1) courses. To put it politely, most CS1 books are less than engaging, and simply fail to capture the imaginations of most of today's students. No matter how often I say it, many of my students never bother to "read the book." Now, these students aren't blameless, but it isn't entirely their fault. Many CS1 books present computer programming in a dry, abstract, mind-numbing way that's great if you're trying to fall asleep, but not so good if you want to learn.

This is a tragedy, because writing software is one of the best opportunities to exercise creativity in today's world. Traditional engineers and scientists are limited in what they can do by the physical laws that govern our world. But if a software engineer can imagine something, he or she can usually make it happen in the virtual world of the computer. In its 2006 "Best Jobs in America" study, *Money Magazine* listed software engineer #1 on its list of best jobs, because of its *creativity*, pay, and prestige. According to the U.S. Bureau of Labor Statistics, software engineering is also expected to be one of the fastest-growing job markets in the next decade.

This growing demand for software engineers poses a problem, because ever since the dot-com bust in 2001-2, fewer and fewer students have been enrolling in CS1 courses. Of those who do enroll, many drop out, at least in part because the subject matter fails to engage them. CS1 courses are the starting point for software engineers; every student who drops out of CS1 is one less prospective software engineer. Those of us who are CS1 instructors need to do everything we can to attract students to CS1, and retain as many of those students as possible. I wrote this book to try to help attract students to and retain students in CS1.

The Advantages of Alice

At the 2003 ACM SIGCSE conference, I saw Carnegie Mellon University's Randy Pausch demonstrate 3D animation software he called Alice. Using Alice, he built a sophisticated 3D animation (like *Shrek* or *Toy Story*, but much simpler) in just a few minutes. To do so, he used the traditional computer programming tools: variables, if statements, loops, subprograms, and so on. But his Alice software offered some startling advantages over traditional programming, including the following:

- *The allure of 3D graphics*. It is difficult to overstate the visual appeal of 3D animations, especially to today's visually-oriented students. When your program works, you feel euphoric! But even when you make a mistake (a logic error), the results are often comical, producing laughter instead of tears.
- *The Alice IDE*. Alice includes a drag-and-drop integrated development environment (IDE) that eliminates syntax errors. This IDE eliminates all of the missing semicolons, curly

braces, and quotation marks; misspelled keywords or identifiers; and other syntax problems that bedevil CS1 students.

- *Object-based programming*. Alice includes a huge library of off-the-shelf 3D objects, ranging from astronauts to ants, cowboys to castles, fairies to farms, mummies to motorboats, ponds to pagodas, robots to rowboats, skyscrapers to space shuttles, turtles to T-rexes, wizards to waterfalls, and zombies to Zambonis, each of which can be animated through a variety of predefined methods. Alice makes it easy to build 3D worlds from these objects. Those objects can then be animated using object-based programming.

By using 3D animation to motivate students, eliminating syntax errors, and turning logic errors into comedy, Alice transforms the CS1 experience from frustration to joy. In short, Alice makes it *fun* to learn object-based programming!

As I watched Professor Pausch's demonstration, it became apparent to me that Alice could solve many of the problems afflicting CS1 courses. If instructors would use Alice to initially *introduce* each programming topic, Alice's engaging environment would help motivate students to master that topic. Then, with that mastery to build upon, the instructor could *review* that topic in a traditional programming language like Java or C++, reinforcing its importance.

Imaginary Worlds

In the summer of 2003, I decided to put some of these ideas to the test, by offering a summer "computer camp" in which we would use Alice to teach some middle school students how to program. Our pilot group of 6th, 7th, and 8th graders learned object-based programming, and had a lot of fun doing so!

Our 2003 results were very encouraging, so in the summer of 2004, we began offering *The Imaginary Worlds Camps*, with 28 middle school boys and 25 middle school girls signing up. The results were amazing. Alice captured their imaginations and wouldn't let them go. Some students wanted to stay at the end of the day, to keep working on their programs—we had to force them to leave! Others wanted to skip the snack break. (My college students have never passed up food to keep working on a project.) At the end of the camp, the feedback was loud and uniformly positive: these students had loved learning how to program with Alice.

The *Imaginary Worlds Camps* gave me the chance to experiment with Alice, trying out different examples, and honing them to teach a concept in the simplest way possible. Many of those examples have made their way into this book, and I owe a debt of gratitude to all of the young boys and girls whose creativity, energy, and enthusiasm made these camps so much fun.

Why This Book?

As I indicated at the beginning of this preface, I think most CS1 textbooks are boring. This is a shame, as software is a wonderful way to express one's creativity. I wrote this book to to engage students—especially at-risk students—by motivating them to keep reading and successfully complete CS1.

To accomplish this challenging goal, this book integrates coverage of Alice with coverage of the Java programming language. The first six chapters use Alice to introduce the central concepts of object-based programming. The last eight chapters use Java to revisit and expand on those concepts, culminating in object-oriented programming. Together, these fourteen chapters provide integrated coverage of Alice and Java within a single book.

I spent the Fall 2004 semester on sabbatical at Carnegie Mellon. Each week, I spent three days working on this book and three days working as a member of the Alice team, helping them find errors in Alice. Working with these people was invaluable, as they helped me better understand Alice's strengths and weaknesses. This in turn helped me decide which Alice features to include in the first part of this book, and which features to exclude.

All the examples in this book were written and quality assurance tested using software that may be downloaded for free. Alice 2.0 can be downloaded from `alice.org`. Java SE can be downloaded from `java.sun.com`. The Eclipse IDE can be downloaded from `www.eclipse.org`. Eclipse contains many features to simplify common programming tasks. Chapter 7 provides extensive coverage of Eclipse 3.1, including nearly 20 screen captures to help students make the transition from Alice to Java. All examples are compatible with Java versions 5 and 6.

Pedagogical Features

To help students master the concepts of programming with objects, this book uses a number of pedagogical features, including the following:

- *Movie Metaphors*. Movies are pervasive in our culture. Since Alice programs are similar to movies, this book uses the language of movies to introduce software design. Using this approach, the book builds a conceptual bridge from a student's existing knowledge of movies to the new ideas of software design.
- *Detailed Diagrams*. This book contains roughly 300 color screen captures. Many of these demonstrate the exact drag-and-drop steps needed to use Alice and Eclipse effectively.
- *Engaging Alice Examples*. Using Alice's rich library of 3D objects, the first six chapters of this book include examples that keep students captivated as they learn the basics of programming. A few examples include:
    - a dragon flapping its wings
    - a scarecrow singing "Old MacDonald Had a Farm"
    - a fish jumping out of the water
    - three trolls facing off against a wizard
    - a girl walking in a spiral to follow a treasure map
    - and many more!
- *Motivating Java Examples*. The last eight chapters of this book include Java examples that students will find fun, socially relevant, or both, including:
    - monitoring a city's air pollution levels
    - displaying a custom logo
    - playing "The Chaos Game"
    - analyzing global warming data from a tropical reef
    - handling orders at a small business that sells t-shirts

  - playing the "Guess My Number" game
  - monitoring pH levels in a lake threatened by acid rain
  - and many more!
- *Integrated Software Design*. Beginning in Chapter 1 and continuing throughout, this book emphasizes software design. Each chapter shows how that chapter's concepts fit into the overall software design methodology. Students following this methodology can never say, "I don't know where to start."
- *Alice Tips*. The first six chapters include special "Alice Tip" sections that cover critical details students need to know to use Alice effectively.
- *Chapter Summaries*. The final section of each chapter includes a bulleted list of the key concepts covered in that chapter, plus a separate list of that chapter's key vocabulary terms.
- *Programming Projects*. Each chapter concludes with 10–12 programming projects, of varying levels of difficulty.

Using This Book

This book is intended for CS1 courses, but it can be used by anyone wishing to learn about object-oriented programming. The first six chapters introduce the central concepts of object-based programming in Alice, as follows:

1. Getting started with Alice: using objects and methods
2. Building Alice methods: using abstraction to hide details
3. Variables, parameters, and functions: computing and storing data for later use
4. Control structures: controlling flow via Alice's **`if`**, **`while`**, and **`for`** statements
5. Data structures: using and processing Alice's arrays and lists
6. Events: handling mouse and keyboard input in Alice

The next eight chapters revisit and expand upon these concepts in Java, so that by the end of the book, the student has been introduced to object-oriented and event-driven programming, as follows:

7. From Alice to Java, using Eclipse
8. Variables, types (including primitive and reference types), and expressions
9. Methods: class and instance methods in Java
10. Control structures: Java's **`if`**, **`switch`**, **`while`**, **`for`**, and **`do`** statements
11. Files, File I/O, and Exceptions in Java
12. Data Structures: Java arrays, **`LinkedList`**s, and **`ArrayList`**s
13. Object-Oriented Programming in Java
14. Event-Driven Programming: Using **`swing`** to build GUIs in Java

These fourteen chapters can be used in different ways, including:

- *The Spiral Approach*: Spend 4-6 weeks introducing all of the programming concepts using Alice (the first spiral). Then spend the remainder of the semester revisiting those same concepts in Java (the second spiral). In this approach, the programming concepts are covered in two distinct "batches": an Alice batch, followed by a Java batch. To use this approach, simply cover the chapters in order:

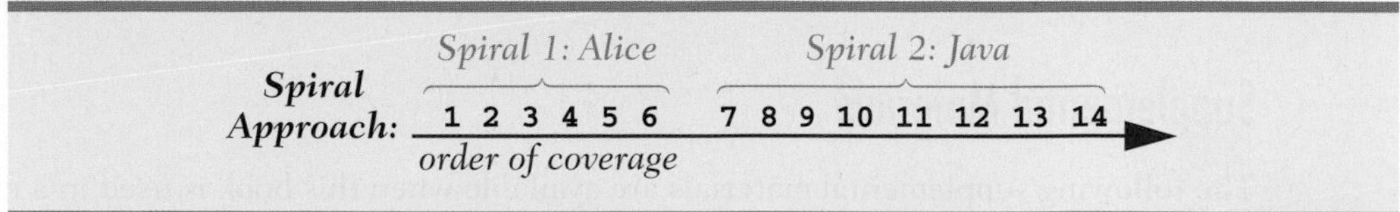

- *The Interleaved Approach*: For each concept (for example, methods), introduce that concept using Alice. After the students have gained hands-on experience with that concept in Alice, immediately revisit that same concept in Java. In this approach, the programming concepts are covered sequentially, with the Alice and Java chapters interleaved, as follows.

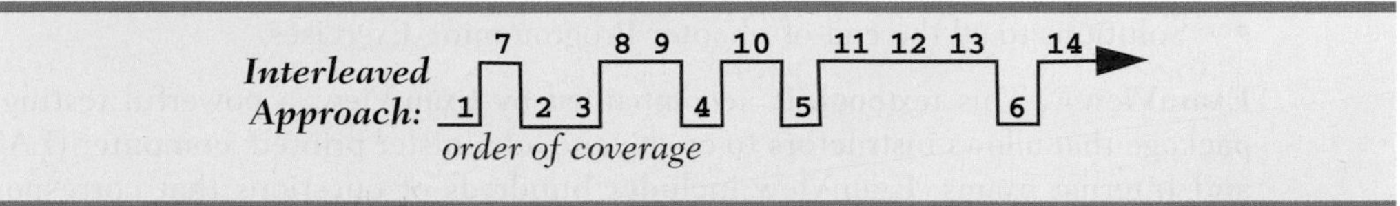

If an instructor does not normally cover event-driven programming, Chapters 6 and 14 may be omitted. However, most students find this material to be *very* engaging, because it allows them to start building graphical applications and games! If an instructor wishes, events may be introduced at any point after Chapters 3 and 8.

Appendices and Cover Material

The appendices provide resources and material supplementing what is covered in the chapters. Appendix A presents an exhaustive list of Alice's standard methods and functions, including detailed behavioral descriptions.

Appendix B provides a "supplemental chapter" on recursion, beginning with Alice examples that help students visualize what happens during recursion, and ending with Java examples that show students the broad range of problems for which recursion can be useful.

Appendix C presents a complete list of Java's keywords. This can help novice Java programmers learn the words they should not use as identifiers.

Appendix D presents the Unicode standard's *Basic Latin* chart, with both the decimal and hexidecimal codes for each symbol. This provides a convenient place for students to look up the decimal and hexidecimal codes Java uses to represent most of the `char` literals used in this book.

The inside covers contain two useful Alice "Quick Reference" pages. Inside the front cover is a complete list of the standard methods and functions that can be applied to an Alice object. Inside the back cover is a complete list of the standard functions that can be applied to an Alice world. Unlike the lists in Appendix A, these "Quick References" display each method, function, and parameter exactly as they appear in Alice. By presenting all of these methods and functions together, a student can see all of the methods and functions at once, and quickly locate a particular method or function.

Supplemental Materials

The following supplemental materials are available when this book is used in a classroom setting. All instructor teaching tools, outlined below, are available with this book on a single CD-ROM. They are also available for download at `www.course.com`.

Electronic Instructor's Manual. The Instructor's Manual that accompanies this textbook includes:

- Additional instructional material to assist in class preparation, including suggestions for lecture topics.
- Solutions to all the end-of-chapter Programming Exercises.

ExamView®. This textbook is accompanied by ExamView, a powerful testing software package that allows instructors to create and administer printed, computer (LAN-based), and Internet exams. ExamView includes hundreds of questions that correspond to the topics covered in this text, enabling students to generate detailed study guides that include page references for further review. These computer-based and Internet testing components allow students to take exams at their computers, and save the instructor time because each exam is graded automatically.

PowerPoint Presentations. This book comes with Microsoft PowerPoint slides for each chapter. These are included as a teaching aid for classroom presentations, either to make available to students on the network for chapter review, or to be printed for classroom distribution. Instructors can add their own slides for additional topics that they introduce to the class.

Distance Learning. Course Technology is proud to present online test banks in WebCT and Blackboard to provide the most complete and dynamic learning experience possible. For more information on how to bring distance learning to your course, contact your local Course Technology sales representative.

Source Code. All necessary source code is available for students and instructors at the Course Technology Web site (`www.course.com`), at the author's website (`alice.calvin.edu`), and on the Instructor Resources CD-ROM.

The author's site also provides a feedback link and errata list. If you find a mistake, or want to point out a feature that works especially well, please use that feedback link. Such feedback will help me improve future editions of the book.

Solution Files. The solution files for all programming exercises are available for instructors at `www.course.com`, and on the Instructor Resources CD-ROM.

Acknowledgments

A book cannot be developed without the help and support of many people. My heartfelt thanks go to *Randy Pausch* of Carnegie Mellon University for creating Alice, and pursuing his vision to its fruition. I would also like to thank the Alice team: *Dennis Cosgrove*, *Dave Culyba*, *Mike Darga*, *Caitlin Kelleher*, and *Gabe Yu*. Each person patiently answered my questions and made me feel welcome at Carnegie Mellon.

The following people served as reviewers, whose careful reading of early drafts and constructive criticism helped make this book what it is. My thanks to: *Gian Mario Besana*, DePaul University; *Barbara Boucher Owens*, Southwestern University; *Nan Schaller*, Rochester Institute of Technology; *Mark Shwayder*, University of Montana; and *Leila Wallace*, Geneva College.

A number of people at Course Technology also played important roles. My thanks to *Alyssa Pratt*, Senior Product Manager, *Amy Jollymore*, Acquisitions Editor, *Mary Franz*, Senior Acquisitions Editor, and *Jill Klaffky*, Content Project Manager for helping me produce the book, as well as *Peter Stefanis*, and *Chris Scriver*, who checked and rechecked each chapter and program for quality assurance. I am especially grateful to *John Bosco*, of Green Pen Quality Assurance, who helped me polish the manuscript. This book would not be what it is without the careful attention to detail of all of these people.

I would also like to thank the staff at GEX Publishing Services, especially *Gina Dishman*, who smoothly guided the production process.

A special "thank you" goes to numerous *Imaginary Worlds Camps* students, who inspired some of the examples in this book; and the *Department of Computer Science* at *Calvin College*, whose support made it possible.

I also wish to thank my wife *Barbara*, and my sons *Roy* and *Ian*, for their patience, understanding, and support over many months of writing. Their love and encouragement sustained me through the process.

Last in order but first in importance, I wish to thank *God*, the original creative Person. I believe that the joy we experience in being creative is the result of our bearing His image. To Him be the glory.

-Joel C. Adams

In memory of William E. Ewing III,
whose dry humor never failed to "jar your preserves."

Chapter 1

Getting Started With Alice

The computer programmer ... is a creator of universes for which he [or she] alone is the lawgiver ... universes of virtually unlimited complexity can be created in the form of computer programs. Moreover ... systems so formulated and elaborated act out their programmed scripts. They compliantly obey their laws and vividly exhibit their obedient behavior. No playwright, no stage director, no emperor, however powerful, has ever exercised such absolute authority to arrange a stage or a field of battle and to command such unswervingly dutiful actors or troops.

JOSEPH WEIZENBAUM

If you don't know where you're going, you're liable to wind up somewhere else.

YOGI BERRA

Louis, I think this is the beginning of a beautiful friendship.

RICK (HUMPHREY BOGART) TO CAPTAIN RENAULT (CLAUDE RAINS), IN *CASABLANCA*

Objectives

Upon completion of this chapter, you will be able to:

- ❑ Design a simple Alice program
- ❑ Build a simple Alice program
- ❑ Animate Alice objects by sending them messages
- ❑ Use the Alice **`doInOrder`** and **`doTogether`** controls
- ❑ Change an object's properties from within a program
- ❑ Use Alice's **`quad view`** to position objects near one another

Welcome to the fun and exciting world of computer programming! In this chapter, we are going to build our first computer program using **Alice**, a free software tool for creating virtual worlds.

1.1 Getting and Running Alice

1.1.1 Downloading Alice

Alice can be freely downloaded from the Alice website at **`http://alice.org`**. For the Windows version, clicking the download link begins the transfer of a compressed archive file named **`Alice.zip`** to your computer. (For MacOS, the file is named **`Alice.dmg`**.) Save this file to your computer's desktop.

1.1.2 Installing Alice

Alice does not have a special installer like other programs you might have used. When the download has finished, double-click the **`Alice.zip`** (or **`Alice.dmg`**) file to open the archive file. Your computer will open a window containing a folder named **`Alice`**. Drag that **`Alice`** folder from the window onto your computer's desktop.

If you'd rather not have the **`Alice`** folder on your desktop, open a window to the folder in which you wish to store **`Alice`** (for example, **`C:\Program Files\`**). Then drag the **`Alice`** folder from your desktop into that window.

Once the **`Alice`** folder is where you want it, open the **`Alice`** folder, and locate the file named **`Alice.exe`** (or just **`Alice`** in MacOS). In Windows, right-click the file, and from the menu that appears, choose **`Create Shortcut`** to create a shortcut (alias) to **`Alice.exe`**. (MacOS users, select the file and choose **`File->Make Alias`**.) Drag the resulting shortcut to your desktop and rename it **`Alice`**, so that you can launch Alice conveniently.

1.1.3 Running Alice

To start Alice, just double-click the **`Alice`** icon on your desktop. Congratulations!

1.2 The Alice Tutorials

As shown in Figure 1-1, when you start Alice for the first time, Alice gives you the option of working through a set of interactive tutorials. These excellent tutorials cover the basics of using Alice while giving you hands-on practice working in the Alice environment. Because they are such effective learning tools, we are going to let these tutorials teach you the basics of Alice. This chapter will concentrate on aspects of Alice *not* covered in the tutorials.

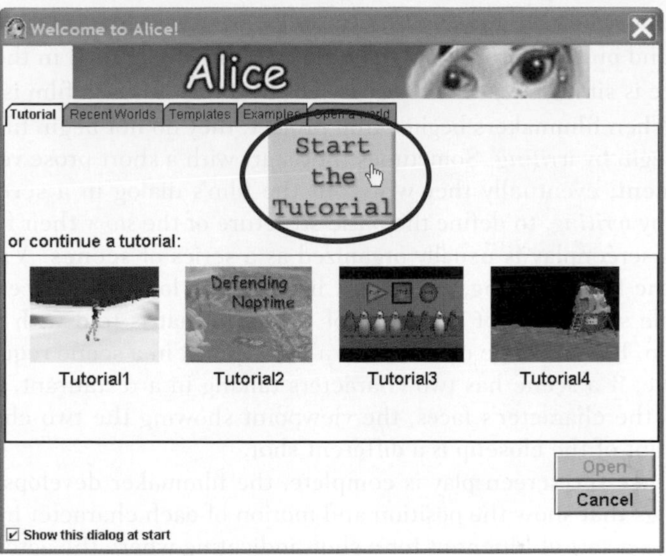

FIGURE 1-1 The Alice Tutorial window

(If this window does not appear, you can make it appear by clicking on Alice's **`Help`** menu and then selecting the **`Tutorial`** choice.) To activate the tutorials, click the **`Start the Tutorial`** button, and then work your way through the four tutorials. Remember, the point of these tutorials is to learn how to use Alice, not to see how fast you can finish them. Read carefully, taking special note of *what* you are doing at each step, *how* you are doing it, and *why* you are doing it. Close Alice when you are finished with the tutorials.

The rest of this chapter assumes you have completed the tutorials, so if you have not yet done so, you should *complete the tutorials now, before proceeding further.* If for some reason you cannot complete the tutorials right away, feel free to keep reading, but I strongly encourage you to complete the tutorials as soon as possible, and then *re-read this chapter.*

Developing programs to solve problems is a complex process that is both an art and a science. It is an art in that it requires a good deal of imagination, creativity, and ingenuity. But it is also a science in that it uses certain techniques and methodologies. In this chapter, we're going to work through the *thought process* that goes into creating computer software.

If you can manage it, the very best way to read this book is at a computer, doing each step or action as we describe it. By doing so, you will be engaging in *active learning*, which is a much better way to learn than by trying to absorb the ideas through passive reading.

1.3 Program Design

Now that you have finished the tutorials, we are ready to build our first computer program and put into practice several of the skills you learned in the tutorials. Programming in Alice is similar to *filmmaking*, so let's begin with how a film is put together.

When filmmakers begin a film project, they do not begin filming right away. Instead, they begin by *writing*. Sometimes they start with a short prose version of the film called a **treatment**; eventually they write out the film's dialog in a **screenplay**, but they always begin by *writing*, to define the basic structure of the *story* their film is telling.

A screenplay is usually organized as a series of **scenes**. A scene is one piece of the story the film is telling, usually set in the same location. A scene is usually made up of multiple **shots**. A shot is a piece of the story that is told with the **camera** in the same position. Each change of the camera's **viewpoint** in a scene requires a different shot. For example, if a scene has two characters talking in a restaurant, followed by a closeup of one of the character's faces, the viewpoint showing the two characters is one shot; the viewpoint of the closeup is a different shot.

Once the screen play is complete, the filmmaker develops **storyboards**, which are drawings that show the position and motion of each character in a shot. Each storyboard provides a sort of blueprint for a shot, indicating where the actors stand, where the camera should be placed with respect to them, and so on. (You may have seen storyboards on the extras that come with the DVD version of a film.)

Creating an Alice program is much like creating a film, and modern computer software projects are often managed in a way that is quite similar to film projects.

1.3.1 User Stories

A modern software designer begins by writing a prose description of what the software is to do, from the perspective of a person using the software. This is called a **user story**. For example, here is a user story for the first program we are going to build:

> When the program begins, Alice and the White Rabbit are facing each other, Alice on the left and the White Rabbit on the right. Alice turns her head and then greets us. The White Rabbit also turns and greets us. Alice and the White Rabbit introduce themselves. Simultaneously, Alice and the White Rabbit say "Welcome to our world."

A user story provides several important pieces of information, including:

- A basic description of what happens when the user runs the program
- The *nouns* in the story (for example, Alice, the White Rabbit) correspond to the **objects** we need to place in the Alice world. Objects include the characters in the story — background items like plants, buildings, or vehicles, and so on.
- The *verbs* in the story (for example, turns, says) correspond to the *actions* we want the objects to perform in the story.
- The chronological *flow* of actions in the story tells us what has to happen *first*, what happens *next*, what happens *after that*, and so on. The *flow* thus describes the *sequence of actions* that take place in the story.

By providing the objects, behaviors, sequence of actions, and description of what the program will do, a user story provides an important first step in the software design process, upon which the other steps are based. The user story is to a good software product as the screenplay is to a good film.

It is often useful to write out the flow of the story as a numbered sequence of objects and actions. For example, we can write out the flow in the user story as shown in Figure 1-2:

Scene: Alice is on the left, the White Rabbit is on the right.

1. Alice turns her head toward the user.
2. Alice greets the user.
3. The White Rabbit turns to face the user.
4. The White Rabbit greets the user.
5. Alice introduces herself.
6. The White Rabbit introduces himself.
7. Simultaneously, Alice and the White Rabbit say "Welcome to our world".

FIGURE 1-2 First program flow (algorithm)

A **flow** is thus a series of steps that precisely specify (in order) the behavior of each object in the story. In programming terminology, a flow — a sequence of steps that solve a problem — is called an **algorithm**.

1.3.2 Storyboard-Sketches

When they have a completed screenplay, filmmakers often hire an artist to sketch each shot in the film. For each different shot in each scene, the artist creates a drawing (in consultation with the filmmaker) of that shot, with arrows to show movements of the characters or camera within the shot. These drawings are called **storyboards**. When completed, the collection of storyboards provides a graphical version of the story that the filmmaker can use to help the actors visualize what is going to happen in the shot, before filming begins.

To illustrate, Figure 1-3 shows a pair of storyboards for a scene we will develop in Section 2.4.1. The first storyboard frames the scene, showing three trolls menacing a wizard, with the wizard's castle in the background. In the second storyboard, we zoom in on the wizard to get a better view of his reaction. The progression of storyboards thus serves as a kind of cartoon version of the story, which the filmmaker uses to decide how the film will look, before the actual filming begins. By first trying out his or her ideas on paper, a filmmaker can identify and discard bad ideas early in the process, before time, effort, and money are wasted filming (or in our case, programming) them.

FIGURE 1-3 A storyboard and corresponding scene

In a similar fashion, the designers of modern computer software draw sketches of what the screen will look like as their software runs, showing any changes that occur. Just as each distinct shot in a film scene requires its own storyboard, each distinct screen in a computer application requires a different sketch, so we will call these **storyboard-sketches**. Since our first program has just one scene, it has just one storyboard-sketch, as shown in Figure 1-4.

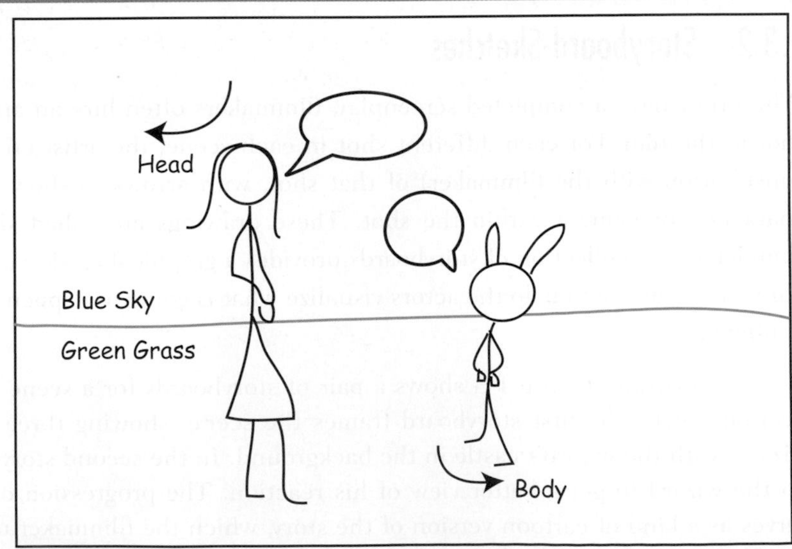

FIGURE 1-4 Storyboard-sketches

In Alice programming, the storyboard-sketches provide important information for the programmer about each object visible on the screen, including:

- Its **position** (where it is with respect to the other objects)
- Its **pose** (what are the positions of its limbs, if it has any)
- Its **orientation** (what direction it is facing)

Storyboard-sketches also indicate where Alice's **camera** object should be positioned, whether it is stationary or moving during the shot, and so on.

1.3.3 Transition Diagrams

When a program has multiple scenes, it has multiple storyboards. When all the storyboard-sketches are completed, they are linked together in a **transition diagram** that shows any special events that are required to make the transition from one sketch to the next. In a movie, there are no special events, so the transition diagram is a simple linear sequence, as shown in Figure 1-5.

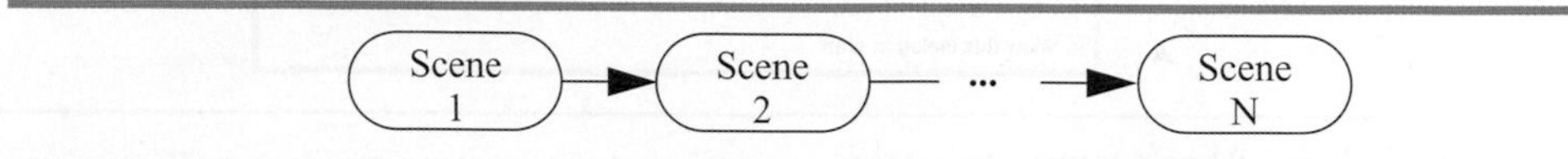

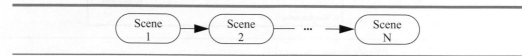

FIGURE 1-5 A movie's transition diagram

1.4 Program Implementation In Alice

With a user story, storyboard-sketches, and transition diagram in hand, the program's **design** is done, and we are ready to build it in Alice. We begin by starting Alice. Alice displays a **`Welcome to Alice`** window that allows us to choose a **`Template`** (background and sky) for the world, as shown in Figure 1-6.

FIGURE 1-6 Alice's template worlds

(You can also get this window to appear by clicking Alice's **`File`** menu, and then choosing **`New World`**.) Double-click the template you want to use (we will choose the **`grass`** template here), and Alice will create a pristine[1] three-dimensional world for you, using that template, as shown in Figure 1-7. (Your screen may look slightly different.) For consistency with the tutorials, we have added the names for the various areas in Alice to Figure 1-7.

1. Here and elsewhere, we will use the word *pristine* to describe an Alice world in its beginning state — before any objects have been added to it.

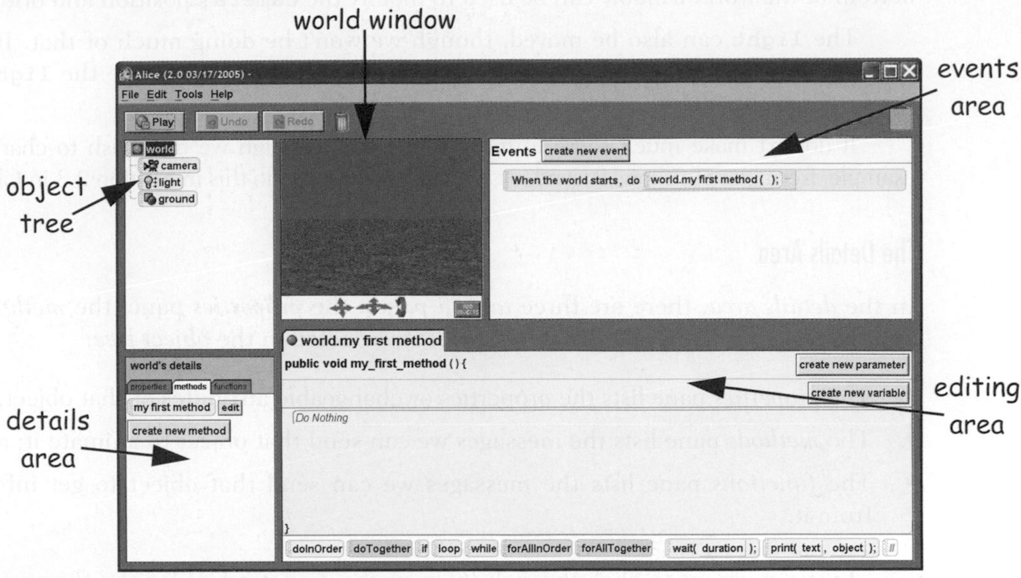

FIGURE 1-7 A pristine Alice world

Menus

At the top of the Alice window are four menus:

- **`File`** lets you load and save your Alice programs/worlds (and other things).
- **`Edit`** lets you change your preferences.
- **`Tools`** lets you examine your world's statistics, error console, and so on.
- **`Help`** lets you access the Alice tutorials, some example worlds, and so on.

Buttons

Below Alice's menus are three buttons:

- **`Play`** runs the program associated with the current world.
- **`Undo`** undoes your most recent action (this is very handy!).
- **`Redo`** redoes the most recently undone action.

If you are like me, you will find yourself using the **`Play`** button frequently (every time you want to run your program); the **`Undo`** buton when using trial-and-error to find just the right effect, and the **`Redo`** button very rarely.

The Object Tree

The *object tree* is where the objects in your world are listed. Even in a pristine world, the *object tree* contains several objects, namely the **`camera`**, the **`light`**, and the **`ground`**. Like other objects in Alice, the **`camera`** can be moved within the world. Its position determines what is seen in the *world window*. As you saw in the tutorials, the blue arrow-controls at the bottom of the *world window* can be used to modify the **camera**'s position and orientation.

The **light** can also be moved, though we won't be doing much of that. If you are working on a shot and find that you need more light, you can change the **light**'s position, orientation, color, and brightness.

It doesn't make much sense to move the ground, though we may wish to change it (for example, from grass to snow, or sand, or ...). We'll see how to do this in Section 2.3 in Chapter 2.

The Details Area

In the *details area*, there are three *tabbed panes*: the *properties* pane, the *methods* pane, and the *functions* pane. For whatever object is selected in the *object tree*:

- The *properties* pane lists the properties or changeable attributes of that object;
- The *methods* pane lists the messages we can send that object to animate it; and
- The *functions* pane lists the messages we can send that object to get information from it.

Take a moment to click through these panes, to get a feel for the things they contain. We'll present an overview of them in Section 1.5.

The Editing Area

The *editing area* is where we will edit or build the program that controls the animation. As can be seen in Figure 1-7, the *editing area* of a pristine world contains a method named **World.my first method** that is empty, meaning it contains no *statements*. Very shortly, we will see how to build our first program by adding statements to this method.

At the bottom of the *editing area* are *controls* (**doInOrder**, **doTogether**, **if**, **loop**, and so on) that can be used to build Alice statements. We will introduce these controls one by one, as we need them, throughout the next few chapters.

The Events Area

The *events area* is where we can tell Alice what to do when special actions called **events** occur. A pristine world contains just one event, as can be seen in Figure 1-7. This event tells Alice to send the **my first method** message to the **World** object when the world starts (that is, when the user clicks the **Play** button). Clicking the **Play** button thus causes **my first method** to **run**, meaning any statements within it are performed. Programmers often use the phrases ***run* a program** and ***execute* a program** interchangeably.

1.4.1 Program Style

Before we begin programming, you may want to alter the *style* in which Alice displays the program. Click the **Edit** menu, followed by the **Preferences** choice, and Alice will display the *Preferences* window shown in Figure 1-8.

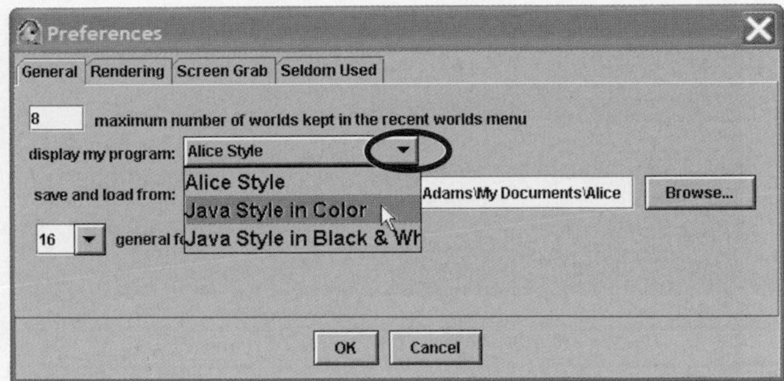

FIGURE 1-8 Using Java style

Since Java is a popular programming language, we will be displaying our programs using Alice's *Java style in Color*. By doing so, Alice will provide us with an introduction to the Java we will learn later in the course. If you want your programs to look consistent with those in the text, please make this change on your copy of Alice. You will then need to restart Alice for the changes to take effect.

1.4.2 Adding Objects to Alice

Once we have a pristine world, the next step is to populate it with objects using the skills you learned in the Alice tutorials. By clicking the **`ADD OBJECTS`** button below the *world window*, locating **`Class AliceLiddell`** and **`Class WhiteRabbit`** in the Alice Gallery (under **`People`** and **`Animals`**, respectively), adding them to the world, and repositioning and rotating them, we can build the scene from our first storyboard-sketch, as shown in Figure 1-9.

FIGURE 1-9 Alice Liddell and the White Rabbit

The items in the Alice Gallery are not objects but are like blueprints that Alice uses to build objects. Such blueprints are called **classes**. Whenever we drag a class from the Gallery into the *world window*, Alice uses the class to build an object for the world.

For example, when we drag the **AliceLiddell** and **WhiteRabbit** classes to the world, Alice adds two new objects to the world, and lists them in the *object tree*: **aliceLiddell** and **whiteRabbit**. If we were to drag **Class WhiteRabbit** into the world again, Alice would again use the class to create an object for the world, but this object would be named **whiteRabbit2**. Feel free to try this; you can always delete **whiteRabbit2** (or any object in the *object tree*), either by dragging it to the **Trash**, or by right-clicking it and selecting **delete** from the menu that appears.

The key idea is that each object is made from a class. Even though the world might contain ten **whiteRabbit** objects, there would still be just one **WhiteRabbit** class from which all of the **whiteRabbit** objects were made.

To distinguish objects from classes, Alice follows this convention: each word in the name of a *class* is capitalized (for example, **AliceLiddell**, **WhiteRabbit**); but for an *object*, each word in the name *except the first* is capitalized (for example, **aliceLiddell**, **whiteRabbit**).

If you don't like the name Alice gives an object, you can always rename it by (1) right-clicking the object's name in the *object tree*, and (2) choosing **rename** from the menu that appears, and (3) typing your new name for the object. Alice will then update all statements that refer to the object to use the new name.

With the objects **aliceLiddel** and **whiteRabbit** in place, we are almost ready to begin programming! In Alice, programming is accomplished mainly in the *object tree* (to select the object being animated), the *details area* (the **properties** or characteristics of an object are listed under the *properties* tab, and the **messages** we can send an object are listed under the *methods* and *functions* tabs), and the *editing area* (to add statements to the program that animate the selected object).

1.4.3 Accessing Object Subparts

In the user story, the first action is that Alice should seem to see us (the user) and turn her head toward us. To make this happen, we will use skills from the Alice tutorials.

If we click on **aliceLiddell** in the *object tree*, then we select all of **aliceLiddell**. However, the user story says that Alice is to turn her head, so we just want to select that part of her. To do so, we click the **+** sign next to **aliceLiddell** in the *object tree* to view her subparts, and then do the same on her **neck**, exposing her **head**, which we then select as shown in Figure 1-10.

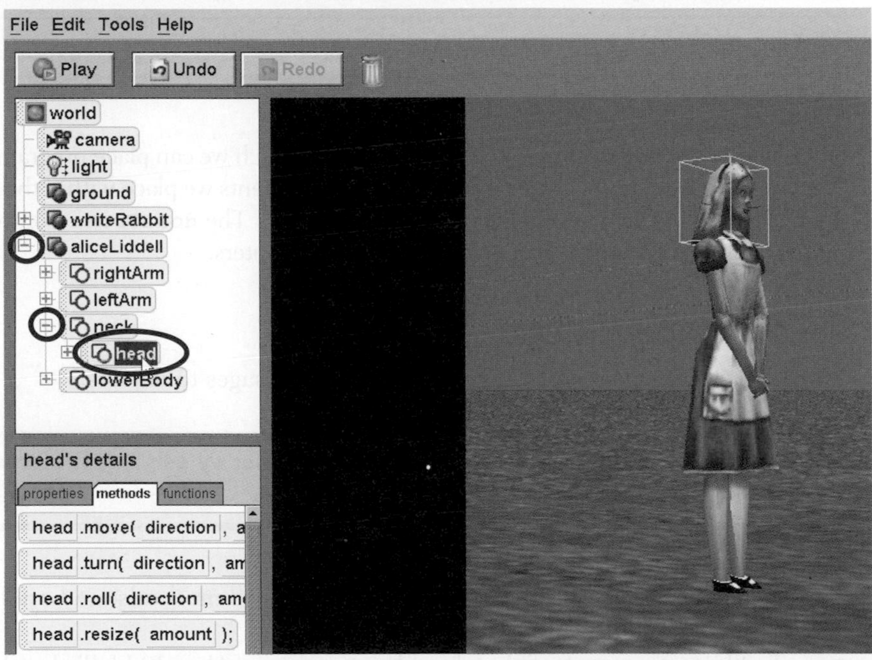

FIGURE 1-10 Accessing an object's subparts

As can be seen in Figure 1-10, when we click on an object in the *object tree* (for example, Alice Liddell's **head**), Alice draws a box around that object in the *world window*, to highlight it and show its boundaries. This box is called an object's **bounding box**, and every Alice object has one.

Selecting an object's subpart in the *object tree* also changes the *details area* to indicate the *properties*, *methods*, and *functions* for that subpart.

Since the steps in a flow or algorithm need to be performed in a specified order, we begin programming by dragging a **doInOrder** control from the bottom of the *editing area*, as shown in Figure 1-11.

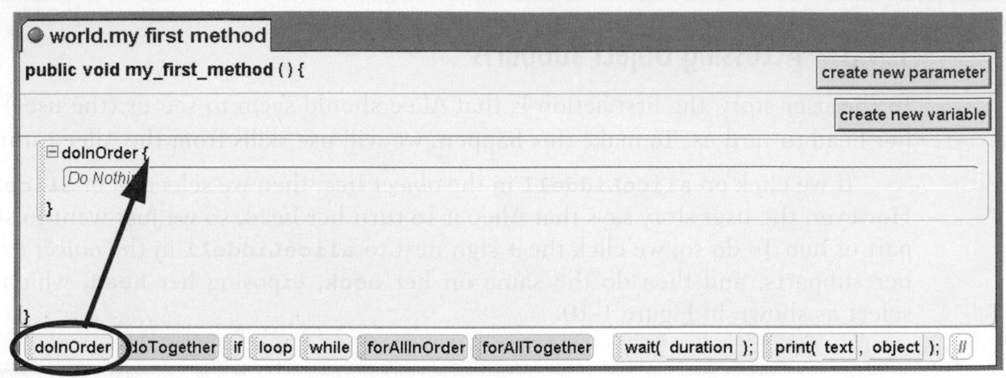

FIGURE 1-11 Dragging the **doInOrder** control

The **doInOrder** control is a structure within which we can place program statements (see Section 1.4.7 below). As its name suggests, any statements we place within the **doInOrder** will be performed in the order they appear, top-to-bottom. The **doInOrder** control also has additional convenient features that we will see in later chapters.

1.4.4 Sending Messages

Alice programming consists largely of sending messages to objects.

> You can get an object to perform a desired behavior by sending the object a **message** that asks the object to produce that behavior.

In Alice, behavior-producing messages are called **methods**, and are listed under the *methods pane* of the *details area*.

To illustrate, step 1 of the algorithm is to make Alice Liddell's head turn to look at the user. To accomplish this, we can send **aliceLiddell.neck.head** the **pointAt()** message, and specify the **camera** as the thing her head is to face. (Similarly, to make the White Rabbit say "Hello", we can send **whiteRabbit** the **say()** message, and specify **Hello** as the thing we want him to say.) With Alice Liddell's **head** selected in the *object tree*, we scan through the methods in the *details area* until we see **pointAt()**. We then click on **pointAt()**, drag it into the *editing area*, and drop it.

As we drag a method, Alice surrounds it with a red border so long as the mouse is in a place where dropping it has no benefit. When the mouse moves into an area where we can drop the method beneficially, Alice changes the method's border's color from red to green. Alice consistently uses the color red to warn you that you *should not* do something (for example, drop the method), and uses the color green to indicate when you *may* do something.

The **pointAt()** message requires that we specify a **target** — the thing at which we want Alice Liddell's head to point. When you drop the **pointAt()** method in the *editing area*, Alice displays a menu of the objects in your world, from which you can choose the **target**, as shown in Figure 1-12.

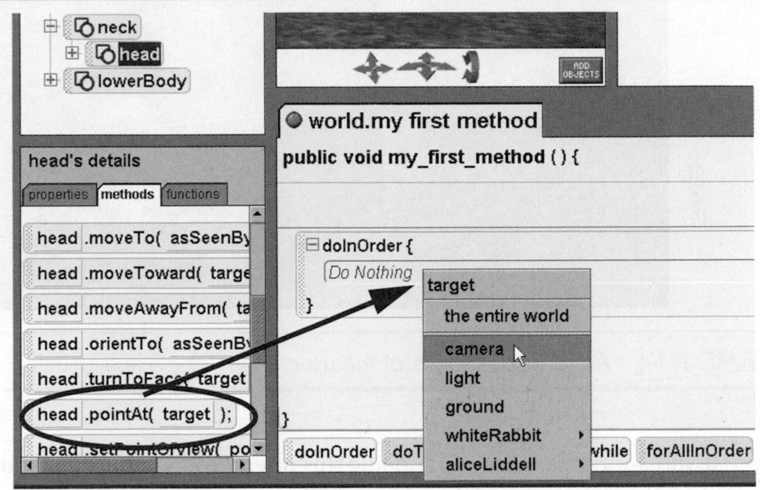

FIGURE 1-12 Dragging the **pointAt()** message

When we select the **camera**, Alice redraws the *editing area* as shown in Figure 1-13.

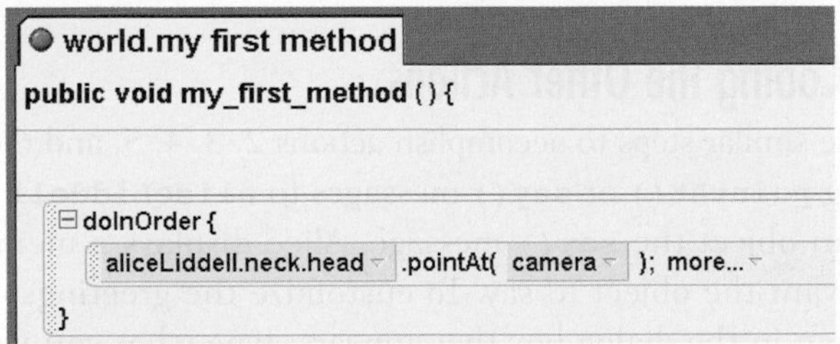

FIGURE 1-13 Our first message

1.4.5 Testing and Debugging

If we now click the **Play** button, you will see **aliceLiddell**'s head turn and seem to look at you (the user)! Figure 1-14 shows the end result.

FIGURE 1-14 Alice Liddell looks at the user

(If you are not at a computer doing this interactively, compare Figure 1-14 to Figure 1-9 to see the effect of sending Alice's **head** the **pointAt(camera)** message.)

By clicking the **Play** button, we are **testing** the program, to see if it produces the desired result. If the program does something other than what we wanted, then it contains an **error** or **bug**. Finding and fixing the error is called **debugging** the program. If you have followed the steps carefully so far, your program should have no bugs, so let's continue. (If your program does have a bug, compare your editing area against that shown in Figure 1-13 to see where you went wrong.)

1.4.6 Coding the Other Actions

We can use similar steps to accomplish actions 2, 3, 4, 5, and 6 of the algorithm in Figure 1-2 by sending **pointAt()** or **say()** messages to **aliceLiddell** or the **whiteRabbit**. When we send an object the **say()** message, Alice displays a menu from which we can select what we want the object to say. To customize the greetings, select the **other...** menu-choice; then in the dialog box that appears, type what you want the object to say. After a few minutes of clicking, dragging, and dropping, we can have the partial program shown in Figure 1-15.

```
world.my first method
public void my_first_method ( ) {

  doInOrder {
    aliceLiddell.neck.head  .pointAt( camera  ); more...
    aliceLiddell  .say( Oh, hello there!  ); duration = 2 seconds  fontSize = 30  more...
    whiteRabbit  .pointAt( camera  ); more...
    whiteRabbit  .say( Uhm, yes. Hello there!  ); duration = 2 seconds  fontSize = 30  more...
    aliceLiddell  .say( My name is Alice Liddell.  ); duration = 2 seconds  fontSize = 30  more...
    whiteRabbit  .say( And I am the White Rabbit.  ); duration = 2 seconds  fontSize = 30  more...
  }
```

FIGURE 1-15 A partial program

By clicking on the **more...** to the right of a message in the *editing area*, we can customize various attributes of that message. For example, in Figure 1-15, we have increased the **duration** attribute of each **say()** message (depending on the length of what is being said), to give the user sufficient time to read.

> **For say() messages, set the duration to 2–3 seconds per line of text being displayed, to give the user time to read what is being said.**

You can also adjust the **fontSize** (and other attributes) to specify the appearance of a **say()** message's letters. We will always use a **fontSize** of at least **30**, to ensure that the letters display well on high-resolution computer screens (see Figure 1-15).

1.4.7 Statements

Most of the lines in the program have the same basic structure:

```
object.message(value); more...
```

In programming terminology, such a line is sometimes called a **statement**. A computer program consists of a collection of statements, the combination of which produce some desirable behavior. The basic structure shown above is quite common, and is what we will use most often.

The **doInOrder** control is also a statement; however it is a statement that controls *how other statements are performed* (that is, one at a time, top-to-bottom).

1.4.8 The Final Action

We are nearly done! All that is left is the final step in the algorithm, in which Alice Liddell and the White Rabbit say "Welcome to our world" simultaneously. It should be evident that we can accomplish this in part by sending **`say()`** messages to **`aliceLiddell`** and the **`whiteRabbit`**. For both objects, the value accompanying the **`say()`** message should be the same value: **`Welcome to our world`**.

As we have seen, the **`doInOrder`** control performs the first statement within it, then the next statement, then the next statement, and so on. This is sometimes called **sequential execution**, meaning the statements are performed in order or *in sequence*. Sequential execution means that if we were to send **`aliceLiddell`** the **`say()`** message, and then send **`whiteRabbit`** the **`say()`** message, the message to the White Rabbit would not be performed until after the message to Alice Liddell had been completed.

To achieve the effect specified in the user story, we must send **`say()`** messages to **`aliceLiddell`** and the **`whiteRabbit`** *simultaneously*. We can accomplish this using the **`doTogether`** control, located at the bottom of the *editing area*. To use this control, we click on **`doTogether`**, drag it upwards into the *editing area*, and drop it when the green bar appears below the last statement in the program, producing the program shown in Figure 1-16.

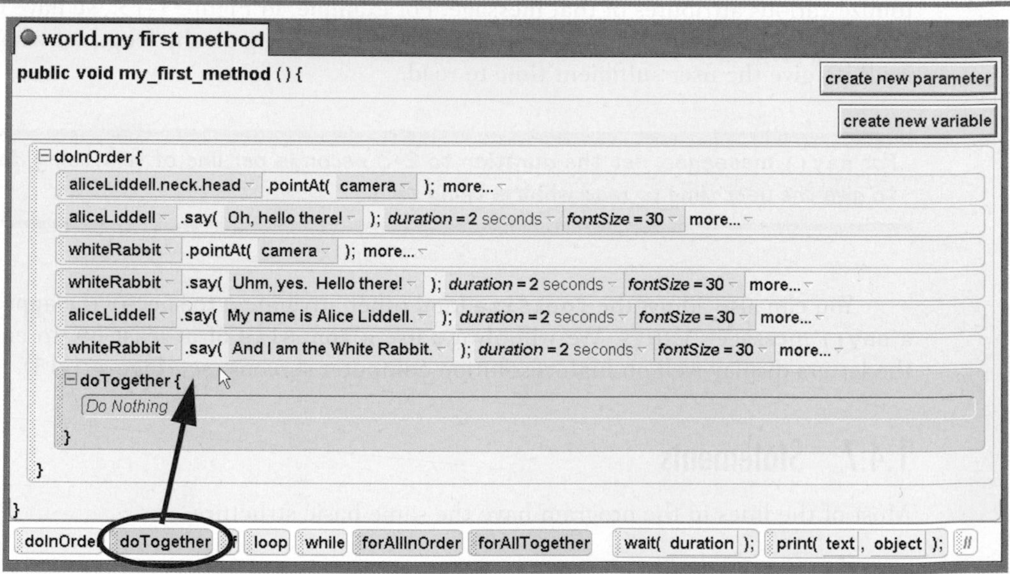

FIGURE 1-16 Dragging the **`doTogether`** control

The **`doTogether`** control is another Alice statement. Like the **`doInOrder`**, it has a form different from the **`object.message()`** structure we saw previously. When the program performs a **`doTogether`** statement, all statements within it are performed simultaneously, so it should provide the behavior we need to finish the program.

Using the same skills we used earlier, we can send **say()** messages to **aliceLiddell** and to the **whiteRabbit**. However, now we drop these messages inside the **doTogether** statement, yielding the final program, shown in Figure 1-17.

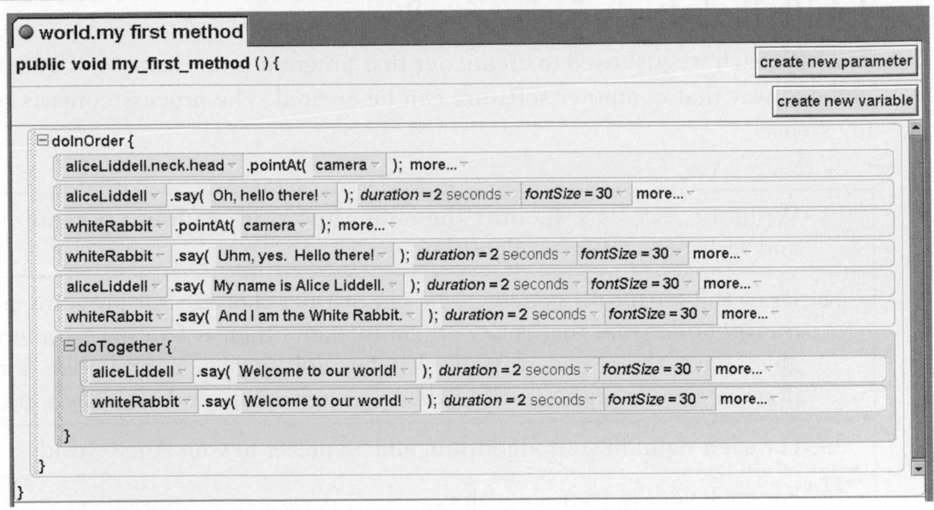

FIGURE 1-17 Our first program

1.4.9 Final Testing

When we run the program, the final scene appears as shown in Figure 1-18.

FIGURE 1-18 Alice Liddell and the White Rabbit speaking together

We saw earlier that the Alice **doInOrder** statement performs the statements within it *sequentially*. By contrast, the **doTogether** statement performs the statements it contains *simultaneously* or *concurrently*.

1.4.10 The Software Engineering Process

The approach we just used to create our first program is an example of a methodical, disciplined way that computer software can be created. The process consists of the following steps:

1. Write the *user story*. Identify the nouns and verbs within it. Organize the nouns and verbs into a *flow* or *algorithm*.
2. Draw the *storyboard-sketches*, one per distinct shot in your program, and create a *transition diagram* that relates them to each other. If you have some users available, have them review your sketches for feedback, and take seriously any improvements they suggest. Update your user story and algorithm, if necessary.
3. For each noun in your algorithm: add an *object* to your Alice world.
4. For each verb in your algorithm:
   a. Find a *message* that performs that verb's action, and send it to the verb's object. (If the object has no message that provides that verb's action, we'll see how to build our own methods in Chapter 2.)
   b. Test the message sent in Step 4a, to check that it produces the desired action. If not, either alter how the message is being sent (with its **more...** attributes), or find a different message (and if you cannot find one, build your own).

Steps 1 and 2 of this process are called **software design**. Steps 3 and 4 — in which we build the program and then verify that it does what it is supposed to do — are called **software implementation and testing**. Together, software design, implementation, and testing are important parts of **software engineering** — a methodical way to build computer programs.

We will use this same basic process to create most of the programs in this book. You should go through each of these steps for each program you write, because the result will be better-crafted programs.

1.5 Alice's Details Area

As mentioned earlier, Alice's *details area* provides three tabbed panes. Whenever an object is selected in the *object tree*, these three panes list the properties or characteristics of that object, the methods for that object, and the functions, or questions that we can ask that object. In this section, we provide an overview of this *details area*.

1.5.1 The *properties* Pane

To see the properties of an object, first click on that object in the *object tree*, and then click the *properties* tab in the *details area*, as shown in Figure 1-19.

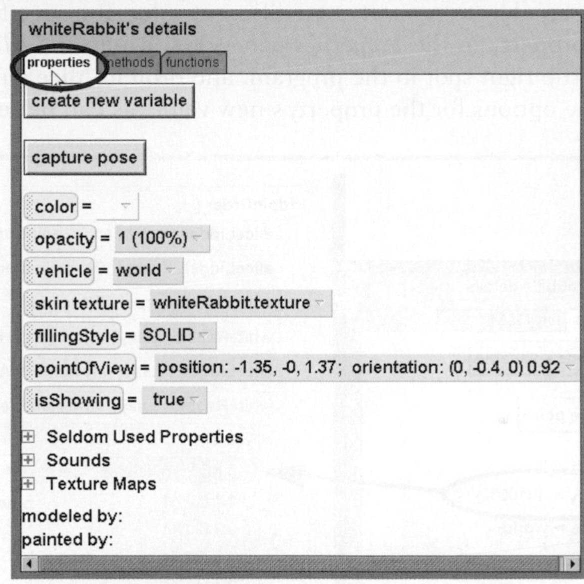

FIGURE 1-19 The *properties* pane

Here, we can see an object's properties, including its color, opacity, vehicle, skin texture, fill style, point of view (position + orientation), and whether or not it is showing.

The values of an object's properties determine the object's appearance and behavior when you run your program. Feel free to experiment with these settings, to see what they do. (You can always use Alice's **Undo** button if you make a mistake.) For example, if the White Rabbit's ghost were an object in the story, we might add a **whiteRabbit** to the world, and change its opacity to 30%, so that 70% of the light in the world passes through him. The result would be a ghostly translucent **whiteRabbit** in the program.

Changing A Property From Within A Program

When you set an object's property to a value within the *properties* pane, that property has that value when your program begins running, and will keep that value unless your program causes it to change. For example, suppose that we wanted the White Rabbit to magically disappear after he and Alice have greeted us, and Alice to then say, "Now where did he go this time?" We can easily elicit the required behavior from **aliceLiddel** by sending her a **say()** message; but how do we get the **whiteRabbit** to disappear before she says it?

There are actually two ways to accomplish this special effect. If we desire the White Rabbit to disappear instantly, we can do this by setting his **isShowing** property to **false** at the right place in the program. If we want him to disappear slowly (say, over the course of a few seconds), we can do this by setting his **opacity** property to **0** at the right place in the program, and then modifying the statement's **duration** attribute to the required length of time. Either approach requires that we learn how to set one of the **whiteRabbit**'s properties, so we will use the latter approach, and leave the use of the first approach as an exercise.

To set an object's property to a different value at a specific point in the program, we click that property in the *properties* pane, drag it into the *editing area* until a green bar appears at the right spot in the program, and drop it. Alice will then display a drop-down menu of the options for the property's new value, as can be seen in Figure 1-20.

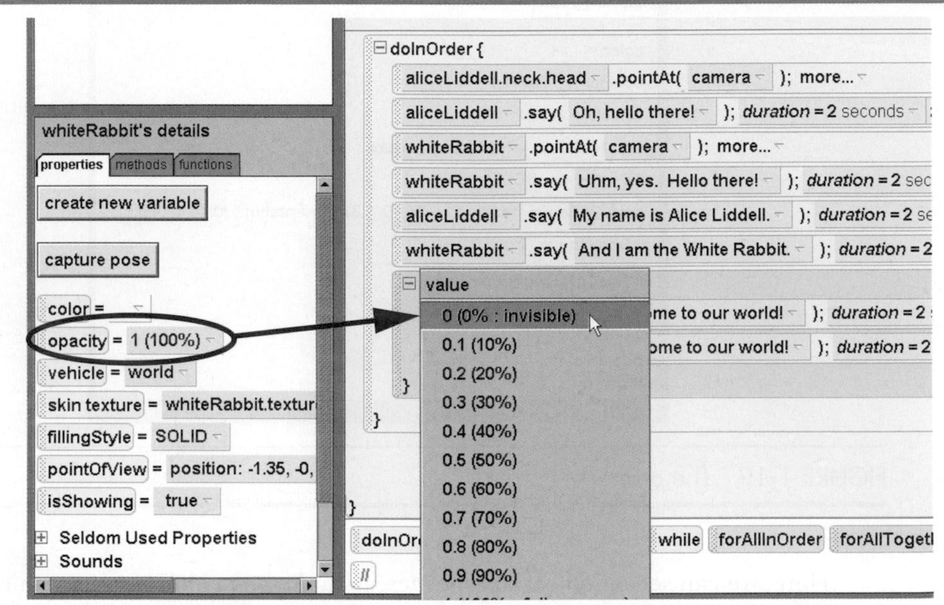

FIGURE 1-20 Setting a property by dragging it into the editing area

When we select a value from that menu, Alice inserts a new statement into the *editing area*. This statement sends a special **set()** message to the **whiteRabbit**, telling it to set its **opacity** property to the value we selected from the menu. By default, the **duration** of this **set()** message is one second, so to make the White Rabbit disappear more slowly, we set it to two seconds, yielding the statement shown in Figure 1-21.

```
doTogether {
    aliceLiddell .say( Welcome to our world! ); duration = 2 seconds  fontSize = 30  more...
    whiteRabbit .say( Welcome to our world! ); duration = 2 seconds  fontSize = 30  more...
}
whiteRabbit .set( opacity, 0 (0%) ); duration = 2 seconds  more...
}
```

FIGURE 1-21 The special `set()` message Alice generates to set a property

Adding the statement to make Alice say "Now where did he go this time?" is straightforward, and is left as an exercise.

1.5.2 The *methods* Pane

Click the *methods* tab of the *details area* and you will see the behavior-generating messages that you can send to the object selected in the *object tree*. Figure 1-22 shows some of the behavior-generating messages that are common to all Alice objects; a complete list is given in Appendix A.

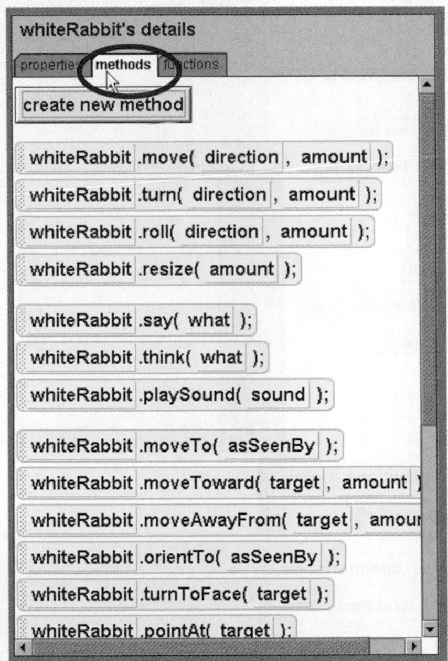

FIGURE 1-22 The *methods* pane

These messages provide a rich set of operations that, together with the **doTogether** and **doInOrder** controls, let us build complex animations. Since we can send these messages to any Alice object, they allow us to build worlds containing talking animals, dancing trees, singing buildings, and just about anything else we can imagine!

The **resize()** message is especially fun, as it lets you make an object change size (for example, **resize(2)** to grow twice as big, or **resize(0.5)** to shrink to half size) as your program runs. The **resize()** message's **more...** menu includes a **dimension** choice that you can use to change an object's *width* (**LEFT_TO_RIGHT**), *height* (**TOP_TO_BOTTOM**), or *depth* (**FRONT_TO_BACK**), letting you create some interesting visual effects as your program runs.

In addition to these basic messages, some Alice objects respond to additional (non-basic) messages. For example, in the **People** folder of the Alice Gallery are tools called the **heBuilder** and **sheBuilder** that allow you to build custom male and female characters for your world. Each "person" built using one of these tools will respond to the additional messages. Figure 1-23 shows a person built using the **heBuilder**, whom we have renamed **bob**, and the non-basic messages that can be sent to such a person.

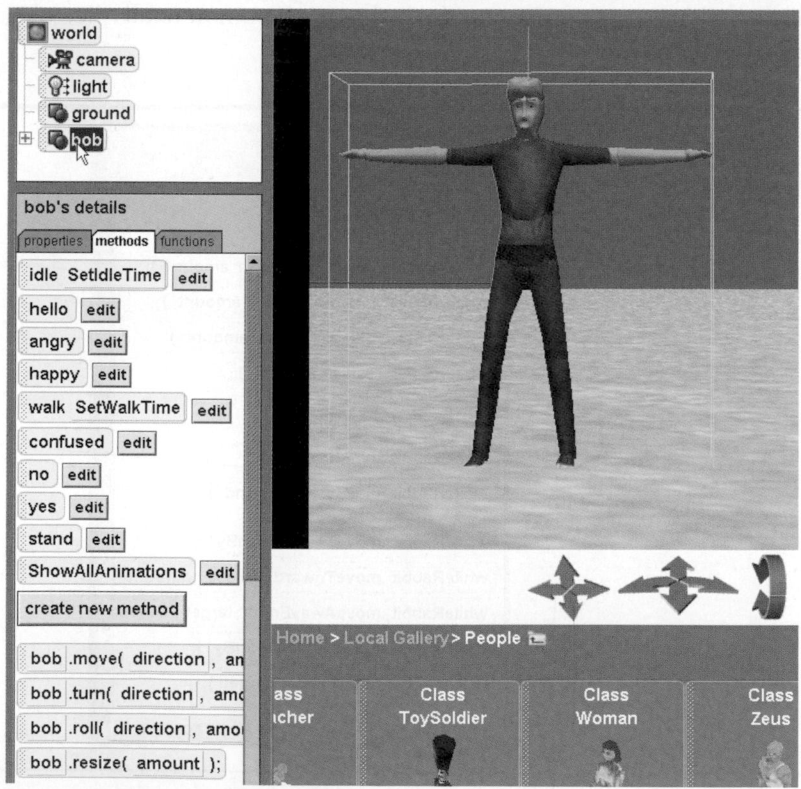

FIGURE 1-23 Non-basic methods

Other Alice classes (for example, **`Frog`**, **`Monkey`**, **`Penguin`**) provide different non-basic methods. To discover them, just add an object to your world and see what methods appear in the *details area*.

1.5.3 The *functions* Pane

If we click the *functions* tab in the *details area* as shown in Figure 1-24, we will see the list of functions or question messages that we can send to the object selected in the *object tree*.

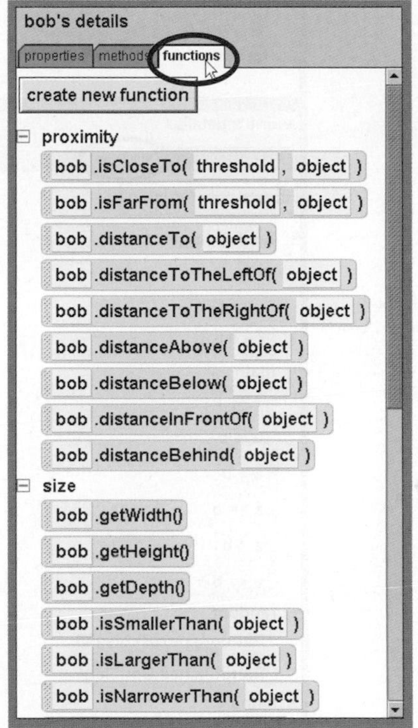

FIGURE 1-24 The *functions* pane

Functions are messages that we can send to an object to retrieve information from it. Where the *methods* tab provides standard behavior-generating messages, the *functions* tab provides a set of standard messages that we can send to an object to "ask it a question." The standard Alice functions let us ask an object about its:

- **proximity** to another object (that is, how close or how far the other object is)
- **size** (its *height*, *width*, or *depth*, and how these compare to another object)
- **spatial relation** to another object (*position* or *orientation* with respect to the other object)
- **point of view** (*position* and *orientation* within the world)
- **subparts**

Many of these standard functions refer to an object's bounding box (or one of its edges) that we saw in Section 1.4.3.

Alice also provides a different group of function messages we can send to the world. That is, if we select the **world** object and then the *functions* tab, Alice displays a group of world functions, some of which are shown in Figure 1-25.

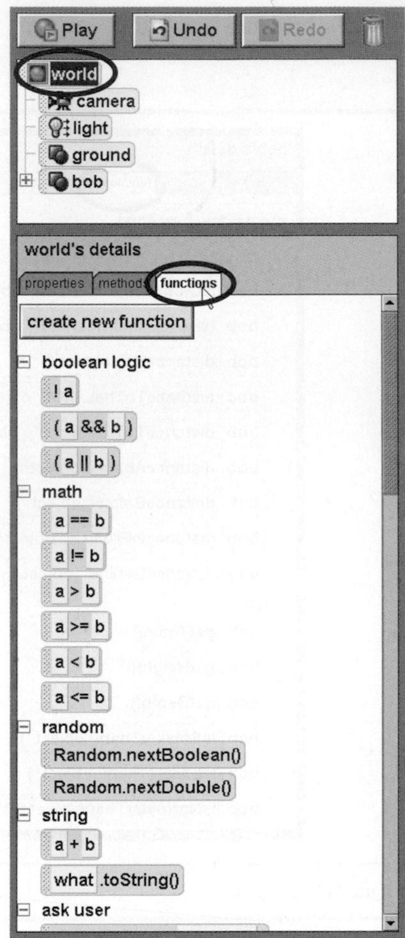

FIGURE 1-25 The *world functions* pane

We will see how to use these different kinds of messages in the coming chapters.

1.6 Alice Tip: Positioning Objects Using Quad View

In the Alice tutorials, we saw how the **ADD OBJECTS** button in the *world window* lets us navigate the Alice Gallery, locate classes, and use them to add objects to the world.

By default, **ADD OBJECTS** displays just the *world window*. However, trying to position two objects in close proximity to one another (for example, trying to position a person on the back of a horse) can be difficult using this single window, since it offers just one view. For such situations, Alice has the **quad view** that provides the *world window*, plus views from the top, right, and front of the scene. To use it, click the **quad view** radio button near the top of the window, as shown in Figure 1-26.

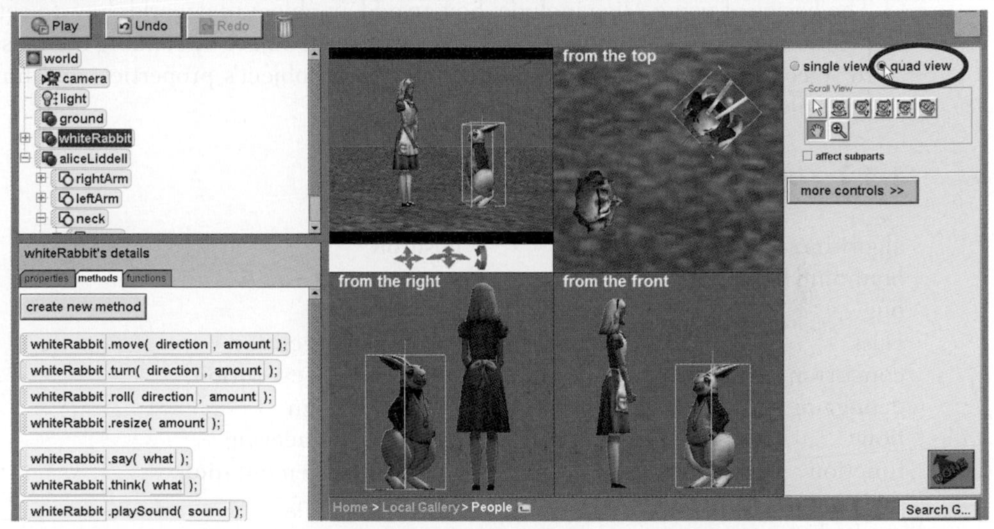

FIGURE 1-26 The quad view

As can be seen above, the quad view provides two additional controls:

- a "hand" control that lets you (within any of the views) drag the mouse to move the camera left, right, up, or down to view a different part of the scene
- a "magnifying glass" control that lets you drag the mouse *down* to zoom the camera *in* on some detail of the scene, or drag *up* to zoom the camera *out* to see more of the scene

These additional controls are very useful when you shift to the quad view and the characters you wanted to see are nowhere to be seen. When this happens, just click the magnifying glass and then drag *up* within the view to zoom out until the characters become visible (probably very small), switch to the hand control and move the camera until the characters are centered, then switch back to the magnifying glass and drag *down* within the view to zoom back in.

1.7 Chapter Summary

- The *user story* describes the behavior of a computer program.
- *Storyboard-sketches* indicate the appearance of each of the program's scenes.
- *Transition diagrams* relate the storyboard-sketches to one another.
- A *flow* or *algorithm* provides a concise summary of the user story.
- The basics of using Alice include: how to add an object to a world; how to set its initial position, orientation, and pose; how to animate an object by sending it a message; how to select an object's subparts; how to change an object's properties; and how to send multiple messages simultaneously.

1.7.1 Key Terms

algorithm
bounding box
bug
class
concurrent execution
debugging
flow
function
message
method
object
orientation
point of view
position
pose
property
sequential execution
simultaneous execution
software design
software engineering
software implementation
software testing
statement
storyboard-sketches
user story

Programming Projects

1.1 Modify the world we created in Section 1.4 so that, after Alice and the White Rabbit introduce themselves, Alice tells the user she and the White Rabbit would like to sing a duet, after which they sing a simple song, such as *Mary Had A Little Lamb*. Have Alice and the White Rabbit sing alternate lines of the song.

Mary had a little lamb, *little lamb,* *little lamb.* *Mary had a little lamb* *it's fleece was white as snow.*	*And everywhere that Mary went,* *Mary went,* *Mary went.* *And everywhere that Mary went* *the lamb was sure to go.*
It followed her to school one day, *school one day,* *school one day.* *It followed her to school one day* *which was against the rules.*	*It made the children laugh and play,* *laugh and play,* *laugh and play.* *It made the children laugh and play* *to see a lamb at school.*

1.2 Finish the world we modified in Section 1.5.1, so that the movie ends with **aliceLiddell** saying, *Now where did he go this time?* Modify the world so that the **whiteRabbit** disappears instantly. Modify the world to make a **pop** sound when the **whiteRabbit** disappears.

1.3 If your computer has a microphone, modify the world we created in Section 1.4, using **doTogether** controls and **playSound()** messages to record voices for Alice and the White Rabbit, so that the user can hear what each character says instead of having to read it. Alter your voice for each character.

1.4 Using any two characters from the Alice Gallery, design and build a world in which one tells the other a knock-knock joke. (If you don't know any knock-knock jokes, see **www.knock-knock-joke.com**). Make your story end with both characters laughing.

1.5 Using the **heBuilder** or **sheBuilder** (under **People** in the **Local Gallery**), build a superhero named **Resizer**, who can alter his or her size at will. Build a world in which **Resizer** demonstrates his or her powers to the user by growing and shrinking. Make sure that **Resizer** tells the user what he or she is going to do before doing it.

1.6 Build a world containing one of the hopping animals (for example, a bunny or a frog). Write a program that makes the animal hop once, as realistically as possible (that is, legs extending and retracting, head bobbing, and so on). Bonus: Send your animal **playSound()** messages, so that the predefined sound **thud1** is played as it leaves the ground, **whoosh2** is played while it is in the air, and **thud2** is played when it lands.

1.7 Using the **heBuilder** or **sheBuilder** (under **People** in the **Local Gallery**), build a person. Place the person in a world containing a building. Using the **walk()**, **move()**, and **turn()** messages, write a program that makes him or her walk around the building.

1.8 Using the **heBuilder** or **sheBuilder** (under **People** in the **Local Gallery**), build a person. Then build a world containing your person and one of the items from the **Sports** section of the Gallery (for example, a baseball or a basketball). Write a program in which your person uses the item for that sport (for example, pitches the baseball or dribbles the basketball).

1.9 Choose one of your favorite movie scenes that contains just two or three characters. Use Alice to create an animated version of that scene, substituting characters from the Alice Gallery for the characters in the movie.

1.10 Write an original short story (10-20 seconds long), and use Alice to create an animated version of it. Your story should have at least two characters, and each character should perform at least five actions that combine to make an interesting story.

1.11 *Mules* is a silly (and confusing!) song with the lyrics shown below (sung to the tune of *Auld Lang Syne*). Build a world containing a horse (the closest thing in the Alice Gallery to a mule) and a person. Build a program that animates the person and horse appropriately while the person "sings" the lyrics to the song. For example, the person should point to the different legs (front or back) as he or she sings about them, move to the back of the horse when the song calls for it, get kicked as the sixth line is sung, and so on.

On mules we find two legs behind,
and two we find before.
We stand behind before we find,
what the two behind be for!

When we're behind the two behind,
we find what these be for —
so stand before the two behind,
behind the two before!

Chapter 2
Methods

Great things can be reduced to small things, and small things can be reduced to nothing.

CHINESE PROVERB

Weeks of programming can save you hours of planning.

ANONYMOUS

When do you show the consequences? On TV, that mouse pulled out that cat's lungs and played them like a bagpipe, but in the next scene, the cat was breathing comfortably.

MARGE SIMPSON (JULIE KAVNER), IN "ITCHY AND SCRATCHY LAND," *THE SIMPSONS*

Objectives

Upon completion of this chapter, you will be able to:

- ❑ Build world-level methods to help organize a story into scenes and shots
- ❑ Build class-level methods to elicit desirable behaviors from objects
- ❑ Reuse a class-level method in multiple worlds
- ❑ Use dummies to reposition the camera for different shots within a scene
- ❑ Understand how an object's *position*, *orientation*, and *point of view* are determined

In the last chapter, we saw how to design and build computer programs. We also saw how Alice lets us build programs consisting of *statements*, in which we often send *messages* to *objects*. Finally, we saw that Alice provides us with a rich set of predefined messages that let us create programs to generate fun and interesting animations.

Alice's predefined messages provide an excellent set of *basic operations* for animation. However, for most Alice objects, these basic operations are *all* that are predefined. (The people we can create using the **`heBuilder`** and **`sheBuilder`** tools are unusual in providing methods beyond the basic ones.) The result is that for many of the behaviors we might want Alice objects to exhibit, there are no predefined methods to elicit those behaviors. For example, a horse should be able to walk, trot, and gallop, but there are no predefined **`Horse`** methods for these behaviors. A dragon or pterodactyl should at least be able to flap its wings (if not fly), but the **`Dragon`** and **`Pterodactyl`** classes do not provide methods for such behavior. A wizard should be able to cast a spell, but the **`Wizard`** class does not contain a **`castSpell`** message.

When an Alice class does not provide a method for a behavior we need, Alice lets us create a new method to provide the behavior. Once we have created the method, we can send the corresponding message to the object to elicit the behavior.

There are actually two quite different reasons for building your own methods. The first reason is to divide your story into manageable pieces to help keep it more organized. The second reason is to provide an object with a behavior it should have, but does not. In this chapter, we will examine both approaches. As we shall see, the motivation, thought process, and circumstances are quite different for these two different approaches.

2.1 World Methods for Scenes and Shots

As we mentioned in Chapter 1, films (and by extension, animations) are often broken down into **scenes**, with each scene making up one piece of the story. Scenes can be further broken down into **shots**, with each shot consisting of a set and whatever characters are in the shot, filmed from a particular camera position. When a film crew has finished one shot, they begin work on the next one. When all the shots for a particular scene are finished, the shots are combined to form the scene and that scene is done. Work then begins on the next scene.

Scenes and shots thus provide a logical and convenient way to break a big film project down into smaller, more manageable pieces. We can use the same approach in Alice. By organizing your user story into a series of scenes, and organizing each complex scene into a series of shots, you can work through the story shot by shot and scene by scene, without being overwhelmed by the size of the project. This approach — in which you solve a "big" problem by (1) breaking it into "small" problems, (2) solving each "small" problem, and (3) combining the "small" problem solutions into a solution to the "big" problem — is called **divide and conquer**.

2.1.1 Methods For Scenes

To illustrate how this approach can be used in Alice, suppose that we have a user story consisting of three scenes. When we first start Alice (even before we have added any objects to the world), we can organize our Alice program to reflect the scene structure of our user story. To create a method for our first scene, we first select **world** in the *object tree*, make certain that the *methods* tab is selected in the *details area*, and then click the **create new method** button there, as shown in Figure 2-1.

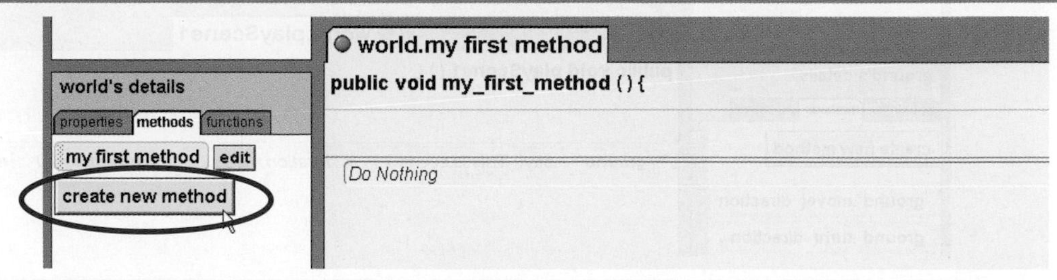

FIGURE 2-1 The **create new method** button

Clicking this box pops up a small **New Method** dialog box into which we can type the name we wish to give the new method. A method name should usually be (1) a *verb* or *verb phrase*, and (2) descriptive of what it does. Since we are creating a method to play the first scene, we will choose the name **playScene1**.

> Method names should begin with a lowercase letter and contain no spaces. If a name consists of multiple words, capitalize the first letter of each word after the first.

When we click the **New Method** dialog box's **OK** button, Alice does two things:

1. Alice creates a new pane in the *editing area*, labeled **world.playScene1**, containing an empty method definition for the **playScene1()** method.
2. Alice updates the *details area*, adding **playScene1** to the world's list of methods.

If you compare Figure 2-2 (below) to Figure 2-1, you will see both of these changes.

FIGURE 2-2 A new **playScene1()** method

One way to check that the method is working is to send a **say()** message to the world's **ground** object in **playScene1()**, as shown in Figure 2-3.[1]

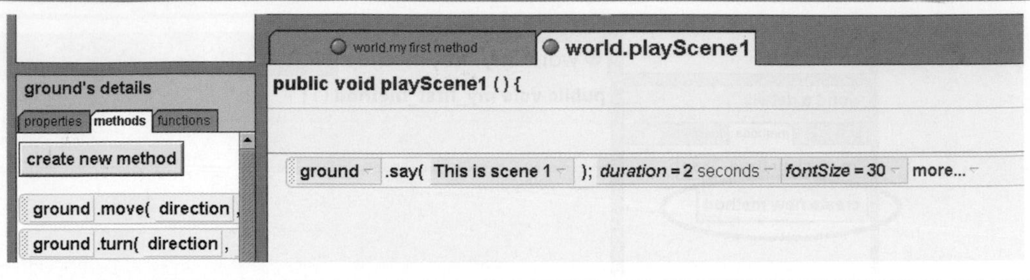

FIGURE 2-3 A simple method test

However, when we click Alice's **Play** button, the warning dialog box in Figure 2-4 appears.

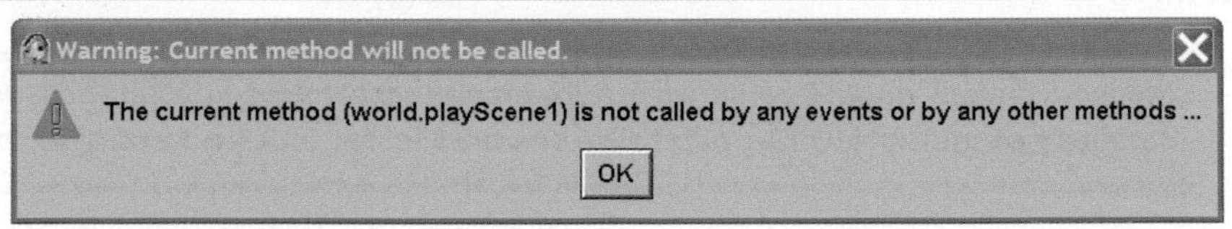

FIGURE 2-4 The "Method Not Called" warning

Alice is warning us that although we have *defined* a new method, there are no statements in the program that send the corresponding message. The problem is that **my_first_method()** is empty, and since that is where the program begins running, we need to send the **playScene1()** message from within **my_first_method()**.

After carefully reading the warning, we click the **OK** button to close that window, and then close the **World Running** window that appears. We then click on the tab for **my_first_method** in the *editing area*, drag a **doInOrder** control up from the bottom of the pane, click on **world** in the *object tree*, and then drag the **playScene1()** message from the *details area* into the **doInOrder** statement, giving us the (short) program shown in Figure 2-5.

1. Another approach is to have the method perform a **print()** statement, which is at the bottom of the *editing area*. When performed, this statement displays a message at the bottom of the **World Running** window, but it is awkward to view. (We had to resize the window and then scroll up to see the message.) The **print()** statement can also be used to view the value of a variable or parameter (see Chapter 3) when the statement is performed.

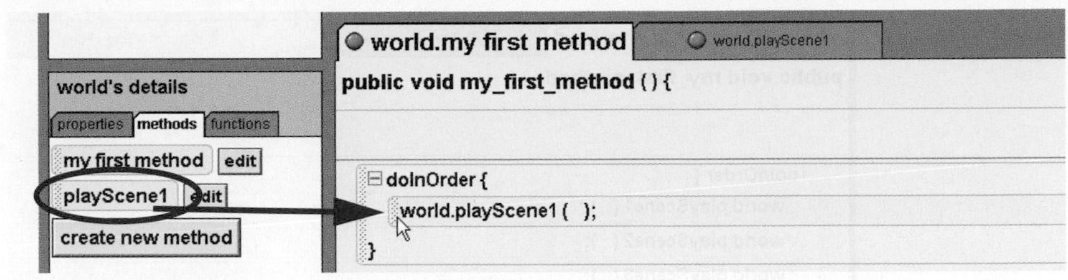

FIGURE 2-5 Sending **playScene1()** from **my_first_method()**

Now, when we click Alice's **Play** button, **world.my_first_method()** begins running. It sends the **playScene1()** message to **world**, which sends the **say()** message to the **ground**. If we've done everything correctly, we will see the **ground** "speak," as can be seen in Figure 2-6.

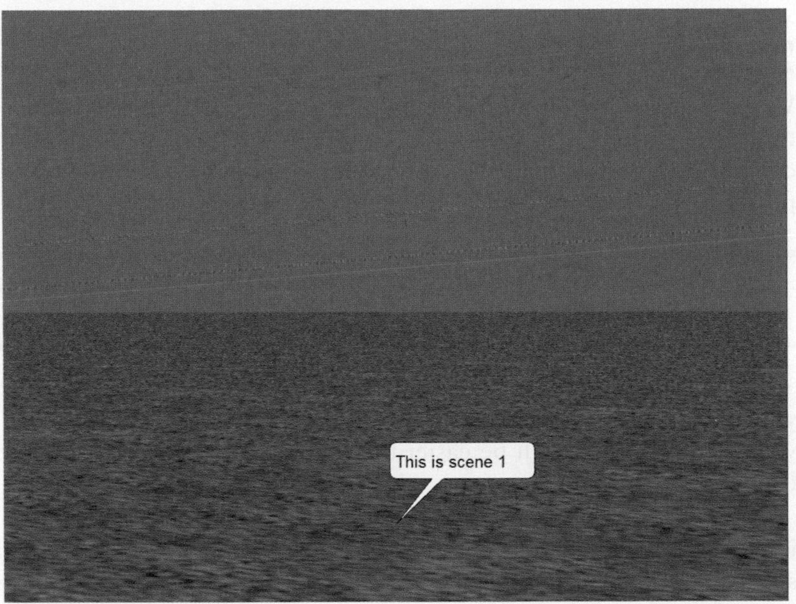

FIGURE 2-6 The **ground** speaks

Since the user story consists of three scenes, we can use this same approach to create new methods for the remaining two scenes, giving us the **my_first_method()** shown in Figure 2-7.

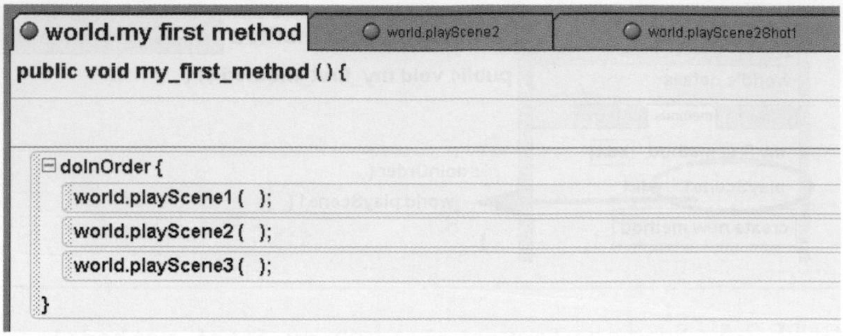

```
world.my first method | world.playScene2 | world.playScene2Shot1
public void my_first_method () {

  doInOrder {
    world.playScene1 ( );
    world.playScene2 ( );
    world.playScene3 ( );
  }
```

FIGURE 2-7 Three new **playScene()** methods

Inside each new **playScene** method, we can send the **ground** a distinct **say()** message (for example, naming that scene). Clicking Alice's **Play** button should then display those messages in order. This is a simple way to test that the new methods are working properly. When we are confident that all is well, we can begin adding statements to **playScene1()** to perform the first scene, adding statements to **playScene2()** to perform the second scene, and so on.

2.1.2 Methods For Shots

We have just seen how a big, complicated project can be broken down into smaller, easier-to-program scenes. However in a *very* big project, a scene itself may be overwhelmingly complicated! In such situations, complex scenes can be divided into simpler (easier-to-program) **shots**. One good rule of thumb is:

> If you must use the scroll bar to view all the statements in a scene method, divide it into two or more shot methods.

The idea is that long methods are complicated, and therefore more error prone. If you keep your methods short and sweet, you'll be less likely to make a mistake — and if you do make one, it will be easier to find, since you won't have to scroll back and forth through lots of statements.

To illustrate this idea, suppose that the first scene is reasonably simple, and can be implemented in a method that requires no scrolling. However, suppose that the second scene is quite complicated, and we estimate that building it would require four or more screenfuls of statements. We can use an approach similar to what we did in Section 2.1.1 to create a method for each shot. Being systematic, we might name these methods **playScene2Shot1**, **playScene2Shot2**, **playScene2Shot3**, and **playScene2Shot4**.

As before, we select **world** in the *object tree*, and then click the **create new method** button in the *details area*. When asked to name the first method, we name it **playScene2Shot1**. As before, Alice (1) updates the *editing area* with a new pane containing an empty definition for the new method, and (2) adds the new method to the list of methods in the *details area*. To test that it works, we can again send the **ground** object a **say()** message, as shown in Figure 2-8.

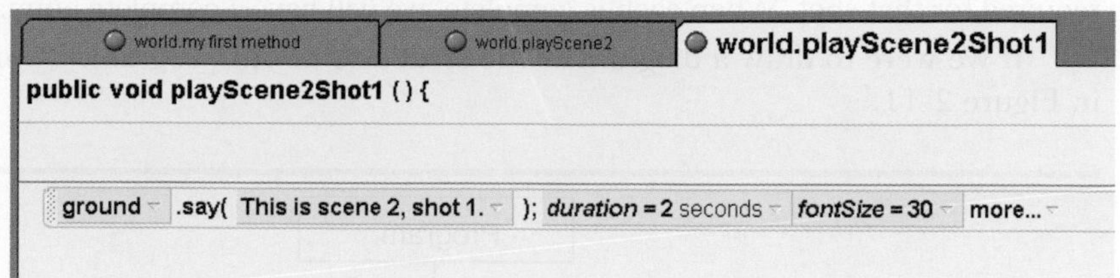

FIGURE 2-8 Testing a shot method

We can then select **`world`** in the *object tree*, click on the **`world.playScene2`** tab in the *editing area*, delete the **`ground.say()`** message from **`playScene2()`**, drag a **`doInOrder`** control into **`playScene2()`**, and finally drag the **`playScene2Shot1()`** message from the *details area* into the **`doInOrder`** statement, yielding the definition found in Figure 2-9.

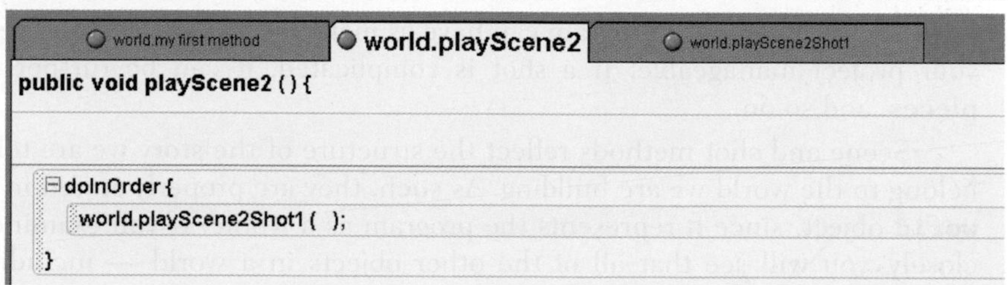

FIGURE 2-9 Calling a shot method from a scene method

If we repeat this for each of the remaining shots in the scene, we get the definition shown in Figure 2-10.

```
world.playScene2Shot2    world.playScene2Shot3    world.playScene2Shot4
world.my first method    world.playScene2    world.playScene2Shot1
public void playScene2 () {                 create new parameter
                                            create new variable
doInOrder {
  world.playScene2Shot1 ( );
  world.playScene2Shot2 ( );
  world.playScene2Shot3 ( );
  world.playScene2Shot4 ( );
}
```

FIGURE 2-10 A scene method built from shot methods

Now we can add statements to each of the four shot methods to produce the animation required for that shot. When each is complete, we will have a complete animation for Scene 2!

If we were to draw a diagram of the structure of our program, it would be as shown in Figure 2-11.

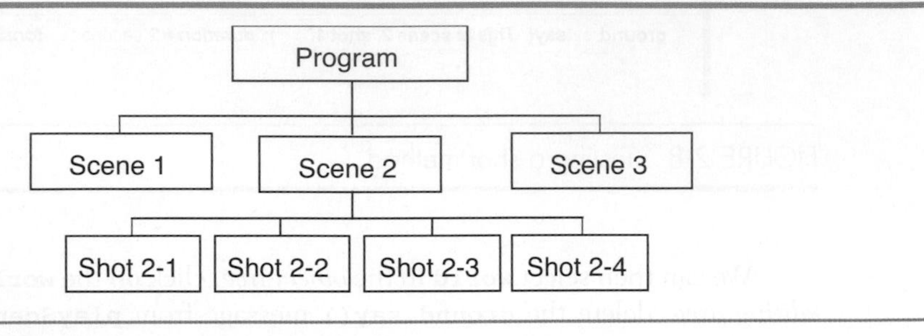

FIGURE 2-11 Structure diagram

Such a diagram or program can have as many pieces and levels as necessary to make your project manageable. If a shot is complicated, it can be further subdivided into **pieces**, and so on.

Scene and shot methods reflect the structure of the story we are telling, and hence belong to the world we are building. As such, they are properly stored in the *object tree*'s **`world`** object, since it represents the program as a whole. If you examine the *object tree* closely, you will see that all of the other objects in a world — including the **`camera`**, **`light`**, **`ground`**, and anything else we add to the world — are parts of the **`world`**. Because we store scene and shot messages in the **`world`** object, these messages must be sent to it, as we see in Figure 2-10.

In Alice, methods stored in the **`world`** are called **world methods**, because they define a message that is sent to the **`world`**. A method that affects the behavior of *multiple objects* (like a scene) should be defined as a world method.

2.2 Object Methods for Object Behaviors

An alternative to the world method is the **object method**, which is used to define a complex behavior for a *single object*. Where a world method usually controls the behavior of multiple objects (for example, each character in a scene), an object method controls the behavior of just one object — the object to which the corresponding message will be sent.

2.2.1 Example 1: Telling a Dragon to Flap Its Wings

To illustrate how to build an object method, let's create a new story starring a dragon who lives in the desert, as shown in Figure 2-12. Suppose that in one or more of this story's scenes, the dragon must flap its wings. Wing-flapping is a reasonably complex behavior, and it would be convenient if we could send a **`flapWings()`** message to a **`dragon`** object, but class **Dragon** does not provide a **flapWings()** method. In general, the following rule of thumb should be used in defining methods:

Methods that control the behavior of a single object should be stored in that object.

From another perspective, a dragon is responsible for controlling its wings, so a **flapWings()** message should also be sent to a **dragon**. To do so, the **flapWings()** method must be stored in the **dragon** object. Conversely, it makes no sense to send the **world** a **flapWings()** message (since it has no wings to flap), so **flapWings()** should *not* be defined as a world method.

Assuming that we have added a **dragon** to the **world**, we can define a **dragon** method named **flapWings()** as follows. We first select **dragon** in the *object tree*, and click the *methods* tab in the *details area*. Above the list of **dragon** methods, we see the **create new method** button, as can be seen in Figure 2-12.

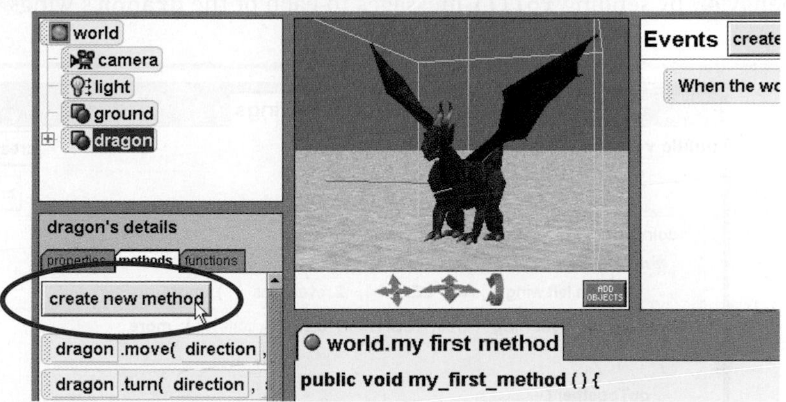

FIGURE 2-12 Creating a new class-level method

As we have seen before, clicking this button generates a dialog box asking us for the name of the new method, in which we can type **flapWings**. Alice then (1) creates a new tabbed pane in the *editing area* labeled **flapWings** containing an empty definition of a **flapWings()** method, and (2) creates an entry for the new method in the *details area* above the **create new method** button, as shown in Figure 2-13.

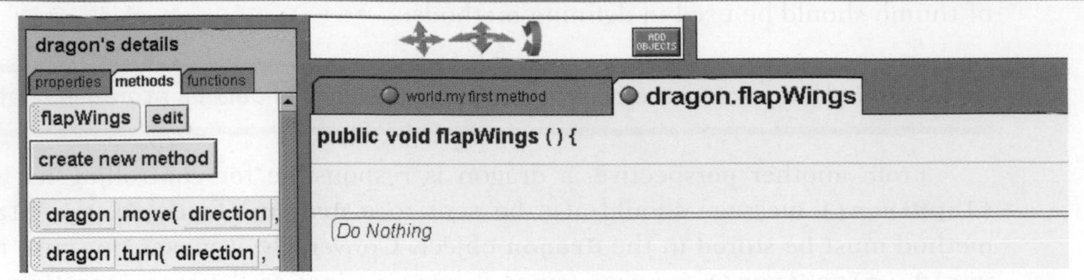

FIGURE 2-13 The empty `flapWings()` method

We can then fill this empty method definition with the statements needed to elicit the desired wing-flapping behavior. Figure 2-14 shows one way we might define such behavior, by sending **`roll()`** messages to each of the **`dragon`**'s wings.

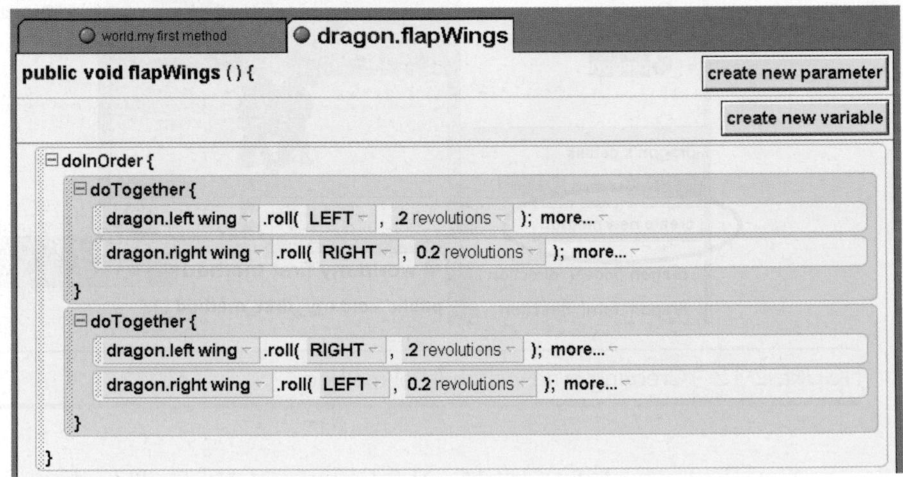

FIGURE 2-14 One way to define a `flapWings()` method

Comments

It may take you some time to figure out why each statement that appears in Figure 2-14 is there. Puzzling out the purpose of statements consumes time that could be better spent on other activities.

To help human readers understand why a method's statements are there, good programmers insert **comments** into their methods to explain the purpose of tricky statements. Comments are ignored by Alice, so you can write whatever is needed by way of explanation.

To add a comment to a method in Alice, click on the *comment control* at the bottom of the *editing area*, drag the control upwards until the green bar appears above the statements you want to explain, and then drop the control, as shown in Figure 2-15.

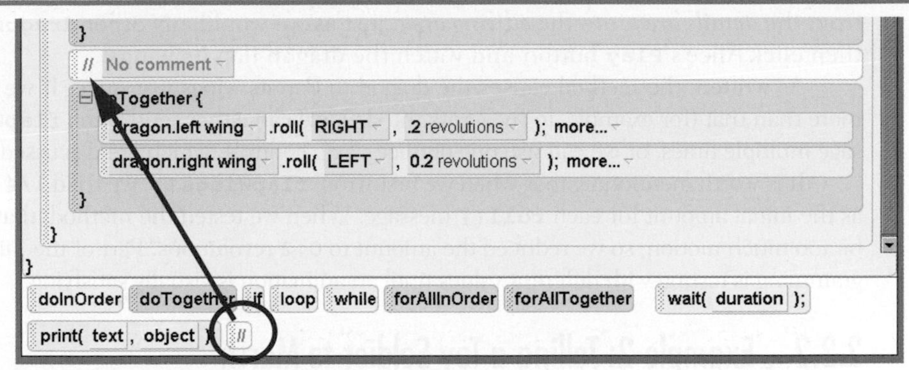

FIGURE 2-15 Dragging a comment

When you drop the comment, Alice gives it a **No comment** label. To edit a comment's explanation, you can either double-click its text, or click its list arrow and choose **other** from the menu that appears. Figure 2-16 shows a final, commented version of the **flapWings()** method.

```
world.my first method    dragon.flapWings
public void flapWings ( ) {                create new parameter
                                           create new variable
  doInOrder {
    // Downstroke: make both wings flap DOWN together
    doTogether {
      dragon.left wing .roll( LEFT , .2 revolutions ); more...
      dragon.right wing .roll( RIGHT , 0.2 revolutions ); more...
    }
    // Upstroke: make both wings flap UP together
    doTogether {
      dragon.left wing .roll( RIGHT , .2 revolutions ); more...
      dragon.right wing .roll( LEFT , 0.2 revolutions ); more...
    }
  }
}
```

FIGURE 2-16 Final **flapWings()** method

Testing

To test the **flapWings()** method, we switch to **my_first_method()** — or to a world method that **my_first_method()** invokes, such as the scene method in which the dragon flaps its wings — select **dragon** in the *object tree*, and then drag **flapWings()** from the *details area* into the *editing area*, just as we would any other **dragon** method. We then click Alice's **Play** button and watch the dragon flap its wings!

As written, the method causes the dragon to flap its wings just once. If we need it to flap more than that (for example, to fly across the sky), we can either send it the **flapWings()** message multiple times, or we can use one of Alice's *loop* controls, which are discussed in Chapter 4.

It is worth mentioning that when we first wrote **flapWings()**, we tried **1/4 revolution** as the initial amount for each **roll()** message. When we tested the method, that seemed like a bit too much motion; so we reduced the amount to **0.2** revolutions. Part of the "art" of Alice programming is testing with different values until an animation is visually satisfying.

2.2.2 Example 2: Telling a Toy Soldier to March

Suppose we have a different story,[2] containing a scene in which a toy soldier is to march across the screen. There is a **ToySoldier** class in the Alice Gallery; unfortunately, this class contains no **march()** method. So let's build one! We can do so by defining an object method named **march()** in the **toySoldier**.

Design

It is always a good idea to spend time designing before we start programming, especially with a complex behavior like marching. If we think this behavior through step-by-step (Ha, ha! Get it? Step? Marching?), we might break it down into the following algorithm:

ALGORITHM 2-1 Behavior: The ToySoldier should:

```
1 move forward 1/4 step; simultaneously his left leg rotates forward,
  his right leg rotates backward, his left arm rotates backward, his
  right arm rotates forward;

2 move forward 1/4 step; simultaneously his left leg rotates backward,
  his right leg rotates forward, his left arm rotates forward, his
  right arm rotates backward;

3 move forward 1/4 step; simultaneously his right leg rotates forward,
  his left leg rotates backward, his right arm rotates backward, and
  his left arm rotates forward;

4 move forward 1/4 step; simultaneously his right leg rotates back-
  ward, his left leg rotates forward, his right arm rotates forward,
  and his left arm rotates backward.
```

We can figure out just how much each arm or leg needs to rotate later, when we test the method. The thing to notice is that, because the actions within each step are occuring simultaneously, *Steps 1 and 4, and Steps 2 and 3 describe exactly the same behaviors*! For

2. Whenever we begin a new story or change to a different story, you will need to save your current world (using **File -> Save World**), and then open a new world (using **File -> New World**).

lack of better names, we might call Step 1 *marchLeft* and call Step 2 *marchRight*. If we were to write methods for these two steps, then the algorithm simplifies to this:

```
marchLeft;
marchRight;
marchRight;
marchLeft.
```

To move the soldier forward, we send him the **move()** message. To make his arms and legs rotate appropriately, we send **turn()** messages to his subparts. After some trial-and-error to find good **move()** and **turn()** distances, we get a definition like the one shown in Figure 2-17.

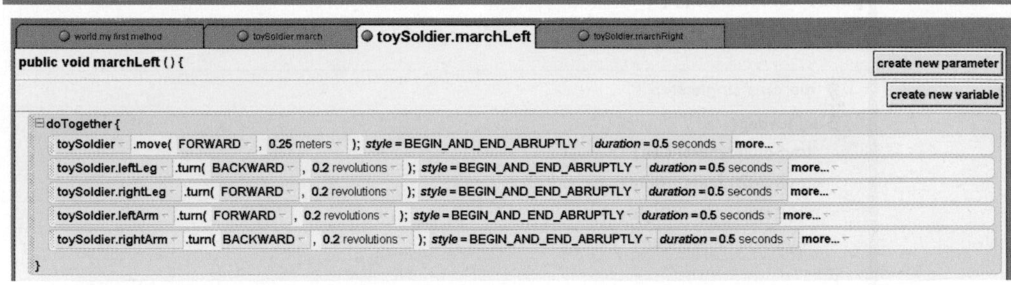

FIGURE 2-17 The **marchLeft()** method

The **marchRight()** method is similar, but with the behaviors reversed, as given in Figure 2-18.

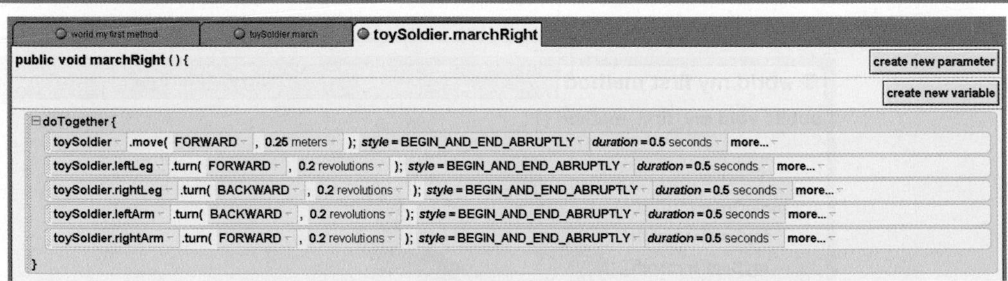

FIGURE 2-18 The **marchRight()** method

You may be wondering why in Figure 2-17 and Figure 2-18 we set each **move()** and **turn()** message's **style** attribute to **BEGIN_AND_END_ABRUPTLY**. The reason is that using this **style** smooths out the animation and makes it less "jerky." More precisely, by using this **style**, the first sending of **marchLeft()** will end abruptly, and since **marchRight()** begins abruptly, it will commence *immediately*. When it ends (abruptly), the second sending of **marchRight()** will begin without delay. And when it ends (abruptly), the second sending of **marchLeft()** will begin with no delay.

> *If you find that your animations are moving in a "jerky" fashion, try setting the* **style** *of the animation's messages to* **BEGIN_AND_END_ABRUPTLY**.

With these two methods in place, the **march()** method is quite simple, as shown in Figure 2-19.

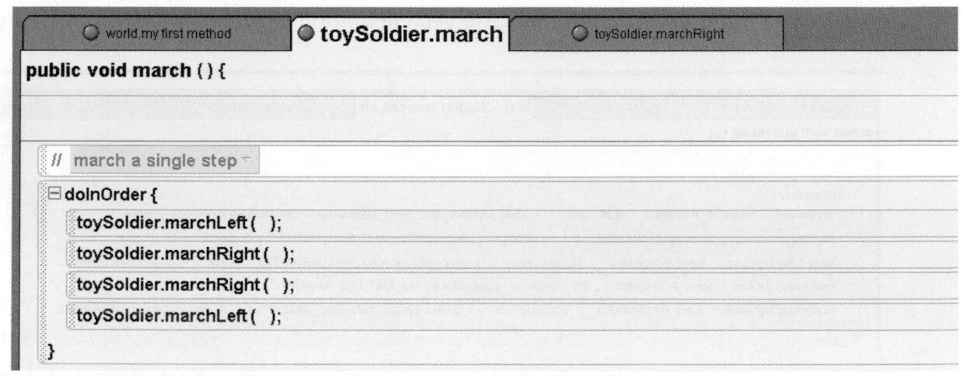
world.my first method
toySoldier.march
toySoldier.marchRight
public void march () {
// march a single step
doInOrder {
toySoldier.marchLeft ( );
toySoldier.marchRight ( );
toySoldier.marchRight ( );
toySoldier.marchLeft ( );
}

FIGURE 2-19 The **march()** method

To test the **march()** method, we can send the **toySoldier** the **march()** message, either from the scene in which it is needed or from **my_first_method()**. Figure 2-20 shows the latter.

world.my first method
toySoldier.march
toySoldier.marchRight
public void my_first_method () {
doInOrder {
toySoldier.march ( );
toySoldier.march ( );
toySoldier.march ( );
toySoldier.march ( );
}

FIGURE 2-20 Testing the **march()** method

Now, when we click Alice's **Play** button, the soldier marches across the scene!

2.3 Alice Tip: Reusing Your Work

If you right-click on a statement, Alice displays a menu containing a **`make copy`** choice. Selecting this choice duplicates that statement. For example, in creating the program in Figure 2-20, we dragged **`toySoldier.march();`** into the *editing area* just once, and then used this right-click **`make copy`** mechanism to rapidly duplicate that statement three times.

This mechanism can also save time when you need to do similar, but not identical, things in a method. For example, to build the **`flapWings()`** method shown in Figure 2-16, we first built the top **`doTogether`** statement that makes the dragon's wings move down. We then made a copy of that statement, and in that copy, reversed the direction of the **`roll()`** messages, changing **`LEFT`** to **`RIGHT`** in the first message, and **`RIGHT`** to **`LEFT`** in the second message. This was much easier (and faster) than building the bottom **`doTogether`** statement from scratch.

In the rest of this section, we examine two other ways you can reuse existing work.

2.3.1 Using the Clipboard

The right-click **`make copy`** mechanism is useful when you have a statement that you want to duplicate *within* a particular method. But suppose you have written a statement in one method that you want to reuse in a different method.

For example, suppose you are programming a scene method, and producing the desired behavior takes more statements than anticipated. Viewing the method requires you to scroll back and forth, so you decide to break the scene up among two or more shot methods. How can you move the statements already in your scene method into a new (empty) shot method?

The answer is the **Alice clipboard**, located above the *events area* in the upper-right corner of the screen. From the *editing area*, you can drag any statement onto the clipboard and Alice will store a copy of it there for you, as shown in Figure 2-21.

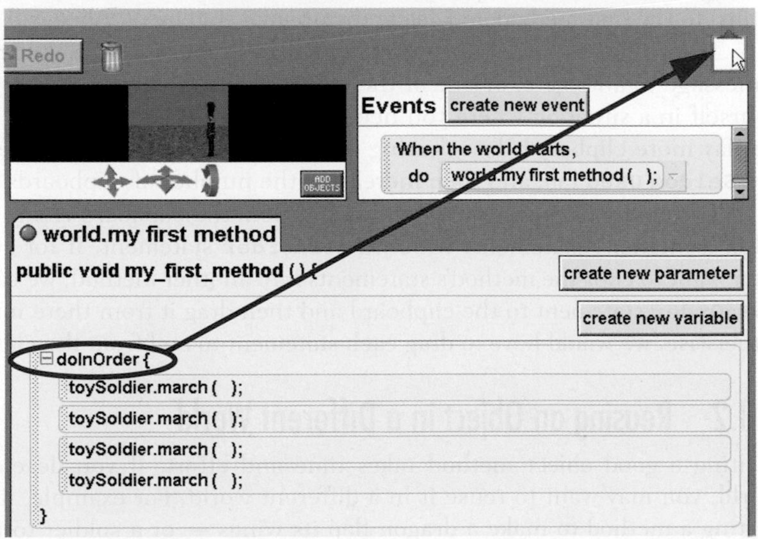

FIGURE 2-21 Dragging a statement to the clipboard

If we then create a new method (that is, for a scene or shot), we can drag the statement from the clipboard and drop it into that method, as shown in Figure 2-22.

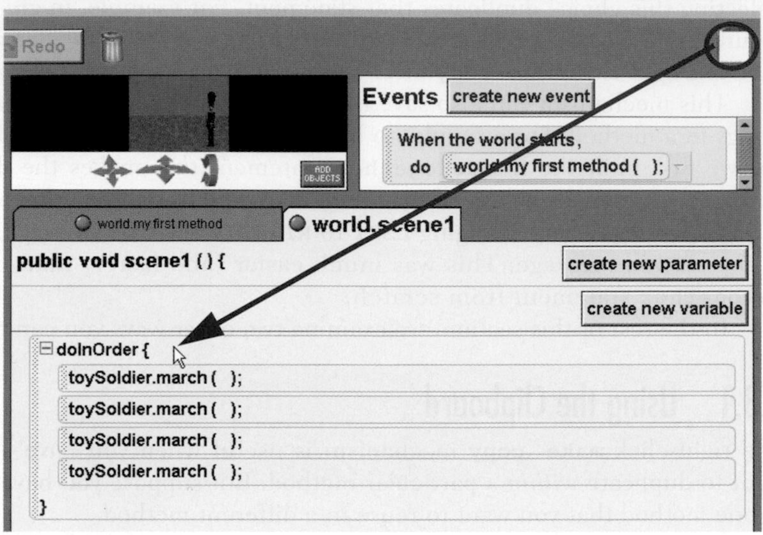

FIGURE 2-22 Dragging a statement from the clipboard

When we drag a statement from the clipboard and drop it in the *editing area*, Alice *copies* the statement from the clipboard. That is, a statement copied to the clipboard remains there until we replace it by dragging another statement onto the clipboard. In this case — where we are *moving* a statement from one method to another — we must then return to the first method and *delete* the original statement; Alice will not delete it for us.

The clipboard holds just one statement, whether it be a **doInOrder**, a **doTogether**, a message to an object, or one of the other Alice statements we will see later. If you find yourself in a situation where you need to store multiple statements, you can tell Alice to display more clipboards by selecting the **Edit -> Preferences** menu choice, selecting the **Seldom Used** tab, and then increasing the number of clipboards as necessary.

The ability to copy a statement to and from the clipboard is one advantage of placing all of a method's statements within a **doInOrder** statement. If for any reason we should later want to copy the method's statements into another method, we can just drag the outer **doInOrder** statement to the clipboard and then drag it from there into the other method. Otherwise, we would have to drag each statement to and from the clipboard individually.

2.3.2 Reusing an Object in a Different World

Writing a good object method takes time and effort. If you develop an object in one world, you may want to reuse it in a different world. For example, if we have spent time writing a method to make a dragon flap its wings — or a soldier to march, or a horse to gallop, or whatever — and we want to reuse that same character with the same behavior in a different world, we do not want to have to redo the work all over again.

Thankfully, Alice lets us reuse an object in different worlds. To do so, follow these steps:

1. In the world containing the original object, right-click it and **rename** it, choosing a new name that describes how it differs from the old object (for example, **marchingSoldier**).
2. Right-click the object again, but this time choose **save object...** Use the **Save Object** dialog box to save the object to your desktop (or anywhere you can find easily).
3. Open the world where you want to reuse the object.
4. Choose **File -> Import...** In the dialog box that appears, navigate to your saved object, select it, and click the **Import** button.

Let's go through these steps using the dragon we modified in Section 2.2.1.

1. First, we give the **dragon** a new name by right-clicking it, choosing **rename**, and then giving it a descriptive name, as shown in Figure 2-23.

FIGURE 2-23 Renaming an object

2. We right-click again, but, as shown in Figure 2-24, this time we choose **save object...** from the menu that appears:

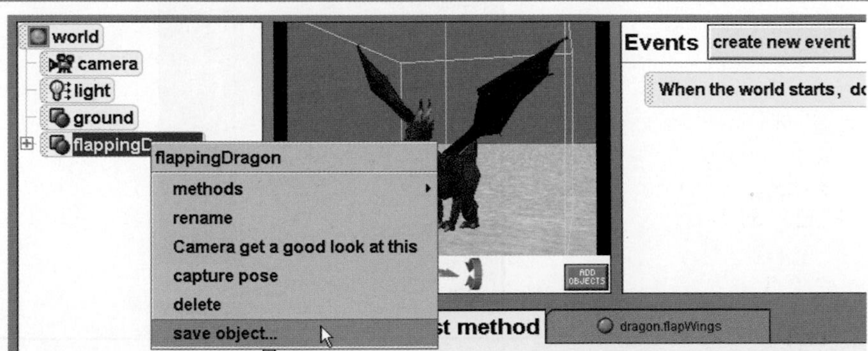

FIGURE 2-24 Saving an object

As shown in Figure 2-25, a **Save Object** dialog box appears, with which we navigate to where we want to save the object (for example, the **Desktop**).

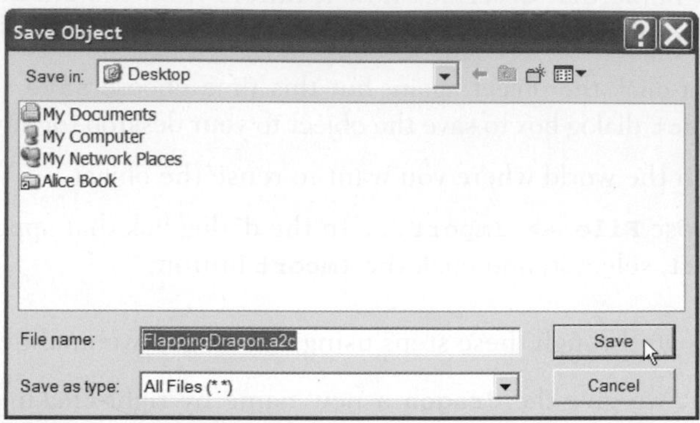

FIGURE 2-25 Saving an object

When we click the **Save** button, Alice saves the object in a special *.a2c* file (*a2c* stands for *a*lice-2.0-*c*lass). In our example, the file will be saved as **FlappingDragon.a2c**.[3]

3. Using Alice's **File** menu, we open the world into which we want to reuse the object. This can be either a new world, or an existing world. We will use a new, snowy world here.
4. With the new world open, we choose **Import...** from the **File** menu, as shown in Figure 2-26.

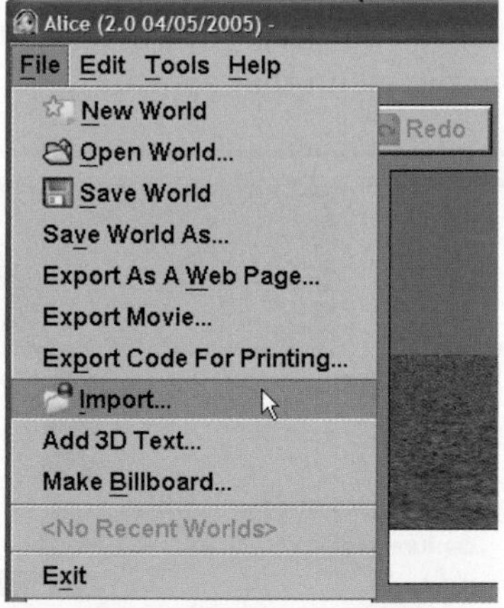

FIGURE 2-26 Importing an object

3. The first letter of a *class* is capitalized, to help distinguish it from an *object*, whose first letter is lowercase.

In the dialog box that appears, we navigate to where we saved the object (for example, the **`Desktop`**), select the *.a2c* file we saved in Step 2, and click the **`Import`** button, as shown in Figure 2-27.

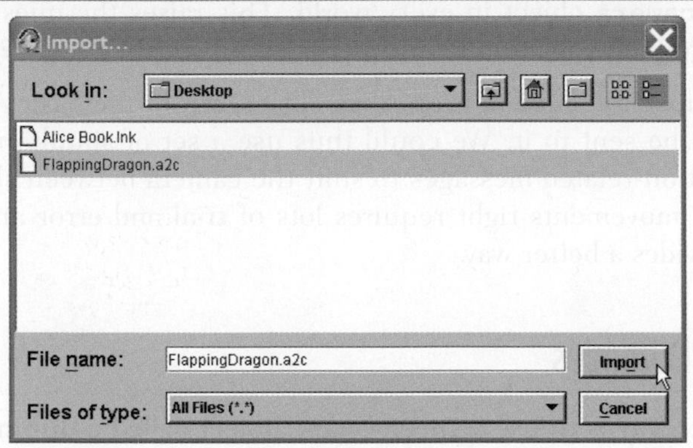

FIGURE 2-27 The import dialog box

Voila! the new world contains a copy of the **`flappingDragon`**, as shown in Figure 2-28!

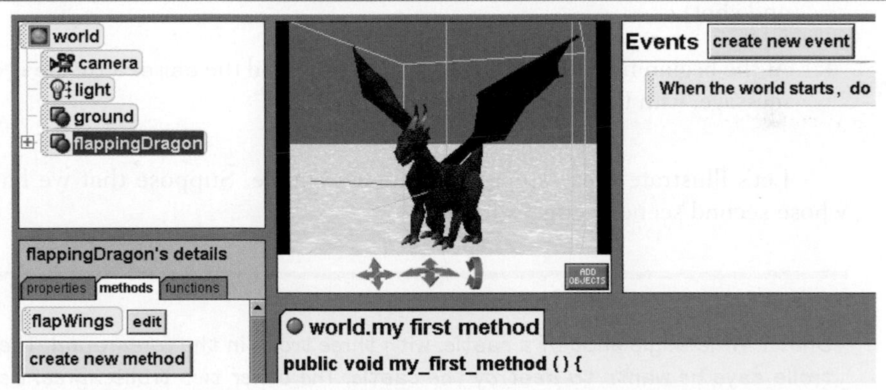

FIGURE 2-28 A reused object

As shown in Figure 2-28, the dragon in this new world includes the **`flapWings()`** method.

By saving an object from one world, and importing it into another, Alice provides us with a means of reusing the work we invest in building object methods.

2.4 Alice Tip: Using Dummies

As we mentioned earlier, scenes are often divided into shots, with each shot being a piece of a scene filmed with the camera in a different position. We have also seen that Alice places a **camera** object in every world. This raises the question: How do we move the camera from one position to another position within a scene?

Because the **camera** is an Alice object, any of the basic Alice messages from Appendix A can be sent to it. We could thus use a set of simultaneous **move()**, **turn()**, and other motion-related messages to shift the camera between shot methods. However, getting such movements right requires lots of trial and error and gets tedious. Thankfully, Alice provides a better way.

2.4.1 Dummies

The better way is to use a special Alice object called a **dummy**. A dummy is an invisible *marker* in your world that has a position and an orientation. The basic idea is as follows:

1. Manually move the camera (using the controls below the *world window*) until it is in the position and orientation where you want it for a given shot.
2. Drop a dummy at the **camera**'s position. This dummy has the **camera**'s point of view.
3. Rename the dummy something descriptive (for example, the number of the scene and shot).
4. At the beginning of the method for that shot, send the **camera** the **setPointOfView()** message, with the dummy as its target.

Let's illustrate these steps with a new example. Suppose that we have a user story whose second scene begins as follows:

Scene 2: The Wizard and the Trolls.

Shot 1: Wide-angle shot of a castle, with three trolls in the foreground. The leader of the trolls says he wants to destroy the castle. The other two trolls agree. Before they can act, a wizard materializes between them and the castle.

Shot 2: Zoom in: a half-body shot of the wizard. He cries, "YOU SHALL NOT PASS!"

Shot 3: Zoom out: the same wide angle shot as before. The trolls turn to the wizard ...

We can start by creating a new world, and creating empty world methods named **playScene2Shot1()**, **playScene2Shot2()**, **playScene2Shot3()**, and **playScene2()**, with this latter method invoking the first three. We then invoke **playScene2()** from **my_first_method()**, as we did in Section 2.1. We can then add the **castle**, **wizard**, and **trolls** to build the scene, as shown in Figure 2-29.

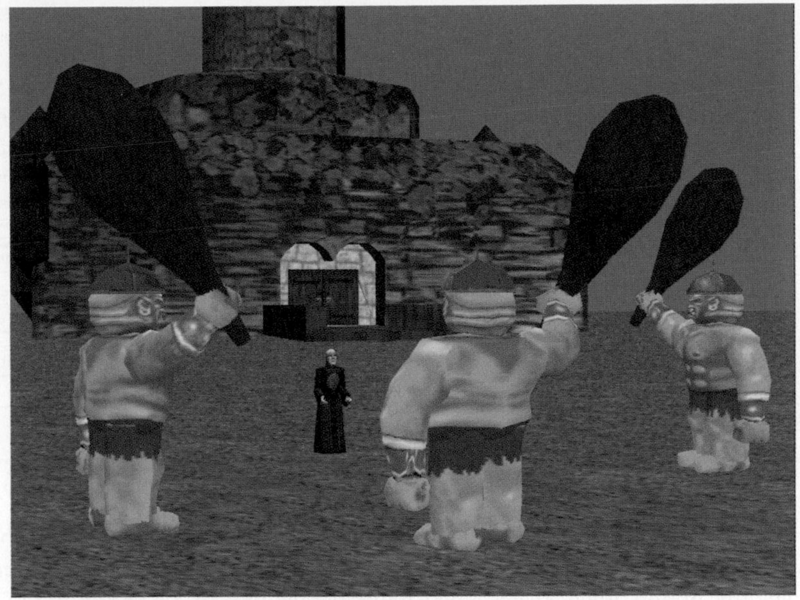

FIGURE 2-29 The set of "The Wizard and the Trolls"

With the *Add Objects* window still open, we click the **more controls** button, as shown in Figure 2-30.

FIGURE 2-30 The **more controls** button

Among the additional controls this button exposes is the **drop dummy at camera** button, as can be seen in Figure 2-31.

FIGURE 2-31 More controls

When we click this button, Alice adds a **dummy** object — an invisible marker — to the world, with the same position and orientation (point of view) as the **`camera`**. The first time we click this button, Alice creates a new folder named **`Dummy Objects`** in the *object tree*, in which all dummies are stored. If we open this folder (Figure 2-32), we can see the **`Dummy`** object inside it.

FIGURE 2-32 A dummy object

Since the name **`Dummy`** is not very descriptive, we can right-click on the object, select **`rename`** from the menu that appears, and rename the dummy **`scene2Shot1`**, as shown in Figure 2-33.

FIGURE 2-33 A renamed dummy

By doing so, we will know exactly which scene and shot this dummy is for, and not confuse it with the dummies we create for other scenes and shots.

Now that we have a dummy in place for the first shot, the next step is to manually position the **camera** where we want it for the second shot, using the controls beneath the *world window*. Using these controls, we can zoom in until we get a nice half-body shot of the wizard, leaving space above his head for his dialog-balloon to appear. See Figure 2-34.

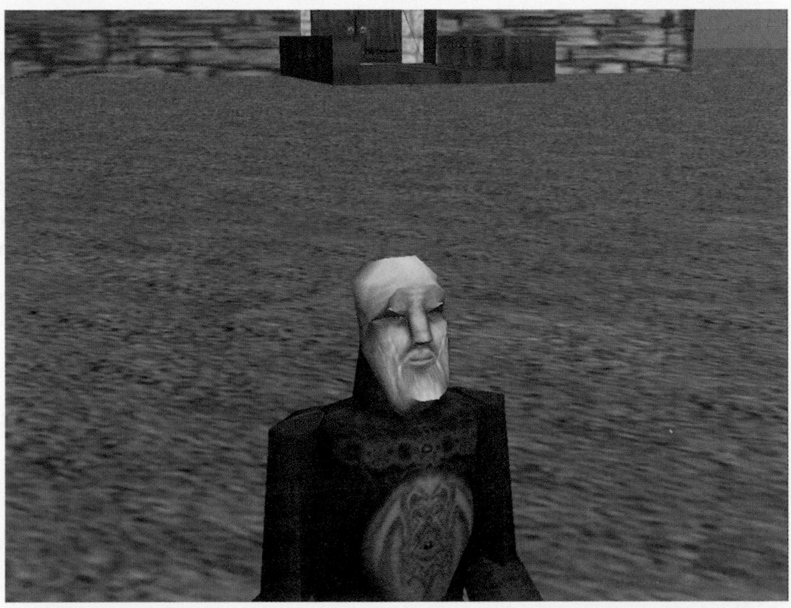

FIGURE 2-34 A half-body shot of the wizard

When we have the **camera** just where we want it, we again press the **drop dummy at camera** button to drop a second dummy at the **camera**'s current position. As before, we rename it, as shown in Figure 2-35.

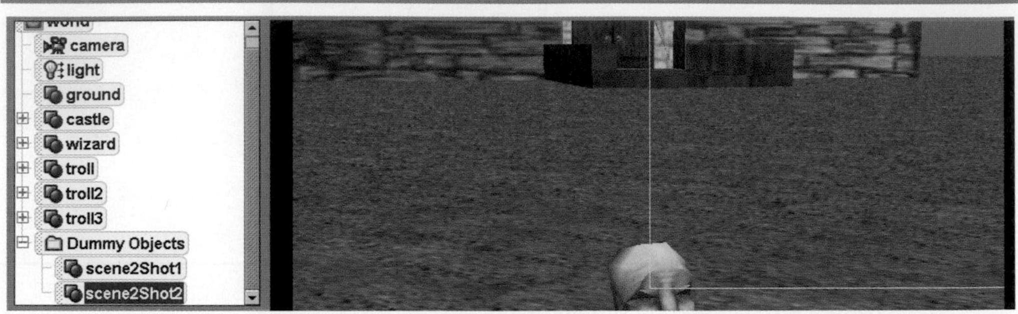

FIGURE 2-35 A second dummy

Since the third shot is back in the camera's original position, we can reuse the **scene2Shot1** dummy for the third shot and avoid creating an additional dummy.

With dummies for all three of the shots, we then click the *Add Objects* window's **DONE** button and turn our attention to programming these shots.

2.4.2 Using `setPointOfView()` to Control the Camera

Now that we have dummies for each of the shots, how do we make use of them? The key is the method ***obj*.setPointOfView(*obj2*)**, which changes the position and orientation of **obj** to that of **obj2**. If we send the message **setPointOfView(*aDummy*)** to the **camera**, then the **camera**'s position and orientation will change to that of ***aDummy***!

Back in the *editing area* with the **playScene2Shot1()** method open, we start by dragging a **doInOrder** statement into the method. We then click on the **camera** in the *object tree*, scroll down to the **setPointOfView()** method in the *details area*, and then drag **setPointOfView()** to make it the first statement in the **playScene2Shot1()** method. For its target, we select **Dummy Objects -> scene2Shot1**, as shown in Figure 2-36.

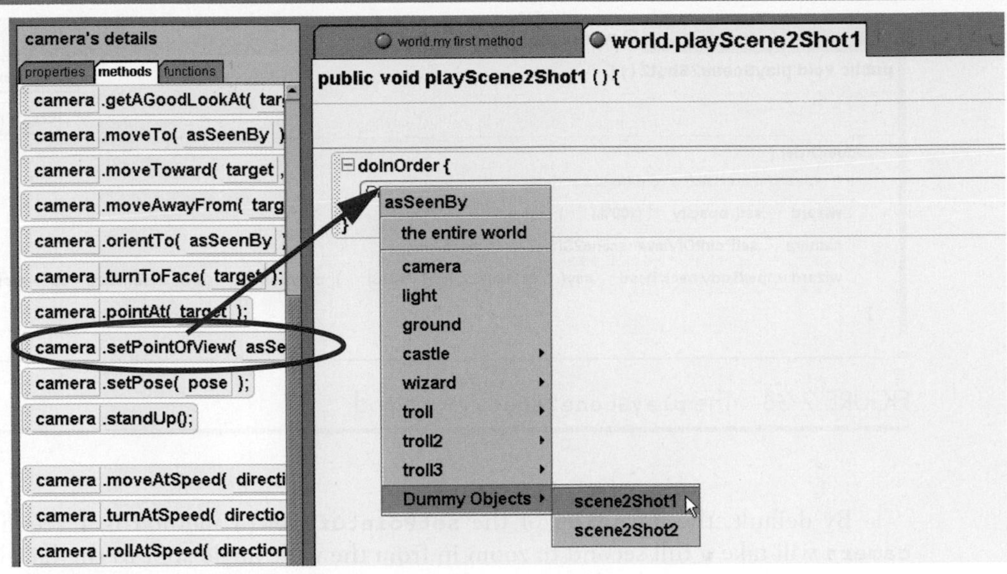

FIGURE 2-36 Setting the **camera**'s point of view to a dummy

When we have chosen **scene2Shot1** as its target, we then set the statement's **duration** to zero (so that the camera moves to this position and orientation instantly). We can then add the rest of the statements for the shot, resulting in a method definition like that shown in Figure 2-37.

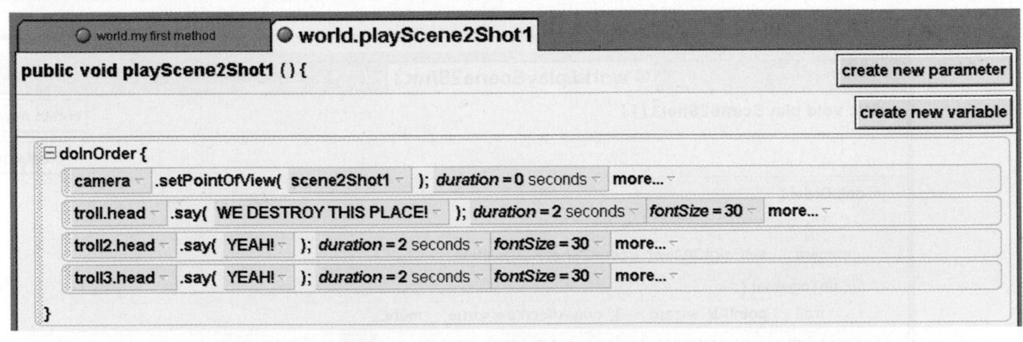

FIGURE 2-37 Using the **setPointOfView()** method with a dummy

We then use the same approach in **playScene2Shot2()** to move the **camera** to the position and orientation of the **scene2Shot2** dummy near the start of that method (Figure 2-38).

```
world.my first method | world.playScene2Shot2
public void playScene2Shot2 () {                create new parameter
                                                create new variable
  doInOrder {
    // wizard materializes to defend castle
    wizard .set( opacity, 1 (100%) ); more...
    camera .setPointOfView( scene2Shot2 ); more...
    wizard.upperBody.neck.head .say( YOU SHALL NOT PASS! ); duration = 2 seconds fontSize = 30 more...
  }
```

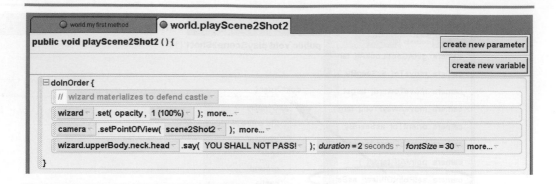

FIGURE 2-38 The **playScene2Shot2()** method

By default, the **duration** of the **setPointOfView()** method is 1 second, so the **camera** will take a full second to zoom in from the wide angle shot to the half-body shot of the wizard. If we want a faster zoom, we can reduce the **duration** (for example, 0 seconds causes an instantaneous cut). If we want a slower zoom, we can set the **duration** to 2 or more seconds.

Note also that to make the **wizard** materialize, the **playScene2Shot2()** method sets his **opacity** property to 1, using the approach described in Section 1.5.1. To make him initially invisible, we manually set his **opacity** to 0 in the *properties* pane.

For the third shot, we use the **setPointOfView()** message to reset the **camera**'s position and orientation back to the wide-angle shot, using the **scene2Shot1** dummy. Figure 2-39 shows the code at this point.

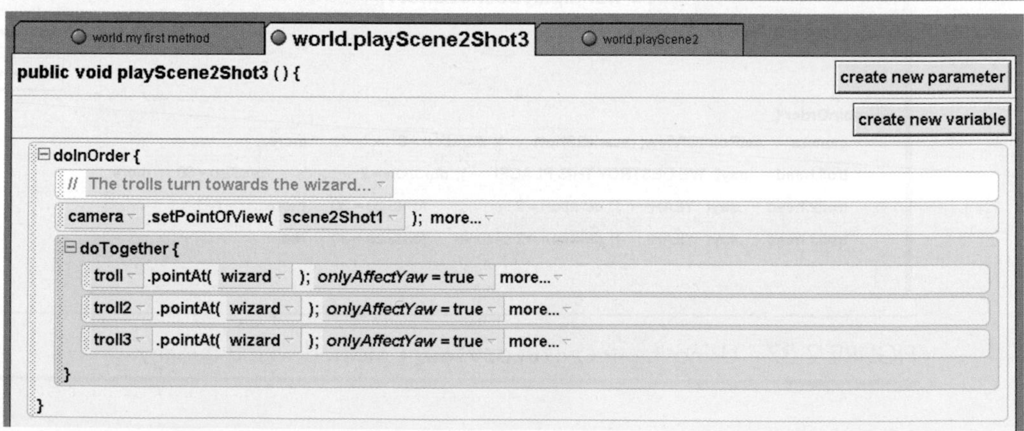

FIGURE 2-39 The **playScene2Shot3()** method

Now, when we click the **Play** button, we see the first shot from the wide angle view and see the trolls speak. The camera then zooms in to the half-body view of the wizard, and we see his dialog. The camera then zooms back out to the wide-angle view, and the trolls turn toward the wizard.... What happens next? It's up to you! (See the Chapter 3 problems for one possibility.)

You may have noticed that when we used the **pointAt()** message to make the trolls turn to the wizard, we set that message's **onlyAffectYaw** attribute to **true**. Every object in a 3D world has six attributes that determine its position and orientation in the world. **Yaw** is one of these six attributes, which we examine in the next section.

2.5 Thinking in 3D

Most of us are not used to thinking carefully about moving about in a three-dimensional world, any more than we think carefully about grammar rules when we speak our native language. However, to use Alice well and understand the effects of some of its methods, we need to conclude this chapter by thinking about how objects move in a 3D world.

Every object in a 3D world has the following two properties:

- An object's **position** determines its *location* within the 3D world.
- An object's **orientation** determines *the way it is facing* in the 3D world, determining what is in front of and behind the object, what is to the left and right of the object, and what is above and below the object.

In the rest of this section, we will explore these two properties in detail.

2.5.1 An Object's Position

Pretend that you are a pilot flying the seaplane in Figure 2-40.

FIGURE 2-40 A seaplane

As you fly the seaplane, it can move along any of the arrows shown in Figure 2-41.

FIGURE 2-41 The seaplane and 3D axes

Each pair of opposite-facing arrows (from the pilot's perspective: *LEFT-RIGHT* [red], *UP-DOWN* [green], *FORWARD-BACKWARD* [blue]) is called an **axis**. Two or more of these arrows are called **axes**.

Every Alice object has its own three axes. For example, from a "downward-looking" angle, we might imagine the three axes of our three-dimensional world as shown in Figure 2-42.

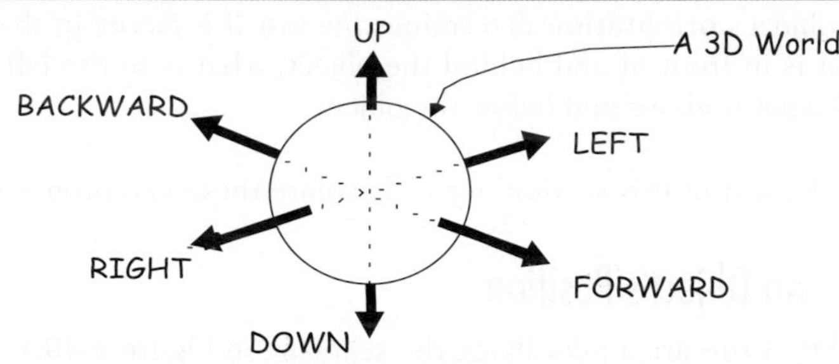

FIGURE 2-42 The three-dimensional world

Once we create a world and start adding objects to it, every object is located somewhere within that 3D world. To determine each object's exact location, we can use the world's axes.

To illustrate, the seaplane's position along the world's *LEFT-RIGHT* axis specifies its location in the world's *width* dimension. We will call this axis the **LR axis**.

Similarly, the seaplane's position along the world's *UP-DOWN* axis specifies its location in the world's *height* dimension. We will call this axis the **UD axis**.

Finally, the seaplane's position along the world's *FORWARD-BACKWARD* axis specifies its location in the world's *depth* dimension. We will call this axis the **FB axis**.

An object's **position** within a three-dimensional world thus consists of three values — *lr*, *ud*, and *fb* — that specify its location measured using the world's three axes.[4]

4. These axes are usually called the X, Y, and Z axes, but we'll use the more descriptive LR, UD, and FB.

Changing Position

To change an object's position, Alice provides a method named **move()** (see Appendix A). When we drop Alice's **move()** method into the *editing area*, Alice displays a menu of the directions the object may move, shown in Figure 2-43.

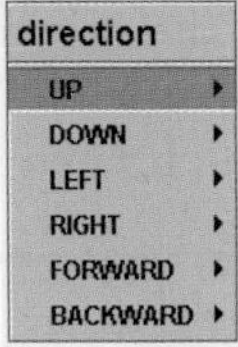

FIGURE 2-43 The directions an object may move

If you compare Figure 2-41 and Figure 2-43, you'll see that Alice's **move()** message allows an object to move along any of that object's three axes:

- Moving **LEFT** or **RIGHT** changes the object's location along its LR-axis.
- Moving **UP** or **DOWN** changes the object's location along its UD-axis.
- Moving **FORWARD** or **BACKWARD** changes its location along its FB-axis.

Alice's **move()** message thus changes the *position* of the object to which the message is sent with respect to the world's axes, but the directional values that we specify for the movement (**LEFT**, **RIGHT**, **UP**, **DOWN**, **FORWARD**, and **BACKWARD**) are given with respect to *that object's axes*, not the world's axes.

2.5.2 An Object's Orientation

When an object moves, its axes move with it. For example, if we send the seaplane of Figure 2-41 the message **turn(RIGHT, 0.25)**, the picture would change to that shown in Figure 2-44.

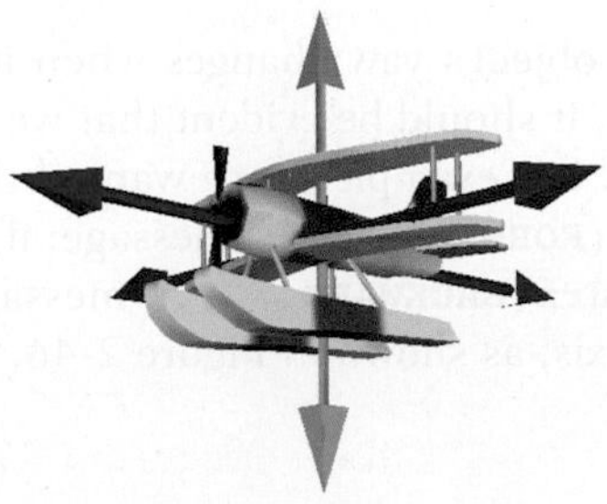

FIGURE 2-44 The seaplane turned 1/4 revolution right

If we now send the turned seaplane a message to **move(FORWARD, ...)**, the seaplane will move forward according to the new direction its FB axis points.

Yaw

If you compare the axes in Figure 2-41 and Figure 2-44 carefully, you'll see that a **turn(RIGHT, 0.25)** message causes the seaplane to *rotate* about its UD-axis. A **turn(LEFT, 0.25)** message causes a rotation about the same axis, but in the opposite direction. If we were to position ourselves "above" the plane's UD-axis and look down, we might visualize the effects of such **turn()** messages as shown in Figure 2-45.

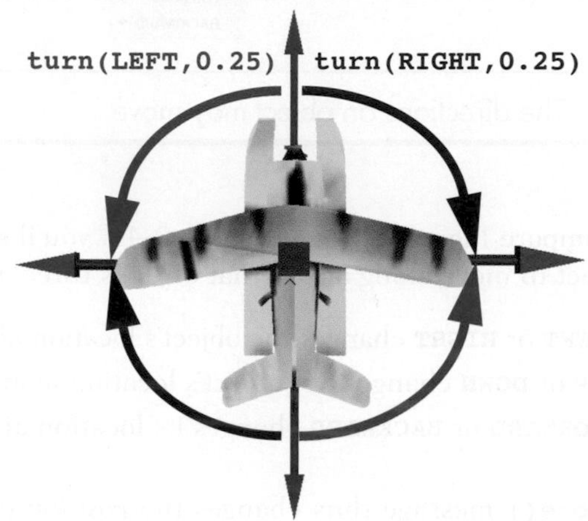

FIGURE 2-45 Changing yaw: turning left or right

In 3D terminology, an object's **yaw** is how much it has rotated about its UD axis from its original position. For example, when you shake your head "no," you are changing your head's yaw. Alice's **turn(LEFT, ...)** and **turn(RIGHT, ...)** messages change an object's yaw.

Pitch

We just saw that an object's yaw changes when it rotates around its UD axis. Since an object has three axes, it should be evident that we could also rotate an object around one of its other two axes. For example, if we wanted the seaplane to dive toward the sea, we could send it a **turn(FORWARD, ...)** message; if we wanted it to climb toward the sun, we could send it a **turn(BACKWARD, ...)** message. These messages cause an object to rotate about its LR-axis, as shown in Figure 2-46.

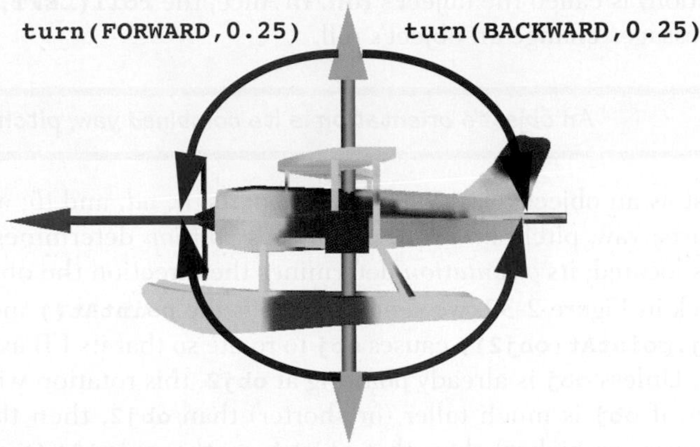

FIGURE 2-46 Turning forward or backward

An object's **pitch** is how much it has rotated about its LR axis from its original position. For example, when you shake your head "yes," you change your head's pitch. In Alice, a **turn(FORWARD, ...)** or **turn(BACKWARD, ...)** message changes an object's pitch.

Roll

An object can also rotate around its FB axis. For example, if we were to send the seaplane the **roll(LEFT, 0.25)** or **roll(RIGHT, 0.25)** message, it would rotate as shown in Figure 2-47.

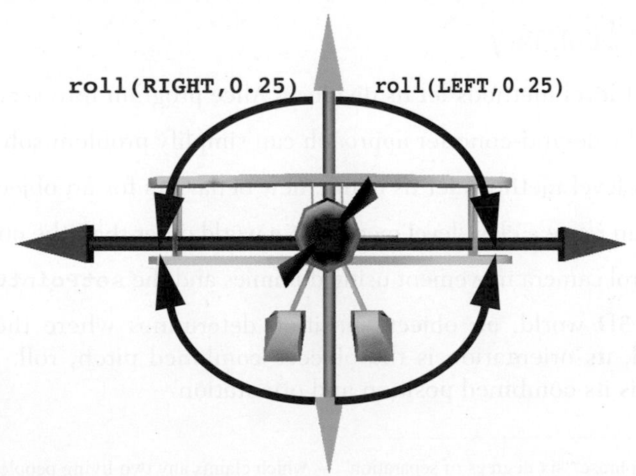

FIGURE 2-47 Rolling left or right

The amount by which an object has rotated about its FB axis (compared to its original position) is called the object's **roll**. In Alice, the `roll(LEFT, ...)` and `roll(RIGHT, ...)` messages change an object's roll.

An object's orientation is its combined yaw, pitch, and roll.

Just as an object's *position* has three parts: *lr*, *ud*, and *fb*; an object's *orientation* has three parts: yaw, pitch, and roll. An object's *position* determines where in the world that object is located; its *orientation* determines the direction the object is facing.

Back in Figure 2-39, we sent three trolls the `pointAt()` message. By default, a message `obj.pointAt(obj2);` causes `obj` to rotate so that its FB axis is pointing at the *center* of `obj2`. Unless `obj` is already pointing at `obj2`, this rotation will change the yaw of `obj`. However, if `obj` is much taller (or shorter) than `obj2`, then the center of `obj2` will be much lower (or higher) than that of `obj`, so the `pointAt()` message will also change `obj`'s pitch. This would cause the trolls to lean forward at an unnatural angle. By setting the message's `onlyAffectYaw` attribute to `true`, we ensured that each troll's pitch remained unchanged.

The message `obj.turnToFace(obj2);` is a shorthand for `obj.pointAt(obj2)` with `onlyAffectYaw=true`, and we will use it in future examples.

2.5.3 Point of View

In Alice, an object's combined position and orientation are called that object's **point of view**. An object's point of view thus consists of six values: [(*lr*, *ud*, *fb*), (yaw, pitch, roll)]. Alice's `move()`, `turn()`, and `roll()` messages let you change any of these six values for an object, giving Alice objects *six degrees of freedom*.[5] Alice's `setPointOfView()` message (see Appendix A) lets you set an object's point of view.

2.6 Chapter Summary

- ❏ World-level methods let us divide an Alice program into scenes and shots.
- ❏ The divide-and-conquer approach can simplify problem solving.
- ❏ Class-level methods let us define new behaviors for an object.
- ❏ We can reuse a class-level method in a world other than the one where we defined it.
- ❏ Control camera movement using dummies and the `setPointOfView()` message.
- ❏ In a 3D world, an object's position determines where the object is located in the world; its orientation is the object's combined pitch, roll, and yaw; and its point of view is its combined position and orientation.

5. The phrase "six degrees of separation" — which claims any two living people are connected by a chain of six or fewer acquaintances — is derived from this phrase "six degrees of freedom." The "Six Degrees of Kevin Bacon" game — that claims that the actor Kevin Bacon and any other actor are linked by a chain of six or fewer film co-stars — is further derived from "six degrees of separation." See `www.cs.virginia.edu/oracle/`.

2.6.1 Key Terms

axis
comment
divide and conquer
dummy
object method
orientation
pitch
point of view
position
reusable method
roll
scene
shot
world method
yaw

Programming Projects

2.1 Revisit the programs you wrote for Chapter 1. If any of them require scrolling to view all of their statements, rewrite them using divide-and-conquer and world-level methods whose statements can be viewed without scrolling.

2.2 The director Sergio Leone was famous for the extreme closeups he used of gunfighters' eyes in "western" movies like *For a Fistful of Dollars*; *The Good, the Bad, and the Ugly*; and *Once Upon a Time in the West*. Watch one of these films; then modify the **playScene2()** method we wrote in Section 2.4, using Leone's camera techniques to heighten the drama of the wizard's confrontation with the trolls.

2.3 Build an undersea world containing a **goldfish**. Build a **swim()** method for the **goldfish** that makes it swim forward one meter in a realistic fashion. Add a **shark** to your world, and build a similar **swim()** method for it. Build a program containing a scene in which the **shark** chases the **goldfish**, and the **goldfish** swims to its giant cousin goldfish that chases the **shark** away. (Hint: Make the giant cousin goldfish by Saving and Importing your modified **goldfish**.)

2.4 Choose a hopping animal from the Alice Gallery (for example, a frog, a bunny, etc.). Write a **hop()** method that makes it hop in a realistic fashion. Add a building to your world, then write a program that uses your **hop()** method to make the animal hop around the building. Write your program using divide-and-conquer so that **my_first_method()** contains an **Inorder** control and no more than four statements.

2.5 Build a world containing a flying vehicle (for example, a biplane, a helicopter, etc.). Build a class-level **loopDeeLoop()** method for your flying vehicle that makes it move in a vertical loop. Using the Torus class (under Shapes), build a world containing a giant arch. Then write a program in which your flying vehicle does a **loopDeeLoop()** through the arch.

2.6 *Boom, Boom, Ain't It Great To Be Crazy* is a silly song with the lyrics on the next page. Create an Alice program containing a character who sings this song. Use divide-and-conquer to write your program as efficiently as possible.

A horse and a flea and three blind mice *sat on a curbstone shooting dice.* *The horse he slipped and fell on the flea.* *"Whoops," said the flea, "there's a horse on me."* *Boom, boom, ain't it great to be crazy?* *Boom, boom, ain't it great to be crazy?* *Giddy and foolish, the whole day through,* *boom, boom, ain't it great to be crazy?*	*Way down south where bananas grow,* *a flea stepped on an elephant's toe.* *The elephant cried, with tears in his eyes,* *"Why don't you pick on someone your size."* *Boom, boom, ain't it great to be crazy?* *Boom, boom, ain't it great to be crazy?* *Giddy and foolish, the whole day through,* *boom, boom, ain't it great to be crazy?*
Way up north where there's ice and snow, *there lived a penguin whose name was Joe.* *He got so tired of black and white,* *he wore pink pants to the dance last night.* *Boom, boom, ain't it great to be crazy?* *Boom, boom, ain't it great to be crazy?* *Giddy and foolish, the whole day through,* *boom, boom, ain't it great to be crazy?*	

2.7 Using appropriately colored `Shapes` from the Alice Gallery, build a checker-board. Then choose an object from the Gallery to serve as a checker. Build class-level methods named `moveLeft()`, `moveRight()`, `jumpLeft()`, and `jumpRight()` for the character. Then make copies of the object for the remaining checkers. Build a program that simulates the opening moves of a game of checkers, using your board and checkers.

2.8 Using the `heBuilder` or `sheBuilder` (or any of the other persons with enough detail in the Alice Gallery), build a person and add him or her to your world. Using your person, build an aerobic exercise video in which the person leads the user through an exercise routine. Use world- and/or class-level methods in your program, as appropriate.

2.9 In Section 2.4, we developed a program consisting of Scene 2, in which a wizard faces off against three trolls. Create your own Scene 1 and Scene 3 for this program to show what happened before and after the scene we developed.

2.10 Write an original story consisting of at least two characters, three scenes, and dummies to position your characters in the different scenes. Each scene should have multiple shots. Use world- and class-level methods to create your story efficiently.

Chapter 3
Variables and Functions

The first step towards wisdom is calling things by their right names.

OLD CHINESE PROVERB

Figuratively speaking, killing two birds with one stone may be good, but killing three, four, or even more birds with one stone is even better.

V. OREHCK III

Stop! Who would cross the Bridge of Death must answer me these questions three, ere the other side he see.

THE BRIDGEKEEPER (TERRY GILLIAM), IN *MONTY PYTHON AND THE HOLY GRAIL*

Objectives

Upon completion of this chapter, you should be able to:

- ❑ Use variables to store values for use later in a method
- ❑ Use a variable to store the value of an arithmetic expression
- ❑ Use a variable to store the value produced by a function
- ❑ Use parameters to write methods that are more broadly useful
- ❑ Define and access property variables
- ❑ Use the **`vehicle`** property to synchronize the movements of two objects
- ❑ Create functions — messages that return a value to their sender

In Chapter 2, we saw how to define world and object methods. In this chapter, we turn our attention to **variables**, the use of which can make it easier to define methods. In computer programming, *a variable is a name that refers to a piece of the program's memory, in which a value can be stored, retrieved, and changed.*

Alice provides several different kinds of variables that we will examine in this chapter. The first kind is the **method variable**, which lets us store a value within a method for later use. The second kind is the **parameter**, which lets us write methods that are more broadly useful. These first two kinds of variables are created using the two buttons that appear on the right edge of every Alice method, as shown in Figure 3-1.

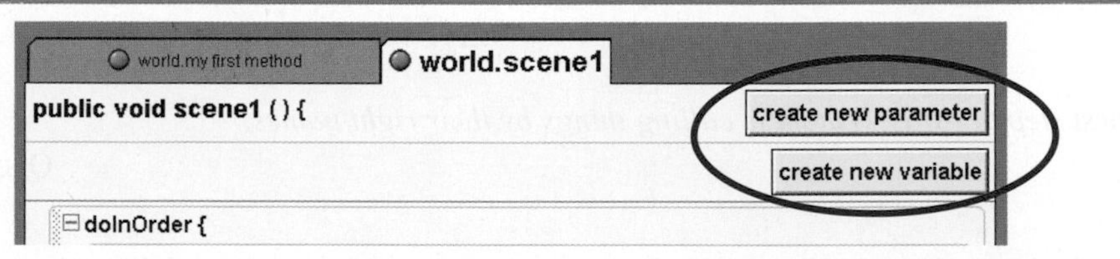

FIGURE 3-1 The buttons to create variables and parameters

The third and final kind of variable is the **object variable** or **property variable**, which lets us store a property of an object. Object variables are created using the **`create new variable`** button under the *properties* pane of the *details area*.

In this chapter, we'll see how to create and use all three kinds of variables.

3.1 Method Variables

Method variables are names defined within a method that refer to program memory in which values can be stored. When we click the **`create new variable`** button within a method, Alice asks us what we want to *name* the variable, the *type* of information we want to store in it, and its initial value. When we have told it these things, Alice reserves as much program memory as is needed for that type of information, and associates the name with that memory, which is called **defining** the variable. Method variables are often called **local variables**, because they can only be accessed from within the method in which they are defined — they are *local* to it.

One common use of method variables is to compute and store values that will be used later, especially values that will be used more than once. Another common use is to store values that the user enters. In the rest of this section, we present these two uses.

3.1.1 Example 1: Storing a Computed Value

Suppose that in Scene 2 of a story, a girl and a horse are positioned as seen in Figure 3-2.

FIGURE 3-2 Girl and horse: initial positions

Suppose our scene calls for the girl to move toward the horse and stop when she is directly in front of it. We can send the girl the **`move()`** message to move her toward the horse, but how far should we ask her to move? One way would be to use trial-and-error to find a suitable value. But trial-and-error is tedious, especially when there is a better way. The better way is to:

1. Define a variable to store the distance from the girl to the horse.
2. Ask the girl how far she is from the horse, and store her reply in the variable.
3. Use that variable in the **`move()`** message to get her to move the right distance.

To accomplish the first step, we just click the **`create new variable`** button we saw in Figure 3-1. To get the information it needs to define the variable, Alice pops up a **`Create New Local Variable`** dialog box in which we can enter the variable's **name**, **type**, and **initial value**.

A variable's name should be a noun that describes the value it stores.

For example, this variable is storing the distance from the girl to the horse, so we will **name** it **`distanceToHorse`**. Like method names, variable names always use lower-case letters, capitalizing the first letter of words after the first word.

A variable's **type** describes the kind of value we intend to store in it. Alice provides four basic types:

- `Number`, for storing numeric values (for example, `-3`, `-1.5`, `0`, `1`, `3.14159`, and so on)
- `Boolean`, for storing logical (`true` or `false`) values
- `Object`, for storing references to Alice objects (for example, `troll`, `wizard`, `castle`, and so on)
- `Other`, for storing things like `String`s, `Color`s, `Sound`s, and other kinds of values

Since the distance from the girl to the horse is a numerical value, `Number` is the appropriate type for this variable.

As its name suggests, the **initial value** is the value the variable will contain when the method begins. We will usually use a value like 0 or 1, as shown in Figure 3-3.

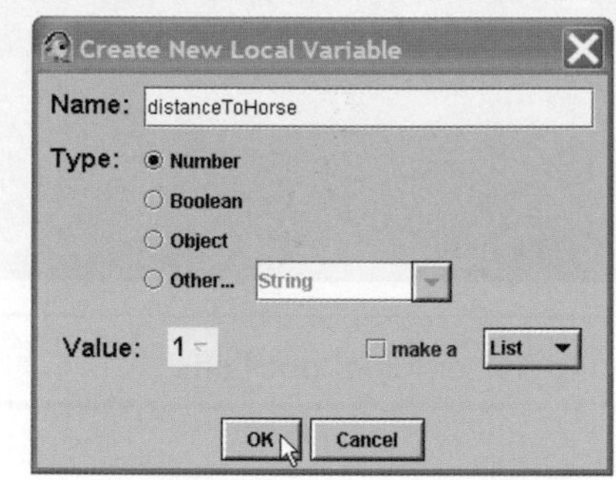

FIGURE 3-3 The `Create New Local Variable` dialog box

When we click the `OK` button, Alice defines a new variable in the method, in the space above the *editing area*, as shown in Figure 3-4.

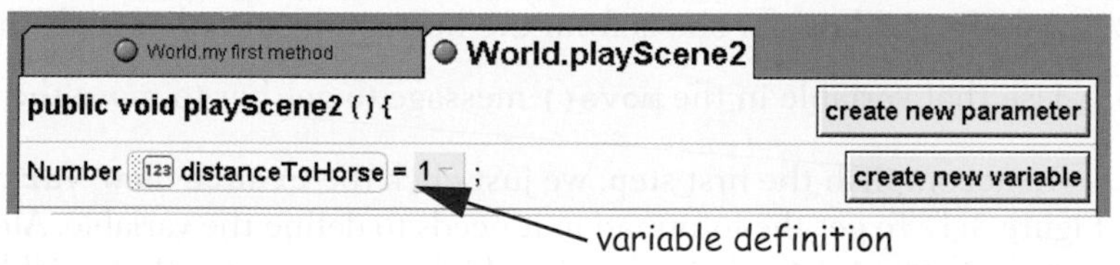

FIGURE 3-4 The `distanceToHorse` variable

Next, we want to ask the girl how far she is from the horse, and set the value of this variable to her response. In Alice, it is easiest to do these steps in reverse order.

Setting the value of a variable is done in a way similar to how we set the value of a property back in Chapter 1: we drag its definition into the *editing area*, and Alice generates a menu of potential values, as shown in Figure 3-5.

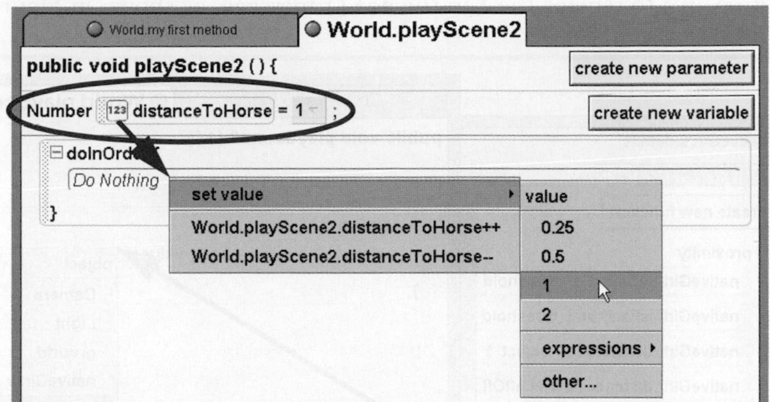

FIGURE 3-5 Setting a variable's value (part I)

If we wished to add 1 to **`distanceToHorse`**, we would choose **`World.playScene2.distanceToHorse++`** from the menu (**++** is called the **increment operator**). If we wanted to subtract 1 from its value, we would choose **`World.playScene2.distanceToHorse--`** (**--** is called the **decrement operator**). Since we want to *set* the variable's value, we choose the **`set value`** choice.

The value to which we want to set **`distanceToHorse`** is the result of asking the girl how far she is from the horse. Unfortunately, this value is not present in the menu. In this situation, we can choose any value from the menu to act as a **placeholder** for the function. (In Figure 3-5, we are choosing **`1`** as the placeholder.) The result is the **`set()`** statement shown in Figure 3-6.

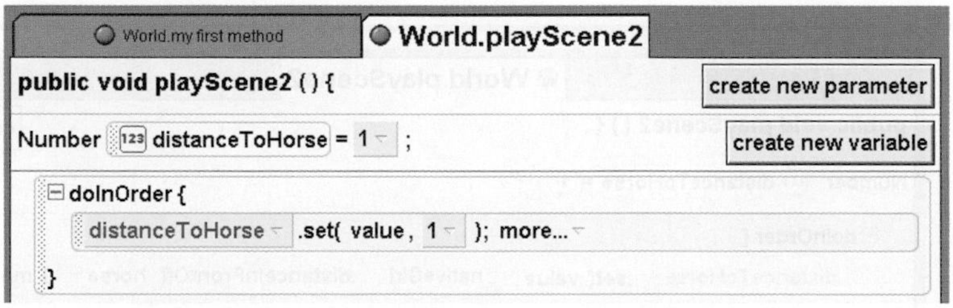

FIGURE 3-6 Setting a variable's value using a placeholder

With a **`set()`** statement in place, we are ready to ask the girl how far she is from the horse. To do so, we make sure we have the girl selected in the *object tree*, and then click the *functions* tab in the *details area*. "How far are you from the horse?" is a proximity question, so we look in the proximity section of the functions. Since the girl is in front of the horse and we see a **distanceInFrontOf()** proximity function, we drag it into the *editing area* to replace the **1** in the **set()** message, as shown in Figure 3-7.

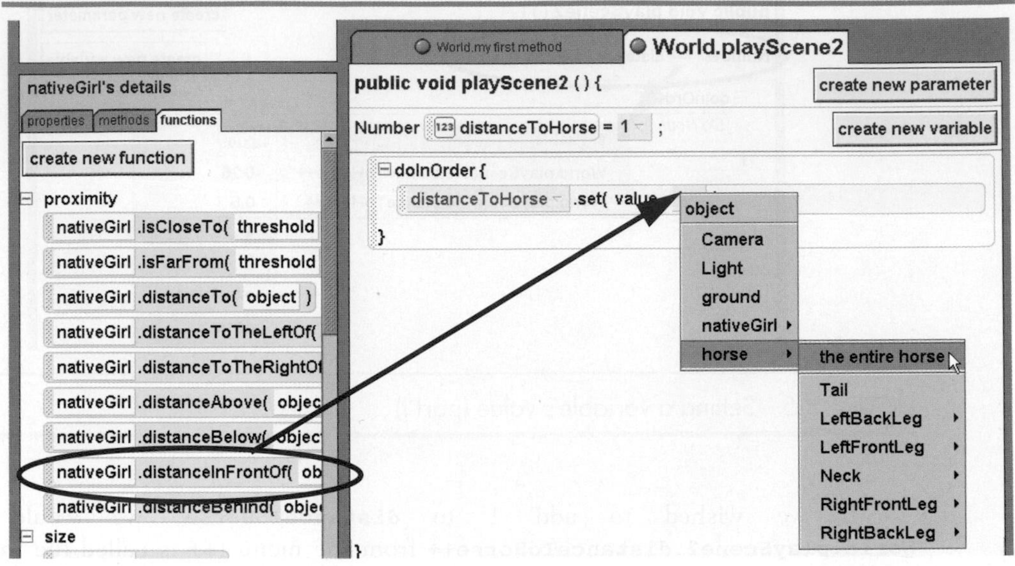

FIGURE 3-7 Setting a variable's value to a function's answer

When we drag the function onto the placeholder (**1**), the box around the **1** turns green, indicating we can drop it. Alice then asks us for the object whose distance we want to compute, and displays a menu of the available options. When we select **horse -> the entire horse** (see Figure 3-7), Alice replaces the placeholder **1** with the function, as can be seen in Figure 3-8.

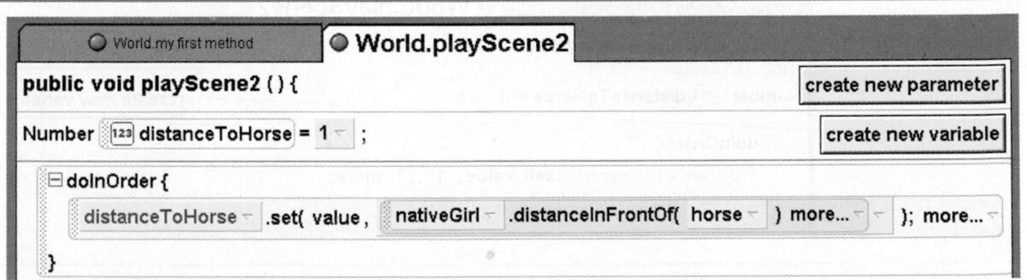

FIGURE 3-8 Setting a variable's value (part III)

You may be wondering why we used the **distanceInFrontOf()** function instead of the **distanceTo()** function. The reason is that the **distanceTo()** function returns the distance from the *center* of one object to the *center* of the other object. If we moved the girl that far, she and the horse would occupy the same space, which looks really weird! (Try it and see.) By contrast, the other proximity methods all measure from the *outer edge* of one object's bounding box to the *outer edge* of the other object's bounding box.

Once we have a variable containing the distance from the girl to the front of the horse, we can use it in the **move()** message. When we drag the **move()** message into the *editing area*, we can specify that we want the girl to move forward the value of the variable by selecting **expressions -> distanceToHorse**. Alice's **expressions** menu usually contains a list of all the variables (and parameters, and functions we define) that are available for use within the current method. Figure 3-9 illustrates this.

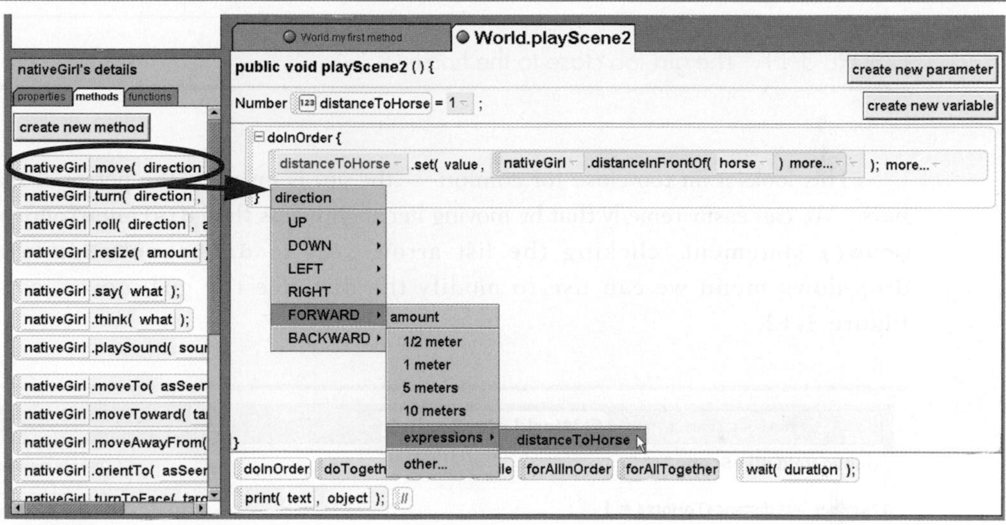

FIGURE 3-9 Using a variable's value in a message (part I)

Figure 3-10 shows the statement Alice generates when we select **distanceToHorse**.

```
World.my first method    World.playScene2
public void playScene2 () {                                  create new parameter
Number distanceToHorse = 1 ;                                  create new variable
  doInOrder {
    distanceToHorse .set( value, nativeGirl .distanceInFrontOf( horse ) more... ); more...
    nativeGirl .move( FORWARD , distanceToHorse meters ); more...
  }
```

FIGURE 3-10 Using a variable's value in a message (part II)

When we play this method, we get the result shown in Figure 3-11.

FIGURE 3-11 The girl too close to the horse

This looks a bit too close for comfort — the girl is invading the personal space of the horse! We can easily remedy that by moving her slightly less than **distanceToHorse**. In the **move()** statement, clicking the list arrow next to **distanceToHorse** reveals a drop-down menu we can use to modify the distance the girl moves, as shown in Figure 3-12.

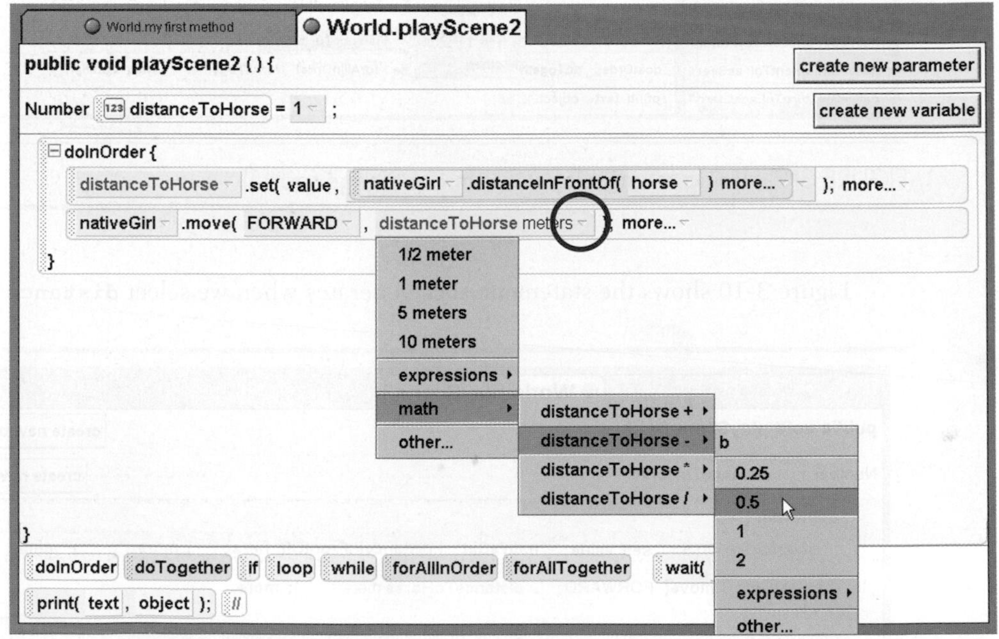

FIGURE 3-12 Adjusting a value in a message

As can be seen in Figure 3-12, Alice's **math** menu choice provides the basic arithmetic calculations of addition, subtraction, multiplication, and division. Selecting **distanceToHorse - 0.5** produces the statement shown in Figure 3-13.

```
World.my first method | World.playScene2
public void playScene2 () {                                  create new parameter
Number 123 distanceToHorse = 1 ;                             create new variable
  doInOrder {
    distanceToHorse .set( value, nativeGirl .distanceInFrontOf( horse ) more... ); more...
    nativeGirl .move( FORWARD , ( distanceToHorse - 0.5 ) ); more...
  }
```

FIGURE 3-13 Decreasing how far she moves

Now, when we play the method, the girl stops a comfortable distance from the horse, as shown in Figure 3-14.

FIGURE 3-14 Stopping a comfortable distance from the horse

Using functions and variables has a major advantage over trial-and-error: it yields the right behavior even if we reposition the girl or the horse! If we had used trial-and-error to find the exact distance to move the girl, and then later repositioned the girl or horse, the value we had found using trial-and-error would no longer be correct, so we would have to fix it (either with another round of trial-and-error, or by getting smart and using a variable and a function).

Once you get used to using variables and functions, they often provide a much better way to make a character move a distance relative to another object.

3.1.2 Example 2: Storing a User-Entered Value

Another common use of variables is to store values that the user enters, for later use. To illustrate, suppose your geometry teacher gives you a list of right triangles' leg-lengths, and tells you to calculate each triangle's hypotenuse length using the Pythagorean Theorem:

$$c = \sqrt{a^2 + b^2}$$

We could either get out our calculators and grind through the list, or we could write an Alice program to help us. Which sounds like more fun? (Writing an Alice program, of course!)

As always, we start with a user story. We might write something like this:

> Scene: There is a girl on the screen. She says, "I can calculate hypotenuse-lengths in my head!" Then she says, "Give me the lengths of the two edges of a right triangle..." A dialog box appears, prompting us for the first edge length. When we enter it, a second dialog box appears, prompting us for the second edge length. When we enter it, the girl says, "The hypotenuse-length is X." (Where X is the correct answer.)

The nouns in our story include girl, hypotenuse-length, first edge length, second edge length, and two dialog boxes. For the girl, we will use the **`skaterGirl`** from the Alice Gallery. For the hypotenuse-length, first edge length, and second edge length, we will create **`Number`** variables named **`hypotenuse`**, **`edge1`**, and **`edge2`**, respectively. For the dialog boxes, Alice provides a function that will build and display dialog objects for us (see below).

Since the scene has just one object (girl), we will create a **`skaterGirl`** object method named **`computeHypotenuse()`** to animate her with the desired behavior. Within this method, we declare the three **`Number`** variables, and then begin programming the desired behavior. Using what we have seen so far, we can get to the point shown in Figure 3-15:

world.my first method
skaterGirl.computeHypotenuse
public void computeHypotenuse () {
Number hypotenuse = 1 ; Number edge1 = 1 ; Number edge2 = 1 ;
doInOrder {
skaterGirl .say(I can calculate hypotenuse lengths in my head!); duration = 3 seconds fontSize = 30 more...
skaterGirl .say(Give me the lengths of two edges of a right triangle); duration = 3 seconds fontSize = 30 more...
edge1 .set(value , 1); more...
}

FIGURE 3-15 Getting started

But how do we generate a dialog box to set the value of **`edge1`**? The trick is to look in the **`World`**'s functions! The **`World`**'s *functions* pane provides an entirely different set of function-messages from those we can send to an object. If we scroll down a bit, we find the **`NumberDialog`** function that we can drag over to replace the **`1`** placeholder, as we saw in Figure 3-7. When we drop it on the **`1`**, Alice displays a menu of questions we can have the dialog box ask, as shown in Figure 3-16.

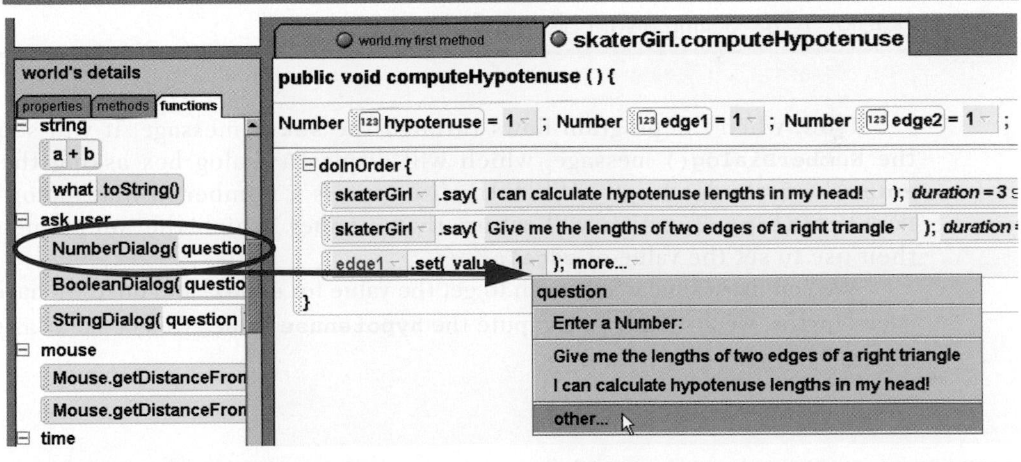

FIGURE 3-16 Dragging a dialog function

In this case, we want the dialog box to ask for the length of one edge of a right triangle, so we choose **`other...`** Alice then lets us enter the prompt to be displayed, as shown in Figure 3-17.

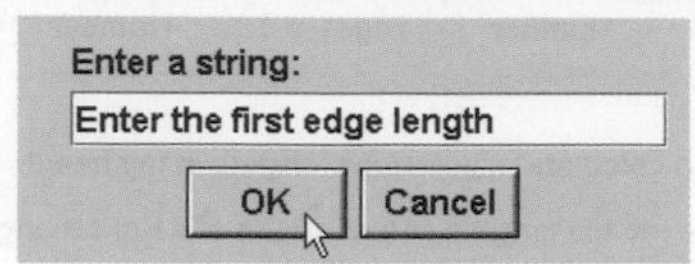

FIGURE 3-17 Customizing a dialog box's prompt message

This yields the **`set()`** message shown at the bottom of Figure 3-18.

```
World.my first method    skaterGirl.computeHypotenuse
public void computeHypotenuse ( ) {                                                    create new parameter
Number hypotenuse = 1 ; Number edge1 = 1 ; Number edge2 = 1 ; String hypotString = default string ;   create new variable
doInOrder {
  skaterGirl .say( I can calculate hypotenuse lengths in my head! ); duration = 3 seconds fontSize = 30 more...
  skaterGirl .say( Give me the lengths of two edges of a right triangle: ); duration = 3 seconds fontSize = 30 more...
  edge1 .set( value , NumberDialog( question = Enter the first edge length: ) more... ); more...
}
```

FIGURE 3-18 Setting a variable to a dialog box's result

Now, when the program flows through the **`set()`** message, it will send **`World`** the **`NumberDialog()`** message, which will display a dialog box asking the user to enter the first edge length. When the user enters a number in that dialog box, the **`NumberDialog()`** function will return that number, which the **`set()`** method will then use to set the value of **`edge1`**.

We can use a similar approach to get the value for **`edge2`**, and once we have the two edge lengths, we are ready to compute the **`hypotenuse`** value. We get as far as shown in Figure 3-19 before we hit a snag.

```
World.my first method | skaterGirl.computeHypotenuse
public void computeHypotenuse ( ) {                                              create new parameter
Number 123 hypotenuse = 1 ; Number 123 edge1 = 1 ; Number 123 edge2 = 1 ; String hypotString = default string ; create new variable
  doInOrder {
    skaterGirl .say( I can calculate hypotenuse lengths in my head! ); duration = 3 seconds fontSize = 30 more...
    skaterGirl .say( Give me the lengths of two edges of a right triangle: ); duration = 3 seconds fontSize = 30 more...
    edge1 .set( value, NumberDialog( question = Enter the first edge length: ) more... ); more...
    edge2 .set( value, NumberDialog( question = Enter the second edge length: ) more... ); more...
    hypotenuse .set( value, 1 ); more...
  }
}
```

FIGURE 3-19 How to compute the hypotenuse

Looking back at the Pythagorean Theorem, we see that we need the square root function. Like the dialog box function, square root is available in the **World**'s *functions* pane, under the *advanced math* category. We thus drag and drop **Math.sqrt()** to replace the placeholder **1** in the **set()** message. From there, we can use the list arrow, the **expressions** menu choice, and the **math** menu choice several times to build the **set()** statement shown in Figure 3-20.

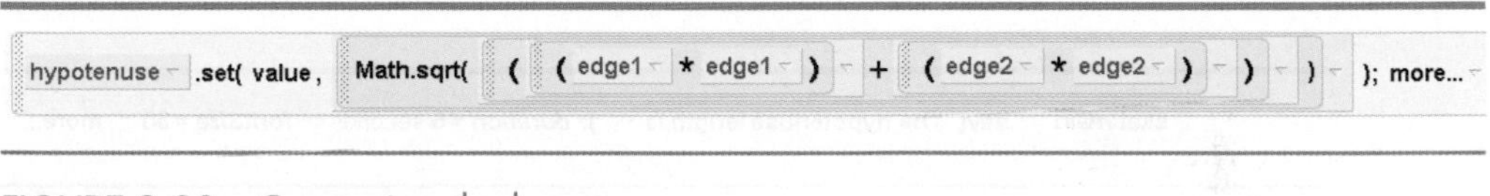
hypotenuse .set(value, Math.sqrt(((edge1 * edge1) + (edge2 * edge2)))); more...

FIGURE 3-20 Computing the hypotenuse

Now that we have the **hypotenuse** calculated, how do we get the **skaterGirl** to say it? We can easily get her to say "**The hypotenuse length is** ", but how do we get her to say the value of **hypotenuse** at the same time? The answer has to do with *types*. As you know, the type of hypotenuse is **Number**. The type of the value we send with the **say()** message must be a **String**. Resolving this dilemma takes several steps.

The first step is to declare a new variable that will contain the value of **hypotenuse**, converted to a **String**. We'll call it **hypotString**, make its type **String**, and leave its initial value as **<None>**. We can then set its value to a placeholder value, like any other variable.

```
hypotenuse .set( value, Math.sqrt( ( ( edge1 * edge1 ) + ( edge2 * edge2 ) ) ) ); more...
hypotString .set( value, default string ); more...
```

FIGURE 3-21 Converting the hypotenuse to a string (part I)

The next step is to use this variable to store a **String** representation of the (**Number**) value of **hypotenuse**. To do this, we go back to the **World**'s *functions* pane again, and under *string operations* we find a function named **toString()**. We drag this function into the **set()** statement to replace its **default string** value. When we drop it, Alice displays a menu from which we can choose **expressions -> hypotenuse** as the thing that we convert to a **String**. The result is the statement in Figure 3-22.

```
hypotString .set( value , hypotenuse .toString() ); more...
```

FIGURE 3-22 Converting the hypotenuse to a string (part II)

We now have a **String** version of the **hypotenuse**. The next step in the algorithm is for the **skaterGirl** to say "The hypotenuse length is X" where X is **hypotString**. To make this happen, we need a way to combine **"The hypotenuse is "** with **hypotString**. In programming, combining two strings **a** and **b** into a single string **ab** is called **concatenating** the strings, and for **String** values, the **+** sign is called the **concatenation operator**. In a concatenation **a + b**, the order of **a** and **b** matters: **"en" + "list"** makes **"enlist"**, but **"list" + "en"** makes **"listen"**.

We can start by having **skaterGirl** say the first part of what we want her to say: **"The hypotenuse length is "**. It doesn't show up well in Figure 3-23, but we must take care to leave a space after the word **is**, to separate it from the next part.

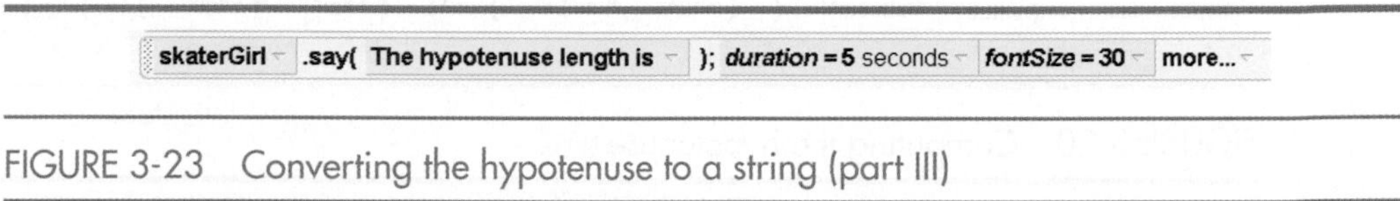

FIGURE 3-23 Converting the hypotenuse to a string (part III)

To make her also say the second part, we make a final trip to the **World**'s *functions* pane, from which we drag the other **String** function (**a+b**) onto **"The hypotenuse length is "** in the **set()** statement. When we drop the **a+b** function onto **"The hypotenuse length is "** in Figure 3-23, Alice takes the **String** that's there (**"The hypotenuse length is "**) as its **a** value. Alice then displays the menu we have seen before, from which we can select **expressions -> hypotString** as the (**a+b**) function's **b** value, as shown in Figure 3-24.

```
skaterGirl .say( The hypotenuse length is + hypotString ); duration = 5 seconds fontSize = 30 more...
```

FIGURE 3-24 Concatenating two strings

Since that is the last step, the method is done! The complete method is shown in Figure 3-25.

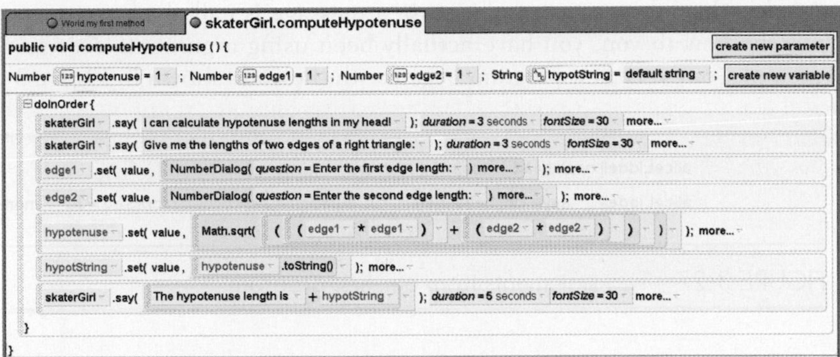

FIGURE 3-25 The **computeHypotenuse()** method (final version)

We then send **skaterGirl** the **computeHypotenuse()** message in **my_first_method()** to finish the program.

To test our work, we enter commonly known values. Figure 3-26 shows the result after we have entered edge lengths of 3 and 4 (the corresponding hypotenuse length is 5).

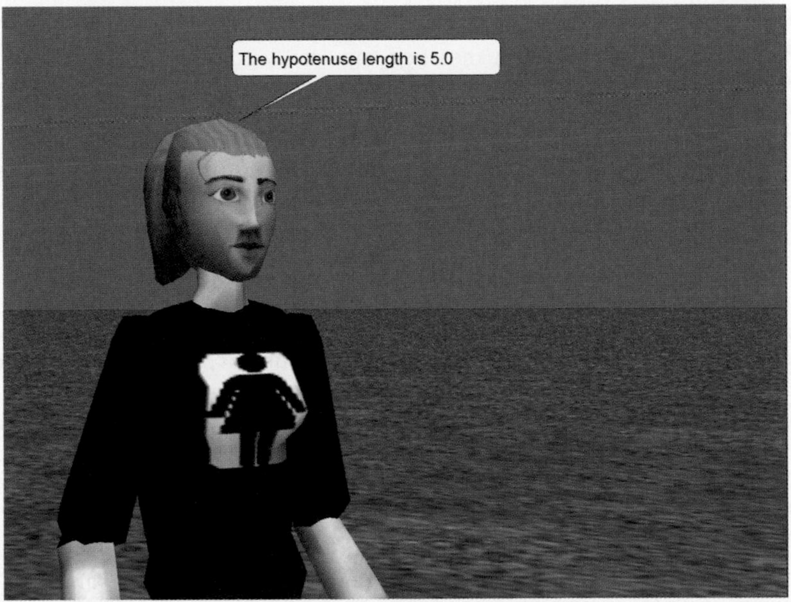

FIGURE 3-26 Testing **computeHypotenuse()**

Variables thus provide a convenient way to store values for later use in a program.

3.2 Parameters

A value that we pass to an object via a message is called an **argument**. While the word may be new to you, you have actually been using arguments ever since Chapter 1. For example, our very first program began with the code shown in Figure 3-27.

```
aliceLiddell.neck.head .pointAt( camera ); more...
aliceLiddell .say( Oh, hello there! ); duration = 2 seconds fontSize = 30 more...
```

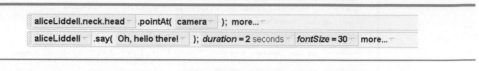

FIGURE 3-27 Two statements from our first program

In the first statement, **`camera`** is an argument being passed to **`aliceLiddell.neck.head`** — the *value* at which **`aliceLiddell.neck.head`** should point. Each of the statements in Figure 3-27 has a single argument: **`camera`** (an **`Object`**) in the first statement, and **`Oh, hello there!`** (a **`String`**) in the second statement. Other methods we have seen require us to pass multiple arguments, as shown in Figure 3-28.

```
flappingDragon.left wing .roll( LEFT , .2 revolutions ); more...
flappingDragon.right wing .roll( RIGHT , 0.2 revolutions ); more...
```

FIGURE 3-28 The `roll()` message requires two arguments

Here, we see that the **`roll()`** message requires two arguments: the *direction* the object is to roll, and the *amount* it is to roll.

When you send an object a message accompanied by an argument, that argument must be stored somewhere so that the receiving object can access it.

> **A parameter is a variable that stores an argument, so that the receiver of the message can access it!**

Thus, the **`pointAt()`** and **`say()`** methods each have a single parameter, while the **`roll()`** method has two parameters. There is no limit to the number of parameters a method can have.

To make all of this a bit more concrete, let's see some examples.

3.2.1 Example 1: Old MacDonald Had A Farm

Suppose we have a user story containing a scene in which a scarecrow is supposed to sing the song "Old MacDonald," one line at a time. Some of the lyrics to this song are below:

Old MacDonald had a farm, E-I-E-I-O. And on this farm he had a cow, E-I-E-I-O. With a moo-moo here, and a moo-moo there, here a moo, there a moo, everywhere a moo-moo. Old MacDonald had a farm, E-I-E-I-O.	*Old MacDonald had a farm, E-I-E-I-O. And on this farm he had a duck, E-I-E-I-O. With a quack-quack here, and a quack-quack there, here a quack, there a quack, everywhere a quack-quack. Old MacDonald had a farm, E-I-E-I-O.*
Old MacDonald had a farm, E-I-E-I-O. And on this farm he had a horse, E-I-E-I-O. With a neigh-neigh here, and a neigh-neigh there, here a neigh, there a neigh, everywhere a neigh-neigh. Old MacDonald had a farm, E-I-E-I-O.	*Old MacDonald had a farm, E-I-E-I-O. And on this farm he had a dog, E-I-E-I-O. With a ruff-ruff here, and a ruff-ruff there, here a ruff, there a ruff, everywhere a ruff-ruff. Old MacDonald had a farm, E-I-E-I-O.*

Subsequent verses introduce other farm animals (for example, chicken, cat, pig, etc.). For now, we will just have the character sing these four verses.

Clearly, we *could* use divide-and-conquer to have the scarecrow sing four verses; in each verse we send the scarecrow five **say()** messages. For example, **singVerse1()** would contain statements like these:

```
scarecrow.say("Old MacDonald had a farm, E-I-E-I-O.");
scarecrow.say("And on this farm he had a cow, E-I-E-I-O.");
scarecrow.say("With a moo-moo here and a moo-moo there,");
scarecrow.say("here a moo, there a moo, everywhere a moo-moo.");
scarecrow.say("Old MacDonald had a farm, E-I-E-I-O.");
```

However, this approach has several disadvantages. One is that if later we want to add a fifth verse, then we must write a new method, containing five more **say()** messages, and add it to the program. With this approach, every new verse we want the scarecrow to sing will require a new method containing five more statements. This seems like a lot of repetitious work.

A related disadvantage of this approach is that each verse-method we write is identical, except for (1) the animal, and (2) the noise it makes.

> **Whenever you find yourself programming the same thing more than once, there is usually a better way to write the program.**

In this case, the better way is to write a single "generic" **singVerse()** method, to which we can pass a given animal and its noise as arguments. That is, we want a message like this:

```
scarecrow.singVerse("cow", "moo");
```

to make the scarecrow sing the first verse; a message like this:

```
scarecrow.singVerse("horse", "neigh");
```

to make him sing the second verse, and so on.

The trick to making this happen is to build a method with a generic *animal* parameter to store whatever animal we want to pass, and a generic *noise* parameter to store the noise it makes. The statements of this method then contain the lyrics that are common to each verse, but using the *animal* parameter in place of the specific cow, duck, horse, or dog; and using the *noise* parameter in place of the specific moo, quack, neigh, or ruff.

Assuming we have created a world containing a **scarecrow** (from Alice's Web Gallery) and whatever other farm-related objects we desire, we can start by creating a new **scarecrow** method named **singVerse()**. With this method open, we click the **create new parameter** button we saw back in Figure 3-1. When clicked, this button generates a **Create New Parameter** dialog box similar to the **Create New Local Variable** dialog box we saw in Figure 3-3. As in that dialog box, we can specify the *name* of the parameter and its *type*. When we click this dialog box's **OK** button, it defines a new parameter with the given *name* and *type* between the method's parentheses. In Figure 3-29, we have used this button to create the **animal** and **noise** parameters.

world.my first method | scarecrow.singVerse

public void singVerse (String animal , String noise) {

create new parameter

create new variable

FIGURE 3-29 Parameters for animal and noise

With the parameters defined, we can proceed to add statements to the method to make the scarecrow sing a verse. Like a variable, a parameter's name appears in the **expressions** menu choice that appears when we drag and drop a statement into the method. Figure 3-30 shows one way we might define the **singVerse()** method.

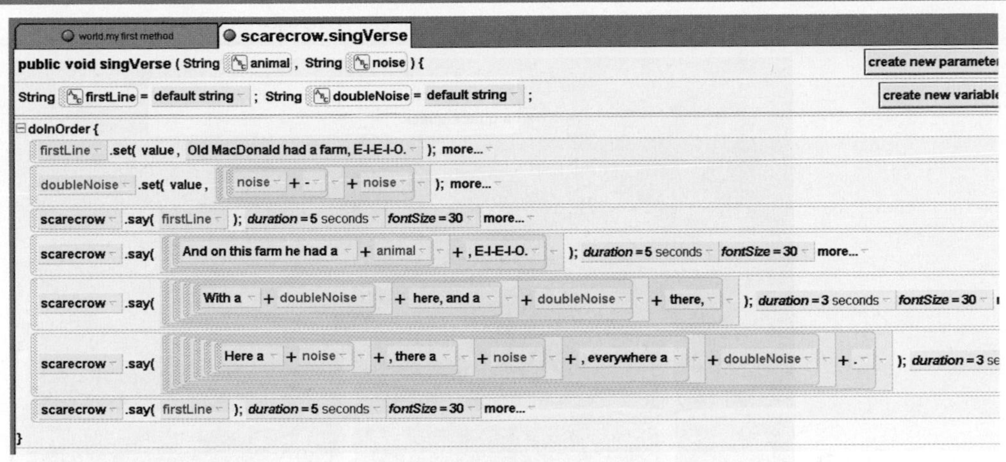

FIGURE 3-30 The **singVerse()** method

Recognizing that the first and last lines are the same, we defined a variable named **firstLine** to store those lines, so that we need not write them twice. Also, seeing that a verse uses the string *noise-noise* three times, we defined a variable named **doubleNoise**, and defined its value as **noise + "-" + noise**, using the string concatenation operator (+) we saw in the last section. In fact, we used the concatenation operator *14 times* in building this method, most often in the statements in which the scarecrow sings the 3rd and 4th lines of the verse.

Given this method, we can now define a **singOldMacDonald()** method quite simply (Figure 3-31).

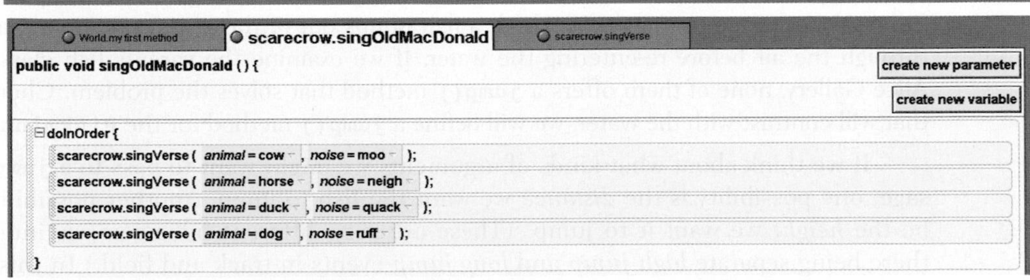

FIGURE 3-31 The **singOldMacDonald()** method

Figure 3-32 presents the program running, partway through its third verse.

Here a quack, there a quack, everywhere
a quack-quack.

FIGURE 3-32 Testing **singOldMacDonald()**

If we should subsequently decide to add a new verse, doing so is as easy as sending the **scarecrow** another **singVerse()** message, with the desired *animal* and *noise* arguments.

3.2.2 Example 2: Jumping Fish!

Suppose we have a user story in which a fish jumps out of the water, tracing a graceful arc through the air before re-entering the water. If we examine the various fish classes in the Alice Gallery, none of them offers a **jump()** method that solves the problem. Choosing one that will contrast with the water, we will define a **jump()** method for the **Pinkminnow** class.

If we think about what kinds of arguments we might want to pass to a **jump()** message, one possibility is the *distance* we want the fish to jump. Another possibility would be the *height* we want it to jump. (These are very different behaviors, as indicated by there being separate *high jump* and *long jump* events in track and field.) In this section, we will have the fish do the equivalent of the long jump, and pass the *distance* we want it to jump.

If we think through the behavior this method should provide, we might sketch it as the sequence of steps shown in Figure 3-33.

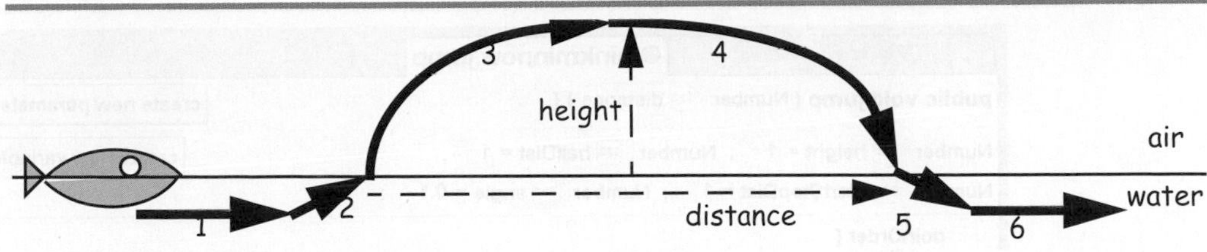

FIGURE 3-33 Sketching a fish's jumping behavior

We can write out these steps as an algorithm as follows:

```
1 fish swims forward a starting distance (to get its speed up)
2 fish angles upward
3 fish moves upward the height and half the distance, angling upward
4 fish moves downward the height and forward half the distance, angling downward
5 fish angles upward (levels off)
6 fish swims forward a stopping distance (coasting to a stop)
```

If we consider how an animal jumps, when an animal jumps a short distance, it doesn't spring very high; but if it jumps a longer distance, it springs higher. The height and distance of an animal's jump are thus related. For the sake of simplicity, we will approximate the height as 1/3 of the distance. (If this proves too simplistic, we can always change it.) Similarly, if a fish is to jump farther, it may need a longer starting distance to get its speed up, and the distance it glides before it stops will be greater. For simplicity's sake, we will assume that the starting and stopping distances are 1/4 of the distance to be jumped.

Using our algorithm and our sketch, we might identify these objects: fish, height, distance, half the distance, angle, starting distance, and stopping distance. We have already selected the **Pinkminnow** class for the fish. Since we intend to pass the distance to be jumped as an argument, and such a value is numeric, we will create a **Number** parameter to store this value using the **create new parameter** button. The remaining objects are all numeric values, so we will define a **Number** variable for each of them, using the **create new variable** button we saw in Figure 3-1. We will use the names **height**, **halfDist**, and **angle** for three of these objects. If we assume that the starting and stopping distances are the same, we can use one variable for both, which we will name **startStopDist**, as shown in Figure 3-34.

```
World.my first method | pinkminnow.jump
public void jump ( Number 123 distance ) {                    create new parameter
Number 123 height = 1 ; Number 123 halfDist = 1 ;             create new variable
Number 123 startStopDist = 1 ; Number 123 angle = 0.1 ;
⊟ doInOrder {
```

FIGURE 3-34 The `jump()` parameter and variables

Given our algorithm and these variables, building the method consists of setting their values appropriately, and then dragging the right statements into the method to elicit the behavior required by our algorithm. Figure 3-35 shows the completed definition.

```
World.my first method | pinkminnow.jump
public void jump ( Number 123 distance ) {                                                                  create
Number 123 height = 1 ; Number 123 halfDist = 1 ; Number 123 startStopDist = 1 ; Number 123 angle = 0.1 ;    cre
⊟ doInOrder {
  height .set( value, ( distance / 3 ) ); more...
  halfDist .set( value, ( distance / 2 ) ); more...
  startStopDist .set( value, ( distance / 4 ) ); more...
  pinkminnow .move( FORWARD , startStopDist meters ); more...
  pinkminnow .turn( BACKWARD , angle revolutions ); duration = 0.1 seconds style = BEGIN_AND_END_ABRUPTLY more...
  ⊟ doTogether {
    pinkminnow .move( FORWARD , halfDist meters ); style = BEGIN_AND_END_ABRUPTLY more...
    pinkminnow .move( UP , height meters ); style = BEGIN_AND_END_ABRUPTLY more...
    pinkminnow .turn( FORWARD , angle revolutions ); style = BEGIN_AND_END_ABRUPTLY more...
  }
  ⊟ doTogether {
    pinkminnow .move( FORWARD , halfDist meters ); style = BEGIN_AND_END_ABRUPTLY more...
    pinkminnow .move( DOWN , height meters ); style = BEGIN_AND_END_ABRUPTLY more...
    pinkminnow .turn( FORWARD , angle revolutions ); style = BEGIN_AND_END_ABRUPTLY more...
  }
  pinkminnow .turn( BACKWARD , angle revolutions ); duration = 0.1 seconds style = BEGIN_AND_END_ABRUPTLY more...
  pinkminnow .move( FORWARD , startStopDist meters ); style = BEGIN_AND_END_ABRUPTLY more...
}
}
```

FIGURE 3-35 The `jump()` method (complete)

We can see in Figure 3-35 that each variable's value is accessed multiple times. One of the benefits of using variables this way is that if we later decide to change a value (for example the height of the jump, or its angle), we only have to change it in one place, instead of in several places. This can be a big time-saver when you are using trial-and-error to find just the right value.

To test our program, we send **pinkminnow** the **jump()** message. To test it thoroughly, we use a variety of argument values (for example, 0.25, 0.5, 1, 2, ...), to check that its behavior is appropriate in each case. Figure 3-36 shows a test using one of these values.

```
World.my first method    pinkminnow.jump
public void my_first_method (){

   pinkminnow.jump( distance = 1 );
```

FIGURE 3-36 Testing the `jump()` method

Figure 3-37 is a montage of snapshots, showing the behavior produced by the **jump()** method.

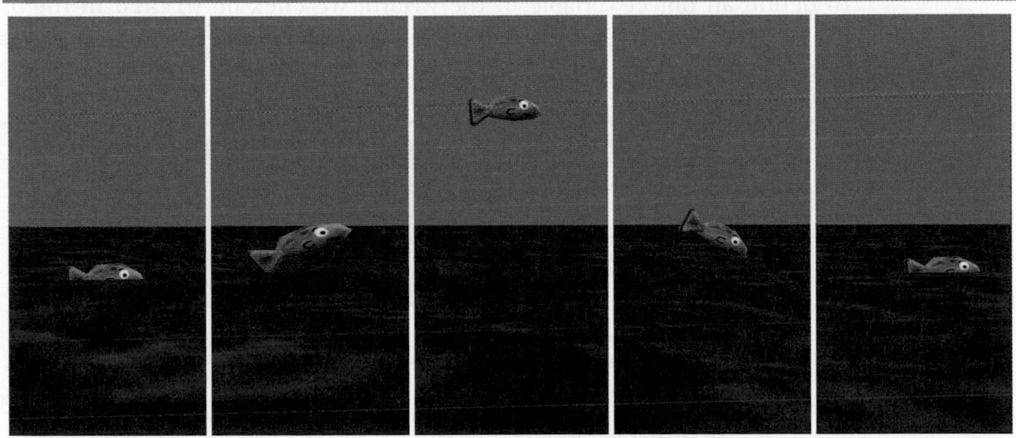

FIGURE 3-37 A jumping fish

Parameters are thus variables through which we can pass arguments to a method. By passing different arguments to the same method, that method can produce different (related) behaviors. For example, the **singVerse()** method allows the **scarecrow** to sing different verses of the same song, depending on what *animal* and *noise* values we pass it. Similarly, the **jump()** method makes the **pinkminnow** jump different distances, depending on what *distance* we pass it.

The key to using parameters well is to anticipate that you will want to pass different values to the method as arguments, and then create a parameter to store such values. A well-written method with parameters is like a stone that (figuratively speaking) lets you kill multiple birds.

3.3 Property Variables

Now that we have seen method variables and parameters, it is time to take a brief look at Alice's third kind of variable: **object variables**, which are also known as **instance variables** or **properties**. Whereas method variables and parameters are defined within a method, an object variable is defined within an object. More precisely, an object variable is defined within the *properties* pane of an object's *details area*.

An object variable allows an object to *remember* one of its properties. Each object has its own variable for the property, in which it can store a value distinct from any other object.

To clarify this, let's look at a concrete example. Suppose a user story calls for twin wizards named *Jim* and *Tim*, and each wizard needs to know his own name. One way to make this happen is to add a **`wizard`** to our world and define within it an object variable whose name is **`myName`**, whose type is **`String`**, and whose value is **`"Jim"`**. If we then make a copy of the **`wizard`**, the new wizard will have its own **`myName`** variable, whose value we can change to **`"Tim"`**.

To define an object variable in the wizard, we click on **`wizard`** in the *object tree*, click the *properties* tab in the *details area*, and then click the **`create new variable`** button we see there[1], as shown in Figure 3-38.

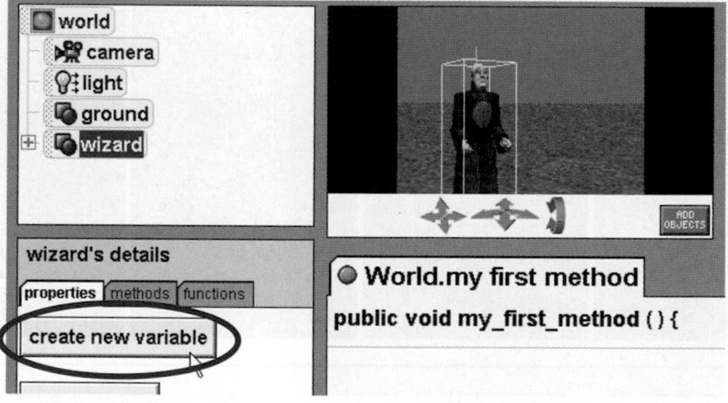

FIGURE 3-38 The properties pane's **`create new variable`** button

1. Just below the **`create new variable`** button is a **`capture pose`** button. When pressed, this button saves the object's current *pose* (the positions+orientations of its subparts) in a new property variable of type **`Pose`**. If you want to pose your character manually before running your program, this button lets you save such poses. You can use the **`setPose()`** method within your program to change an object's pose to a saved pose. (The **`getCurrentPose()`** function can be used to retrieve an object's current pose while your program is running.)

Clicking this button causes the **create new variable** dialog box to appear, which is almost identical to the **Create New Local Variable** dialog box we saw back in Figure 3-3. In it, we enter **myName** for the name, select **Other -> String** as its type, and enter **Jim** for its value. When we click the dialog box's **OK** button, Alice creates a new **String** variable named **myName** whose value is **Jim** in the wizard's *properties* pane, as shown in Figure 3-39.

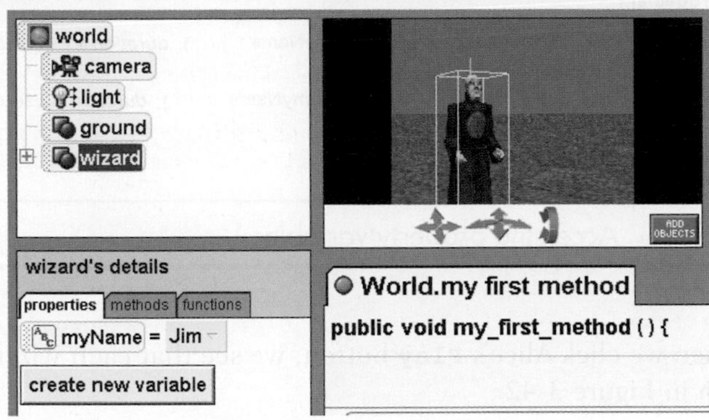

FIGURE 3-39 A new property variable

To make the wizard's twin, we can use the **copy** button (the rightmost control in the **Add Objects** window), as was covered in the Alice Tutorial. Copying the wizard this way gives us two wizards named **Jim**, so we close the **Add Objects** window, click on the second wizard in the *object tree*, click the *properties* tab in the *details area*, and there change the value of the new wizard's **myName** property from **Jim** to **Tim**. See Figure 3-40.

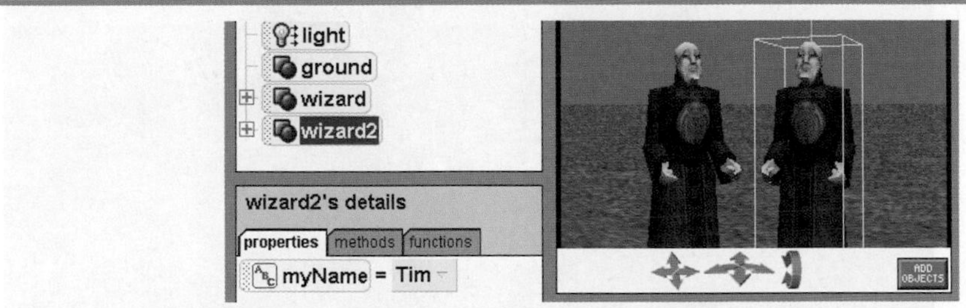

FIGURE 3-40 Twin wizards

A program can now access each wizard's name, as shown in Figure 3-41.

```
World.my first method
public void my_first_method () {

  doTogether {
    wizard .say( My name is + wizard.myName ); duration = 2 seconds fontSize = 30 more...
    wizard2 .say( My name is + wizard2.myName ); duration = 2 seconds fontSize = 30 more...
  }
```

FIGURE 3-41 Accessing property variables

When we click Alice's **Play** button, we see that each wizard "knows" his own name, as shown in Figure 3-42.

FIGURE 3-42 The twin wizards introduce themselves

A property variable thus provides a place for us to store an *attribute* of an object, such as its name, its size, its weight, and anything else we want an object to know about itself.

As we have seen, each Alice object has a number of predefined property variables. These variables store the object's **color** (essentially a filter through which we see the object), its **opacity** (what percentage of light the object reflects), its **vehicle** (what can move this object?), its **skinTexture** (the graphical appearance of the object), its **fillingStyle** (how much of the object gets drawn), its **pointOfView** (the object's position and orientation), and its **isShowing** property (whether or not the object is visible). If you have not done so already, take the time to experiment with each of these properties, to get a feel for what role each plays.

In the next section of this chapter, we will take a closer look at the **vehicle** property.

3.4 Alice Tip: Using the Vehicle Property

In some user stories, it may be desirable to **synchronize** the movements of two objects, so that when one of the objects moves, the other moves with it. To illustrate, let us return to the example from Section 3.1.1, in which Scene 2 had a girl approaching a horse. Suppose that Scene 4 calls for her to ride the horse across the screen. We might set the scene as shown in Figure 3-43.

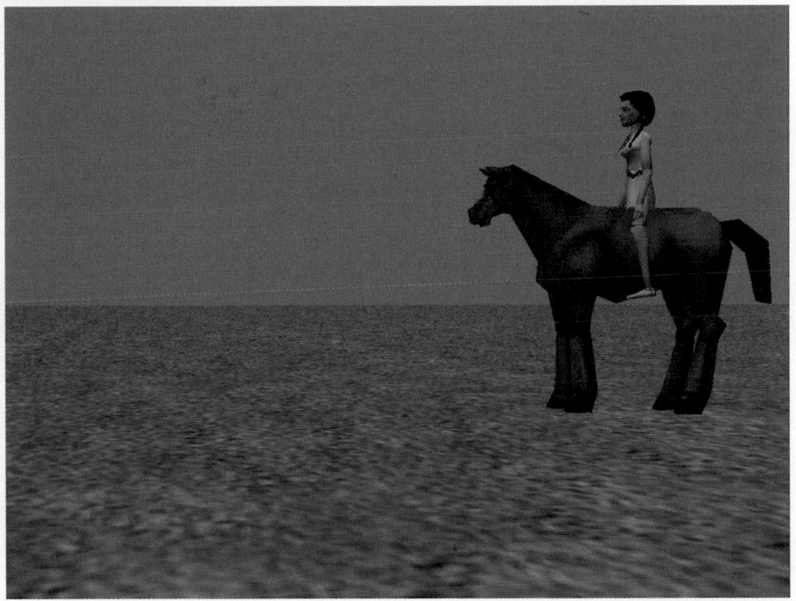

FIGURE 3-43 The girl on the horse

With the girl on the horse, we can use a **move()** message to move the horse across the screen (Figure 3-44).

```
World.my first method | world.playScene4
public void playScene4 () {

  doInOrder {
    horse .move( FORWARD , 5 meters ); more...
  }
```

FIGURE 3-44 Moving the horse across the screen

However, as shown in Figure 3-45, when we do so, the horse moves, leaving the girl hanging suspended in mid-air!

FIGURE 3-45 Moving the horse leaves the girl hanging

We could solve this problem using a **doTogether** block, in which we make the girl and the horse move together. But doing so would force us to write twice as many statements anytime we wanted her to ride the horse, and the additional statements to move the girl will be virtually identical to those we are using to move the horse. It would be much better if we could somehow make the girl "ride" the horse, so that if the horse moves, the girl moves with it.

The way to achieve this better solution is by using the **vehicle** property. As its name implies, an object's **vehicle** is the thing on which it "rides," which is by default, the **world**. If we want the girl to ride the horse, we need to change her **vehicle** property. This can be done by setting her **vehicle** property (using the approach we saw back in Section 1.5.1) at the beginning of the scene, as shown in Figure 3-46.

```
World.my first method | world.playScene4
public void playScene4 () {

  doInOrder {
    nativeGirl .set( vehicle, horse ); more...
    horse .move( FORWARD , 5 meters ); more...
  }
```

FIGURE 3-46 Changing the girl's **vehicle** property

As soon as we have made this change, playing the scene causes the girl to "ride" the horse across the screen, as shown in Figure 3-47.

FIGURE 3-47 The girl rides the horse across the screen

By setting the **vehicle** of the girl to the horse, any **move()** messages we send to the horse will cause her to move as well, effectively synchronizing her movements with those of the horse.

Note that if a subsequent scene calls for the girl and the horse to move independently, we will need to reset her **vehicle** to be the **World**. If we neglect to do this, then **move()** messages we send to the horse will make her move too, since their movements will still be synchronized.

3.5 Functions

We have seen how to use a function to send an object a message in order to get information from it. Suppose we wanted to be able to get information from an object, but there was no predefined function providing that information? In such circumstances, we can define our own function.

3.5.1 Example: Retrieving an Attribute From an Object

Let us return to the twin wizards we met in Section 3.3. Suppose that in addition to their names, the wizards have titles that, together with their names, they use on formal occasions. For example, suppose that the wizard *Jim* goes by the title *The Enchanter*, while the wizard *Tim* goes by the title *The Magus*. (Yes, these sound pretentious to me, too.) It should be evident that we can use the same approach we used in Section 3.3 to define a second property variable for each of the wizards to store his title. We will name this property variable **myTitle**, and define it to be of type **String**. Once we have defined this property, we can set its value to the appropriate value in each of the wizards, as shown in Figure 3-48.

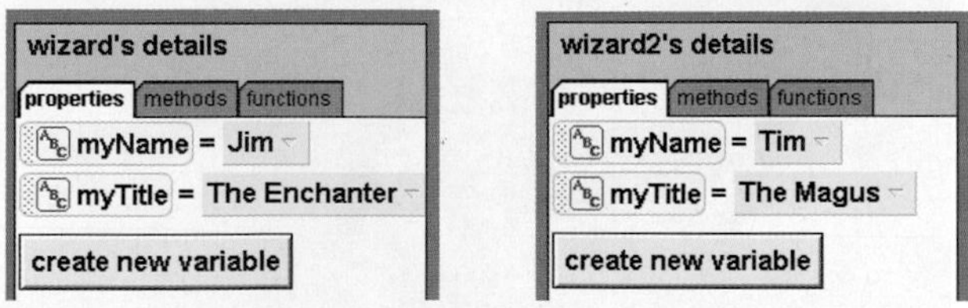

FIGURE 3-48 The wizards' **myTitle** properties

Now suppose that, at times, we need to access a wizard's name, at other times we need to access a wizard's title, and at other times we need to access a wizard's full name (that is, title plus name). In the first case, we can retrieve the wizard's name using the **myName** property. In the second case, we can retrieve the wizard's title using the **myTitle** property. But how can we access the wizard's full name?

One approach would be to concatenate **myTitle** and **myName** with a space in between:

```
wizard.say("I am " + myTitle + " " + myName);
```

This approach is okay, so long as we don't have to access the full name very often. If we have to access it frequently, it can get tiresome to have to repeatedly rebuild the wizard's full name. In such a situation, we can define a function that, when sent to a wizard, produces his full name as its value. To do so, we select the wizard in the *object tree*, click the *functions* tab in the *details area*, and then click the **create new function** button, as shown in Figure 3-49.

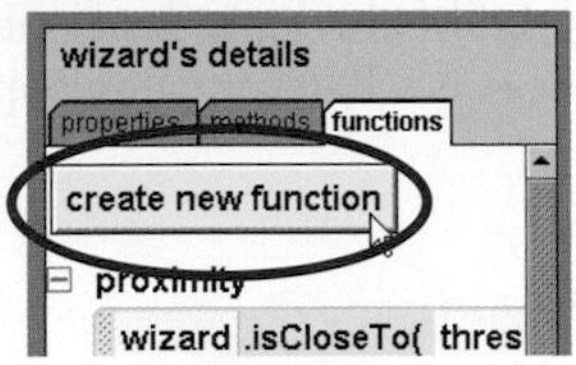

FIGURE 3-49 The **create new function** button

Alice then displays a **New Function** dialog box in which we can enter the name of the function and select the type of value it should produce. We will call the function *getFullName*, and the value it produces is a **String**, as shown in Figure 3-50.

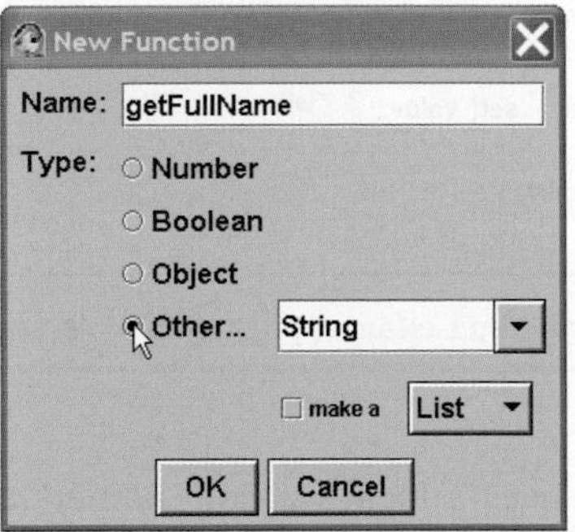

FIGURE 3-50 The **New Function** dialog box

When we click the **OK** button, Alice adds the new function to the wizard's *functions* in the *details area* and opens this function in the *editing area*, as shown in Figure 3-51.

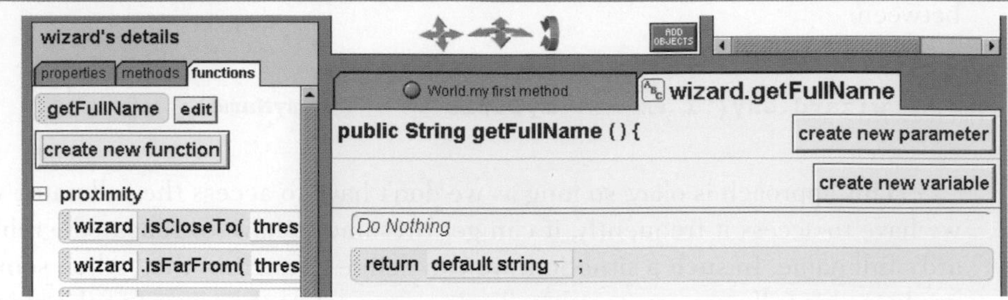

FIGURE 3-51 An "empty" string-returning function

Unlike an Alice method (which produces no value), *a function produces a value*. The value the function produces is whatever value appears in the function's **`return`** **statement**, whose form is:

```
return Value ;
```

When Alice performs this statement, the function produces **`Value`**, sending it back to the place from which the function-message was sent. Note that when Alice defines an "empty" function, it supplies the **`return`** statement with a default **`Value`** appropriate for the function's type.

Figure 3-52 shows one way we could define the function.

FIGURE 3-52 The `getFullName()` function (version 1)

This approach uses a local variable named **`fullName`** to store the computation of concatenating the wizard's title, a space, and the wizard's name, and then returns the value of **`fullName`**. Alternatively, we can eliminate the local variable and just return the value produced by the concatenation operators. Figure 3-53 uses this approach to define **`getFullName()`** for **`wizard2`**.

FIGURE 3-53 The **`getFullName()`** function (version 2)

This version is equivalent to that in Figure 3-52, but it requires no local variable. Now, we can use these functions in a program like that shown in Figure 3-54.

FIGURE 3-54 The wizards introduce themselves

The behavior these functions produce can be seen in Figure 3-55.

FIGURE 3-55 The wizards introducing themselves

3.5.2 Functions With Parameters

Like methods, functions can have parameters to store arguments passed by the sender of the message. The arguments can then be accessed through the parameters. To illustrate, recall that in Section 3.1.2, we built a world in which **skaterGirl** could compute hypotenuse-lengths in her head. The method we wrote there inputs values for the two leg lengths, computes the hypotenuse, and then outputs the result. There might be situations where we just want to calculate the numerical hypotenuse-length, without the input or output:

```
hypotenuse.set(value, skaterGirl.calculateHypotenuse(3, 4) );
```

To define such a function, we make sure **skaterGirl** is selected in the *object tree*, click the *functions* tab in the *details area*, and then click the **create new function** button as before. When the **New Function** dialog box appears, we enter its name (*calculate-Hypotenuse*), but this time we select **Number** as the type of value it produces, as shown in Figure 3-56.

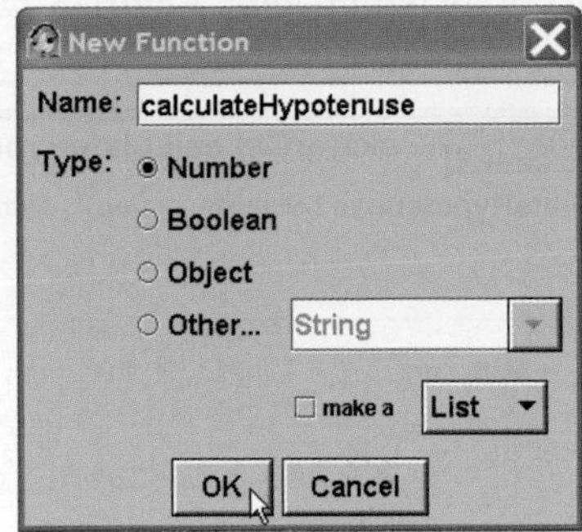

FIGURE 3-56 Creating a number-producing function

When we click the **OK** button, Alice adds **calculateHypotenuse** to **skaterGirl**'s *functions* in the *details area*, and opens the new function in the *editing area*, as shown in Figure 3-57.

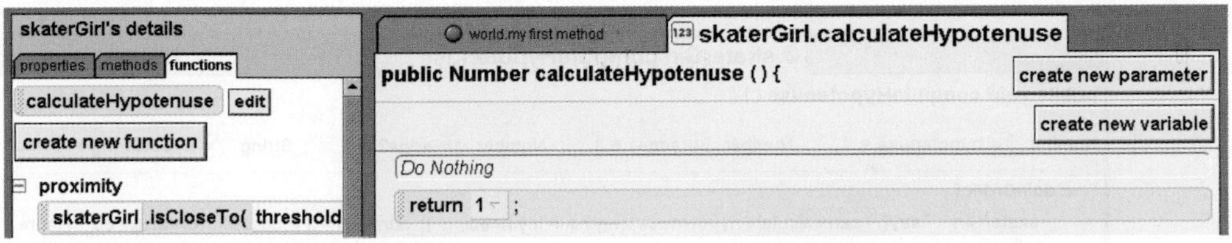

FIGURE 3-57 An empty number-returning function

To store whatever arguments the sender of this message passes for the two leg lengths, we need two parameters, which we can make using the function's **create new parameter** button. This displays a dialog box like the one shown in Figure 3-3, in which we can enter a parameter's name and its type. Doing this for each of the two parameters gives us the function shown in Figure 3-58.

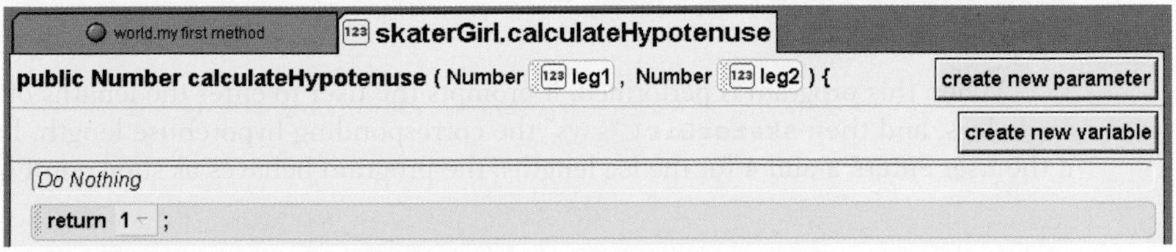

FIGURE 3-58 A function with parameters

To finish the function, we add the necessary operations to make it compute the hypotenuse length using its parameters. Figure 3-59 shows one way to do so.

```
world.my first method | skaterGirl.calculateHypotenuse
public Number calculateHypotenuse ( Number leg1 , Number leg2 ) {
Number hypot = 1 ;
  hypot .set( value , Math.sqrt( ( ( leg1 * leg1 ) + ( leg2 * leg2 ) ) ) );
  return hypot ;
```

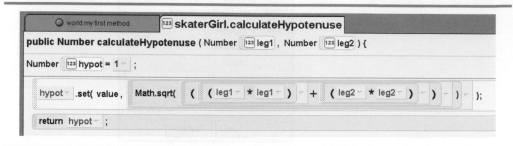

FIGURE 3-59 Calculating the hypotenuse

Given this function, we can now send **skaterGirl** the **calculateHypotenuse()** message, and pass it arguments for the leg lengths. Figure 3-60 shows a revised version of Figure 3-25.

```
world.my first method | skaterGirl.computeHypotenuse
public void computeHypotenuse ( ) {
Number hypotenuse = 1 ; Number edge1 = 1 ; Number edge2 = 1 ; String hypotString = default string ;
  doInOrder {
    skaterGirl .say( I can calculate hypotenuse lengths in my head! ); duration = 3 seconds fontSize = 30 more...
    skaterGirl .say( Give me the lengths of two edges of a right triangle: ); duration = 3 seconds fontSize = 30 more...
    edge1 .set( value , NumberDialog( question = Enter the first edge length ) more... ); more...
    edge2 .set( value , NumberDialog( question = Enter the second edge length ) more... ); more...
    hypotenuse .set( value , skaterGirl.calculateHypotenuse ( leg1 = edge1 , leg2 = edge2 ) ); more...
    hypotString .set( value , hypotenuse .toString() ); more...
    skaterGirl .say( The hypotenuse length is + hypotString ); duration = 5 seconds fontSize = 30 more...
  }
}
```

FIGURE 3-60 Sending a function-message

When this program is performed, it prompts the user to enter the lengths of the two triangle legs, and then **skaterGirl** "says" the corresponding hypotenuse length. For example, if the user enters **3** and **4** for the leg lengths, the program behaves as shown in Figure 3-61.

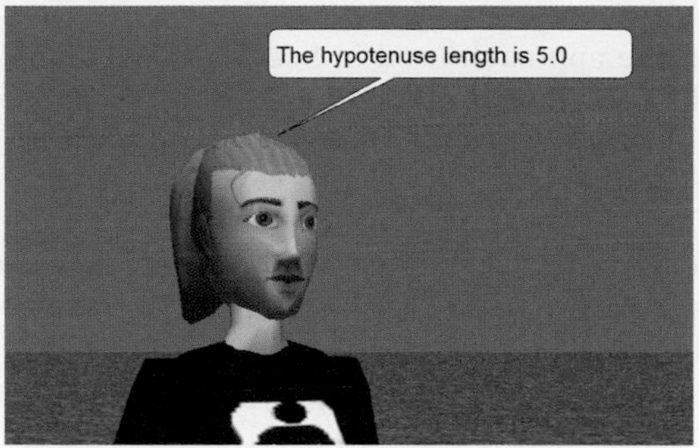

FIGURE 3-61 Testing the function

Functions are thus much like methods. We can create parameters and local variables within each of them, and perform just about any computation we can envision. The difference between the two is that a function-message returns a value to its sender, while a method-message does not. Because of this difference, a function-message must be sent from a place where a *value* can appear, such within a **set()** statement. By contrast, a method-message can only be sent from a place where a *statement* can appear.

Being able to define messages — both method and function — is central to object-based programming. In the chapters to come, we will see many more examples of each.

3.6 Chapter Summary

- ❑ Method variables let us store computed and user-entered values for later use.
- ❑ Parameters let us store and access arguments passed by the sender of a message.
- ❑ Properties (object variables) let us store and retrieve an object's attributes.
- ❑ Alice's **vehicle** property lets us synchronize the movements of two objects.
- ❑ A function lets us send a message to an object, and get a value in response.

3.6.1 Key Terms

argument	placeholder
concatenation	property variable
define a variable	**return** statement
function	synchronized movements
initial value	variable
local variable	variable name
method variable	variable type
object variable	vehicle
parameter	world functions

Programming Projects

3.1 Following the approach used in Section 3.1.1, build a scene containing two people who walk toward each other from opposite sides of the screen. When they meet, they should turn and walk off together toward a building, and enter the building when they get there.

3.2 Using the horse we used in Section 3.4, build a **`gallop()`** method for the horse that makes its legs move realistically through the motions for one stride of a gallop. Then modify the **`playScene4()`** method so that the horse gallops across the screen. (For now, you may send the **`gallop()`** message multiple times.)

3.3 Using the **`heBuilder`** or **`sheBuilder`**, build a person. For your person, define an object method named **`walkInSquare()`** that has a parameter named **`edgeLength`**. When **`walkInSquare(`*`dist`*`)`** is sent to your person, he or she should walk in a square with edges that are each ***`dist`*** meters long. Make certain your person begins and ends at the same spot. When the person is done, have the person say the area and perimeter of the square.

3.4 Using the ideas in this chapter, build a world containing a person who can calculate Einstein's formula $e = m^*c^2$ in his or her head, where the user enters the m value (mass, in kilograms), and c is the speed of light (299,792,458 meters per second). Define descriptive variables for each quantity, and use the **`World`** function **`pow()`** to compute c^2.

3.5 Choose a hopping animal from the Alice Gallery (for example, a frog, a bunny, etc.). Write a **`hop()`** method that makes it hop in a realistic fashion, with a parameter that lets the sender of the message specify how far the animal should hop. Using your **`hop()`** method, have your animal hop around a building in four hops.

3.6 *The Farmer in the Dell* is an old folk song with the lyrics below. Create an Alice program containing a character who sings this song. Use a **`singVerse()`** method, parameters, and variables to write your program efficiently.

The farmer in the dell. The farmer in the dell. Heigh-ho, the derry-o. The farmer in the dell.	*The farmer takes a wife. The farmer takes a wife. Heigh-ho, the derry-oh. The farmer takes a wife.*
The wife takes a child. The wife takes a child. Heigh-ho, the derry-oh. The wife takes a child.	*The child takes a nurse. The child takes a nurse. Heigh-ho, the derry-oh. The child takes a nurse.*
The nurse takes a cow. The nurse takes a cow. Heigh-ho, the derry-oh. The nurse takes a cow.	*The cow takes a dog. The cow takes a dog. Heigh-ho, the derry-oh. The cow takes a dog.*

The dog takes a cat. *The dog takes a cat.* *Heigh-ho, the derry-oh.* *The dog takes a cat.*	*The cat takes a rat.* *The cat takes a rat.* *Heigh-ho, the derry-oh.* *The cat takes a rat.*
The rat takes the cheese. *The rat takes the cheese.* *Heigh-ho, the derry-oh.* *The rat takes the cheese.*	*The cheese stands alone.* *The cheese stands alone.* *Heigh-ho, the derry-oh.* *The cheese stands alone.*

3.7 Using the **heBuilder** or **sheBuilder** (or any of the other persons in the Alice Gallery with enough detail), build male and female persons and add them to your world. Using your persons, build a program in which your people dance the waltz (or a similar dance in which the partners' movements are synchronized). Have your world play music while your people dance.

3.8 Build a world in which two knights on horseback joust, using the techniques from this chapter.

3.9 In Section 2.4, we developed Scene 2 of a program, in which a wizard confronts three trolls. Write a wizard method **castChangeSizeSpell(*obj*, *newSize*)**, that takes an object ***obj*** and a number ***newSize*** as arguments. The method should cause the wizard to turn towards ***obj***, raise his arms, say a magic word or phrase, and then lower his arms. The method should resize ***obj*** the amount specified by ***newSize***, and then make certain ***obj*** is standing on the ground. Create a scene 3 in which the wizard uses the **castChangeSizeSpell()** message to defeat the trolls by shrinking most of them to 1/10 their original size.

3.10 Alice provides the **Pose** type, which can be used to store the position of each of an object's subparts. Under the *properties* pane, the **capture pose** button allows you to save an object's current **Pose** in a property variable before the program is run. The function named **getCurrentPose()** can be used (as the value of a **set()** message) to save an object's pose in a **Pose** variable as the program is running. The **setPose()** method can be used to set an object's pose to a pose stored in a **Pose** variable. Rewrite the **march()** method we wrote in Section 2.2.2. Discard the **moveLeftLegForward()** and **moveRightLegForward()** methods we used, using three **Pose** variables instead.

Chapter 4
Flow Control

Controlling complexity is the essence of computer programming.

BRIAN KERNIGHAN

When you get to the fork in the road, take it.

YOGI BERRA

If you build it, he will come.

THE VOICE (JAMES EARL JONES), IN *FIELD OF DREAMS*

While you're at it, why don't you give me a nice paper cut and pour some lemon juice on it?

MIRACLE MAX (BILLY CRYSTAL), IN *THE PRINCESS BRIDE*

Objectives

Upon completion of this chapter, you will be able to:

- ❑ Use the **`Boolean`** type and its basic operations
- ❑ Use the **`if`** statement to perform some statements while skipping others
- ❑ Use the **`for`** and **`while`** statements to perform (other) statements more than once
- ❑ Use **`Boolean`** variables and functions to control **`if`** and **`while`** statements
- ❑ Use the **`wait()`** message to temporarily suspend program execution

In Chapter 1, we saw that the flow of a program is the sequence of steps the program follows in performing a story. From the perspective of an Alice program, we can think of a flow as the sequence of statements that are performed when we click the **Play** button.

In the preceding chapters, the programs we have written have mostly used the **doInOrder** statement, which produces a sequential execution. However, we sometimes used a **doTogether** statement, which produces a parallel execution. If we consider a group of *N* statements within a **doInOrder** statement compared to a **doTogether** statement, we can visualize the difference in behavior of these two statements in a **flow diagram** like the one shown in Figure 4-1.

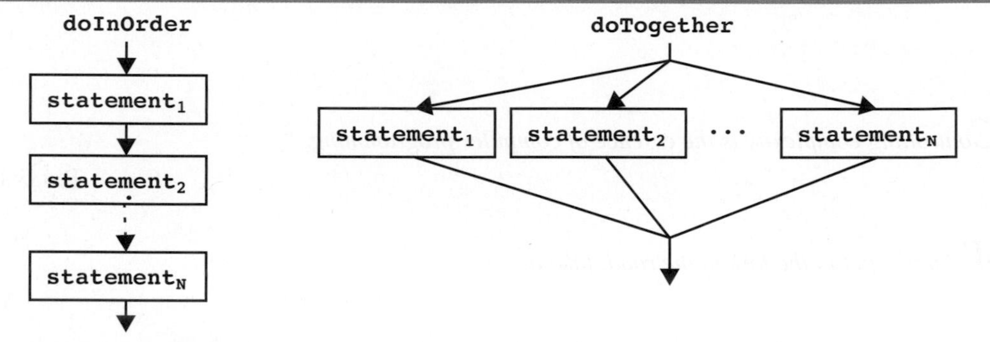

FIGURE 4-1 The flows produced by the **doInOrder** and **doTogether** statements

The **doInOrder** and **doTogether** are thus **flow control** statements, because their effect is to *control the flow* of the program through the statements within them. Computer scientists often describe flow control statements as **control structures**.

In this chapter, we will examine several of Alice's flow control statements, including the following:

- the **if** statement, which directs the flow through one group of statements and away from another group of statements
- the **for** statement, which directs the flow through a group of statements a fixed number of times
- the **while** statement, which directs the flow through a group of statements an arbitrary number of times

Before we examine these statements, let's briefly look at a related topic: the **Boolean** type.

4.1 The Boolean Type

You may recall from Chapter 3 that **Boolean** is one of Alice's basic types (for defining variables). The **Boolean** type is named after George Boole, a 19th century English mathematician who studied *true/false* values and the kinds of operations that can be used with them.

Whereas a **Number** variable can have any of millions of (numeric) values, and an **Object** variable can refer to any Alice object, a **Boolean** variable can have either of just two values: **true** or **false**. At first, this may seem rather limiting: what good is a type that only provides two values? As we shall see, the **Boolean** type is extremely useful when we want the program to make decisions. Decision-making depends on current circumstances or *conditions*, so a piece of a program that produces a **true** or **false** value is called a **boolean expression** or **condition**.

4.1.1 Boolean Functions

The *functions* pane of Alice's *details area* contains questions we can ask an object. When the answer to a question is **true** or **false**, the function is a condition. Many of the questions we can ask an object produce a **Boolean** value for their answer, including those shown in Figure 4-2.

Function	Value Produced
***obj*.isCloseTo(*dist*, *obj2*)**	**true**, if ***obj2*** is within ***dist*** meters of ***obj***; **false**, otherwise.
***obj*.isFarFrom(*dist*, *obj2*)**	**true**, if ***obj2*** is at least ***dist*** meters away from ***obj***; **false**, otherwise.
***obj*.isSmallerThan(*obj2*)**	**true**, if ***obj2***'s volume exceeds that of ***obj***; **false**, otherwise.
***obj*.isLargerThan(*obj2*)**	**true**, if ***obj***'s volume exceeds that of ***obj2***; **false**, otherwise.
***obj*.isNarrowerThan(*obj2*)**	**true**, if ***obj2***'s width exceeds that of ***obj***; **false**, otherwise.
***obj*.isWiderThan(*obj2*)**	**true**, if ***obj***'s width exceeds that of ***obj2***; **false**, otherwise.
***obj*.isShorterThan(*obj2*)**	**true**, if ***obj2***'s height exceeds that of ***obj***; **false**, otherwise.
***obj*.isTallerThan(*obj2*)**	**true**, if ***obj***'s height exceeds that of ***obj2***; **false**, otherwise.

FIGURE 4-2 Boolean functions

continued

Function	Value Produced
***obj*.isToTheLeftOf(*obj2*)**	**true**, if ***obj***'s position is beyond ***obj2***'s left edge; **false**, otherwise.
***obj*.isToTheRightOf(*obj2*)**	**true**, if ***obj***'s position is beyond ***obj2***'s right edge; **false**, otherwise.
***obj*.isAbove(*obj2*)**	**true**, if ***obj***'s position is above ***obj2***'s top edge; **false**, otherwise.
***obj*.isBelow(*obj2*)**	**true**, if **obj**'s position is below ***obj2***'s bottom edge; **false**, otherwise.
***obj*.isInFrontOf(*obj2*)**	**true**, if ***obj***'s position is before ***obj2***'s front edge; **false**, otherwise.
***obj*.isBehind(*obj2*)**	**true**, if ***obj***'s position is beyond ***obj2***'s rear edge; **false**, otherwise.
***obj*.isToTheLeftOf(*obj2*)**	**true**, if ***obj***'s position is beyond ***obj2***'s left edge; **false**, otherwise.

FIGURE 4-2 Boolean functions *(continued)*

Note that most of these functions refer to an object's bounding box. For example, the function ***obj*.isBehind(*obj2*)** uses the rear edge of ***obj2***'s bounding box.

These functions can be used with an **if** or **while** statement (see below) to make a decision or otherwise control an object's behavior.

4.1.2 Boolean Variables

Another kind of condition is the **Boolean** variable or parameter. **Boolean** variables, parameters, or properties can be created by clicking the appropriate **create new variable** (or **parameter**) button, and then specifying **Boolean** as the type of the new variable (or parameter). Such variables can be used to store **true** or **false** values until they are needed, and can serve as a condition in an **if** or **while** statement, which we describe below.

4.1.3 Relational Operators

Another kind of condition is produced by an *operator* that computes a **true** or **false** value. The six most common operators that produce **Boolean** values are called the **relational operators**, and they are shown in Figure 4-3.

Relational Operator	Name	Value Produced
`val1 == val2`	equality	**true**, if **val1** and **val2** have the same value; **false**, otherwise.
`val1 != val2`	inequality	**true**, if **val1** and **val2** have different values; **false**, otherwise.
`val1 < val2`	less-than	**true**, if **val1** is less than **val2**; **false**, otherwise.
`val1 <= val2`	less-than-or-equal	**true**, if **val1** is less than or equal to **val2**; **false**, otherwise.
`val1 > val2`	greater-than	**true**, if **val1** is greater than **val2**; **false**, otherwise.
`val1 >= val2`	greater-than-or-equal	**true**, if **val1** is greater than or equal to **val2**; **false**, otherwise.

FIGURE 4-3 The relational operators

In Alice, the six relational operators are located in the *functions* pane of the **world**'s *details area*. These are most often used to compare **Number** values. For example, suppose a person is to receive overtime pay if he or she works 40 hours or more in a week. If **hoursWorked** is a **Number** variable in which a person's weekly working hours are stored, then the condition

```
hoursWorked > 40
```

will produce **true** if the person should receive overtime pay, and **false** if he or she should not. Relational operators compare two values and produce an appropriate **true** or **false** value.

Beyond numeric values, the equality (**==**) and inequality (**!=**) operators can be used to compare **String**, **Object**, and **Other** values. We will see an example of this in Section 4.2.

4.1.4 Boolean Operators

The final three conditional operators are used to combine or modify relational operations. These are called the **boolean operators**, and they are shown in Figure 4-4.

Boolean Operation	Name	Value Produced
val1 && val2	AND	**true**, if **val1** and **val2** are both **true**; **false**, otherwise.
val1 || val2	OR	**true**, if either **val1** or **val2** is **true**; **false**, otherwise.
!val	NOT	**true**, if **val** is **false**; **false**, if **val** is **true**.

FIGURE 4-4 The boolean operators

Like the relational operators, Alice provides the boolean operators in the *functions* pane of the **World**'s *details area*. To illustrate their use, suppose we want to know if a person is a teenager, and their age is stored in a **Number** variable named **age**. Then the condition

```
age > 12 && age < 20
```

will produce the value **true** if the person is a teenager; otherwise it will produce the value **false**. Similarly, suppose that a valid test score is in the range 0 to 100, and we want to guard against data-entry mistakes. If the score is in a **Number** variable named **testScore**, then we can decide if it is invalid with the condition

```
testScore < 0 || testScore > 100
```

since the condition will produce **true** if either **testScore < 0** or **testScore > 100** is **true**, but will produce **false** if neither of them is **true**.

Now that we have seen the various ways to build a condition, let's see how we can make use of them to control the flow of a program.

4.2 The `if` Statement

4.2.1 Introducing Selective Flow Control

Suppose we have a user story in which the following scene occurs:

> Scene 3: A princess meets a mute dragon, and says "Hello." The dragon just looks at her. She asks it, "Can you understand me?" The dragon shakes its head up and down to indicate *yes*. She says, "Can you speak?" The dragon shakes its head sideways to indicate *no*. She says, "Can you only answer yes or no questions?" The dragon shakes its head *yes*. She says, "Are you a tame dragon?" The dragon shakes its head *no*.

The co-star of the scene is a mute dragon, who answers yes-or-no questions by shaking his head up and down for *yes*, and shaking it sideways for *no*. We could write two separate **dragon** methods, one named **shakeHeadYes()**, and another named **shakeHeadNo()**. Instead, let's "kill two birds with one stone" and write one **shakeHead()** method providing both behaviors.

As we saw in Chapter 3, the key to making one method do the work of two (or more) is to use a parameter to produce the different behaviors. In this case, we will pass the argument **yes** when we want the dragon to shake its head up and down, and pass the argument **no** when we want it to shake its head sideways. To store this argument, we will need a parameter whose type is **String**. For lack of a better name, we will name the parameter **yesOrNo**.

If we write out the behavior this method should produce, we might write the following:

Parameter: yesOrNo, a String.

If *yesOrNo* is equal to "yes", the dragon shakes his head up and down;

Otherwise, the dragon shakes his head sideways.

The key idea here is that if the parameter has one value, we want one thing to happen; otherwise, we want something else to happen. That *if* is the magic word. Any time we use the word *if* to describe a desired behavior, we can use Alice's **if statement** to produce that behavior.

To build this method in Alice, we might start by opening a world, adding a **playScene3()** method to the world, adding a dragon to the world; positioning the camera so that we can see the dragon's head clearly; selecting **dragon** in the *object tree*; creating a new method named **shakeHead()**; and then within this method, creating a new parameter named **yesOrNo**, whose type is **String**. The result is shown in Figure 4-5.

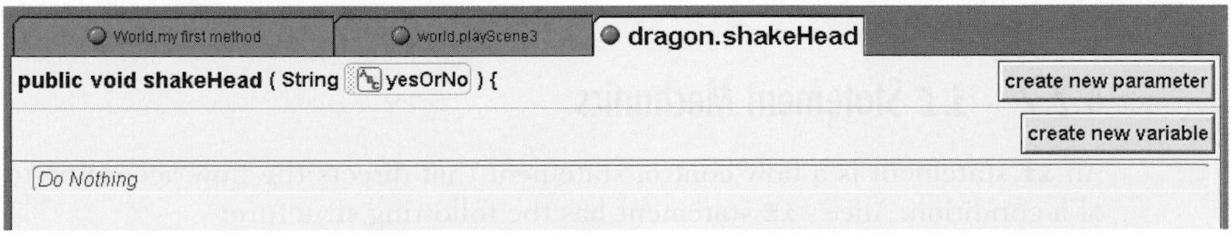

FIGURE 4-5 The empty **shakeHead()** method

Looking at the algorithm for this method, we see the magic word *if*. There is a control named **if** at the bottom of Alice's *editing area*, so we drag it into the method. When we drop it, Alice produces a **condition** menu, with the choices **true** or **false**, as shown in Figure 4-6.

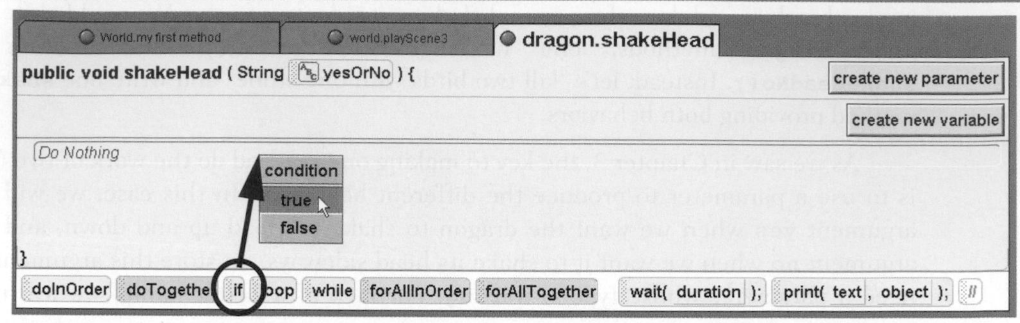

FIGURE 4-6 Dragging the `if` control

For the moment, we will just choose **`true`** as a *placeholder* value. Alice then generates an **`if`** statement in the method, as shown in Figure 4-7.

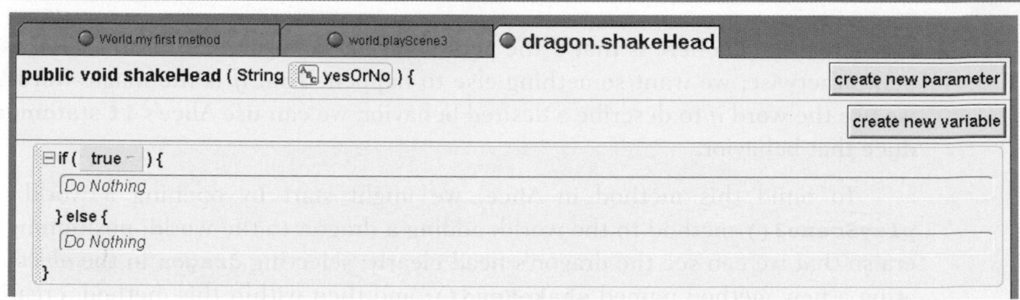

FIGURE 4-7 The Alice `if` statement

4.2.2 `if` Statement Mechanics

An **`if`** statement is a flow control statement that directs the flow according to the value of a condition. Alice's **`if`** statement has the following structure:

```
if ( Condition ) {
    Statements1
} else {
    Statements2
}
```

and we might visualize the **`if`** statement's flow-behavior as shown in Figure 4-8.

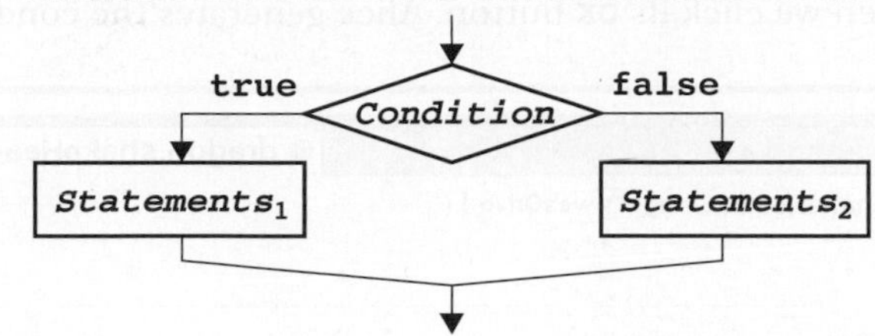

FIGURE 4-8 Flow through an `if` statement

Figure 4-8 shows that when the flow reaches an **`if`** statement, it reaches a "fork" in its path. Depending on its ***`Condition`***, the flow proceeds one way or the other, but not both. That is, when the flow first reaches an **`if`** statement, its ***`Condition`*** is evaluated. If the value of the ***`Condition`*** is **`true`**, then the flow is directed through the first group of statements (and the second group is ignored); if the ***`Condition`***'s value is **`false`**, then the flow is directed through the second group of statements (ignoring the first group). Put differently, when the **`if`** statement's ***`Condition`*** is **`true`**, then the first group of statements is *selected* and the second group is skipped; otherwise, the second group of statements is *selected* and the first group is skipped. The **`if`** statement's behavior is sometimes called **selective flow**, or **selective execution.**

4.2.3 Building `if` Statement Conditions

Back in the user story, we want the dragon to shake its head up and down if **`yesOrNo`** is equal to **`yes`**; otherwise, it should shake its head sideways. We saw in Figure 4-3 that the **equality operator** is **`==`**, so that is what we need. To use it, we can click on the **`yesOrNo`** parameter, drag it into the *editing area*, and drop it on the placeholder in the **`if`** statement's condition. Alice will display a menu from which we can choose **`yesOrNo ==`** , followed by a second menu from which we can choose the **`b`**-value, as shown in Figure 4-9.

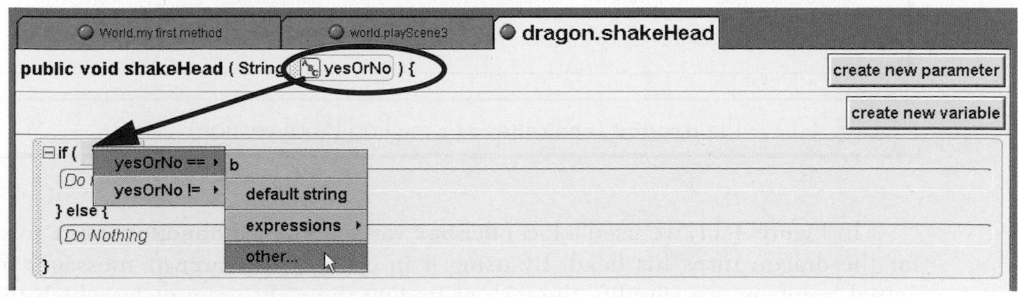

FIGURE 4-9 Dragging a parameter to an `if` statement's condition

Choosing **other** for the **b**-value produces a dialog box into which we can type **"yes"**. When we click its **OK** button, Alice generates the condition shown in Figure 4-10.

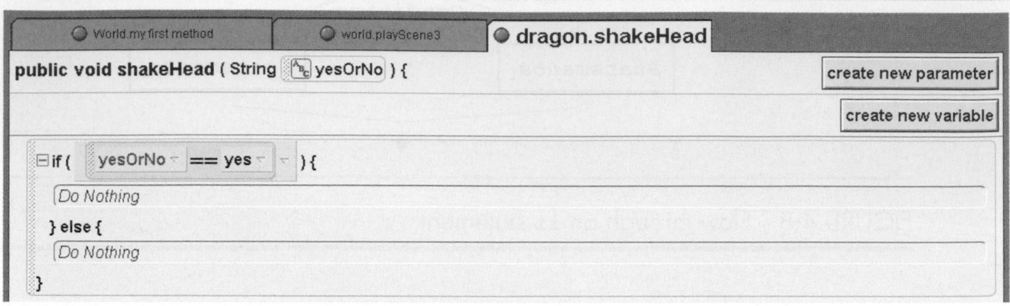

FIGURE 4-10 An **if** statement's condition using a parameter

With the condition in place, finishing the method consists only of placing messages in the top *Do Nothing* area to shake the dragon's head up and down, and placing messages in the bottom *Do Nothing* area to shake its head sideways. Figure 4-11 shows the finished method.

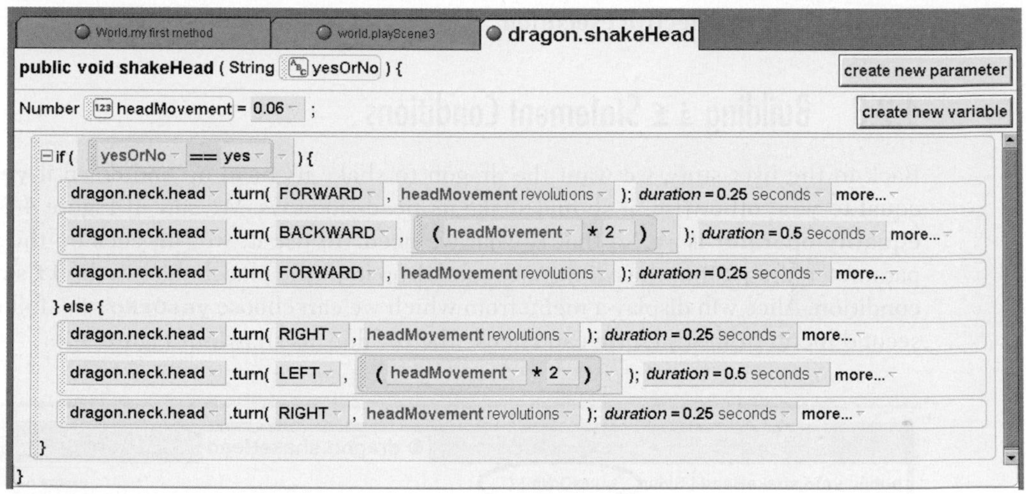

FIGURE 4-11 The **dragon.shakeHead()** method (final version)

In Figure 4-11, we used a local **Number** variable named **headMovement** to store how far the dragon turns his head. By using it in each of the **turn()** messages instead of actual numbers, we simplify the task of finding the right amount by which the dragon should shake his head, since trying a given value only requires one change (to the variable) instead of six changes.

To test the **shakeHead()** method, we build the scene method, as shown in Figure 4-12.

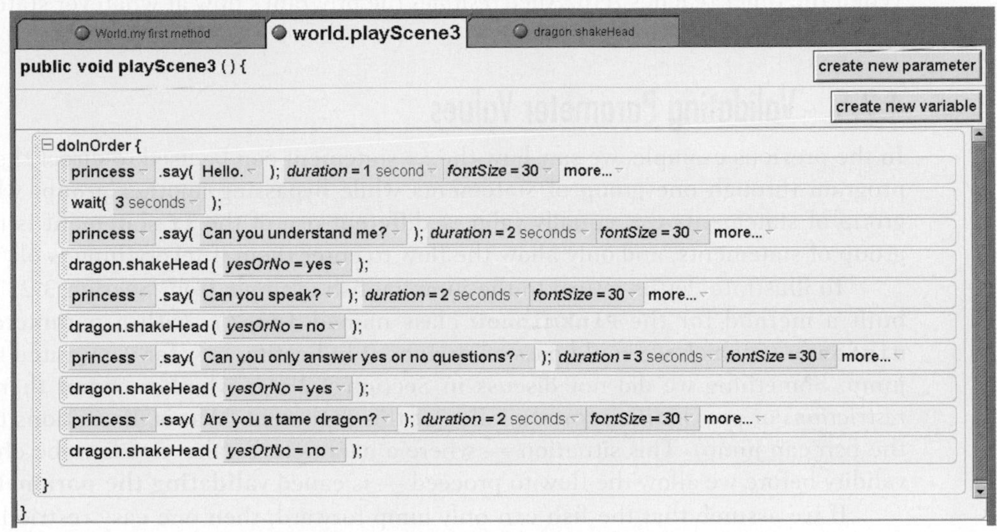

FIGURE 4-12 Testing **shakeHead()** in **playScene3()**

When we click Alice's **Play** button, we see that the **shakeHead()** method works as intended, as shown in Figure 4-13.

FIGURE 4-13 Testing the **shakeHead()** method

4.2.4 The `wait()` Statement

To introduce a time delay between the princess's first and second statements in Figure 4-12, we used another flow control statement named **wait()**, whose form is as follows:

```
wait(numSecs);
```

When the flow reaches this statement, Alice *pauses* the program's flow, sets an internal timer to **numSecs** seconds, and starts this timer counting down towards zero. When the timer reaches zero, Alice *resumes* the program's flow at whatever statement follows the **wait()**.

4.2.5 Validating Parameter Values

In the previous example, we saw how the **if** statement can be used to direct the flow of a program through one group of statements while bypassing another group, where each group of statements was equally valid. A different use of the **if** statement is to *guard* a group of statements, and only allow the flow to enter them if "everything is ok."

To illustrate, let us return to the jumping fish example from Section 3.2. There, we built a method for the **Pinkminnow** class named **jump()**, with a parameter named **distance** to which we could pass an argument indicating how far we wanted the fish to jump. Something we did not discuss in Section 3.2 was whether or not there are any *restrictions* or *preconditions* on the value of this argument (that is, limitations to how *far* the fish can jump). This situation — where a parameter's value needs to be checked for validity before we allow the flow to proceed — is called **validating the parameter**.

If we assume that the fish can only jump forward, then one easy restriction is that the argument passed to **distance** must be positive. We can check this with the condition **distance > 0**. Passing an argument that is 0 or less can be treated as an error.

There may also be an upper bound on how far a **PinkMinnow** can jump, but identifying such a bound is more difficult. Minnows are rather small fish, so 2 meters might be a reasonable upper bound. However if a minnow were bigger than normal, or were super-strong, maybe it could jump farther, so we want to make this upper bound easy to change. We can do so by defining a variable named **MAX_DISTANCE**, and then using the condition **distance <= MAX_DISTANCE** to check that the argument passed to parameter **distance** is within this bound.

> If a variable's value will not change, and its purpose is to improve a program's readability, name it with all uppercase letters, to distinguish it from normal variables.

We now have two conditions that need to be met in order for the argument passed to the parameter to be deemed valid: **distance > 0** and **distance <= MAX_DISTANCE**. Since *both* of these must be true in order for our argument to be acceptable, we use the boolean AND operator (**&&**) to combine them: **distance > 0 && distance <= MAX_DISTANCE**.

We will use these ideas to revise the **jump()** method, as follows:

```
if (distance > 0 && distance <= MAX_DISTANCE) {
   // ... statements performed when distance is valid
   // (make the fish jump)
} else {  // ... distance is invalid
   if (distance <= 0) {
      // ... statements performed when distance is too low
   } else {
      // ... statements performed when distance is too high
   }
}
```

Here, we are using an **`if`** statement with a second **`if`** statement nested within its **`else`** statements. The first **`if`** is often called the **outer `if`**, and the second **`if`** is often called the **inner `if`**, or the **nested `if`**.

Figure 4-14 presents a revised version of the **`jump()`** method, using this approach to validate the parameter.

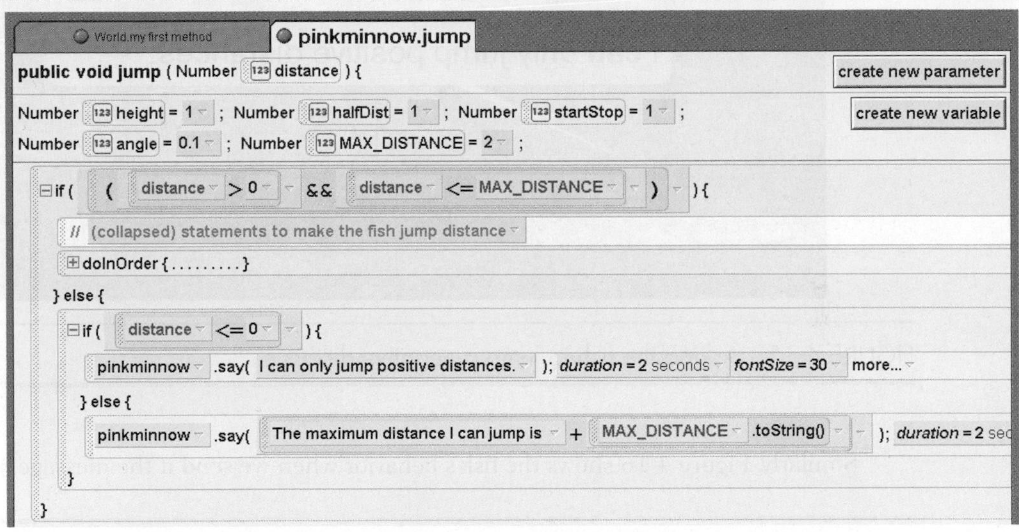

FIGURE 4-14 Validating a parameter's value with nested `if` statements

To save space, we have collapsed the **`doInOrder`** statement that contains the statements that make the fish jump, using the plus (+) sign at the beginning of the statement.

Let us take a moment to trace the program flow through the revised method:

- When **`distance`** is valid, the outer **`if`**'s condition will be **`true`**, so flow will proceed into the statements that make the fish jump, as we saw in Figure 3-36 in Chapter 3.
- When **`distance`** is invalid, the first condition will be **`false`**, so flow will proceed into the **`else`** statements of the outer **`if`**. The only statement there is the inner **`if`** statement, which determines *why* **`distance`** is invalid (too small or too large?):
  - If **`distance`** is zero or less, the flow proceeds to the statement in which we send the fish the first **`say()`** message.
  - Otherwise, **`distance`** must be greater than **`MAX_DISTANCE`**, so the flow proceeds to the statement in which we send the fish the second **`say()`** message.

To illustrate, Figure 4-15 shows the fish's behavior when we send it the message **`jump(-2)`**.

FIGURE 4-15 Asking the fish to jump a negative distance

Similarly, Figure 4-16 shows the fish's behavior when we send it the message **`jump(3)`**.

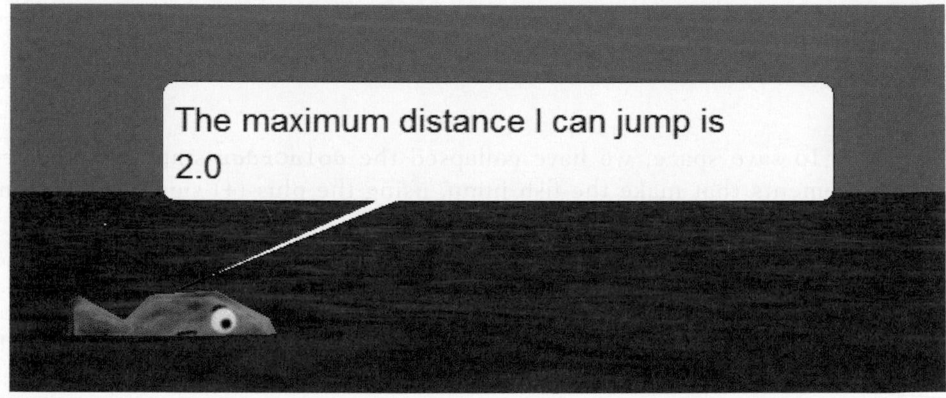

FIGURE 4-16 Asking the fish to jump too far

When building a method with a parameter, think about whether there are any "bad" arguments that could be passed to the parameter. If so, use an **`if`** statement to guard against such values.

The **`if`** statement thus provides a way to build **if-then-else logic** into a method. When such logic uses a method's parameter for its condition, then the method can produce different behaviors, based on what argument is passed to that parameter when the message is sent.

4.3 The `for` Statement

4.3.1 Introducing Repetition

In Section 2.2.1, we built a **`flapWings()`** method for the dragon, and in Section 2.3, we saw how to rename, save, and import the dragon as a **`flappingDragon`**. One drawback to the **`flapWings()`** method is that the **`flappingDragon`** will only flap its wings once. Now that we have learned about parameters, we might improve this method by passing it an argument specifying how many times the dragon should flap its wings. To store this argument, we will need a **`Number`** parameter, which we will name **`numTimes`**. We might describe the behavior we want this way:

> Parameter: *numTimes*, a Number.
>
> *For each value count* = 1, 2, ..., *numTimes*:
>
> The dragon flaps its wings once.

Since we already know how to make the dragon flap its wings once, the idea is to have the method redirect the flow so as to *repeat* the wing-flapping behavior **`numTimes`** times.

We can start by opening the **`flapWings()`** method from Figure 2-16. To make the dragon's wing-flapping seem more realistic, we might adjust the **`duration`** values of the wing movements, so that downstrokes (that is, beating against the air) take longer than upstrokes (that is, resetting for a downstroke). In the version below, we've made the complete cycle (down-stroke and up-stroke) require 1 second.

To make the **`flapWings()`** method flap the dragon's wings more than once, we define a **`Number`** parameter named **`numTimes`**, as shown in Figure 4-17. Next, we drag the **`loop`** control from the bottom of the *editing area* into the method. Since we want to repeat the method's wing-flap behavior, we drop the **`loop`** control at the very beginning of the method. When we drop it, Alice displays an **`end`** menu from which we can choose the number of repetitions we want, as shown in Figure 4-17.

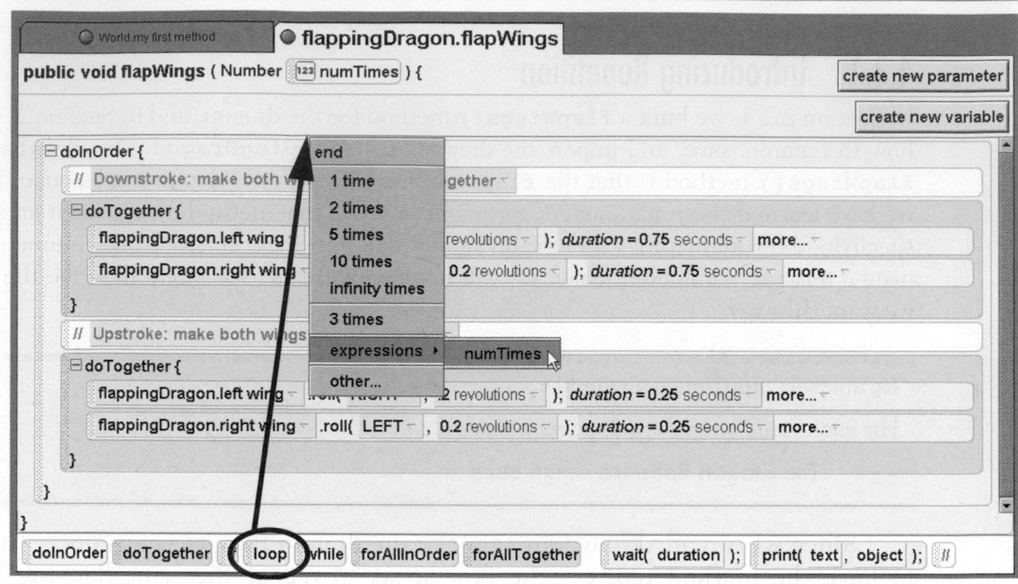

FIGURE 4-17 Dragging the **loop** control

When we select **numTimes**, Alice inserts an empty **for statement** in the method, as shown in Figure 4-18.

FIGURE 4-18 An empty **for** loop

To finish the method, we drag the **doInOrder** statement below the **for** statement into the **for** statement, resulting in the method definition shown in Figure 4-19.

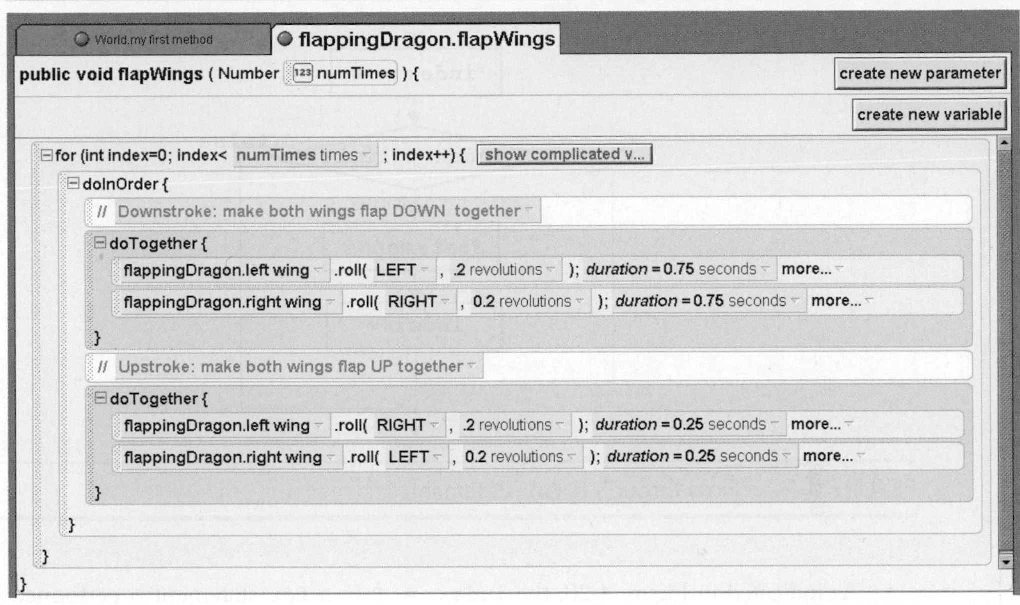

FIGURE 4-19 The revised `flapWings()` method

With this definition, if we send the **dragon** the message **flapWings(3)**, then it will flap its wings three times. If we send it the message **flapWings(8)**, it will flap its wings eight times.

4.3.2 Mechanics of the `for` Statement

The **for** statement is a flow control statement whose purpose is to direct the program's flow through the statements within it, while *counting* through a range of numbers. For this reason, it is sometimes called a **counting loop**. If we were to send the **dragon** the message **flapWings(3);** then the **for** statement would count **0, 1, 2** (performing the statements within it once for each number), and then quit. If we were to send **dragon.flapWings(8);** then the **for** statement would count **0, 1, 2, 3, 4, 5, 6, 7** (again, performing the statements within it once for each number), and then quit. More generally, the **for** statement in **flapWings()** will always count from **0** to **numTimes-1**.

How does it work? Alice's "simple" **for** statement has the structure shown below:

```
for (int index = 0; index < limit; index++ ) {
   Statements
}
```

When the program's flow reaches this statement, the flow behaves as shown in Figure 4-20.

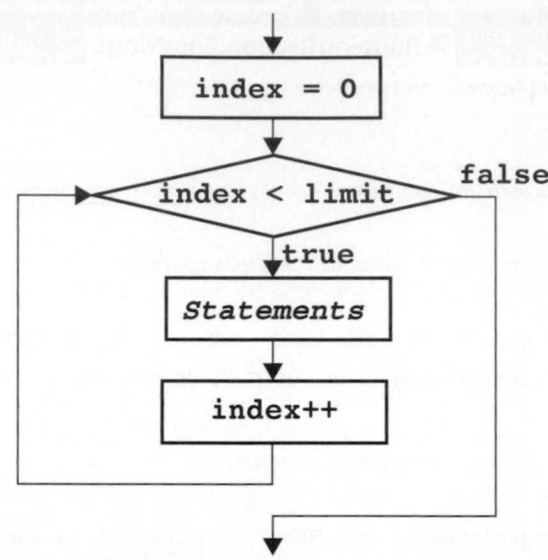

FIGURE 4-20 Flow through a **for** statement

As indicated in Figure 4-20, the **index = 0** in a **for** statement is performed just once, when the flow first reaches the statement. The **for** statement's condition **index < limit** is then checked. If the condition is **false**, then the flow is directed *around* the ***Statements*** within it to whatever statement follows the **for** statement. If the condition is **true**, then the ***Statements*** within the **for** statement are performed, followed by the **index++** (recall that **++** is the **increment operator**). The flow is then redirected *back* to the condition, restarting the cycle.

In Figure 4-21, we trace the behavior of the **for** statement in Figure 4-19 when we send **dragon** the message **flapWings(3)**.

Step	Flow is in...	Effect	Comment
1	**index = 0;**	Initialize **index**	**index**'s value is **0**
2	**index < numTimes (0 < 3)**	The condition is **true**	Flow is directed into the loop
3	**doInOrder**	Flap wings	The first repetition
4	**index++**	Increment **index**	**index**'s value changes from **0** to **1**
5	**index < numTimes (1 < 3)**	The condition is **true**	Flow is directed into the loop
6	**doInOrder**	Flap wings	The second repetition
7	**index++**	Increment **index**	**index**'s value changes from **1** to **2**

FIGURE 4-21 Tracing the flow of **flapWings(3)**

continued

Step	Flow is in...	Effect	Comment
8	**`index < numTimes (2 < 3)`**	The condition is **`true`**	Flow is directed into the loop
9	**`doInOrder`**	Flap wings	The third repetition
10	**`index++`**	Increment **`index`**	**`index`**'s value changes from 2 to 3
11	**`index < numTimes (3 < 3)`**	The condition is **`false`**	Flow is directed *out of* the loop
12	Flow leaves the **`for`** statement, moving to the end of the method		

FIGURE 4-21 Tracing the flow of **`flapWings(3)`** *(continued)*

The simple version of the Alice **`for`** statement always begins counting with **`0`**, uses **`index < limit`** as the condition (for whatever **`limit`** value we specify), and uses **`index++`** as the way to increase the index. If we want different values for any of these, we can click the **`show complicated version`** button on the first line of the **`for`** statement. (The button appears as **`show complicated v...`** in Figure 4-19). Clicking this button "expands" the first line of the **`for`** statement into the form shown in Figure 4-22.

```
for (int 123 index = 0 ; index< numTimes times ; index += 1 ){ show simple version
```

FIGURE 4-22 The complicated **`for`** loop

Where the simple version just lets you modify the **`limit`** value, the complicated version also lets you set the initial value of **`index`** to a value other than zero, and increase **`index`** by a value other than **`1`** each repetition.

In our experience, the simple version of the **`for`** loop is sufficient most of the time, but Alice provides the complicated version for situations where the simple version is inadequate. Both versions will only count up; if you need to count down, you will need to use a **`while`** statement (see Section 4.4) with a **`Number`** variable that you explicitly set, test, and decrement.

4.3.3 Nested Loops

Suppose the first scene of a user-story is as follows:

> A castle sits in a peaceful countryside. A dragon appears, flying toward the castle. When it gets close, it circles the castle's tower three times, and then descends, landing on the castle's drawbridge.

Using divide-and-conquer, we might divide this scene into three shots:

1. A castle sits in a peaceful countryside. A dragon appears, flying toward the castle.
2. When it gets close, it circles the castle's tower three times.
3. It then descends, landing on the castle's drawbridge.

The first shot can be built several ways. One way is to position the dragon off-screen, store the distance from the dragon to the castle's drawbridge in a variable, and then use a **move()** statement to move the dragon that distance, as we have seen before. Another way is to go into the **Add Objects** window, position the dragon above the castle's drawbridge, move it upwards until it is even with the castle's tower, and then (using **more controls**) click the **drop dummy at selected object** button. If we then drag the dragon off-screen, the program can move it to the dummy's position above the drawbridge using the **setPointOfView()** message.

The third shot can also be built in several ways. Section 4.4 presents one approach.

To build the second shot, we will use a **for** statement controlling other statements that make the dragon fly around the castle tower, as shown in Figure 4-23.

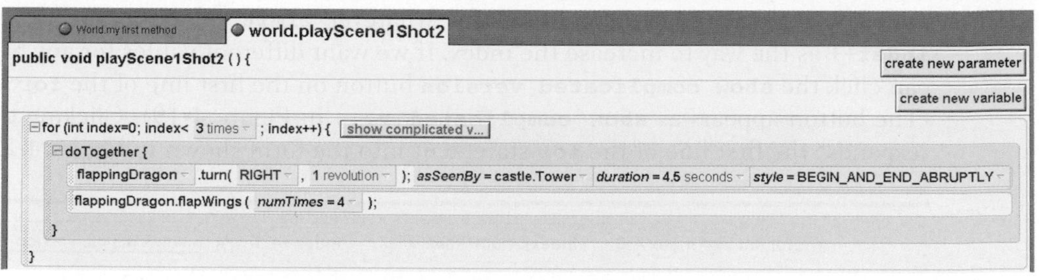

FIGURE 4-23 Making the dragon circle the castle

As defined in Figure 4-23, the **for** statement contains a **doTogether** statement that causes the dragon to simultaneously fly around the castle (taking 4.5 seconds per circuit), and flap its wings four times. As shown above, this behavior will repeat three times. If, after testing the method, we were to decide that two circuits around the castle tower would be preferable, all we need to do is change the **for** statement's **limit** value from **3** to **2**.

Figure 4-23 is deceptively simple. It contains several subtleties that we discuss next.

Nested for Statements

One subtlety is that this method is actually using *two* **for** statements: the one visible in Figure 4-23, plus the one that is hidden within the **flapWings()** method. This situation — where one **for** statement is controlling another **for** statement — is called **nested for statements**, because one **for** statement is nested within another.

In Figure 4-23, the **inner for statement** (the one hidden within **flapWings()**) repeats 4 times for every 1 repetition of the **outer for statement** (the one that is visible). With the outer statement repeating 3 times, the dragon flaps its wings a total of 3 × 4 = 12 times. Nested loops thus have a **multiplying effect**: if the outer loop repeates **i** times and the inner loop repeats **j** times, then the statements in the inner loop will be repeated a total of **i × j** times.

The **asSeenBy** Attribute

The second subtlety is how the **turn()** message in Figure 4-23 causes the dragon to circle the tower. Alice's **turn()** message has a special **asSeenBy** attribute. Normally, this attribute is set to **None**, in which case **turn()** just causes its receiver to revolve about its **LR** axis or its **FB** axis. However, if we specify another object (like **castle.tower**) as the value of the **asSeenBy** attribute, then the **turn()** message causes its receiver to *revolve around that object*. Figure 4-23 uses this trick to make the dragon revolve around the castle tower once for each repetition of the outer **for** statement.

The **duration** Attribute

In testing the method, we initially set the **duration** of the **turn()** message to **4** seconds, to match the dragon's 4 wing-flaps (1 per second) per circuit of the tower. This produced a "hitch" in the animation as the dragon finished each circuit. The problem is that while each wing-flap takes 1 second to complete, the **flapWings(4)** message consumes slightly longer than 4 seconds.[1] As a result, the 4-second **turn()** message was finishing before the 4 wing-flaps. We were able to smooth the animation by increasing the **duration** of the **turn()** message slightly, and setting the message's **style** attribute to **BEGIN_AND_END_ABRUPTLY**, as shown in Figure 4-23.

4.4 The **while** Statement

The **for** statement is a means of causing flow to repeatedly move through the same group of statements a fixed number of times. For this reason, the **for** statement is often called a counting statement, or a **counting loop**. The program must "know" (that is, be able to compute) how many repetitions are needed when flow reaches the **for** statement, to set its **limit** value.

This raises a problem: What do we do when we encounter a situation for which we need repetitive flow-behavior, but we do not know in advance how many repetitions are required? For such statements, Alice (and other programming languages) provides the **while** statement.

4.4.1 Introducing the **while** Statement

In Section 4.3.3, we began work on a scene consisting of three shots:

1. A castle sits in a peaceful countryside. A dragon appears, flying toward the castle.
2. When it gets close, it circles the castle's tower three times.
3. It then descends, landing on the castle's drawbridge.

---

1. For each repetition of a **for** statement, its **index++** statement and the **index < limit** condition must be processed, which consumes time. A **flapWings(*n*)** message thus consumes more than ***n*** seconds.

We have seen how to build the first two shots, and it is possible to build the third shot using a variable, a function, and a **doTogether** statement containing a **move()** message and the **flapWings()** method. The drawback to this approach is that we must coordinate the **move()** and **flapWings()** messages, so that the duration of the **move()** (that is, how long the descent will take) coincides with the wing-flaps of the dragon. If we later change the elevation of the dragon above the drawbridge, we will have to recoordinate the **move()** and **flapWings()** messages.

In this section, we will see an alternative way to build this shot, using a **while** statement, a function, and a **doTogether** statement containing a **move()** message and the **flapWings()** message. The idea is to repeatedly (1) have the dragon flap its wings, and (2) move it downwards whatever distance it drops in one wing-flap, so long as it is above the drawbridge.

We begin by moving the camera closer (via a dummy we'll rename shot1-3, using the techniques described in Section 2.4.), to better see the dragon's descent, as shown in Figure 4-24.

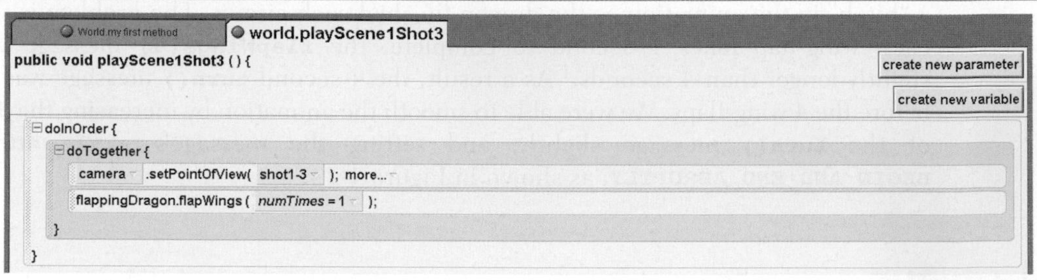

FIGURE 4-24 Moving the camera closer

With the camera in position, we are ready to make the dragon descend. To do so, we click the **while** control at the bottom of the *editing area*, drag it into the method, and drop it at the last position within the **doInOrder** statement. See Figure 4-25.

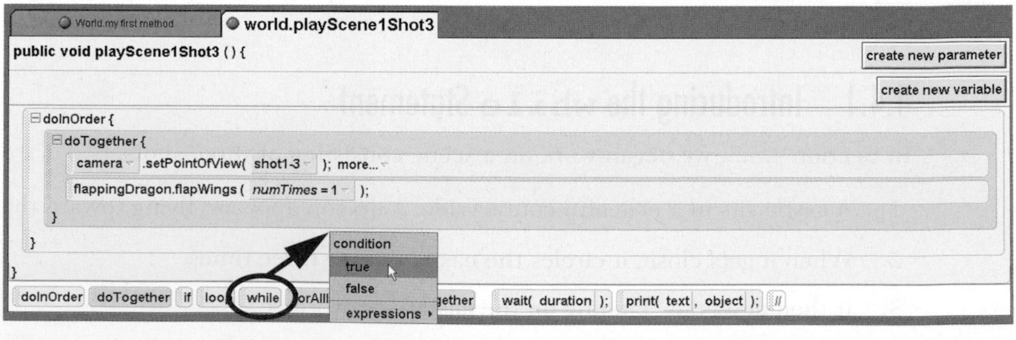

FIGURE 4-25 Dragging the **while** control

When we drop it there, Alice generates a **condition** menu from which we can choose a condition to control the **while** statement. For the moment, we just choose **true** as a *placeholder*. Alice then generates the empty **while** statement shown in Figure 4-26.

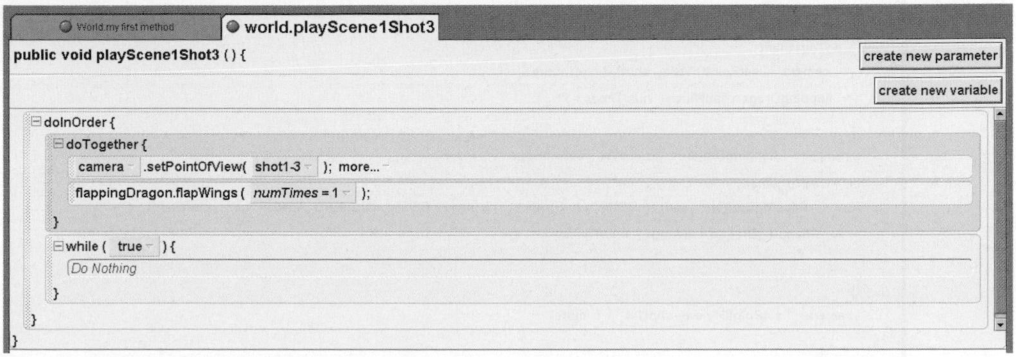

```
World.my first method | world.playScene1Shot3
public void playScene1Shot3 () {                    create new parameter
                                                    create new variable
  doInOrder {
    doTogether {
      camera .setPointOfView( shot1-3 ); more...
      flappingDragon.flapWings ( numTimes = 1 );
    }
    while ( true ){
      Do Nothing
    }
  }
}
```

FIGURE 4-26 An empty **while** statement

For each repetition of the **while** statement, we want the dragon to flap its wings once and move downward a short distance (still to be determined). We want this behavior to repeat as many times as necessary, so long as the dragon is above the drawbridge. For the **while** statement's condition, we can thus drag the dragon's **isAbove()** function into the **while** statement's placeholder condition, and when we drop it, choose the castle's drawbridge as its argument, as shown in Figure 4-27.

```
while ( flappingDragon .isAbove( castle.bridge ) more... ){
  Do Nothing
}
```

FIGURE 4-27 Repeating so long as the dragon is above the drawbridge

Any statements we place within the **while** statement will be repeated so long as the condition **flappingDragon.isAbove(castle.Bridge)** produces the value **true**. Those statements must ensure that the condition eventually becomes **false**, or else an **infinite loop** will result. That is, if the flow reaches the **while** statement shown in Figure 4-27, the flow will remain there sending **flappingDragon** the **isAbove()** message over and over forever, or until we terminate the program, whichever comes first. Any time the flow reaches a **while** loop whose statements do not cause its condition to eventually become **false**, this infinite looping behavior is the result.

To avoid an infinite loop, the loop's statements should flap the dragon's wings and move it down a small distance, so that its bounding box eventually touches that of the bridge. When that happens, the **isAbove()** condition will become **false** and the loop will terminate. We can use these ideas to complete the method as shown in Figure 4-28.

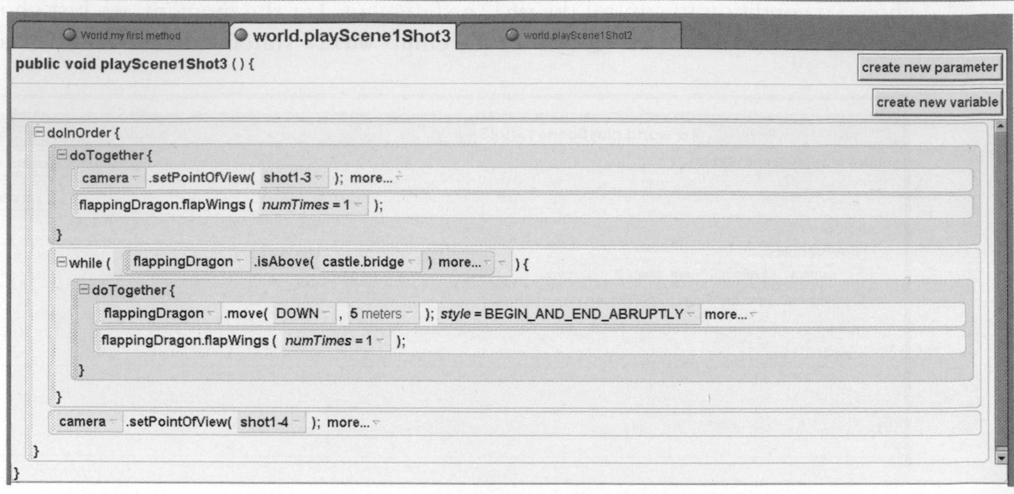

FIGURE 4-28 The `playScene1Shot3()` method (final version)

Each repetition of the **`while`** statement in Figure 4-28 takes 1 second, during which the dragon simultaneously flaps its wings and moves down 5 meters. If we decide this descent is too slow, we can double its descent rate by changing the **`5`** to a **`10`**; or if it seems too fast, we can slow the descent by changing the **`5`** to a **`4`**, a **`2`**, or a **`1`**. The key decision in this approach is how far a dragon should descend in 1 second (which is simpler than the use-a-variable approach).

The final statement in the method zooms the camera in (using another dummy) for a closer shot of the dragon on the bridge after its descent, yielding the shot in Figure 4-29.

FIGURE 4-29 The dragon on the drawbridge

4.4.2 `while` Statement Mechanics

Where the **`for`** statement is a counting loop, the **`while`** statement is a **general**, or **indefinite loop**, meaning the number of repetitions to be performed need not be known in advance. The structure of the Alice **`while`** statement is as follows:

```
while ( Condition ) {
   Statements
}
```

When flow reaches a **`while`** statement, it proceeds as shown in Figure 4-30.

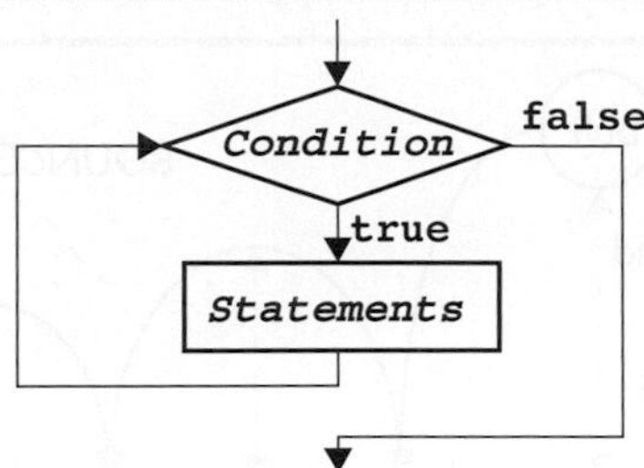

FIGURE 4-30 Flow through a `while` statement

In Figure 4-30, when flow first reaches a **`while`** statement, its ***`Condition`*** is evaluated. If it is **`false`**, then the flow leaves the **`while`** statement, bypassing its ***`Statements`***. However, if it is **`true`**, then the ***`Statements`*** within the **`while`** statement are performed, after which the flow is redirected back to recheck its ***`Condition`***, where the process begins again.

4.4.3 Comparing the `for` and `while` Statements

If you compare Figure 4-30 to Figure 4-20, you will see that the **`while`** statement's behavior is actually much simpler than that of the **`for`** statement. This is because the **`while`** is the more general flow-control statement; whereas the **`for`** statement is useful mainly in counting situations, the **`while`** statement can be used in any situation where repetition is required.

So when should you use each statement? Whenever you are working to produce a behavior that needs to be repeated, ask yourself this question: "Am I counting something?" If the answer is "yes," then use a **`for`** statement; otherwise, use a **`while`** statement. For example, in Figure 4-19 and Figure 4-23, we counted wing-flaps and tower-circuits, respectively. By contrast, in Figure 4-28, we were not counting anything, just controlling the dragon's descent.

Both the **`while`** and the **`for`** statements test their condition *before* the statements within the loop are performed. In both cases, if the condition is initially **`false`**, then statements within the loop will be bypassed (that is, not performed). If you write a program containing a loop statement that seems to be having no effect, it is likely that the loop's condition is **false** when flow reaches it. To remedy this, either choose a different condition, or ensure that its condition is **true** before flow reaches the loop.

4.4.4 A Second Example

As a second example of the **while** statement, suppose that Scene 1 of a story has a girl named Jane dropping a soccer ball (that is, a football everywhere outside of the U.S.). Jane lets it bounce until it stops on its own. Our problem is to get it to bounce realistically.

When dropped, a ball falls until it strikes a surface beneath it. It then rebounds upwards some distance (depending on some bounce factor that combines its elasticity, the hardness of the surface it hits, etc.), drops again, rebounds again, drops again, rebounds again, and so on. We can sketch the behavior as being something like that shown in Figure 4-31.

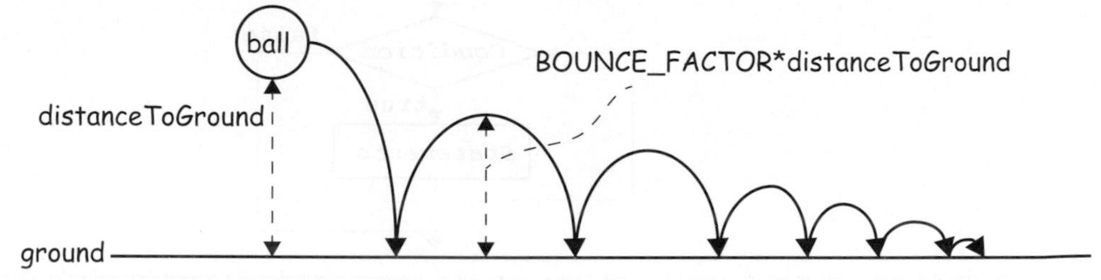

FIGURE 4-31 Sketch of the up-down motion of a bouncing ball

For simplicity, we will just have the soccer ball bounce straight up and down.

Using the **sheBuilder** (located in the **People** folder in the Alice Gallery), the **SoccerBall** class from Alice's **Web Gallery**, and the **quad-view** window, we might start by building a scene like the one shown in Figure 4-32.

FIGURE 4-32 Jane with the soccer ball

To produce the desired bouncing behavior, we can write a **dropAndBounce()** method for the **soccerBall**, which is shown in Figure 4-33.

```
public void dropAndBounce () {
Number distanceToGround = 0 ; Number BOUNCE_FACTOR = 0.67 ;
doInOrder {
  distanceToGround .set( value, soccerBall .distanceAbove( ground ) more... ); more...
  while ( distanceToGround > 0 ) {
    soccerBall .move( DOWN , distanceToGround meters ); duration = distanceToGround seconds style = BEGIN_GENTLY_AND_END_ABRUPTLY m
    distanceToGround .set( value, ( distanceToGround * BOUNCE_FACTOR ) ); more...
    soccerBall .move( UP , distanceToGround meters ); duration = distanceToGround seconds style = BEGIN_ABRUPTLY_AND_END_GENTLY more
  }
}
```

FIGURE 4-33 Method **soccerBall.dropAndBounce()**

When Jane drops the ball, we do not know in advance how many times it is going to rebound, so we have used a **while** statement instead of a **for** statement. The condition controlling the loop is this: the ball should continue to bounce so long as its distance above the ground exceeds zero.

We have assumed that on each bounce, the ball will rebound to 2/3 of the distance it fell previously. (If this proves to be a poor assumption, we have made it easy to change by storing the 2/3 in a variable called **BOUNCE_FACTOR**.) By storing the (initial) distance from the ball to the ground in a variable named **distanceToGround**, then for each repetition of the loop, we

1. move the ball *down* **distanceToGround** meters
2. change the value of **distanceToGround** to **distanceToGround*BOUNCE_FACTOR**
3. move the ball *up* **distanceToGround** meters (which is now 2/3 of its previous value)

To make the ball's behavior seem more realistic, we set the **duration** of each bounce-movement to the current value of the **distanceToGround** variable. Thanks to this, each successive bounce-movement will occur faster as **distanceToGround** gets smaller.

Another refinement to increase the realism was to set the style of the **move()** causing the ball's drop to **BEGIN_GENTLY_AND_END_ABRUPTLY**, and set the style of the **move()** causing the ball's rebound to **BEGIN_ABRUPTLY_AND_END_GENTLY**. The net effect is to make a fast down-to-up transition when the ball bounces, and to make a slow up-to-down transition as the ball reaches the peak of its bounce.

Given the method in Figure 4-33, we can easily build a world method (since it animates two different objects) in which Jane drops the ball, as shown in Figure 4-34.

FIGURE 4-34 Method `world.janeDropsBall()`

Try this yourself, and experiment with the statements and settings shown in Figure 4-33, to see how each one affects the ball's behavior. (There's always the **Undo** button!)

4.5 Flow-Control in Functions

At the end of Chapter 3, we saw that if we want to ask an object a question for which there is not already a function, we can define our own function to provide the answer. The functions we wrote there used sequential flow, and were fairly simple. The flow-control statements we have seen in this chapter allow us to build functions that answer more complex questions.

4.5.1 Spirals and the Fibonacci Function

Suppose that we have a story in which a girl finds an old book. The book tells her that there is a treasure hidden near a certain palm tree in the middle of the desert. The book contains a map showing how to find the tree, plus instructions for locating the treasure from the tree. Suppose that Scene 1 of the story has the girl finding the old book and reading its contents. In Scene 2, the girl uses the map to locate the palm tree. In Scene 3 she follows the instructions:

> Scene 3: The girl is at the tree, her back to the camera. She says, "Now that I am at the tree, I turn to face North." She turns to face the camera. "Then I walk in a spiral of six quarter turns to the left, and then say the key phrase." She walks in a spiral of six quarter turns to her left, says a key phrase, and an opening appears in the ground at her feet.

The main challenge in building this user story is getting the girl to move in a spiral pattern. Mathematicians have discovered that many of the spirals that occur in nature — for example, the spiraling chambers inside a nautilus shell, the spiral of petals in a rose, and the spiraling seeds in sunflowers and pinecones — all use a pattern given in the following numbers:

1, 1, 2, 3, 5, 8, 13, 21, 34, 55, 89, 144, ...

Can you see a pattern in these numbers? The first known mention of them is by the Indian scholar Gospala sometime before 1135 AD. The first European to discover them was Leonardo Pisano, a 13th century mathematician who found that they predict the growth of rabbit populations. Leonardo was the son of Guglielmo Bonaccio, and often called himself Fibonacci (short for "son of Bonaccio"). Today, these numbers are called the **Fibonacci series.**

To draw a spiral from the series, we draw a series of squares whose lengths and widths are the Fibonacci numbers. Starting with the smallest square, we draw a series of quarter turn arcs, crossing from one corner of the square to the opposite corner, as shown in Figure 4-35.

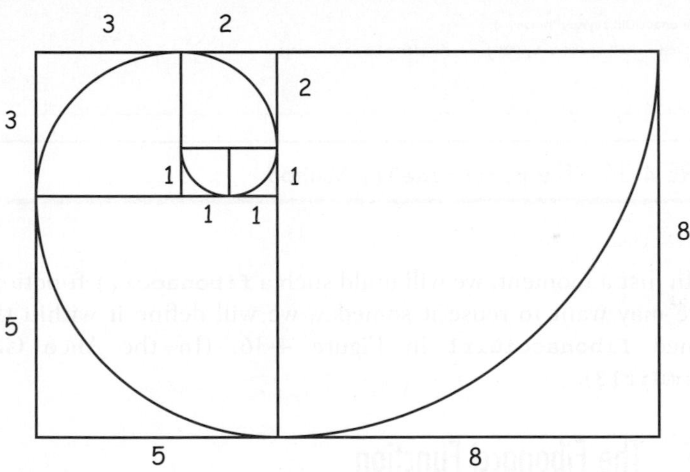

FIGURE 4-35 A Fibonacci spiral pattern

To move the girl in the story in a spiral pattern, we can use a similar approach. More precisely, we can move her in a close approximation of the Fibonacci spiral as follows:

1. move her forward 1 meter while turning left 1/4 revolution
2. move her forward 1 meter while turning left 1/4 revolution
3. move her forward 2 meters while turning left 1/4 revolution
4. move her forward 3 meters while turning left 1/4 revolution
5. move her forward 5 meters while turning left 1/4 revolution
6. move her forward 8 meters while turning left 1/4 revolution

More concisely, we can have her move 6 times, each time moving a distance equal to the next Fibonacci number while turning left 1/4 revolution. That is, if we had a function that, given a positive number i, computes the ith Fibonacci number, we could write the **playScene3()** method as shown in Figure 4-36.

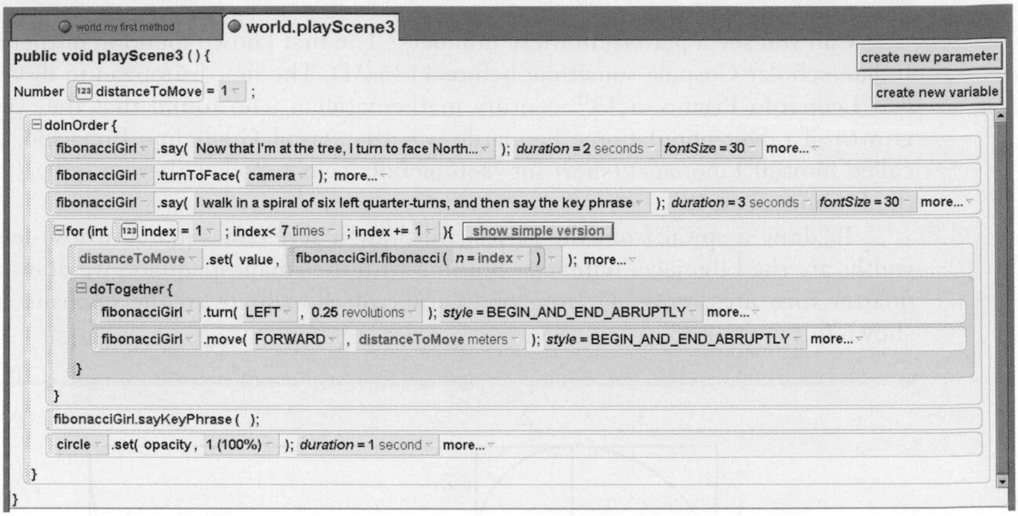

```
world.my first method | world.playScene3
public void playScene3 () {                                   create new parameter
Number 123 distanceToMove = 1 ;                               create new variable
  doInOrder {
    fibonacciGirl .say( Now that I'm at the tree, I turn to face North... ); duration = 2 seconds fontSize = 30 more...
    fibonacciGirl .turnToFace( camera ); more...
    fibonacciGirl .say( I walk in a spiral of six left quarter-turns, and then say the key phrase ); duration = 3 seconds fontSize = 30 more...
    for (int 123 index = 1 ; index< 7 times ; index += 1 ){ show simple version
      distanceToMove .set( value, fibonacciGirl.fibonacci ( n = index ) ); more...
      doTogether {
        fibonacciGirl .turn( LEFT , 0.25 revolutions ); style = BEGIN_AND_END_ABRUPTLY more...
        fibonacciGirl .move( FORWARD , distanceToMove meters ); style = BEGIN_AND_END_ABRUPTLY more...
      }
    }
    fibonacciGirl.sayKeyPhrase ( );
    circle .set( opacity, 1 (100%) ); duration = 1 second more...
  }
}
```

FIGURE 4-36 The **playScene3()** Method

In just a moment, we will build such a **fibonacci()** function. Since it seems possible we may want to reuse it someday, we will define it within the girl, whom we have renamed **fibonacciGirl** in Figure 4-36. (In the Alice Gallery, her name was **RandomGirl3**).

4.5.2 The Fibonacci Function

To create the **fibonacci()** function that is invoked in Figure 4-36, we select the girl in the *object tree*, click the *functions* tab in her *details area*, and then click the **create new function** button. Alice prompts us for the name of the function, so we enter **fibonacci**.

To invoke this function, we must pass it a positive **Number** argument indicating which Fibonacci number we want it to return. To store this argument, the function must have a **Number** parameter. We will name this parameter **n**.

Design

The question the function must answer is this: Given n, what is the nth Fibonacci number? If we look at the series carefully

1, 1, 2, 3, 5, 8, 13, 21, 34, 55, 89, 144, ...

we can see this pattern: after the initial two 1s, every subsequent number is the *sum of the preceding two numbers*. That is, there are two cases we must deal with:

> if (n is 1 or n is 2) the function's result is 1;
>
> otherwise, the function's result is the sum of the preceding two values in the series.

The tricky part is figuring out "the preceding two values in the series." As we have seen before, let's first try doing this by hand. For example, to compute **fibonacci(9)**:

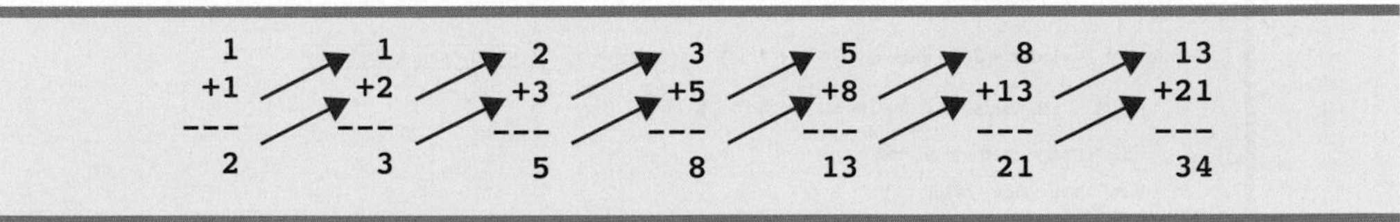

Since we are doing the same thing over and over, we can do this using a loop. To do so, we store each value used per iteration in a variable: one for the next-to-last term, one for the last term, and one for the result; we can then use a **for** loop to count from 3 to **n**. When **n** is 9:

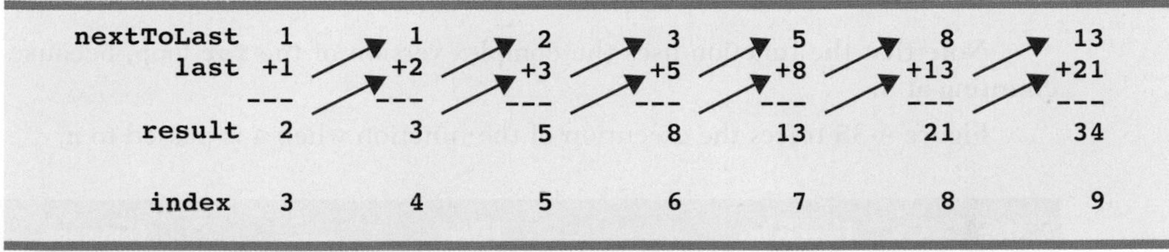

Putting all of this together yields the following algorithm for the function:

```
Parameter: n, a Number.
Number result = 0; Number nextToLast = 1; Number last = 1;
if (n == 1 or n == 2) {
   result = 1;
} else {
   for (int index = 3; index < n+1; index++) {
      result = last + nextToLast;
      nextToLast = last;
      last = result;
   }
}
return result;
```

Coding in Alice

We can encode the algorithm in Alice as shown in Figure 4-37.

```
world.my first method | world.playScene3 | fibonacciGirl.fibonacci

public Number fibonacci ( Number n ) {                    create new parameter
Number result = 0 ; Number last = 1 ; Number nextToLast = 1 ;   create new variable
  if ( ( n == 1 || n == 2 ) ){
    result .set( value, 1 );
  } else {
    for (int index = 3 ; index< ( n + 1 ) ; index += 1 ){  show simple version
      result .set( value, ( nextToLast + last ) );
      nextToLast .set( value, last );
      last .set( value, result );
    }
  }
  return result ;
```

FIGURE 4-37 The **fibonacci()** function

Note that the function uses the complex version of the **for** loop, because it begins counting at 3.

Figure 4-38 traces the execution of the function when **4** is passed to **n**.

Step	Flow is in...	Effect	Comment
1	**if *Condition***	***Condition*** is **false**	Control flows to the **if**'s **else** branch
2	**index = 3**	For loop is initialized	**index** is **3**
3	**index < n+1**	The condition is **true**	Flow is directed into the loop
4	**result = ...**	Compute fibonacci(3)	**result** is **2**
5	**nextToLast = ...**	Update **nextToLast**	**nextToLast** is **1**
6	**last = ...**	Update **last**	**last** is **2**
7	**index++**	Increase **index**	**index** is **4**
8	**index < n+1**	The condition is **true**	Flow is directed into the loop
9	**result = ...**	Compute fibonacci(4)	**result** is **3**

FIGURE 4-38 Tracing the **fibonacci()** function

continued

Step	Flow is in...	Effect	Comment
10	**nextToLast = ...**	Update **nextToLast**	**nextToLast** is 2
11	**last = ...**	Update **last**	**last** is 3
12	**index++**	Increase **index**	**index** is 5
13	**index < n+1**	The condition is **false**	Flow is directed out of the loop
14	**return result;**	The function terminates	**result** is 3, the 4th Fibonacci number
15	Flow leaves the function, returning **result** to the point where the function was invoked.		

FIGURE 4-38 Tracing the **fibonacci()** function *(continued)*

Note that we initialize **result** to zero. If the user passes an invalid argument (for example, zero or a negative number), then the function returns this zero. First, control flows into the **if** statement's **else** branch. However when its **for** loop tests the condition **(3 < (n+1))**, that condition will be **false** if **n** is negative or zero, so the body of the **for** loop will be skipped. Control then flows to the **return** statement, and since **result** has not been modified, the function returns zero.

Using this function, the **for** loop in Figure 4-35 will cause **fibonacciGirl** to move in a spiral pattern, after which she says the key phrase and a dark opening appears in the ground at her feet. What happens next? It's up to you!

4.6 Chapter Summary

- **Boolean** operators allow us to build *conditions*.
- The **if** statement uses a condition to direct program flow *selectively* through one group of statements while bypassing others.
- The **for** statement uses a condition to direct program flow through a group of statements *repeatedly*, a fixed number of times.
- The **while** statement uses a condition to direct program flow through a group of statements *repeatedly*, where the number of repetitions is not known in advance.
- The **wait()** message lets us suspend a program's flow for a fixed length of time.
- The **asSeenBy** attribute alters the behavior of the **turn()** message.

4.6.1 Key Terms

boolean expression
boolean operators
(&&, ||, !)
Boolean type
boolean variables
condition
control structure
counting loop
flow control
flow diagram
general loop
if-then-else logic
if statement
indefinite loop
infinite loop
nested statement
(inner statement, outer statement)
relational operators
(==, !=, <, >, <=, >=)
repetitive control
selective control
selective execution
selective flow
validating parameter values
wait() statement
while statement

Programming Projects

4.1 Choose a hopping animal from the Alice Gallery (for example, a frog or a bunny). Write a **hop()** method that makes it hop in a realistic fashion, with a (validated) parameter that lets the sender of the message specify how far the animal should hop. Then build a method containing just one **hop()** message that causes your animal to hop around a building.

4.2 *Johnny Hammers* is a traditional song with the lyrics below. Create an Alice program containing a character who sings this song. Write your program using as few statements as possible.

Johnny hammers with 1 hammer, 1 hammer, 1 hammer. Johnny hammers with 1 hammer, all day long.	*Johnny hammers with 2 hammers, 2 hammers, 2 hammers. Johnny hammers with 2 hammers, all day long.*
Johnny hammers with 3 hammers, 3 hammers, 3 hammers. Johnny hammers with 3 hammers, all day long.	*Johnny hammers with 4 hammers, 4 hammers, 4 hammers. Johnny hammers with 4 hammers, all day long.*
Johnny hammers with 5 hammers, 5 hammers, 5 hammers. Johnny hammers with 5 hammers, all day long.	*Johnny's very tired now, tired now, tired now. Johnny's very tired now, so he goes to sleep.*

4.3 Using the horse we used in Section 3.4, build a **gallop()** method for the horse that makes its legs move realistically through the motions of a gallop, with a (validated) parameter that specifies the number of strides (or alternatively, the distance to gallop). Then create a story containing a scene that uses your method to make the horse gallop across the screen.

4.4 *The Song That Never Ends* is a silly song with the lyrics below. Create an Alice program containing a character who sings this song, using as few statements as possible. (If your computer has a microphone, get your character to "sing" a recording of the song as well as "say" the lyrics. If you do not know the tune, find and listen to the song on the World Wide Web.)

This is the song that never ends, and it goes on and on my friends. Some people started singing it not knowing what it was, and now they'll keep on singing it forever just because.	*This is the song that never ends, and it goes on and on my friends. Some people started singing it not knowing what it was, and now they'll keep on singing it forever just because.*
This is the song that never ends, and it goes on and on my friends. Some people started singing it not knowing what it was, and now they'll keep on singing it forever just because.	*... (ad infinitum, ad annoyeum, ad nauseum)*

4.5 Build a world containing a person who can calculate the average of a sequence of numbers in his or her head. Have the person ask the user how many numbers are in the sequence, and then display a **`NumberDialog`** that many times to get the numbers from the user. When all the numbers have been entered, have your person "say" the average of those numbers.

4.6 Proceed as in Problem 4.5, but instead of having your person ask the user in advance how many numbers are in the sequence, have your person and each **`NumberDialog`** tell the user to enter a special value (for example, -999) after the last value in the sequence.

4.7 *99 Bottles of Pop* is a silly song with the lyrics below. Create an Alice program in which a character sings this song. Use as few statements as possible. (Hint: Even though this is a counting problem, you will need to use a **`while`** statement instead of a **`for`** statement. Why?)

99 bottles of pop on the wall, 99 bottles of pop, take one down, pass it around, 98 bottles of pop on the wall.	*98 bottles of pop on the wall, 98 bottles of pop, take one down, pass it around, 97 bottles of pop on the wall.*
(96 verses omitted) ...	*1 bottle of pop on the wall, 1 bottle of pop, take one down, pass it around 0 bottles of pop on the wall.*

4.8 Using the **`heBuilder`** or **`sheBuilder`** (or any of the other persons in the Alice Gallery with enough detail), build a person and add him or her to your world. Using your person, build an aerobic exercise video in which the person leads the user through an exercise routine. Using repetition statements, your person should do each exercise a fixed number of times. (Hint: Use **`Pose`** variables and the **`capture pose`** button.)

4.9 Proceed as in Problem 4.8, but at the beginning of the program, ask the user to specify the difficulty level of the workout (1, 2, 3, 4, or 5). If the user specifies 1, have your person do each exercise 10 times. If they specify 2, 20 times. If they specify 3, 40 times, If they specify 4, 80 times. If they specify 5, 100 times.

4.10 From the Alice Gallery, choose a clock class that has subparts for the minute and hour hands.

a. Build a clock method named **`run()`** that moves the minute and hour hands realistically (that is, each time the minute hand completes a rotation, the hour hand should advance 1 hour). Define a parameter named **`speedUp`** that controls the **`duration`**s of the hand movements, such that **`run(0)`** will make the clock run at normal speed, **`run(60)`** will make the clock run at 60 times its normal speed, **`run(3600)`** will make the clock run at 3600 times its normal speed, and so on.

b. Build a clock method **`setTime(h, m)`** that sets the clock's time to **`h:m`** (**`m`** minutes after hour **`h`**).

c. Build three functions for your clock: one that returns its current time (as a **`String`**), one that returns its current hours value (as a **`Number`**), and one that returns its current minutes value (as a **`Number`**).

d. Build a clock method **`setAlarm(h, m)`** that lets you set the clock's alarm to **`h:m`**. Then modify your **`run()`** method so that when the clock's current time is equal to **`m`** minutes after hour **`h`**, the clock plays a sound (for example, Alice's **`gong`** sound).

4.11 Using appropriately colored **`Shapes`** from the Alice Gallery, build a chessboard. Then choose objects from the Gallery to serve as chess pieces. Build a class-level method named **`chessMove()`** for each piece that makes it move appropriately (for example, a bishop should move diagonally). For pieces that can move varying distances, the definition of **`chessMove()`** should have a (validated) parameter indicating the distance (in squares) of the move, plus any other parameters necessary. When your "pieces" are finished, build a program that simulates the opening moves of a game of chess, using your board and pieces.

4.12 Design an original 3–5 minute story that uses each of the statements presented in this chapter at least once.

Chapter 5
Lists and Arrays

He's making a list, checking it twice. 'Gonna find out who's naughty or nice ...

SANTA CLAUS IS COMING TO TOWN

For seven men she gave her life. For one good man she was his wife. Beneath the ice by Snow White Falls, there lies the fairest of them all.

VIRGINIA (KIMBERLY WILLIAMS), IN *THE 10TH KINGDOM*

The generation of random numbers is too important to be left to chance.

ROBERT R. COVEYOU

When a cat is dropped, it always lands on its feet, and when toast is dropped, it always lands with the buttered side down. I propose to strap buttered toast to the back of a cat; the 2 will hover, inches above the ground. With a giant buttered-cat array, a high-speed monorail could easily link New York with Chicago.

JOHN FRAZEE

Objectives

When you complete this chapter, you will be able to:

- ❑ Use a list to store multiple items
- ❑ Use Alice's **`forAllInOrder`** and **`forAllTogether`** statements
- ❑ Use random numbers to vary the behavior of a program
- ❑ Use an array to store multiple items

In the preceding chapters, we have often used variables to store values for later use. Each variable we have seen so far has stored a *single* value, which might be a **Number**, a **Boolean**, a **String**, an **Object**, a **Sound**, a **Color**, or any of the other types that Alice supports. For example, if we have three variable definitions like this in our program:

```
Number result = 0.0;
Boolean done = false;
String name = "Jo";
```

then we might (simplistically) visualize these three variables as shown in Figure 5-1.

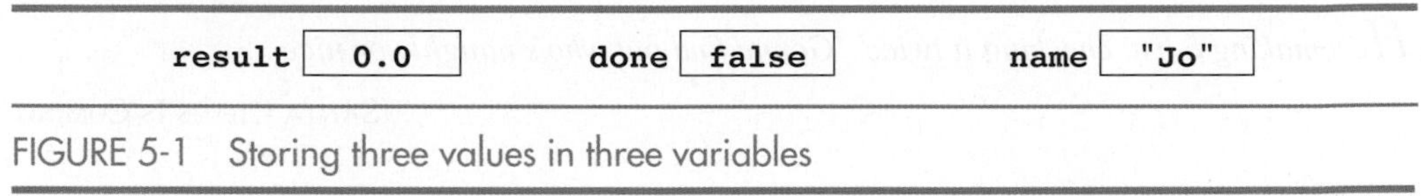

FIGURE 5-1 Storing three values in three variables

Each variable stores a single value (of a given type) that can be changed by the program.

It is sometimes convenient to be able to define a variable that can store *multiple* values. For example, suppose you have 12 songs (call them $s_0 ... s_{11}$) in your music player that you want to represent in a program. You could define 12 single-value variables (for example, **song**$_0$, **song**$_1$, **song**$_2$, ..., **song**$_{10}$, **song**$_{11}$), but it would be more convenient if you could define one variable capable of storing all 12 songs, as shown in Figure 5-2.

playList	s_0	s_1	s_2	s_3	s_4	s_5	s_6	s_7	s_8	s_9	s_{10}	s_{11}

FIGURE 5-2 Storing 12 values in one variable

One advantage of this approach is that if I need to pass my song collection to a method, I only have to pass one argument (**playList**) instead of 12. Also, my method needs only one parameter.

A variable like this is called a **data structure** — a structure for storing a group of data values. In this chapter, we will examine two data structures that are available in Alice:

- The **list**, which stores a group of values where the group's size changes frequently
- The **array**, which stores a group of values where the group's size does not change

Each structure is used for storing *sequences* of values, but the two have very different properties.

5.1 The List Structure

5.1.1 List Example 1: Flight of the Bumble Bees

Suppose Scene 2 of a story requires a dozen bees to take off, one at a time, to defend the honor of their queen bee. We might begin by using the Alice Gallery to build the scene as shown in Figure 5-3.

FIGURE 5-3 The queen and her 12 bees

To make the bees take off one at a time, we could use 12 separate statements:

```
bee.move(UP, verticalDistance);
bee2.move(UP, verticalDistance);
...
bee12.move(UP, verticalDistance);
```

Note, however, that although the bee to which we are sending the **`move()`** message changes, each statement is otherwise the same. Remember: *any time you find yourself programming the same thing over and over, there is usually a better way.* In this case, the better way is to create a data structure variable named **`bees`** that stores references to the 12 bees, and which we might visualize as shown in Figure 5-4.

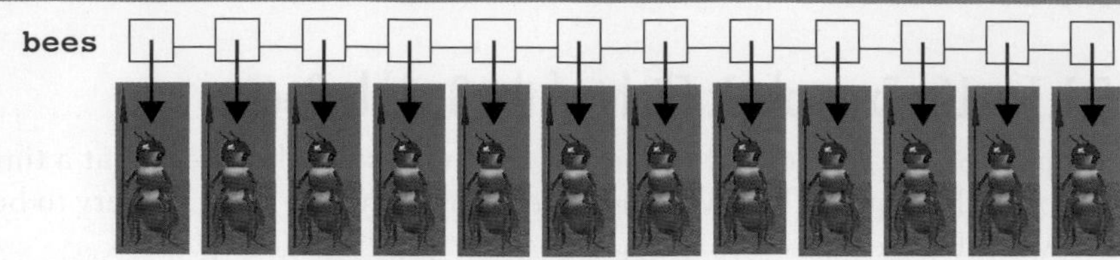

FIGURE 5-4 A list of 12 bees

As indicated in the caption of Figure 5-4, this kind of data structure is called a **list**, as in *shopping list*, *guest list*, or *play list*. Alice's list data structure can store a sequence of **items**, which can be any Alice type (for example, **Number**, **Boolean**, **Object**, **String**, **Color**, etc.).

Given a list variable, we can use Alice's **forAllInOrder** statement to send each item in the list the message **move(UP, verticalDistance)**:

```
for all bees, one item_from_bees at a time {
   item_from_bees.move(UP, verticalDistance);
}
```

We will look at each of these steps separately.

Defining a List Variable

We can begin by defining a **playScene2()** method, and then defining a list variable within it. To create a list variable, we click the **create new variable** button as usual. Because the things we want to store in the list (bees) are objects, we select **Object** as the type in the dialog box that appears. We then click the checkbox labeled **make a List**, which expands the dialog box with a **Values** pane, as shown in Figure 5-5.

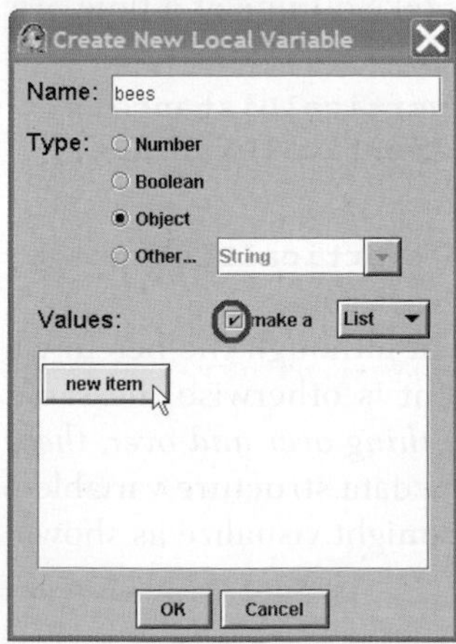

FIGURE 5-5 Creating a list variable

To store the bees in the list, we click the **new item** button visible in Figure 5-5. Alice then adds an item to the list whose value is **<None>**, as shown in Figure 5-6 (left side).

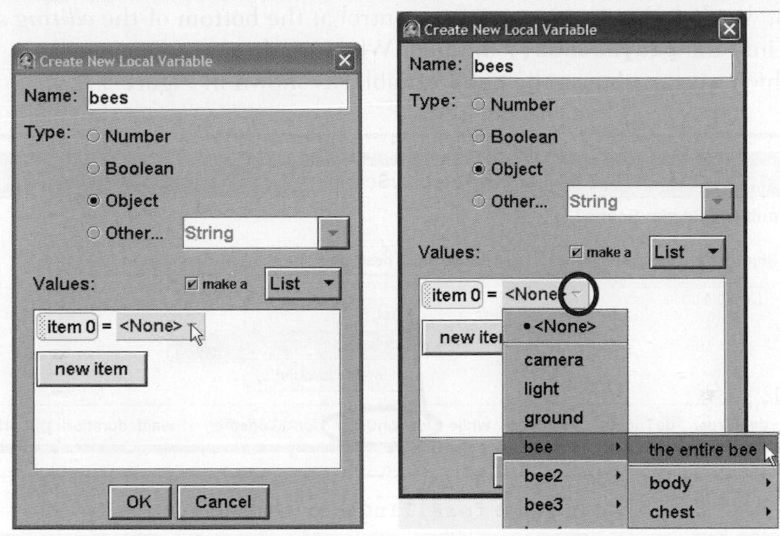

FIGURE 5-6 Defining initial values in a list variable

To make the value of this new item the first bee, we click the list arrow next to **<None>**, choose the **bee** from the menu that appears, and select **the entire bee**, as shown in Figure 5-6 (right side). We then repeat these steps to create new items for each additional bee in the story, and finally click the dialog's **OK** button. The result is the list variable shown in Figure 5-7.

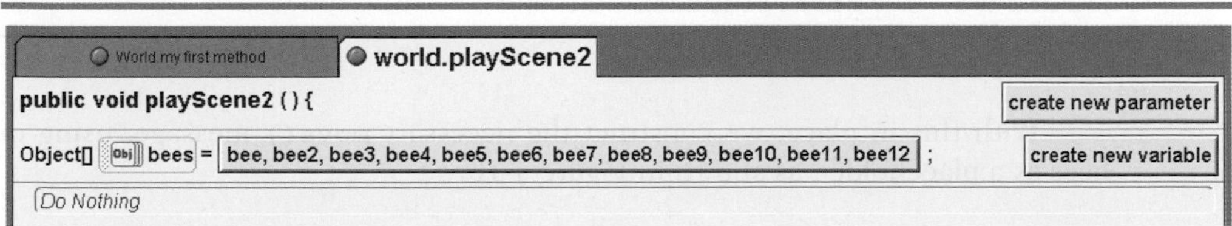

FIGURE 5-7 A list variable definition

While Alice's choice of font makes it a bit difficult to see, the form of this definition is:

```
Object [] bees = bee, bee2, ... bee12;
```

Alice uses square brackets (**[** and **]**) to distinguish data structures from "normal" variables.

Processing List Entries

Now that we have defined a list variable, the next step is to use a new Alice statement — the **forAllInOrder** statement — to send the **move()** message to each of its items. To do so, we click the **forAllInOrder** control at the bottom of the *editing area*, and then drag it into the **playScene2()** method. When we drop it, Alice generates a **list** menu from which we can choose the **bees** variable, as shown in Figure 5-8.

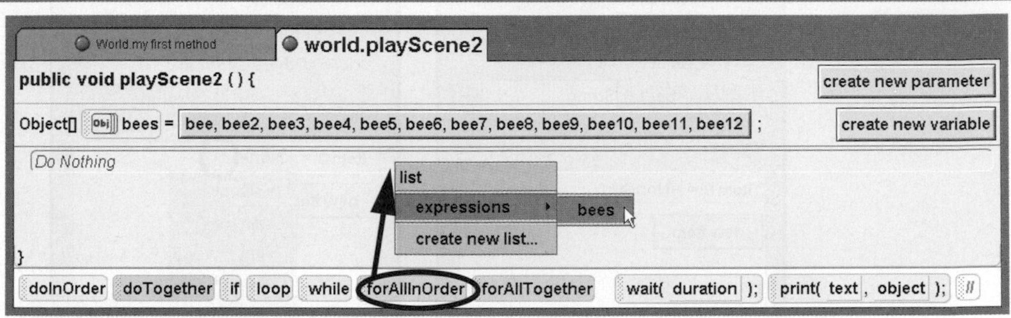

FIGURE 5-8 Dragging the **forAllInOrder** statement

When we choose **bees** from this menu, Alice generates the **forAllInOrder** statement shown in Figure 5-9.

```
For all bees , one item_from_bees at a time {
  Do Nothing
}
```

FIGURE 5-9 The **forAllInOrder** statement

With this in place, we construct the necessary **move()** message, using one of the bees as a placeholder, as shown in Figure 5-10.

```
For all bees , one item_from_bees at a time {
  bee2 .move( UP , 5 meters ); more...
}
```

FIGURE 5-10 The **forAllInOrder** statement with a bee placeholder

We then replace the placeholder with an item from the **bees** list. To do so, we drag **item_from_bees** onto the placeholder and drop it, as shown in Figure 5-11.

```
For all bees , one item_from_bees at a time {
  item_from_bees .move( UP , 5 meters ); more...
}
```

FIGURE 5-11 The **forAllInOrder** statement with an item from **bees**

The resulting loop will send the **move()** message to each bee in the list, one at a time, causing them to "take off." We can similarly add statements to make the queen bee turn to face each bee and order it to take off. Figure 5-12 shows the completed scene method.

```
World.my first method | world.playScene2
public void playScene2 () {                                   create new parameter
Object[] bees = bee, bee2, bee3, bee4, bee5, bee6, bee7, bee8, bee9, bee10, bee11, bee12 ;   create new variable
  For all bees , one item_from_bees at a time {
    queenBee .turnToFace( item_from_bees ); more...
    queenBee .say( GO! ); fontSize = 30 more...
    item_from_bees .move( UP , 5 meters ); more...
  }
```

FIGURE 5-12 The **playScene2()** method (final version)

With Figure 5-4 as the starting scene, we can trace the flow through this loop as follows:

- In the first repetition of this loop, the **queenBee** faces **bee** and says **Go!**; then **bee** moves up five meters, because **item_from_bees** refers to **bee**.
- In the second repetition of the loop, the **queenBee** faces **bee2** and says **Go!**; then **bee2** moves up five meters, because **item_from_bees** refers to **bee2**.
- In the third repetition of the loop, the **queenBee** faces **bee3** and says **Go!**; then **bee3** moves up five meters, because **item_from_bees** refers to **bee3**.
- This process repeats for each bee, up to the eleventh bee.
- In the eleventh repetition of the loop, the **queenBee** faces **bee11** and says **Go!**; then **bee11** moves up five meters, because **item_from_bees** refers to **bee11**.
- In the twelfth (and final) repetition of the loop, the **queenBee** faces **bee12** and says **Go!**; then **bee12** moves up five meters, because **item_from_bees** refers to **bee12**.

Figure 5-13 shows the scene during the loop's first, third, and last repetitions.

FIGURE 5-13 Repetitions 1, 3, and 12 of the loop

The code shown in Figure 5-12 thus achieves the effect of 12 **turnToFace()** messages, 12 **say()** messages, and 12 **move()** messages. However it does so using only one **turnToFace()** statement, one **say()** message, one **move()** message, a **forAllInOrder** statement, and a list!

Moreover, suppose later on we decide that, to be more convincing, the scene needs more bees taking off (for example, positioned behind those already in the scene). All we have to do is (1) add the new bees to the world, and (2) add them to the **bees** list.[1] We need not add any new **turnToFace()**, **say()**, or **move()** statements to **playScene2()**.

In any situation for which you need to do the same thing to multiple items, a data structure can save you a lot of work!

5.1.2 List Operations

The preceding example illustrates how the **forAllInOrder** statement can be used to process each of the items in a list in turn. It provides a very simple way to **iterate** (or loop) through the entries in the list, doing the same thing to each item in the list.

You may have noticed that there is also a **forAllTogether** control at the bottom of the editing pane. This can be used to create **forAllTogether** statements. Like the **forAllInOrder** statement, the **forAllTogether** statement operates on a list. However, where the **forAllInOrder** statement performs the statements within it once for each item in the list *sequentially*, the **forAllTogether** statement performs the statements within it once for each item in the list *simultaneously*, or in parallel.

To illustrate, if we wanted all of the bees in Figure 5-3 to take off at the same time instead of one at a time, we could rewrite the **playScene2()** method using the **forAllTogether** statement, as shown in Figure 5-14.

1. To add new values to a list variable, just click the box of values (for example, **bee**, **bee2**, ... **bee12**) in its definition.

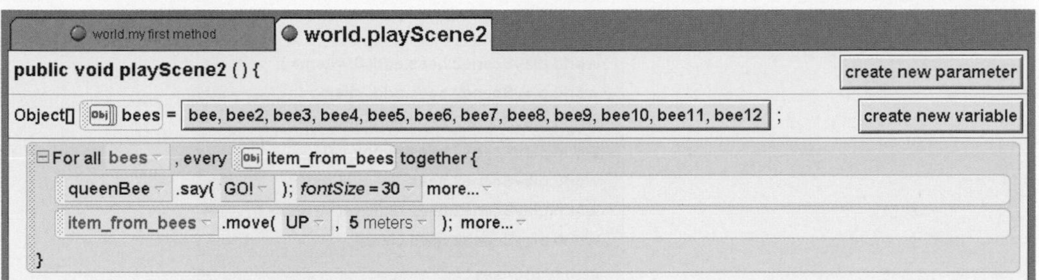

FIGURE 5-14 Making the bees take off together

Using this version of **playScene2()**, clicking Alice's **Play** button produces the screen shown in Figure 5-15.

FIGURE 5-15 The bees take off together

Alice provides the **forAllInOrder** and **forAllTogether** statements to simplify the task of processing all of the values in the list data structure. In addition to these *statements*, Alice provides *messages* that you can send to a list variable to modify it or its items. More precisely, if you drag a list variable into the *editing area* and drop it anywhere a *statement* can appear, Alice generates the menu shown in Figure 5-16.

set value
world.playScene2.bees.add(0, <item>);
world.playScene2.bees.add(<item>);
world.playScene2.bees.add(<index>, <item>);
world.playScene2.bees.remove(0);
world.playScene2.bees.removeLast();
world.playScene2.bees.remove(<index>);
world.playScene2.bees.clear();
item responses

FIGURE 5-16 The list methods menu

The three sections in this menu let you:

- Set the value of the list to another list (the **set value** choice)
- Send a message to the list (the middle portion of the menu)
- Send a message to any of the items in the list (the **item responses** choice)

Because the middle portion of the menu is unique to lists, we will examine it next.

List **Methods**. The messages you can send to a list include those shown in Figure 5-17.

Alice List Method	Behavior
`aList.add(0, val);`	Create a new item containing ***val*** at ***aList***'s beginning
`aList.add(i, val);`	Insert a new item containing ***val*** at position ***i*** in ***aList*** (the item at position ***i*** shifts to position ***i+1***, and so on)
`aList.add(val);`	Create a new item containing ***val*** at ***aList***'s end
`aList.remove(0);`	Remove the first item from ***aList***
`aList.remove(i);`	Remove the item at position ***i*** from ***aList*** (the item at position ***i+1*** moves to position ***i***, and so on)
`aList.removeLast();`	Remove the last item from ***aList***
`aList.clear();`	Remove all items from ***aList***

FIGURE 5-17 List methods

Figure 5-6 showed how to initially define a list with a group of values. However, there are situations in which a program needs to modify the contents of a list *as it is running*. For example, once the bees are in the air, we might want to have the queen take off too, and add her to the **bees** list. The messages in Figure 5-17 allow a program to modify a list by adding and/or removing items.

Each item in a list has a **position**, or **index**, by which it can be accessed. The index of the first item is always zero, the index of the second item is always one, and so on. To illustrate, Figure 5-18 shows **bees** again, but this time showing the index of each list item.

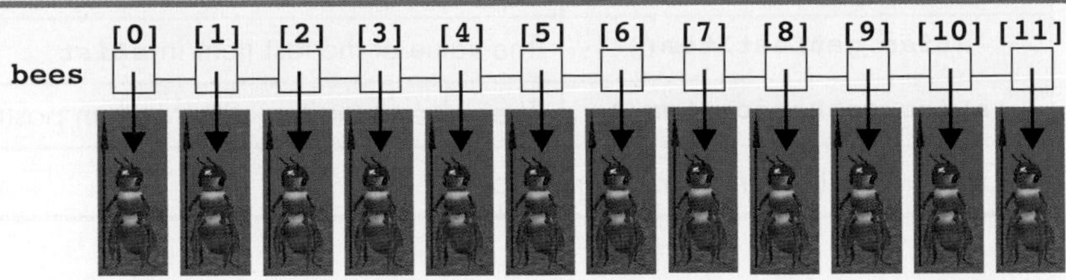

FIGURE 5-18 The list of 12 bees with index values

In the list messages **add(i, val)** and **remove(i)**, the value of **i** is the position or index at which the value will be added or removed. To illustrate, suppose we have the following list:

```
List aList = 2, 8, 4;
```

Suppose we then perform the following statements:

```
aList.remove(1);     // remove the item at index 1 (the 8)
aList.add(0, 1);     // insert 1 at the beginning
aList.add(2, 3);     // insert 3 at index 2
aList.add(5);        // append 5
```

As a result, the contents of **aList** will be **1, 2, 3, 4, 5**.

List Functions

Alice also provides function messages that we can send to a list to get information from it, as shown in Figure 5-19.

List Function	Return Value
***aList*.size()**	The number of items in ***aList***
***aList*.firstIndexOf(val)**	The position of the first item containing ***val*** in ***aList*** (or -1 if ***val*** is not present in ***aList***)
***aList*.lastIndexOf(val)**	The position of the last item containing ***val*** in ***aList*** (or -1 if ***val*** is not present in ***aList***)
***aList*[0]**	The value of the first item in ***aList***

FIGURE 5-19 List functions

continued

List Function	Return Value
***aList*[*i*]**	The value of the item at position ***i*** in ***aList***
***aList*.getLastItem()**	The value of the last item in ***aList***
***aList*.getRandomItem()**	The value of an item at a random position in ***aList***

FIGURE 5-19 List functions *(continued)*

To use these functions, you must drag a list definition into the *editing area* and drop it onto a *placeholder whose type is the function's return type*. For example, the top three functions — **size()**, **indexOf()**, and **lastIndexOf()** — each return a **Number**, so if you drop a list onto a **Number** placeholder, Alice will display a menu whose choices are these messages, as shown in the *left-hand* menu in Figure 5-20.

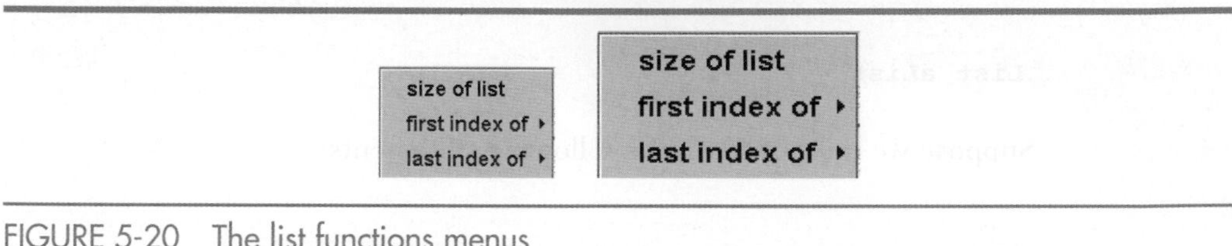

FIGURE 5-20 The list functions menus

However, if you drop a list onto a placeholder whose type is the type of item in the list (for example, **Object**), Alice will display the *right-hand* menu in Figure 5-20, from which you can choose one of the bottom four functions of Figure 5-19.

5.1.3 List Example 2: Buying Tickets

Suppose Scene 3 of a story has a line of people waiting for something (for example, to buy tickets to a film). After the first person has been served, she turns and walk away. The remaining people in the line then move forward, so that the person who was second is the new first person in line.

We might begin by building the scene shown in Figure 5-21.

FIGURE 5-21 People waiting in a line

Alice's list data structure makes it fairly easy to animate such a scene. The basic idea is to represent the line of people with a list containing each of the people in the scene. Then we can use the list methods and functions to move them around, using an algorithm like this:

```
personList = isis, randomGuy2, skaterGirl, skaterGuy, cleo;
while personList is not empty {
   Set firstPerson to the first item in personList
   Have firstPerson say "Two tickets please", and then "Thank you"
   Have firstPerson turn left
   Have firstPerson move off-screen
   Remove the first item from personList
   Advance the line, moving each person in personList forward
}
```

To determine whether a list is empty, we can compare its **size()** to zero. To get the first item in the list, we can use the **[0]** function. To "advance the line" we can either use a **forAllTogether** statement or a **forAllInOrder** statement. To remove the first item from the list, we can use the **remove(0)** method.

Figure 5-22 presents an Alice version of this algorithm, using a **forAllInOrder** statement to "advance the line."

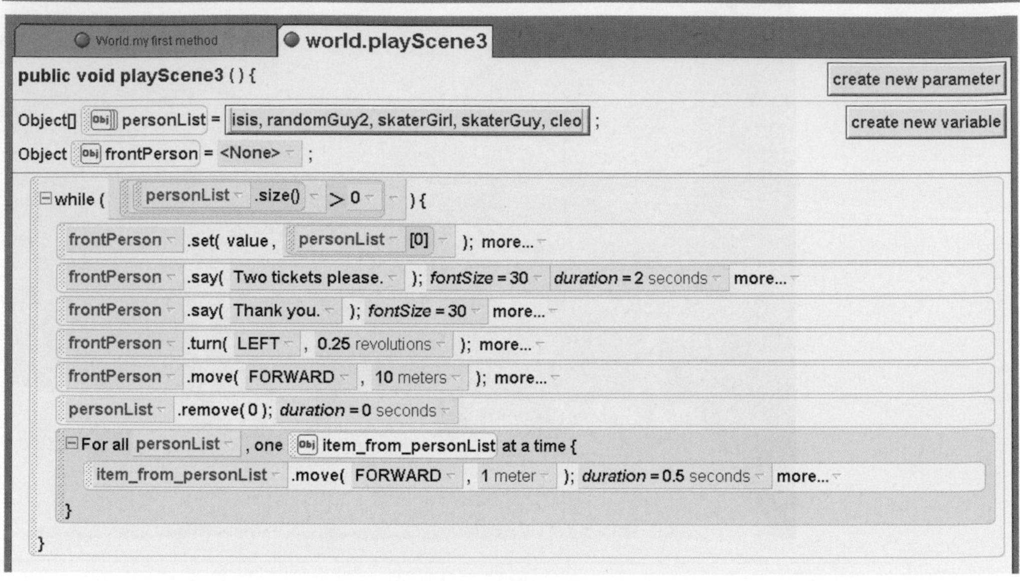

FIGURE 5-22 Animating a line of people

Figure 5-23 shows three screen shots of this scene, all taken during the first pass through the **while** statement in **playScene3()**.

FIGURE 5-23 Screen captures from **playScene3()**

To see how the people in line are moving, compare their positions against the background in each screen capture. For example, **cleo** is in front of the rounded window in the leftmost capture; in the rightmost capture, she and the others have moved forward.

The list is one of the two data structures available in Alice. The other is called the array, and we examine it next.

5.2 The Array Structure

Alice's second data structure is called the **array**. Like an Alice list, an array can store a group of values, each of which can be accessed through its position or index. However, unlike the list, the array is a *fixed-sized data structure*, meaning it cannot grow or shrink as your program runs. You can still change the values of the items in an array, but once your program begins running, its *capacity* (the maximum number of values it can store) cannot change. An array is thus a somewhat less flexible data structure than a list.

Why would anyone want to use an array instead of a list? There are two answers:

1. In Alice and most other programming languages, it takes less of a computer's memory to store a group of items in an array than it does to store the same group of items in a list. Put differently, if you have a group of items to store and the size of the group never changes, it is more *memory-efficient* to store the group in an array instead of a list.
2. In most other programming languages, items in a list cannot be accessed via index values. Instead, only the first and last item in the list can be accessed. The exact reason is beyond the scope of our discussion, but accessing an arbitrary item from a list is *much* more time-consuming than accessing an arbitrary item from an array, so most languages don't let you do it. So, if the solution to a problem requires a program to access arbitrary values from a group, then it's better to store the group in an array instead of a list. Put differently, to access an arbitrary group item, an array is more *time-efficient* than a list.

To see the Alice array in action, let's see an example.

5.2.1 Array Example 1: The Ants Go Marching

Suppose a user story has an ant marching along, singing the song "The Ants Go Marching." The lyrics to the song are as follows:

<table>
<tr>
<td>The ants go marching one-by-one
Hurrah! Hurrah!
The ants go marching one-by-one
Hurrah! Hurrah!
The ants go marching one-by-one,
the little one stopped to suck his thumb,
and they all went marching
down to the ground
to get out of the rain
BOOM! BOOM! BOOM!</td>
<td>The ants go marching two-by-two
Hurrah! Hurrah!
The ants go marching two-by-two
Hurrah! Hurrah!
The ants go marching two-by-two,
the little one stopped to tie his shoe,
and they all went marching
down to the ground
to get out of the rain
BOOM! BOOM! BOOM!</td>
</tr>
<tr>
<td>…
The ants go marching three-by-three,
the little one stopped to climb a tree,
…</td>
<td>…
The ants go marching four-by-four,
the little one stopped to shut the door,
…</td>
</tr>
</table>

. .. *The ants go marching five-by-five* *The little one stopped to take a dive,* ...	... *The ants go marching six-by-six* *The little one stopped to pick up sticks,* ...
... *The ants go marching seven-by-seven* *The little one stopped to pray to heaven,* ...	... *The ants go marching eight-by-eight* *The little one stopped to shut the gate,* ...
The ants go marching nine-by-nine *Hurrah! Hurrah!* *The ants go marching nine-by-nine* *Hurrah! Hurrah!* *The ants go marching nine-by-nine,* *the little one stopped to check the time,* *and they all went marching* *down to the ground* *to get out of the rain* *BOOM! BOOM! BOOM!*	*The ants go marching ten-by-ten* *Hurrah! Hurrah!* *The ants go marching ten-by-ten* *Hurrah! Hurrah!* *The ants go marching ten-by-ten,* *the little one stopped to say, 'THE END',* *and they all went marching* *down to the ground* *to get out of the rain* *BOOM! BOOM! BOOM!*

One way to build this story would be to send the ant 10 **`say()`** messages per verse times 10 verses = 100 **`say()`** messages. But many of the song's lines are exactly the same from verse to verse, so this approach would result in lots of wasteful, replicated effort.

Another way would be to recognize that this is basically a *counting problem*: the song is counting from 1 to 10. So perhaps we could use a **`for`** statement to count through the verses, and put statements within the **`for`** statement to make the ant sing a verse? This is good thinking; the difficulty is that each verse differs from the others in *two* ways:

- the number being sung (*one, two, ..., nine, ten*); and
- what the little ant does (*suck his thumb, tie his shoe, ..., check the time, say* "THE END").

One solution is to make two indexed groups, one for each way the verses differ, as shown in Figure 5-24.

Group 1	
Index	**Numbers**
0	one
1	two
2	three
3	four

Group 2	
Index	**What the little ant does**
0	suck his thumb
1	tie his shoe
2	climb a tree
3	shut the door

FIGURE 5-24 Groups of strings

continued

Group 1	
Index	**Numbers**
4	five
5	six
6	seven
7	eight
8	nine
9	ten

Group 2	
Index	**What the little ant does**
4	take a dive
5	pick up sticks
6	pray to heaven
7	shut the gate
8	check the time
9	say 'THE END'

FIGURE 5-24 Groups of strings *(continued)*

If we defined two data structures (one for each group), then the **for** statement could count from 0 to 9, and on repetition *i*, retrieve the value associated with index *i* from each data structure.

Because the number of verses in the song is fixed, it makes sense to use array data structures to store the two groups. Defining an array variable is similar to defining a list variable, which we saw in Figures 5-5 and 5-6. The only difference is that we must specify that we want an **Array** variable instead of a **List** variable, as shown in Figure 5-25.

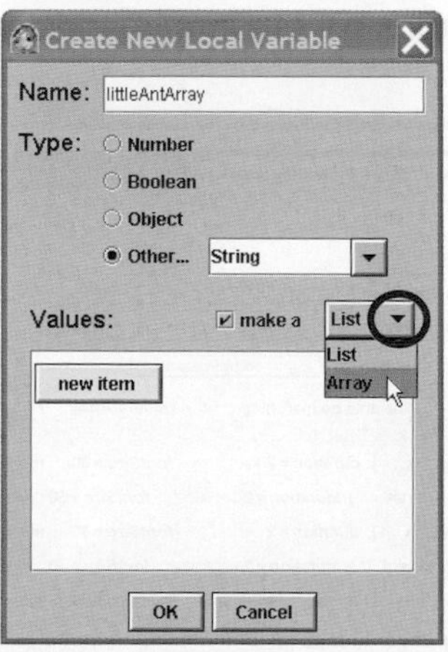

FIGURE 5-25 Creating an **Array** variable

Once we have created the array variable, we can fill it with values in exactly the same way as we would a list (see Figure 5-6).

Given the ability to define arrays, we can build this algorithm to solve the problem:

```
Define numberArray = one, two, three, four, five, six, seven, eight,
nine, ten;
Define littleAntArray = suck his thumb, tie his shoe, climb a tree,
shut the door, take a dive, pick up sticks, pray to heaven, shut the
gate, check the time, say 'THE END',
for each index 0 through 9 {
   repeatedLine = "The ants go marching " + numberArray[index] + "-by-"
   + numberArray[index];
   ant.say(repeatedLine);
   ant.say("Hurrah! Hurrah!");
   ant.say(repeatedLine);
   ant.say("Hurrah! Hurrah!");
   ant.say(repeatedLine);
   ant.say("The little one stopped to " + littleAntArray[index]);
   ant.say("and they all went marching");
   ant.say("down to the ground");
   ant.say("to get out of the rain.");
   ant.say("BOOM! BOOM! BOOM!);
}
```

Using this algorithm, we can build the program, as shown in Figure 5-26.

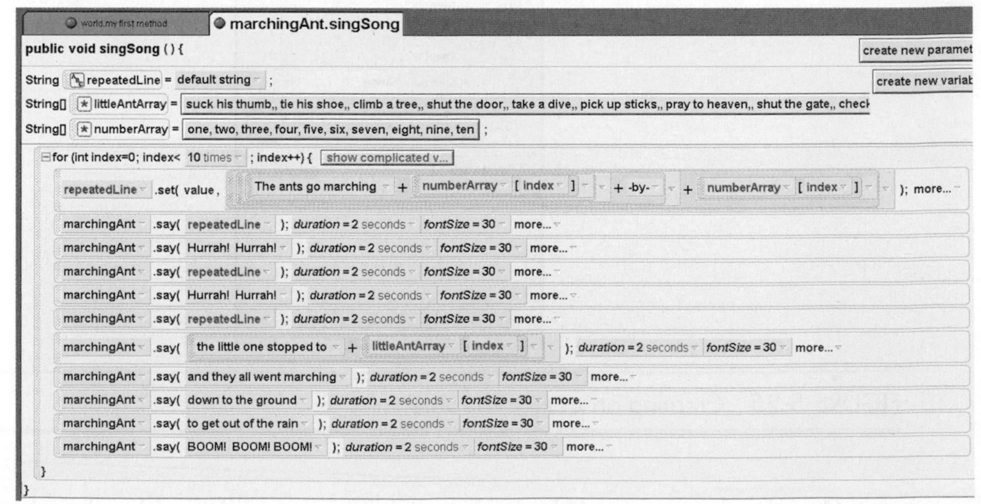

FIGURE 5-26 Singing "The Ants Go Marching"

When performed, this method (using just 12 statements and three variables) causes the **marchingAnt** to "sing" the entire 10-verse, 100-line song!

If we add a method that makes the ant march, and then have the ant sing the song as it marches, the result will appear something like what is shown in Figure 5-27.

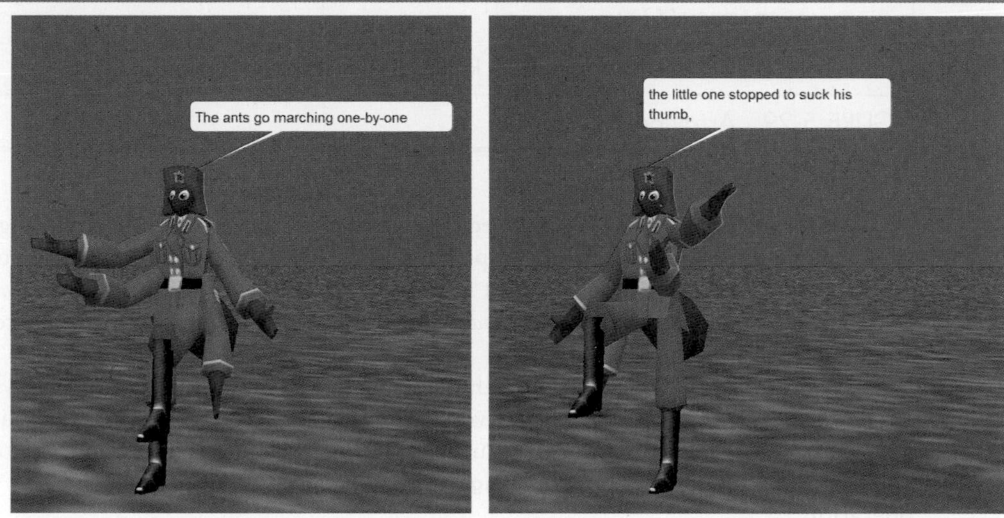

FIGURE 5-27 The singing ant in action

5.2.2 Array Operations

Like lists, arrays are **indexed variables**, meaning their items can be accessed using an index value. For example, we could have written the "bees" program in Figure 5-12 using an array instead of a list. If we had done so, we could have drawn the **bees** group as shown in Figure 5-28:

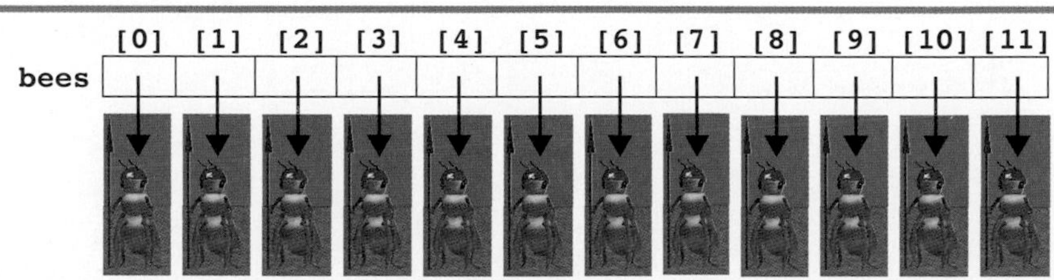

FIGURE 5-28 An array of 12 bees

We saw in Section 5.1.2 that Alice provides a variety of predefined operations that can be used with list variables. By contrast, there are only a few operations for array variables. These are listed in Figure 5-29.

Alice Array Operation	Behavior
`anArray[i] = val;`	Change the value at position **`i`** in **`anArray`** to **`val`**
`val.set(value, anArray[i]);`	Retrieve the value at position **`i`** in **`anArray`**
`anArray.length`	Retrieve the number of values in **`anArray`**

FIGURE 5-29 Array operations

The notation **`anArray[i]`** is called the **subscript operation**. As shown in Figure 5-29, there are two versions of the subscript operation. The first one is sometimes called the *write version*, because it changes (that is, writes) the value of item **`i`** of the array. The second one is sometimes called the *read version*, because it retrieves (that is, reads) the value of item **`i`** of the array.

If an array variable is dropped where a *statement* can appear, Alice displays a menu from which you can select the write version of the subscript operation. If an array variable is dropped onto a *placeholder* variable or value, Alice displays a menu from which you can select either the array's **`length`** attribute or the read version of the subscript operation.[2]

At the time of this writing, the Alice **`forAllInOrder`** and **`forAllTogether`** statements can only be used on a list, not on an array. Until this changes, if you want to process each of the values in an array, you must use a **`for`** statement like this:

```
for (int index = 0; index < anArray.length; index++) {
        // do something with anArray[index]
}
```

To illustrate, Figure 5-30 presents an alternative version of Figure 5-12 using an array.

2. When this was written, Alice was very inconsistent in displaying these menus, for both arrays and lists. Hopefully, these problems will be fixed by the time you read this!

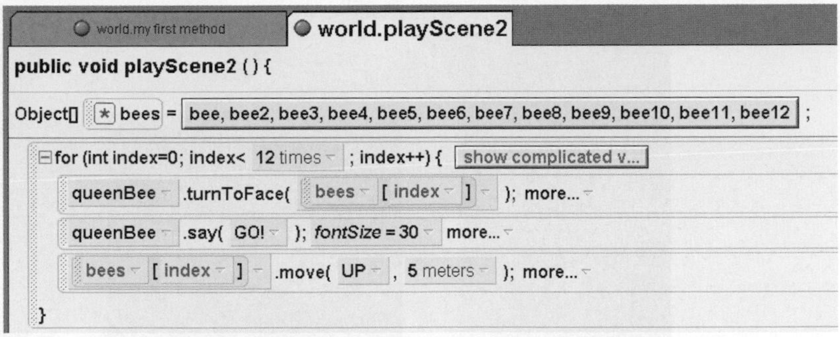

```
world.my first method | world.playScene2
public void playScene2 () {
Object[] bees = bee, bee2, bee3, bee4, bee5, bee6, bee7, bee8, bee9, bee10, bee11, bee12 ;
  for (int index=0; index< 12 times ; index++) {  show complicated v...
    queenBee .turnToFace( bees [ index ] ); more...
    queenBee .say( GO! ); fontSize = 30 more...
    bees [ index ] .move( UP , 5 meters ); more...
  }
```

FIGURE 5-30 The bees take off using an array

This method produces exactly the same behavior as that of Figure 5-12. However, note that because we cannot use a **forAllTogether** statement on an array, we cannot use an array to produce the simultaneous behavior shown in Figure 5-14 and Figure 5-15.

5.2.3 Array Example 2: Random Access

Suppose we want to build the following simple story:

> Scene: A castle has two magical doors. The left door tells the right door a random knock-knock joke.

If the left door told the right door the same joke every time, then this story would quickly become boring and the user would not want to play the story more than twice. However, if each time the scene is played, the left door tells a *random* (that is, potentially different) knock-knock joke, we make the scene more interesting and worth revisiting.

We can begin by positioning the **camera** and **castle** as shown in Figure 5-31.

FIGURE 5-31 The castle doors

Our next problem is to figure out how to make the doors tell a knock-knock joke. Let's look at several jokes, to see what is the same and what is different about each one:

Joke 1	Joke 2	Joke 3
L: Knock-knock	L: Knock-knock	L: Knock-knock
R: Who's there?	R: Who's there?	R: Who's there?
L: Boo.	L: Who.	L: Little old lady.
R: Boo who?	R: Who who?	R: Little old lady who?
L: Don't cry, it's just a joke.	L: Is there an owl in here?	L: I didn't know you could yodel!

Comparing these (lame) jokes, we see that knock-knock jokes have the following structure:

L: Knock-knock
R: Who's there?
L: *name*
R: *name* who?
L: *punchline*

where *name* and *punchline* are the parts that vary from joke to joke.

If we make *name* and *punchline* array variables, then we can store multiple jokes in them. For example, to store the three jokes above, we would define *name* and *punchline* as follows:

```
String [] name = {"Boo", "Who", "Little old lady" };
String [] punchline = {"Don't cry, it's just a joke.",
                       "Is there an owl in here?",
                       "I didn't know you could yodel!"};
```

Such definitions create parallel data structures in which **punchline[0]** corresponds to **name[0]**, **punchline[1]** corresponds to **name[1]**, and so on. We can visualize them as shown in Figure 5-32.

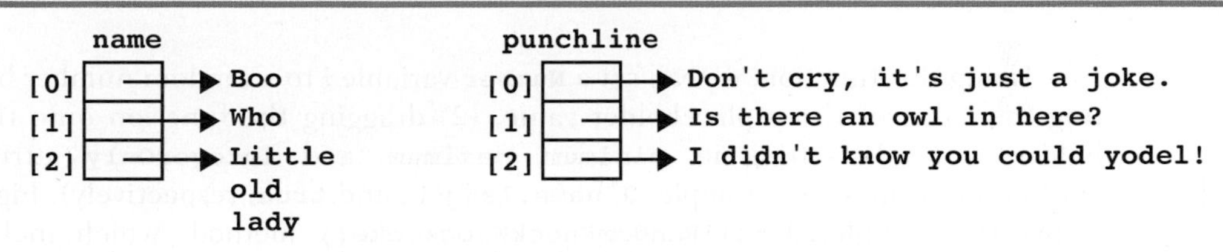

FIGURE 5-32 The **name** and **punchline** arrays

Once we have the parts of the jokes stored in arrays, we can tell the joke at index *i* as follows:

L: Knock-knock

R: Who's there?

L: *name[i]*

R: *name[i]* who?

L: *punchline[i]*

That is, if *i* has the value 0, then this will tell the "Boo who" joke; if *i* has the value 1, then it will tell the "Who who" joke, and so on.

Generating Random Numbers

To tell a random joke from the array, we need to generate a **random number** for the index *i*. That is we need to set *i* to a value that is randomly selected from the range of possible index values for the array. Fortunately, Alice makes this fairly easy by providing a **world** function named **Random.nextDouble()**, as shown in Figure 5-33.

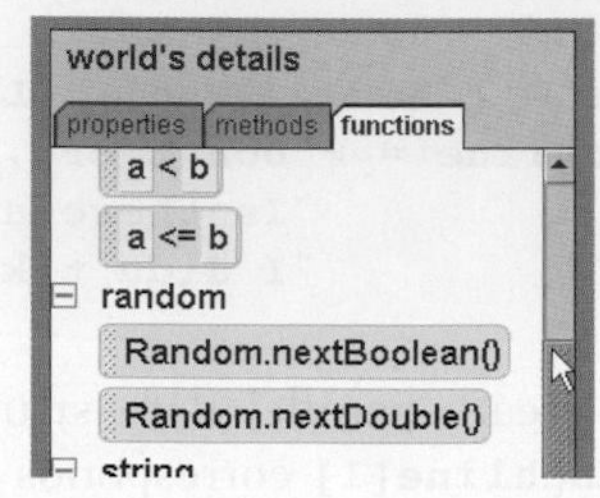

FIGURE 5-33 The world function **Random.nextDouble()**

Using this function, we can set a **Number** variable *i* to a random number by (1) setting the value of i to a placeholder value, (2) dragging the function onto the placeholder, and (3) setting its **minimum**, **maximum**, and **integerOnly** attributes to appropriate values (for example, **0**, **name.length**, and **true**, respectively). Figure 5-34 shows the completed **tellRandomKnockKnockJoke()** method, which includes the jokes above, plus two others.

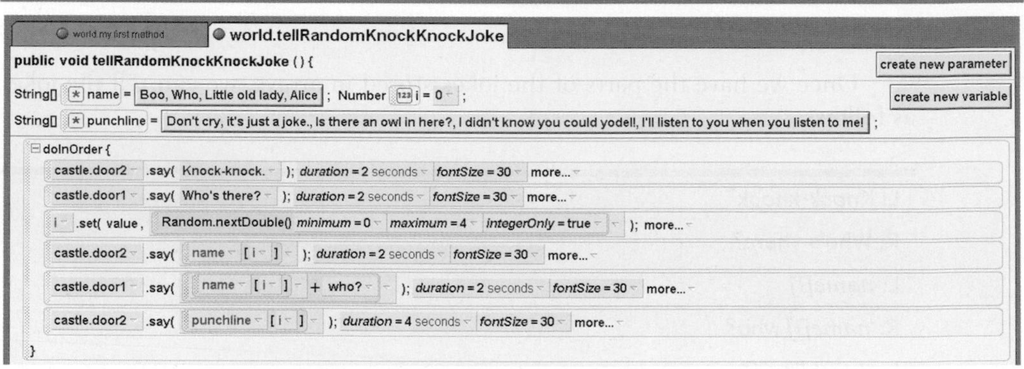

FIGURE 5-34 The **tellRandomKnockKnockJoke()** method

Each time this method is performed, it tells a knock-knock joke selected at random from the **name** and **punchline** arrays. By randomly generating the value of **i**, and then using that same value as the index for both **name[i]** and **punchline[i]**, we ensure that the name and punchline for a given joke match one another.

Random Details

The **`Random.nextDouble()`** function has two quirks to keep in mind:

- If you wish to generate an *integer* (that is, a whole number without decimal places like -1, 0, 1, or 1234), be sure to set the **`integerOnly`** attribute to **`true`**, or else the function will produce a *real* number (that is, a number with decimal places like -1.25, 0.05, 98.7654, etc.).
- In Figure 5-34, the arrays contain 4 items, indexed 0, 1, 2, and 3. To generate a random index value from the group {0, 1, 2, 3}, we specified a minimum value of 0, but a maximum value of 4. In general, if we want to generate a random number from the range **`a`** through **`b`**, then we should specify **`a`** as the minimum value and **`b+1`** as the maximum value. Put differently, whatever minimum value we specify is *included* in the range of randomly generated values, but whatever maximum value we specify is *excluded* from the range of randomly generated values.

Recall that in Figure 5-19, we saw that one of the messages we can send to an Alice list is the **`getRandomItem()`** function. In situations where we just need to retrieve one random item from a data structure, a list and this function provide an easy way to solve the problem.

However, we cannot use a list and the **`getRandomItem()`** function to solve the random knock-knock joke problem (at least not as easily). Do you see why not? The issue is that the problem has *two* data structures: one containing the names and one containing the corresponding punchlines. If we were to store the names and punchlines in two lists and then send each list the **`getRandomItem()`** function, the randomly selected punchline would be unlikely to correspond to the randomly selected name.[3]

5.3 Alice Tip: Using the `partNamed()` Function

Suppose that Scene 1 of a story begins as follows:

> Scene: The court of the fairy queen is crowded with fairy-courtiers talking amongst themselves. One of the fairies announces, "Her majesty, the Queen!" The fairy queen enters her court, and all the courtiers turn toward her. As she moves along the promenade leading to her throne, each courtier in succession turns to her and bows. Upon reaching her throne, the queen turns and says "Please rise." As one, the courtiers turn toward her and rise from their bows.

Looking over the nouns in the story, we might begin building this scene by creating a "fairy court" in a woodland setting, with a promenade leading to a throne, and a crowd of fairies flanking each side of the promenade. Figure 5-35 shows one possible realization of this scene using various fairy, forest, and other classes from the Alice Web Gallery.

3. We could replace the two arrays in Figure 5-34 with two lists. Because Alice lists support the subscript operation, we could randomly generate an index *i* and then access the item at position *i* in each list. However, because the data structures' sizes remain fixed as the program runs, using an array is preferable.

FIGURE 5-35 The court of the fairy queen

We also chose class **OliveWaterblossom** as the fairy queen, added her to the world, and positioned her behind the camera (13 meters from the throne) to set up her entry to the court.

With the scene set, we are ready to think about generating the behavior required by the user story. We might break the actions down into the following sequence of steps:

1. One of the fairies announces, "Her majesty, the Queen!"
2. As the queen enters the court, each courtier simultaneously turns to face the camera.
3. Do together:
    a. Move the queen 13 meters forward (down the promenade, toward her throne).
    b. Make the queen's wings flap.
    c. As she passes each courtier, have him or her turn toward the queen and bow.
4. The queen turns 1/2 revolution (so that she is facing her courtiers).
5. The queen says "Please rise."
6. Together each courtier turns toward the queen and rises from his or her bow.

Together, these steps make up an algorithm we can use for the **playScene1()** method.

Defining The Method

What is the best way to implement this algorithm? Steps 1 and 5 require all courtiers to take a simultaneous action, and Step 2c requires each courtier to take an action one at a time. One way to elicit these simultaneous and one-at-a-time actions is to place the courtiers into a list data structure. Given such a list, we can use the **`forAllTogether`** statement to make all courtiers do the same thing simultaneously in Steps 1 and 5, and we can use the **`forAllInOrder`** statement to make them all do the same thing one at a time in Step 2c.

With this approach, we can revise the algorithm as follows:

1. Let **`courtierList`** be a list of all the courtier fairies.
2. The courtier nearest the throne announces the queen.
3. For all items in **`courtierList`** together:
   Each item in **`courtierList`** turns to face the camera.
4. Do together:
   a. The queen moves 13 meters forward (down the promenade, toward her throne).
   b. The queen's wings flap.
   c. For each item in **`courtierList`**, one at a time:
      The item in **`courtierList`** turns toward the queen and bows.
5. The queen turns 1/2 revolution.
6. The queen says "Please rise."
7. For all items in **`courtierList`** together:
   Each item in **`courtierList`** turns toward the queen and rises from his/her bow.

Most of these steps are straightforward to program in Alice. However, there are two subtle points to keep in mind as we do so.

Defining The List

One subtle part is that when we define the **`courtierList`** variable as a list of **`Object`** and then add fairies to it, the order of the fairies in the list is significant. That is, because we are using the **`forAllInOrder`** statement in Step 3c and this statement goes through the items in the list from first to last, we must be careful to add the fairies to the list so that those closest to the camera are earlier in the list and those who are farthest from the camera are later in the list. Otherwise, the fairies will not turn toward the queen and bow to her as she moves past them. Figure 5-36 presents a fragment of this list from the **`playScene1()`** method.

```
Object[] courtierList = shadeAniseed, petalBeamweb, sprightlyReedsmoke, mabHazelnut, meadSeafeather, lichenZenspider, leafFlameglimmer, h
```

FIGURE 5-36 Defining the courtier list

Making A Fairy Bow

The second subtle part is generating the bowing and rising behaviors for the courtiers. It is easy to make an individual fairy-courtier bow and rise, by "opening" the individual in the *object tree*, selecting their **upperBody** component, and then sending this component the **turn()** message, as shown in Figure 5-37.

```
cordFlamewand.upperBody .turn( FORWARD , 0.25 revolutions ); more...
```

FIGURE 5-37 Making an individual courtier bow

The difficulty arises when we seek to use this approach with an item from the list within a **forAllInOrder** or **forAllTogether** statement. Although each item in the list is a fairy that has an **upperBody** component, we defined the **courtierList** variable as a list of **Objects**. Because not all Alice **Objects** have **upperBody** components (for example, buildings, fish, trees, etc.), Alice will not let us access the **upperBody** component of an item from the list. So we *can* make each courtier turn and face the queen by programming:

```
for all courtierList, one item_from_courtierList at a time:
    item_from_courtierList.turnToFace(oliveWaterblossom);
```

But we *cannot* make each courtier bow to the queen by programming:

```
for all courtierList, one item_from_courtierList at a time:
    item_from_courtierList.upperBody.turn(FORWARD, 0.25); // NO!
```

Because the lists are lists of **Objects**, we can only send a list item a message (or select a component) that is common to all **Objects**.

For this situation, every Alice object provides a function message called **partNamed(component)** that can be sent to that object to retrieve its part named **component**. In our situation, we know that every fairy in the list contains a component named **upperBody**, so we can send each fairy the **partNamed(upperBody)** message to retrieve its **upperBody** part, and then send that part the **turn()** message to make the fairy bow.

To use the **partNamed()** function, we begin with the statement shown in Figure 5-37, using the courtier's **upperBody** component as a placeholder. We then drag the courtier's **partNamed()** function onto the placeholder, yielding the statement shown in Figure 5-38.

```
cordFlamewand .partNamed( ) .turn( FORWARD , 0.25 revolutions ); more...
```

FIGURE 5-38 Using the **partNamed()** function

If we click the list arrow for **partNamed()**'s argument, and choose **other...** from the menu that appears, Alice displays a dialog box where we can type the name of the part we wish to access (**upperBody** in this case). When we do this, we get the statement shown in Figure 5-39.

```
cordFlamewand .partNamed( upperBody ) .turn( FORWARD , 0.25 revolutions ); more...
```

FIGURE 5-39 The **partNamed()** function

In the statement in Figure 5-39, **cordFlamewand** is a placeholder that we need to replace with an item from the list. To do so, we can drag and drop this statement into a **forAllInOrder** (or **forAllTogether**) statement, specify the **courtierList** as the **forAllInOrder** statement's list variable, and then drag the loop's **item_from_courtierList** variable onto the placeholder to replace it. The resulting statement is shown in Figure 5-40.

```
cordFlamewand .partNamed( upperBody ) .turn( FORWARD , 0.25 revolutions ); more...
```

FIGURE 5-40 Replacing the placeholder with a list item

Using this same approach, we can make the courtiers rise at the end of the scene. Figure 5-41 shows the completed **playScene1()** method.

```
world my first method | world.playScene1
public void playScene1 () {                                    create new parameter
Object[] courtierList = shadeAniseed, petalBeamweb, sprightlyReedsmoke, mabHazelnut, meadSeafeather, lichenZenspider, leafFlameglimm   create new variable
;
  cordFlamewand .say( Her majesty, the Queen! ); duration = 2 seconds fontSize = 40 more...
  For all courtierList , every item_from_courtierList together {
    item_from_courtierList .turnToFace( camera ); more...
  }
  doTogether {
    For all courtierList , one item_from_courtierList at a time {
      item_from_courtierList .pointAt( oliveWaterblossom ); duration = 0.25 seconds onlyAffectYaw = true more...
      item_from_courtierList .partNamed( upperBody ) .turn( FORWARD , 0.25 revolutions ); more...
    }
    oliveWaterblossom .move( FORWARD , 13 meters ); duration = 16 seconds more...
    oliveWaterblossom.flapWings ( duration = 16 , amount = 1 );
  }
  oliveWaterblossom .turn( LEFT , 0.5 revolutions ); more...
  oliveWaterblossom .say( Please rise. ); duration = 2 seconds fontSize = 30 more...
  For all courtierList , every item_from_courtierList together {
    item_from_courtierList .turnToFace( oliveWaterblossom ); more...
    item_from_courtierList .partNamed( upperBody ) .turn( BACKWARD , 0.25 revolutions ); more...
  }
}
```

FIGURE 5-41 The **playScene1()** method (final version)

When we run the program, we get the desired behavior. Figure 5-42 presents three screen captures: one partway through the **forAllInOrder** statement, one after all have bowed and the queen says "Please rise.", and one at the end of the scene.

FIGURE 5-42 Screen captures from **playScene1()**

Components Are Objects

The **partNamed()** function thus provides a means of retrieving a component of an object. The components of an object are themselves objects, so in **playScene1()**, we could have defined an **Object** variable named **torso**, and then used it in the **forAllInOrder** statement as follows:

```
for all courtierList, one item_from_courtierList at a time {
    item_from_courtierList.turnToFace(oliveWaterblossom);
    torso.set(value, item_from_courtierList.partNamed(upperBody));
    torso.turn(FORWARD, 0.25);
}
```

Either approach is okay. The point is that the components of an Alice **Object** are **Object**s, and can be referred to by **Object** variables.

Sending Messages to null

What happens if the object to which we send the **partNamed(component)** function does not have a part named **component**? For example, suppose we defined two **Object** variables, one named **part1**, the other named **part2**, and then set their values as follows:

```
part1.set(value, OliveWaterblossom.partNamed(upperBody));
part2.set(value, OliveWaterblossom.partNamed(xyz));
```

Because **OliveWaterblossom** does not have a component named **xyz**, the **partNamed()** function returns a special "zero" value named **null**, that denotes the absence of an **Object**. This value **null** is stored in variable **part2**, instead of a reference to a component. We can envision these two variables as shown in Figure 5-43.

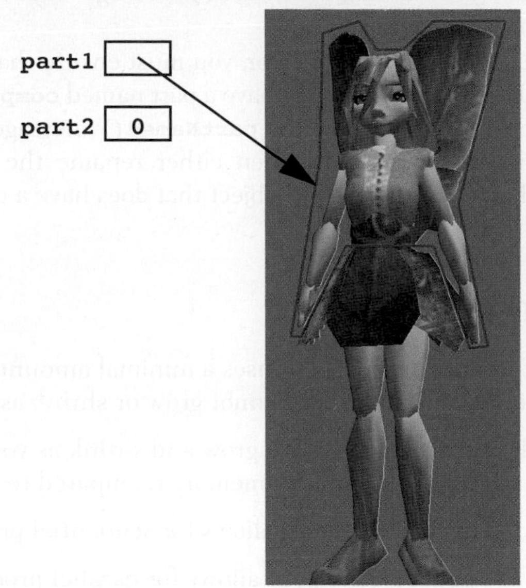

FIGURE 5-43 Variables with non-**null** and **null** values

Where **part1** refers to the queen from the waist up, **part2** refers to *nothing*. If the program then erroneously tries to send a message to **part2**:

```
part2.turn(FORWARD, 0.25);
```

Alice will generate an error message:

```
Alice has detected a problem with your world:
subject must not be null.
```

Alice will display this error any time a message is sent via a variable whose value is **null**, which Alice usually displays as **<None>**. This error may appear for a variety of reasons, including the following:

- You deleted an object from your world to which your program was sending a message.
- You deleted a variable from a method or world through which a message was being sent.
- You misspelled the name of the component in the **partNamed()** function.
- You sent the **partNamed(component)** function to an object that does not have a part named **component**.

To correct the first two kinds of errors (which are by far the most common), look through your program's methods for statements in which a message is sent to **<None>**. When you find such a statement, either replace **<None>** with a valid object or delete/disable the statement.

To correct the second kind of error, check the spelling of the component in each statement where you send a **partNamed()** message. If you find one that is incorrect, correct its spelling.

To correct the third kind of error, you must ensure that the **partNamed(component)** function is only sent to objects that have a part named **component**. Check the parts of each object to which you are sending the **partNamed()** message. If you find one that does not have a part named **component**, then either rename the component in that object, or replace that object with a different object that does have a component named **component**.

5.4 Chapter Summary

- An array is a data structure that uses a minimal amount of your computer's memory to store a sequence of items, but cannot grow or shrink as your program runs.
- A list is a data structure that can grow and shrink as your program runs, at the cost of using some additional computer memory (compared to the array).
- The **forAllInOrder** statement allows for sequential processing of the items in a list.
- The **forAllTogether** statement allows for parallel processing of the items in a list.
- The **Random.nextDouble()** function provides a way to generate random numbers.
- The **partNamed(component)** function lets us retrieve a part of an object (usually so that we can send it a message).
- The **null** value is a special "zero" value used to indicate the *absence* of an object. In the *editing area*, Alice usually displays **<None>** to represent the **null** value.

5.4.1 Key Terms

array
data structure
forAllInOrder statement
forAllTogether statement
index
item
iterate
list
null
partNamed() function
position
random number

Programming Projects

5.1 Using the **Cheerleader** class from the Alice Gallery, build a world containing 5–6 cheerleaders who lead a cheer at a sporting event. Your cheer can be either funny or serious, and it can either be a cheer unique to your school or a standard cheer (for example, "The Wave").

5.2 *This Old Man* is a silly song with the lyrics below. Create an Alice program containing a character who sings this song, using as few statements as possible.

This old man, he played one. He played knick-knack on my drum, with a knick-knack paddy-wack give a dog a bone. This old man came rolling home.	*This old man, he played two. He played knick-knack on my shoe, with a knick-knack paddy-wack give a dog a bone. This old man came rolling home.*
This old man, he played three. He played knick-knack on my knee, ...	*This old man, he played four. He played knick-knack on my door, ...*
This old man, he played five. He played knick-knack on my hive, ...	*This old man, he played six. He played knick-knack on my sticks, ...*
This old man, he played seven. He played knick-knack up in heaven, ...	*This old man, he played eight. He played knick-knack on my gate, ...*
This old man, he played nine. He played knick-knack on my spine, with a knick-knack paddy-wack give a dog a bone. This old man came rolling home.	*This old man, he played ten. He played knick-knack once again, with a knick-knack paddy-wack give a dog a bone. This old man came rolling home.*

5.3 Create a city scene featuring a parade. Store the paraders (that is, vehicles, people, etc.) in a data structure and use it to coordinate their movements. Make your parade as festive as possible.

5.4 Build a world containing a person who can calculate the average, minimum, and maximum of a group of numbers in his or her head. Use a **`NumberDialog`** to get the numbers from the user. Have your person and each **`NumberDialog`** tell the user to enter a special value (for example, -999) after the last value in the sequence has been entered. Store the group of numbers in a data structure, and write three new world functions — **`average()`**, **`minimum()`**, and **`maximum()`** — that take a data structure as their argument and return the average, minimum, and maximum value in the structure, respectively. When all the numbers have been entered, have your person "say" the group's average, minimum, and maximum values.

5.5 Create a scene in which a group of Rockettes do a dance number (for example, the Can-Can). Store the Rockettes in a data structure, and use **`forAllInOrder`** and/or **`forAllTogether`** statements to coordinate the movements of their dance routine.

5.6 Create a "springtime" scene that runs for a minute or so, starting with an empty field but ending with the field covered with flowers. The flowers should "grow" out of the ground as your scene plays. Make your program as short as possible by storing the flowers in a data structure.

5.7 Proceed as in Problem 5.6, but use random-number generation to make the flowers appear in a different order or pattern every time your program is run.

5.8 Create a scene in which two people are talking near a not-very-busy intersection, which uses four stop signs to control the traffic. Build the intersection using buildings and roads. Define two data structures: one containing a group of vehicles, and one containing the four directions a vehicle can move through the intersection (for example, north, south, east, and west). As your characters talk, use random numbers to select a vehicle and its direction.

5.9 Choose an old pop song that has several unique arm or body motions and whose lyrics are available on the Internet (for example, *YMCA* by the Village People, *Walk Like An Egyptian* by the Bangles, etc.). Using Alice, create a "music video" for the song, in which several people sing the song and use their arms or bodies to make the motions. Make your video as creative as possible, but try to avoid writing the same statements more than once. If you have access to a *legal* digital copy of the song, use the **`playSound()`** message to play it during your video.

5.10 Create a scene containing a group of similar creatures from the Alice gallery (for example, a herd of horses, a school of fish, a pack of wolves, etc.). Store your group in a data structure, and write a method that makes the group exhibit *flocking behavior*, in which the behavior of one member of the group causes the rest of the group to behave in a similar fashion. (Hint: designate one member of the group as the leader, and make the leader the first item in the data structure.)

Chapter 6
Events

It's not the events of our lives that shape us, but our beliefs as to what those events mean.

Anthony Robbins

Often do the spirits
Of great events stride on before the events,
And in to-day already walks to-morrow

Samuel Taylor Coleridge

To understand reality is not the same as to know about outward events. It is to perceive the essential nature of things. The best-informed man is not necessarily the wisest. Indeed there is a danger that precisely in the multiplicity of his knowledge he will lose sight of what is essential. But on the other hand, knowledge of an apparently trivial detail quite often makes it possible to see into the depth of things. And so the wise man will seek to acquire the best possible knowledge about events, but always without becoming dependent upon this knowledge. To recognize the significant in the factual is wisdom.

Dietrich Bonhoeffer

In the event of a water landing, I have been designed to act as a flotation device.

Data (Brent Spiner), in *Star Trek: Insurrection*

Objectives

Upon completion of this chapter, you will be able to:

- ❑ Create new events in Alice
- ❑ Create handler methods for Alice events
- ❑ Use events to build interactive stories

Most of the programs we have written so far have been scenes from stories that, once the user clicks Alice's **Play** button, simply proceed from beginning to end. For some of our **interactive programs**, the user must enter a number or a string, but entering such values via the keyboard has been all that we have required of the user in terms of interaction with the program.

When a user clicks Alice's **Play** button for a program, it *triggers* a change in the program — usually creating a flow that begins at the first statement in **world.my_first_method()**. An action by the user (or the program) that causes a change in the program is called an **event**. For example, clicking Alice's **Play** button triggers a **When the world starts** event.

Alice supports a variety of events, including those listed in Figure 6-1.[1]

Alice Event	Triggered By	Triggered When
When the world starts	the user	the user clicks Alice's **Play** button
***While the world is running**		the world is running
When a key is typed	the user	the user releases a keyboard key
***While a key is pressed**		the user holds down a keyboard key
When the mouse is clicked on something	the user	the user clicks the left mouse button while pointing at an object
***While the mouse is pressed on something**		the user holds down the left mouse button while pointing at an object
While something is true	the program	a condition remains true
***When something becomes true**		a condition becomes true
When a variable changes	the program	a variable changes its value
Let the mouse move <objects>	the user	the user moves the mouse
Let the arrow keys move <subject>	the user	the user presses one of the arrow keys
Let the mouse move the camera	the user	the user moves the mouse
Let the mouse orient the camera	the user	the user moves the mouse

FIGURE 6-1 Alice events

1. An event marked with an asterisk (*) is accessible by (1) creating the event above it in Figure 6-1, (2) right-clicking on that event, and then (3) choosing **change to ...** from the menu that appears.

There are two steps to making a program respond when an event occurs:

1. Choose (or define) a method providing the behavior to occur in response to the event.

2. Tell Alice to invoke that method whenever the event occurs.

Invoking a method in response to an event is called **handling the event**, and a method that is invoked in response to an event is often called an **event handler**. A program that solves a problem or tells a story mainly through events and handlers is called an **event-driven program**.

In the rest of this chapter, we will see how to build event-driven programs. While we will not cover all Alice events, we will provide a representative introduction to what they can do.

6.1 Handling Mouse Clicks: The Magical Doors

To let us see how an event-driven world differs from those we have built before, let us revise the scene-story from Section 5.2.3 as follows:

> Scene: A castle has two magical doors. When the user clicks on the right door, it opens; but when the user clicks on the left door, it tells the right door a random knock-knock joke.

Because some of the behavior is the same as in the world we built in Section 5.2.3, we will begin with that world. As before, the initial shot is as shown in Figure 6-2.

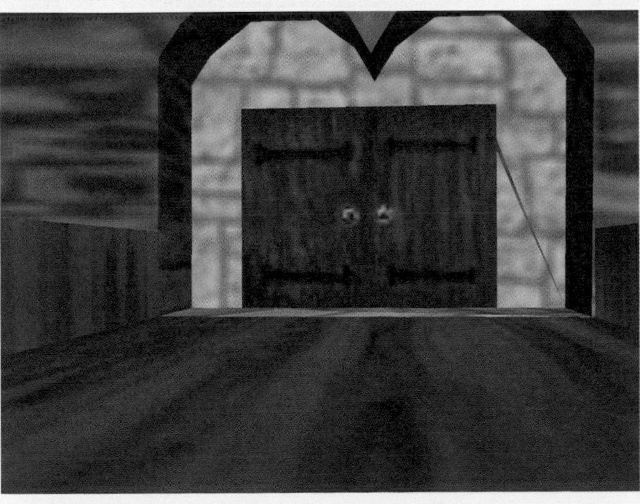

FIGURE 6-2 The castle doors

We will deal with each door separately. However, before we begin, we should prevent the left door from telling jokes when we run the world. To do so, we delete the **`tellRandomKnockKnockJoke()`** message from **`my_first_method()`**.[2]

6.1.1 The Right Door

You may recall from the Alice tutorials that handling mouse clicks is easy in Alice. To do so, we follow two steps:

1. If the event should trigger behavior that requires more than one message, we define a method that produces that behavior. This method will be the handler.
2. We create a new event in the *events area* that invokes the handler — either the method we defined in Step 1, or the single message that produces the required behavior.

To illustrate, the behavior to make the right door open can be elicited with a single message, **`turn()`**, so we need not create a new method. Instead, we proceed to Step 2 by clicking the **`create new event`** button and choosing **`When the mouse is clicked on something`** from the menu that appears, as shown in Figure 6-3.

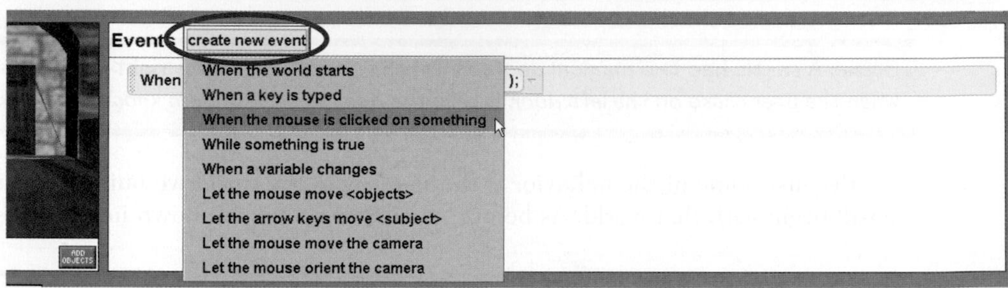

FIGURE 6-3 Creating a new mouse event

When we select this choice, Alice creates a new event in the *events area*, as shown below.

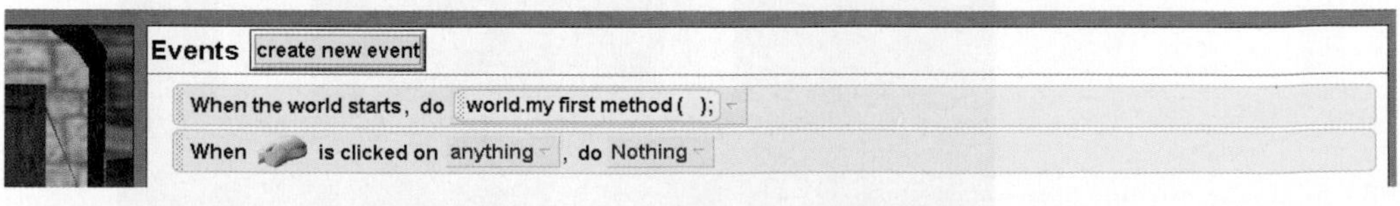

FIGURE 6-4 A new mouse event

2. Alternatively, we could achieve the same effect by deleting **`When the world starts do world.my_first_method()`** from the *events area*.

To satisfy the user story, we need this event to be triggered by clicking on the right door (**castle.door1**), rather than **anything**. To make this happen, we click the list arrow next to **anything** and select **castle->door1**, modifying the event as shown in Figure 6-5.

When is clicked on castle.door1, do Nothing

FIGURE 6-5 A mouse event for the right door

The object from which an event originates — **castle.door1** in this case — is called the **event source**.

To handle this event, we can replace **Nothing** with the message **castle.door1.turn(LEFT, 0.25);** by opening up the **castle** in the *object tree*, selecting **door1**, and then from the *methods* pane of the *details area*, dragging the **turn()** message to the *events area* and dropping it on **Nothing**. Figure 6-6 shows the resulting event.

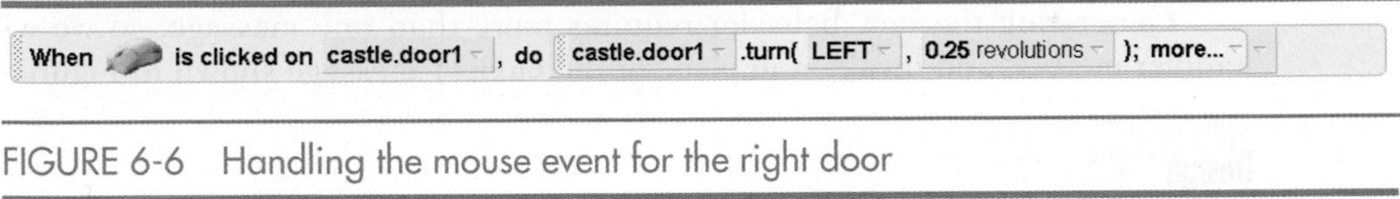
When is clicked on castle.door1, do castle.door1 .turn(LEFT , 0.25 revolutions); more...

FIGURE 6-6 Handling the mouse event for the right door

Congratulations — you have just handled your first event! When we click Alice's **Play** button, nothing happens until the user clicks the right door, at which point it swings open.

6.1.2 The Left Door

Dealing with the left door is nearly as easy as the right door, but only because we already have a method that makes the left door tell a random knock-knock joke (see Figure 5-33). That is, if we had not already written **world.tellRandomKnockKnockJoke()**, we would have to write a handler method for this event, as described in Step 1 above.

Since we already have a method to serve as a handler, we can proceed to Step 2 of the event steps. To do so, we use the same approach we saw in Figure 6-3 through Figure 6-6, but specifying **castle.door2** as the source of this event, and dragging-and-dropping **world.tellRandomKnockKnockJoke()** as its handler. This is shown in Figure 6-7.

Events create new event
When the world starts, do world.my first method( );
When is clicked on castle.door1, do castle.door1 .turn(LEFT , 0.25 revolutions); more...
When is clicked on castle.door2, do world.tellRandomKnockKnockJoke( );

FIGURE 6-7 Handling the mouse event for the left door

That's it! Now, when we click Alice's **Play** button, clicking on the left door produces a random knock-knock joke, while clicking on the right door causes that door to open.

Note that, unlike past worlds we have built, **world.my_first_method()** does nothing in this new world. Instead, all of the interesting behavior lies in the handler methods, which are triggered by the event of the user clicking the mouse.

6.1.3 The Right Door Revisited

If we test the world thoroughly, we find that the right door opens correctly *the first time* we click on it. However if we subsequently click on the right door again, it turns left *again* (precisely what we told it to do). The mistake lies in the *logic* we used in defining how that door should behave. Such mistakes are called **logic errors**. A better response to a mouse click on the right door would be to open the door if it is closed and to close the door if it is open.

It is important to see that it is okay to revise the user story when testing reveals a weakness. Just as a filmmaker may rewrite a scene the night before it is shot, a programmer may have to rewrite a part of the user story to improve the overall program.

Generating the new behavior requires more than one message, so we will write a handler method and invoke it in place of the **turn()** message shown in Figure 6-6.

Design

To design this method, we can revise the right door part of the user story as follows:

> When the user clicks on the right door, if it is closed, it opens; otherwise, it closes.

Notice that the revised story contains the magic word *if*. This strongly suggests that the method will need an **if** statement.

Programming: Storing the Door's State

One way to produce this new behavior is to add a new property to the castle, to indicate whether or not its right door is closed.[3] To do so, we select **castle** in the *object tree*, click the *properties* tab in the *details area*, and then click the **create new variable** button, as we saw back in Section 3.3.

The right door is in one of two states: either it is *closed* or it is *open*. This means that we can represent whether or not the right door is closed with a **Boolean** variable named **rightDoorClosed**, using **true** to represent the *closed* state and **false** to represent the *open* state. Since the door is closed at the outset, its initial value should be **true**, as shown in Figure 6-8.

---

3. Since this is a characteristic of the right door, such a property really should be defined in **castle.door1**. Unfortunately, Alice only lets you add properties, methods, and questions to an object at the "top" level of the *object tree*, so the best available place to store this property is **castle**.

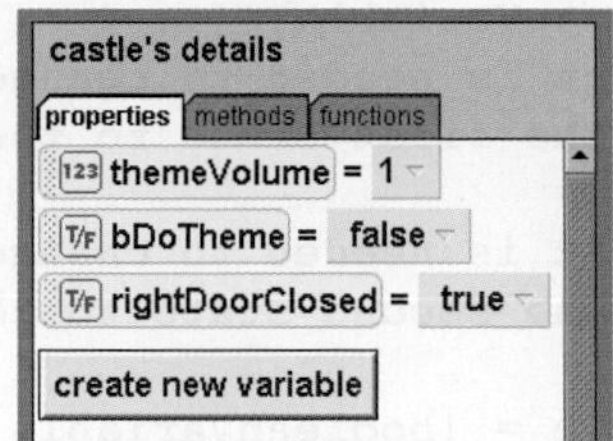

FIGURE 6-8 Storing the state of the castle's right door

When the user clicks on the right door, the handler method for that event can use an **`if`** statement to determine which way to **`turn()`** it (**`LEFT`** or **`RIGHT`**), and then update the value of **`rightDoorClosed`** from **`true`** to **`false`** (or vice versa) to reflect the door's changed state.

Programming: Defining the Handler

We create a handler method the same way as any other method: by choosing the *methods* tab in the *details area*, clicking the **`create new method`** button, naming the method, and then defining its behavior. As usual, if a handler method affects the behavior of a single object, it should be defined within that object; otherwise it should be stored in the **`world`**. Figure 6-9 shows the **`castle.openOrCloseRightDoor()`** method.

```
world.my first method | castle.openOrCloseRightDoor
public void openOrCloseRightDoor ( ) {          create new parameter
                                                create new variable
  doInOrder {
    if ( castle.rightDoorClosed ) {
      castle.door1 .turn( LEFT , 0.25 revolutions ); more...
    } else {
      castle.door1 .turn( RIGHT , 0.25 revolutions ); more...
    }
    castle.rightDoorClosed .set( value , ! castle.rightDoorClosed ); more...
  }
}
```

FIGURE 6-9 Handling clicks on the castle's right door

The last statement in Figure 6-9 uses the logical *not* operator (`!`) we saw in Section 4.1.4 to invert the value of **`rightDoorClosed`** from **`true`** to **`false`** when opening the door, and from **`false`** to **`true`** when closing the door.

The approach shown in Figure 6-9 can be generalized into a standard pattern for situations in which an object can be in one of two states (for example, *open-closed*, *in-out*, *on-off*, etc.) to switch the object from one state to the other. We can generalize the pattern for such **two-state behavior** as follows:

```
if (booleanStateVariable) {
     // do what is needed to change the object
     // from the first state to the second state
} else {
     // do what is needed to change the object
     // from the second state to the first state
}
booleanVariable = !booleanVariable. // update the state variable
```

Programming: Handling the Event

Given the **openOrCloseRightDoor()** handler method shown in Figure 6-9, we can finish the program by specifying that it be the handler for the **When the mouse is clicked on castle.door1** event, by dragging the new method and dropping it on top of the previous handler (the **castle.door1.turn()** message). Figure 6-10 shows the resulting *events area*.

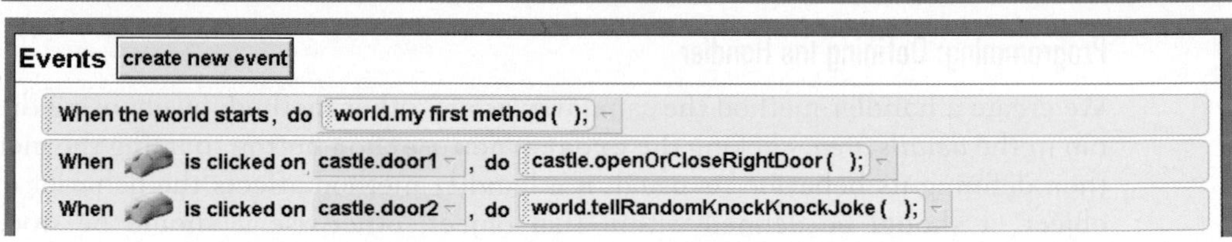
Events
create new event
When the world starts, do world.my first method ( );
When is clicked on castle.door1 , do castle.openOrCloseRightDoor ( );
When is clicked on castle.door2 , do world.tellRandomKnockKnockJoke ( );

FIGURE 6-10 The (revised) *events area*

Now, a click on the closed right door opens it, and a click on the open right door closes it.

6.1.4 Event Handling Is Simultaneous

One tricky thing about events is that two events can occur almost simultaneously, requiring their handlers to run at the same time. For example, in the "castle doors" program we wrote in this section, a user could click on the left door and then click on the right door, before the left door finishes the joke. Figure 6-11 shows two screen captures under these circumstances.

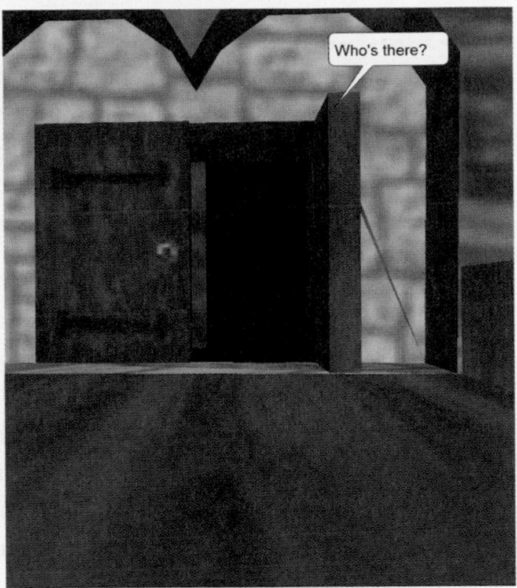

FIGURE 6-11 Handling simultaneous events

As shown in Figure 6-11, Alice handles such simultaneous events quite well. The first (left) screen capture shows the left door beginning its knock-knock joke while the right door is opening. The handlers for the left and right doors thus run simultaneously. When the right door's handler finishes, the left door's handler keeps running, as seen in the second screen capture.

Handlers running simultaneously usually work well, but if two running handlers both modify the same property of an object, a conflict may arise. For example, to tell a knock-knock joke, the left door's handler sends both doors **say()** messages. If the right door's handler also sent either door a **say()** message, then the simultaneous performance of both handlers would interfere with the joke and create a conflict. To avoid such conflicts, avoid designing programs in which two different events simultaneously modify the same property of the same object.

6.1.5 Categorizing Events

In this section, we have seen how to handle a **mouse event** — an event that is triggered when the user moves the mouse or clicks a mouse button. A **keyboard event** is triggered when the user presses a keyboard key. Because they are initiated by a user action, mouse and keyboard events are both known as **user events**. By contrast, a **program event** is triggered when the world starts running, or the program changes the value of a variable or condition.

6.2 Handling Key Presses: A Helicopter Flight Simulator

Now that we have seen how mouse click events can be handled, let's look at keyboard events.

6.2.1 The Problem

> Scene: *Catastrophe!* The mayor's cat is lost, bringing your city's government to a halt. As the city's only helicopter pilot, you have been asked to help find the mayor's cat. You find yourself in the cockpit of a running helicopter at an airport outside the city. Fly the helicopter and find the mayor's cat.

6.2.2 Design

We can build the scene using the classes from the Alice Gallery (see below), but let's first spend a few minutes thinking what the user must do: how he or she will fly the helicopter.

Flying a helicopter is complicated: the user needs to be able to make the helicopter move *up*, *down*, *forward*, *backward*, and turn *left* or *right*. It would be difficult to elicit all six of these behaviors using a mouse, so we will instead use keyboard keys for each of them. After a bit of thought, we might decide to operate the helicopter as follows:

> To make the helicopter ascend (take off), use the 'a' key. To descend (land), use the 'd' key. When the helicopter is in the air, use the up and down arrow keys to move it forward and backward. Similarly, when the helicopter is in the air, use the left and right arrow keys to turn it left and right.

These keys are chosen for their:

- **Mnemonic values**: 'a' is the first letter in *ascend*, and 'd' is the first letter in *descend*, making these keys easy to remember. Likewise, the up, down, left, and right arrow keys point in the directions we want the helicopter to move, making their meanings easy to remember.
- **Convenient positions**: 'a' and 'd' are near one another on most keyboards, allowing the user to easily control the helicopter's elevation with two fingers of one hand. Likewise, the four arrow keys are usually grouped together, allowing the user to easily control the helicopter's forward, backward, left, and right motion with the fingers on the other hand.

It is important to consider *human factors* when building interactive stories. If the story requires complex behaviors, make the controls for your user as convenient and easy to use as possible. Making programs easy to use is an important aspect of programming known as **usability**.

6.2.3 Programming in Alice

To construct the scene, we can build an Alice world containing an airport, a city terrain, an assortment of buildings, a helicopter, and a (Cheshire) cat. After arranging the buildings to resemble a small city, we place the cat somewhere within the city (exactly where is for you to find out), position the helicopter at the airport, and then position the camera to be peering out the front of the helicopter. We then set the `camera`'s `vehicle` property to be the **helicopter**, so that any message that moves the **helicopter** will also move the **camera**.

Making the Helicopter's Propellor Spin

The helicopter's engine is running when the story begins, so its propellor should be spinning when the world starts. The **Helicopter** class has a method named **heli blade()** that continuously spins its **propellor** and **rotor**. By using this method as the handler for Alice's default **When the world starts** event (see Figure 6-12), the helicopter's propellor begins spinning as soon as we press Alice's **Play** button.

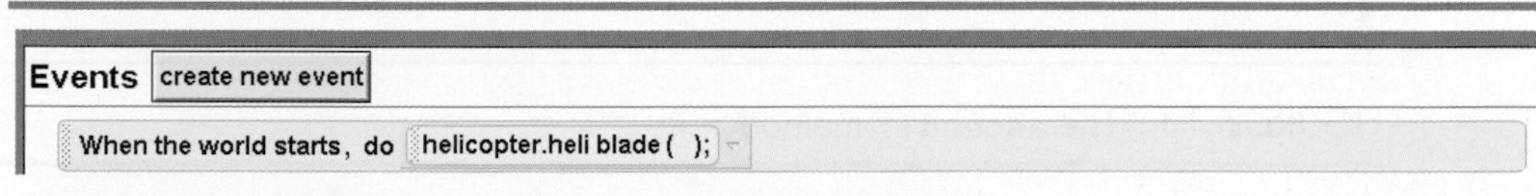

FIGURE 6-12 Making the helicopter's propellor spin

Making the Helicopter Ascend

A helicopter must be in the air before it can go forward or backward, turn left or right, or descend. As a result, it makes sense to define the **helicopter.ascend()** method first, while keeping those other operations in mind.

Our other five operations must to be able to determine if the helicopter is in the air. (If it is not, those operations should do nothing.) To store this information, we can create a **Boolean** property for the **helicopter** named **inTheAir**, initially **false**, as shown in Figure 6-13.

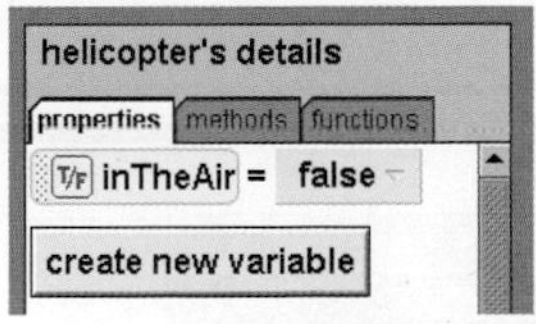

FIGURE 6-13 The **helicopter.inTheAir** property

With this property in place, we can define the **ascend()** method as shown in Figure 6-14.

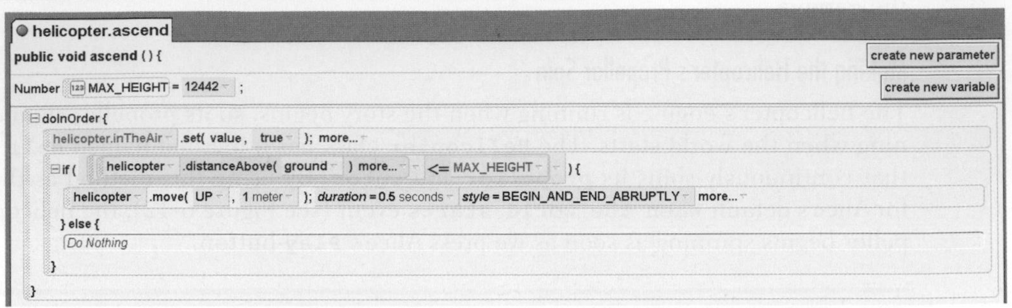

FIGURE 6-14 The **ascend()** method

Since helicopters cannot fly infinitely high, we first define a constant named **MAX_HEIGHT** and set its value to the maximum altitude a helicopter has attained (according to the Internet, 12,442 meters). The body of the method then sets **helicopter.inTheAir** to **true**, and moves the helicopter up 1 meter if it has not already attained the maximum altitude. To smooth the animation, we set the **move()** message's ***style*** attribute to **BEGIN_AND_END_ABRUPTLY**. To make it move upwards at a reasonable rate, we set its ***duration*** attribute to **0.5** seconds, which effectively makes the helicopter ascend at 2 meters per second.

With the **ascend()** method defined, our next task is to associate it with the **'a'** keyboard event. To do so, we click the **create new event** button in the *events area*, and select **When a key is typed**, as shown in Figure 6-15.

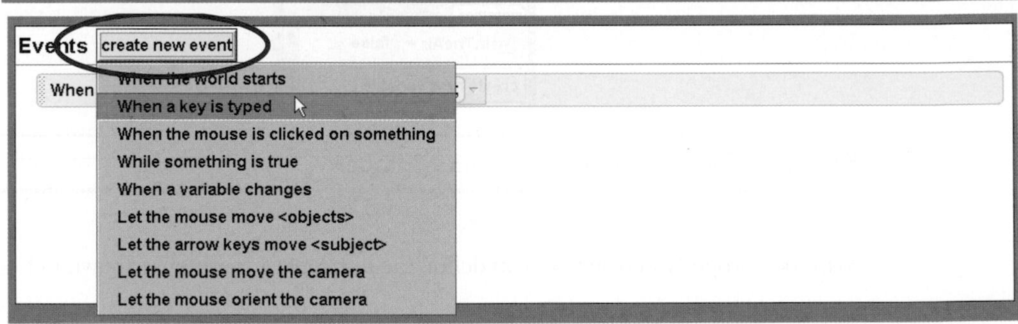

FIGURE 6-15 Creating a new keyboard event

Alice then generates the **When a key is typed** event shown in Figure 6-16.

When any key is typed, do Nothing

FIGURE 6-16 The `when a key is typed` event

If we use this event to make the `'a'` key trigger the **`ascend()`** method, then each press of the `'a'` key will move the helicopter up 1 meter. Put differently, to climb just 100 meters, the user would have to press the `'a'` key 100 times, which is no fun for the user!

A better approach is to use the **`While a key is pressed`** event from Figure 6-1. As indicated there, we can convert a **`When a key is typed`** event to a **`While a key is pressed`** event by right-clicking on the **`When a key is typed`** event, and then selecting **`change to -> While a key is pressed`** from the menu, as shown in Figure 6-17.

FIGURE 6-17 Changing `When a key is typed` into `While a key is pressed`

Selecting this choice causes Alice to replace the **`When a key is typed`** event with a **`While a key is pressed`** event, as shown in Figure 6-18.

While any key is pressed
Begin: <None>
During: <None>
End: <None>

FIGURE 6-18 The `While a key is pressed` event

As seen in Figure 6-18, this event allows *three* different handlers to respond to one key event:

- **`Begin`**: a handler here is performed *once*, when the key is first pressed.
- **`During`**: a handler here is performed *continuously*, as long as the key remains down.
- **`End`**: a handler here is performed *once*, when the key is released.

For the problem at hand, we will only need one of these parts: the **`During`** part.

To specify that we want the `'a'` key to trigger this event, we click the list arrow next to **`any key`** and choose **`letters->A`** from the menu that appears, as shown in Figure 6-19.

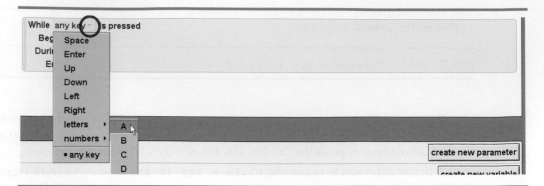

FIGURE 6-19 Making `'a'` trigger an event

We then make the **`ascend()`** method the handler for the **`During`** part of this event, as shown in Figure 6-20.

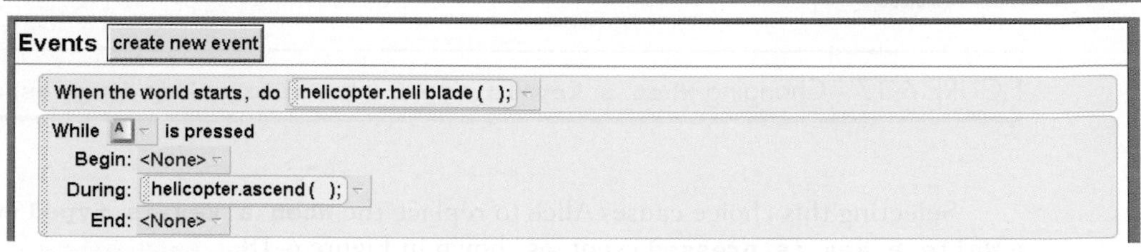

FIGURE 6-20 Associating `'a'` with **`helicopter.ascend()`**

With this event defined, holding down the `'a'` key will make the **`helicopter`** ascend smoothly into the air, and set **`helicopter.inTheAir`** to **`true`**.

Making the Helicopter Descend

To make the helicopter descend, we write a **`descend()`** method to serve as a handler for the **`'d'`** keyboard event. If we think through its behavior, it has two things to accomplish:

1. If the **`helicopter`** is above the ground, the **`helicopter`** should move down 1 meter.
2. Otherwise, the **`helicopter.inTheAir`** property should be set to **`false`**.

Figure 6-21 presents a definition for **descend()** that achieves both of these goals.

```
helicopter.ascend | helicopter.descend
public void descend () {                         create new parameter
                                                 create new variable
  if( helicopter .distanceAbove( ground ) more... > 0 ){
    helicopter .move( DOWN , 1 meter ); duration = 0.25 seconds  style = BEGIN_AND_END_ABRUPTLY  more...
  } else {
    helicopter.inTheAir .set( value , false ); more...
  }
}
```

FIGURE 6-21 The **descend()** method

Our method first checks to see if the helicopter is above the ground. If not, it sets the **inTheAir** property to **false**. Since the **ascend()** and **descend()** methods control the helicopter's vertical movement, they are responsible for changing the value of **inTheAir** when necessary. No other methods should modify this property (though they will read its value).

If the helicopter is above the ground, our method moves it down 1 meter. As in **ascend()**, we set the ***style*** of the **move()** method to **BEGIN_AND_END_ABRUPTLY** to smooth the animation. Unlike **ascend()**, we set its ***duration*** to **0.25** seconds, so that the helicopter descends at a rate of 4 meters per second (to simulate the effect of gravity on its descent).

We can associate the **descend()** method with the **'d'** event using the same approach we used for **'a'** in Figure 6-15 through Figure 6-19. The result is the event shown in Figure 6-22.

```
While D is pressed
  Begin: <None>
  During: helicopter.descend( );
  End: <None>
```

FIGURE 6-22 Associating **'d'** with **helicopter.descend()**

With this event in place, we can now use **'d'** key to land the helicopter!

The Arrow Keys

As we saw in Figure 6-1, Alice provides a **Let arrow keys move <subject>** event. You might be tempted to use this event to control the **helicopter** in the program, by creating an event like that shown in Figure 6-23.

FIGURE 6-23 Control using the arrow keys?

This kind of an event works great in many situations, and it would be nice if it worked in ours. The problem for us is that a helicopter should *not* move unless it is in the air. If we were to use this event, then the arrow keys *would* cause the **helicopter** to move, even when it is "parked" on the ground! Moreover, Alice provides no easy way to modify the behavior triggered by this event. As a result, we will not use this event in the program. Instead, we will define four separate events: one for each of the four arrow keys.

The good news is that we will not need four separate event handlers. As we shall see, two methods are all we need to handle all four arrow events.

Making the Helicopter Turn

To make the helicopter turn left or right, we could define two separate methods like we did for ascending and descending. However, these methods would be nearly identical, differing only in the direction we want the helicopter to turn. Instead of defining separate methods, we will use a single method, and pass an argument (**LEFT** or **RIGHT**) to specify the direction we want the helicopter to turn. The basic logic is as shown in Figure 6-24.

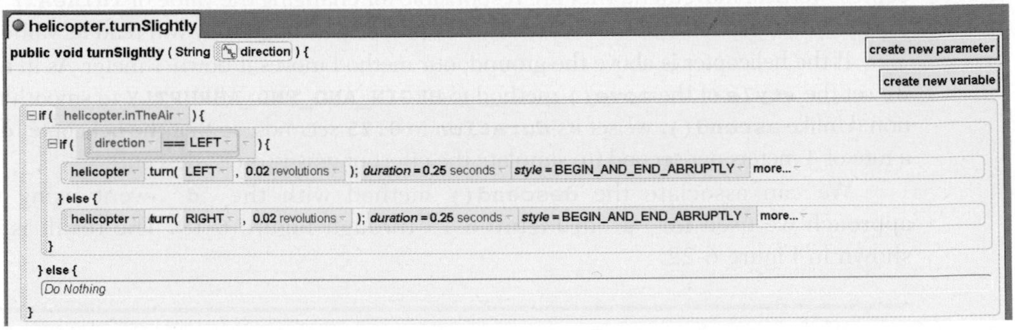

```
helicopter.turnSlightly
public void turnSlightly ( String direction ) {                create new parameter
                                                               create new variable
  if ( helicopter.inTheAir ){
    if ( direction == LEFT ){
      helicopter .turn( LEFT , 0.02 revolutions ); duration = 0.25 seconds style = BEGIN_AND_END_ABRUPTLY more...
    } else {
      helicopter .turn( RIGHT , 0.02 revolutions ); duration = 0.25 seconds style = BEGIN_AND_END_ABRUPTLY more...
    }
  } else {
    Do Nothing
}
```

FIGURE 6-24 The **turnSlightly()** method

We named the method **turnSlightly()**, to keep it distinct from the existing **turn()** method, and because it only turns the **helicopter** a small, fixed amount (**0.02** revolutions).

With this definition to serve as a handler, we can associate it with the left and right arrow keys using the approach shown in Figure 6-15 through Figure 6-19, but passing **Left** as an argument to the handler for the left arrow key event, and **Right** as an argument to the handler for the right arrow key event. Doing so produces the two events shown in Figure 6-25.

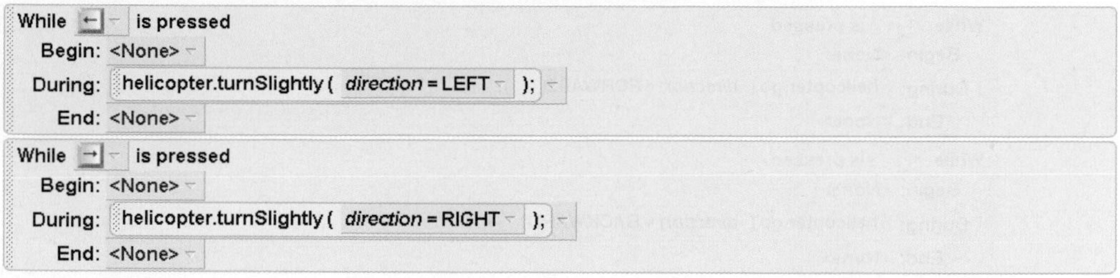

```
While ← is pressed
  Begin: <None>
  During: helicopter.turnSlightly( direction = LEFT );
  End: <None>
While → is pressed
  Begin: <None>
  During: helicopter.turnSlightly( direction = RIGHT );
  End: <None>
```

FIGURE 6-25 The left and right arrow events

Using these events, we can turn the helicopter left or right, but only when it is in the air.

Moving the Helicopter Forward or Backward

Our final operations are to move the helicopter forward or backward in response to the up and down arrow keys. As with turning the helicopter, we can do both of these in a single method, by passing **FORWARD** or **BACKWARD** as an argument to specify which direction to go. As in **turnSlightly()**, this method must only let the helicopter move if it is in the air. Figure 6-26 presents a definition for this method, which we have named **go()**.

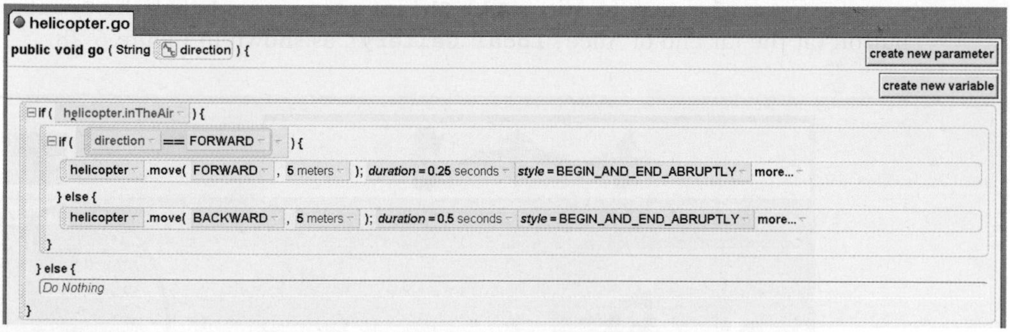

```
helicopter.go
public void go ( String direction ) {                    create new parameter
                                                          create new variable
  if ( helicopter.inTheAir ){
    if ( direction == FORWARD ){
      helicopter .move( FORWARD , 5 meters ); duration = 0.25 seconds style = BEGIN_AND_END_ABRUPTLY more...
    } else {
      helicopter .move( BACKWARD , 5 meters ); duration = 0.5 seconds style = BEGIN_AND_END_ABRUPTLY more...
    }
  } else {
    Do Nothing
  }
}
```

FIGURE 6-26 The **go()** method

To make the helicopter move forward twice as fast as it goes backward, we use a ***distance*** of **5** meters for each, but a ***duration*** of **0.25** seconds for forward and **0.5** seconds for backward. In each case, we use the **BEGIN_AND_END_ABRUPTLY style** to smooth the animation.

With a handler in place, all we have to do is associate it with the appropriate up and down arrow key events, using the same approach we have seen before, as shown in Figure 6-27.

```
While ↑ is pressed
   Begin: <None>
   During: helicopter.go( direction = FORWARD );
   End: <None>
While ↓ is pressed
   Begin: <None>
   During: helicopter.go( direction = BACKWARD );
   End: <None>
```

FIGURE 6-27 The up and down arrow events

At this point, our program is operational, provided there is someone there to explain to users what they are supposed to do. In the next section, we will see how to add instructions.

6.3 Alice Tip: Using 3D Text

In the last section, we built a working helicopter flight simulator. However, for a program with such a complex user interface (the user must use both hands and operate six keys), it is a good idea to present some operating instructions when the program begins.

To do so, we return to Alice's **Add Objects** screen, and click the **Create 3D Text** button (at the far end of Alice's **Local Gallery**), as shown in Figure 6-28.

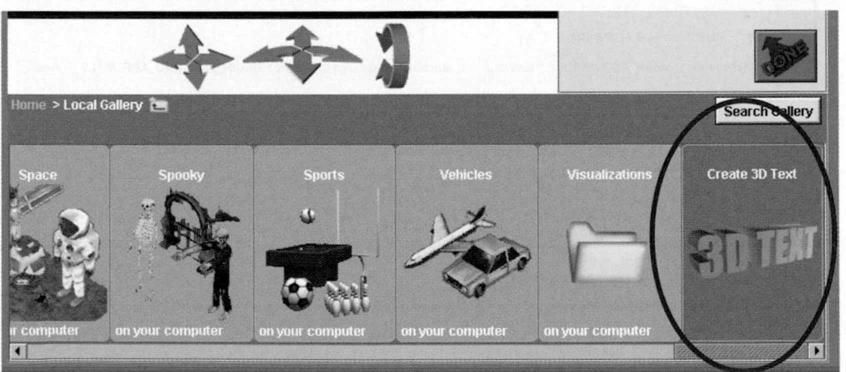

FIGURE 6-28 The create 3D text button

When this button is clicked, Alice displays the **Add 3D Text** dialog box shown in Figure 6-29.

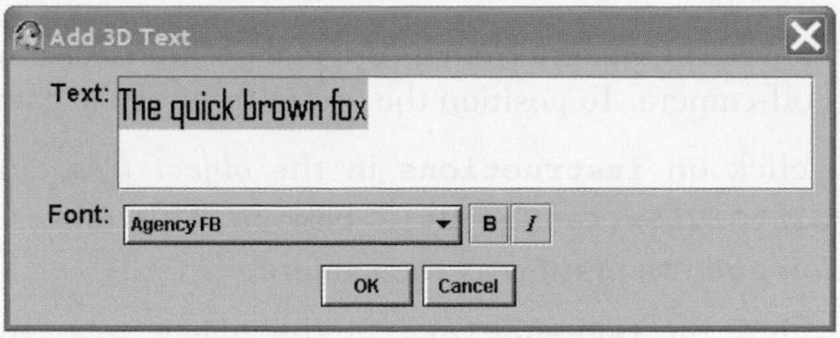

FIGURE 6-29 The **Add 3D Text** dialog box

Using this dialog box, we can replace **The quick brown fox** with any textual information we want to appear in our world, such as:

- *instructions* for the user
- an *opening title* for the story
- *closing credits* for the story

and so on. We can specify that the text be displayed in a particular font using the **Font** drop-down box, and make the text bold or italic using the **B** and ***I*** buttons.

To make the instructions for the helicopter, we can type the text shown in Figure 6-30.

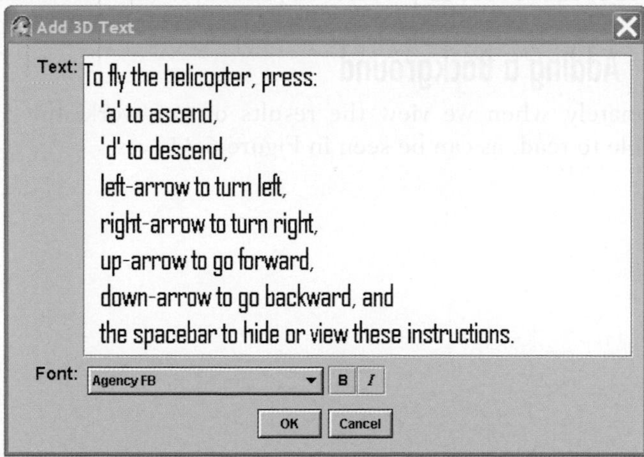

FIGURE 6-30 Instructions for the flight simultor

When we click the **OK** button, Alice inserts a three-dimensional version of these instructions into the world, and names it **To fly the helicopter**. To discuss it more conveniently, we will right-click on it and rename it **instructions**.

6.3.1 Repositioning Text that Is Off-Camera

If we have moved the camera from its original position, Alice will add new 3D text at a position that is off-camera. To position the text in front of the camera, we can use these steps:

1. Right-click on **instructions** in the *object tree*, and then choose **methods-> setPointOfView(<asSeenBy)->camera**. This moves the text to be in the same position and orientation as the camera.
2. Right-click on **instructions** in the *object tree*, and then choose **methods-> move(<direction>,<amount>)->FORWARD->10 meters**. This moves the text forward so that we can see it. However since its point of view is like that of the camera, its front is facing away from us, making it backwards to our view.
3. Right-click on **instructions** in the *object tree*, and then choose **methods-> turn(<direction>,<amount>)->LEFT->1/2 revolution**. This spins the text 180 degrees, making it readable to us.

From here, we can use the controls at the upper right of the **Add Objects** window to resize and reposition the text as necessary to make the **instructions** fit the screen.

We will make the instructions appear or disappear whenever the user presses the spacebar. One way to make this occur is to make the **instructions** *move with the camera*, so that the spacebar event handler just has to make them visible to make them appear, or invisible to make them disappear.[4] To make them move with the camera, we set the **instructions.vehicle** property to **camera** in the *details area*. At the same time, we set the **instructions.color** property to **yellow**, to (in theory) make them show up well.

6.3.2 Adding a Background

Unfortunately, when we view the results of our work, the **instructions** are nearly impossible to read, as can be seen in Figure 6-31.

4. This approach is simple because the camera moves with the helicopter which flies throughout the world. For text that should only appear once (like titles or credits), it makes more sense to build a dedicated scene for displaying the text, and then moving the camera to and from that scene when necessary.

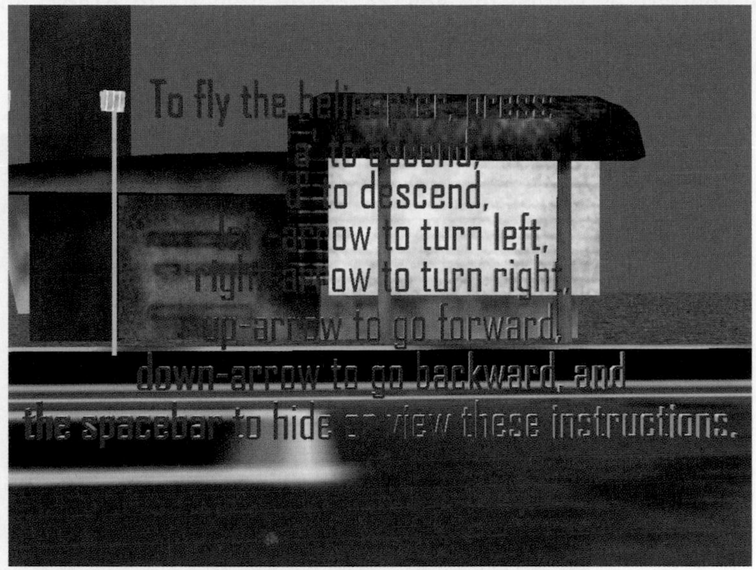

FIGURE 6-31 Instructions that are hard to read

To improve their visibility we can add a *background* behind the **`instructions`**. To make such a background, we can add an object from the **`Shapes`** folder in Alice's **`Local Gallery`**, as shown in Figure 6-32.

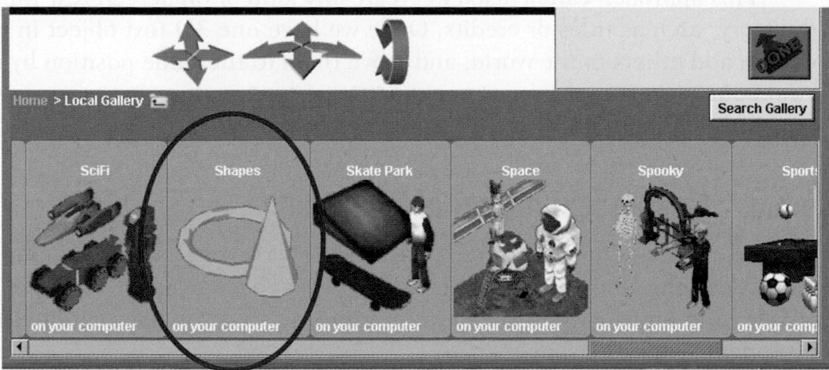

FIGURE 6-32 Alice's **`shapes`** folder

There, we find a **`Square`** class that (since our view is rectangular) we can use as a background for the **`instructions`**. If we drag and drop it into the world, we can use the controls at the upper right of the **`Add Objects`** window to resize the **`square`** to fill the screen, and reposition the **`square`** so that it is behind the **`instructions`**. (Or reposition the **instructions** to be in front of the **square**.) When we are finished, we can increase the contrast by setting the **square.color** property to **black**, and using right-click->**methods** to make the **light** turn to face these instructions.[5] The result is the easier-to-read screen shown in Figure 6-33.

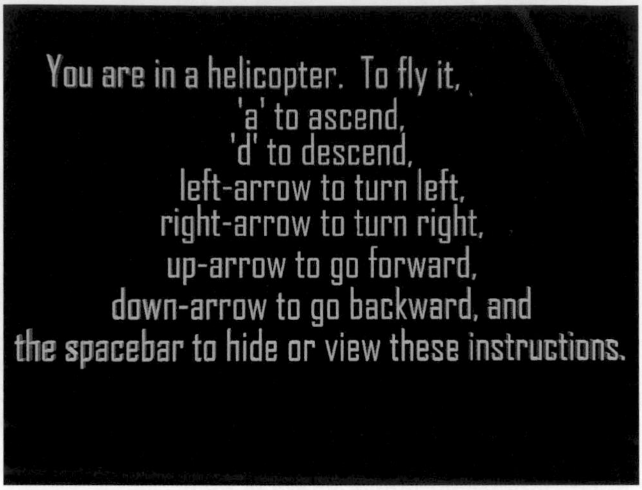

You are in a helicopter. To fly it,
'a' to ascend,
'd' to descend,
left-arrow to turn left,
right-arrow to turn right,
up-arrow to go forward,
down-arrow to go backward, and
the spacebar to hide or view these instructions.

FIGURE 6-33 Instructions that are easy to read

Since we want the background to move with the **instructions**, we set the **square.vehicle** property to be **instructions**.

This approach can be used to create any kind of on-screen text we want to appear in the story, such as titles or credits. Once we have one 3D text object in the right position, we can add others to the world, and move them to the same position by using right-click->**methods->*objectName*.setPointOfView(<asSeenBy>)** to move new text to the position and orientation of the existing 3D text.

6.3.3 Making Text Appear or Disappear

We are almost done! Our next task is to write an event handler that makes the **instructions** and **square** (the instructions' background) disappear when they are visible, and appear when they are invisible, so that the user can make them appear or disappear using the spacebar.

This is another example of the two-state behavior we saw back in Figure 6-9. However, **instructions** and **square** already have an **isShowing** property that indicates whether or not they are visible, so we need not define any new properties. Instead, we can just toggle **instructions.isShowing** and **square.isShowing** to elicit the desired behavior, as shown in the **toggleInstructionVisibility()** method in Figure 6-34.

5. If we leave the light as it is, some portions of the 3D text may be darker than others, if the text is in the shadows. By making the light face the instructions, we illuminate the text uniformly, eliminating such shadows.

```
world.toggleInstructionVisibility
public void toggleInstructionVisibility ( ) {                create new parameter
                                                             create new variable
  doTogether {
    square .set( isShowing , ! square propertyName = isShowing ); duration = 0 seconds more...
    instructions .set( isShowing , ! instructions propertyName = isShowing ); duration = 0 seconds more
  }
```

FIGURE 6-34 Toggling the visibility of **`instructions`** and **`square`**

When this method is performed, it uses the **`!`** (NOT) operator to invert the **`square`** and **`instruction`** objects' **`isShowing`** properties. That is, if **`isShowing`** were **`true`** for each object *before* the method was performed, **`isShowing`** is **`false`** for each of them *after* the method finishes. Conversely, if **`isShowing`** was **`false`** for each of them *before* the method runs, **`isShowing`** is **`true`** for each *after* the method finishes.

To finish the program, we must make this method the handler for spacebar events. To do so, we can use the **`When a key is typed`** event shown in Figure 6-16, replace **`any`** with **`Space`**, and then drag the **`world.toggleInstructionVisibility()`** method onto **`Nothing`** to make it the event's handler. The result is the event shown in Figure 6-35.

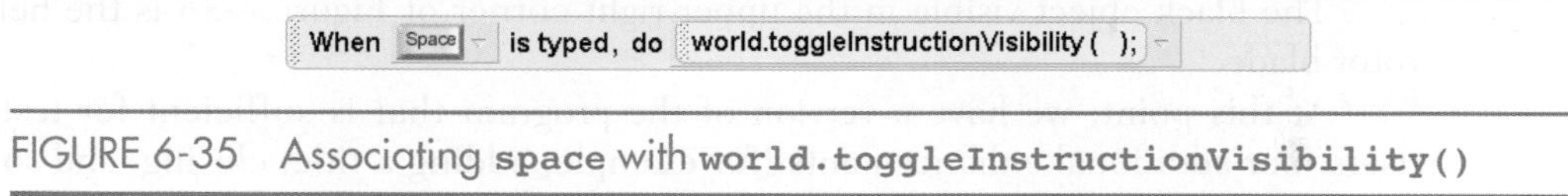
When Space is typed, do world.toggleInstructionVisibility( );

FIGURE 6-35 Associating **`space`** with **`world.toggleInstructionVisibility()`**

Now, when the program begins running, the **`instructions`** appear as shown in Figure 6-33. When the user is ready and presses the spacebar, the instructions and background disappear, revealing the scene behind them. The scene that appears depends on the position and orientation of the **`camera`**. Figure 6-36 shows the scene.

FIGURE 6-36 After the user presses the spacebar

The black object visible in the upper-right corner of Figure 6-36 is the helicopter's rotor blade.

At this point, we have a version of the program that is sufficient for testing with users. For additional enhancements (for example, adding a title, closing, and so on), see the Programming Problems at the end of the chapter.

If 3D text objects or backgrounds are to be fixed in place in front of the camera, they should be the **last** objects you add to a world or scene. The reason is that they will usually lie between the camera and any objects you subsequently place in the world; if you try to click on these latter objects, the 3D text or background will intercept your click.

6.4 Alice Tip: Scene Transitional Effects for the Camera

In Section 2.4, we saw how to use **`Dummies`** to mark camera positions, and how to use the **`setPointOfView()`** message to change the position of the **`camera`** to that of a dummy. This approach provides a convenient way to shift the camera from its position at the end of a given scene to a new position at the beginning of the next scene.

Instead of instantaneously jumping from the end of one scene to the beginning of the next scene (a transition called a *cut*), filmmakers often use special camera effects like *fades* or *wipes* to smooth the transition between scenes. Such **transition effects** can make the transition between scenes seem less abrupt and jarring to the viewer, or be used to convey a sense of time elapsing between the scenes.

Alice does not provide any built-in transitional effects. However, it does provide us with raw building blocks that we can use to create our own. With a little time and effort, we can build credible transitional effects. In this section, we will see how to do so.

6.4.1 Setup for Special Effects

Before we see how to create the effects themselves, we need to do a bit of setup work. The basic idea is to add four black shutters or "flaps" outside of the camera's viewport, that we can manipulate to create the effects. These shutters should be positioned at the top-left-right-bottom positions outside of the camera's viewing area, as shown in Figure 6-37.

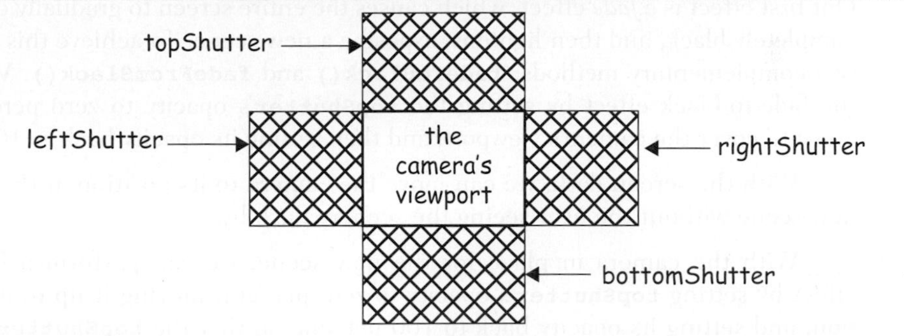

FIGURE 6-37 Surrounding the camera with four shutters

To create such shutters in Alice, we add four **square** objects to a world; change the **color** property of each **square** to **black**; change the **vehicle** property of each **square** to the **camera**; rename them **topShutter**, **leftShutter**, **rightShutter**, and **bottomShutter**; and position them as shown in Figure 6-38.

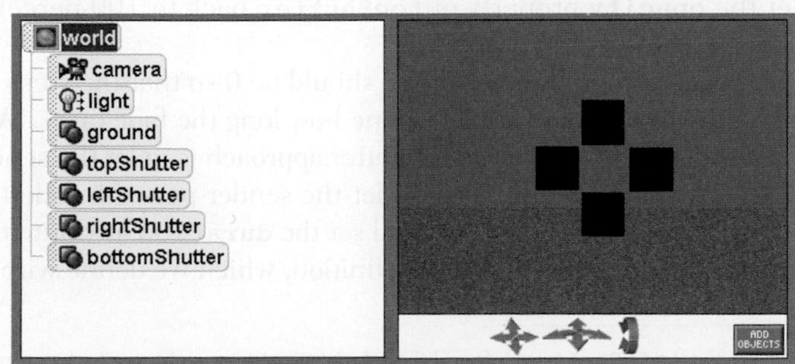

FIGURE 6-38 Using four squares for shutters

Moving each square to a position outside of the camera's viewing area is tricky, because we cannot easily drag them to the right position. Instead, we can position a square at the center of the screen, and then drag it towards the camera until it completely fills the viewing area. We can then use right-click->**methods->*objectName*. move(<direction>,<amount>)** with the appropriate arguments to move the square just outside the viewing area, using trial-and-error to find the right distance. (For us, this distance was about 0.08 meters.[6])

With shutters in place, we can perform a variety of special effects by writing methods that move the shutters. We perform such effects using *complementary pairs* of methods, in which one method "undoes" the actions of the other.

6.4.2 The Fade Effect

Our first effect is a *fade* effect, which causes the entire screen to gradually darken until it is completely black, and then lightens, exposing a new scene. To achieve this effect, we write two complementary methods: **fadeToBlack()** and **fadeFromBlack()**. We can perform the fade-to-black effect by setting the **topShutter**'s opacity to zero percent, moving it down to cover the camera's viewport, and then setting its opacity back to 100 percent.

With the screen dark, we can move the camera to its position at the beginning of a new scene without the user seeing the scenery flash by.

With the camera in place for the new scene, we can perform a fade-from-black effect by setting **topShutter**'s opacity to zero percent, moving it up to its original position, and setting its opacity back to 100 percent, so that the **topShutter** is exactly as it was at the beginning of the fade-to-black effect.

Fade to Black

Using the **topShutter**, we can achieve the fade-to-black effect as follows:

1. Set the **opacity** property of **topShutter** to 0 percent, so that it is invisible.
2. Move **topShutter** down so that it is in front of the camera's viewing area.
3. Set the **opacity** property of **topShutter** back to 100 percent, making it visible.

For Steps 1 and 2, the **duration** should be 0 so that the steps happen instantaneously. For Step 3, the **duration** will determine how long the fade takes. While we could make this duration last a fixed length of time, a better approach is to let the sender of this message specify how long the fade should take. To let the sender pass this fade time as an argument, we must define a parameter to store it, and set the **duration** attribute of Step 3 to that parameter. Figure 6-39 shows the resulting definition, which we define within **camera**.

6. To move the **leftShutter** left and the **rightShutter** right, we had to turn each 180 degrees, as the way they were facing caused the LEFT and RIGHT directions to move them the opposite way.

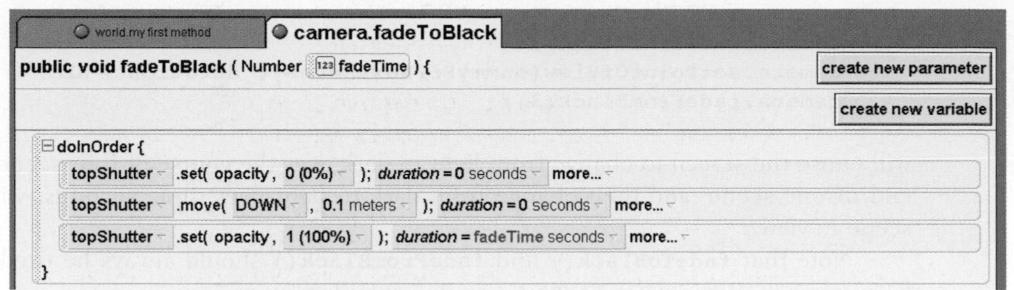

FIGURE 6-39 The **fadeToBlack()** method

With this method, the message **camera.fadeToBlack(5);** will cause the screen to darken over the course of five seconds. You may have to adjust the distance you move **topShutter**, depending on its placement and size with respect to the camera.

Fade From Black

The fade-from-black method has to "undo" everything the fade-to-black method did, in the reverse order, so as to leave the **topShutter** in its original position:

1. Set the **opacity** property of **topShutter** to 0 percent.
2. Move **topShutter** up so that it is out of the camera's viewing area.
3. Set the **opacity** property of **topShutter** to 100 percent.

As before, we should allow the sender to specify the effect's *time*. In this method, it controls the **duration** of Step 1, while Steps 2 and 3 occur instantaneously, as shown in Figure 6-40.

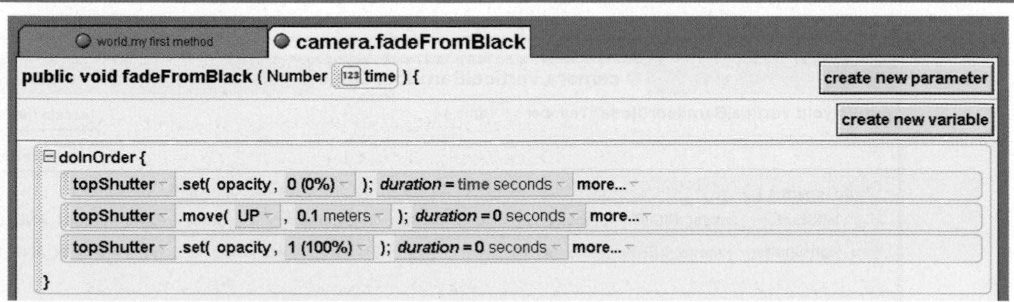

FIGURE 6-40 The **fadeFromBlack()** method

With these two methods, the messages:

```
camera.fadeToBlack(4);
camera.setPointOfView(dummyForNextScene); duration = 0
camera.fadeFromBlack(3);
```

will cause the screen to change from light to dark over the course of four seconds at the end of one scene, and then change from dark to light over three seconds, with a new scene in view.

Note that **fadeToBlack()** and **fadeFromBlack()** should always be used in pairs, because each manipulates **topShutter** in a complementary way.

6.4.3 The Barndoor Edge Wipe Effect

Edge wipe effects are transitions in which one or more edges move across the screen to hide the end of one scene and expose the beginning of the next scene. One kind of edge wipe transition is the *barndoor wipe*, in which the shutters move like the doors of a barn, sliding closed at the end of a scene and then opening on a new scene. Two common barndoor edge wipes are:

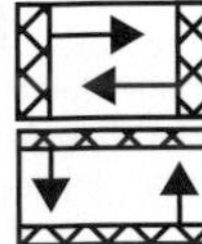

- *vertical*, in which the "doors" close and open from the sides of the screen.
- *horizontal*, in which the "doors" close and open from the top and bottom of the screen.

In this section, we will show how to use the shutters to achieve the vertical effect. The horizontal effect is similar and is left for the exercises.

Vertical Barndoor Effects

We can perform a *vertical barndoor close* effect by simultaneously moving the left and right shutters towards one another. As before, the best approach is to let the sender of the message pass the effect's *time* as an argument, and then use that argument's parameter as the **duration** value for each shutter's movement. We define this method within **camera**, using the definition shown in Figure 6-41.

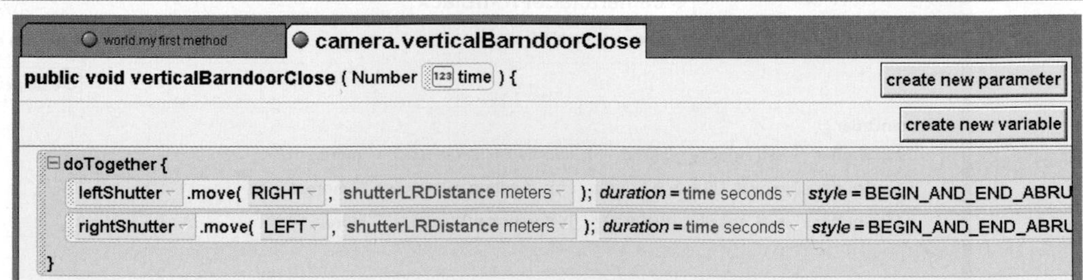

FIGURE 6-41 The **verticalBarndoorClose()** method

To simplify changing the distance the left and right shutters must move, we defined a **camera** property named **shutterLRDistance**, which we then used to control the shutter movements.

The complementary effect — the *vertical barndoor open* effect — can be achieved by simultaneously moving the left and right shutters apart, as shown in Figure 6-42.

```
world.my first method | camera.verticalBarndoorOpen
public void verticalBarndoorOpen ( Number 123 time ) {      create new parameter
                                                            create new variable
  doTogether {
    leftShutter .move( LEFT , shutterLRDistance meters ); duration = time seconds style = BEGIN_AND_END_ABRUP
    rightShutter .move( RIGHT , shutterLRDistance meters ); duration = time seconds style = BEGIN_AND_END_ABR
  }
```

FIGURE 6-42 The `verticalBarndoorOpen()` method

Using these two methods, a programmer can send messages like this:

```
camera.verticalBarndoorClose(4);
camera.setPointOfView(dummyForNextScene); duration = 0
camera.verticalBarndoorOpen(3);
```

to "close the door" over the course of four seconds, shift the camera to the next scene, and then "open the door" over three seconds. Because they act as complementary operations, these methods should be used in pairs, or the shutters will not be in place for subsquent transitions.

The *horizontal barndoor edge wipe* is similar, but involves moving the top and bottom shutters instead of the left and right shutters. Building this effect is left as an exercise.

6.4.4 The Box Iris Wipe Effect

Our last effect is a different wipe effect called an *iris wipe*, in which the screen is darkened except for an area called the *iris* that shrinks (the iris is closing) at the end of a scene, and expands (the iris is opening) to expose a new scene. This effect is usually used to center the viewer's attention on something in the scene, which is encircled by the iris as it closes.

We can define a "box iris close" effect using the shutters, by simultaneously moving all four shutters towards the center of the camera's viewport. As in the preceding effect methods, we let the sender of the message specify the *time* the effect should take. For added flexibility, we also let the sender specify what *percentage* the iris should close, as shown in Figure 6-43.

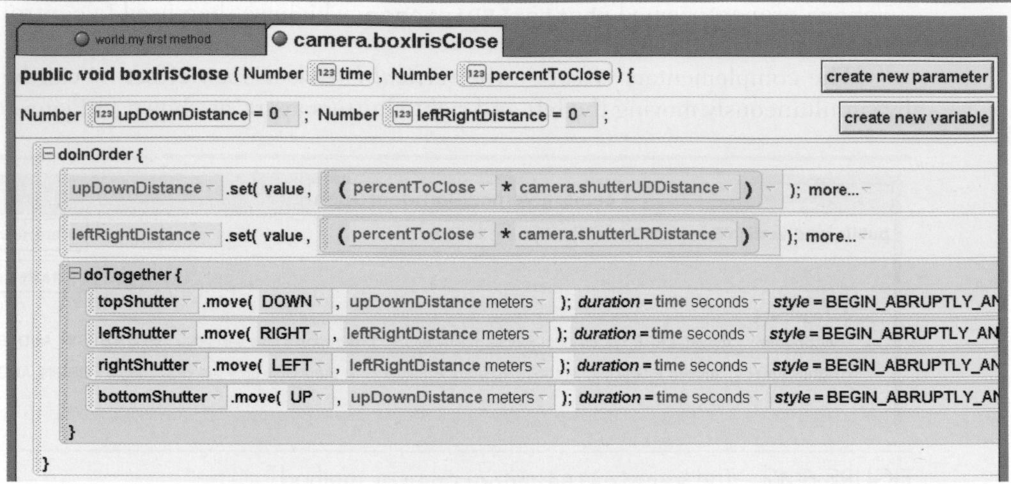

FIGURE 6-43 The `boxIrisClose()` method

We first compute how far to close each shutter, by multiplying the parameter **`percentToClose`** by each shutter's close distance. We then simultaneously move each shutter that distance using the value of parameter **`time`** as the ***`duration`***. As shown in Figure 6-44, when this method runs, the shutters outline a shrinking box that contains roughly **`percentToClose`** of the screen area.

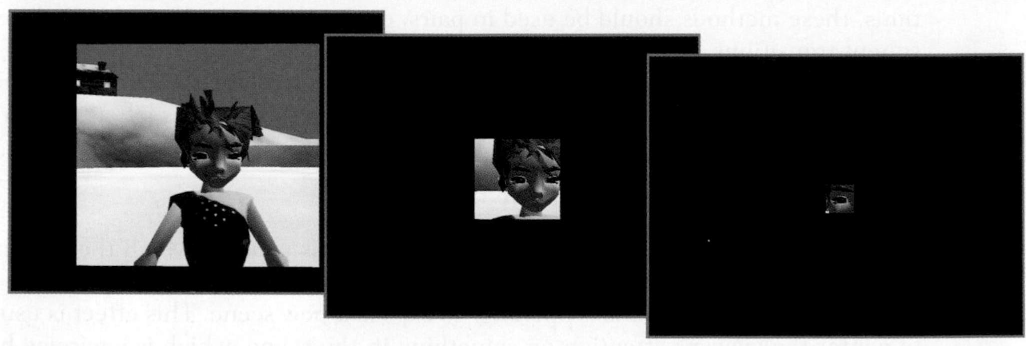

FIGURE 6-44 The box iris effect (closing)

The complementary **`boxIrisOpen()`** method is similar, as shown in Figure 6-45.

```
world.my first method    camera.boxIrisOpen
public void boxIrisOpen ( Number 123 time , Number 123 percentToOpen ) {            create new parameter
Number 123 upDownDistance = 0 ; Number 123 leftRightDistance = 0 ;                  create new variable
  doInOrder {
    upDownDistance .set( value, ( percentToOpen * camera.shutterUDDistance ) ); more...
    leftRightDistance .set( value, ( percentToOpen * camera.shutterLRDistance ) ); more...
    doTogether {
      topShutter .move( UP , upDownDistance meters ); duration = time seconds style = BEGIN_ABRUPTLY_AND_END_GENTLY more...
      leftShutter .move( LEFT , leftRightDistance meters ); duration = time seconds style = BEGIN_ABRUPTLY_AND_END_GENTLY more...
      rightShutter .move( RIGHT , leftRightDistance meters ); duration = time seconds style = BEGIN_ABRUPTLY_AND_END_GENTLY more...
      bottomShutter .move( DOWN , upDownDistance meters ); duration = time seconds style = BEGIN_ABRUPTLY_AND_END_GENTLY more...
    }
}
```

FIGURE 6-45 The **boxIrisOpen()** method

With these methods, we can now create interesting transitions:

```
camera.boxIrisClose(3, 0.75);
// do something interesting inside the iris
camera.boxIrisClose(2, 0.25);
// move camera to the next scene
camera.boxIrisOpen(5, 100);
```

6.4.5 Reusing Transition Effects

If you search on the Internet for terms like *transition*, *effect*, *fade*, and *wipe*, you can find many other transition effects that can be defined using techniques like those we presented in this section. (To define them, you may need to add more shapes to the camera.) We hope that this section has provided you with an introduction into how such effects can be created. However, once we have defined a nice group of transition effects, how do we reuse them in different programs?

Unfortunately, the **save object as...** technique presented in Section 2.3 will not save properties that are objects, so with the **camera**'s shutters being **Square**s, we cannot rename, save, and import the modified **camera** into a different world and have its shutters come with it, even if we were to make the four shutters properties of the **camera**.[7]

Instead, we define all of these transitions in a "template world" we call **TransitionEffects** that contains nothing but the **camera**, the **light**, the **ground**, and the **square**s we use for the transitions. For any story in which we want transitions, we open this **TransitionEffects** world as the starting world for the story, and then use **File->Save world as...** to save it using a name appropriate for that story. Of course, this means that we must plan ahead and know in advance that we will be using transitions in the story. This is one more reason to spend time carefully designing your program before you start programming.

7. This was true when this book was written. It may not be true by the time you read this. Check and see!

6.5 Chapter Summary

- ❑ We can create new events in Alice, including both mouse and keyboard events.
- ❑ We can write methods that act as event handlers.
- ❑ We can associate event handlers with specific events.
- ❑ We can use 3D text to add titles, instructions, and credits to a world.
- ❑ We can use the Alice **`square`** shape as a background for 3D text, and to create "special effects" for transitions between scenes. Alice shapes can be used as "building blocks" to build other structures in Alice.

6.5.1 Key Terms

event	logic error
event-driven program	mouse event
event handler	program event
event source	transition effect
handling an event	two-state behavior
interactive program	usability
keyboard event	user event

Programming Projects

6.1 Choose one of the robots from the Alice Gallery, and provide events and handlers so that the user can control the robot using the keyboard. For example, use the arrow keys to make the robot go forward, backward, left, or right; use other keys to control the robot's arms (or other appendages). Build a world in which the user must navigate the robot through obstacles.

6.2 Using the **`dragon.flapWings();`** method we wrote in Section 2.2.1, build a short story in which a dragon flies from place to place in search of adventure, landing periodically to eat, talk, and anything else required by your story. Make **`dragon.flapWings()`** the handler of a **`While something is true`** event, so that the dragon automatically flaps its wings whenever it is above the ground.

6.3 Build a world containing a puzzle the user must solve. Place characters in the world who can provide hints to the puzzle's solution when the user clicks on them. Let the user navigate through the world using the arrow keys.

6.4 Add the following enhancements to the helicopter flight simulator program we built in Sections 6.2 and 6.3 (in increasing order of difficulty):

a. Add a "title" screen that names the program, and describes the problem to be solved.

b. Add a "congratulations" screen that appears when the user finds and clicks on the cat.

c. Modify the program so that when the helicopter descends over the roof of any of the buildings, it lands on the roof instead of passing right through it.

d. Modify the program so that if the helicopter collides with anything in the world as it moves forward, backward, left, or right, the helicopter "crashes" and the world displays a "better luck next time" screen.

6.5 Build methods to perform the following transition effects:

a. Build a method **fadeTo(*someColor*, *fadeTime*);** that lets the sender specify the color to which the screen should fade, and **fadeFrom(*fadeTime*)** that complements **fadeTo()**. Then revise the **fadeToBlack()** and **fadeFromBlack()** methods so that they use **fadeTo()** and **fadeFrom()**.

b. Build a method **barWipeCover(*direction*, *time*);** that, at the end of a scene, moves a single shutter from one of the edges to cover the screen; and a method **barWipeUncover(*direction*, *time*);** that complements **barWipeCover()**. The direction argument should be either **LEFT**, **RIGHT**, **UP**, or **DOWN**.

c. In a *diagonal wipe*, a shutter crosses the screen from one corner to the opposite corner. Write complementary methods that perform the two parts of a diagonal wipe.

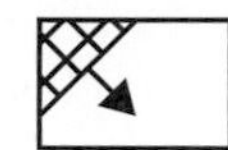

d. A *bowtie wipe* is like a barndoor wipe, but the shutters coming from the sides are wedges that form a bow-tie when they first touch one another. Write complementary methods that perform the two parts of a bowtie wipe.

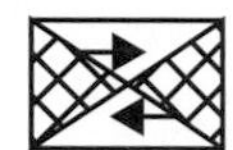

e. A *rotating octagonal iris wipe* is an iris wipe in which the iris is a rotating octagon rather than a rectangle. Write complementary methods that perform the two parts of a rotating octagonal iris wipe.

6.6 Choose a popular game like chess, checkers, mancala, master mind, etc. Create a board and pieces for the game. Add event handlers that allow the user to move the pieces interactively.

6.7 Using the **Carrier** and **FighterPlane** classes from Alice's Web Gallery, create a carrier-jet simulation, in which the user must fly the **fighterPlane**, taking off from and landing on the **carrier**.

6.8 Using the **WhackAMoleBooth** class from the Alice Gallery **Amusement Park** folder, program a whack-a-mole game in which the **mole** pops its head out of a random hole in the booth for a short, random length of time before ducking down again, and the user tries to bop the mole with the **bopper**. Play a sound each time the user successfully bops the mole.

6.9 Proceed as in Problem 6.8, but make your program a continuously running series of games. Limit each game to some fixed length of time (for example, 60 seconds). Have the user enter his or her name at the beginning of a game. Your program should keep track of how many times the user bops the mole during the game, and when the time expires, display (a) that number as the user's score for this game, and (b) the top five scores since the program began running. Play a special sound if the user beats the highest score (becoming the new top score).

6.10 Design and build your own original, interactive computer game.

Chapter 7
From Alice to Java

It [computer programming] is the only job where I get to be both an engineer and an artist. There's an incredible, rigorous, technical element to it, which I like because you have to do very precise thinking. On the other hand, it has a wildly creative side where the boundaries of imagination are the only real limitation.

ANDY HERTZFELD

Be not afraid of going slowly. Be afraid of standing still.

CHINESE PROVERB

Toto, I've got a feeling we're not in Kansas anymore.

DOROTHY GALE (JUDY GARLAND), IN *THE WIZARD OF OZ*

Objectives

Upon completion of this chapter, you will be able to:

❑ Write some first Java programs

❑ Learn the basics of the Eclipse Integrated Development Environment (IDE)

❑ Begin making the transition from Alice to Java

By way of review, computer programming consists of four steps:

1. *Designing* the program
2. *Writing* the program
3. *Running* the program
4. *Testing* the program

For example, to design an Alice program, we write out the user story and draw storyboards. To write an Alice program, we launch Alice, drag objects into the *world window*, and then animate those objects by selecting them in the *object tree* and dragging statements into the *editing area*. To run an Alice program, we click Alice's **`Play`** button and observe the objects' behaviors in the *world window*. To test an Alice program, we verify that the objects are behaving as expected when we run it. If they are not, we fix the program by modifying the statements in the *editing area*. Note that we do not use Alice for Step 1; we only use Alice for Steps 2–4.

Alice is a wonderful way to learn the basic concepts of programming, because its 3D graphics make it easy to visualize many of those concepts. That is, when we use a loop to make a dragon's wings flap several times, we can see the wings flapping as the program flow moves through the loop. Alice's drag-and-drop programming environment also makes it difficult to make typing mistakes when writing a program. This is a *wonderful* feature of Alice.

While Alice is great, other programming languages have benefits of their own. For example, the Java programming language allows us to build new classes that we can then use to create new kinds of objects. Also, a program written in Java will run on any computer on which Java has been installed. In fact, much of Alice is written in Java! Java also lets you create an *applet* — a special kind of Java program that can be downloaded from a remote Web site as part of a Web page, making the page interactive.

In this chapter, we begin our study of programming in Java. Accordingly, this chapter examines designing, writing, running, and testing Java programs. Let's get started!

7.1 Designing a First Java Program

Designing a Java program is similar to designing an Alice program. We begin by writing out the user story — a textual description of what our program should do. To illustrate, suppose we frequently travel between Europe and the United States, and often find ourselves having to convert dollars into euros. Suppose further that we have a handheld computer with us. Then we can design a program for our computer that will do such conversions for us!

We might begin by writing the following user story:

> Our program should ask the user the question, "How many dollars do you want to convert to euros?" Our program should read this dollar amount from the user. The program should then ask the question, "What is the euros-per-dollar exchange rate?" Our program should then read the euros-per-dollar exchange rate from the user. Our program should then compute the corresponding number of euros. Finally, it should display the dollar and (computed) euro values.

7.1.1 The Object List

The next step is to make a list of the noun phrases in our story, omitting the user (who is not a part of our program). These noun phrases will indicate the objects in the program, so we should also indicate the type of value each object stores, and what name it will have in the program. Using the story above, we get the following list.

Noun Phrase	Type of Value	Name
our program	?	*DollarsToEurosConverter*
question	string of characters	none
dollar amount	number (real)	*dollars*
exchange rate	number (real)	*eurosPerDollar*
number of euros	number (real)	*euros*

Names like *DollarsToEurosConverter* and *eurosPerDollar* may seem long-winded, but the more descriptive our names are, the more readable the program will be, which is very important.

> When naming objects, always choose names that are nouns or noun phrases.

The questions we ask a user will appear on the screen as a sequence or **string** of characters. The dollar amount, exchange rate, and number of euros are numbers with a decimal point, which are known as **real numbers**. However, it is not clear how we should describe the type of the program, since it doesn't have a value like the other noun phrases do.

> When a noun phrase cannot be represented using one of the existing types (string, number, and so on), create a *class* to represent such objects.

We must thus create a class to represent our program. As we saw in Alice, classes are the patterns or blueprints from which objects are made, so Java will use the class we create as a pattern for solving dollar-to-euro conversion problems.

In giving names to the items in our program, we will follow this convention:

> *Naming Convention:*
>
> **When naming a class, capitalize each word in the name.**
>
> **When naming a variable or method, capitalize each word except the first.**

7.1.2 The Operations List

The next design step is to list the verb phrases in our story, again ignoring actions taken by the user who is external to the program. These verb phrases correspond to the operations the program must perform. To the right of each verb phrase, we write the corresponding Java operation or message, if we know it. (Learning these messages is a big part of learning to program in Java.) Using the story above, we get the following list:

Verb Phrase
ask the user
read this dollar amount
read ... exchange rate
compute ... euros
display

As it happens, Java makes it fairly easy to perform each of these operations. The only one that is slightly complicated is computing the corresponding number of **euros**. Since *eurosPerDollar* contains the euros-per-dollar exchange rate, we can compute *euros* as follows.

> *euros = dollars * eurosPerDollar;*

7.1.3 The Algorithm

The final design step is to organize the objects and operations into a sequence of steps that, when performed, will solve our problem. As we have seen before, this sequence of steps is called an algorithm. For the problem of converting dollars to euros, we can write the algorithm shown in Figure 7-1.

Algorithm: DollarsToEurosConverter.

```
Display "How many dollars do you want to convert?"
Read dollars.
Display "What is the euros-per-dollar exchange rate?"
Read eurosPerDollar.
Compute euros = dollars * eurosPerDollar.
Display dollars and euros, plus descriptive labels.
```

FIGURE 7-1 Dollars to euros conversion algorithm

Once we have an algorithm, the design is finished, and we can begin writing the program.

7.2 Writing a First Java Program

In programming terminology, Alice's *world window*, *object tree*, *editing area*, **Play** button, and so on are together called an **integrated development environment**, or **IDE**. Most computer programmers today use an IDE to write their programs, because the IDE lets you write, run, and debug a program, all within the same environment.

For example, the programs in this and subsequent chapters were written using Eclipse, a free IDE for Java (and other languages) developed by IBM. In the remainder of this section, we will introduce the use of Eclipse. Feel free to download[1] and install[2] it on your computer before continuing. (If you are already familiar with a different Java IDE, or your instructor wishes for you to use a tool other than Eclipse,[3] use it instead.)

---

1. Eclipse can be downloaded from **www.eclipse.org/downloads/**. Note that, depending on the version of Eclipse available at the time you download it, your screens may differ from those shown in this book. This is okay, as the basic functionality will be the same. See your instructor or technical support person if you have any questions.
2. To install Eclipse, unzip the downloaded file, drag the unzipped folder to a convenient location (for example, **C:\eclipse**), and then create a shortcut to the Eclipse program (**C:\eclipse\eclipse.exe** in this example) on your desktop or the QuickLaunch bar.
3. An IDE is a convenient way to write Java programs, but it is not the only way. You can write a Java program using a text editor like TextEdit or a word processor like Microsoft Word. You can compile a Java program from the command line by typing **javac** followed by the name of the file containing your program (for example, **javac DollarsToEurosConverter.java**). You can run a Java program from the command line by typing **java** followed by the name of the class containing the program's **main()** method (for example, **java DollarsToEurosConverter**). You can debug a Java program from the command line by typing **jdb** followed by the name of the class containing the program's **main()** method (for example, **jdb DollarsToEurosConverter**). The advantage of an IDE is that it lets you do all of these from within the same convenient application.

7.2.1 Starting Eclipse

To launch Eclipse, double-click either **eclipse.exe** or the **eclipse** shortcut you created during the installation. An Eclipse splash screen should appear.[4]

When you launch Eclipse, a dialog box will appear, asking you what folder you wish to use as your workspace. You can either create a special folder to hold your Java programs, or you can just click **Ok** and Eclipse will create a folder named **workspace** for you.

The first time you run Eclipse, the next thing that appears is a special welcome screen, which offers you an overview of Eclipse, tutorials for using Eclipse, some code samples, and a summary of what's new in the current edition. (This screen is something like the tutorials that appear the first time you run Alice.) If you want to browse through some of these, feel free. When you are done, click the Close button on the **Welcome** tab near the top of the screen, and the Eclipse IDE will appear, as shown in Figure 7-2.

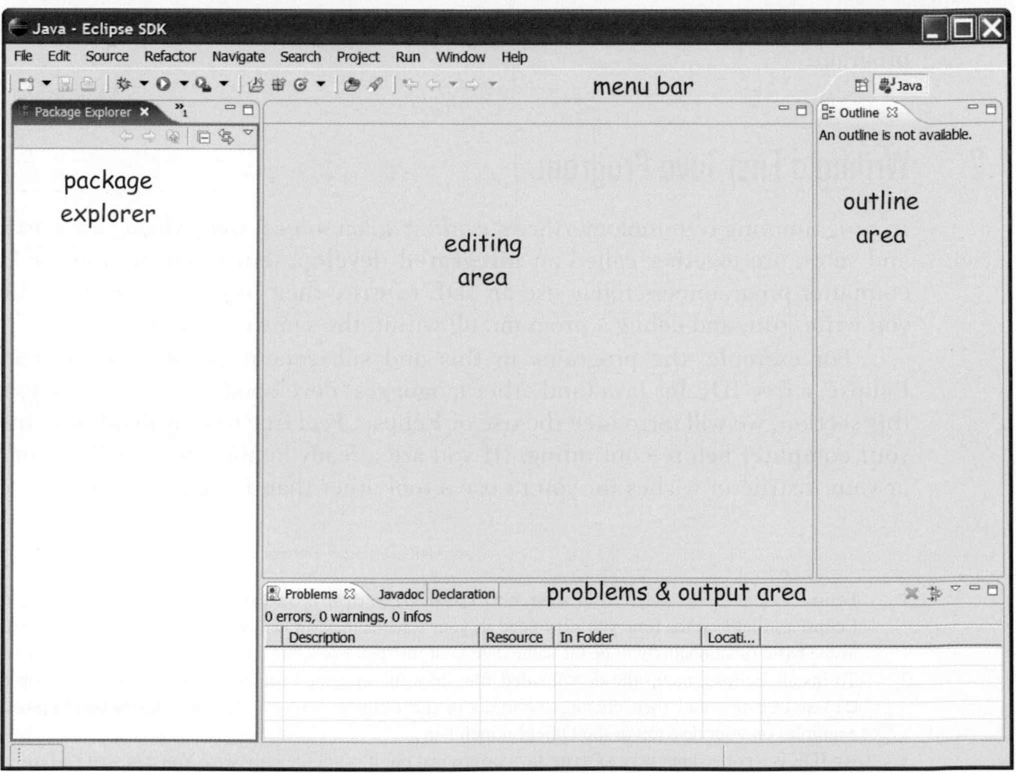

FIGURE 7-2 The initial Eclipse IDE

4. If Eclipse does not launch, make sure you have a Java RunTime Environment (JRE) installed on your system. The latest JRE is available at **http://java.sun.com/j2se/downloads/index.html**.

Like Alice, the Eclipse IDE is divided into several regions. The ones we will use the most are the *menu bar*, the *package explorer*, and the *editing area*, which are labeled in Figure 7-2, along with the *outline area* and *problems & output area*.

7.2.2 Writing a Java Program Using Eclipse

The first step to writing a Java program in Eclipse is to create a **project** — a special folder in which Eclipse will store the program. To create a project, select **`File->New->Project`** from the *menu bar*, as shown in Figure 7-3.

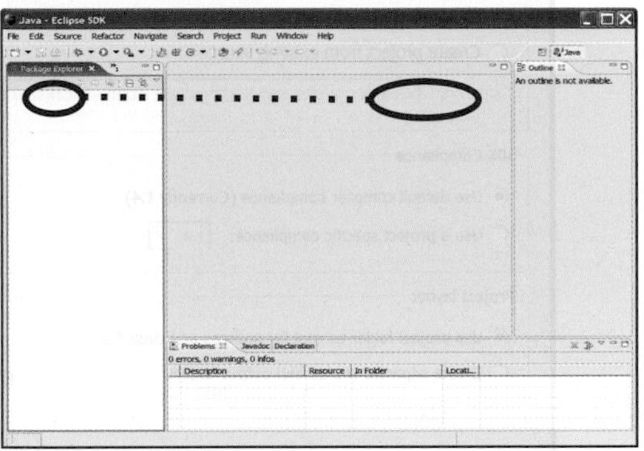

FIGURE 7-3 Creating a new project in Eclipse

Eclipse will respond by opening the **`New Project`** dialog box. Make certain that **`Java Project`** is selected and click the **`Next`** button, as shown in Figure 7-4.

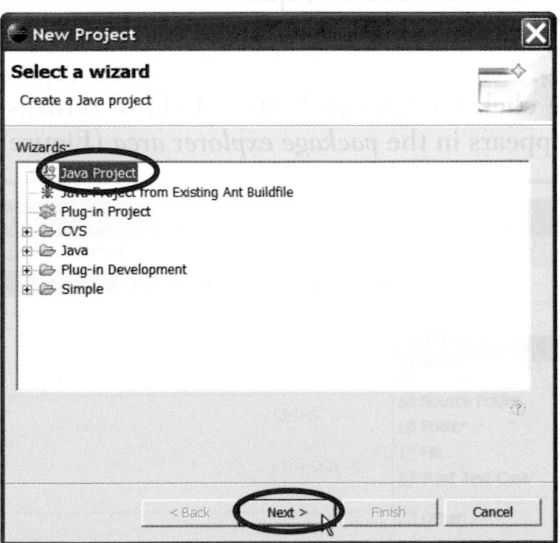

FIGURE 7-4 The New Project — Select a wizard dialog box

Eclipse responds with a dialog box in which we can enter the name of the program. To do so, we type **DollarsToEurosConverter** in the **Name** textbox, as shown in Figure 7-8.

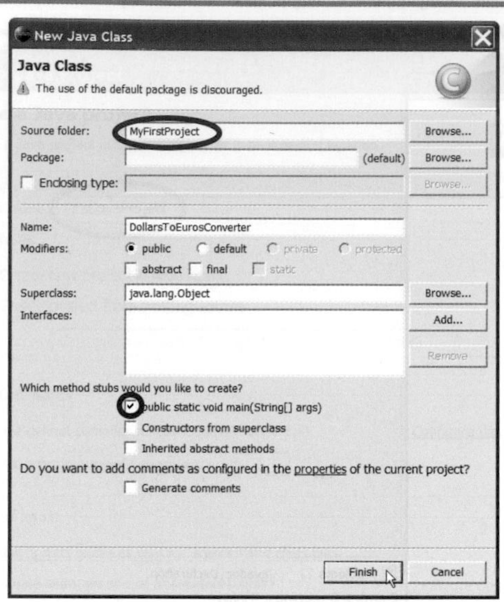

FIGURE 7-8 The New Java Class dialog box

After making certain that the checkbox for **public static void main()** is checked (and none of the others), we can click the **Finish** button. Eclipse then creates a new file named **DollarsToEurosConverter.java**, and opens it in the *editing area*, as shown in Figure 7-9.

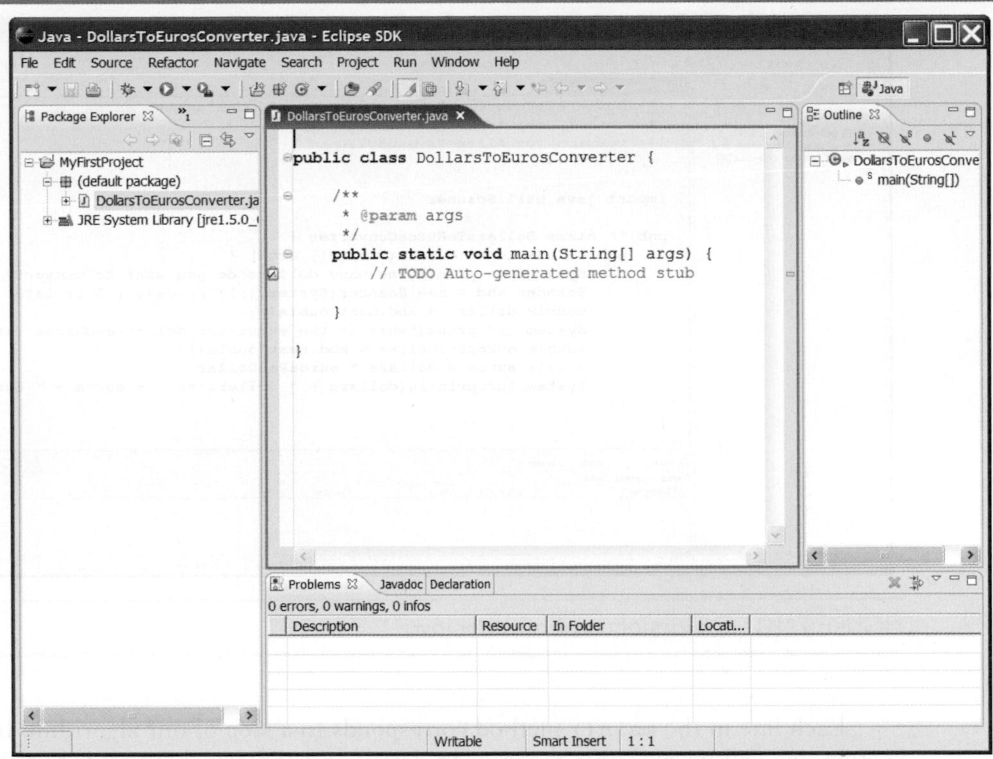

FIGURE 7-9 Ready to edit in Eclipse

Eclipse creates a class with the name of our program, containing a method named **`main()`**. To enter the program, we must modify what Eclipse has generated, removing or replacing comments with Java statements, until the *editing area* is as shown in Figure 7-10.[5] (Do this now.)

5. We will not use Eclipse's *outline area*, so we have closed it in Figure 7-10, to have more room in the *editing area*.

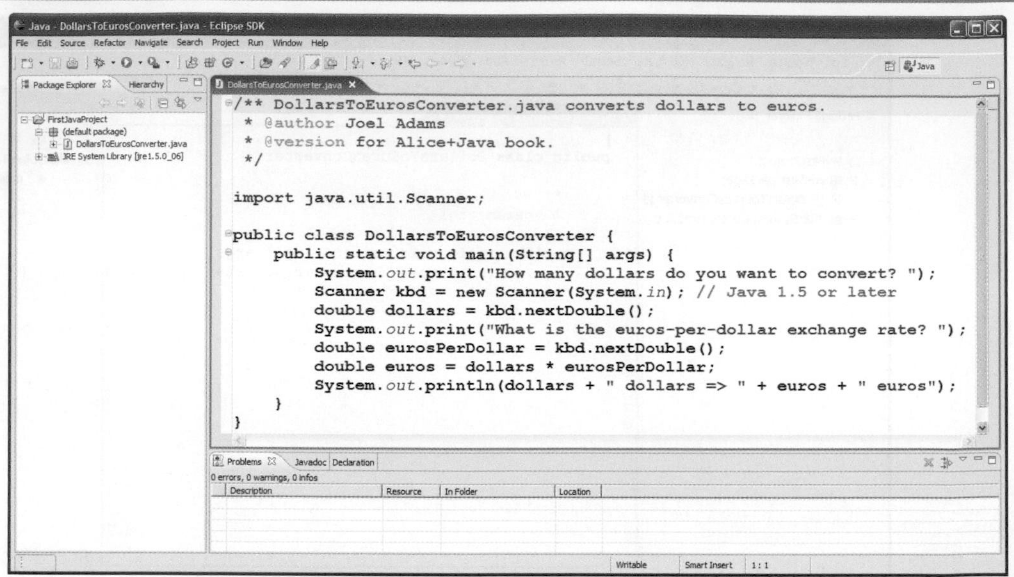

FIGURE 7-10 DollarsToEurosConverter.java

Each line in the **main()** method corresponds to a step of our algorithm. In the next section, we will go over this program in detail, and indicate how each line works. But before we do that, let us see how to compile the program in Eclipse.

7.2.3 Compiling a Java Program Using Eclipse

Once we have typed a Java program in Eclipse's *editing area*, our next step is to **compile** our program, which means have Java check it for syntax errors. To do so, we use a program called the Java **compiler**. Eclipse comes with its own built-in Java compiler; to use it, we just save our program (using **File->Save** or **Ctrl-s**) and Eclipse will automatically invoke its compiler to check what we have written. If the compiler finds any errors, Eclipse will display an error symbol in the *editing area* next to the statement where it discovered the error. Eclipse also creates a list of all the errors. To see it, click the **Problems** tab (if necessary) in the *problems & output area* directly beneath the *editing area*.

To illustrate, if we omit the semicolon at the end of the last statement in the **main()** method and then save our program, Eclipse will mark that line as an error, and describe the problem on the **Problems** tab, as shown in Figure 7-11.

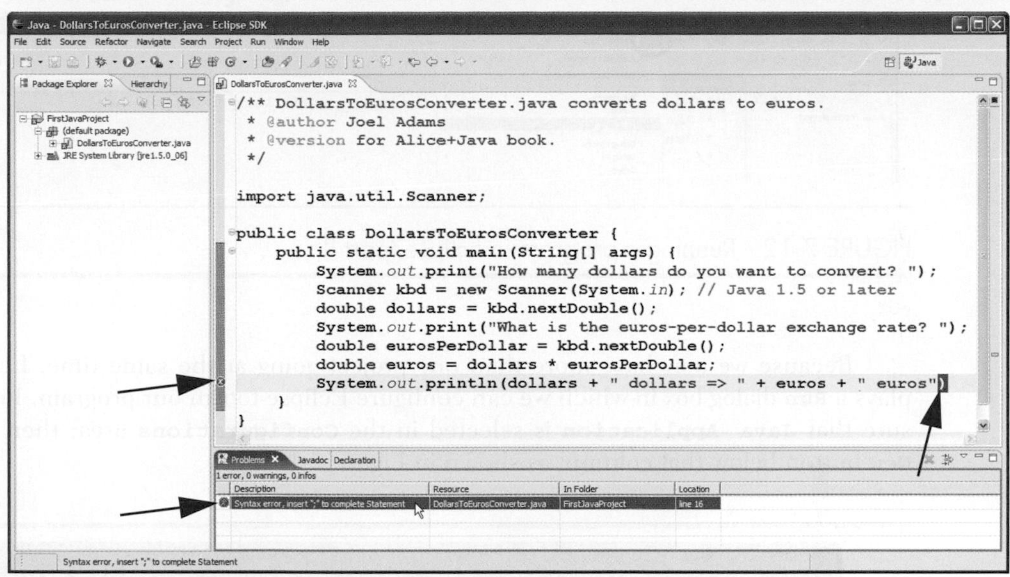

FIGURE 7-11 Eclipse marks errors

Eclipse will also pop up a description of the error if you "hover" the mouse over the error mark in the *editing area*. To fix the error, we add the semicolon at the end of the line, and then save.

If you have different errors, carefully read the message in the *problems & output area* to determine the problem. Then find the line in the *editing area* that produced the error, and change it as suggested by the error message. All errors must be fixed before we can proceed.

Once we have corrected the errors in our program and saved it, we are ready to run it.

7.2.4 Running a Java Program Using Eclipse

Running your program in Eclipse the first time requires some setup. After this setup has been done once, a single mouse-click suffices to run your program. We will present these separately.

Running Your Program the First Time

To run a Java program in Eclipse the first time, choose the **`Run->Run...`** menu choice, as shown in Figure 7-12.

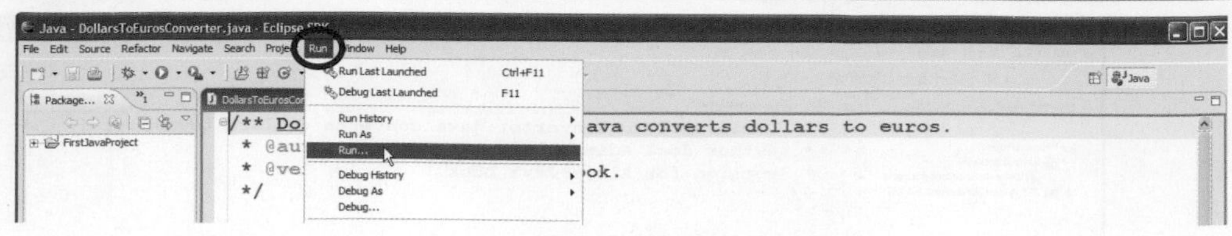

FIGURE 7-12 Running a program in Eclipse (part I)

Because we may have more than one project going at the same time, Eclipse displays a **Run** dialog box in which we can configure Eclipse to run our program. First, make sure that **Java Application** is selected in the **Configurations** area; then click the **New** button below that column, as shown in Figure 7-13.

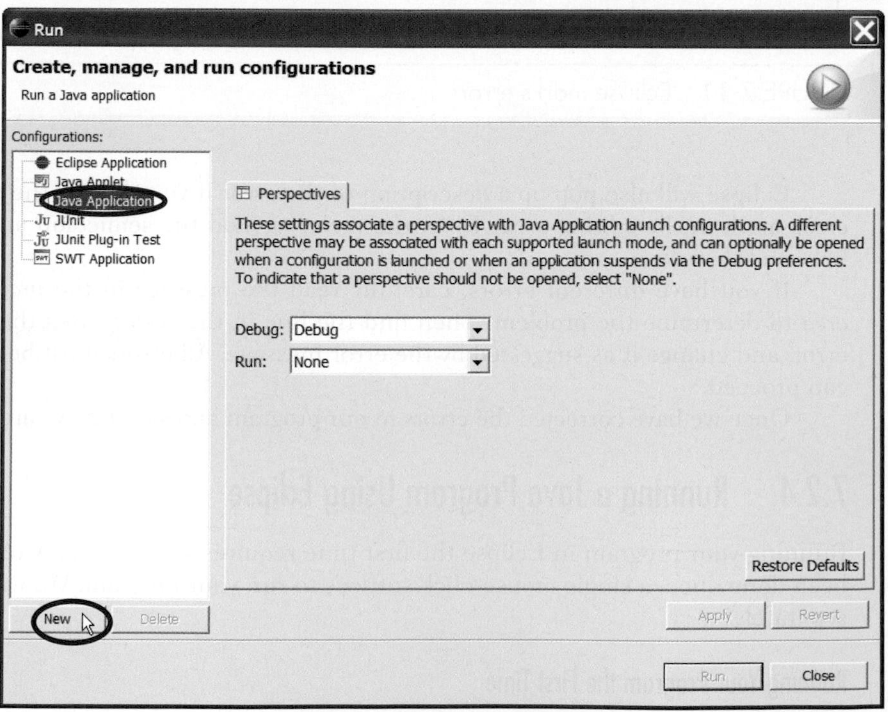

FIGURE 7-13 The Run dialog box

Eclipse adds a new **Java Application** run configuration to that column, and then displays the dialog box shown in Figure 7-14.

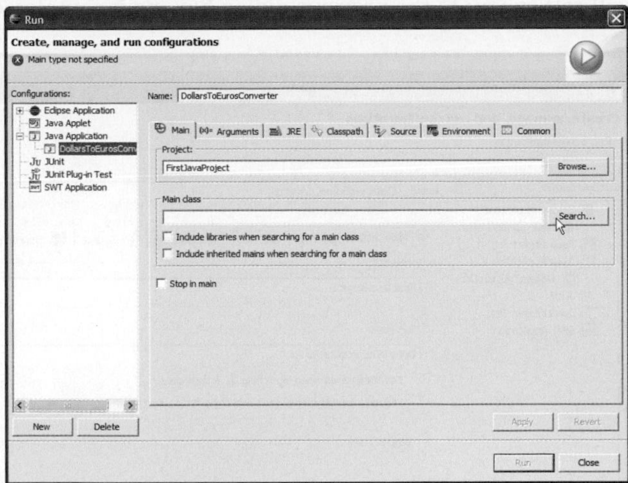

FIGURE 7-14 The main tab on the Run dialog box

Your selected project should be listed in the box below **Project**; if it is not, you can click the **Browse...** button and select it from the list that appears.

When Eclipse runs our program, the flow of execution begins in the **main()** method. Since a project may have several classes, our next step is to tell Eclipse which class contains the **main()** method. Click the **Search...** button and Eclipse will display a list of the classes in the project. (Your class will not appear here until it has compiled correctly.)

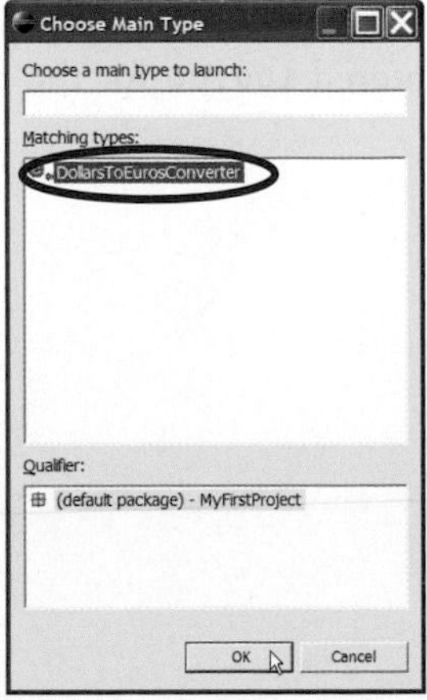

FIGURE 7-15 Selecting the class containing **main()**

Select the name of the class (**`DollarsToEurosConverter`**), and click the **`OK`** button. Eclipse will return you to the previous dialog box, now completed. See Figure 7-16.

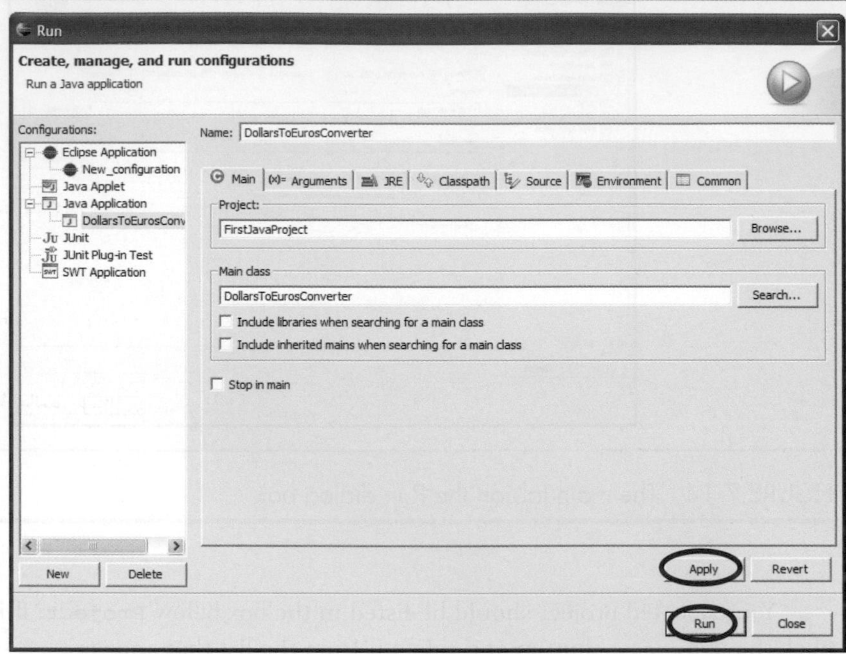

FIGURE 7-16 Running a program the first time in Eclipse

Click the **`Apply`** button and Eclipse will save and remember these settings. Then click the **`Run`** button and Eclipse will run your program in the **`Console`** tab of the *problems and output area*! If we click in that area, we can enter values (shown in green below) in response to our program's questions. For example, Figure 7-17 shows a sample run of our program, in which we entered **`100.00`** for the number of dollars and **`0.85`** for the euros-per-dollar exchange rate.

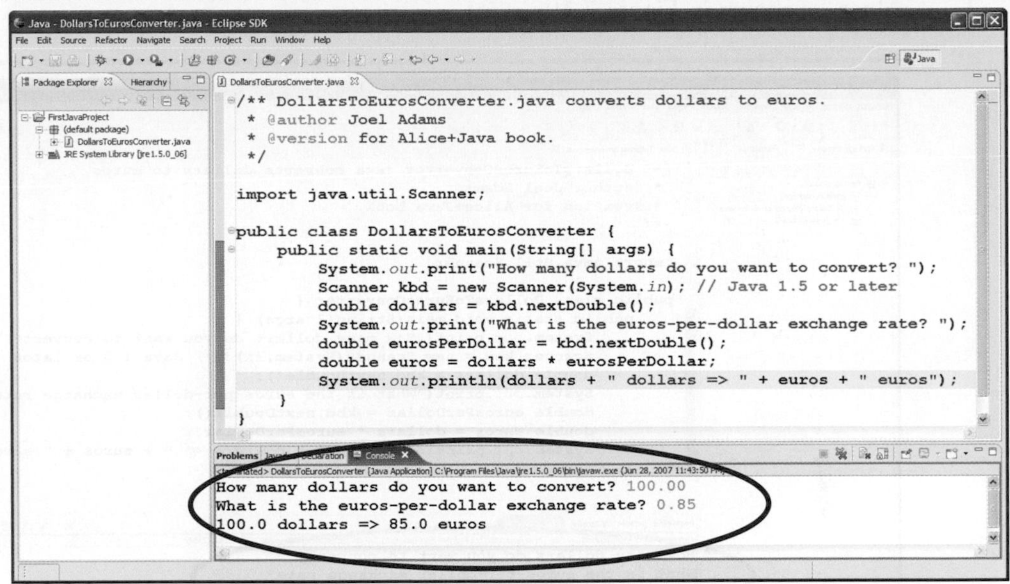

FIGURE 7-17 **DollarsToEurosConverter**: sample run

7.2.5 Testing a Java Program Using Eclipse

Functional Testing

The first few times we run a program, we enter realistic but easily verifiable values. For example, we entered **100** and **0.85** during our first run. Since our program just multiplies these values together, that made it easy to verify that our program was producing the correct result (**85.0**).

However, getting the right answer once is not sufficient to guarantee that your program is correct. Before we can have any confidence that our program works correctly, we must run it multiple times, using a variety of different values. This process is called **functional testing**.

Thankfully, it is much easier to run our program after the first run. To run our program again, we just click the **Run** button on the toolbar, as shown in Figure 7-18.

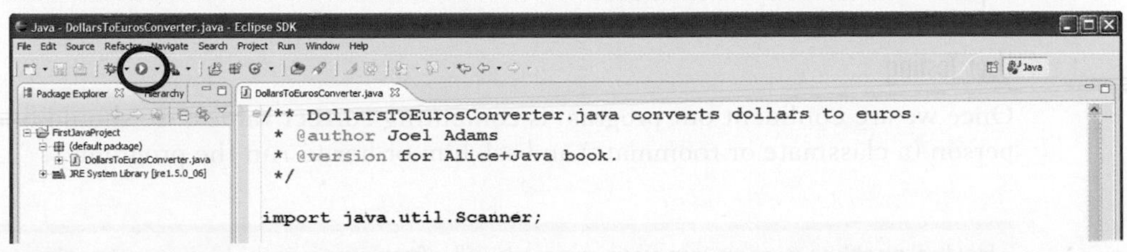

FIGURE 7-18 The **Run** button

Eclipse will then rerun our program without further ado, allowing us to enter new values, as shown in Figure 7-19.

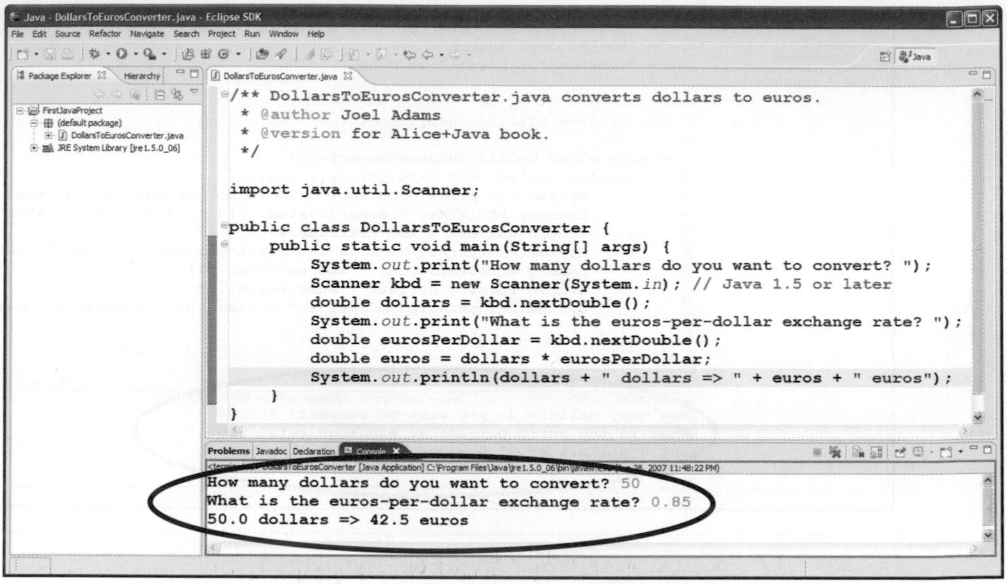
Java - DollarsToEurosConverter.java - Eclipse SDK
File Edit Source Refactor Navigate Search Project Run Window Help
Package Explorer
Hierarchy
FirstJavaProject
(default package)
DollarsToEurosConverter.java
JRE System Library [jre1.5.0_06]
DollarsToEurosConverter.java
/** DollarsToEurosConverter.java converts dollars to euros.
 * @author Joel Adams
 * @version for Alice+Java book.
 */
import java.util.Scanner;
public class DollarsToEurosConverter {
public static void main(String[] args) {
System.out.print("How many dollars do you want to convert? ");
Scanner kbd = new Scanner(System.in); // Java 1.5 or later
double dollars = kbd.nextDouble();
System.out.print("What is the euros-per-dollar exchange rate? ");
double eurosPerDollar = kbd.nextDouble();
double euros = dollars * eurosPerDollar;
System.out.println(dollars + " dollars => " + euros + " euros");
}
}
Problems Javadoc Declaration Console
How many dollars do you want to convert? 50
What is the euros-per-dollar exchange rate? 0.85
50.0 dollars => 42.5 euros

FIGURE 7-19 Running the program (again)

During this second run, we entered **50** and **0.85**. Since 50 is half of 100, this second run should produce half of 85.0 (42.5). By using such easily verified values, we can tell immediately whether or not our program is computing correct values.

Testing a program using easily verified values is sometimes called **sanity checking**. If our program produces "insane" results when we test it, it fails our sanity checks, implying there is something wrong with the logic in the program — our program contains a **logic error**. When this happens, we must review our program and study its logic, to discover where we went wrong. When we find our mistake, we modify the program to correct its logic, recompile it, rerun it, and retest it.

Sanity checking is often sufficient for simple programs. However for a more complex program, we must test the program using a wide range of input values, to check that it performs correctly in each case.

User Testing

Once we are confident our program is computing correct values, we should find another person (a classmate or roommate) and ask him or her to run the program.

> Having another person run your program will often uncover hidden assumptions you have made in writing and testing your program.

To illustrate, suppose we ask our roommate to run the program. After showing her how to start it, she enters the values shown (underlined) below.

```
How many dollars do you want to convert? 100.01
What is the euros-per-dollar exchange rate? 0.84973
100.01 dollars => 84.9814973 euros
```

By testing our program differently than we would have, our roommate has helped us discover a flaw in it: it does not round the value of **euros** to two decimal places. In programming terminology, we say that our program is not properly **formatting euros**, which means controlling the way the value of **euros** is printed or displayed.

For situations like this, Java 1.5 and later provides the **printf()** (print-formatted) method. If we replace the last line of our program with this one:

```
System.out.printf("%.2f dollars => %.2f euros", dollars, euros);
```

then our program formats **euros** properly when we run it:

```
How many dollars do you want to convert? 100.01
What is the euros-per-dollar exchange rate? 0.84973
100.01 dollars => 84.98 euros
```

In the next section, we will explain each line of this program, including the **printf()** method.

7.3 Java Basics

Now that we have walked through the mechanics of using an IDE like Eclipse to write, run, and test a Java program, we are ready to examine the basics of Java programming. To do so, we will use the program we wrote in Section 7.2, comparing it to the algorithm we developed in Section 7.1. We will begin by listing the contents of **DollarsToEurosConverter.java**. The final version is given in Figure 7-20.[6]

---

6. If the **printf()** at the end of Figure 7-20 causes a compilation error, make certain that you are using Java 5.0 or later. To find the Java version in Eclipse, click **Project** on the Eclipse menu bar, click **Properties**, expand **Java Compiler** on the left side of the dialog box, and read the value in the **Compiler compliance level** text box. Numbers like **1.5.0** and **5.0** are different notations for the same version of Java. You must use Java **5.0 (1.5.0)** or higher to run the programs in this book. If yours is lower, click the **Enable project specific settings** checkbox, select **5.0** (or higher) in the **Compiler compliance level** text box, and then click the **Apply** button.

```java
/** DollarsToEurosConverter.java converts dollars to euros.
 * @author Joel Adams, CS Dept, Calvin College
 * @version 1.0, for Alice+Java book.
 */
import java.util.Scanner;

public class DollarsToEurosConverter {
  public static void main(String[] args) {
    System.out.print(
           "How many dollars do you want to convert? ");
    Scanner keyboard = new Scanner(System.in); // Java 1.5 or later
    double dollars = keyboard.nextDouble();
    System.out.print(
           "What is the euros-per-dollar exchange rate? ");
    double eurosPerDollar = keyboard.nextDouble();
    double euros = dollars * eurosPerDollar;
    System.out.printf(
           "%.2f dollars => %.2f euros", dollars, euros);
  }
}
```

FIGURE 7-20 `DollarsToEurosConverter.java`

7.3.1 Comments

The first four lines in the file comprise an opening **comment**. Comments are for the benefit of a person reading the file and are ignored by the Java compiler. Each file you create should have such a comment. It is our practice to include the name of the file and its purpose on the first line, followed by who wrote it, when, where, why, and so on. Your instructor may require other pieces of information in this comment, so be sure to ask what he or she requires.

Java actually supports three different kinds of comments:

- **Inline comments** begin with `//` and end at the end of that line. Inline comments are often used to comment on a single program statement. For example, the **`Scanner`** class was not available in Java prior to version 1.5, so we might add this comment at the end of the statement to warn people not to try to compile this with an older Java compiler.

```java
Scanner keyboard = new Scanner(System.in); // Java 1.5 or later
```

- **Block comments** begin with `/*` and end with `*/`. These are often used for opening comments and other comments that span multiple lines of text. Block comments are sometimes called *C-style comments* because they date back to the C programming language.

- **Javadoc comments** begin with `/**` and end with `*/`. Javadoc comments are block comments containing special **tags** (for example, `@author`, `@version`, `@param`, `@return`). When processed by a free program named `javadoc`, these comments will create a Web page that describes how to use the class in the file containing the comments. Javadoc comments thus do double-duty: they serve to help the reader of a file understand its contents AND they can be used to create online documentation for your software. (The online documentation pages for Java's application programming interface (API) are all generated from Javadoc comments.) See `http://java.sun.com/j2se/javadoc/` for more information.

It is important to make your code readable, and comments are an important tool in writing programs that are easy to read. Inline comments should be used to explain statements that are "tricky" or whose purpose is not obvious.

7.3.2 Import Statements and Packages

The actual program in `DollarsToEurosConverter.java` begins after the opening comment. The first line after the comment is an **import statement**:

```
import java.util.Scanner;
```

There are thousands of predefined classes that come with Java. If, for each use of a class in a program, Java had to search through its thousands of classes, compiling a Java program would take a long time. To organize these classes so that they can be found more quickly, Java stores related classes in groups called **packages**. For example, all of the classes that simplify writing network software are in a package named `java.net`. The `Scanner` class is in a package named `java.util`.

If you want to use a class from one of these packages, you must import it, using an import statement like the one above. If you find yourself importing a lot of classes from the same package, you can either supply an import statement for each class, or you can import all of the classes in the package with a single **wild-card import statement**:

```
import java.util.*;
```

Since some classes are used more often than others, some commonly used classes (for example, the `String` class and the `System` class) are stored in a special package named `java.lang`. The classes in `java.lang` are automatically imported into your program, so you need not do anything special to use them.

It is our practice to place all of the import statements for a program after the opening comment and before that program's class. This keeps the import statements organized in one place.

Online documentation (generated using javadoc) is available for all the Java packages and the classes at Sun's Java Web site, and can be accessed via your browser. To do so, point your browser to `java.sun.com/reference/api/index.html` and click the link for the version of Java you are using. We encourage you to familiarize yourself with this page, and bookmark it in your browser, as it provides you with:

- A list of all of the classes that come with Java
- A list of all of the methods (messages that can be sent to an object) of a given class
- The package in which a given class is stored

7.3.3 The Simplest Java Program

The class that makes up our program follows any import statements the program needs. The simplest Java program (that does nothing) consists of just a class and an empty method named **main()**, as can be seen in Figure 7-21.

```
public class SimplestJavaProgram {
  public static void main(String[] args) {
  }
}
```

FIGURE 7-21 The simplest Java program

Note that this program has no import statements, because it uses no classes or packages.

Since there is no existing type that represents the simplest Java program, we must create a class to represent one. The class declaration begins with the word **public**, which makes the class "visible" to those who might want to use it.[7] Then comes the word **class**, which indicates that whatever comes next is the name of a new type. Next is the name of the class — in this case, the name of our program (**SimplestJavaProgram**) — followed by a pair of curly braces (**{** and **}**). This general pattern:

```
public class NameOfTheClass {
}
```

defines the structure of most of the classes we will create throughout the rest of the book.

Every Java program needs a method named **main()**, where the flow of execution will begin when the program is run. (The **main()** method is like **myFirstMethod()** in Alice.) This method must be defined within the curly braces of the class:

```
public class NameOfTheClass {
    public static void main(String [] args) {
    }
}
```

7. Classes can also be **private**, which limits their accessibility.

The first word in the **main()** method is the word **public**. Used before a method, the word **public** indicates that the method can be invoked outside of the class. When we run our program, Java sends our class the **main()** message, so if **main()** cannot be invoked outside of the class, a runtime error will occur.

Next is the word **static**. This indicates that **main()** is invoked by sending a message to the *class* (for example, **SimplestJavaProgram.main()**), not to an *object*. This distinction will become important in later chapters; for now, just remember that the **main()** method must be a **static** method.

Next is the word **void**. This indicates that **main()** doesn't produce any result when it finishes. We'll see why this is important when we start writing Java methods; for now, just remember that **main()** is a **void** method, meaning it returns nothing to its invoker.

Next comes the name of the method (**main**) followed by a pair of parentheses. The parentheses indicate that this is a method, as opposed to a variable.

Inside the **main()** method's parentheses is **String [] args**. This defines the name **args** as a variable capable of storing an array (sequence) of **String** values. We will not use **args** much in this book, but it provides a way for Java to pass the values to the **main()** method when it is invoked.

Finally, we have a pair of curly braces. These are sometimes called the **body** of the method. When a program is run, the flow of execution begins at the first statement inside these curly braces. Since the curly braces of the **main()** method in Figure 7-21 are empty, nothing happens when we run that program.

If you compare this simplest program to the Java that Eclipse generated for us in Figure 7-9, you'll see that Eclipse generates a minimal program for us when we have it create a new class (along with a Javadoc comment and an inline comment).

Programs that do nothing are not very interesting. To make a Java program do something, we must put **statements** within the curly braces (**{** and **}**) of its **main()** method, as can be seen in Figure 7-20. Java statements are much like statements in Alice using Java mode, except that we must *type* them into Eclipse's *editing area*, rather than drag-and-drop them.

7.3.4 Some Java Statements

One way to write a program is to go through an algorithm step by step, translating each step into the equivalent Java statements. We are going to follow this approach to discuss the purpose of each Java statement in our **DollarsToEurosConverter** program.

Step 1

In the first step of our algorithm, we asked the user a question:

```
1 Display "How many dollars do you want to convert?"
```

For every program, Java defines an object named **System.out** through which textual values (letters, digits, punctuation, and so on) can be displayed on the screen. The messages we can send to **System.out** include the following:

- **System.out.print(*value*);** will display ***value*** on the screen
- **System.out.println(*value*);** will display ***value*** on the screen and then advance the cursor to the next line

We can thus perform Step 1 in Java using the following statement:

```
System.out.print("How many dollars do you want to convert? ");
```

This will display our question, leaving the (blinking) cursor at the end of the question, so that the answer the user types in response will be on the same line as the question.

```
How many dollars do you want to convert? 100.01
```

When the user presses the **Enter** key after typing **100.01**, the cursor will move to the next line, so that the next thing we **print()** to the screen will begin on that line.

Step 2

In the second step of our algorithm, we read the user's response to our question:

```
2 Read dollars.
```

Just as Java provides **System.out** for displaying values on the screen, Java provides an object named **System.in** that is associated with our computer's keyboard. Unfortunately, the class of **System.in** does not provide methods for reading numbers. To do so, we can "wrap" **System.in** within an object called a **Scanner**, which will let us read the numbers easily. The statements to do so look like this:

```
Scanner keyboard = new Scanner( System.in );
double dollars = keyboard.nextDouble();
```

The first line is a **declaration statement** that creates and initializes a variable named **keyboard**. The statement declares a **Scanner** variable named **keyboard**, creates a new **Scanner** object that "wraps up" **System.in**, and then makes **keyboard** refer to the newly created **Scanner** object. A variable like **keyboard** that refers to an object is sometimes called a **handle**, because it is the way we interact with the object (for example **keyboard.nextDouble()**).

The second line is another declaration statement that creates and initializes a variable named **dollars**. This statement creates the variable **dollars**, sends **keyboard** a message named **nextDouble()** that extracts a real number from **System.in**, and then sets **dollars** to the number that **nextDouble()** returns. As indicated in this statement, Java uses the type **double** to store real numbers (numbers with decimal points).

Now that we have seen two declaration statements, a pattern should be evident. Declaration statements have the form:

```
type variableName = initialValue;
```

That is, the first part of a declaration statement is a valid Java type (for example, **Scanner** or **double**). Next is a variable name (for example, **keyboard** or **dollars**). Next is an optional **=** sign followed by an initial value of the same type as the variable (for example, a **Scanner** object, or the value returned by **keyboard.nextDouble()**). Although this initialization portion of the declaration is optional, it is a good practice to always supply an initial value for your variables.

As described previously, Java stores the **Scanner** class in the **java.util** package. In order for the Java compiler to know that the word **Scanner** is a type when it processes this statement, we must have imported this package into our program using the **import** keyword.

Step 3

In the third step of our algorithm, we ask the user another question:

```
3 Display "What is the euros-per-dollar exchange rate?"
```

We can perform this step using the same approach we used for Step 1:

```
System.out.print("What is the euros-per-dollar exchange rate? ");
```

Step 4

In the fourth step of our algorithm, we again read the user's response:

```
4 Read eurosPerDollar.
```

We can perform this step using the same approach as we used in Step 2, using the same **Scanner** object we defined there:

```
double eurosPerDollar = keyboard.nextDouble();
```

This declaration statement declares a variable named **eurosPerDollar** capable of storing a real number, sends **keyboard** the **nextDouble()** message to obtain a real number from **System.in**, and then sets the value of **eurosPerDollar** to that number.

Besides **nextDouble()**, we can send a **Scanner** object these messages:

- the **nextInt()** message returns the next integer (whole number) value
- the **nextBoolean()** message returns the next boolean (true or false) value
- the **nextLine()** message returns a **String** containing all of the characters from the last thing read until the end of the current line

See Sun's online documentation for **java.util.Scanner** for a complete list.

Step 5

In the fifth step of our algorithm, we compute the number of euros:

```
5 Compute euros = dollars * eurosPerDollar.
```

We can perform this step using a declaration statement:

```
double euros = dollars * eurosPerDollar;
```

This statement declares a variable named **euros** capable of storing a real number, multiplies the value in **dollars** times the value in **eurosPerDollar**, and then sets **euros** to that product.

Step 6

In the final step of our algorithm, we display the number of euros:

```
6 Display dollars and euros, plus descriptive labels.
```

In the first version of this program, we performed this step by sending **System.out** the following **println()** message:

```
System.out.println(dollars + " dollars => " + euros + " euros");
```

The **print()** and **println()** methods each take a single **String** as their argument. To display multiple values, it is customary to use Java's concatenation operator (**+**) which, like Alice's concatenation operator, combines two **String** values into one. However, as the statement above indicates, Java's concatenation operator goes even further: When one of the operands of **+** is a **double** (for example, the value of **dollars** or **euros**) and the other operand is a **String** (for example **"dollars => "** or **" euros"**), Java will convert the **double**'s value into the corresponding **String**. (For example, the number **100.01** is converted into the string **"100.01"**, and the number **84.9814973** is converted into the string **"84.9814973"**.) These **String** values are then combined into a single **String**, which the **println()** method displays on-screen.

This makes it easy to display the values of numeric variables with descriptive labels. For example, when our roommate tested our program, the statement

```
System.out.println(dollars + " dollars => " + euros + " euros");
```

performed three concatenation operations to produce the **String**

```
"100.01 dollars => 84.9814973 euros"
```

which the **println()** statement then displayed on the screen.

For readability, we should leave *spaces* at the ends of the descriptive labels. If we had instead written

```
System.out.println(dollars + "dollars =>" + euros + "euros");
```

then the **String** produced by the concatenations would have been

```
"100.01dollars =>84.9814973euros"
```

which is much harder to read.

The printf() Statement

For a real number, the number of digits that appear to the right of the decimal point is called the *precision* of the number. For example, **100.01** has two digits of precision, while **84.9814973** has seven digits of precision.

The number of digits the **println()** method displays varies with the precision of the value being displayed. This is a problem when displaying currency values. Such values should have two digits of precision, but in Figure 7-17 and Figure 7-19, only a single digit is displayed. Similarly, during user testing, **euros** displayed with seven digits of precision.

To control the format of printed values, Java provides the **printf()** method. The second version of our program used this message to display correctly formatted values:

```
System.out.printf("%.2f dollars => %.2f euros", dollars, euros);
```

The **printf()** message must have at least one argument, and the first argument must be a **String** called the **format-string**. In the message above, the format-string is `"%.2f dollars => %.2f euros"`.

After the format-string can come any number of arguments, but for each subsequent argument, there must be a **placeholder** in the format-string. In the example above, there are two subsequent arguments: the variables **dollars** and **euros**. The format-string contains a placeholder for each of these (**%.2f**), shown in red below:

```
"%.2f dollars => %.2f euros"
```

A placeholder always begins with the **%** symbol. In each of the placeholders shown above, the **f** at the end specifies that the argument should be displayed as a fixed-point (real) number.

The `.2` in the middle specifies that the value being displayed should be rounded to two digits of precision. Changing the precision is as simple as changing the `2` to a different value.

The **`printf()`** method works by replacing the placeholders in the format-string with the values of the subsequent arguments, matching them from left to right as shown in Figure 7-22.

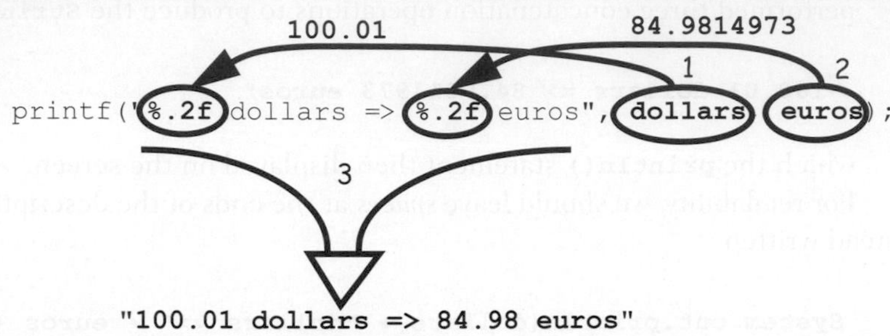

FIGURE 7-22 The `printf()` statement

Understanding how the placeholders work is thus the key to using the **`printf()`** method. Placeholders are very powerful and complex — too complex to cover exhaustively in this introductory chapter. In subsequent chapters, we will revisit the **`printf()`** statement and its placeholders as the need arises.

7.4 A Second Java Program

Suppose you like to eat corn flakes for breakfast. When your supply is running low, you go shopping and find that the grocery store sells two sizes: a "regular" 12-ounce size and an "economy" 15-ounce size. The "regular" size costs $2.90 while the "economy" size costs $4.00. Which is the better deal?

Or suppose you drop and break your out-of-warranty MP3 player, so you go shopping for a replacement. At the store, you find two models by the same manufacturer: a 60-gigabyte model that costs $150, and an 80-gigabyte model that costs $190. Which is the better deal?

Both of these are instances of the same basic problem: finding the *unit price* of an item. In the first version, the unit price is the price per ounce of each size, while in the second version, the unit price is the price per gigabyte of each model. In this section, we will write a program to solve this problem.

7.4.1 Designing the UnitPricer Program

To solve these problems, we might start by writing a user story that describes what should happen in order to solve the problem:

> Our program will ask the user the question, "What is the price of the first item?" The user will enter this first price, which our program will read from the keyboard. The program will then ask the question, "How many units are in the first item?" The user will enter the number of units in the first item, which our program will read. Our program will then ask the user "What is the price of the second item?" The user will enter the second price, and our program will read it. Our program will then ask "How many units are in the second item?" The user will enter the number of units in the second item and our program will read it. Our program will then compute and display the unit prices of the two items, along with descriptive labels.

Instead of referring to corn flakes or MP3 players, we have used the more generic term "items"; and instead of referring to ounces or gigabytes, we have used the more generic term "units." Instead of solving just our corn flakes or MP3 player problems, our program should solve these *and all similar problems*. This ability to **generalize** — to solve broad, generic problems instead of narrow, specific ones — is important, as it results in a more generally useful program.

Once we have our user story, the next step is to locate the noun phrases in it (ignoring the user), and make a list of them.

Noun Phrase	Type of Value	Name
our program	?	*UnitPricer*
questions	String	none
first price	number (real)	*price1*
the keyboard	Scanner	*keyboard*
units in 1st item	number (real)	*units1*
second price	number (real)	*price2*
units in 2nd item	number (real)	*units2*
unit price of 1st item	number (real)	*unitPrice1*
unit price of 2nd item	number (real)	*unitPrice2*
descriptive labels	String	none

Next, we list the verb phrases in our user story (ignoring user actions). Now that we know some Java, we can add a column to this list in which we note how we will accomplish each action.

Verb Phrase	Java Method or Operation
ask the user	`System.out.print();`
read ...	`keyboard.nextDouble()`
compute unit prices	`price1/units1` `price2/units2`
display	`System.out.println();`

The final design step is to build these into an algorithm, as shown in Figure 7-23.

Algorithm: UnitPricer

```
Display "What is the price of the 1st item?" via System.out.
Read price1 from keyboard.
Display "How many units are in the 1st item?" via System.out.
Read units1 from keyboard.
Display "What is the price of the 2nd item?" via System.out.
Read price2 from keyboard.
Display "How many units are in the 2nd item?" via System.out.
Read units2 from keyboard.
Compute unitPrice1 = price1 / units1.
Compute unitPrice2 = price2 / units2.
Display unitPrice1, unitPrice2, and descriptive labels via System.out.
```

FIGURE 7-23 Algorithm for UnitPricer program

With an algorithm in hand to serve as our blueprint, we are ready to write our program.

7.4.2 Writing the UnitPricer Program

Writing the *UnitPricer* program requires that we create a **`UnitPricer`** class, containing a **`main()`** method that contains Java statements corresponding to the steps of the algorithm.

If we use Eclipse to write the program, we must follow steps like those presented in Section 7.2.2 and following. We will not repeat those steps here, except in summary: we must create a new Java project, then create a new class (**`UnitPricer`**). Eclipse will create a file (**`UnitPricer.java`**) to store the class. We must then modify the contents of this file by adding statements that perform the steps of our algorithm. Figure 7-24 presents our version.

```
/** UnitPricer.java calculates the unit prices of two
 *     different items, given their prices and units.
 *     @author Joel Adams, for Alice+Java
 */
import java.util.Scanner;

public class UnitPricer {
  public static void main(String[] args) {
    Scanner keyboard = new Scanner(System.in);

    System.out.print("Enter the price of the 1st item: ");
    double price1 = keyboard.nextDouble();
    System.out.print("How many units are in the 1st item? ");
    double units1 = keyboard.nextDouble();

    System.out.print("Enter the price of the 2nd item: ");
    double price2 = keyboard.nextDouble();
    System.out.print("How many units are in the 2nd item? ");
    double units2 = keyboard.nextDouble();

    double unitPrice1 = price1/units1;
    double unitPrice2 = price2/units2;

    System.out.printf("%nItem 1 unit price: $%7.2f", unitPrice1);
    System.out.printf("%nItem 2 unit price: $%7.2f", unitPrice2);
  }
}
```

FIGURE 7-24 **UnitPricer.java**

For readability, we have added white space that divides our program into sections. These sections correspond roughly to the logical steps of our algorithm.

Our **printf()** messages also use two new features, which we will discuss shortly.

7.4.3 Testing the UnitPricer Program

As before, we will conduct some initial testing on our program using easy-to-verify values. Figure 7-25 shows two testing runs, with the user-entered values underlined.

Result:
Enter the price of the 1st item: 100
How many units are in the 1st item? 10
Enter the price of the 2nd item: 20
How many units are in the 2nd item? 4
Item 1 unit price: $ 10.00
Item 2 unit price: $ 5.00

Result:
Enter the price of the 1st item: 1.00
How many units are in the 1st item? 25
Enter the price of the 2nd item: 0.50
How many units are in the 2nd item? 2
Item 1 unit price: $ 0.04
Item 2 unit price: $ 0.25

FIGURE 7-25 Testing `UnitPricer.java`

The `printf()` Message Revisited

The **`printf()`** message is like the **`print()`** message, in that it does not automatically advance the cursor to the next line. If we want to advance the cursor to the next line, we must specify this in the format-string. To accomplish this, the format-strings in the **`printf()`** messages in Figure 7-24 each begin with a **`%n`** placeholder, which advances the cursor to the next line, in whatever way is appropriate on your computer.[8]

Note that when **`%n`** advances the cursor after the user has entered a value, a blank line results. If the cursor is already at the beginning of a line (for example, after the user presses the **`Enter`** key) then advancing the cursor to the *next* line effectively prints a blank line.

The **`printf()`** messages in Figure 7-24 also use a new placeholder feature:

```
System.out.printf("%nItem 1 unit price: $%7.2f", unitPrice1);
```

8. Different operating systems advance the cursor differently. Unix-based systems such as Linux and MacOS X use a special **linefeed** (**`LF`**) character. MacOS 9 and earlier used a **carriage return** (**`CR`**) character. Microsoft Windows uses both (**`CR+LF`**). A **`printf()`** message translates the **`%n`** placeholder into the one used by your operating system.

The **7** that appears between the **%** and the decimal point specifies the **width** or number of spaces in which the value is to be displayed. When the value being displayed is smaller than this width, the value is *right-justified* within the field, leaving spaces to the left:

```
                          7 spaces wide
                         <------------>
Item 1 unit price: $__ 10.00
Item 2 unit price: $___5.00
```

When combined with a precision value, the effect is to line up the decimal points, making the displayed values easier to read and compare. Generally speaking, a placeholder of the form:

```
%w.pf
```

will display its value in a field of width *w*, with precision *p*.

7.4.4 Solving the Problems

With some degree of confidence that our program is working correctly, we can now use it to solve the problems described at the beginning of this section.

To solve the MP3 player problem (in which the 60-gigabyte model cost $150 and the 80-gigabyte model cost $190), we enter the values shown in Figure 7-26.

```
Enter the price of the 1st item: 150
How many units are in the 1st item? 60
Enter the price of the 2nd item: 190
How many units are in the 2nd item? 80

Item 1 unit price: $    2.50
Item 2 unit price: $    2.38
```

FIGURE 7-26 Solving the MP3 player problem

The 80-gigabyte model is the better buy, assuming we can afford the extra $40 it costs.

To solve the corn flakes problem (in which the 12-ounce "regular" size cost $2.90 and the 15-ounce "economy" size cost $4.00), we enter the values shown in Figure 7-27.

`Enter the price of the 1st item: 2.90`
`How many units are in the 1st item? 12`
`Enter the price of the 2nd item: 4.00`
`How many units are in the 2nd item? 15`
`Item 1 unit price: $    0.24`
`Item 2 unit price: $    0.27`

FIGURE 7-27 Solving the corn flakes problem

The first item has the lower price per ounce. Recalling that it was the "regular" size box and the second item was the "economy" size, the "economy" size is a worse buy in this case!

7.5 The Software Engineering Process

The approach we just used to create our first two Java programs is similar to the approach we used to create Alice programs. The process consists of these steps:

1. Write the *user story*. Identify the nouns and verbs within it.
2. For each noun in your algorithm: Find a *type* to represent that object. If no existing type will adequately represent the object, build a class to create a new type. (We'll see how to build classes to represent non-program objects in Chapter 9.) Use that type to declare the object.
3. For each verb in your algorithm: Find a *message* that performs that verb's action, and send it to the verb's object. If the object has no message that provides that verb's action, define a method to perform that action. (We'll see how to build methods in the next chapter.)
4. Organize your nouns and verbs into an algorithm that solves your problem.
5. Write your program, using your algorithm as a blueprint.
6. Test your program. If it produces incorrect results, return to Step 4.

Steps 1-4 of this process are called **software design**. Steps 5 and 6 are called **software implementation and testing**. Together, software design, implementation, and testing are important pieces of **software engineering**.

We will use this same basic process to create the rest of the programs in this book. You should go through each of these steps for each Java program you write, because the result will be better-crafted programs.

7.6 Chapter Summary

In this chapter, we have begun the transition from Alice to Java. While most of the ideas should seem familiar from Alice, it may take you a while to become accustomed to typing Java statements. Some of the Java ideas we learned about include the following:

- To create a Java program, we create a class containing a method named **`main()`**.
- Java classes are stored in *packages*. Many commonly used classes are in the package **`java.lang`**. To use a class from a package other than **`java.lang`**, you must import that class (or import all the classes in the package using a wildcard).
- A *variable declaration* tells the Java compiler what kind of value we intend to store in a variable, and allows us to give the variable an initial value. Java uses the type **`double`** to declare variables whose values will be real numbers (that is, with a decimal point).
- Java provides **`System.out`**, a predefined object that connects a program to the screen. We can display values on the screen by sending **`print()`**, **`println()`**, or **`printf()`** messages to **`System.out`**.
- Java provides **`System.in`**, a predefined object that connects a program to the keyboard. The **`Scanner`** class from the **`java.util`** package provides convenient methods to read values from **`System.in`**. These methods include **`readDouble()`** for **`double`** values, and **`readLine()`** for **`String`** values.
- *Eclipse* is a free IDE that (once you get used to it) makes it easy to write, compile, debug, and test Java programs.
- *Software engineering* is methodically designing, implementing, and testing software.

7.6.1 Key Terms

algorithm
block comment
class
comment
compile
compiler
declaration statement
error
flow
format-string
functional testing
import statement
inline comment
integrated development environment (IDE)
Javadoc comment
logic error
message
method
object
package
placeholder
project
real numbers
run
sanity checking
software design
software engineering
statement
string
tag
testing
user story

Programming Projects

7.1 Design and write a "greeter" program that asks the user for his or her name, and then displays "Welcome to Java," followed by that name.

7.2 Design and write a "dog years" program that asks the user how old he or she is, and then computes and displays the user's age in dog years. Assume that dog years = person years × 7.

7.3 *Mary Had A Little Lamb* is a traditional children's song. Design and write a program that asks the user his or her first name, and then the name of an animal. The program should then print the lyrics to *Mary Had A Little Lamb*, but with the word *Mary* replaced by the user's first name, and *lamb* replaced by the user's animal, throughout the song. For example, if the user enters *Carol* and *porcupine* for these two values, the program should display:

Carol had a little porcupine, little porcupine, little porcupine. Carol had a little porcupine its fleece was white as snow.	*And everywhere that Carol went, Carol went, Carol went. And everywhere that Carol went the porcupine was sure to go.*
It followed her to school one day, school one day, school one day. It followed her to school one day which was against the rules.	*It made the children laugh and play, laugh and play, laugh and play. It made the children laugh and play to see a porcupine at school.*

7.4 Suppose you are visiting a foreign country. Design and write a "kilometers to miles" converter program that asks the user for a number in kilometers, and then computes and displays the corresponding number in miles.

7.5 Suppose you are visiting a foreign country. Design and write a "liters to gallons" converter program that asks the user for a number of liters, and then computes and displays the corresponding number of gallons.

7.6 Suppose you are visiting a foreign country. Design and write a "mileage" program that asks users the distance they've driven, how much fuel they've used, and then computes and displays the mileage (for example, in miles per gallon or kilometers per liter).

7.7 Suppose you are a small business owner. Design and write a "payroll" program that asks the user for the number of hours worked and the hourly wage, and then computes and displays the user's pay. Assume that pay = hours × wage (no overtime).

7.8 Suppose you are a small business owner. Design and write a "reverse-payroll" program that asks the number of hours you've worked and your weekly net profit, and then computes and displays your wage (in dollars per hour).

7.9 Suppose you want to carpet several rooms in your house. To help you decide how much carpet to buy, design and write a "carpet area" program that asks the user for the length and width of a room (in feet), and then computes and displays the area of the floor of that room (in square yards).

7.10 Suppose you are on vacation and decide to buy each of your friends and family similar souvenirs. Each souvenir comes in a box, and these boxes are all the same size. You need to determine how many souvenirs you can pack into your suitcase. Write a program that asks the user for the length, width, and height of the souvenir; asks the user for the (inner) length, width, and height of your suitcase; and then computes and displays the number of souvenirs that can fit in the suitcase.

7.11 Suppose you are painting the walls in several rooms in your house. To help you decide how much paint to buy, design and write a "wall-paint" program that asks the user for the length, width, and height of a room, and then computes and displays the number of gallons of paint that will be needed for that room. Assume that a gallon of paint will cover 400 square feet of wall surface.

7.12 Body-mass index (BMI) is a simplistic measure that insurance companies sometimes use to calculate a person's health risk. If a person's BMI is less than 18.5 they may be underweight; between 18.5 and 24.9 they may be normal; between 25 and 29.9 they may be overweight; and over 30 they may be obese. Design and write a program to calculate a person's BMI, given his or her weight (in pounds or kilograms) and height (in feet plus inches, or in meters). A person's BMI can be computed using either of the following formulas.

$$BMI = \frac{WeightInPounds}{heightInInches \times heightInInches} \times 703$$

or

$$BMI = \frac{WeightInKilos}{heightInCms \times heightInCms} \times 10000$$

Chapter 8
Types and Expressions

There are two types of people in the world: Those that talk the talk and those that walk the walk. People who walk the walk sometimes talk the talk but most times they don't talk at all, 'cause they walkin'. Now, people who talk the talk, when it comes time for them to walk the walk, you know what they do? They talk people like me into walkin' for them.

KEY (ANTHONY ANDERSON) IN *HUSTLE & FLOW*

There are two kinds of people in the world, those who believe there are two kinds of people in the world and those who don't.

ROBERT BENCHLEY

There are three types of people: Those who see. Those who see when they are shown. Those who never see.

LEONARDO DA VINCI

There are three types of people in the world: those who can count, and those who can't.

ANONYMOUS

There are 10 types of people in the world: those who understand binary and those who don't.

ANONYMOUS

Objectives

After reading this chapter, you should be able to:

- ❑ Use variables and constants
- ❑ Understand the difference between Java's fundamental and class types
- ❑ Build complex Java expressions
- ❑ Better understand and use Java's **`Scanner`** and **`PrintStream`** classes

In the last chapter, we saw that both Alice and Java programming involve sending messages to objects. We also saw that Java uses the type **`double`** to represent real numbers.

In this chapter, we will examine this concept of *type* in greater depth, to see why it is so important in programming. Along the way, we will see how to declare variables and constants, learn how to construct expressions that set their values, learn more about **`printf()`**'s placeholders, and see how to use some of the functions that Java provides.

8.1 Introductory Example: Months from Month Numbers

Suppose we have a friend who teaches English to adults for whom English is not their native language. Our friend tells us that her students are having trouble remembering the English names of the months. She wishes that she had a computer program to help her students recall the names of the months. Being good friends, we volunteer to write such a program!

We start by writing the following user story:

> Our program should display the prompt, "To see the month for a given number, enter a number (1-12):". Our program should then read the month number from the keyboard. It should then use the month number to compute and display the corresponding month abbreviation, with descriptive labels.

Next, we identify the noun phrases in our program.

Noun Phrase	Type of Value	Name
Our program	?	*MonthAbbreviations*
prompt	**`String`**	none
month number	number (**`int`**)	*monthNumber*
the keyboard	**`Scanner`**	*keyboard*
month abbreviation	**`String`**	*monthAbbrev*
descriptive labels	**`String`**	none

Continuing with our design, we identify the verb phrases in our user story:

Verb Phrase	Java Method or Operation
display (various things)	**`System.out.print();`**
read *monthNumber*	**`keyboard.nextInt()`**
compute *monthAbbrev*	**?**
display *monthAbbrev*	**`System.out.println();`**

There are a variety of ways that we might compute *monthAbbrev* from *monthNumber*. One way that does not require us to learn any new statements is to use some of the methods of Java's **`String`** class. The basic idea is to build a **`String`** we will call *monthTable*, containing all of the three-letter month abbreviations. Figure 8-1 shows such a table.

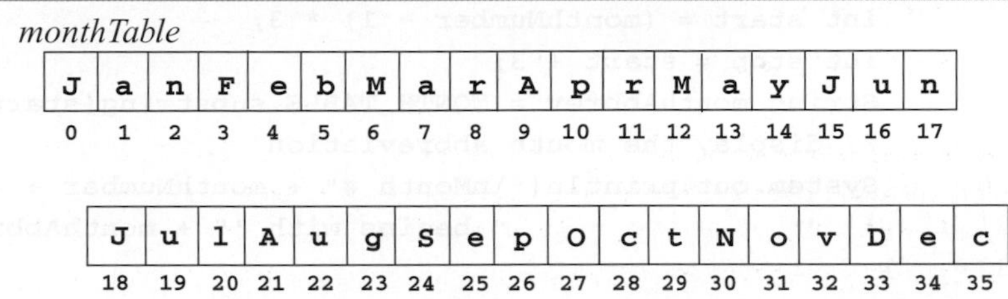

FIGURE 8-1 A table of fixed-size month abbreviations

As can be seen in Figure 8-1, each character in a **`String`** object has a number associated with it. This number is called the character's **index** within the **`String`**. For example, the index of the **`J`** in **`Jan`** is **`0`**, the index of the **`F`** in **`Feb`** is **`3`**, the index of the **`M`** in **`Mar`** is **`6`**, the index of the **`O`** in **`Oct`** is **`27`**, the index of the **`N`** in **`Nov`** is **`30`**, and the index of the **`D`** in **`Dec`** is **`33`**.

Do you see a pattern? The index of the first character in the abbreviation of *monthNumber* is (*monthNumber* - 1) * 3. We can thus use *monthNumber* to compute the index at which the value for *monthAbbrev* begins within *monthTable*.

To extract a copy of the month abbreviation located at index (*monthNumber* - 1) * 3 within *monthTable*, we can send *monthTable* the **`substring()`** message. For example, the message *monthTable*.**`substring(`***0, 3***`)`** will produce the string **`"Jan"`**; the message *monthTable*.**`substring(`***3, 6***`)`** will produce the string **`"Feb"`**; the message *monthTable*.**`substring(`***27, 30***`)`** will produce **`"Oct"`**, and so on. In general, the message *aString*.**`substring(`***start, stop***`)`** produces a copy of the piece of *aString* that begins at index *start* and that ends at index *stop-1*. Since all of the abbreviations in *monthTable* are three characters long, we can use *start*+3 as the *stop* value.

Figure 8-2 presents a Java program that uses this approach to solve the problem.

```
/** MonthAbbreviations.java reads a number from 1-12 and displays
 *    the three-letter abbreviation of the corresponding month.
 */
import java.util.Scanner;

public class MonthAbbreviations {
  public static void main(String[] args) {
   // get the month number
   System.out.println("To see the first three letters of a month,");
   System.out.print(" enter a month number (1-12): ");
   Scanner keyboard = new Scanner(System.in);
   int monthNumber = keyboard.nextInt();
   // compute the month abbreviation
   final String MONTH_TABLE = "JanFebMarAprMayJun" +
                              "JulAugSepOctNovDec";
   int start = (monthNumber - 1) * 3;
   int stop = start + 3;
   String monthAbbrev = MONTH_TABLE.substring(start, stop);
   // display the month abbreviation
   System.out.println("\nMonth #" + monthNumber +
                  " begins with '" + monthAbbrev + "'.");
  }
}
```

FIGURE 8-2 The **MonthAbbreviations** program

Figure 8-3 shows a sample run of this program.

Result:

```
To see the first three letters of a month,
 enter a month number (1-12): 11

Month #11 begins with 'Nov'.
```

FIGURE 8-3 A **MonthAbbreviations** sample run

The program in Figure 8-2 introduces several new Java features, centered around the idea of **type**. In both Alice and Java, every variable has an associated type that is specified when the variable is declared.[1] A variable's type is important because it tells the Java

1. Recall that we introduced declaration statements in Section 7.3.4.

compiler how we intend to use the variable — what kind of values we will store in it, the kind of operations we intend to perform with it, and so on.

Java provides hundreds of predefined types that are useful in solving problems. Java divides these types into two categories:

- The **primitive types** store various kinds of *numbers*, and can be used as "building blocks" to build other types. These types include **`boolean`**, **`char`**, **`int`**, **`double`**, and others.
- The **reference types** store references to *objects*, or instances of classes. Reference types are sometimes called **class types** because they are the names of classes. **`String`**, **`Scanner`**, and **`System`** are all examples of reference types.

There are several differences between these categories. One difference is that there are only eight primitive types in Java, but there are hundreds of reference types. Another difference is that we cannot create new primitive types, but we can create as many reference types as we wish, by building classes. Yet another difference is that the first letter of a primitive type is always lowercase, while the first letter of a reference type is customarily uppercase.

In the rest of this chapter, we will examine these two categories in greater detail.

8.2 Java's Primitive Types

As mentioned above, there are only eight primitive types in Java. Figure 8-4 presents a list of these types, along with information as to how they differ from one another.

Primitive Type	Description	Range of Values
`byte`	small integers	-128 .. 127
`short`	medium integers	-32,768 .. 32,767
`int`	normal integers	-2,147,483,648 .. 2,147,483,647
`long`	large integers	-9,223,372,036,854,775,808 .. 9,223,372,036,854,775,807
`float`	less precise real numbers	± 1.40129846432481707e-45 .. ± 3.40282346638528860e+38
`double`	more precise real numbers	± 4.94065645841246544e-324 .. ± 1.79769313486231570e+308
`boolean`	logical values	**`false, true`**
`char`	single characters	0 .. 65,535

FIGURE 8-4 Java's primitive types

Java's numeric types differ in the magnitude of the values they can store. The reason is that different types use different amounts of memory, so when you declare a variable with a particular type, you are really telling the Java compiler how much memory to associate with the variable.

The smallest unit of memory is the **bit**, which can store a single 0 or 1. You can think of a bit as being like a light switch: when the switch is *off*, that represents 0; when it is *on*, that represents 1. A single bit is all that is needed for a **boolean** variable, since we can use a 0 to represent the value **false** and a 1 to represent the value **true**.[2] 0 and 1 are the two symbols used in the **base-2** or **binary number system**, and the word *bit* is a contraction of ***binary digit***.

By using combinations of bits, we can store numbers larger than 1. For example, if we use 2 bits, there are four different bit patterns we might use to represent the numbers 0 to 3:

00	zero	10	two
01	one	11	three

With 3 bits, there are eight different bit patterns we can use to represent the numbers 0 to 7:

000	zero	100	four
001	one	101	five
010	two	110	six
011	three	111	seven

With N bits, there are 2^N different bit patterns. For example, the **`char`** type uses 16 bits, so it can represent $2^{16} = 65{,}536$ different characters. By contrast, a **`byte`** variable has 8 bits and so can represent just $2^8 = 256$ values. An **`int`** variable has 32 bits, and a **`double`** variable has 64 bits.

A raw value of a given type appearing in a program is called a **literal**. For example, there are only two boolean literals: **`true`** and **`false`**. By contrast, there are many **`int`** literals, such as -5, 0, 12, and so on. Similarly, -2.5, 0.0, and 3.14159 are **`double`** literals. **`'A'`**, **`'1'`**, **`'$'`**, and **`'+'`** are **`char`** literals. We'll discuss literals more when we examine their respective types, below.

While Java provides eight different primitive types, four are most commonly used:

- **`double`**, to store real values
- **`int`**, to store integer values
- **`boolean`**, to store logical values
- **`char`**, to store character values

In the rest of this section, we will focus primarily on these four types.

---

2. Although a single bit is all that is necessary to represent a boolean value, today's computers cannot access individual memory bits quickly. To avoid slowing down a program, most compilers represent boolean variables using the smallest number of bits that can be quickly accessed. On "32-bit" computers, this may be as large as 32 bits!

8.2.1 The **double** Type

As we have seen previously, Java uses the **double** type to represent **real numbers**, that is, numbers that contain a decimal point. Variables of type **double** can be declared as usual:

```
double length = 3.5;
double penalty = -1.5;
```

Numbers in a Java program like **3.5** and **-1.5** are called **fixed-point literals** because the position of the decimal point is fixed within the number. We can visualize such variables as follows:

length	**+3.5**
penalty	**-1.5**

For scientific computing, Java can also represent **scientific notation** values. For example, the speed of light is often given as 2.998×10^8. We can represent such a number in Java using this notation:

```
2.998e8
```

In general, a scientific notation number $A.B \times 10^C$ can be represented in Java as **A.BeC**.

Note that we could represent the same number using either of these equivalent notations:

```
0.2998e9
29.98e7
```

Because the position of the decimal point "floats" within the number depending on the value of the exponent, these kind of values are known as **floating-point literals**. Java treats both fixed-point and floating-point literals as being of type **double**.[3]

3. Java's **float** type uses 32 bits and its **double** type uses 64 bits, so a **double** has about twice the precision of a **float**. If you need to use **float** literals in a program (in situations where memory is limited), append the letter **f** or **F** to a **double** literal. For example, the Java compiler will treat the literals **3.14159F** or **2.998e8f** as **float** values.

Constants

When we need an item in a program, but the program does not change the item's value, we can declare the item to be a **constant** by placing the word **final** before its declaration. For example, the declarations:

```
final double SPEED_OF_LIGHT = 2.998e8;
final double ABSOLUTE_ZERO_CELSIUS = -273.15;
```

declare **SPEED_OF_LIGHT** and **ABSOLUTE_ZERO_CELSIUS** to be constants whose values are **2.998e8** and **-273.15**, respectively. A constant differs from a variable in that its value can be *read*, but *not changed*. For this reason, constants are sometimes called **read-only items**. We might envision the preceding constants as follows:

SPEED_OF_LIGHT	**2.998e8**
ABSOLUTE_ZERO_CELSIUS	**-273.15**

We can use the name of a constant anywhere in a program where we might use its literal. For example, to compute Einstein's formula $e = mc^2$, we might write:

```
double energy = mass * SPEED_OF_LIGHT * SPEED_OF_LIGHT;
```

If we subsequently find that we need greater precision in our calculations, we only have to change the constant declaration:

```
final double SPEED_OF_LIGHT = 2.99792458e8;
```

and all uses of that name throughout the program will automatically use the more precise value.

Another reason to use a constant is to improve a program's **readability**. If we give a constant a name that describes its value, then statements using the constant will be easier to read.

> To distinguish constants from variables, use solely uppercase letters for the name of a constant, and separate words with underscore (_) characters.

Any type of item whose value does not change can be declared a constant. For example, the program in Figure 8-2 declared *monthTable* to be a constant:

```
final String MONTH_TABLE = "JanFebMarAprMayJun" +
                           "JulAugSepOctNovDec";
```

Expressions

An **expression** is a series of operands, operators, objects, and/or messages that combine to produce a value. For example, this is a valid Java expression:

```
6.0 + 5.0 - 4.0 * 3.0 / 2.0
```

because the operands and operators combine to produce the `double` value `5.0`. Likewise, if `a`, `b`, `c`, `d`, and `e` are `double` variables, then this is a valid expression:

```
a / b * c - d + e
```

If `a`'s value is `16`, `b`'s value is `8`, `c`'s value is `4`, `d`'s value is `2`, and `e`'s value is `1`, then this expression produces the value `7`. An expression that produces a `double` value is called a **`double` expression.**

The arithmetic operators: `+`, `-`, `*`, and `/` can be used to perform addition, subtraction, multiplication, and division respectively. These are often used to construct expressions for scientific formulas. To illustrate, Charles's Law relating the volume of a gas to its temperature is:

$$\frac{V_1}{T_1} = \frac{V_2}{T_2}$$

Given any three of these values, we can compute the fourth. For example, how much does a gas expand if we increase its temperature? If we have a value for its original volume (V_1) in a `double` variable named `volume1`, its original temperature (T_1) in a variable named `temperature1`, and the new temperature (T_2) in a variable named `temperature2`, then we can construct this Java expression to compute and store the new volume in a variable named `volume2`:

```
double volume2 = volume1 / temperature1 * temperature2;
```

Assignment Expressions

Suppose that we have been given the problem of computing the sum of three numbers, but we must do it using just two variables. One way to do so is as follows:

```
System.out.print("Enter the first value: ");     // 1
double runningTotal = keyboard.nextDouble();      // 2
System.out.print("Enter the second value: ");    // 3
double nextValue = keyboard.nextDouble();         // 4
runningTotal = runningTotal + nextValue;          // 5
System.out.print("Enter the third value: ");     // 6
nextValue = keyboard.nextDouble();                // 7
runningTotal = runningTotal + nextValue;          // 8
System.out.println("Total: " + runningTotal);    // 9
```

This solution initializes the variable **runningTotal** with the first value, and then uses it to keep a running total as the other values are read. The second variable **nextValue** is used to read in the other values. If the three values being entered are **33.3**, **22.2**, and **11.1**, then following the performance of the statement on line 4 above, these two variables are as follows:

runningTotal	33.3
nextValue	22.2

The next statement on line 5 is new to us:

```
runningTotal = runningTotal + nextValue;          // 5
```

This is called an **assignment statement**, because the = operator *assigns* the sum of **runningTotal** and **nextValue** back to the variable **runningTotal**. Thus, the = operator is called the **assignment operator**. After this statement is performed, the variables change as follows:

runningTotal	55.5
nextValue	22.2

After the prompt for input on line 6, another assignment statement appears on line 7:

```
nextValue = keyboard.nextDouble();                // 7
```

After the user enters the third value (**11.1**), this assignment statement changes the variables as follows:

runningTotal	55.5
nextValue	11.1

Line 8 also contains an assignment statement:

```
runningTotal = runningTotal + nextValue;          // 8
```

This statement updates **runningTotal**, changing the variables as follows:

runningTotal	66.6
nextValue	11.1

The assignment operator is thus the way we change the value of a variable. The general pattern for the assignment statement is as follows:

```
variableName = expression;
```

where ***variableName*** is the variable whose value we are changing, and ***expression*** is any expression that produces a value whose type is compatible with that of ***variableName***.

Java's Math Class

In addition to the arithmetic operators, Java provides a rich set of mathematical functions that can be used to build more complex expressions. These functions are defined as **Math** class methods — messages one sends to the **Math** class. Figure 8-5 presents a complete list of these methods. Unless noted otherwise, method arguments are **double** values.

Math Method	Description
Math.abs(*v*)	Returns the absolute value of ***v***, which can be a **double**, **float**, **int**, or **long**
Math.acos(*v*)	Returns the angle whose cosine is ***v***
Math.asin(*v*)	Returns the angle whose sine is ***v***
Math.atan(*v*)	Returns the angle whose tangent is ***v***
Math.atan2(*y*, *x*)	Converts the rectangular coordinates **(*x*,*y*)** to polar coordinates **(*r*, *theta*)**, and returns the ***theta*** portion
Math.cbrt(*v*)	Returns the cube root of ***v***
Math.ceil(*v*)	Returns the smallest **double** value that is an integer greater than or equal to ***v***
Math.cos(*v*)	Returns the cosine of the angle ***v***
Math.cosh(*v*)	Returns the hyperbolic cosine of ***v***
Math.exp(*v*)	Returns ***e*** to the power ***v***, where ***e*** is Euler's number
Math.expm1(*v*)	Returns e^v-1
Math.floor(*v*)	Returns the largest **double** value that is an integer less than or equal to ***v***
Math.hypot(*x*,*y*)	Returns the square root of $(x^2 + y^2)$
Math.IEEEremainder (*v1*, *v2*)	Returns the remainder of **v1/v2**
Math.log(*v*)	Returns the natural logarithm (base ***e***) of ***v***

continued

Math Method	Description
`Math.log10(v)`	Returns the base-10 logarithm of ***v***
`Math.log1p(v)`	Returns the natural logarithm of the value `(v+1)`
`Math.max(x,y)`	Returns the maximum of ***x*** and ***y***, which can be **`double`**, **`float`**, **`int`**, or **`long`** values
`Math.min(x,y)`	Returns the minimum of ***x*** and ***y***, which can be **`double`**, **`float`**, **`int`**, or **`long`** values
`Math.pow(x,y)`	Returns the value ***x*** to the power ***y***
`Math.random()`	Returns a random value ***x***; `0.0 <= x` and `x < 1.0`
`Math.rint(v)`	Returns a **`double`** value that is the integer closest to ***v***
`Math.round(v)`	If ***v*** is a **`double`**, returns the **`long`** closest to ***v*** If ***v*** is a **`float`**, returns the **`int`** closest to ***v***
`Math.signum(v)`	Returns `0.0` if ***v*** is zero; `1.0` if ***v*** is positive; and `-1.0` if ***v*** is negative. ***v*** may be a **`double`** or a **`float`**
`Math.sin(v)`	Returns the sine of angle ***v***
`Math.sinh(v)`	Returns the hyperbolic sine of ***v***
`Math.sqrt(v)`	Returns the rounded positive square root of ***v***
`Math.tan(v)`	Returns the tangent of angle ***v***
`Math.toDegrees(v)`	Returns the degrees equivalent to angle ***v*** (in radians)
`Math.toRadians(v)`	Returns the radians equivalent to angle ***v*** (in degrees)
`Math.ulp(v)`	Returns the "degenerate" **u**nits in the **l**ast **p**lace of ***v***; the distance between ***v*** and the next largest **`double`** value

FIGURE 8-5 Functions from Java's **`Math`** class

Java's **`Math`** class also defines two constants that are useful for scientific computing:

- **`Math.E`**, the closest-possible **`double`** approximation of Euler's number *e*
- **`Math.PI`**, the closest-possible **`double`** approximation of π

To illustrate the use of the **Math** class, suppose we must write a program to compute the volume of a planet, given its radius. Since planets are roughly spherical, the formula for the volume of a sphere will provide a reasonable approximation:

$$volume = \frac{4}{3} \times \pi \times radius^3$$

Assuming that we have read the planet's radius into a variable named **radius**, we can write the Java equivalent of this formula as follows:

```
double volume = 4.0 / 3.0 * Math.PI * Math.pow(radius, 3.0);
```

The **Math** class is a part of the **java.lang** package, so it need not be imported using the **import** statement.

It is worth mentioning that Java also provides a separate **StrictMath** class, that provides the same functionality as the **Math** class. The difference is that computations using the **StrictMath** class are guaranteed to produce the same results on different platforms (for example, MacOS, Linux, Windows, and so on). Results computed using the **Math** class may differ slightly from one platform to another.

8.2.2 The `int` Type

Some quantities are best expressed as **integers**, or whole numbers that can be positive, zero, or negative. For example, a person's age, IQ, waist size, house number, and post office box number are usually given as integers. Integers are natural to use when counting things that are indivisible; such as the number of animals at the zoo, children in your family, floors in a building, and so on.

Java uses the type **int** to represent integers. That is, if we use whole numbers like **0**, **1**, **5**, **10**, **2000**, or **-3** in a Java program, Java treats such numbers as **int literals.**[4]

The program in Figure 8-2 used the **int** type to store the (1-12) month number:

```
int monthNumber = keyboard.nextInt();
```

Besides declaring an **int** variable, this declaration uses the **Scanner** class's **nextInt()** method to retrieve the next integer from the keyboard.[5] The program then declares two other **int** variables:

```
int start = (monthNumber - 1) * 3;
int stop = start + 3;
```

4. Java's **byte**, **short**, **int**, and **long** type use 8, 16, 32, and 64 bits respectively. If you need to use a **long** literal in a program, append the letter **l** or **L** to an **int** literal. For example, **-15L** or **32L** are valid **long** literals. Also, Java treats literals that begin with **0** as *octal* (base-8) literals, so the innocent-looking literal **010** is actually 8_{10}. Literals that begin with **0x** are taken to be *hexadecimal* (base-16) numbers, so **0x10** is 16_{10}.

5. The **Scanner** class provides methods to retrieve most of the primitive types: **nextBoolean()**, **nextByte()**, **nextDouble()**, **nextFloat()**, **nextInt()**, **nextLong()**, and **nextShort()**.

In the sample run shown in Figure 8-3, we might envision these variables as follows:

monthNumber	11
start	30
stop	33

As shown above, we can build **int** expressions the same way we built **double** expressions. Integer addition, subtraction, and multiplication all work as we might expect, but **integer division** is tricky. To see why, remember back to your primary school days, when you first learned about division. How did you do division before you knew about decimal numbers — when whole numbers were all you knew? I can remember my teacher saying something like this:

3 goes into 2 zero times with a remainder of 2.

3 goes into 3 one time with a remainder of 0.

3 goes into 4 one time with a remainder of 1.

3 goes into 5 one time with a remainder of 2.

3 goes into 6 two times with a remainder of 0.

3 goes into 7 two times with a remainder of 1.

and so on. This is the way integer division works. Unlike division with real numbers, integer division produces *two* distinct results: the **quotient**, and the **remainder**. In Java, using the / operator with two integer operands produces the *quotient* of the division. For example:

```
2 / 3 produces 0        5 / 3 produces 1
3 / 3 produces 1        6 / 3 produces 2
4 / 3 produces 1        7 / 3 produces 2
```

just as my third grade teacher taught me.

Be careful when performing integer division, because given two integer operands, the / operator only produces the quotient of the division.

So if / produces the quotient, how can we get the remainder? To get the *remainder* of an integer division, Java provides the **modulus** or **remainder** (%) operator. For example:

```
2 % 3 produces 2        5 % 3 produces 2
3 % 3 produces 0        6 % 3 produces 0
4 % 3 produces 1        7 % 3 produces 1
```

The modulus operator is surprisingly useful. As a simple illustration, suppose that we have an **int** variable named **num** and we want to know if its value is even or odd. The expression:

```
num % 2
```

produces **1** if **num** is odd, and produces **0** if **num** is even.

Integer Assignment

We can use the assignment operator (**=**) to change the values of **int** variables using the same general pattern we saw before:

```
variableName = expression;
```

For example, if we declare a variable named **count** and initialize it to zero:

```
int count = 0;
```

then we might picture it as follows:

count	0

To add one to this variable, we can use an assignment statement:

```
count = count + 1;
```

and the value of **count** will increase by one. This is known as *incrementing* the variable.

count	1

Assignment to an **int** variable works fine so long as the ***expression*** being assigned produces an **int**. However, care must be taken when mixing **int** and **double** values in the same program. If the type of ***expression*** is not compatible with the type of ***variableName***, the Java compiler will generate an error when it processes this statement. For example, if we write:

```
double decimalNumber;
decimalNumber = 11;  // assign int to double variable - ok
```

then the Java compiler will convert the **int** literal **11** to the double value **11.0** before doing the assignment. But if we write:

```
int wholeNumber;
wholeNumber = 11.1;  // assign double to int variable - error
```

then the Java compiler generates this error:

```
Type mismatch: cannot convert from double to int
```

The problem is that the **double** type has a decimal part and the **int** type doesn't, so Java refuses to perform this conversion to prevent information from being lost. However when asked to assign an **int** value to a **double** variable, no information can be lost when the Java compiler converts the whole number to a real.

Assignment Shortcuts

We have seen that to add one to a variable, we can use an assignment statement like:

```
count = count + 1;
```

This kind of situation (in which we need to *increment* a variable) occurs so often that Java provides a special **increment operator** for it. Instead of the preceding statement, we can write either:

```
count++;
```

or

```
++count;
```

and Java will add 1 to the value of **count**.[6] Java also provides a **decrement operator** (**--**) to conveniently subtract 1 from a variable.

Another common operation is to add a value greater than 1 to a variable. For example, to increase **count** by 2, we could write:

```
count = count + 2;
```

Java provides another shortcut for this and similar operations. We can accomplish the same thing by writing:

```
count += 2;
```

More generally, the statement:

```
variableName += expression;
```

6. When used as a statement, the prefix (**++count;**) and postfix (**count++;**) forms are equivalent. However when used as an expression — for example, **i = ++count;** or **j = count++**; — the prefix form produces **count**'s new value, while the postfix form produces **count**'s original value. For example, if **count**'s value is 0, the statement **i = ++count;** will set **i** to **count**'s new value 1, but the statement **j = count++;** will set **j** to **count**'s old value 0.

will add the value produced by ***expression*** to ***variableName***. Java supports a similar shortcut for each of the arithmetic operators (**+=**, **-=**, ***=**, **/=**, **%=**).[7] For example, to multiply the value in **count** by 10 and store the result back into **count**, we can use this statement:

```
count *= 10;
```

Similarly, to divide **count** by 2 and store the result back into **count**, we can use this statement:

```
count /= 2;
```

8.2.3 The char Type

To store a *single* character efficiently, Java provides the **char** type.[8] A **char** variable can be declared in the usual way, for example:

```
char middleInitial = 'C';
```

We might envision such variables as we have seen before:

middleInitial	'C'

As indicated, a **char** literal consists of a single letter, digit, or other keyboard symbol enclosed within *single quotes*. For example, the following are all distinct **char** literals:

```
'A', 'a', '2', '#', '+', '{', '.'
```

Trying to place multiple characters between the single quotes (such as **'ABC'**) usually produces a compilation error.

However, suppose we wanted to form a literal of the single quote character? For this and similar situations, Java provides **escape sequences**, consisting of a backslash followed by one or more additional characters. Figure 8-6 shows the Java escape sequences.

Escape Sequence	Description
`\b`	Backspace
`\t`	Horizontal tab
`\n`	Newline (Line feed)

continued

7. Shortcuts are also provided for the bit-shift operators (**<<** and **>>**), which are not covered in this text.
8. Java's **String** class is designed to store *multiple* characters efficiently. Because of the extra information needed to store multiple characters, a **String** is not a very efficient way to store *individual* characters.

Escape Sequence	Description
`\r`	Carriage return
`\"`	Double quote
`\'`	Single quote
`\\`	Backslash
`\uhhhh`	Unicode character with hexadecimal code ***hhhh***

FIGURE 8-6 The **char** escape sequences

Thus, the **char** literal `'\''` represents the single quote character. Similarly, `'\t'` represents the TAB character, and `'\n'` represents a newline on many systems. These escape sequences can also be used in **String** literals, as we shall see in Section 8.3.

At the end of Figure 8-6, we see the phrase **Unicode character**. To see what this means, let's return again to primary school. Suppose we want to pass a note to our friend on the other side of the room via our classmates, but we want to prevent any of our classmates from reading the note. One way to solve this problem is to agree with our friend to use a *code*, in which we substitute a number for each letter. If we agree to use the numbers 65 through 90 for A through Z, and the number 32 for spaces, then we could send our friend this *coded message*:

```
77-69-69-84-32-77-69-32-65-70-84-69-82-32-83-67-72-79-79-76
```

from which our friend could *decode* our ultra-important, super-secret message:

```
MEET ME AFTER SCHOOL
```

This is the idea behind Unicode, a standard code that Java uses to represent characters. Each letter, digit, or symbol is represented by a different number using 16 bits, so that it can represent 2^{16} = 65,536 different characters.

The Unicode escape sequence lets a Java **char** represent the symbols used in most of the world's languages. To do so, we just have to look up the (hexadecimal/base-16) number for that symbol at *www.unicode.org*, and then use that code in the Unicode escape sequence shown in Figure 8-6. For example, the Unicode hexadecimal number for the euro symbol (€) is **20ac**, so the escape sequence `'\u20ac'` is a Java **char** literal for this symbol. Thus, in Section 7.2.5, we could have used the following format string:

```
System.out.printf("$%.2f => \u20ac%.2f", dollars, euros);
```

Then the program would display the dollar and euro symbols when we run it:

```
How many dollars do you want to convert? 100.01
What is the euros-per-dollar exchange rate? 0.84973
$100.01 => €84.98
```

Similarly, the author once lived on a street named Þingholtsstræti in Reykjavik, Iceland. This street name has two symbols not found in the English alphabet: the *thorn* character (Þ, the "th" sound in the word "this") and the *ae* character (æ, an "eye" sound). The Unicode hexadecimal numbers for these characters are **00de** and **00e6** respectively, so the statement:

```
System.out.println("\u00deingholtsstr\u00e6ti");
```

displays the name correctly:

```
Þingholtsstræti
```

Thanks to Unicode, Java can display the symbols used in most of the world's languages.[9] Java's support for non-English languages is a feature that has made it popular around the world.

8.2.4 The `boolean` Type

Java's **boolean** type is in some ways its simplest type, as it has just two literals: **false** and **true**. The **boolean** type is useful for writing expressions that capture logic, so that **boolean** expressions are often called **logical expressions**.

Logical expressions are used primarily to control the flow of execution through a program. We will use logical expressions primarily in Chapters 10 and later, but we provide a short introduction to them here.

Relational Operators

Java provides six **relational operators** that produce **boolean** values. These operators are listed in Figure 8-7.

Relational Operator	Produces
`x == y`	`true` if `x` and `y` contain the same values; `false` otherwise.
`x != y`	`true` if `x` and `y` contain different values; `false` otherwise.

continued

9. You may have to install special fonts on your computer in order for some characters to display correctly. Google for *Unicode fonts* and your language to find the ones you need.

Relational Operator	Produces
`x < y`	**true** if **x**'s value is less than **y**'s value; **false** otherwise.
`x > y`	**true** if **x**'s value is greater than **y**'s value; **false** otherwise.
`x <= y`	**true** if **x**'s value is less than or equal to **y**'s value; **false** otherwise.
`x >= y`	**true** if **x**'s value is greater than or equal to **y**'s value; **false** otherwise.

FIGURE 8-7 The relational operators

The relational operators allow us to build simple logical expressions. For example, to determine whether or not a person is a senior citizen, we could use the statements:

```
boolean seniorStatus = age >= 65;
System.out.println("Senior citizen? " + seniorStatus);
```

This will display **Senior citizen?** followed by **true** if **age** is greater than or equal to 65; otherwise it displays **Senior citizen?** followed by **false**.

The Logical Operators

Sometimes one needs to construct more complex logical expressions. For such situations, Java provides three **logical operators**, which take **boolean** values as their operands and produce a **boolean** value. These are shown in Figure 8-8.

Logical Operator	Produces
`a && b`	**true** if **a** and **b** are both **true**; **false** otherwise.
`a || b`	**true** if **a** or **b** is **true**; **false** otherwise.
`!b`	**true** if **b** is **false**; **false** if **b** is **true**.

FIGURE 8-8 The logical operators

For example, water is in its liquid state when its temperature is between 0 and 100 Celsius. If we read a Celsius water temperature into a variable named **waterTemp**, the statements:

```
boolean liquidWater = 0.0 < waterTemp && waterTemp < 100.0;
System.out.println("liquid? " + liquidWater);
```

would display **true** if the the water is in a liquid state; otherwise they will display **false**. That is, if the water is ice, then the subexpression **0.0 < waterTemp** will be **false**, so the entire expression will produce **false**. Similarly, if the water is steam, then the subexpression **waterTemp < 100.0** will produce **false**, making the entire expression **false**. Note that we cannot perform this computation by writing the following:

```
boolean liquidWater = 0.0 < waterTemp < 100.0;   // ERROR!
```

The Java compiler will generate an error because the rightmost **<** operator is trying to compare a **boolean** value (the result of **0.0 < waterTemp**) to a **double** value (**100.0**).

As another example, electromagnetic radiation is invisible to our eyes if its wavelength is less than 400 nanometers or greater than 700 nanometers. If an instrument measures the wavelength of some radiation and stores it in a variable named **wavelength**, then the statements:

```
boolean invisible = wavelength < 400 || wavelength > 700;
System.out.println("not visible? " + invisible);
```

will display **true** if the radiation is outside the 400–700 nanometer range; **false** otherwise.

Figure 8-9 summarizes the behavior of the logical operators with a **truth table**: a table showing the value produced by an operator for each possible combination of operands.

a	b	a && b	a || b	!a
false	false	false	false	true
false	true	false	true	true
true	false	false	true	false
true	true	true	true	false

FIGURE 8-9 Truth table for logical operators

8.3 Reference Types

At the beginning of Section 8.2, we saw a number of differences between primitive types and reference types. We begin this section with two more.

8.3.1 Reference Variable Initialization

One difference is in how we *initialize* variables of reference types. To initialize reference type variables, we usually create an object using the **new** operator. For example, the program in Figure 8-2 used the following declaration to create a **Scanner** object and store a reference to it in the variable named **keyboard**:

```
Scanner keyboard = new Scanner(System.in);
```

The **new** operation asks Java's system to allocate memory for an object of the indicated type, and then returns a reference to that object.[10] Drawing this reference as an arrow, we might envision the result as follows:

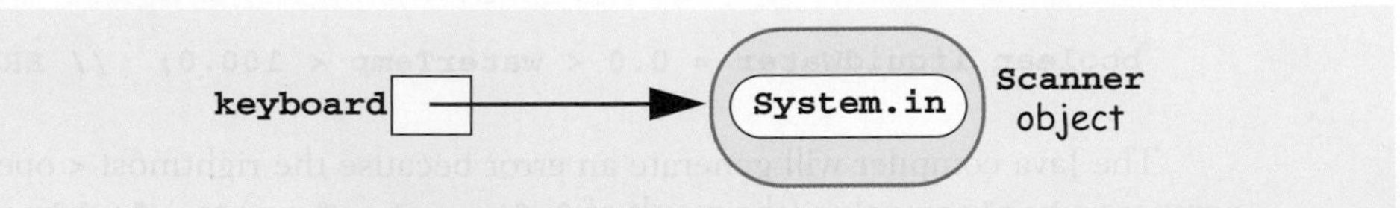

A reference type variable thus stores a reference to an object, not the object itself. By contrast, when the program in Figure 8-2 declares primitive type variables **start** and **stop**:

```
int start = (monthNumber - 1) * 3;
int stop = start + 3;
```

the primitive type values are stored *within* the variable. When **monthNumber** is 11, we can envision these variables as follows:

start	30
stop	33

Most reference types require the **new** operation to create an object, but the **String** type provides a special shortcut. The Java compiler treats a **String** declaration statement:

```
String tongueTwister = "Unique New York"; // say it fast 5 times
```

as a shorthand for the more verbose statement:

```
String tongueTwister = new String("Unique New York");
```

10. In programming, the word reference means *address*, so a reference variable stores the address of an object.

In each case, the result is the same; a new **String** is created with the indicated value, and its reference is stored in the **String** variable:

The `null` Initialization

Reference variables can also be set to a special value **null**:

```
String tongueTwister = null;
```

This initializes the variable to a special "zero reference" that we might visualize as follows:

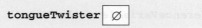

tongueTwister ∅

The word **null** thus has a special meaning:

*A reference type variable whose value is **null** does not refer to any object.*

This allows us to use the equality or inequality operators to test whether or not a reference type variable refers to an object. The statement:

```
System.out.println("Refers to an object? " + tongueTwister != null);
```

will display **true** if **tongueTwister** refers to an object; otherwise, it will display **false**.

8.3.2 Sending Messages

Another important difference between primitive and reference types is that reference types are *classes* that contain *methods*; primitive types are not classes and so do not contain methods. A consequence of this difference is this:

To compute with reference types, we send messages to objects.

For example, the program in Figure 8-2 sends a **Scanner** object the **nextInt()** message:

```
Scanner keyboard = new Scanner(System.in);
int monthNumber = keyboard.nextInt();
```

In this statement, we are sending the **nextInt()** message to the **Scanner** object referenced by **keyboard**. We might visualize the situation as follows:

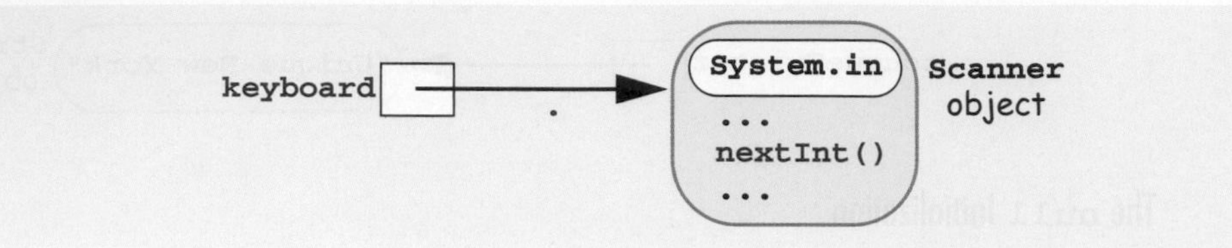

The variable named **keyboard** contains a reference to a **Scanner** object that, as an instance of class **Scanner**, contains a **nextInt()** method. The expression **keyboard.nextInt()** thus invokes the **nextInt()** method in that **Scanner** object. This is generally how we compute with reference type variables; a statement with the form:

```
referenceVariable.methodName()
```

is sending the message named ***methodName()*** to the object to which ***referenceVariable*** refers, not to ***referenceVariable*** itself.

Because reference type variables are the means by which we access objects, a reference type variable is sometimes called a **handle**. In the preceding diagram, **keyboard** is a handle for the **Scanner** object containing **System.in**.

Note that by contrast, we cannot send messages to primitive type variables, because their types are not classes. Put differently, primitive type values do not contain any methods that would allow them to respond to messages.

Objects and Messages

Since computing with reference types is sending messages to objects, the following statement is true:

> **To use a reference type, we must know the messages we can send to its objects.**

In Alice, the messages we can send to an object appear in the *details area* when we highlight that object. In Java, there are two ways to find out what messages we can send to an object:

1. In your integrated development environment (IDE), if you type the name of a handle and then a period to indicate you want to send a message, many IDEs will display a

drop-down menu from which you can choose the message you want to send via that handle. Figure 8-10 illustrates this capability using Eclipse:

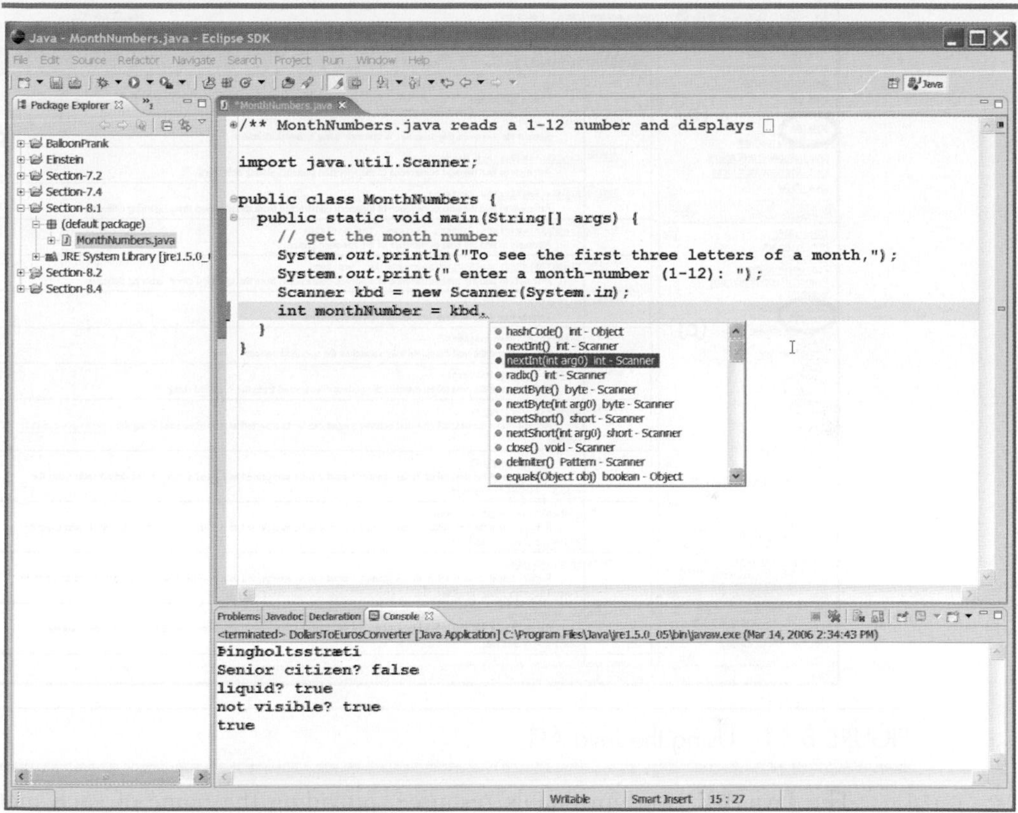

FIGURE 8-10 Using an IDE's drop-down menu

This is very useful when you know you need a method but you cannot remember its exact name. If you can recognize it on the menu, choose it and the IDE will invoke it for you.

2. Look up the object's class in Sun's Java **application programming interface** (API).[11] As shown in Figure 8-11, the Java API organizes Java's classes by package. For example, to find all of the messages that we can send to the `Scanner` class, we (a) navigate to the API in a Web browser; (b) scroll down to the `java.util` package in the package list (upper-left) pane; (c) scroll down to the `Scanner` class in the package (lower-left) pane; and then (d) scroll down until we find the list of methods for that class in the class (right-hand) pane.

11. A link to the API for the latest version of Java can be found at `http://java.sun.com/reference/api/`.

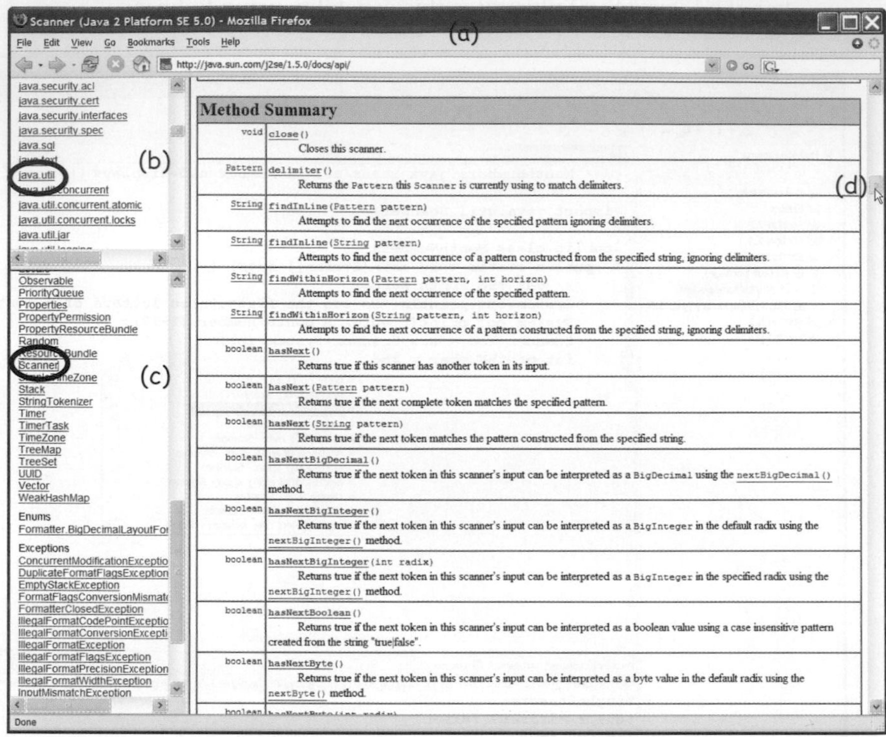

FIGURE 8-11 Using the Java API

The Java API is an invaluable resource, providing the name of each method, any parameters it requires, what type of value it returns, and many other details. Clicking on the name of the method in the *Method Summary* area takes us to a detailed description of that method. Instead of having to remember the details of thousands of methods in Java's hundreds of classes, we can just look them up in the API! If you frequently use a method from a particular class, you will naturally come to remember it. If you forget its details, you can always look it up again. Practice using the Java API. If you bookmark it in your browser, its wealth of information will always be at your fingertips.

Messages and `null`

Since it is *objects* that respond to messages, the following should be evident:

> Sending a message to a handle whose value is **`null`** produces an error.

For example, suppose we were to initialize the **`keyboard`** variable to **`null`**:

```
Scanner keyboard = null;
```

If we then try to send it the **nextInt()** message, we will get an error, because **keyboard** does not refer to a **Scanner** object that can respond to the **nextInt()** message:

keyboard ∅

On our system, trying to do this generates the following error message:

```
Exception in thread "main" java.lang.NullPointerException
```

If you see an error message containing **NullPointerException**, a statement in your program is trying to send a message via a handle whose value is **null**.

Now that we have seen some of the major differences between the primitive and reference types, let us look at some of the reference types in greater detail.

8.3.3 The String Type

As we have seen, the **String** type is used to store sequences of characters. To illustrate, suppose we have these declarations:

```
String lastName      = "Cat";
char   middleInitial = 'E';
String firstName     = "Alan";
String goesBy = firstName;
```

We might envision these variables as follows:

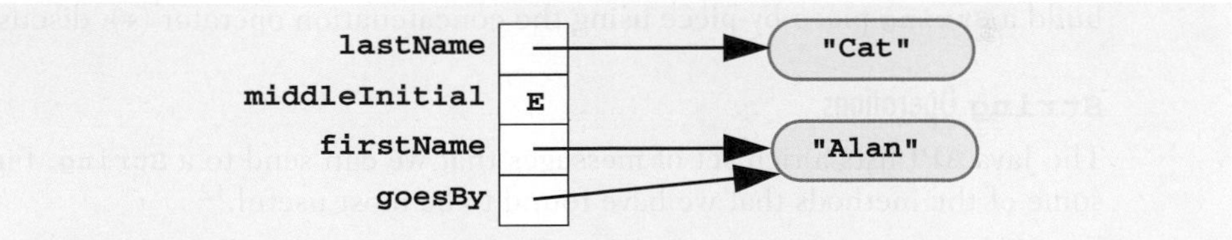

As indicated, different **String** variables can refer to the same **String** object! If we were to subsequently change the value of **goesBy** with a **String** assignment statement:

```
goesBy = "Al";
```

then the picture would change accordingly, since **"Al"** is a new **String** object:

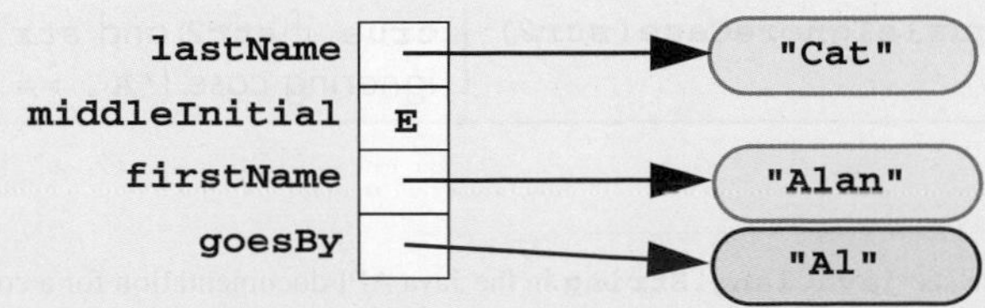

As can be seen in these examples, a **String** literal consists of a pair of double quotes (**"** and **"**) surrounding zero or more characters.

The use of double quotes serves to distinguish **String** literals from **char** literals. It also means that in Java, **"E"** and **'E'** are completely different things!

Escape sequences can also be used in **String** literals. The program in Figure 8-2 used the **\n** escape sequence within a **String** in the statement:

```
System.out.println("\nMonth #" + monthNumber +
                   " begins with '" + monthAbbrev + "'.");
```

All of the escape sequences listed in Figure 8-6 can be used within **String** literals.

The null and Empty Strings

Both of the following are valid **String** handle declarations:

```
String nullString = null;
String emptyString = "";
```

The first statement declares a variable whose value is **null**; the second declares a variable whose value is the reference to a **String** containing zero characters:

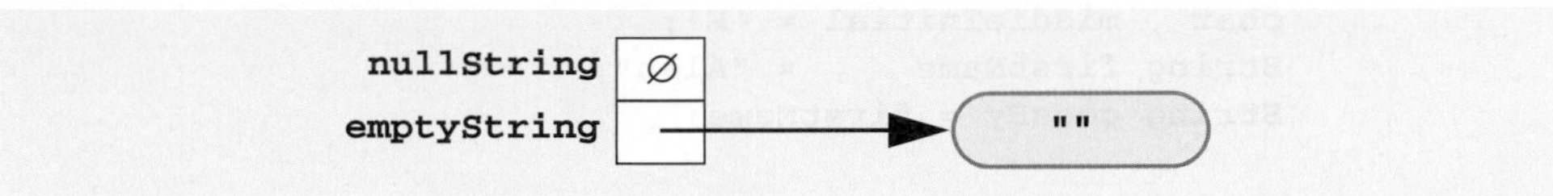

The empty **String** is sometimes a useful initial value, such as when we need to build a **String** piece-by-piece using the concatenation operator (**+**), discussed below.

String Operations

The Java API lists a rich set of messages that we can send to a **String**. Figure 8-12 lists some of the methods that we have found to be most useful.[12]

String Method	Returns
***str*.charAt(*i*)**	the **char** located at index ***i*** within ***str***
***str*.endsWith(*str2*)**	**true**, if ***str2*** is the suffix of **str**; **false** otherwise
***str*.equals(*str2*)**	**true**, if **str2** and ***str*** contain the same characters considering case (**'A' != 'a'**); **false** otherwise
***str*.equalsIgnoreCase(*str2*)**	**true**, if **str2** and ***str*** contain the same characters ignoring case (**'A' == 'a'**); **false** otherwise

continued

12. Please see **java.lang.String** in the Java API documentation for a complete list of the **String** methods.

String Method	Returns
str.indexOf(ch)	the index of the first occurrence of **char ch** within **str**; **-1** if not present
str.indexOf(str2)	the index at which the first occurrence of **String str2** begins within **str**; **-1** if not present
str.lastIndexOf(ch)	the index of the last occurrence of **char ch** within **str**; **-1** if not present
str.lastIndexOf(str2)	the index at which the last occurrence of **str2** begins within **str**; **-1** if not present
str.length()	the number of characters in **str**
str.startsWith(str2)	**true**, if **str2** is the prefix of **str**; **false** otherwise
str.substring(start, stop)	a copy of the portion of **str** that begins at index **start** and that ends at index **stop-1**
str.toLowerCase()	a copy of **str** containing only lowercase characters
str.toUpperCase()	a copy of **str** containing only uppercase characters
str.trim()	a copy of **str**, minus any leading or trailing spaces
String.valueOf(b)	the **String** equivalent of **boolean** value **b**
String.valueOf(c)	the **String** equivalent of **char** value **c**
String.valueOf(d)	the **String** equivalent of **double** value **d**
String.valueOf(i)	the **String** equivalent of **int** value **i**
String.valueOf(o)	the **String** equivalent of the **Object** named **o**

FIGURE 8-12 Some of the **String** methods

To illustrate the use of these methods, suppose we have the following declaration:

```
String lastName = "Cat";
```

Since each character in a **String** has an index, and the index of the first character is always 0, the statement:

```
char lastInitial = lastName.charAt(0);
```

will set **lastInitial** to the **char** value **'C'**. Similarly, the statement:

```
System.out.println( lastName.length() );
```

will display the value `3`. As these examples show, most of the methods in Figure 8-12 are **instance methods** — messages that must be sent to a `String` *object* (that is, an instance of a `String`) via a handle.

The last five methods in Figure 8-12 are **class methods** — messages that must be sent to the `String` *class*, not a `String` object. These five methods are used to convert primitive type values into the corresponding `String` values. To illustrate, the statement:

```
String PI_AS_STRING = String.valueOf(Math.PI);
```

will initialize `PI_AS_STRING` as a handle to a `String` whose characters are the *digits* of `PI`:

```
PI_AS_STRING [ ]------> ("3.141592653589793")
```

The important thing to see is that instance methods are messages that one sends to an object, while class methods are messages that one sends to the class. In the Java API (and elsewhere), class methods are indicated by the special word `static`; for example:

```
static String valueOf(double d);
```

A method without the word `static` is an instance method.[13]

Concatenation

When used with numeric types like `double` or `int`, the plus symbol (`+`) performs *addition*. However when used with the `String` type, the plus symbol performs *concatenation*. For example, the expression:

```
"en" + "list"
```

produces the `String` value `"enlist"`, while the expression:

```
"list" + "en"
```

produces the `String` value `"listen"`. Concatenation thus takes two `String` operands and produces a `String` consisting of the first operand followed by the second operand. For example, if we have these statements:

```
String word = "good";
word = word + "bye";
```

13. Recall that a program's `main()` method is defined using the word `static`. This indicates that `main()` is a *class method*. When you run your program, Java responds by sending the message `main()` to your program class!

then the first statement initializes **word** as the handle for the **String** object **"good"**:

The second statement builds a second **String** consisting of **"good" + "bye"** and stores its reference in **word**:

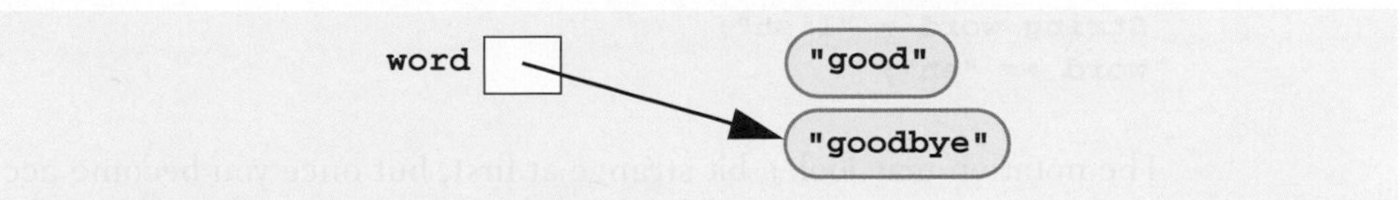

Once there is no handle to an object like **"good"**, a Java component called the **garbage collector** reclaims it, so that its memory can be reused by other objects.

Concatenation can be used with other types besides **String**. So long as one of the operands to **+** is a **String**, the **+** symbol will convert the other operand to a **String** — even if it is a numeric primitive type — and then concatenate the two **String** values. This is why we can write statements like this one from Figure 8-2:

```
System.out.println( "\nMonth #" + monthNumber +
                    " begins with '" + monthAbbrev + "'." );
```

The first **+** converts the **int** value in **monthNumber** (say, **11**) to the corresponding **String** value (**"11"**) and then concatenates it to **"\nMonth #"**, producing **"\nMonth #11"**. The second **+** concatenates **" begins with '"** to that **String**, producing **"\nMonth #11 begins with '"**. The third **+** concatenates the value referred to by **monthAbbrev** (say, **"Nov"**) to that **String**, producing **"\nMonth #11 begins with 'Nov"**. The final **+** concatenates **"'."** to that **String**, producing **"\nMonth #11 begins with 'Nov'."**. This **String** is then passed as the argument to the **println()** message, which is then sent to **System.out**.

The Concatenation-Assignment Shortcut

Previously, we saw that we can write statements like this:

```
String word = "list";
word = word + "en";
```

This kind of situation, in which we have to write a statement of the form:

```
someString = someString + someOtherString;
```

is another surprisingly common task. It is needed so often, Java provides a special **concatenation-assignment shortcut** (`+=`) that eliminates the need to type the variable name twice. Using this shortcut, we can type:

```
someString += someOtherString;
```

and achieve the same result. Using this, we can revise the preceding statements as follows:

```
String word = "list";
word += "en";
```

The notation may look a bit strange at first, but once you become accustomed to it, it is a very convenient way to combine the two operations (`=` and `+`) into one (`+=`).

8.3.4 Performing Input and Output

The `Scanner` Class

In Chapter 7, and again in Section 8.1, we saw that Java's `Scanner` class can be used to read primitive type values from the keyboard. For example, the program in Figure 8-2 uses the statements:

```
Scanner keyboard = new Scanner(System.in);
int monthNumber = keyboard.nextInt();
```

to read a whole number from the keyboard into the `int` variable named `monthNumber`. Figure 8-13 shows some of the `Scanner` class methods for reading values from the keyboard, using a `Scanner` variable named ***keyboard***.

Scanner Method	Reads and Returns
keyboard.next()	a word (String) from *keyboard*
keyboard.nextBoolean()	a boolean (true or false) value from *keyboard*
keyboard.nextByte()	a byte (small integer) value from *keyboard*
keyboard.nextDouble()	a double (large real) value from *keyboard*
keyboard.nextFloat()	a float (small real) value from *keyboard*
keyboard.nextInt()	an int (normal integer) value from *keyboard*

continued

Scanner Method	Reads and Returns
keyboard.nextLong()	a long (large integer) value from *keyboard*
keyboard.nextShort()	a short (medium integer) value from *keyboard*
keyboard.nextLine()	a String value from *keyboard*

FIGURE 8-13 **Scanner** methods for reading primitive types

As can be seen in Figure 8-13, most of the primitive types have their own **Scanner** methods, allowing values of their types to be read conveniently.[14]

The PrintStream Class

Another common task is to display a value on the screen. We have seen that we can do so by sending **print()**, **println()**, or **printf()** messages to **System.out**. The type of **System.out** is a reference type called **PrintStream** from the package **java.io**. As with other reference types, there are many messages we can send to a **PrintStream**, and we encourage you to examine the Java API to see a complete list.

The **PrintStream** API page lists multiple versions of the **print()** method: one for displaying **boolean** values, one for **char** values, one for **double** values, and so on. In programming terminology, we say that the name **print()** is **overloaded**, meaning the name has multiple definitions. When we send a message to an object that has multiple definitions of that method, the Java compiler uses the type of value we pass with the method to determine which method to invoke. Thus, when we write:

```
System.out.print("Enter a month number (1-12): ");
```

Java invokes the method the API lists as **void print(String s)**. But if we write:

```
System.out.print(Math.PI);
```

Java invokes the method listed as **void print(double d)**. Overloading lets you use the same name for methods that perform the same basic operation using different types.

The other **PrintStream** method that we have used is the **printf()** method. We saw in Section 7.3.4 that the **printf()** method can be used to control how values are displayed. We also saw that the first argument we pass to **printf()** must be a *format-string*, in which we embed *placeholders* that provide formatting information. Figure 8-14 presents a partial list of the conversion codes that can be used in placeholders.

14. Individual **char** values can be read by sending the **read()** message directly to **System.in** (that is, without using a **Scanner**). This is a bit beyond us at the moment; we will see how to do it in Chapter 11.

Placeholder	Is Used to Display...
`%b`	a **boolean** (**true** or **false**) value
`%c`	a **char** value
`%d`	an integer value
`%e`	a real value, displayed in floating-point (scientific) notation
`%f`	a real value, displayed in fixed-point notation
`%g`	a real value, displayed in floating- or fixed-point notation, depending on the value's precision and rounding
`%s`	a **String** value
`%n`	a platform-independent newline character
`%%`	the % character

FIGURE 8-14 Format-string placeholder conversion codes

A format-string can contain an arbitrary number of placeholders. For example, the following statements:

```
String lastName       = "Cat";
char   middleInitial = 'E';
String firstName      = "Al";
System.out.printf("My name is %s %c. %s!", firstName,
                            middleInitial, lastName);
```

use the **char** and **String** placeholder codes to display:

```
My name is Al E. Cat!
```

Similarly, if **monthNumber** is **11** and **monthAbbrev** is **"Nov"**, then we could write:

```
System.out.printf("Month #%d is %s.", monthNumber, monthAbbrev);
```

and Java will display:

```
Month #11 is Nov.
```

Java provides several placeholder codes for real values. The statements:

```
System.out.printf("%nUsing f = %f...", 200.0/3.0 );
System.out.printf("%nUsing e = %e...", 200.0/3.0 );
System.out.printf("%nUsing g = %g...", 200.0/3.0 );
```

use the **f**, **e**, and **g**, placeholders, which display this output:

```
Using f = 66.666667...
Using e = 6.666667e+01...
Using g = 66.6667...
```

If we wish to increase the precision, we can do so by altering the placeholder:

```
System.out.printf("%nUsing .10f = %.10f...", 200.0/3.0 );
System.out.printf("%nUsing .10e = %.10e...", 200.0/3.0 );
System.out.printf("%nUsing .10g = %.10g...", 200.0/3.0 );
```

Java will then display the following values:

```
Using .10f = 66.6666666667...
Using .10e = 6.6666666667e+01...
Using .10g = 66.66666667...
```

Note that for the **e** and **f** placeholders, the precision is the number of digits to the right of the decimal point; however, for the **g** placeholder, the precision is the total number of digits.

We also saw that placeholders let us control the width of the field in which a value is displayed. For example, the statement:

```
System.out.printf("%nUsing 12.5f = %12.5f...", 200.0/3.0);
System.out.printf("%nUsing 13.5f = %13.5f...", 200.0/3.0);
System.out.printf("%nUsing 14.5f = %14.5f...", 200.0/3.0);
```

will display its values in increasingly wide fields:

```
Using 12.5f =     66.66667...
Using 13.5f =      66.66667...
Using 14.5f =       66.66667...
```

Finally, before we specify the width of a field, we can use one or more flags to further control its format. To illustrate two of these flags (**-** and **0**), we can write:

```
System.out.printf("%nUsing  12.5f = %12.5f...", 200.0/3.0);
System.out.printf("%nUsing -12.5f = %-12.5f...", 200.0/3.0);
System.out.printf("%nUsing 012.5f = %012.5f...", 200.0/3.0);
```

and Java will display:

```
Using  12.5f =      66.66667...
Using -12.5f = 66.66667     ...
Using 012.5f = 000066.66667...
```

The - flag thus causes a value to be left-justified within its field, and the 0 flag causes leading blanks to be replaced by zeros. Other flags include +, which causes a sign to appear for both positive and negative values; and (, which causes negative values to be displayed surrounded by parentheses. See the Java API for a complete list.

Now that we have seen these examples, this general pattern for the placeholder should make sense:

```
% [flags] [width] [.] [precision] conversionCode
```

(The square brackets [and] are used to indicate that an item is optional.) Thus, the placeholder **%(012.5f** will display a real value with five decimal digits of precision in a field 12 spaces wide in which leading blanks are replaced by zeros, and if the value is negative it will be surrounded by parentheses. Whew!

8.3.5 Expression Details

Let's conclude our introduction to Java types with a look at how Java processes expressions.

Operator Precedence

Consider the following expression:

```
2.0 + 2.0 * 2.0 - 2.0 / 2.0
```

If Java were to simply process the expression from left to right, it would produce the value **3.0**. However when Java processes this expression, it produces **5.0**. Why is this? The answer is that different operators are given different priorities or **precedence levels**. That is, in an arithmetic expression, multiplication and division have higher precedence than addition and subtraction, meaning * and / are applied before + or /. When two arithmetic operators have the same precedence, Java processes them from left to right. Java thus performs the operations in the preceding expression in this order:

```
     3        1       4      2
2.0 + 2.0 * 2.0 - 2.0 / 2.0
```

The result produced is thus **2.0 + 4.0 - 1.0 == 5.0**.

Parentheses (`(` and `)`) have even higher precedence than `*` and `/`, so they can be used to alter the order in which operators are applied. For example:

```
(2.0 + 2.0) * (2.0 - 2.0) / 2.0
```

Because of the parentheses, Java will perform the operations in this order:

```
     1       3      2      4
2.0 + 2.0  *  2.0 - 2.0  / 2.0
```

The result produced is thus `4.0 * 0.0 / 2.0 == 0.0`.

Figure 8-15 presents a list of all of the operators we have seen thus far, ranked according to their precedence levels (higher to lower).

Operator	Precedence	Description
`()`, `.`, `++`, `--`	higher	parentheses, object-access, post-increment, post-decrement
`++`, `--`, `+`, `-`, `!`		pre-increment, pre-decrement, plus sign, negative sign, boolean NOT
`new`		object creation
`*`, `/`, `%`		arithmetic multiplication, division
`+`, `-`		arithmetic addition, subtraction, `String` concatenation
`<`, `>`, `<=`, `>=`		relational operators except `==` and `!=`
`==`, `!=`		equality, inequality
`&&`		boolean AND
`||`		boolean OR
`=`, `+=`, `-=`, `*=`, `/=`, `%=`	lower	assignment, assignment shortcuts

FIGURE 8-15 Operator precedence

Note that the arithmetic operators are all higher precedence than the relational operators. This ensures that if we write an expression like this:

```
x + 1 < y - 1
```

the addition and subtractions will be performed first, followed by the less-than operation.

Note also that the relational operators are all higher precedence than the boolean operators. This ensures that if we write an expression like this:

```
x < y && x < z
```

the two less-than operations will be performed before the boolean AND, without having to use parentheses.

Finally, note that assignment is the lowest precedence operation. This ensures that if we write an assignment statement with this form:

```
variableName = expression;
```

any and all operations in ***expression*** will be performed before the assignment operation.

Operator Associativity

Precedence lets us determine the order of evaluation among different operators. But what determines the order in which operators of the same precedence are performed? To illustrate, consider the expression:

```
8 - 4 - 2
```

If the left subtraction is performed first, the result is `4 - 2 == 2`. If the right subtraction is performed first, the result is `8 - 2 == 6`. Which is it?

The answer depends on a concept called **operator associativity**. In situations like this, if the left operation is performed first, then we say that the operator is **left-associative**; if the right operation is performed first, then we say that it is **right-associative**. All of Java's arithmetic, relational, and logical operators are left-associative, so the actual result of this expression is `2`.

However, a few Java operators are right-associative, as shown in Figure 8-16.

Operator	Associativity	Description
`()`, `.`, `++`, `--`	left	parentheses, object-access, post-increment, post-decrement
`++`, `--`, `+`, `-`, `!`	right	pre-increment, pre-decrement, plus sign, negative sign, boolean NOT
`new`	right	object creation
`*`, `/`, `%`	left	arithmetic multiplication, division
`+`, `-`	left	arithmetic addition, subtraction, `String` concatenation
`<`, `>`, `<=`, `>=`	left	relational operators except `==` and `!=`
`==`, `!=`	left	equality, inequality

continued

`&&`	left	boolean AND
`||`	left	boolean OR
`=, +=, -=, *=, /=`	right	assignment, assignment shortcuts

FIGURE 8-16 Operator associativity

For example, consider the assignment operator (**=**). Because it is right-associative, we can build assignment expressions like the one below:

```
double w, x, y, z;
w = x = y = z = 0.0;
```

When this statement is performed, the assignments are performed in the order shown below:

```
4    3    2    1
w = x = y = z = 0.0
```

First **z** is assigned 0.0, then **y** is assigned **z**'s value (0.0), then **x** is assigned **y**'s value (0.0), and finally **w** is assigned **x**'s value (0.0).

8.4 Example: Computing Loudness

Suppose we are considering buying a house that is about 200 meters from a busy highway. The real estate agent tells us that it is a "very quiet" neighborhood, and while it seems quiet as we tour the house, it isn't rush hour. Is the agent's claim reasonable?

We decide to consult with a friend who is a physics major. She tells us that what most of us call "loudness," physicists called "sound pressure level" (SPL) and that SPL is relative to our distance to the object generating the sound. So what we really want to know is the SPL of the rush hour traffic at a distance of 200 meters. She gives us this formula:

$$SPL_2 = SPL_1 - 20 \times \log_{10}\left(\frac{\text{distance}_2}{\text{distance}_1}\right)$$

That is, we can compute how loud the rush hour traffic is at any distance (distance_2), provided we have a reference loudness (SPL_1), and the distance at which it was measured (distance_1).

SPL is measured in decibels, which are usually integers.

8.4.1 Designing the SoundLevel Program

As usual, we begin by writing a user story:

> Our program should ask the user the question, "What is the sound's reference loudness (decibels)?" It should then read the reference loudness from the keyboard. It should then ask "What is its reference distance (meters)?" It should then read the reference distance from the keyboard. It should ask, "What is the new distance?" It should read the new distance from the keyboard. It should then compute and display the new loudness, along with descriptive labels.

We could "hard-wire" values like the desired distance (200 meters) and the source of the sound ("rush hour traffic") into the program. However by having the user enter these values, we generalize the program, making it useful for computing the loudness of any noise at any distance.

Next, we locate the noun phrases in the story and make a list of them.

Noun Phrase	Type of Value	Name
our program	?	*SoundLevel*
questions	`String`	none
reference loudness	`int`	*loudness1*
the keyboard	`Scanner`	*keyboard*
reference distance	`double`	*distance1*
new distance	`double`	*distance2*
new loudness	`int`	*loudness2*
descriptive labels	`String`	none

Next, we list the verb phrases, noting how we will accomplish each action in Java.

Verb Phrase	Java Method or Operation
ask the user ...	`System.out.print();`
read *loudness1* read *distance1, distance2*	`keyboard.nextInt()` `keyboard.nextDouble()`
compute *loudness2*	`=, -, *, /, Math.log10(), ...`
display	`System.out.println();`

Finally, we organize the objects and operations into an algorithm that solves our problem, as shown in Figure 8-17.

Algorithm: SoundLevel

```
Display "What is the reference loudness (decibels)?" via System.out
Read loudness1 from keyboard
Display "What is the reference distance (meters)?"
Read distance1
Display "What is the new distance?"
Read distance2
Compute loudness2 = loudness1 - 20 * log10(distance2/distance1)
Display loudness2 and descriptive labels
```

FIGURE 8-17 Algorithm for *SoundLevel* program

8.4.2 Writing the Program

Our next step is to create a **SoundLevel** class containing a **main()** method, and add to that method Java statements corresponding to our algorithm. Figure 8-18 presents such a program.

```
/** SoundLevel.java computes the loudness of a sound at one
 *    distance, given its loudness at a different distance.
 */
import java.util.Scanner;

public class SoundLevel {
 public static void main(String[] args) {
   System.out.println("To find a sound's SPL at a distance:");
   Scanner keyboard = new Scanner( System.in );
   // read loudness1, distance1, distance2
   System.out.print("- what is the ref. loudness (decibels)? ");
   int loudness1 = keyboard.nextInt();
   System.out.print("- what is the ref. distance (meters)? ");
   double distance1 = keyboard.nextDouble();
   System.out.print("- what is the new distance? ");
   double distance2 = keyboard.nextDouble();
   // compute loudness2
   long loudness2 = loudness1 -
              Math.round( 20 * Math.log10(distance2/distance1) );
   // display result
   System.out.println("\nThe SPL of the sound at distance "
                  + distance2 + " is " + loudness2 + " db");
```

continued

```
23      }
24   }
```

FIGURE 8-18 **SoundLevel.java**

Decibel values are usually integers. However, the subexpression on line 19:

```
20 * Math.log10(distance2/distance1)
```

produces a **double** value. Since **double** values are bigger than **int** (or **long**) values, trying to assign a **double** value to an **int** variable results in a compilation error. To prevent this error, line 19 uses the **Math.round()** method to round that **double** value to the nearest integer. However, **Math.round()** returns a **long**, not an **int**. Because of this, line 18 declares **loudness2** to be of type **long** rather than type **int**.

8.4.3 Testing the Program

As before, we will conduct some initial testing on the program using easily verifiable values. The $log_{10}(10)$ is 1.0, so we might enter values for *distance1* and *distance2* such that the quotient of *distance2/distance1* is 10. Then the *log(distance2/distance1)* subexpression will produce 1.0, the *20 * log(distance2/distance1)* subexpression will produce *20.0*, and the result should be 20 less than the reference loudness. Figure 8-19 shows a test run using this approach.

```
Result:
To find a sound's SPL at a distance:
- what is the ref. loudness (decibels)? 50
- what is the ref. distance (meters)? 10
- what is the new distance? 100

The SPL of the sound at distance 100.0 is 30 db
```

FIGURE 8-19 Testing **SoundLevel.java**

Since the resulting loudness (30) is 20 less than the reference loudness (50), the program seems to be working correctly. We then repeat this process using other easily verifiable values.

8.4.4 Solving the Problem

When we have some degree of confidence that the program is working correctly, we can use it to solve the problem described at the beginning of this section. After a short Google session, we find that rush hour traffic measured from 5 meters away produces an SPL of 70 db, while the SPL in a quiet neighborhood is about 40 db. Figure 8-20 shows the program in action.

Result:
To find a sound's SPL at a distance:
- what is the ref. loudness (decibels)? 70
- what is the ref. distance (meters)? 5
- what is the new distance? 200
The SPL of the sound at distance 200.0 is 38 db

FIGURE 8-20 Solving the sound level problem

Since a quiet neighborhood has an SPL of 40 db, and the program indicates that the SPL from the highway is 38 db, the real estate agent's claim is quite reasonable.

8.5 Chapter Summary

- A Java type is either a primitive type or a reference type.
- A primitive type variable stores values of that type.
- A reference type variable or handle stores a reference to an object. Messages sent to a handle are delivered to the handle's object.
- An expression is a sequence of operands and operations that combine to produce a value.
- Operator precedence and associativity determine the order in which operators are applied in an expression.

8.5.1 Key Terms

API
assignment operator
assignment statement
base-2
binary number
bit
boolean
boolean operator
byte
char
class method
concatentation-assignment shorcut
constant
decrement
double
double expression
escape sequence
expression
fixed-point literals
float
floating-point literals
garbage collector
handle
increment
index
instance method
int
integers
integer division
left associativity
literal
logical expression
logical operators
long
Math class
null
object
operator associativity
operator precedence
overloaded
precedence levels
primitive type
PrintStream class
quotient
read-only items
real numbers
reference type
remainder
relational operator
right associativity
Scanner class
scientific notation
short
truth table
type
Unicode

Programming Projects

8.1 Modify the program we developed in Figure 8-18 so that it first asks the user what is making the sound, and then reads the user's response into a **String** variable named *soundSource*. Then modify the subsequent output statements so that they refer to *soundSource* when asking the user a question or displaying the result of the computation.

8.2 Design and write an "Einstein" program that asks the user for a mass in kilograms, and then computes the energy that can be obtained from that mass using Einstein's formula $e = mc^2$. Use the **pow()** method from Java's **Math** class to compute c^2.

8.3 Modify the program in Figure 8-2 so that it displays a month's full name instead of its abbreviation. (Hint: "Pad" each month in *monthTable* with spaces so that all months are the same length. Then use the **String** method **trim()** to remove leading or trailing spaces from the extracted month.)

8.4 Design and write a "Hypotenuse" program that asks the user for the lengths of two legs of a right triangle, and displays the length of the triangle's hypotenuse using the **`Math.hypot()`** method.

8.5 Proceed as in Project 8.4, but instead of using **`Math.hypot()`**, use **`Math.sqrt()`**, **`Math.pow()`**, and the Pythagorean Theorem to calculate the hypotenuse length:

$$hypotenuse = \sqrt{leg1^2 + leg2^2}$$

8.6 Design and write a program that asks the user for three numbers and displays the maximum and minimum of the three, using the **`Math.max()`** and **`Math.min()`** methods. (Hint: You may invoke the methods more than once.)

8.7 Design and write a program that asks the user to enter a positive number, and then displays the number of digits in that number. (Hint: Read it in as something other than a number.)

8.8 Design and write a program that asks the user to type a word, reads the word, and then displays **`Contains uppercase: true`** if the word contains one or more uppercase letters, and displays **`Contains uppercase: false`** if the word contains no uppercase letters. (Hint: Look in the **`String`** API; use two of the methods there and a logical expression to solve the problem.)

8.9 Design and write a program that computes the volume of a cylinder, using the formula below. Use your program to measure the volume of (a) a soup can, and (b) a propane tank.

$$cylinderVolume = \pi \times radius^2 \times height$$

8.10 Design and write a program that computes the volume of a sphere using the formula below. Compute the volume twice, once using the **`Math`** class and again using the **`StrictMath`** class. Use **`printf()`** to display the volumes at high precision, and see if you get the same results. Use your program to compute the volume of (a) a basketball, and (b) our planet.

$$sphereVolume = \frac{4}{3} \times \pi \times radius^3$$

8.11 Design and write a program that uses Charles's Law to compute how much the volume of a gas decreases when its temperature is reduced. Inflate a balloon, measure the balloon's radius, and calculate its volume. (Hint: Use the sphere volume formula from Project 8.10.) Record the room temperature. Then find a freezer and record the temperature inside. Put the balloon in the freezer overnight. Using your program, predict the volume of a balloon when it reaches the temperature in the freezer. In the morning, measure the balloon's new radius and calculate its new volume. How well did your program predict the outcome?

8.12 At a grocery store, find a food item that comes in two different box sizes (for example, breakfast cereal). Measure and record the dimensions of each box, as well as the mass of the food inside. Then design and write a program that determines which box size is packaged more efficiently. (Hint: Compute the *density* = *mass* / *volume* for each box size.)

Chapter 9
Methods

What is the difference between method and device? A method is a device which you used twice.

George Polya

There was a most ingenius architect, who had contrived a new method for building houses, by beginning at the roof and working downward to the foundation; which he justified to me by the like practice of those two prudent insects, the bee and the spider.

Jonathan Swift, *Gulliver's Travels*

Like other occult techniques of divination, the statistical method has a private jargon deliberately contrived to obscure its methods from non-practitioners.

G. O. Ashley

Tonight, we are taking care of Mortimer. And just for him, we'll have something special. I plan on using the Melbourne Method.

Jonathan Brewster (Raymond Massey) in *Arsenic and Old Lace*

Objectives

Upon completion of this chapter, you should be able to:

- ❑ Build your own Java methods
- ❑ Define parameters and pass arguments to them
- ❑ Distinguish between class and instance methods
- ❑ Build a method library

We have seen that when we send a message to an object or class, the corresponding method is performed. In Alice, building a method consisted of clicking the **`create new method`** button, and then dragging statements into the method to provide the required behavior. In this chapter, we will learn how to build methods in Java.

9.1 Introductory Example: The Hokey Pokey Song

The *Hokey Pokey* is a fun song in which people stand in a circle and "dance" by acting out the lyrics. One version of the song uses the following lyrics:

You put your right foot in, you put your right foot out; you put your right foot in, and you shake it all about. You do the Hokey Pokey, and you turn yourself around. That's what it's all about!	*You put your left foot in, you put your left foot out; you put your left foot in, and you shake it all about. You do the Hokey Pokey, and you turn yourself around. That's what it's all about!*
You put your right hand in, you put your right hand out; you put your right hand in, and you shake it all about. You do the Hokey Pokey, and you turn yourself around. That's what it's all about!	*You put your left hand in, you put your left hand out; you put your left hand in, and you shake it all about. You do the Hokey Pokey, and you turn yourself around. That's what it's all about!*
You put your nose in, you put your nose out; you put your nose in, and you shake it all about. You do the Hokey Pokey, and you turn yourself around. That's what it's all about!	*You put your backside in, you put your backside out; you put your backside in, and you shake it all about. You do the Hokey Pokey, and you turn yourself around. That's what it's all about!*
You put your head in, you put your head out; you put your head in, and you shake it all about. You do the Hokey Pokey, and you turn yourself around. That's what it's all about!	*You put your whole self in, you put your whole self out; you put your whole self in, and you shake it all about. You do the Hokey Pokey, and you turn yourself around. That's what it's all about*

Our first problem is to write a Java program that displays the lyrics to this song.

The Brute Force Approach

The following user story gives one way to solve this problem:

> *Our program should display the lyrics of the Hokey Pokey song.*

This story has one object, the lyrics of the song (a `String`), and one action, displaying those lyrics. We could thus write a `main()` method containing a `println()` message, using lots of concatenation operators to build a single, very long character string for the song's lyrics:

```
public class BruteForceHokeyPokey {
  public static void main(String [] args) {
    System.out.println("You put your right foot in,\n"
                      + "you put your right foot out;\n"
                      + "you put your right foot in,\n"
                      + "and you shake it all about.\n"
                      + "You do the Hokey Pokey,\n"
                      + "and you turn yourself around.\n"
                      + "That's what it's all about!\n\n"
                      + "You put your left foot in;\n"
                      + "you put your left foot out;\n"
                      // ... 40 lines omitted ...
                      + "You put your whole self in,\n"
                      + "you put your whole self out;\n"
                      + "You put your whole self in\n"
                      + "and you shake it all about.\n"
                      + "You do the Hokey Pokey,\n"
                      + "and you turn yourself around.\n"
                      + "That's what it's all about!\n");

  }
}
```

Using this approach, the program will be about 60 lines long. This approach is sometimes called a **brute force approach**, because it solves the problem using lots of effort, rather than insight.

A Better Approach

While the brute force approach solves the problem, it isn't a very good solution. It requires a lot of work because it ignores the *structure* of the song. Each verse of the song is identical, except for the body part being put in, put out, and shaken all about:

> You put your <u>bodyPart</u> in,
> you put your <u>bodyPart</u> out;
> you put your <u>bodyPart</u> in,
> and you shake it all about.
> You do the Hokey Pokey,
> and you turn yourself around.
> That's what it's all about!

Thus, a better solution is to write a user story that takes advantage of this structure:

> Our program should display the lyrics of the "right foot" verse, display the lyrics of the "left foot" verse, display the lyrics of the "right hand" verse, display the lyrics of the "left hand" verse, display the lyrics of the "nose" verse, display the lyrics of the "backside" verse, display the lyrics of the "head" verse, and display the lyrics of the "whole self" verse.

Since each "display" operation is the same except for the body part being displayed, we can write a **`printVerse()`** method that displays one verse of the song, and pass to this method an argument consisting of the body part it should mention (see Figure 9-1).

As we saw in Chapter 3, if we wish to pass an argument to a method, that method must contain a parameter to store the argument. The **`printVerse()`** method will thus need a parameter capable of storing a **`String`**, which we will call **`bodyPart`**, as shown in Figure 9-1.

```
/** HokeyPokey.java displays the lyrics of the Hokey Pokey song.
 *   ...
 */

public class HokeyPokey {
 public static void main(String[] args) {
   printVerse("right foot");
   printVerse("left foot");
   printVerse("right hand");
   printVerse("left hand");
   printVerse("nose");
   printVerse("backside");
   printVerse("head");
   printVerse("whole self");
 }
```

continued

```

/** Display a verse of the Hokey Pokey song, given a body part.
 *  @param bodyPart, a String.
 */
 public static void printVerse(String bodyPart) {
   System.out.println("You put your " + bodyPart + " in,\n"
   + "you put your " + bodyPart + " out;\n"
   + "you put your " + bodyPart + " in,\n"
   + "and you shake it all about.\n"
   + "You do the Hokey Pokey,\n"
   + "and you turn yourself around.\n"
   + "That's what it's all about!\n");
 }
}
```

FIGURE 9-1 **HokeyPokey.java**

The resulting program (ignoring comments) is just 21 lines long — about 1/3 of the size of the brute force approach — yet it displays the entire song. This is another case where devoting some time to a careful design results in a program that is a lot less work to write!

9.2 Methods

The program in Figure 9-1 contains two methods: **main()**, and **printVerse()**. The **main()** method uses the **printVerse()** method to build and display each of the verses in the song.

The problem this program solves is similar to the one we solved in Section 3.2.1. Let's compare the definition of **printVerse()** in Figure 9-1 with the definition of **printVerse()** in Figure 3-30. The first line of the method in Figure 3-30 looks like this:

```
public void printVerse(String animal, String noise) {
```

while the first line of the method in Figure 9-1 looks like this:

```
public static void printVerse(String bodyPart) {
```

Comparing these lines one item at a time, we see:

- Each method definition begins with the word **public**. This means the method can be invoked by other classes. That is, if another program needed to display a verse of the Hokey Pokey song (unlikely, but possible), it could use this method to do so. If we wanted to prevent other programs from invoking this method, we could have used the words **private** or **protected**, and the program would behave exactly the same.
- The method from Figure 9-1 contains the word **static**; the Alice method does not. The word **static** tells the Java compiler that this is a **class method**, like the **main()**

method. By contrast, the method from Figure 3-30 does not contain the word **static**. When the word **static** is omitted, that means the method is an **instance method** — a message that must be sent to an object (like **scarecrow**), not a class.

- Both methods contain the word **void**. This indicates the method *returns nothing* when it is invoked. Put differently, a **void** method does not behave like a function, because it produces no result. We will shortly see how to define a method that returns a value.
- **printVerse** is the name of each method; the parentheses that follow the name tell the Java compiler that **printVerse** is a method, not a variable or constant.
- Inside the parentheses are the parameters for the method. If there are multiple parameters, they must be separated by commas. When the corresponding message is sent, an argument must be passed for each parameter in a method's definition. Thus a single **String** argument is required for the **printVerse()** in Figure 9-1; two **String** arguments are required to invoke the **printVerse()** in Figure 3-30.
- In both methods, the open curly brace (**{**) indicates the beginning of the statements the method will perform when it is invoked. The statements within a method's curly braces determine the **behavior** of that method.

Using square brackets (**[** and **]**) to denote optional items, a simplified pattern for a method definition is as follows:

Simplified Pattern for a Java Method

```
[AccessMode] [static] ReturnType MethodName ( Params ) {
    Statements
}
```

where:

AccessMode is either **public**, **private**, or **protected**. A **public** method can be invoked from other classes; a **private** method can only be invoked by methods from the same class; a **protected** method can be invoked by methods from the same class or its subclasses (see Chapter 14). If omitted, the default ***AccessMode*** is **private**.

static indicates this is a class method — a message that must be sent to a class instead of an object. If omitted, the method is an instance method — a message that must be sent to an object instead of a class.

ReturnType is the type of value this method returns when it is done. This may be any primitive type, any reference type, or **void**. If **void**, the method returns nothing; otherwise, the method must return a value of the given type using a **return** statement (see below).

MethodName is the name of the method.

Params is a comma-separated list of parameter declarations for this method.

Statements is the sequence of statements this method performs when it is invoked.

In the remainder of this section, we will focus on the ***ReturnType*** of a method.

9.2.1 Non-`void` vs. `void` Methods

Recall that Alice makes a distinction between two kinds of messages:

1. *Methods* are messages that can be sent anywhere a *statement* may occur.
2. *Functions* are messages that can be sent anywhere an *expression* may occur.

In Java, all messages are called methods, but they are distinguished by their ***ReturnType***. What Alice calls a method is called a **void method** in Java, and what Alice calls a function is called a **non-void method** in Java. That is, a method whose ***ReturnType*** is **void** can be used like a statement, and a method whose ***ReturnType*** is a type other than **void** can be used anywhere an expression of that type may appear.

The **printVerse()** methods of Figure 9-1 and Figure 3-30 are thus both **void** methods. **void** methods are somewhat simpler than non-**void** methods, because they simply perform the statements within them, without returning a value to the sender of the message.

Because **void** methods are invoked like statements, creating a **void** method is like adding a new kind of statement to Java. For example, the programs in Figure 9-1 and Figure 3-30 are both written as though **printVerse()** were a new kind of Java statement.

9.2.2 Non-`void` Methods

The user story in Section 9.1 is quite verbose. Here is a more succinct version:

> Our program should display the lyrics of the "right foot" verse, the "left foot" verse, the "right hand" verse, the "left hand" verse, the "right side" verse, the "left side" verse, the "nose" verse, the "backside" verse, the "head" verse, and the "whole self" verse.

With just one "display" verb, a program written using this user story will have just one **println()** message, and will use a **getVerse(*bodyPart*)** method to build and return the verse for the given ***bodyPart***, as shown in Figure 9-2.

```
/** HokeyPokey.java displays the lyrics of the Hokey Pokey song.
 *   ...
 */
public class HokeyPokey {
  public static void main(String[] args) {
     System.out.println( getVerse("right foot") + "\n"
                        + getVerse("left foot") + "\n"
                        + getVerse("right hand") + "\n"
                        + getVerse("left hand") + "\n"
                        + getVerse("nose") + "\n"
                        + getVerse("backside") + "\n"
                        + getVerse("head") + "\n"
```

continued

```
                           + getVerse("whole self") );
 }

/** Build a verse of the Hokey Pokey song for a given body part.
 *  @param bodyPart, a String.
 *  @return a verse of the Hokey Pokey song for bodyPart.
 */
 public static String getVerse(String bodyPart) {
   return "You put your " + bodyPart + " in,\n"
   + "you put your " + bodyPart + " out;\n"
   + "you put your " + bodyPart + " in,\n"
   + "and you shake it all about.\n"
   + "You do the Hokey Pokey,\n"
   + "and you turn yourself around.\n"
   + "That's what it's all about.\n";
 }
}
```

FIGURE 9-2 **HokeyPokey.java** (using a non-void method)

The program in Figure 9-2 produces the same result as that in Figure 9-1. However, the **getVerse()** method in Figure 9-2 is more flexible than the **printVerse()** method in Figure 9-1. That is, **printVerse()** can be used for one thing: displaying a verse of the song. However, **getVerse()** returns a verse as a **String**, letting the *sender* decide what to do with it. The program in Figure 9-2 is preferable because it offers more options to the sender of the message.

A non-**void** method like **getVerse()** uses Java's **return** statement to produce its result.

Simplified Pattern for a return Statement

```
return Expression ;
```

where:

Expression is an expression producing a value whose type matches the return type of the method. When performed, ***Expression*** is evaluated, and the value it produces is returned to the sender of the message. The value produced is called the method's return value.

The **getVerse()** method in Figure 9-2 returns a **String**. However, any Java type can be used as the return type of a non-**void** method.

9.2.3 Method Design

Once we have determined that we want to build a method, how do we go about designing it?

Designing a method is much like designing a program: we write a user story; identify the nouns (objects); identify the verbs (operations); and organize them into an algorithm. To illustrate, we might write the following user story for the **getVerse()** method from Figure 9-2:

> The method should return:
>
> *You put your bodyPart in,*
>
> *you put your bodyPart out;*
>
> *you put your bodyPart in,*
>
> *and you shake it all about.*
>
> *You do the Hokey Pokey,*
>
> *and you turn yourself around.*
>
> *That's what it's all about!*

Since the method is returning a sequence of characters, it is natural to use **String** for its return type. Since *bodyPart* is the only thing that changes from one verse to another, and since it is a value to be supplied by the sender of the message, we make it a parameter of the method.

> If an item in a method's user story is a variable that must be supplied by the sender, define that item as a parameter of the method; otherwise, define that item locally, within the method.

Variables and constants that are declared within a method are called **local variables**, or **locals**, because they exist only within that method.

9.2.4 Einstein's Formula

As another example, let's look at Einstein's formula:

$$e = m \times c^2$$

For simple, formula-based methods like this, the formula itself can serve as the user story, because the method will just return an expression for the right side of the formula.

Since the formula produces a number that is not necessarily an integer, we will choose **double** for the method's return type.

To identify the parameters, we examine the right side of the formula (user story). There, we see one variable (m, the *mass*), and one constant (c, the *speed of light*). Since the speed of light is constant, the only thing that the user needs to pass when he or she sends this message is the *mass* value. We therefore declare a parameter to store the *mass* value the user will pass, and declare **SPEED_OF_LIGHT** as a constant, local to the method, as can be seen in Figure 9-3.

```
public static double massToEnergy(double mass) {
    final double SPEED_OF_LIGHT = 2.99792458e8;
    return mass * Math.pow(SPEED_OF_LIGHT, 2.0);
}
```

FIGURE 9-3 A Java method for Einstein's formula

When defined within a class, another method in that same class — or a method in a different class[1] — can use the **massToEnergy()** method. For example, to compute the energy that can be obtained from one kilogram (2.2 pounds) of mass from within the same class, we can write:

```
double energy = massToEnergy(1.0);
```

When performed, this statement behaves as shown in Figure 9-4.

```
double energy = massToEnergy(1.0);
            D                        A

       public static double massToEnergy(double mass) {  B
          final double SPEED_OF_LIGHT = 2.99792458e8;
       C  return mass * Math.pow(SPEED_OF_LIGHT, 2.0);
       }
```

FIGURE 9-4 Performing **massToEnergy()**

First (Step A), the argument **1.0** is copied into the parameter **mass**, and control is transferred from the method sending the message to method **massToEnergy()**. Next (Step B), the statements within **massToEnergy()** are performed. The first statement initializes **SPEED_OF_LIGHT** to its value; the second statement is a **return** statement. Its expression

```
mass * Math.pow(SPEED_OF_LIGHT, 2.0)
```

is evaluated, producing a value (89,875,517,873,681,764). Next (Step C), the method produces this value as its return value, and control is transferred back to the sender of

1. Suppose **massToEnergy()** is stored in a class named **Formulas**. To invoke **massToEnergy()** from a different class, (1) **Formulas** should be in the same folder as the class wanting to use its method; and (2) the message must be sent to the class, as follows: **double energy = Formulas.massToEnergy(1.0);**

the message. Finally (Step D), the method's return value is stored into the variable named **energy**.

9.2.5 Computing Initials

If several people are working together on a group project, and a person makes a change to one of the project's documents, it is good practice to *initial* the change, to indicate who made it. If the document was altered using a word processor like Microsoft Word that "knows" the name of the person using it, the word processor can automatically compute the person's initials and record them with the change. To illustrate such a computation, Figure 9-5 presents a method that, given a person's name, returns his or her first initial.

```
public static char firstInitial(String name) {
    return name.charAt(0);   // return the first character
}
```

FIGURE 9-5 The **firstInitial()** method

Because an initial is a single letter, the return type of this method is **char**. Since it needs to receive the person's name from the sender, it has a **String** parameter named **name**. The method assumes that the first thing in **name** is the person's first name. Since the first character in any **String** has index 0, 0 should be the index of the person's first initial. The method thus uses the **charAt()** method from class **String** to access and return the character at index 0.

Using this method within the class where it is defined, we can write:

```
char initial1 = firstInitial("Homer Jay Simpson");
```

and the value of **initial1** will be set to the letter **'H'**.

To compute a person's last initial, we could write the method given in Figure 9-6.

```
public static char lastInitial(String name) {
int indexOfSpace = name.lastIndexOf(' ');
return name.charAt(indexOfSpace + 1);
}
```

FIGURE 9-6 The **lastInitial()** method

As with **firstInital()**, this method returns a **char**, and it has one **String** parameter named **name**. This method assumes that **name** ends with a last name preceded by a space character. It finds the index of that space character using the **lastIndexOf()** method, and then uses the **charAt()** method to access and return the letter *after* that space.

Using this method within the class where it is defined, if we write:

```
char initial2 = lastInitial("Homer Jay Simpson");
```

then the value of **initial2** will be set to the letter **'S'**.

To compute a person's first and last initials, we can write the method given in Figure 9-7.

```
public static String twoInitials(String name) {
  String result = "";               // start with empty string
  result += firstInitial(name);    // append first initial
  result += lastInitial(name);     // append last initial
  return result;                    // we're done!
}
```

FIGURE 9-7 The **twoInitials()** method

Since this method needs to return multiple characters (the two initials), its return type must be **String**. As before, the sender must supply the name, so we have a **String** parameter named **name**. To build the return value, we define a local **String** variable named **result** and initialize it to the empty string. We do this so that we can concatenate characters to it, as one of the operands of the concatenation operator (+) must be a **String**. We then concatenate the **char** returned by **firstInitial(name)**, followed by the char returned by **lastInitial(name)**, and return the resulting **String**.

Using this method within the class where it is defined, if we write:

```
System.out.println( twoInitials("Homer Jay Simpson") );
```

then **HS** will be displayed.

9.2.6 Sound Level Program Revisited

In Section 8.4, we wrote a program to compute the loudness (sound pressure level) of a sound, given a reference loudness, the distance at which that reference loudness was measured, and the distance at which we desire to know the loudness. To make this computation reuseable, we could instead write a method for that formula. The program in Figure 9-8 uses this approach.

```
/** SoundPressureLevel.java computes the loudness of a sound
 *   at one distance, given its loudness at a different distance.
 */
import java.util.Scanner;

public class SoundPressureLevel {
```

continued

```
  public static void main(String[] args) {
     System.out.println(
            "To find the SPL of a sound at a distance:");
     Scanner keyboard = new Scanner( System.in );
     // read loudness1, distance1, distance2
     System.out.print(
            "- what is the reference loudness (decibels)?");
     int loudness1 = keyboard.nextInt();
     System.out.print(
            "- what is the reference distance (meters)? ");
     double distance1 = keyboard.nextDouble();
     System.out.print("- what is the new distance? ");
     double distance2 = keyboard.nextDouble();
     // compute loudness2
     long loudness2 = newSPL(loudness1, distance1, distance2);
     // display result
     System.out.println("\nThe SPL of the sound at distance "
                        + distance2 + " meters is "
                        + loudness2 + "db");
  }

  // Compute SPL at dist2, using spl1 and dist1

  public static long newSPL(int spl1, double dist1,
                                      double dist2) {
     return spl1 - Math.round( 20.0 * Math.log10(dist2/dist1) );
  }
}
```

```
Result:
To find the SPL of a sound at a distance:
- what is the reference loudness (decibels)? 70
- what is the reference distance (meters)? 5
- what is the new distance? 200

The SPL of the sound at distance 200.0 meters is 38 db
```

FIGURE 9-8 `SoundPressureLevel.java`

Note that the program in Figure 9-8 produces exactly the same results as that of Figure 8-18. However, because the new version uses a method to compute the desired loudness, other programs can make use of the `newSPL()` method, provided they are in the same folder as this class. Methods thus provide a way to make a computation *reuseable*.

To illustrate, Figure 9-9 presents a simple class named **MethodTester** that invokes the **newSPL()** method from class **SoundPressureLevel**. Since **newSPL()** is a **static** method, we must send the **newSPL()** message to the **SoundPressureLevel** class.

```
/** MethodTester.java invokes a method from a different class.
 */
public class MethodTester {
  public static void main(String[] args) {
    long testResult = SoundPressureLevel.newSPL(70, 5, 200);
    System.out.println(testResult);
  }
}
```

```
Result:
38
```

FIGURE 9-9 Invoking a class method from a different class

When solving a problem, spend some time thinking about what pieces of your solution might be reuseable in the future. If you solve the problem by building methods to perform those pieces, you will have less work to do when a future problem requires one of those pieces.

9.3 Method Libraries

Now that we have seen how to build a method, let us turn our attention to their use with classes. Looking at Java's **Math** class, we see classes can be used to store a group of related methods. Such a class is known as a **method library**. The idea is to build a class that contains a group of methods that are related in some way, usually with no **main()** method.

For example, a programmer needing to calculate the logarithm of a variable **x** can do so by sending the **log10(x)** message to the **Math** class; and a programmer needing to calculate x^y can do so by sending the **pow(x,y)** message to the **Math** class. Classes like Java's **Math** class are thus repositories for related methods.

In the rest of this section, we will build two simple method libraries as illustrations.

9.3.1 Problem Description: Ballooning a Bedroom

Suppose that you live in an apartment with a friend who likes to play practical jokes on people. One weekend, she goes away and you and your other friends decide to get her back by filling her bedroom with balloons. How many balloons should you purchase? Since this is a computational question, we decide to write a program to help us answer it.

9.3.2 Program Design

Preliminary Ideas

With a bit of thought, it should be evident that this is a problem of *volumes*: we need to determine how many balloon volumes fit within our roommate's bedroom volume.

One way to proceed is to use the volume of a sphere as an approximation for the volume of a balloon. The volume of a sphere can be computed using the following formula:

$$volume_{sphere} = \frac{4}{3} \times \pi \times radius^3$$

Since there is just one variable on the right side of this formula, the only piece of information we need to compute the approximate volume of a balloon is its radius. The radius of a balloon depends on how much we inflate it; a small balloon might have a radius of two inches, while a large balloon might have a radius of six inches. If you've ever blown up a balloon, you know that it takes more time and effort to inflate a balloon with a larger radius; this favors using small balloons. On the other hand, if we use large balloons, we will need to buy and inflate fewer balloons to fill the room. Perhaps our program can help us decide which is preferable.

We can use the volume of a box as an approximation for the volume of our roommate's bedroom. The formula for the volume of a box is as follows:

$$volume_{box} = length \times width \times height$$

This tells us we will need the bedroom's length, width, and height to compute its volume. Knowing what we need to compute these volumes, we are ready to write the user story.

User Story

We might write the following user story for this problem:

> Our program should display a prompt asking the user to enter the radius of a balloon, and then read this radius from the keyboard. It should then use this radius to compute the volume of one balloon. Next, it should compute the volume of our roommate's bedroom. It should then compute the number of balloons required to fill the bedroom using the volume of the bedroom and the volume of one balloon. Finally, it should display the required number of balloons, with suitable labels.

Note that we do not enter the dimensions of our roommate's room. Once our roommate leaves for the weekend, we can easily measure the dimensions of her bedroom. Since these values will not change from one execution of the program to another, we can define these dimensions as constants within the program.

Next, we identify the noun phrases in the program.

Noun Phrase	Type of Value	Name
Our program	?	*BalloonPrank*
prompt	`String`	none
radius of a balloon	`double`	*balloonRadius*
the keyboard	`Scanner`	*keyboard*
volume of one balloon	`double`	*balloonVolume*
volume of the bedroom	`double`	*bedroomVolume*
required # of balloons	`int`	*balloonsRequired*

Continuing with our design, we identify the verb phrases in the user story.

Verb Phrase	Java Method or Operation
display ...	`System.out.print()` or `println()`
read radius	`balloonRadius = keyboard.nextDouble()`
compute volume of a balloon	`balloonVolume = ?`
compute volume of bedroom	`bedroomVolume = ?`
compute balloons required	`balloonsRequired = bedroomVolume / balloonVolume`

We can now organize the objects and operations into an algorithm, as given in Figure 9-10.

Algorithm: BalloonPrank

1. Define constants LENGTH, WIDTH, HEIGHT
2. Display "Enter the radius of a balloon" via *System.out*
3. Read *balloonRadius* from *keyboard*
4. Compute *balloonVolume* from *balloonRadius*
5. Compute *bedroomVolume* from *LENGTH, WIDTH, HEIGHT*
6. Compute *balloonsRequired* = *bedroomVolume* / *balloonVolume*
7. Display *balloonRadius*, *balloonsRequired*, and descriptive labels.

FIGURE 9-10 Algorithm for the `BalloonPrank` program

9.3.3 Program Implementation

Now that we have an algorithm, we have to decide how to perform Steps 4 and 5. One approach is to encode the formulas as expressions within the **main()** method.

However, if we think about **reusability**, the ability to reuse code from one program in a different program, it should be evident that we might again someday need to compute the volume of a sphere, or the volume of a box. This suggests we should write methods for these formulas, as do our design steps.

Having decided to build methods, the second decision is where to store them. We could store them in the **BalloonPrank** class. But let's imagine for a moment that Java provides **Sphere** and **Box** classes, each containing a **volume()** method, such that the expression:

```
Sphere.volume(balloonRadius)
```

produces the value required for Step 4 of the algorithm; and the expression:

```
Box.volume(LENGTH, WIDTH, HEIGHT)
```

produces the value required for Step 5 of the algorithm. Given such methods, we could write the program as shown in Figure 9-11.

```
/** BalloonPrank.java reads a balloon's radius
 *   and displays the number of balloons needed to fill a bedroom.
 */
import java.util.Scanner;

public class BalloonPrank {
   public static void main(String[] args) {
     final double LENGTH = 9.0;  // bedroom dimensions (in feet)
     final double WIDTH  = 8.0;
     final double HEIGHT = 7.0;
     // get the balloon radius
     System.out.print("Enter a balloon radius (inches): ");
     Scanner keyboard = new Scanner(System.in);
     double balloonRadius = keyboard.nextDouble();
      balloonRadius /= 12.0;            // convert inches to feet
     // compute the balloon and bedroom volumes
     double balloonVolume = Sphere.volume(balloonRadius);
     double bedroomVolume = Box.volume(LENGTH, WIDTH, HEIGHT);
     // compute balloons in bedroom
     double balloonsRequired = bedroomVolume / balloonVolume;
     System.out.printf("Using balloons of radius %.0f inches,"
                         + " you will need %.0f balloons",
```

continued

```
                           balloonRadius*12, balloonsRequired);
   }
}
```

```
Result:
Enter a balloon radius (inches): 6
Using balloons of radius 6 inches, you will need 963 balloons
```

```
Result:
Enter a balloon radius (inches): 4
Using balloons of radius 4 inches, you will need 3249 balloons
```

FIGURE 9-11 The **BalloonPrank.java** program

Unfortunately, Java does not provide **Sphere** or **Box** classes. So let's write our own! Figure 9-12 presents such a **Sphere** class, containing a **volume()** method.

```
/** Sphere.java provides sphere-related methods.
 */
public class Sphere {
   /** volume of a sphere (class method)
     * @param radius, the (double) radius of the sphere
     * @return the volume of a sphere with that radius
     */
   public static double volume(double radius) {
      return 4.0 / 3.0 * Math.PI * Math.pow(radius, 3.0);
   }
   // ... other sphere-related methods omitted ...
}
```

FIGURE 9-12 A partial **Sphere.java** class library

Building a **Box** class is similar, as can be seen in Figure 9-13.

```
/** Box.java provides box-related methods.
 */
public class Box {
   /** volume of a box (class method)
     * @param length, the (double) length of the box
     * @param width, the (double) width of the box
```

continued

```
    * @param height, the (double) height of the box
    * @return the volume of a box with these dimensions
    */
   public static double volume(double length, double width,
                                                   double height) {
      return length * width * height;
   }
   // ... other box-related methods omitted ...
}
```

FIGURE 9-13 A partial **Box.java** library

As described previously, the number of variables on the right side of a method's formula determines the number of parameters required. That is, the right side of the sphere volume formula has a single variable, *radius*, so the **Sphere.volume()** method requires just one parameter. By contrast, the right side of the box volume formula has three variables — *length*, *width*, and *height* — so **Box.volume()** has three parameters.

With these classes in the same folder as the **BalloonPrank** class, the **BalloonPrank** class in Figure 9-11 will produce the results shown at the end of the figure. If balloons come in packages of 100, we will need to buy ten packages (1000 balloons) to fill our roommate's bedroom, assuming that we can inflate them to a 6-inch radius.

Figures 9-12 and 9-13 contain just the methods needed to compute the volumes to solve our immediate problem. However, as indicated near the end of each class, we can add other methods to each class as time and opportunity permit. (See Project 9.6.)

9.3.4 Unit Testing

Recall that we cannot have confidence that a program is producing correct results until we have tested it. When writing methods, a special approach is often used for testing. The idea is to create a special **test class**, whose sole purpose is to test the methods in the program or library and make certain that they work as they should. One way to do this is by using these steps:

To test a class (program or library) named **C**:

1. Build a separate class named **CTester**, to test the methods in **C**.
2. Within **CTester**, build an empty **main()** method.
3. For each method **m()** in **C**:
   a. Within **CTester**, build a void method named **testM()**.
   b. Within **testM()**, add statements that test method **m()**.
   c. Within **main()**, invoke **testM()**.
4. Run **CTester**.

This approach — in which we build a test class containing a test method for each method in our program or library, and then run its test methods — is called **unit testing.**[2]

To illustrate this approach, Figure 9-14 presents a test class named **BoxTester**. It contains a test method named **testVolume()**, that tests the **volume**() method of the **Box** class.

```
/** BoxTester.java tests the methods of Box.java.
 */
public class BoxTester {
  public static void main(String[] args) {
     testVolume();
     // add tests for other Box methods here
  }

  public static void testVolume() {
     System.out.print("Testing Box.volume(): ");
     double vol = Box.volume(2.0, 3.0, 4.0);   // test 1
     assert vol == 24.0;
     System.out.print(" 1 ");
     vol = Box.volume(6.0, 5.0, 4.0);          // test 2
     assert vol == 120.0;
     System.out.print(" 2 ");
     System.out.println(" Passed!");
  }
}
```

```
Result:
Testing Box.volume():  1  2  Passed!
```

FIGURE 9-14 **BoxTester.java**

A **SphereTester** class is similar. Building it is left as an exercise.

2. To facilitate unit testing in Java, there is a special unit testing tool called **JUnit**. For those who would like to go beyond the simple approach we present here, see **www.junit.org**.

Our test methods use Java's **assert statement**,[3] which can be used to verify that something is true at a given point in a program. This statement behaves as follows:

Pattern for Java's **assert** *Statement*

```
assert BooleanExpression ;
```

Behavior:

If ***BooleanExpression*** *is* **true**, *execution proceeds to the next statement. Otherwise, the program halts and displays an error message.*

The **assert** *statement is used to verify that something is true when execution reaches a specific position in the program.*

The **assert** statement is not to be used casually, because if its ***BooleanExpression*** is **false**, the program halts. However, for our situation — where we want to test the value returned by a method — this behavior is exactly what we want.

To illustrate, let's trace the execution of **testVolume()**. The first statement is this:

```
System.out.print("Testing Box.volume(): ");
```

This statement displays the name of the method we are testing, so that if **testVolume()** uncovers a problem, we'll know the problem is in **Box.volume()**, not somewhere else. Next are these statements:

```
double vol = Box.volume(2.0, 3.0, 4.0);
assert vol == 24.0;
System.out.print(" 1 ");
```

These three statements constitute the first test for the **Box.volume()** method. The first statement invokes the **volume()** method from the **Box** library, passes it arguments that produce an easily verifiable result, and stores that result into a variable named **vol**. The **assert** statement then uses the equality operator to compare the value stored in **vol** against the value we expect the **volume()** method to produce. If they do not match (that is, **vol == 24.0** is **false**), then the program displays an error message like this and then halts:

```
Exception in thread "main" java.lang.AssertionError
   at BoxTester.testVolume(BoxTester.java:35)
      at BoxTester.main(BoxTester.java:8)
```

If we see **"Testing Volume.box():"** followed by this error, we know that the **volume()** method failed the first test. However, if **vol == 24.0** is **true**, then execution

3. To use the **assert** statement, Java programs must be run using the **-ea** (*e*nable *a*ssertions) switch. To do so in Eclipse, choose **Run->Run...**, click the **Arguments** tab, type **-ea** in the **VM Arguments** text box, and click the **Run** button. To do so from the command line, type **-ea** between the word **java** and the name of the class you are running (for example, **java -ea BoxTester**). Otherwise, Java will ignore all **assert** statements.

proceeds to the next statement, which displays `" 1 "`, indicating that **`Box.volume()`** has passed the first test.

From there, execution proceeds to the second test, performed by these statements:

```
vol = Box.volume(6.0, 5.0, 4.0);
assert vol == 120.0;
System.out.print(" 2 ");
```

Once again, we invoke method **`volume()`**, passing it arguments that produce a result that is easy to verify, and store that result into variable **`vol`**. We then use a second **`assert`** statement to verify that the result is what we expected (**`120.0`**). If not, the **`assert`** will display an error message; otherwise, execution will flow to the third statement, which will indicate **`volume()`** has passed our second test.

If **`volume()`** passes all of the tests, then the final statement in **`testVolume()`** displays **`"Passed!"`**, yielding this cumulative display from **`testVolume()`**:

```
Testing Box.volume(): 1  2  Passed!
```

How many tests should a test method contain? The answer is *at least two*, and perhaps more, depending on the complexity of the method being tested. In general, the more complex a method is, the greater the number of tests required to thoroughly test it. For a simple method like **`Box.volume()`**, two tests are probably sufficient. The **`Sphere.volume()`** method is slightly more complex, so we might add a third test, just to be certain it is working correctly.

Like programming in general, building good tests is a skill that improves with practice.

9.3.5 Test-Driven Development

Program testing is very important. It is so important, a growing number of programmers make it their *starting point* when writing methods. That is, when they need to build a method, these programmers follow this approach:

To build a method `m()` for a program:

1. If we haven't already done so, build a test class for the program.
2. Write a method named `testM()` that thoroughly tests method `m()`, and invoke `testM()` in the main() method of the test class.
3. Write method `m()` for the program.
4. Run the test class to test method `m()`; when it passes all tests, use method `m()` in the program.

Do you see the difference between this approach and the approach we have been using? In this approach, a programmer builds a test method *first*, before building the method for the program! This approach is called **test-driven development**, because it starts with the test, and the test "drives" the subsequent development of the method by focusing our efforts on passing the test.

Though it may seem backward, test-driven development is actually a good way to write methods, because it forces us to think carefully about how we will invoke the method and what it will return, before we begin building the method. This offers these advantages:

- If we know how we will invoke a method, we know how many arguments we will pass it.
- If we know how we many arguments we will pass a method, we know how many parameters we must declare when we build the method.
- If we know what value the method should return for a given group of arguments, we know the method's return type.

Thus, a test like this:

```
double volume = Box.volume(2.0, 3.0, 4.0);
assert volume == 24.0;
```

tells us that we will need to define three **double** parameters for **Box.volume()**, and that its return type is **double**. In a similar fashion, suppose that we store the **firstInitial()** and **lastInitial()** methods in a library named **Initials**. Then tests like these:

```
char ch1 = Initials.firstInitial("John Ronald Ruel Tolkien");
assert ch1 == 'J';
char ch2 = Initials.lastInitial("John Ronald Ruel Tolkien");
assert ch2 == 'T';
```

tells us that methods **firstInitial()** and **lastInitial()** each require a single **String** parameter, and that each method's return type is **char**.

From a different perspective, imagine your reaction if, the day before your final exam, your teacher gives you a copy of thc exam! You would know exactly what you need to do to pass the exam! Building the test method first, and then writing the method, is like having a copy of the exam in advance. You know exactly what your method must do to pass the test.

9.4 Instance Methods

We have seen that a method library is a class containing a group of related class methods. Such a library makes its methods reusable, but it doesn't really use the full capabilities of a class.

Object-based and object-oriented programming are, by definition, programming with objects, which involves sending messages to objects. To send messages to objects, we must learn how to define instance methods, which are the focus of the rest of this chapter.

9.4.1 Box Objects

Suppose that in addition to its **volume()** class method, the **Box** class contained a **surfaceArea()** class method. (See Project 9.6.) To use these class methods in a program, we must type something like this:

```
double boxVol = Box.volume(9.0, 8.0, 7.0);
double boxSurfArea = Box.surfaceArea(9.0, 8.0, 7.0);
```

The problem with using class methods is that we have to pass the dimensions of the box as arguments each time we invoke a method — we're doing the same work, multiple times.

Using Objects

An alternative approach would be to revise the **Box** class in such a way that we can build a **Box** *object* and pass these dimensions *once*, when we define the object:

```
Box aBox = new Box(9.0, 8.0, 7.0);
```

If a **Box** object "remembers" its dimensions by storing them in variables named **myLength**, **myWidth**, and **myHeight**, we can visualize the result of this statement as shown in Figure 9-15.

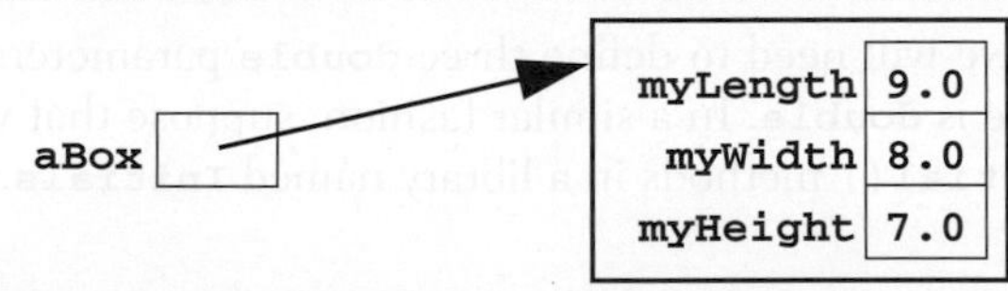

FIGURE 9-15 A **Box** handle and object

Given such a **Box** object that "knows" its dimensions, we might then ask it questions like "What is your volume?":

```
double vol = aBox.volume();
```

or "What is your surface area?":

```
double surfArea = aBox.surfaceArea();
```

Because the **Box** object "knows" its length, width, and height, we need not pass any dimensions with these messages. Instead, a method can compute its result using the stored dimensions:

```
public double volume() { return myLength * myWidth * myHeight; }
```

Figure 9-16 presents another version of the **Box** class, revised to support this approach.

```
/** Box.java provides box-related methods.
 */
public class Box {
   // instance variables to "remember" dimensions
   private double myLength, myWidth, myHeight;
```

continued

```
6
7      // Box constructor
8      public Box(double length, double width, double height) {
9         myLength = length;
10        myWidth = width;
11        myHeight = height;
12     }
13
14     // volume of a Box (instance method)
15     public double volume() { return myLength *
                                        myWidth * myHeight; }
16
17     // accessor methods for instance variables
18     public double getLength() { return myLength; }
19     public double getWidth()  { return myWidth;  }
20     public double getHeight() { return myHeight; }
21
22     // volume of a box (class method)
23     public static double volume(double length, double width,
                                     double height) {
24        return length * width * height;
25     }
26     // ... other methods omitted ...
27  }
28
```

FIGURE 9-16 The **Box** class, revised to support **Box** objects

Instance Variables

The first statement in Figure 9-16 (line 5) declares **myLength**, **myWidth**, and **myHeight**, the variables in which a **Box** object will "remember" its dimensions:

```
private double myLength, myWidth, myHeight;
```

Each instance of the **Box** class — each **Box** object — will have its own copies of these variables, to keep its dimensions distinct from those of other **Box** objects. Because of this, they are known as **instance variables** in Java terminology. An instance variable is a variable defined within a class, outside of a method, without the word **static**. (By contrast, variables defined within a class, outside of the methods, and using the word

static, are **class variables.** A class variable is associated with a class, and all objects of that class will *share* that variable.)

Like methods, instance variables are declared with an **access specifier**, which can be **private**, **protected**, or **public**. Unlike methods, instance variables should always be declared to be **private**. Doing so prevents programmers from accessing them directly, and potentially changing their values in unexpected ways.

Instance variables can be given whatever names one likes. However, the name should include that characteristic of the object that the variable is being used to "remember" (for example, *length* or *width*).

It is our practice to prepend the word "**my**" to the names of our instance variables. Doing so serves to distinguish instance variables from other variables, and can be helpful when we start defining methods. For example, pretend with me for a moment that I am a **Box** object. How do I respond if a program asks me, "What is your width?" Return **myWidth**, of course.

Constructors

Once we have instance variables in which an object can "remember" things, we need a way to initialize those variables to user-supplied values. That is the role of the next item in Figure 9-16, on lines 8-12:

```
public Box(double length, double width, double height) {
    myLength = length;
    myWidth = width;
    myHeight = height;
}
```

This item is called a **constructor**, because when an object is constructed using the **new** operator, this item is used to initialize the new object's instance variables.

> The name of a constructor is always the name of its class.
>
> A constructor has no return type (not even **void**).

To illustrate, if we were to write:

```
Box box1 = new Box(1.1, 2.2, 3.3);
Box box2 = new Box(9.9, 8.8, 7.7);
```

then

1. In the first statement, the **new** operator:
    d. Allocates the memory for a new **Box** object.
    e. Invokes the **Box** constructor, passing **1.1** to parameter **length**, **2.2** to parameter **width**, and **3.3** to parameter **height**. The **Box** constructor then runs, which sets that object's instance variables (**myLength**, **myWidth**, and **myHeight**) to the corresponding parameter values (**1.1**, **2.2**, and **3.3**, respectively).
    f. Returns a reference to the new **Box** object, which is stored in the **Box** handle **box1**.

2. Then in the second statement, the **new** operator:

   a. Allocates the memory for a new **Box** object;
   b. Invokes the **Box** constructor, passing **9.9** to parameter **length**, **8.8** to parameter **width**, and **7.7** to parameter **height**. The **Box** constructor then runs, which sets that object's instance variables to the parameter values (**9.9**, **8.8**, and **7.7**, respectively).
   c. Returns a reference to the new **Box** object, which is stored in the **Box** handle **box2**.

   Following these two statements, we can visualize **box1** and **box2** as seen in Figure 9-17.

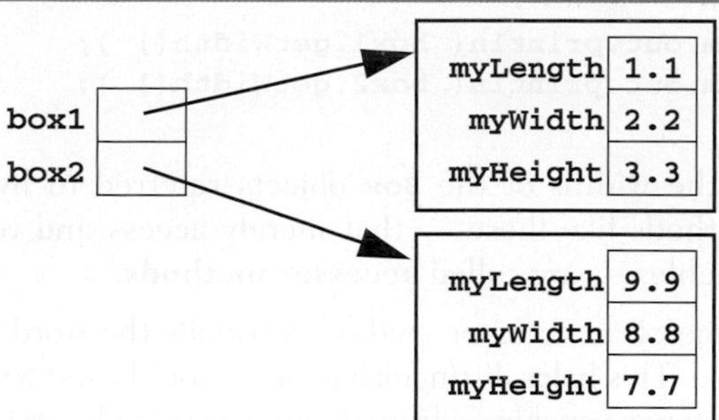

FIGURE 9-17 **Box** handles and objects

Instance Methods

With the ability to initialize objects, we are ready for a method that asks a **Box** object "What is your volume?" Such a method is shown in Figure 9-16, line 15.

```
public double volume() { return myLength * myWidth * myHeight; }
```

Note that this method is *not* defined with the word **static**. The absence of **static** makes this an **instance method** — a message we send to an instance of a class (that is, an object). To illustrate, given this method and the two **Box** objects shown in Figure 9-17, we can write:

```
double box1Vol = box1.volume();
double box2Vol = box2.volume();
```

The first statement sends the **volume()** message via the **box1** handle to the top **Box** in Figure 9-17, which computes **1.1 * 2.2 * 3.3**, and then returns the result, **7.986**, which is then stored in the variable **box1Vol**. The second statement sends the **volume()** message via the **box2** handle to the bottom box in Figure 9-17, which computes **9.9 * 8.8 * 7.7**, and then returns the result, **670.824**, which is then stored in the variable **box2Vol**. The key point is that because each **Box** object has its own copies of the instance variables, sending the same **volume()** message to each object produces a different result.

Lines 18-20 of Figure 9-16 define three more instance methods:

```
public double getLength() { return myLength; }
public double getWidth()  { return myWidth; }
public double getHeight() { return myHeight; }
```

These simple methods allow a programmer to ask a **Box** object, "What is your length?", "What is your width?", and "What is your height?", respectively. That is, given the **Box** objects shown in Figure 9-17, the statements:

```
System.out.println( box1.getWidth() );
System.out.println( box2.getWidth() );
```

will display the widths of the **Box** objects referred to by **box1** (**2.2**) and **box2** (**8.8**). Instance methods like these — that merely access and return the values of an object's instance variables — are called **accessor methods**.

The name of an accessor method is usually the word "**get**" followed by the attribute being retrieved. This helps distinguish an accessor like **getWidth()** — that just accesses and returns an instance variable — from a non-accessor like **volume()**, which actually performs a computation. This convention is so common, accessor methods are often called **getters**.

9.4.2 Sphere Objects

We can use these same ideas to revise the **Sphere** class, as shown in Figure 9-18.

```
/** Sphere.java provides sphere-related methods...
 */
public class Sphere {
   // instance variable
   private double myRadius;

   // constructor
   public Sphere(double radius) { myRadius = radius; }

   // volume of a Sphere (instance method)
   public double volume() { return volume(myRadius); }

   // accessor method for myRadius
   public double getRadius() {return myRadius; }

   // volume of a sphere (class method)
   public static double volume(double radius) {
      return 4.0 / 3.0 * Math.PI * Math.pow(radius, 3.0);
```

continued

```
    }
    // ... other sphere-related methods omitted ...
}
```

FIGURE 9-18 The **Sphere** class, revised to support **Sphere** objects

As before, we begin by declaring an instance variable for each characteristic that distinguishes one object of this type from another. For a sphere, there is just one thing to "remember":

```
private double myRadius;
```

We then define a constructor to initialize this instance variable:

```
public Sphere(double radius) { myRadius = radius; }
```

Given this much, a programmer can write:

```
Sphere sphere1 = new Sphere(4.0);
Sphere sphere2 = new Sphere(5.5);
```

and **sphere1** and **sphere2** will refer to two distinct **Sphere** objects, as seen in Figure 9-19.

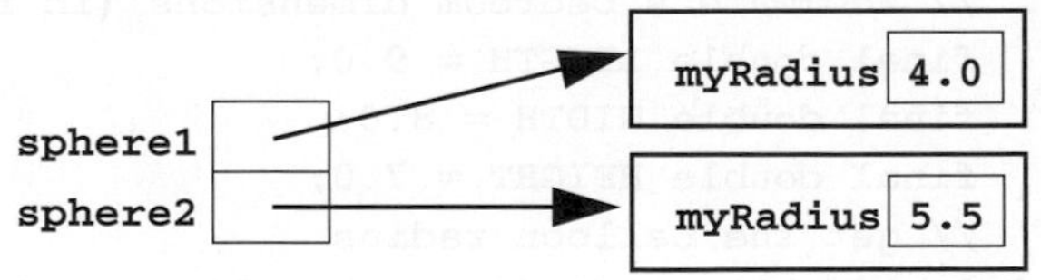

FIGURE 9-19 **Sphere** handles and objects

To compute a **Sphere** object's volume, we can invoke **Sphere.volume()** from Figure 9-12.

```
public double volume() { return volume(myRadius); }
```

That is, rather than rewriting the sphere volume formula using **myRadius**, we can return the result of passing **myRadius** to the **volume()** class method.

We can now send **volume()** messages to the objects in Figure 9-19:

```
System.out.println( sphere1.volume() );
System.out.println( sphere2.volume() );
```

The top **Sphere** object will compute and return its volume using its value for **myRadius** (**4.0**). The bottom object will perform the same computation, but using its own **myRadius** value (**5.5**). Each object thus responds to the same message by computing a different result, because their instance variables have different values.

The last revision to the **Sphere** class is an accessor method to retrieve the sphere's radius:

```
public double getRadius() { return myRadius; }
```

Once again, pretend with me that I am a **Sphere** object receiving the **getRadius()** message. What do I do? Return **myRadius**. What could be more natural?

9.4.3 The BalloonPrank Program Using Objects

Given revised **Sphere** and **Box** classes, we can revise the **BalloonPrank** program in a way that uses objects. Figure 9-20 presents the revised version.

```
/** BalloonPrank.java reads a balloon's radius and
 *   displays the number of balloons needed to fill a bedroom.
 */
import java.util.Scanner;

public class BalloonPrank {
   public static void main(String[] args) {
      // roommate's bedroom dimensions (in feet)
      final double LENGTH = 9.0;
      final double WIDTH = 8.0;
      final double HEIGHT = 7.0;
      // get the balloon radius
      System.out.print("Enter a balloon radius (inches): ");
      Scanner keyboard = new Scanner(System.in);
      double balloonRadius = keyboard.nextDouble();
      balloonRadius /= 12.0;            // convert inches to feet
      // build balloon and bedroom models
      Sphere balloon = new Sphere(balloonRadius);
      Box bedroom = new Box(LENGTH, WIDTH, HEIGHT);
      // compute balloons in bedroom
      double balloonsRequired = bedroom.volume() /
                                    balloon.volume();
      System.out.printf("Using balloons of radius %.0f inches,"
                        + " you will need %.0f balloons",
                        balloonRadius*12, balloonsRequired);
   }
```

continued

```
26  }
    Result:
    Enter a balloon radius (inches): 6
    Using balloons of radius 6 inches, you will need 963 balloons
    Result:
    Enter a balloon radius (inches): 4
    Using balloons of radius 4 inches, you will need 3249 balloons
```

FIGURE 9-20 The revised **BalloonPrank** program

As can be seen, the resulting program produces the same results as that of Figure 9-11. However, this version uses **Sphere** and **Box** objects to model a balloon and bedroom, respectively. Using this approach, we have **Sphere** and **Box** classes that can be reused for a wide variety of problems. For example, to compute the volume of our planet, a programmer can type:

```
Sphere earth = new Sphere(6356.75);  // quadratic mean radius in km
double earthVolume = earth.volume(); // cubic km
```

9.5 Program Design Revisited

9.5.1 Classes, Methods, and Design

In Section 7.5, we saw that we can design software using these steps:

1.	Write the user story. Identify the nouns and verbs within it.
2.	For each noun in your algorithm: Find a type to represent that object. If no existing type will adequately represent the object, build a class to create a new type. Use that type to declare the object.
3.	For each verb in your algorithm: Find a message that performs that verb's action, and send it to the verb's object. If no existing message that provides that verb's action, define a method to perform that action.
4.	Organize your nouns and verbs into an algorithm that solves your problem.
5.	Write your program, using your algorithm as a blueprint.
6.	Test your program. If it produces incorrect results, return to Step 4.

Note the last two sentences in Step 2.

> **If no existing type will adequately represent the object, build a class to create a new type. Use that type to declare the object.**

This was the case with the final version of the **`BalloonPrank`** program in Figure 9-20. With no existing type being adequate to represent a *bedroom* or a *balloon*, we built generalized classes (**`Box`** and **`Sphere`**) for such objects, and then used these types to declare the objects.

The last sentence in Step 3 is also worth noting. We can paraphrase it as follows:

> **If no existing message provides a verb's action, define a method to perform it.**

This also occurred with the program in Figure 9-20. Having no existing message to compute the volume of a box or sphere, we built **`volume()`** methods for each class. Such methods may be class or instance methods, but instance methods are generally more convenient to use.

Classes and methods hide low-level implementation details. For example, **`Math.sqrt(x)`** calculates the square root of **`x`**. So long as it produces correct results and doesn't take too long to do so, we don't worry about *how* it calculates its result. Similarly,

```
System.out.print("Hi!");
```

makes **`"Hi!"`** appear on the screen — the details of how it accomplishes this remain hidden.

This concept of using a method or class to hide low-level details is called **abstraction**. Thinking in terms of abstractions frees us from having to worry about low-level details. This in turn lets us focus on the higher-level behavior needed to solve a problem.

9.5.2 Keywords, Identifiers, and Scope

There are different kinds of words in a Java program, including:

- Words whose meanings are predefined, such as **`class`**, **`int`**, **`void`**, **`double`**, **`return`**, **`final`**, **`static`**, and many others. These kind of words are known as **keywords**, and they cannot be used to name variables, constants, methods, or classes. A complete list of Java's keywords is given in Appendix C.
- Words whose meanings are defined by the programmer, such as the names of classes, methods, variables, and constants. These are known as **identifiers**.

When the Java compiler processes a keyword, the meaning of that word is built into the compiler. However, when the Java compiler processes an identifier, its meaning is not built in; it is the responsibility of the programmer to *declare* the meaning of that word for the compiler. This is the purpose of a declaration statement; when we declare a class, a variable, a constant, or a method, we are telling the Java compiler that word's meaning in the program.

To illustrate, if we type the following method:

```
public static double massToEnergy(double mass) {
   final double SPEED_OF_LIGHT = 2.99792458e8;
   return mass * Math.pow(SPEED_OF_LIGHT, 2.0);
}
```

we are telling the Java compiler several things, including:

1. The identifier **massToEnergy** is the name of a class method whose return type is **double**, and that must be passed a single argument whose type is **double**-compatible.
2. The identifier **mass** is the name of a **double** parameter in method **massToEnergy()**.
3. The identifier **SPEED_OF_LIGHT** is the name of a **double** constant whose value is **2.99792458e8** in **massToEnergy()**.

So far so good. Where things get tricky is when we use the same identifier in different ways in the same class. For example, we might build the **Initials** class library shown in Figure 9-21, to store the initials-related methods we built in Section 9.2.5.

```
public class Initials {
  // get the first initial of a name
  public static char firstInitial(String name) {
     char result = name.charAt(0);
     return result;
  }

   // get the last initial of a name
   public static char lastInitial(String name) {
     int indexOfSpace = name.lastIndexOf(' ');
     return name.charAt(indexOfSpace + 1);
   }

  // get the first and last initials of a name
   public static String twoInitials(String name) {
     String result = "";          // start with empty string
     result += firstInitial(name); // append first initial
     result += lastInitial(name);  // append last initial
     return result;                // we're done!
   }
}
```

FIGURE 9-21 An **Initials** class

Here, we see that the identifier **result** is used twice in the same class, and it has two different meanings! The **firstInitial()** method declares **result** to be a **char** variable, while the **twoInitials()** method declares **result** to be a **String** variable. When the Java compiler processes the word **result**, how does it know which meaning to use?

To answer this question, it is helpful to know that a Java **block** is a pair of matching curly braces (**{** and **}**), plus any declarations or statements within them. There are four blocks in Figure 9-21, three of them nested inside the fourth, as shown in Figure 9-22.

```
public class Initials {

   public static char firstInitial(String name) {
      char result = name.charAt(0);
      return result;
   }

   public static char lastInitial(String name) {
      int indexOfSpace = name.lastIndexOf(' ');
      return name.charAt(indexOfSpace + 1);
   }

   public static String twoInitials(String name) {
      String result = "";
      result += firstInitial(name);
      result += lastInitial(name);
      return result;
   }
}
```

FIGURE 9-22 Some Java blocks

When the Java compiler processes an identifier's declaration, it records the information about that identifier. When the compiler subsequently processes an identifier in a statement, it must look up that word's meaning. To do so, it first looks for a declaration of that identifier within the current block. If it does not find a declaration there, it looks in a surrounding block; if not found there, it looks in a surrounding block; and so on, until it reaches the outermost class.[4] The Java compiler uses the first declaration it finds; if it cannot find a declaration of that word, it generates an error message.

To illustrate, when method **firstInitial()** performs the statement:

```
return result;
```

it does so within the block of **firstInitial()**. In processing this statement, the Java compiler searches the current block, and finds a declaration of **result** whose type is **char**.

By contrast, when method **twoInitials()** performs the identical statement:

```
return result;
```

4. Actually, the search for a declaration continues from the class to the superclass, to that class's superclass, and so on, until the **Object** class is reached. We'll learn about superclasses and the **Object** class in Chapter 14.

it does so within the block of **twoInitials()**. To process this statement, the Java compiler searches the current block, and finds a declaration of **result** whose type is **String**.

It may seem strange, but the same word — **result**, in this case — can have different meanings at different places in a program! That part of a program where a particular declaration of a word provides its meaning is called the **scope** of that declaration.

For local identifiers — variables or constants declared in a block within a method — the scope begins at the identifier's declaration and ends at that block's closing curly brace (**}**). For example, the scope of the **char** variable **result** begins at its declaration and ends at the closing curly brace of method **firstInitial()**. The scope of the **String** variable **result** begins at its declaration, and ends at the closing curly brace of method **twoInitials()**. If we attempt to access a local identifier before its declaration, or past the end of the block in which it is declared, the Java compiler will generate an error. To illustrate, if we were to write:

```
public static String twoInitials(String name) {
   result += firstInitial(name); // ERROR! result is used here,
   String result = "";           //  before its declaration.
   result += lastInitial(name);  // OK - use after declared
   return result;
}
```

the Java compiler will generate an error for the first statement, because it uses **result** before it is has been declared, outside of its scope.

Parameters are treated in a similar fashion. A parameter's scope begins at the beginning of its method, and ends at its method's closing curly brace. If we attempt to access a parameter outside of the method in which it is declared, the Java compiler will generate an error.

By contrast, the scope of an identifier declared in a class — a method, class variable, or instance variable — begins at the beginning of the class, and ends at the end of the class. Such identifiers can thus be accessed anywhere within the class, without generating an error. To illustrate, instead of writing the **Initials** class of Figure 9-21 the way we did, we could have instead written it as shown in Figure 9-23, with the definition of **twoInitials()** preceding the definitions of **firstInitial()** and **lastInitial()**.

```
public class Initials {

   public static String twoInitials(String name) {
      String result = "";
      result += firstInitial(name);   // used before declared - OK
      result += lastInitial(name);    // used before declared - OK
      return result;
   }

   public static char firstInitial(String name) {
      char result = name.charAt(0);
      return result;
   }

   public static char lastInitial(String name) {
      int indexOfSpace = name.lastIndexOf(' ');
      return name.charAt(indexOfSpace + 1);
   }
}
```

FIGURE 9-23 An **Initials** class (alternative version)

Method **twoInitials()** can invoke methods **firstInitial()** and **lastInitial()**, even though their definitions follow its definition! Because the identifiers **firstInitial** and **lastInitial** are declared in a *class* (as opposed to in a *method*), their scope begins at the beginning of the class, not at their declaration, and ends at the end of the class.

The same is true of instance variables. In writing the **Sphere** class of Figure 9-18, we could declare **myRadius** at the bottom of the class instead of at the top:

```
public class Sphere {
   public Sphere(double radius) { myRadius = radius; }
   public double volume() { return volume(myRadius); }
   public static double volume(double radius) {
      return 4.0 * Math.PI * Math.pow(radius, 3.0) / 3.0;
   }

   private double myRadius;    // declaration following uses
}
```

and the Java compiler will not generate an error. However, an organization (for example, a company or school) may require that a convention be followed, for consistency and readability.

9.6 Chapter Summary

- To make a group of statements reusable, place them within a method.
- In Java, a method is either a class method or an instance method.
  - A class method is a message that is sent to a class. A class method is defined by placing the word **`static`** before the method's return type.
  - An instance method is a message that is sent to an instance of a class — an object. If a method is *not* defined using the word **`static`**, it is an instance method.
- In Java, a method is either **`void`** or non-**`void`**, depending on its return type.
  - **`void`** methods correspond to Alice methods, and are defined by using the word **`void`** for the method's return type. A **`void`** method produces no value, so it is used like a statement.
  - non-**`void`** Java methods correspond to Alice functions, and are defined by using a primitive or reference type for the method's return type. A non-**`void`** method produces a value, the type of which must match the method's return type, so a non-**`void`** method can be used anywhere an expression of that type can occur. Non-**`void`** methods use a **`return`** statement to produce the method's value.
- For each argument that is passed when a message is sent, there must be a parameter of that type in the corresponding method; and vice versa. Arguments are matched against parameters from left to right.
- A method library is a class whose purpose is to store class methods, so that they can be conveniently reused by different programs.
- When none of the existing types are adequate to represent an object in a problem, build a class to represent such objects, and use it to declare the objects in your program.
- Testing is very important when it comes to methods. Unit testing and test-driven development are two (related) approaches to method testing.
- The scope of a declaration is that part of a program in which the identifier being declared has a particular meaning.
  - If an identifier is declared in a block within a method, its scope begins at its declaration and ends at the end of the block.
  - The scope of a parameter begins at the beginning of its method, and ends at the end of that method.
  - If an identifier is declared in a class, its scope begins at the beginning of the class and ends at the end of the class.

9.6.1 Key Terms

abstraction
access specifier
accessor method
argument
assert statement
behavior
block
brute force approach
class method
constructor
getter
identifier
instance method
instance variable
keyword
local
method
method library
non-**void** method
parameter
return statement
return type
reuseability
scope
static
test class
test-driven development
unit testing
void
void method

Programming Projects

9.1 Write a method that, given a `String` containing the name of a month (for example, `"January"`), returns the three-letter abbreviation for that month (for example `"Jan"`).

9.2 Given three numbers `a`, `b`, and `c`, design and write two functions: `max(a, b, c)`, which returns the maximum of these three numbers, and `min(a, b, c)`, which returns the minimum of these three numbers. Then write a program that asks the user for three numbers and uses your methods to compute and display the maximum and minimum of the three. Your methods should use the `Math.max()` and `Math.min()` methods. (Hint: You may invoke the methods more than once.)

9.3 Using an approach similar to that of the program in Figure 9-2, write a program that displays the lyrics of the song "Old MacDonald," as given in Section 3.2.1. Your program should use a non-`void` method to compute and return a `String` for each verse.

9.4 On the Yoyodyne 9000 computer system, usernames consist of the first letter of a person's first name, followed by the first four letters of his or her last name. Design and write a method that, given a person's name, computes and returns his or her username. For example, given the names `"Ada Lovelace"`, `"Homer Jay Simpson"`, or `"John Ronald Ruel Tolkien"`, your method should return `"alove"`, `"hsimp"`, and `"jtolk"`, respectively. Then write a program that prompts the user for that person's full name and displays his or her username. Your program and method may assume that a person's last name contains at least four letters.

9.5 Design and write a method named `containsUppercase()` that, given a `String`, returns `true` if the `String` contains one or more uppercase letters; otherwise, the method should return `false`. (Hint: Look in the `String` API; use two of the methods there and a logical expression to solve the problem.)

9.6 The surface areas of a sphere and a box are given by the formulas below. Using these formulas, design and write **`surfaceArea()`** methods for the **`Sphere`** and **`Box`** classes given in Section 9.3.3. Then write two programs, one that uses **`surfaceArea()`** to compute the surface area of a sphere whose radius is given by the user, and the other that uses **`surfaceArea()`** to compute the area of a box whose dimensions are given by the user.

$$sphereSurfaceArea = \pi \times radius^2 \times 4$$
$$boxSurfaceArea = 2 \times length \times width + 2 \times length \times height + 2 \times width \times height$$

9.7 The volume and surface area of a cylinder can be computed using the formulas below. Design and write a **`Cylinder`** class containing methods for each of these formulas. Then write a program that, given a *radius* value and a *height* value, uses your methods to compute the volume and surface area of a cylinder with those dimensions. Write a program that uses your methods, and use it to compute the volume and surface area of a can of soda.

$$cylinderVolume = \pi \times radius^2 \times height$$
$$cylinderSurfaceArea = 2 \times \pi \times radius^2 + 2 \times \pi \times radius \times height$$

9.8 The quadratic formula — which computes the roots of a quadratic equation $y = ax^2 + bx + c$ — is given below. Design and write a **`Quadratic`** class containing two class methods: **`plusRoot()`**, which returns the root when the plus sign is applied; and **`minusRoot()`**, which returns the root when the minus sign is applied. Then write a **`main()`** method that gets *a*, *b*, and *c* values from the user, and uses your methods to compute the roots of that quadratic equation.

$$quadratic_{roots} = \frac{-b \pm \sqrt{b^2 - 4ac}}{2a}$$

9.9 The mathematician Gauss discovered that the summation from 1 to *n*:

$$summation(n) = 1 + 2 + \ldots + (n-1) + n$$

and the summation from *a* to *b*:

$$summation(a, b) = a + (a+1) + \ldots + (b-1) + b$$

can be computed using the formulas below. Write methods for each of these formulas, and store them in a class named **`Gauss`**. Then write a test class containing test methods for each method.

$$summation(n) = \frac{n \times (n+1)}{2}$$

$$summation(a, b) = \frac{(b - a + 1) \times (a + b)}{2}$$

9.10 Proceed as in Project 9.6, 9.7, or 9.8, but build a constructor and instance methods for the class(es), and use them to solve the problem.

9.11 Proceed as in Project 9.4, 9.5, 9.6, 9.7, 9.8, 9.9, or 9.10, but also build unit tests for each method.

9.12 Proceed as in Project 9.4, 9.5, 9.6, 9.7, 9.8, 9.9, or 9.10, but use test-driven development.

Chapter 10
Flow Control in Java

If you kill him with the pill from the till by making with it the drug in the jug, you need not light the candle with the handle on the gâteau from the château.

CAPT. HANS GEERING (SAM KELLY), IN *'ALLO 'ALLO*

You switch the switch marked "switch."

TREVOR CHAPLIN (JAMES BOLIN) IN *THE BEIDERBECKE AFFAIR*

The only good books she ever wrote were when she was with me: every morning, while she was sleeping, I'd cross out half her adjectives.

ALFRED DE MUSSET (MANDY PATINKIN) IN *IMPROMPTU*

Oh dear, she's stuck in an infinite loop and he's an idiot! Oh well, that's love for you, I guess.

PROFESSOR HUBERT FARNSWORTH (BILLY WEST II), IN *FUTURAMA*

Objectives

Upon completion of this chapter, you should be able to use the following control structures in Java:

- ❑ `if` statement
- ❑ `switch` statement
- ❑ `while` loop
- ❑ `for` loop
- ❑ `do` loop

In the last chapter, we saw how to define Java methods that run sequentially from beginning to end. In this chapter, we introduce Java's **`if`**, **`switch`**, **`while`**, **`for`**, and **`do`** statements; and use them to write methods that provide more complex behaviors.

10.1 Introductory Example: pH

Gardeners, chemists, and lifeguards all deal with *pH* — a value between 0 and 14 that indicates the concentration of hydrogen ions in a solution. Solutions with a pH in the bottom half of the scale are *acidic*, solutions in the top half are *alkaline* (or basic), and solutions in the middle are *neutral*. For example, a strong acid has pH 2 or lower (the pH of our stomach acids is about 2), lemon juice has pH 2.3, orange juice has pH 3.5, pure rain water has pH 5.6, pure water has pH 7; sea water has pH 8.5, household ammonia has pH 11.9, lime (calcium hydroxide) has pH 12.4, and some drain cleaners have pH values of 13 and higher.

pH is important to life because water can become too acidic or too alkaline. For example, a typical lake might have pH values ranging from 6.5 to 8.5, depending on the time of year, the depth at which samples were taken, and so on. As lake water becomes more acidic (at or below pH 6.5), whether due to acid rain or the local geology, the ability of fish to reproduce decreases; if the pH drops enough, the lake becomes devoid of life. If detected in time, such acidity can be countered by adding lime or other water-soluble alkaline substances to the lake, to raise its pH.

Suppose you are monitoring the pH in various lakes by taking water samples from them and recording their pH. If a lake is becoming acidic, such sampling may help us find the source of the acid. In big lakes, you take many samples; in small lakes, you take a few samples. Our first problem is to write a program that, given the pH values of a batch of samples, correctly labels them as *acidic*, *alkaline*, or *neutral*.

We might divide this problem into these subproblems:

1. Build a class to model pH values and operations, including:
   a. a constructor to build pH objects, given a valid pH value (0-14)
   b. a **`label()`** method that returns *acidic*, *alkaline*, or *neutral*, as appropriate
2. Write a program that uses this class to label the pH values from a given lake.

10.1.1 Subproblem 1: A `PH` Class

To model and operate on pH values, we will build a class named **`PH`**. (Recall that class names start with a capital letter.) As indicated above, this class will need a constructor and a **`label()`** method. We consider each of these in turn.

The `PH` Class

If we consider what a pH object needs to "remember," one obvious thing is its pH value. With that as a starting point, we can begin by building a minimal class, containing an instance variable named **`myValue`**:

```
public class PH {
    private double myValue;
}
```

The Constructor

To initialize the instance variable **myValue**, the class needs a constructor. Thinking through what this constructor must do, we can write the following user story:

> **PH** *Constructor.*
>
> *Given: pH, a real number.*
>
> If *pH* < the minimum pH value or *pH* > the maximum pH value, our method should display an error message and terminate; otherwise, it should save *pH* in **myValue**.

When a user story contains the word "if", it usually implies that we only want to do something *when certain conditions are true*. For example, we only want to initialize **myValue** to the value of parameter *pH* when its value is a valid pH value. Similarly, we only want our error message to display (and our program to terminate) when the value of parameter *pH* is invalid. From these observations, we might expand our **PH** class as follows:

```
public class PH {
   public static double MIN = 0.0;
   public static double MAX = 14.0;

   public PH(double pH) {
      if (pH < MIN || pH > MAX) {
         System.err.println("PH(): received invalid pH: " + pH);
         System.exit(1);
      } else {
         myValue = pH;
      }
   }

   private double myValue;
}
```

Just like Alice, Java has an **if statement** that will *guard* a group of statements, and only perform them when a condition is true. Our **PH()** constructor method uses an **if** statement to validate the value of parameter **pH**, before saving it in **myValue**.

Note also that instead of using the literal values **0.0** and **14.0**, we declare constants **MIN** and **MAX**. By making these public class (**static**) constants, the users of this class can use the expressions **PH.MIN** and **PH.MAX** to improve the readability of their programs.

The `label()` Method

The last piece of our **PH** class (for now) is a **label()** method. The basic idea is that upon receiving a **label()** message, a **PH** object will respond with *acidic*, *alkaline*, or *neutral*, as appropriate. If we think through the required behavior, we might write the following user story:

> **label() Method.**
>
> *If* **myValue** *< the minimum pH value or* **myValue** *> the maximum pH value, our method should return "error"; otherwise, if* **pH** *< the neutral value, it should return "acidic"; otherwise, if* **pH** *> the neutral value, it should return "alkaline"; otherwise, it should return "neutral".*

Once again, we see that magic word "if" in our user story, so we know our **label()** method will need an **if** statement. Figure 10-1 presents the complete **PH** class (minus documentation), including the **label()** method that behaves as specified in this user story.

```
// PH.java models pH values and operations.

public class PH {
  public static final double MIN = 0.0;
  public static final double MAX = 14.0;
  public static final double NEUTRAL = 7.0;

  public PH(double pH) {
     if (pH < MIN || pH > MAX) {
       System.err.println("PH(): bad argument received: " + pH);
       System.exit(1);
     } else {
       myValue = pH;
     }
  }

  public String label() {
   if (myValue < MIN || myValue > MAX) { // double-check validity
      return "error";
    } else if (myValue < NEUTRAL) {       // see if it's acidic
      return "acidic";
    } else if (myValue > NEUTRAL) {       // see if it's alkaline
      return "alkaline";
    } else {                              // if none of the above
      return "neutral";                   // it must be neutral
    }
  }

  private double myValue;
}
```

FIGURE 10-1 The **PH** class

To test the **PH** class in Figure 10-1, we might use the following tests:

```
String aLabel = new PH(0.0).label();
assert aLabel.equals("acidic");
aLabel = new PH(6.99).label();
assert aLabel.equals("acidic");
aLabel = new PH(7.0).label();
assert aLabel.equals("neutral");
aLabel = new PH(7.01).label();
assert aLabel.equals("alkaline");
aLabel = new PH(14.0).label();
assert aLabel.equals("alkaline");
```

In each of these tests, we (1) use an expression like **new PH(0.0)** to build a new **PH** object, (2) immediately send that **PH** object the **label()** message, and (3) store the character string returned by **label()** in a **String** variable named **aLabel**. The tests then test whether or not the character string in **aLabel** is correct using the **equals()** method.

Note that in a condition **str1 == str2**, where **str1** and **str2** are **String** handles, the **==** operator compares the *handles*, not the **String**s to which the handles refer.

The **equals()** method should be used to test the equality of **String** values.

10.1.2 Subproblem 2: Processing Multiple pH Values

Our second subproblem is to use the class in Figure 10-1 to display the correct labels for a sequence of pH values. For now, we will assume that such values will be entered at the keyboard; we will see how to read such values from a file in Chapter 11.

This program must read and process multiple pH values. Since different-sized lakes produce differing numbers of samples, the program cannot know in advance how many pH values the method will have to process. For situations where (1) repetition is required, but (2) the number of repetitions is not known in advance, Java supplies a **while statement** (or **while loop**).

To avoid an infinite loop, we must ensure that the **while** statement eventually terminates. In problems like this, where the values being read are constrained to some range of valid values (0-14 in this case), we can ask the user to enter *a value from outside that range* to indicate he or she is done (for example, -1). We use this approach in the following algorithm:

1. Set **boolean** variable *done* to **false**.
2. While NOT *done*:
   a. Prompt the user to enter a pH value (-1 to quit);
   b. Read *ph* from the keyboard;
   c. If *ph* < the minimum pH value: set *done* to **true**;
   d. Else: display **phLabel(*ph*)**.

This algorithm repeats Steps 2a, 2b, 2c, and 2d so long as *done* remains **false**. Since the **if** statement in Step 2c guards the change to *done*, *done* will remain **false** until the user enters a negative value. This provides a means of avoiding an infinite loop.

Figure 10-2 performs these steps in the **main()** method.

```
/* PhLabeler.java labels a sequence of pH values.
 */
import java.util.Scanner;

public class PhLabeler {
 public static void main(String[] args) {
   Scanner keyboard = new Scanner(System.in);
   boolean done = false;
   while (!done) {
      System.out.print("Enter a pH value (-1 to quit): ");
      double phValue = keyboard.nextDouble();
      if (phValue < PH.MIN) {
          done = true;
      } else {
          PH pH = new PH(phValue);
          System.out.println(" --> " + pH.label() );
      }
   }
 }
}
```

```
Result:
Enter a pH value (-1 to quit): 0.0
 --> acidic
Enter a pH value (-1 to quit): 6.9
 --> acidic
Enter a pH value (-1 to quit): 7.0
 --> neutral
Enter a pH value (-1 to quit): 7.1
 --> alkaline
Enter a pH value (-1 to quit): 14.0
 --> alkaline
Enter a pH value (-1 to quit): -1
```

FIGURE 10-2 A program to label pH values

The **main()** method in Figure 10-2 uses Java's **while** loop to produce repetitive behavior. Java provides three different loop statements, each with its own use. We will take a detailed look at each of them in Section 10.3.

10.2 Selective Execution

The program in Figure 10-2 uses Java's **if** statement to perform statements *selectively*, based on the value of a boolean expression or condition. That is, within the **if** statement:

```
if (phValue < PH.MIN) {
   done = true;
} else {
   PH ph = new PH(phValue);
   System.out.println(" --> " + ph.label() );
}
```

when the condition **phValue < PH.MIN** is **true**, this statement is performed:

```
done = true;
```

but when the condition **ph < PH.MIN** is **false**, these statements are performed:

```
PH ph = new PH(phValue);
System.out.println(" --> " + ph.label() ) ;
```

As we saw in Alice, this kind of execution — where we select one group of statements to be performed to the exclusion of another group of statements — is called **selective execution**. There are two Java statements that provide selective execution: the **if** statement and the **switch** statement. In this section, we examine both of these statements.

10.2.1 Java's if Statement

Java's **if** statement is a very flexible statement. For example, the **if** statement in the **main()** method of Figure 10-2 selects one of two groups of statements to perform:

```
if (phValue < PH.MIN) {
   done = true;                                     // group 1
} else {
   PH ph = new PH(phValue);                         // group 2
   System.out.println(" --> " + ph.label() );
}
```

By contrast, the **if** statement in the **label()** method selects one of four groups to perform:

```
if (myValue < MIN || myValue > MAX) {
    return "error";                                   // group 1
} else if (myValue < NEUTRAL) {
    return "acidic";                                  // group 2
} else if (myValue > NEUTRAL) {
    return "alkaline";                                // group 3
} else {
    return "neutral";                                 // group 4
}
```

An **if** statement can select from among one or more groups of statements, because the **else** portion of the statement is optional.

To illustrate, consider that the time of day can be expressed in either 12-hour format (for example, 2:59 AM, 2:59 PM) or 24-hour format (for example: 2:59, 14:59). Given an hour value in 24-hour format, the following method returns the corresponding 12-hour value:

```
public static int convert24To12(int hour24Value) {
    int hour12Value = hour24Value;
    if (hour24Value > 12) {
       hour12Value -= 12;
    }
    return hour12Value;
}
```

This method uses an **if** statement to selectively perform a subtraction statement. We can envision the method's behavior as a *branching flow*, as shown in Figure 10-3.

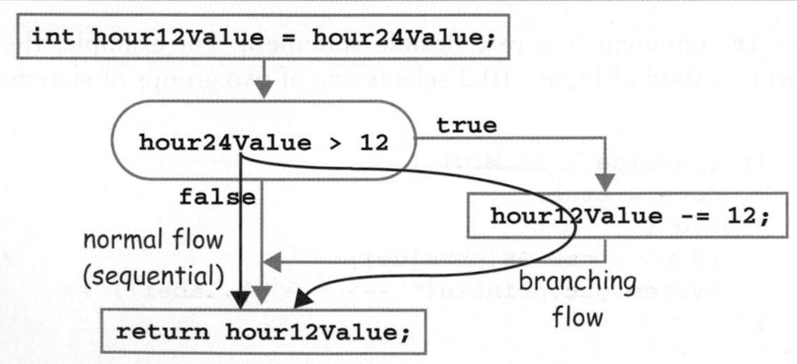

FIGURE 10-3 Flow through **convert24To12()**

Given values like 1, 2, 3, ..., 12, the method returns the given value; but given values like 13, 14, 15, ..., 24, it returns 1, 2, 3, ..., 12, respectively. Such **if** statements, that have no **else** portion, are sometimes called **one-branch if statements** because they provide a **branch** in the normal sequential flow through the method, as can be seen in Figure 10-3.

An **`if`** statement like that in the **`main()`** method of Figure 10-2 is called a **two-branch `if` statement**:

```
if (phValue < PH.MIN) {
    done = true;                                   // branch 1
} else {
    PH ph = new PH(phValue);                       // branch 2
    System.out.println(" --> " + ph.label() );
}
```

When this statement is performed, the flow follows one of the branches shown in Figure 10-4.

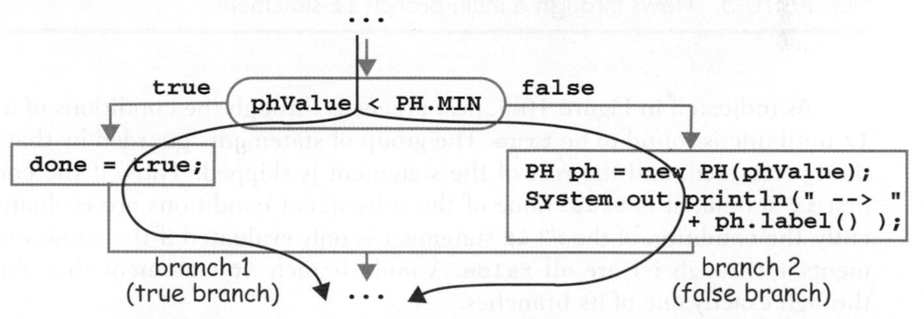

FIGURE 10-4 Flows through a two-branch `if` statement

Such statements are called **two-branch `if` statements** because the statement selects and performs one of the two branches, bypassing the other branch. The first branch is sometimes called the **`true` branch** because it is selected when the **`if`** statement's condition is **`true`**; the second branch is correspondingly called the **`false` branch**.

By contrast, the **`label()`** method in Figure 10-1 contains a **multi-branch if statement**:

```
if (myValue < MIN || myValue > MAX) {
    return "error";                                // branch 1
} else if (myValue < PH_NEUTRAL) {
    return "acidic";                               // branch 2
} else if (myValue > PH_NEUTRAL) {
    return "alkaline";                             // branch 3
} else {
    return "neutral";                              // branch 4
}
```

When performed, the flow can follow any of the multiple branches shown in Figure 10-5.

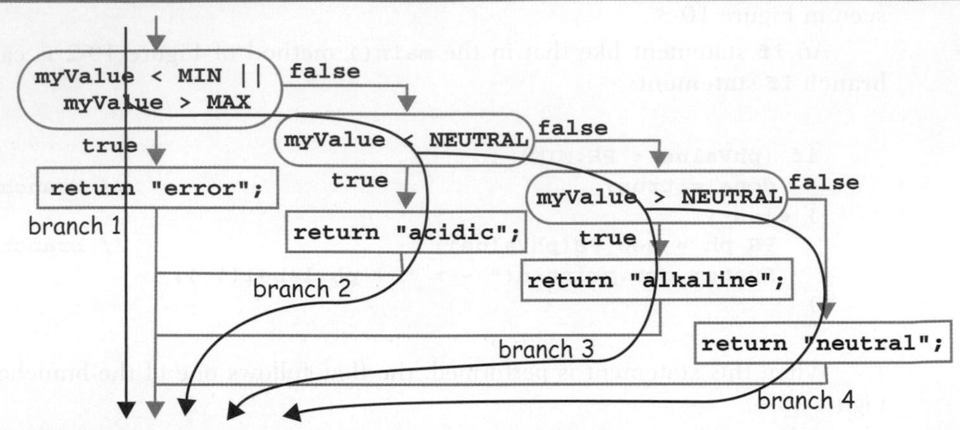

FIGURE 10-5 Flows through a multi-branch **if** statement

As indicated in Figure 10-5, flow proceeds through the conditions of a multi-branch **if** until one is found to be **true**. The group of statements guarded by that condition are then performed, and the rest of the statement is skipped. Thus, if the condition of the first **if** statement is **true**, none of the subsequent conditions are evaluated. Put differently, the condition of the ith **if** statement is only evaluated if the conditions of **if** statements 1 through i-1 are all **false**. A multi-branch **if** statement thus directs the flow through exactly one of its branches.

It might appear that Java provides three different **if** statements, but the one-, two-, and multi-branch **if** statements are all built from the same statement.

Pattern for Java's **if** statement:

```
if ( Condition ) Statement1
[ else Statement2 ]
```

where:

Condition is any boolean expression.

Each ***Statement$_i$*** is either a single Java statement, or a group of statements surrounded by curly braces ({ and }).

When execution reaches an **if** statement, its ***Condition*** is evaluated. If it is **true**, ***Statement$_1$*** is performed and ***Statement$_2$*** (if present) is skipped. If it is **false**, ***Statement$_1$*** is skipped and ***Statement$_2$*** (if present) is performed.

Thus, when we write an **if** statement that guards a single statement:

```
if (hour24Value > 12) {
   hour12Value -= 12;
}
```

the curly braces are not strictly necessary. However, it is good practice to always include the braces, because doing so makes it clear what statement(s) the **if** is guarding, and makes it easy to add more statements to that branch at a later date, should the need arise.

Note also that when we write a multi-branch **if** statement, the second **if** corresponds to ***Statement***$_2$ of the first **if** statement, the third **if** statement corresponds to ***Statement***$_2$ of the second **if** statement, and so on. That is, we could have written the multi-branch **if** statement of the **label()** method in Figure 10-2 as follows:

```
if (myValue < MIN || myValue > MAX)
     return "error";
else
     if (myValue < NEUTRAL)
          return "acidic";
     else
          if (myValue > NEUTRAL)
               return "alkaline";
          else
               return "neutral";
```

Although this format clarifies which **else** goes with which **if**, it tends to produce "code creep," in which the indentation of the nested **if** statements causes the code to "creep" across the screen. We believe the format used in Figure 10-2 is more readable, and it avoids "code creep."

The **if** statement is the most general way to achieve selective execution in Java, as it can always be used to select or guard a group of statements. Under limited circumstances, Java's **switch** statement can be used instead. We now turn our attention to it.

10.2.2 Java's switch Statement

In some circumstances, Java's **if** statement can be a bit verbose. For example, suppose you work for the city pet licensing bureau, and the vast majority of the visitors to your office want to know how much a license costs for their pet. To serve these people and streamline your office, you decide to write a program that visitors can use to get an answer to this question.

Imagine that your city's pet licensing fees are as follows: horses - $10.00, dogs - $10.00, cats - $5.00, birds - $5.00, reptiles - $5.00, and fish - $1.00.

To represent pet licenses in this city, we can build a **PetLicense** class. To initialize a **PetLicense** object, we might define a constructor that uses a character as a code for that pet: *h* for horse, *d* for dog, *c* for cat, *b* for bird, *r* for reptile, *f* for fish, and *o* for other. If we define instance variables to store the code and the fee, we can start with this minimal class:

```
public class PetLicense {
  private char    myCode;
  private double myFee;
}
```

To initialize these instance variables, we could write the following constructor:

```
public class PetLicense {
   public PetLicense(char petCode) {
      if (petCode == 'd' || petCode == 'h') {
         myFee = 10.00;
      } else if (petCode == 'b' || petCode == 'c' ||
                 petCode == 'r') {
         myFee = 5.00;
      } else if (petCode == 'f') {
         myFee = 1.00;
      } else if (petCode == 'o') {
         myFee = 0.00;
      } else {
         System.err.println("licenseFee(): code '" + petCode
                               + "' is invalid");
         System.exit(1);
      }
      myCode = petCode;
   }
   private char   myCode;
   private double myFee;
}
```

This method works correctly, validating parameter **petCode** using a multi-branch **if** statement. However, in each condition after the first, we must retype **else if (petCode ==**, and in the conditions that use the OR operator (||), we must repeatedly retype **petCode ==**. All of this redundant typing can be a nuisance.

When selective execution is needed and the following are true about that selection's conditions, we can use Java's **switch** statement instead of its **if** statement:

- The equality operator (**==**) is being used.
- The type of the variable or expression being compared is integer-compatible (that is, **boolean**, **byte**, **char**, **int**, **long**, **short**, or anything that can be turned into an integer).

Figure 10-6 presents a **PetLicense** class whose constructor uses the **switch** statement.

```
public class PetLicense {
  public PetLicense(char petCode) {
    switch (petCode) {
    case 'd': case 'h':
       myFee = 10.00;
       break;
    case 'b': case 'c': case 'r':
       myFee = 5.00;
```

continued

```
            break;
        case 'f':
            myFee = 1.00;
            break;
        case 'o':
            myFee = 0.00;
            break;
        default:
            System.out.println("License(code): code '"
                                      + petCode + "' is invalid");
            System.exit(1);
        }
        myCode = petCode;
    }

    public double getFee() { return myFee; }

    private char   myCode;
    private double myFee;
}
```

FIGURE 10-6 Defining **PetLicense()** using a **switch** statement

This method will pass the following tests:

```
assert new PetLicense('d').getFee() == 10.00;
assert new PetLicense('c').getFee() == 5.00;
assert new PetLicense('f').getFee() == 1.00;
assert new PetLicense('o').getFee() == 0.00;
```

The **switch** statement thus lets us perform multi-branch selection in a way that can be more convenient and readable than a multi-branch **if** statement.

One tricky aspect of the **switch** statement is that you usually need a **break** or **return** statement at the end of each branch, except the last branch. Since the **break** statement is new to us, let's look at it briefly:

Pattern for Java's **break** statement:

```
break;
```

Behavior:

When a **break** statement is performed within a **switch** statement or a loop statement, execution proceeds immediately to the first statement after the **switch** or loop statement.

The **break** statement thus causes the flow to "break out" of a **switch** statement.

If you neglect to put a **break** *statement at the end of a branch of a* **switch**, *the flow will proceed into the next branch!*

To illustrate, suppose we forgot the **break** statements in Figure 10-6, and wrote:

```
private PetLicense(char petCode) {
      switch (petCode) {
         case 'd': case 'h':
            myFee = 10.00;
         case 'b': case 'c': case 'r':
            myFee = 5.00;
         case 'f':
            myFee = 1.00;
         case 'o':
            myFee = 0.00;
         default:
            System.out.println("licenseFee(petCode): petCode '"
                                    + petCode + "' is invalid");
            System.exit(1);
      }
      myCode = code;
}
```

Now, when the following test is performed:

```
assert new PetLicense('c').getFee() == 5.00;
```

(1) the test invokes the **PetLicense()** constructor, passing argument **'c'** to **petCode**; (2) the **switch** statement in **PetLicense()** transfers the flow to case **'c'**, setting **myFee** to **5.00**; (3) in the absence of a **break** statement, the flow proceeds into case **'f'**, resetting **myFee** to **1.00**; (4) the flow proceeds into case **'o'**, resetting **myFee** to **0.00**; and (5) the flow proceeds into the **default** case, which displays the error message and terminates the program! To avoid such behavior, place a **break** statement at the end of each branch of a **switch** statement.

We can summarize the behavior of the **switch** statement as follows:

Pattern for Java's switch statement:

```
switch ( IntegerCompatibleExpression ) {
       CaseList1 StatementList1
       CaseList2 StatementList2
       ...
       CaseListN StatementListN
       default: StatementListN+1
}
```

where:

IntegerCompatibleExpression is an expression producing a value of type **boolean**, **byte**, **char**, **int**, **long**, or **short**.

Each $CaseList_i$ consists of one or more cases, each having the form:

```
case LiteralValue :
```

where *LiteralValue* is a literal whose type is the same as that of *IntegerCompatibleExpression*

When the flow reaches a **switch** statement, its ***IntegerCompatibleExpression*** is evaluated, producing a value ***v***. If ***v*** is present in a given $CaseList_i$, the flow jumps to $StatementList_i$, and then proceeds sequentially until a **break**, a **return**, or the end of the **switch** statement is reached. If ***v*** is not present in any $CaseList_i$ and a **default:** branch is present, the flow jumps to $StatementList_{N+1}$. If ***v*** is not present in any $CaseList_i$ and no **default:** branch is present, the flow jumps to whatever statement follows the **switch** statement. The **default**: thus serves as a "catch-all" case, when none of the other cases are matched.

It is good programming practice to supply a **default:** branch (if for no other reason than to display an error or warning message on an invalid value).

The **default:** branch can be placed anywhere in the **switch** statement. However, because it acts like the final **else** in a multi-branch **if** statement, it is customary to make **default:** the final branch in a **switch** statement.

Nested Switch Statements

One **switch** statement can be nested within another. To illustrate, suppose you and your friends decide to print and sell some cool t-shirts. The shirts differ in price by size: XS - \$9.00; S, M, L - \$10.00; and XL - \$11.00. Figure 10-7 presents a class that models such T-shirts. Its constructor takes a **String** containing the size of a t-shirt, and then uses nested **switch** statements to set an instance variable named **myPrice**.

```
1  public class TShirt {
2   public TShirt(String size) {
3     switch ( size.charAt(0) ) {
4        case 'S': case 'M': case 'L':
5           myPrice = 10.00;
6           break;
7        case 'X':
8           switch ( size.charAt(1) ) {
9              case 'S':
10                myPrice = 9.00;
11                break;
12             case 'L':
13                myPrice = 11.00;
14                break;
15             default:
16                System.err.println("TShirt(size): size \""
17                                    + size + "\" is invalid");
18                System.exit(1);
19          }
20          break;
21       default:
22          System.err.println("TShirt(size): size \""
23                              + size + "\" is invalid");
24          System.exit(1);
25    }
26  }
27
28  public String getSize() { return mySize; }
29  public double getPrice() { return myPrice; }
30
31  public String toString() { return mySize + " ($"
                                    + myPrice + ")"; }
32
33  private String mySize;
34  private double myPrice;
35 }
```

FIGURE 10-7 Pricing t-shirts with nested **switch** statements

If **size** is **"S"**, **"M"**, or **"L"**, the flow jumps from the outer **switch** to line 5, setting **myPrice** to **10.00**. The **break;** on line 6 then transfers the flow to the end of the constructor.

However, given a size of **"XS"** or **"XL"**, the flow jumps to line 8, which uses the second character in the string to branch. If that character is **"S"**, flow jumps to line 10, setting **myPrice** to **9.00**; if it is **"L"**, flow jumps to line 13, setting **myPrice** to **11.00**. The **break**s on lines 11 and 14 transfer the flow to the **break;** on line 20, and from there to the end of the constructor.

Java's **if** and **switch** statements thus provide two different ways to perform selective execution. The **if** statement can be used in *any* situation requiring selective execution. The **switch** statement can only be used when each condition uses the equality operator, and when the type of the item being compared is integer-compatible.

> A **switch** statement cannot be used to compare **double** or **String** values.

The toString() Method

Our **TShirt** class defines a method named **toString()**, which builds and returns a **String** representation of a **TShirt**. If an object has a natural **String** representation, it is a good idea to build it in a **toString()** method, because many of Java's string-related operations will then use that method. To illustrate, if we write:

```
TShirt shirt = new TShirt("M");
System.out.println(shirt);          // invokes shirt.toString()
```

the **println()** message sends **shirt** the **toString()** message, and then displays the resulting **String**. Put differently, defining a **toString()** method lets us display an object using the customary **print()** or **println()** messages!

10.3 Repetitive Execution

We have seen that by default, execution flows through a method's statements *sequentially*. We have also seen that Java's **if** and **switch** statements perform statements *selectively*, causing the flow to branch under specific conditions. In this section, we turn our attention to **repetitive execution**, a third mode of execution that allows us to perform a group of statements *repeatedly*.

Where Alice provided two loop statements, Java provides three: the **while** loop, the **for** loop, and the **do** loop. In the remainder of this section, we examine these three statements.

10.3.1 Java's while Statement

We saw an example of Java's **while** loop in the **main()** method of Figure 10-2. That loop was used to read and label a series of water samples' pH values. Loops like this — intended to read and process a series of values — are called **input loops**.

There are several different kinds of input loops, one of which is shown in Figure 10-2. That loop uses a value from outside the range of valid pH values (a negative value) to mark the end of the values. Because it serves to "guard" the end of the series of values, such an invalid value is called a **sentinel**, and input loops that use this approach are called **sentinel-controlled input loops**. The pattern for a sentinel-controlled input loop is as follows:

Pattern for a Sentinel-Controlled Input (`while`) Loop:

1. *define boolean variable done, initially* `false`;
2. `while (!`*done*`) {`

    a. *read a value v;*

    b. `if (`*v is the sentinel*`) {`

        set done to `true`;

    `} else {`

        do whatever is needed to process v;

    `}`

`}`

Purpose:

Read and process a series of input values.

This pattern can be used to read any series of values whose range is restricted in some way, since a sentinel value can be chosen from outside that range.

Besides input loops, the **`while`** loop can be used in any situation where we need to process a series of values. To illustrate, in Section 9.2.5, we examined the problem of computing a person's initials from a name, and saw how we could compute a person's first initial, or their last initial. But suppose we wanted to build a **`String`** containing all of the person's initials? If we build a class to model and retrieve a person's initials, then a statement like

```
String str = new Initials("Dilbert").getInitials();
```

should set **`str`** to the string **`"D"`**; a statement like

```
String str = new Initials("Albert Einstein").getInitials();
```

should set **`str`** to the string **`"AE"`**; a statement like

```
String str = new Initials("Homer Jay Simpson").getInitials();
```

should set **`str`** to the string **`"HJS"`**; a statement like

```
String str = new Initials("John Ronald Ruel Tolkien").
                    getInitials();
```

should set **`str`** to the string **`"JRRT"`**; and so on. These are the "tests" our class must pass in order for it to be considered correct.

If we think for a moment about what such a class must do, it should be evident from the preceding "tests" that our class needs a constructor to which we pass a name. Given such a parameter named *name*, we might develop the following algorithm:

Initials Constructor

Parameter: *name*, a `String`.

1. Set *result* to `""` (the empty string)
2. Build *names*, by splitting *name* into the sequence of words it contains
3. While *names* still has a word to be processed:
   a. Build *word*, the next word from *names*
   b. Append the first character of *word* to *result*
4. Save *result*

The idea is to take a **String** like **"Homer Jay Simpson"**; split it into three separate substrings: **"Homer"**, **"Jay"**, and **"Simpson"**; and then use a **while** loop to process the series of the substrings. This sounds complicated, and in many languages, it would be. However, Java provides a class named **StringTokenizer** (in the **java.util** package), whose sole purpose is to make it easy to split a **String** in this manner. To illustrate, the statement:

```
StringTokenizer names = new StringTokenizer("Homer Jay Simpson");
```

will build **names** as a handle for a **StringTokenizer** object like that depicted in Figure 10-8.

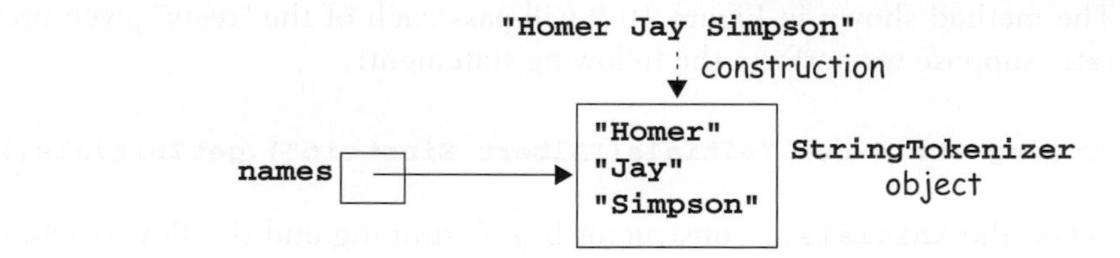

FIGURE 10-8 Visualizing a **StringTokenizer** object

That is, the **StringTokenizer** object constructor uses the spaces that separate words to split its **String** argument into substrings, and then stores each substring. We can then send that object any of the **StringTokenizer** messages listed in the Java API, including:

- **names.hasMoreTokens()**. This method returns **true** if there are any unprocessed substrings in the object referred to by **names**, and returns **false** otherwise.
- **names.nextToken()**. This method returns the next unprocessed substring from the object referred to by **names**.

We can use these methods in a class that solves our initials problem, as shown in Figure 10-9.

```
import java.util.StringTokenizer;

public class Initials {
    public Initials(String name) {
       myName = name;
       myInitials = "";
       StringTokenizer names = new StringTokenizer(name);
       String word = null;
       while ( names.hasMoreTokens() ) {
          word = names.nextToken();
          myInitials += word.charAt(0);
       }
    }

    public String getInitials() { return myInitials; }

    public String getName() { return myName; }

    private String myName;
    private String myInitials;
}
```

FIGURE 10-9 Computing a person's initials

The method shown in Figure 10-9 will pass each of the "tests" given previously. To illustrate, suppose we perform the following statement:

```
String str = new Initials("Albert Einstein").getInitials();
```

When the **Initials()** constructor begins running and the flow reaches its **while** loop, we might envision its variables as shown in Figure 10-10.

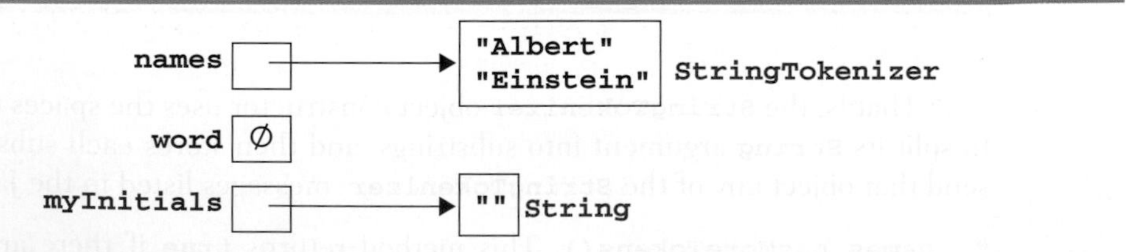

FIGURE 10-10 Visualizing the **Initials()** constructor (part I)

Since there are unprocessed substrings in the **StringTokenizer**, **names.hasMoreTokens()** returns **true**, and flow enters the loop. The handle **word** is then set to the first substring in the **StringTokenizer**, which marks that word as processed. The last statement in the loop sets **result** to itself plus the first character in **word** (**"A"**), as shown in Figure 10-11.

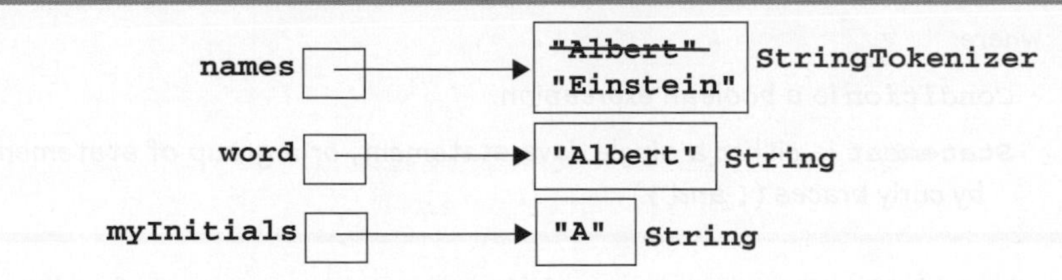

FIGURE 10-11 Visualizing the **Initials()** constructor (part II)

The flow returns to the **while** loop's condition. Since there are unprocessed strings in the **StringTokenizer**, **names.hasMoreTokens()** returns **true**, and flow enters the loop. The handle **word** is then set to the first string in the **StringTokenizer**, which marks that word as processed. The last statement in the loop sets **result** to itself (**"A"**) plus the first character in **word** (**"E"**), as shown in Figure 10-12.

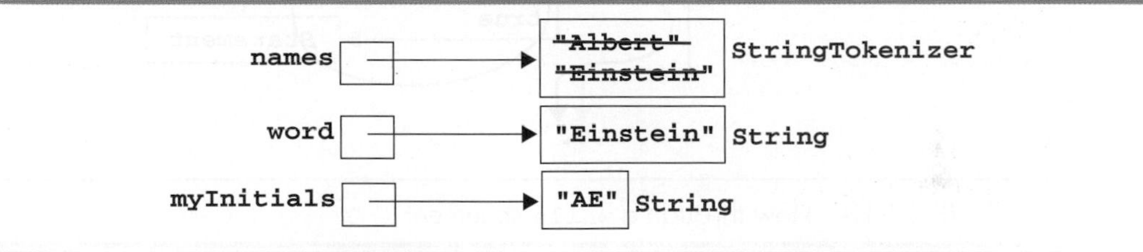

FIGURE 10-12 Visualizing the **Initials()** constructor (part III)

Flow then returns to the **while** loop's condition. Since no substrings remain unprocessed in the **StringTokenizer** object, **names.hasMoreTokens()** returns **false**, and flow moves from the loop to the end of the constructor, which terminates, with **myInitials** correctly initialized.

Summary

We can describe the general pattern for a **while** loop as follows:

> Pattern for Java's **while** statement:
>
> **while (*Condition*) *Statement***
>
> where:
>
> ***Condition*** is a boolean expression.
>
> ***Statement*** is either a single Java statement, or a group of statements surrounded by curly braces (**{** and **}**).

As with the **if** statement, curly braces are not required if only one statement is being repeated. However, it is good practice to always include them, as doing so improves readability by clearly indicating what is within the loop, and makes it easy to add other statements to the loop.

When flow reaches a **while** loop, it follows one of the branches shown in Figure 10-13.

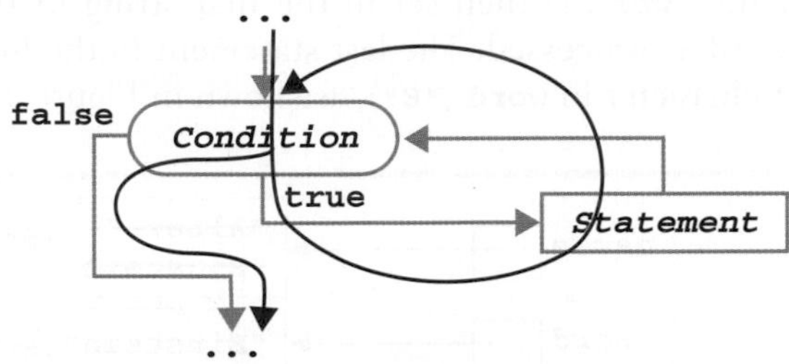

FIGURE 10-13 Flow through a **while** statement

Note that a **while** loop's ***Condition*** is evaluated *before* the ***Statement*** within it is performed, so if the ***Condition*** is initially **false**, the ***Statement*** within it will not be performed. Put differently, a **while** loop performs the ***Statement*** within it *zero or more times*. This form of repetition is called **zero-trip behavior**. As we shall see in Section 10.3.3, this behavior is what distinguishes Java's **while** loop from its **do** loop.

Note also that the ***Statement*** controlled by a **while** loop must eventually cause its ***Condition*** to become **false**, or an **infinite loop** will result; for example:

```
int count = 1;
while (count < 10) {                              // infinite loop!
   System.out.println("Oh no! I can't get out of here!");
}
```

This is usually not a good thing, so make certain that your **while** loops contain statements that ensure that the loop's ***Condition*** will eventually become **false**.

10.3.2 Java's `for` Statement

In Chapter 4, we saw that Alice provides the **for** loop for solving **counting problems** — problems whose solutions require repeating some statements while counting through a range of numbers. Java also supplies a **for** loop, and it is much more flexible than that of Alice.

To illustrate, suppose you live in a city that has five stations to monitor air pollution: four at the north, south, east, and west compass points around the city's perimeter, plus one at the city's center. To compute the city's air pollution index, a meteorologist measures the air pollution level at each of the five stations, and then manually computes the average of the five values. Our task is to write a program to compute this average.

If air pollution readings can never be negative, we could read and compute the average using a sentinel-based input loop, like we saw in Figure 10-2. However, unlike that problem — in which we did not know in advance the number of samples — this problem has a fixed number of measurements (5) to average. This extra information turns this into a counting problem that we can solve using a **for** loop, as shown in Figure 10-14.

```
/** AirPollutionIndex.java averages five air pollution readings.
 */
import java.util.Scanner;

public class AirPollutionIndex {
  public static void main(String[] args) {
   final int NUM_READINGS = 5;
   double sum = 0.0;
   Scanner keyboard = new Scanner(System.in);
   System.out.println("To compute the air pollution index...");
   for (int count = 1; count <= NUM_READINGS; count++) {
    System.out.print("enter reading #" + count + " of " +
                     NUM_READINGS + ": " );
    double reading = keyboard.nextDouble();
    sum += reading;
   }
   double pollutionAverage = sum / NUM_READINGS;
   System.out.printf("The average is %.3f", pollutionAverage);
   }
}
```

```
Result:
To compute the air pollution index...
 enter reading #1 of 5: 11
 enter reading #2 of 5: 12
 enter reading #3 of 5: 13
 enter reading #4 of 5: 13
 enter reading #5 of 5: 11
The average is 12.000
```

FIGURE 10-14 Reading and averaging a series of values with a `for` loop

Figure 10-14 illustrates an alternative form of input loop — a **counting input loop** — that can be used when a program "knows" in advance the number of values to be processed. Figure 10-14 uses this extra information to control a `for` loop that counts from `1` to `NUM_READINGS`. Each repetition of this loop reads a reading and adds it to a `double` variable named `sum`. Upon leaving the loop, the program computes and displays `sum / NUM_READINGS`.

Since the number of repetitions is known in advance, our program makes use of this information (as well as the `count`) when it prompts the user. This approach also frees the user from having to enter a sentinel value at the end of the series of values (though that is not much of an inconvenience). The loop itself is much simpler, because no `if` statement is needed to check for the sentinel value. The `for` loop thus provides an alternative way to build an input loop, provided the number of values to be entered is known in advance.

Counting Loops

The `for` loop in Figure 10-14 counts upward from `1` to `numValues` by ones. However, Java's `for` loop is very flexible, and can be structured to count in a variety of ways. For example, to count upward from `-10` to `+10` by ones, we could write:

```
for (int count = -10; count <= 10; count++) {
   System.out.println(count);
}
```

This statement will display the integers `-10`, `-9`, ..., `-1`, `0`, `1`, ..., `9`, `10`, each on a separate line. If we instead wanted to count upward from `-100` to `+100` by tens, we could write:

```
for (int count = -100; count <= 100; count += 10) {
   System.out.println(count);
}
```

This statement will display the integers `-100`, `-90`, ..., `-10`, `0`, `10`, ..., `90`, `100`, each on its own line. If we instead wanted to count downward from `'Z'` to `'A'` by ones, we could write:

```
for (char ch = 'Z'; ch >= 'A'; ch--) {
   System.out.print(ch);
}
```

This statement will display the characters `Z`, `Y`, `X`, ..., `B`, `A`, all on the same line. If we instead wanted to count downward from `1.0` to `0.0` by `0.1`, we could write:

```
for (double count = 1.0; count >= 0.0; count -= 0.1) {
   System.out.println(count);
}
```

This statement will display the real numbers **1.0**, **0.9**, ..., **0.1**, **0.0**, each on its own line. Java's **for** loop is thus very flexible, and can be used in any situation requiring counting.

When using a **for** loop to count through a range of **double** values, using the **==** or **!=** operators to control the loop can result in problems. To illustrate, what will this loop do?

```
for (double count = 0.0; count != 1.0; count += 0.1) {
   System.out.println(count);
}
```

This innocent-looking loop is an infinite loop! The problem is that the binary (base-2) representation of the real number 0.1 is 0.000110011... (the 0011 repeats infinitely many times). Since a computer uses a finite number of bits to store a real number, it cannot store 0.1 exactly. Because the loop repeatedly adds an inexact **0.1** to **count**, **count**'s value never becomes equal to **1.0**, so the condition **count != 1.0** remains true "forever." Try it and see for yourself!

> When using a **for** loop to count through a range of **double** values, avoid using the **==** or **!=** operators to control the loop's repetition.

Example 1: 99 Bottles of Pop

The lyrics of the silly song "99 Bottles of Pop" are given in Programming Project 4.7. Alice's **for** loop lacks the flexibility to "count down" from 99 to 0, but this is an easy task for Java's **for** loop.

Figure 10-15 presents a class that models this song, with an instance variable named **myLyrics**, initially the empty string. The class constructor builds the song's lyrics by using a **for** loop to count from 99 down to 0, appending the verse for a given **count** to an instance variable named **myLyrics**.

```
/** NinetyNineBottlesSong.java ...
 */

public class NinetyNineBottlesSong {
   public NinetyNineBottlesSong() {
      myLyrics = "";
      for (int count = 99; count > 0; count--) {
         myLyrics += ( getVerse(count) + "\n" );
      }
   }
```

continued

```

   public String getVerse(int numBottles) {
      String result = numBottles
                      + " bottles of pop on the wall,\n"
                      + numBottles + " bottles of pop,\n"
                      + "take one down, pass it around\n"
                      + (numBottles-1)
                      + " bottles of pop on the wall.\n";
      return result;
   }

   public String getLyrics() { return myLyrics; }

   private String myLyrics;

   public static void main(String[] args) {
      System.out.println( new NinetyNineBottlesSong().
                             getLyrics() );
   }
}
```

```
Result:
99 bottles of pop on the wall,
99 bottles of pop
take one down, pass it around
98 bottles of pop on the wall.

98 bottles of pop on the wall,
98 bottles of pop
take one down, pass it around
97 bottles of pop on the wall.
... 97 other verses omitted ...
```

FIGURE 10-15 The "99 Bottles of Pop" song

The **main()** method in Figure 10-15 is notable for its simplicity. It just creates a new instance of its class, sends that instance the **getLyrics()** message, and displays the result.

That said, the program contains a grammatical flaw: on the last verse, it displays "*1 bottles of pop*" instead of "*1 bottle of pop*" — a special case. Fixing this flaw is not difficult, and is left as an exercise.

Example 2: Plotting a Function

Plotting the points of a function lets us visualize that function, helping us to better understand the function's behavior. For functions of the form:

$$y = f(x)$$

this can be done by using a **for** loop to iterate through a range of *x* values. For each *x* value, we use *f*(*x*) to compute the corresponding *y* value, and then plot the point (*x*, *y*).

Java does not provide a standard class to make point-plotting simple, so we have built one named **Plotter**, available on this book's Web site.[1] This class includes:

- A **Plotter(screenX, screenY, xMin, yMin, xMax, yMax, title)** constructor, which lets you build a **Plotter** object at screen coordinates (**screenX**, **screenY**), specifying the minimum and maximum (*x*, *y*) values of the plot's axes, plus its *title*.
- **drawPoint(x,y)**, which plots a point (**x**, **y**)
- **setPenColor(col)**, which plots subsequent points using **Color col**
- **hideAxes()**, which hides the x and y axes
- **showAxes()**, which makes the x and y axes visible (this is the default)
- **minX()**, **minY()**, **maxX()**, and **maxY()**, which return the minimum and maximum **x** and **y** values capable of being plotted by a given **PointPlotter** object
- **deltaX()**, which returns the change in **x** in moving one column across the screen
- **deltaY()**, which returns the change in **y** in moving one row on the screen

plus other methods. Figure 10-16 presents a program that uses the **Plotter** class to plot a function two different ways. Both methods plot the **sin(*x*)** function using a **for** loop to iterate through a range of values for ***x***. The first method — **plotSine1()** — plots **sin(*x*)** by varying ***x*** through the range -π to +π in increments of 0.1. The second method — **plotSine2()** — also plots **sin(*x*)**, but varies ***x*** through the range **minX()** to **maxX()** in increments of **deltaX()**. By comparing the approaches and the plots they produce (see below), you can get a sense of the relative advantages and disadvantages of each approach.

```
/** SineWaves.java uses a for loop and the Plotter class...
 */
import java.awt.Color;      // for Color.RED, etc.

public class SineWaves {
  public static void main(String[] args) {
    SineWaves self = new SineWaves();
    self.run();
  }

  public void run() {
```

continued

1. **http://alice.calvin.edu/books/alice+Java/.**

```
        plotSine1();
        plotSine2();
    }

    public void plotSine1() {
        Plotter plot = new Plotter(100, 100,            // position
                                -4, -1.5, 4, 1.5,  // axes limits
                                "Sine 1");         // title
        plot.setPenColor(Color.RED);
        for (double x = -Math.PI; x <= Math.PI; x += 0.1 ) {
            double y = Math.sin(x);
            plot.drawPoint(x, y);
        }
    }

    public void plotSine2() {
        Plotter plot = new Plotter(120, 120, -4, -1.5, 4, 1.5,
                                                  "Sine 2");
        plot.setPenColor(Color.BLUE);
        for (double x = plot.minX(); x <= plot.maxX();
                                     x += plot.deltaX()){
            double y = Math.sin(x);
            plot.drawPoint(x, y);
        }
    }
}
```

Results:

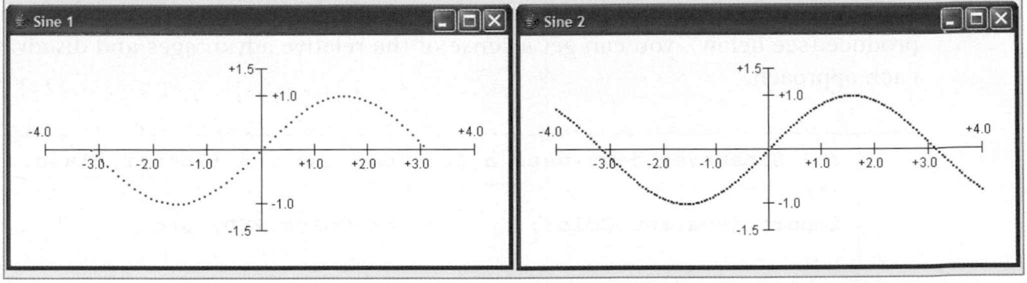

Sine 1

Sine 2

FIGURE 10-16 Plotting the sine function

In the left plot at the bottom of Figure 10-16, we started **x** at **-Math.PI**, ended when **x** surpassed **+Math.PI**, and incremented its value by **0.1** each repetition. In the right plot, we started **x** at **plot.minX()**, ended when **x** surpassed **plot.maxX()**, and varied its value by **plot.deltaX()** each repetition.

Java's **for** loop is amazingly flexible. It can be used to iterate through any sequence of values, provided the is a way to get from one value to the next.

Nested for Loop

All of Java's control statements can be nested. However, in practice, the **for** loop seems to be nested more frequently than the other loops.

To illustrate the use of nested loops, Figure 10-17 presents a **drawBox(*h*, *w*)** method that draws a textual "box" of height ***h*** and width *w*, plus a **main()** method to test its performance.

```
/** TextGraphics.java provides methods for 'drawing'
textual graphics.
 */
public class TextGraphics {
   public void drawBox(int height, int width) {
      for (int count1 = 1; count1 <= height; count1++) {
         for (int count2 = 1; count2 <= width; count2++) {
            System.out.print('*');
         }
         System.out.println();
      }
   }

   public static void main(String[] args) {
      TextGraphics self = new TextGraphics();
      self.drawBox(3, 8);
      System.out.println();
      self.drawBox(4, 4);
   }
}
```

```
Result:
********
********
********

****
****
****
****
```

FIGURE 10-17 A **drawBox(*h*, *w*)** method

The **main()** method begins by creating an instance of the **TextGraphics** class named **self**. It then sends **self** the **drawBox(3, 8)** message. The result is a "box" of 24 asterisks, arranged in 3 rows and 8 columns. After a **println()** message to print a blank line, it then sends **self** the message **drawBox(4, 4)**, and the result is a "box" of 16 asterisks, arranged in 4 rows and 4 columns. However, when we examine the definition of **`drawBox()`**, we find just one **`print('*')`** message! Where are all of the asterisks coming from?

The key is the use of nested **`for`** loops. The inner loop (shown in red) counts from 1 to **`width`**, repeating the **`print()`** message each repetition, so when **`width == 8`**, this loop displays 8 asterisks; when **`width == 4`**, this loop displays 4 asterisks. Flow then leaves the inner loop, and passes to the **`println()`** message, ending that line. However, both the inner loop and the **`println()`** message are "wrapped" in an outer loop (shown in blue), which counts from 1 to **`height`**. That means that the inner loop and the **`println()`** message are repeated **`height`** times, so when **`height == 3`**, the outer loop performs the inner loop and **`println()`** 3 times, displaying 3 rows of asterisks; and when **`height == 4`**, the outer loop performs the inner loop and **`println()`** 4 times, displaying 4 rows of asterisks. More generally, a **`drawBox(h, w)`** message will draw a "box" of ***h*** $\times$ ***w*** asterisks, arranged in ***h*** rows, each having ***w*** columns.

Summary

The general pattern for Java's **`for`** loop is as follows:

> Pattern for Java's **`for`** statement:
>
> **`for (`*`InitialExpr`*`; `*`Condition`*`; `*`ChangeExpr`*`) `*`Statement`***
>
> where:
>
> ***InitialExpr*** is an arbitrary Java expression
>
> ***Condition*** is a boolean expression
>
> ***ChangeExpr*** is an arbitrary Java expression
>
> ***Statement*** is either a single Java statement, or a group of statements surrounded by curly braces ({ and })

When flow reaches a **`for`** loop, it follows one of the branches shown in Figure 10-18.

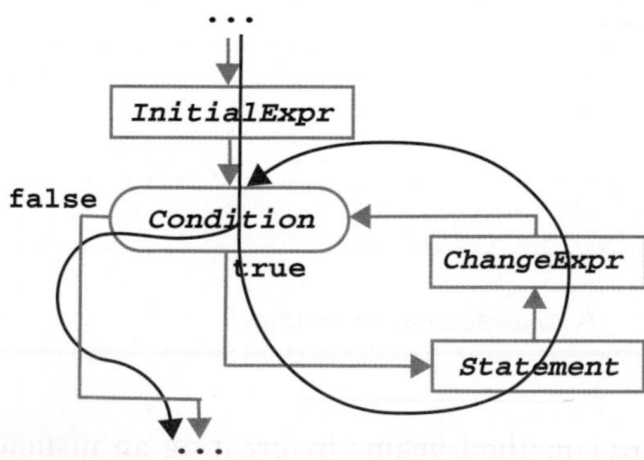

FIGURE 10-18 Flow through a **`for`** statement

Note that the loop's ***InitialExpr*** is performed just once, when flow first reaches the loop. As we have seen, it is usually used to initialize a counter variable. Next, the loop's ***Condition*** is tested, usually comparing the loop's counter variable against some limit value. If the ***Condition*** is **true**, the flow continues to the loop's ***Statement***; then to ***ChangeExpr*** — which usually increases or decreases the loop's counter variable — and then back to the loop's ***Condition*** where the cycle starts anew. But if the loop's ***Condition*** is **false**, flow bypasses the loop's ***Statement*** and ***ChangeExpr*** and proceeds instead to the statement following the loop. Like the **while** loop, the **for** loop provides zero-trip behavior.

Loop Control Variables and Scope

The "counter" variables that control a **for** loop's repetitions are called **loop control variables.** These variables are commonly declared within the loop, as shown in the preceding examples. It is important to remember this about such variables:

> The scope of a loop control variable declared in the ***InitialExpression*** of a **for** loop ends at the end of the loop.

That is, a variable declared in the loop's ***InitialExpression*** cannot be accessed beyond the end of the loop. If a problem requires that the loop control variable be accessed past the loop's end, it should be declared *before* the loop, as follows:

```
int count;   // declaring it here
for (count = 1; count <= LIMIT; count++) {
   // statements to be repeated
}
// makes it still accessible here
```

By declaring **count** outside the loop, its scope extends to the end of the block surrounding it.

10.3.3 Java's do Statement

Unlike Alice, Java provides a third repetition statement known as the **do statement** or **do** loop. The general pattern for this loop is as follows:

> Pattern for Java's do statement:
>
> ```
> do
>      Statement
> while (Condition);
> ```
>
> where:
>
> ***Statement*** is either a single Java statement, or a group of statements surrounded by curly braces ({ and })
>
> ***Condition*** is a boolean expression

When flow reaches a **do** loop, it follows one of the branches shown in Figure 10-19.

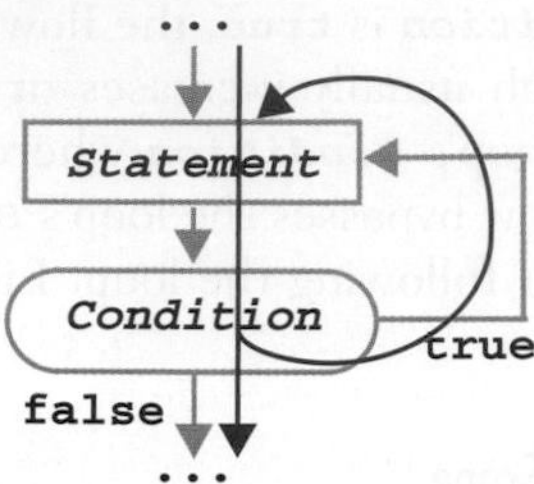

FIGURE 10-19 Flow through a **do** statement

Like the **while** loop, the number of repetitions of a **do** loop is controlled by a ***Condition***. However, a **while** loop tests its ***Condition*** *before* performing its ***Statement***, making it a **test-at-the-top**, or **pretest loop** (see Figure 10-13). By contrast, a **do** loop tests its ***Condition*** *after* its ***Statement*** has been performed, making it a **test-at-the-bottom**, or **posttest loop**. A **do** loop's ***Statement*** will thus be performed *at least once*. This is called **one trip behavior**, and it is the main difference between Java's two general loops. Another difference is this:

> You must type a semicolon at the end of a do loop, to end the statement.

Like a **while** loop, a **do** loop repeats its ***Statement*** so long as its ***Condition*** remains **true**; it is the responsibility of that ***Statement*** to ensure that ***Condition*** eventually becomes **false**, or else an infinite loop will result.

Example: The Guessing Game

The **do** loop is designed for situations where the statements to be repeated must be performed at least once. For example, when a person runs a game program, he or she usually wants to play the game at least once, so the **do** loop is the appropriate choice for such a situation. For a generic "game," we might start with this user story:

> Our program should (1) play the game with the user, (2) ask the user if he or she wants to play again, (3) read the response from the keyboard, and (4) repeat Steps 1-3, so long as the response is affirmative.

Given a generic **Game** object named **aGame**, containing a method named **play()** that plays a game, we could perform this story using a **do** loop, as shown below.

```
char answer;
do {
    aGame.play();
    System.out.print("\nDo you want to play again (y or n): ");
    answer = keyboard.next().charAt(0);
} while (answer == 'y' || answer == 'Y');
```

When the flow reaches this **do** loop, it sends **aGame** the **play()** message. When **play()** ends, the next statement asks the user if he or she wants to play again. The last statement in the loop reads the user's response into a **char** variable named **answer** by (1) sending a **Scanner** object the **next()** message; and (2) sending the resulting **String** the **charAt(0)** message, to retrieve its first character. The loop then checks its condition, and if **answer** is **'y'** or **'Y'**, flow goes back to the beginning of the loop; otherwise, flow leaves the loop.

Note that **answer** must be declared outside of the loop in order for the loop's condition to be able to access it; if **answer** is declared within the loop's curly braces, its scope will end at the closing curly brace (**}**), so it will not be visible when flow reaches the loop's condition.

This provides a new kind of *input loop*, distinct from the sentinel-controlled and counting input loops. This **query-controlled input loop** is extremely general, in that (unlike a sentinel-controlled loop) it can be used in situations where there are no invalid input values to use as sentinels, and (unlike a counting loop) it can be used when the number of values is not known in advance. Its only downside is that the user must respond to the query by entering **'y'** or **'Y'** after each input value, which can become tiresome when there are many input values.

Pattern for a Query-Controlled Input (**do**) Loop:

1. define **char** variable **answer**;
2. **do {**
    a. prompt for, read, and process a value *v*
    b. ask the user if they want to continue (y or n)
    c. read the user's response into **answer**

   } while (answer == 'y' || answer == 'Y');

Purpose:

Read and process a series of input values when any value is permissible.

Now that we have a loop that lets us play a game more than once, we just need to build a **Game** class that models a game. The game we will model is the "Guess My Number" game, in which one player (here, the computer) chooses a number between 1 and

100, and the other person tries to guess it in as few guesses as possible. If we write a description of how this game is played, we might produce this user story:

To play the "Guess My Number" game

Our game should generate a random number from 1 to 100, and initialize a guessCounter to zero. It should then repeatedly (1) increment the guessCounter, (2) ask the user to enter a guess, (3) read his or her guess from the keyboard, (4) if the number is less than the guess, display "Lower"; otherwise if the number is greater than the guess, display "Higher"; otherwise (the user guessed our number), display a congratulatory message indicating how many guesses it took the user to guess our number.

The **GuessingGame** class in Figure 10-20 defines a **play()** method that uses this approach. Since the user needs at least one guess to win the game, it uses a **do** loop to control the repetition.

```
/** GuessingGame.java is a "guess the number" game...
 */
import java.util.*;           // Scanner, Random

public class GuessingGame {
    public void play() {
        Scanner keyboard = new Scanner(System.in);
        Random randNumGen = new Random();
        int number = randNumGen.nextInt(100) + 1;
        int guessCounter = 0;
        boolean done = false;
        do {
            guessCounter++;
            System.out.print("Enter your guess: ");
            int guess = keyboard.nextInt();
            if (number < guess) {
                System.out.print("Lower...   ");
            } else if (number > guess) {
                System.out.print("Higher... ");
            } else {
                System.out.println("You guessed my number in "
                          + guessCounter + " guesses!");
                done = true;
            }
        } while (!done);
    }
}
```

FIGURE 10-20 A "Guess the Number" game class

This is a minimalist model for the game. By building the game as a class, we can in the future easily add more features, such as recording the number of times the user has played the game, the average number of guesses a player takes, and so on. These changes are left as an exercise.

It is worth mentioning that generating a truly random number in software is very difficult, because computers are *deterministic*, and random behavior is (by definition) *non-deterministic*. However, **pseudo-random numbers** — numbers that seem to be random, but are produced by a deterministic mathematical function — can be generated. Alice's random number functions and Java's **`Random`** class (from the **`java.util`** package) both produce such numbers.

As described in the Java API, once we have constructed a **`Random`** object, we can send it a **`nextDouble()`** or **`nextInt()`** message to generate a pseudo-random **`double`** or **`int`** value, respectively. The **`play()`** method in Figure 10-20 uses a version of **`nextInt()`** that, given an argument *n*, returns a pseudo-random number from the range 0..*n-1*. Since the message **`nextInt(100)`** generates a psuedo-random number in the range 0..99, line 9 adds 1 to this number, to make it a random number in the range 1..100.

Figure 10-21 presents a program that uses our **`Game`** class to play the game.

```
/** GameController.java plays a game repeatedly
 */
import java.util.Scanner;

public class GameController {
   public static void main(String[] args) {
      Scanner keyboard = new Scanner(System.in);
      GuessingGame aGame = new GuessingGame();
      System.out.println(
                "I'll think of a number between 1 and 100;"
      + "\n see how long it takes you to guess it.");
      char answer;
      do {
         aGame.play();
         System.out.print(
                 "\nDo you want to play again (y or n)?");
         answer = keyboard.next().charAt(0);
      } while (answer == 'y' || answer == 'Y');
   }
}
```

```
Result:
I'll think of a number between 1 and 100;
 see how long it takes you to guess it.
Enter your guess: 50
Higher... Enter your guess: 75
Lower...  Enter your guess: 62
Lower...  Enter your guess: 56
Higher... Enter your guess: 59
```

continued

```
You guessed my number in 5 guesses!

Do you want to play again (y or n)? n
```

FIGURE 10-21 A "Guess the Number" game program

When a class has no instance variables (like **GuessingGame**), and so needs no constructor to initialize them, Java provides a **default constructor**, so that the programmer need not define one. Line 8 of Figure 10-21 uses such a default constructor to build a **GuessingGame** object.

10.3.4 Choosing the Right Loop

With three different loops to choose, how can we know when to use which loop?

Choosing a loop:

1. *If the problem is a counting problem, where the required number of repetitions can be determined in advance, use the **for** loop.*
2. *Otherwise (the problem is not a counting problem):*
   a. *If the problem is such that the loop's statement should always be performed at least once, then use the **do** loop.*
   b. *Otherwise, use the **while** loop.*

The **while** loop is thus the "default" choice for a loop, when neither condition 1 nor 2a holds.

To illustrate, let's apply these steps to the "initials" problem we solved in Figure 10-9. Since we cannot determine in advance the number of words in a person's name, the problem is not a counting problem, so we do not choose the **for** loop. To choose between the **do** or **while** loops, we must think carefully about the statements that are to be repeated. Figure 10-22 presents the **Initials()** constructor, with the statements to be repeated highlighted.

```
public Initials(String name) {
   myName = name;
   myInitials = "";
   StringTokenizer names = new StringTokenizer(name);
   String word = null;
   while ( names.hasMoreTokens() ) {
       word = names.nextToken();
       myInitials += word.charAt(0);
   }
}
```

FIGURE 10-22 The **Initials()** class constructor

Should the highlighted statements *always* be performed at least once — will performing them be problem-free under all possible circumstances? The answer is *no*, which is why we chose the **while** loop instead of the **do** loop.

The answer is *no* because a user could pass the empty string (**""**) as the argument to parameter **name**. The **StringTokenizer** object built from **name** on line 4 would then contain no strings, and sending it the **nextToken()** message on line 7 would produce a fatal error! By using a **while** loop that bypasses lines 7 and 8 when **hasMoreTokens()** is **false**, the method in Figure 10-9 simply returns the empty string if it is given an empty string.

10.4 Example: The Chaos Game

As a final example of Java's flow-control statements, we will build a program that plays the Chaos Game. This is a game that you can play with pencil and paper (if you have a lot of time). One version of the game can be played as follows:

Chaos Game: Given *numPoints*, the number of points to draw:

1. On a page, draw a triangle's three vertices: red, green, and blue
2. Pick a random point *p1* somewhere within the triangle's boundaries
3. Roll a die, to generate a number from 1–6
4. If the die-roll is 1 or 2:
   a. Find *p2*, the halfway point between *p1* and the red vertex
   b. Draw a red point at *p2*
5. Else, if the die-roll is 3 or 4:
   a. Find *p2*, the halfway point between *p1* and the green vertex
   b. Draw a green point at *p2*
6. Else, if the die-roll is 5 or 6:
   a. Find *p2*, the halfway point between *p1* and the blue vertex
   b. Draw a blue point at *p2*
7. Replace *p1* with *p2*
8. Perform Steps 3 through 7, *numPoints* times

The game requires thousands of points to see its object, so it is faster to write a computer program to play it than for us to play it with pencil and paper!

Using the topics from this chapter, and the preceding steps as an algorithm, we can build a class that uses our **Plotter** class to play the game, as shown in Figure 10-23.

```
import java.awt.Color;
import java.util.Random;

public class ChaosGame {
   public ChaosGame(int numPoints) {
      if (numPoints <= 0) {
```

continued

```
          System.err.println("ChaosGame(reps): "
                             + "reps must be positive");
          System.exit(1);
       }
       myPlot = new Plotter(0, 0, 1, 1, "Chaos");
       myPlot.hideAxes();
       drawVertices();
       drawPoints(numPoints);
    }

    private void drawVertices() {
       myRedVertex = new Point(0.5, 1.0);
       myPlot.setPenColor(Color.RED);
       myPlot.drawPoint(myRedVertex.x, myRedVertex.y);
       myGreenVertex = new Point(0.0, 0.0);
       myPlot.setPenColor(Color.GREEN);
       myPlot.drawPoint(myGreenVertex.x, myGreenVertex.y);
       myBlueVertex = new Point(1.0, 0.0);
       myPlot.setPenColor(Color.BLUE);
       myPlot.drawPoint(myBlueVertex.x, myBlueVertex.y);
    }

    private void drawPoints(int numPoints) {
       Random rng = new Random();
       Point p1 = new Point( rng.nextDouble(),
                             rng.nextDouble()  );
       Point p2 = null;
       for (int i = 0; i < numPoints; i++) {
          int dieRoll = rng.nextInt(6);
          switch (dieRoll) {
            case 0: case 1: // go towards red vertex at (0.5, 1)
              p2 = findPointHalfwayBetween(p1, myRedVertex);
              drawPoint(p2, Color.RED, i);
              break;
            case 2: case 3: // go towards green vertex at (0, 0)
              p2 = findPointHalfwayBetween(p1, myGreenVertex);
              drawPoint(p2, Color.GREEN, i);
              break;
            case 4: case 5: // go towards blue vertex at (1, 0)
              p2 = findPointHalfwayBetween(p1, myBlueVertex);
              drawPoint(p2, Color.BLUE, i);
              break;
            default:
              System.err.println("run(): bad roll value: "
                                 + dieRoll);
```

continued

```
            System.exit(1);
         }
         p1 = p2;
      }
   }

   private void drawPoint(Point p, Color color,
                                    int pointNumber) {
      final int START_DRAWING_AT = 5;
      if (pointNumber > START_DRAWING_AT) {
         myPlot.setPenColor(color);
         myPlot.drawPoint(p.x, p.y);
      }
   }

   private Point findPointHalfwayBetween(Point p1, Point p2) {
      return new Point((p1.x + p2.x) / 2.0,
                       (p1.y + p2.y) / 2.0);
   }

   private class Point {
      public Point(double xVal, double yVal) { x = xVal;
                                               y = yVal; }
      public double x, y;
   }

   private Plotter myPlot = null;
   private Point    myRedVertex, myGreenVertex, myBlueVertex;

   public static void main(String[] args) {
      ChaosGame game1000 = new ChaosGame(1000);
      ChaosGame game10000 = new ChaosGame(10000);
   }
}
```

Results:

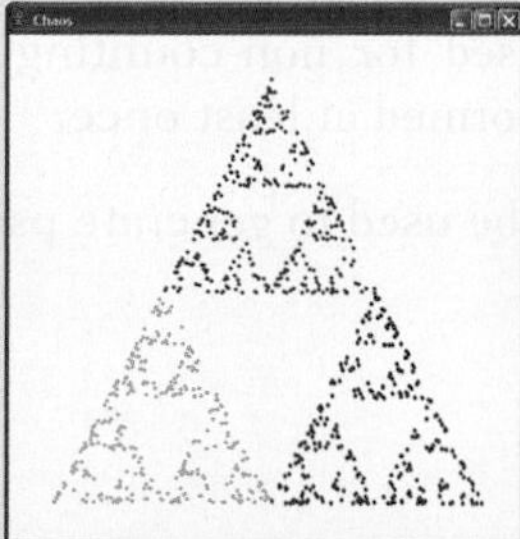

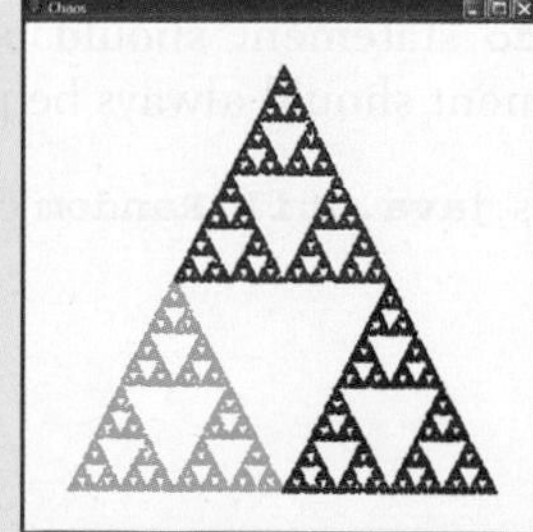

FIGURE 10-23 `ChaosGame.java`

Because it uses random numbers, directions, and colors, you might expect the Chaos Game to produce a chaotic cloud of red, green, and blue points, but this is not the case. Figure 10-23 produces two different runs of the game, one using 1000 points and one using 10,000 points, which are shown at the bottom of the figure.

What's interesting is that given enough points, the game produces this same diagram — known as the *Sierpinski Triangle* — every time, regardless of one's random starting point! Structure emerges from seemingly random behavior; and order emerges out of chaos.

This example illustrates two of the strengths of computers:

1. They can very quickly perform a task that would take a person hours to complete.
2. They help people visualize patterns in data that cannot easily be seen in the data alone.

If you're interested in learning more about the Chaos Game, use a search engine to search for more information on the World Wide Web.

10.5 Chapter Summary

- By default, execution flows through a program *sequentially*.
- Java's **`if`** and **`switch`** statements direct the flow of execution *selectively*.
  - The **`if`** statement can be used in any situation that requires selective execution.
  - The **`switch`** statement is sometimes a more readable way to perform selective execution, but it can only be used when using the equality operation to compare integer-compatible values. A **`break`** or **`return`** statement is usually needed at the end of each of the **`switch`** statement's branches, or execution will flow to the next branch.
- Java's **`while`**, **`for`**, and **`do`** statements direct the flow of execution *repetitively*.
  - The **`for`** statement should be used for counting problems — problems in which the number of repetitions can be determined in advance.
  - The **`while`** statement should be used for non-counting problems, where the loop's statement should not be performed if the loop's condition is initially **`false`**.
  - The **`do`** statement should be used for non-counting problems, where the loop's statement should always be performed at least once.
- The class **`java.util.Random`** can be used to generate pseudo-random numbers.

10.5.1 Key Terms

branch
break statement
counting input loop
default constructor
do statement or loop
false branch
for statement or loop
if statement
infinite loop
input loop
loop control variable
multi-branch **if** statement
one-branch **if** statement
one-trip behavior
posttest loop
pretest loop
pseudo-random number
selective execution
sentinel-controlled input loop
switch statement
test-at-the-bottom loop
test-at-the-top loop
true branch
two-branch **if** statement
while statement or loop
zero-trip behavior

Programming Projects

10.1 pH values can be categorized as follows: values from 0.0 to 2.0 are *strongly acidic*, 2.1 to 4.0 are *acidic*, 4.1 to 6.0 are *weakly acidic*, 6.1 to 6.99 and 7.01 to 8.0 are *near neutral*, 7.0 is *neutral*, 8.1 to 10.0 are *weakly alkaline*, 10.1 to 12.0 are *alkaline*, and 12.1 to 14.0 are *strongly alkaline*. Modify the class in Figure 10-1 so **label()** incorporates these labels. Add a **toString()** method to the **PH** class so that labeled **PH** objects can be displayed via **print()** and **println()** messages.

10.2 Proceed as in Project 10.1; then modify the program in Figure 10-2 so that it computes and displays the average pH for a lake, correctly labeled.

10.3 Build an **LED_Digit** class that, given a single non-negative integer digit (0, 1, 2, ..., 8, or 9), builds a **String** "LED" representation of that digit, as shown below. Define a **toString()** method in your class that returns the **String** representation. Then write a program that reads a digit from the user and displays its "LED" representation.

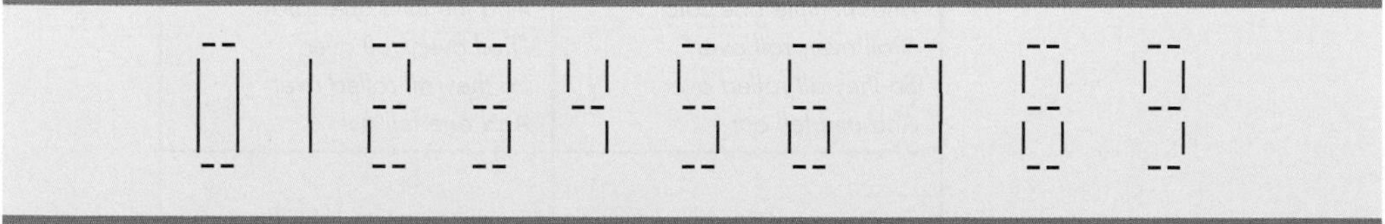

10.4 Proceed as described in Project 10.3; then build a second `LED_Number` class that, given an integer, builds a `String` "LED" representation of that number. Define a `toString()` method that returns that `String` representation. Then write a program that reads a series of numbers and displays the "LED" representation of each. For example, if the user enters -123, your program should produce the output shown below. (Hint: review integer division.)

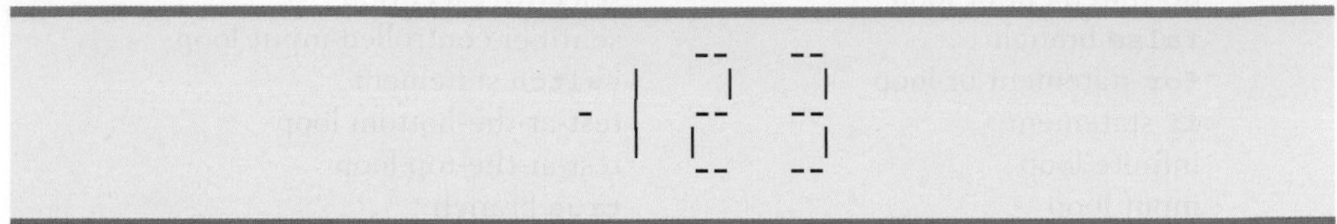

10.5 "Ten in a Bed" is a silly song with the lyrics below. Write a program to display the lyrics efficiently.

<table>
<tr><td>There were 10 in a bed
And the little one said
"Roll over, roll over"
So they all rolled over
And one fell out</td><td>There were 5 in a bed
And the little one said
"Roll over, roll over"
So they all rolled over
And one fell out</td></tr>
<tr><td>There were 9 in a bed
And the little one said
"Roll over, roll over"
So they all rolled over
And one fell out</td><td>There were 4 in a bed
And the little one said
"Roll over, roll over"
So they all rolled over
And one fell out</td></tr>
<tr><td>There were 8 in a bed
And the little one said
"Roll over, roll over"
So they all rolled over
And one fell out</td><td>There were 3 in a bed
And the little one said
"Roll over, roll over"
So they all rolled over
And one fell out</td></tr>
<tr><td>There were 7 in a bed
And the little one said
"Roll over, roll over"
So they all rolled over
And one fell out</td><td>There were 2 in a bed
And the little one said
"Roll over, roll over"
So they all rolled over
And one fell out</td></tr>
<tr><td>There were 6 in a bed
And the little one said
"Roll over, roll over"
So they all rolled over
And one fell out</td><td>There was 1 in a bed
And the little one said
"Good night!"</td></tr>
</table>

10.6 Modify the **PetLicense** class in Figure 10-6, as follows:

- ❑ Modify the class so that pet aardvarks (code 'a') are assessed a fee of $2.00, pet gerbils (code 'g') are assessed a fee of $1.00, pet pigs (code 'p') are assessed a fee of $8.00, and pet monkeys (code 'm') are assessed a fee of $12.00.
- ❑ Add a **getKind()** method that returns a **String** indicating the **PetLicense**'s animal (that is, horse, dog, cat, and so on).
- ❑ Add a **toString()** method that returns a **String** representation of a **PetLicense**.

Then write a program that repeatedly displays a menu of the accepted codes and animals plus 'q' to quit, reads a code from the user, and displays the fee for that animal, until the user enters 'q'.

10.7 Expand the **TShirt** class from Figure 10-7 by adding a **Color** instance variable, modifying the constructor to accept a **Color**, writing an accessor method to retrieve a **TShirt** object's **Color**, and updating the **toString()** method to include a **TShirt**'s **Color**. Then write a **TShirtsOrder** program that reads one or more shirt values from the keyboard, and then prints an invoice, listing the number of shirts of each size, the subtotal, any sales tax (for example, 6%), and the total.

10.8 Write a program that reads an arbitrary number of real numbers from the user, and displays the minimum, maximum, and average of the numbers. Allow the user to enter any values for the numbers.

10.9 Write a program that, using the **Plotter** class from Figure 10-16, displays a menu consisting of a subset of the functions provided by Java's **Math** class, reads a user's choice from the menu, and displays a plot of the function chosen by the user.

10.10 The factorial function *n!* can be computed as shown below. Write a method **factorial(*n*)** that computes and returns ***n***!. Then write a program that repeatedly prompts the user for a value, reads his or her value ***v***, and displays **factorial(*v*)**. Use a sentinel to terminate the program.

$$n! = 1 \times 2 \times \ldots \times (n-1) \times n$$

10.11 A word-palindrome is a simple or compound word that reads the same forward or backward. Some examples of word-palindromes include *wow*, *noon*, *civic*, *kayak*, *tut-tut*, *racecar*, *deified*, and *aibohphobia* (supposedly the fear of palindromes). Write a method named **isPalindrome()** that, given a **String**, returns **true** if that **String** is a word-palindrome, and returns **false** if it is not. Then write a program that reads a series of words from the user and indicates which are palindromes and which are not. Use the word "quit" as a sentinel.

10.12 *2-3 Person Group Project*. Add the following methods to the **TextGraphics** class from Figure 10-17: **drawPyramid()**; **drawDiamond()**; **drawRightTriangle()**; **drawParallelogram()**; **drawInvertedPyramid()**. The methods should produce figures something like those shown below, but should allow the user to specify the dimensions of each figure. Divide the work evenly among the members of your group.

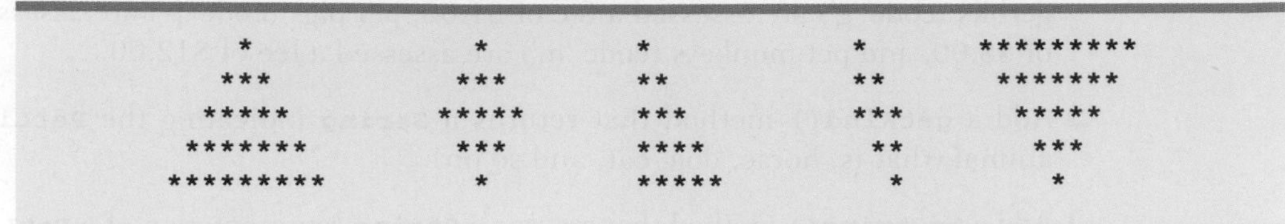

10.13 Write a "Police Sketch Artist" program. The program should display a series of menus, each with at least four choices: a menu of hair styles (for example, *bald*, *spikey*, *bangs*, or *parted*), a menu of eye styles (for example, *beady*, *normal*, *bug-eyed*, *glasses*), a menu of nose styles (for example, *small*, *pointy*, *pug*, *big*), and a menu of facial hair styles (for example, *none*, *mustache*, *beard*, *goatee*). The program should record each of the user's menu choices, and then use those choices to build a "sketch" of the individual like those shown below. Use a query-controlled loop to let the user create multiple sketches if he or she wishes.

```
 ---         \|||/          ---          ---
/   \        \   /         /|||\        ////\
|. .|        |o o|         |O O|        -O-O-
| ! |        | 7 |         | ^ |        | | |
| - |        |/-\|         //-\\        |/-\|
 ---          ---         //|||\\        \|/
```

Chapter 11
Files and Exceptions

Oh don't listen to him. I read his file. It said he suffers from, um, oh, acute paranoia.

SQUID (JAKE M. SMITH), IN *HOLES*

It's not my fault that Buttle's heart condition didn't appear on Tuttle's file!

JACK LINT (MICHAEL PALIN), IN *BRAZIL*

I will not be pushed, filed, stamped, indexed, briefed, debriefed, or numbered.

NO. 6 (PATRICK MCGOOHAN), IN *THE PRISONER*

Mulder: You solved the X-file!
Scully: Yes, except it's not an X-file, Mulder.

MULDER (DAVID DUCHOVNY) AND SCULLY (GILLIAN ANDERSON), IN *THE X-FILES*

No! No exceptions! I want this job, I need it, I can do it. Everywhere I've been today there's always been something wrong, too young, too old, too short, too tall. Whatever the exception is, I can fix it. I can be older, I can be taller, I can be anything.

BRANTLEY FOSTER (MICHAEL J. FOX) IN *THE SECRET OF MY SUCCESS*

Objectives

Upon completion of this chapter, you should be able to:

- ❑ Open and close text files
- ❑ Read values from, and write values to, text files
- ❑ Catch, handle, and throw exceptions

In the preceding chapters, we have written programs that read values from the keyboard and write values to the screen. In this chapter, we will see how to read values from and write values to text files. In the process, we will learn about Java's exception mechanism, which provides a better way of dealing with problems that occur as a program is running.

11.1 Introductory Example: Monitoring Acid Rain Revisited

In Section 10.1, we built a class to model pH values and operations, and then used this class to label a series of lake samples that were entered from the keyboard. Suppose a friend who is an acid rain researcher has collected nine samples — from positions in the northwest, north, northeast, west, center, east, southwest, south, and southeast areas of Blue Lake — and has recorded the pH values in a text file named **`blueLakePhSamples.txt`**, as shown in Figure 11-1.

```
6.6   6.5    6.6
6.8   6.9    6.8
6.9   7.1    7.2
```

FIGURE 11-1 Contents of the file **`blueLakePhSamples.txt`**

Requiring the user to re-enter these values at the keyboard is inefficient, as it forces the user to rekey data that someone has already entered, and it increases the likelihood of a data entry error occurring, since the user could mistype one of the values.

A better approach is to revise our program to read the pH values directly from the file, and to write the results to a second file. A file from which a program reads is called an **input file**, and a file to which it writes is called an **output file**. We can summarize the basic behavior of the revised program as follows:

Purpose: Label pH values that are stored in a file.

1. Prompt for and read *inFileName*, a `String`
2. Open *inFile*, the file whose name is *inFileName*
3. Build *fin*, a `Scanner` for *inFile*.
4. Prompt for and read *outFileName*, a `String`
5. Open *outFile*, the file whose name is *outFileName*
6. Build *fout*, a `PrintWriter` for *outFile*
7. While *fin* contains unread numbers:
    a. Read a number from *fin*, storing it in *phValue*
    b. Build a `PH` object named *ph* from *phValue*
    c. Write *phValue* and *ph.label()* to *fout*
8. Close *fin* and *fout*

Figure 11-2 presents a Java program that performs these steps.

```
// PhLabeler.java reads & labels pH values using file I/O.
import java.util.Scanner;
import java.io.*;              // File, PrintWriter, ...

public class PhLabeler {
   public static void main(String[] args) {
      try {
         // build Scanner for input file
         System.out.print("Enter name of the input file: ");
         Scanner keyboard = new Scanner(System.in);
         String inFileName = keyboard.nextLine();
         File inFile = new File(inFileName);
         Scanner fin = new Scanner(inFile);
         // build PrintWriter for output file
         System.out.print("Enter name of the output file: ");
         String outFileName = keyboard.nextLine();
         File outFile = new File(outFileName);
         PrintWriter fout = new PrintWriter(outFile);
         // read from input file, writing results to output file
         while ( fin.hasNextDouble() ) {
            double phValue = fin.nextDouble();
            PH pH = new PH(phValue);
            fout.println(phValue + " --> " + pH.label() );
         }
         // cleanup
         fin.close();
         fout.close();
         System.out.print("Done. See '" + outFileName + "'.");
      } catch (Exception e) {
         e.printStackTrace();
      }
   }
}
```

```
Result:
Enter name of the input file: blueLakePhSamples.txt
Enter name of the output file: blueLakeOutput.txt
Done. See 'blueLakeOutput.txt'.
```

FIGURE 11-2 The revised `PhLabeler` program

Following the run in Figure 11-2, the file `blueLakeOutput.txt` contains the values shown in Figure 11-3.

```
6.6 --> acidic
6.5 --> acidic
6.6 --> acidic
6.8 --> acidic
6.9 --> acidic
6.8 --> acidic
6.9 --> acidic
7.1 --> alkaline
7.2 --> alkaline
```

FIGURE 11-3 Contents of the file **blueLakeOutput.txt**

To accomplish this, the program in Figure 11-2 uses three new classes: the **File**, **PrintWriter**, and **Exception** classes. In the rest of this chapter, we will explore their use.

11.2 Files

When a computer's power is turned off and on, the contents of its **main memory** — the memory in which a program runs, and where all a program's variables are stored — is erased, because such memory requires electricity to maintain its values.

For example, suppose that you have purchased several songs from Apple's iTunes store. If these songs were only stored in your computer's main memory, and if your computer's power were turned off (whether accidently or intentionally), you would lose all of your songs!

To avoid losing all of your songs when your computer is turned off, we need a different kind of memory, one that does not depend on electricity to maintain its values. Devices like this are called **secondary memory**. DVDs, CDs, hard drives, and USB flash drives are all examples of secondary memory devices. Such devices use different technologies to store information in the absence of electricity. However, reading information from (or writing information to) such devices can take up to 1,000 times as long as reading from (or writing to) a computer's main memory. That is why we run programs in main memory instead of in secondary memory.

To make it easy to save and retrieve information (such as your songs) from a secondary memory device, a computer's operating system builds a **file system** on that device. Like an office filing system, the computer's file system organizes secondary memory and provides operations that a program can use to save and retrieve information. For example, if you have an Apple iPod and you view the list of songs it contains, you are interacting with its file system.

A file system lets a program save or retrieve information in units called (you guessed it) **files**. There are many different kinds of files, including binary files for storing programs, audio files for storing music, video files for storing movies, and text files for storing characters. While each of these files stores different information, a program interacts with them in the same way:

- Open a file (for reading or writing)
- Read information from (or write information to) the file, usually using a loop
- Close the file

For example, when you play a song file on your iPod or other MP3 player, the player

1. Opens that song file for reading
2. Uses a loop to repeat the following steps, until all sounds have been read from the file:
   a. read a sound from the file
   b. play that sound
3. Closes the song file

In the rest of this section, we examine how to perform similar steps using text files.

11.2.1 Opening a File

Preparing a file for reading or writing is called **opening a file**. Opening a file for reading is slightly different from opening one for writing, so we will examine these two operations separately.

Opening a File for Reading

Prior to Java 1.5, opening a text file for reading was complicated, requiring three new classes: **BufferedReader**, **InputStreamReader**, and **InputStream**. Thankfully, opening a text file for reading is much simpler now, requiring just the (familiar) **Scanner** class and the (new to us) **File** class.

To illustrate, the program in Figure 11-2 begins by reading the name of the input file from the user into a **String** variable named **inFileName**. In the sample run, this name is **blueLakePhSamples.txt**. The program then uses Java's **File** class to open this file:

```
File inFile = new File(inFileName);
```

The **File** class provides a connection between our program and the file residing on the secondary memory device, which we might visualize as shown in Figure 11-4.

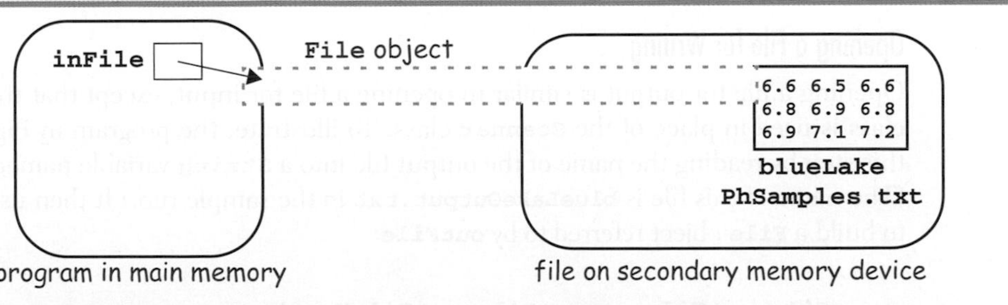

FIGURE 11-4 A **File** links main and secondary memory

However, the **File** class cannot know if we intend to read from or write to the file, so it does not provide methods for these operations. Since there is a **Scanner** constructor to build a **Scanner** from a **File** (see the Java API), we can "wrap" this **File** object in a **Scanner**:

```
Scanner fin = new Scanner(inFile);
```

Assuming that the file referred to by **inFile** exists and is readable[1], this **Scanner** object takes all necessary steps to prepare for reading, as shown in Figure 11-5.

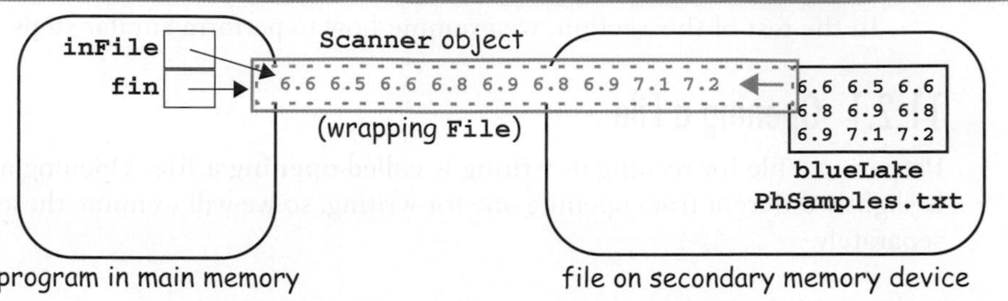

FIGURE 11-5 Wrapping a **File** in a **Scanner**

As we shall see in Section 11.2.2, a program can now read the values from the file via **fin**, using the same operations we have previously used to read from the keyboard.

Recall that the time needed to read from secondary memory can be as much as 1,000 times longer than the time needed to read from main memory. To keep such operations from slowing a program down, the **Scanner** may read several of the values from the file when it accesses the device. As indicated in Figure 11-5, the **Scanner** stores these values in a data structure, so that subsequent read operations can quickly retrieve the values from that data structure, instead of slowing down to access secondary memory. This data structure is called a **buffer**, and the process of storing multiple values in a buffer in main memory to improve program performance is called **buffering**.

Opening a File for Writing

Opening a file for output is similar to opening a file for input, except that the **PrintWriter** class is used in place of the **Scanner** class. To illustrate, the program in Figure 11-2 begins this step by reading the name of the output file into a **String** variable named **outFileName**. (The name of this file is **blueLakeOutput.txt** in the sample run.) It then uses **outFileName** to build a **File** object referred to by **outFile**:

```
File outFile = new File(outFileName);
```

If a file with the name stored in **outFileName** already exists, then **outFile** will be a connection to it, as we saw in Figure 11-4. However, if there is no file with the name in

1. If the file does not exist, or is unreadable, the **Scanner** constructor throws a **FileNotFoundException**. This is a checked exception, so this statement must be performed in a **try-catch** block. (See Section 11.3.)

outFileName, the **File** constructor will try to create an empty file on the secondary memory device, yielding the diagram in Figure 11-6.

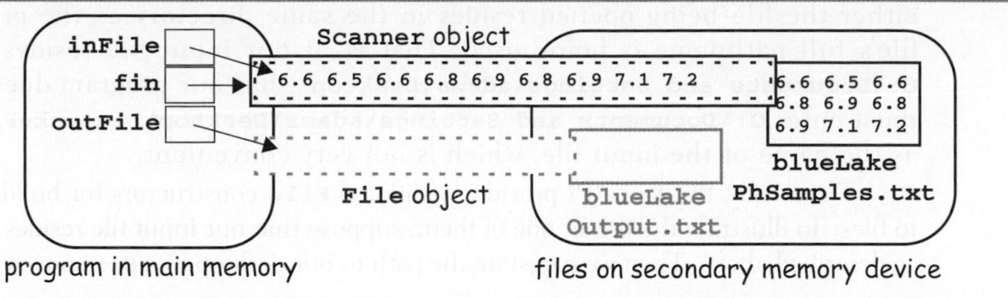

FIGURE 11-6 Creating a new file

Since a **File** object does not provide methods to write information to the file, but the **PrintWriter** class does, and it provides a constructor for building a **PrintWriter** from a **File** (see the Java API), we then "wrap" this **File** object in a **PrintWriter**:

```
PrintWriter fout = new PrintWriter(outFile);
```

Assuming that our program is permitted to write to the file,[2] this statement erases any previous information it contains. Our program now has a writable connection to the (empty) output file, as shown in Figure 11-7.

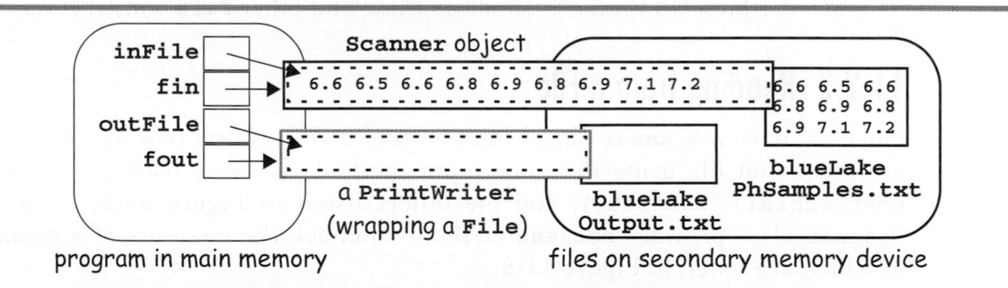

FIGURE 11-7 Wrapping a **File** in a **PrintWriter**

As we shall see in Section 11.2.3, we can now write to the file using the same output methods we have used previously to write to **System.out**.

2. If the program is not permitted to write to the file, the **PrintWriter** constructor throws a **FileNotFoundException**. This is a checked exception, so this statement must be performed in a **try-catch** block. (See Section 11.3.)

File Constructors

The program in Figure 11-2 uses the simplest of the **File** constructors, which takes a **String** parameter giving the name of the file. This constructor assumes that either the file being opened resides in the same directory as the program, or the file's full pathname is being used. That is, if our input file resides in the folder **C:\Documents and Settings\adams\Desktop**, but our program does not, then we must enter **C:\Documents and Settings\adams\Desktop\blueLakePhSamples.txt** as the name of the input file, which is not very convenient.

Thankfully, the Java API provides additional **File** constructors for building connections to files. To illustrate the use of one of them, suppose that our input file resides on our desktop, as described above. Then we can store the path to our desktop in a **String** variable:

```
String pathToFile = "C:/Documents and Settings/adams/Desktop";
```

Note that since Java uses the backslash character (****) for **String** escape sequences, Java uses the forward slash character (**/**) to separate the folder names in a **String**.

We can then use the same statements as before, which prompt for and read the name of the input file into the **String** variable named **inFileName**. However, to build the **File**, we use a different **File** constructor, which allows us to pass a file's full pathname via two separate **String**s:

```
File inFile = new File(pathToFile, inFileName);
```

Now our program will read from the input file located on our desktop!

The same approach can be used to write the output file to a folder different from the one in which the program resides.

See the Java API for more details on these and other **File** constructors.

11.2.2 Reading from a File

Once we have a **Scanner** object built around a connection to a file, we can read values from that file using the same input methods we have used previously: **next()**, **nextDouble()**, **nextInt()**, and the others listed in Figure 8-13. In addition, the **Scanner** class provides **boolean** methods to check the contents of a **Scanner**, some of which are listed in Figure 11-8.

Scanner method	Returns **true** if _____; returns **false** otherwise
***fin*.hasNext()**	there is an unread word of text in ***fin***
***fin*.hasNextBoolean()**	there is an unread **true/false** value in ***fin***
***fin*.hasNextByte()**	there is an unread **byte** value in ***fin***
***fin*.hasNextDouble()**	there is an unread **double** value in ***fin***

continued

Scanner method	Returns `true` if ______; returns `false` otherwise
***fin*.hasNextFloat()**	there is an unread **float** value in ***fin***
***fin*.hasNextInt()**	there is an unread **int** value in ***fin***
***fin*.hasNextLong()**	there is an unread **long** value in ***fin***
***fin*.hasNextShort()**	there is an unread **short** value in ***fin***
***fin*.hasNextLine()**	there is an unread line of text in ***fin***

FIGURE 11-8 Methods for checking the contents of a **Scanner**

Since an input file may be empty, these methods are commonly used to control input loops, as we saw in Figure 11-2.

```
while ( fin.hasNextDouble() ) {
    double phValue = fin.nextDouble();
    PH ph = new PH(phValue);
    fout.println(phValue + " --> " + pH.label() );
}
```

If the input file is initially empty, or contains no **double**-compatible values, the condition **fin.hasNextDouble()** returns **false**, and flow bypasses the body of the loop. However, if the input file contains one or more **double**-compatible values, **fin.hasNextDouble()** returns **true**, and flow enters the loop.

Once inside the loop, the loop reads and processes each **double** value in the input file, and then rechecks the loop's condition. When the final **double** value has been read and processed, the condition **fin.hasNextDouble()** returns **false**, and flow leaves the loop.

The **Scanner** class provides additional methods that can be useful in specialized circumstances. Please see the Java API for their details.

11.2.3 Writing to a File

Writing to a file is simple once we have built a **PrintWriter** between our program and the file. The reason is that we can write values to a file via a **PrintWriter** using the same **print()**, **println()**, and **printf()** methods that we use to write to **System.out** and **System.err**.

Thus, the program in Figure 11-2 displays **phValue** and its label using the statement:

```
fout.println(phValue + " --> " + pH.label() );
```

Alternatively, we could have accomplished the same thing using the **`printf()`** method:

```
fout.printf( "%.1f --> %s%n", phValue, pH.label() );
```

Thus, writing values to a file is just as easy as displaying values on the screen.

11.2.4 Closing a File

An open file consumes memory, and some operating systems limit the number of files that can be open simultaneously. For these reasons, it is good programming practice to have your program inform Java when it is done using a file, so that it can free up the memory for other uses. For both **`Scanner`** and **`PrintWriter`** objects, this is done by sending the object the **`close()`** message. Thus, when flow has left the input loop in Figure 11-2, it reaches the statements:

```
fin.close();
fout.close();
```

The first statement closes the connection between our program and the input file. Once this statement has been performed, any subsequent attempts to read from the **`Scanner`** (for example, using **`nextDouble()`**) will trigger an error.

The second statement closes the connection between our program and the output file, freeing up the memory associated with the **`File`** and **`PrintWriter`** objects.

As with reading, the time needed to write to secondary memory can be as much as 1,000 times longer than the time to write to main memory. To keep such write operations from slowing down a program, a **`PrintWriter`** temporarily stores the values being written in a buffer, in main memory. The **`PrintWriter`** keeps accumulating values in its buffer until one of the following happens:

- The buffer becomes full
- The **`PrintWriter`** receives a **`close()`** message
- The **`PrintWriter`** receives a **`flush()`** message (see the Java API)

When any of these occurs, the **`PrintWriter`** writes all the unwritten values in its buffer to the file. This operation is called **flushing** the buffer. The **`PrintWriter`** class provides a **`flush()`** method that can be used to tell a **`PrintWriter`** to flush its buffer.

11.3 Exceptions

In the last section, we saw the basics of opening, reading from, writing to, and closing files. Our presentation of these topics assumed that nothing goes wrong, and if we lived in a perfect world, we could leave it at that. However, in the real world, all sorts of things go wrong. People enter data incorrectly, electronic circuits fail, and secondary memory devices malfunction. The challenge is to write a program that deals with such occurrences gracefully.

When something "bad" happens as a Java program is running, Java creates an object that models the "bad" thing that occurred. Java calls these objects **exceptions**, and defines a variety of different classes to model the many things that can go wrong while a program is running.

To illustrate, the program in Figure 11-2 tries to open an input file on lines 12 and 13. There are many things that could go wrong in this operation, including the following:

- The input file does not exist.
- The input file exists, but is not in the correct folder.
- The input file is in the correct folder, but the user entered its name incorrectly.
- The input file is in the correct folder, and the user entered its name correctly, but the user is not permitted to read it.

If any of these problems occurs, Java generates an exception that models the problem.

Exceptions are not limited to programs that use files, but can occur in most programs. For example, if a program tries to read a **double** from the keyboard but the user enters a letter of the alphabet such as **z**, Java generates an exception. Similarly, Java generates an exception if we try to send a message via a handle whose value is **null**.

Because there are so many different things that can go wrong when we run a program, Java models such problems using **exception classes**. Some of these classes model very general problems, for example, **Exception**, **IOException**, and **RuntimeException**; other classes model very specific problems such as **FileNotFoundException**, **IllegalArgumentException**, and **NullPointerException**.

Just as biologists have organized all living things into a *kingdom, phylum, class, order, family, genus, species* hierarchy, Java organizes the exception classes into a hierarchy, as can be seen in Figure 11-9.

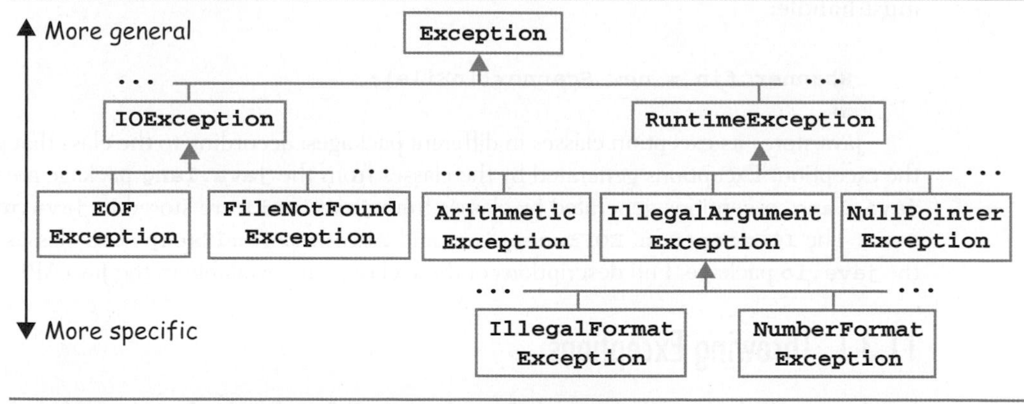

FIGURE 11-9 A part of Java's **Exception** hierarchy

As in the biological hierarchy, the idea in a **class hierarchy** is to place the most general class at the top of the hierarchy, containing attributes all the subsequent layers have in common. The successive layers are then increasingly specialized classes, with arrows connecting two classes that are related.

To illustrate, any methods that would do the same thing in the **IOException** and **RunTimeException** classes are located within the **Exception** class. The **IOException** and **RuntimeException** classes are then defined so as to **inherit** those methods from the

Exception class, so any message we can send to an **Exception** object can also be sent to an **IOException** or **RuntimeException** object. Likewise, methods that do the same thing in **EOFException** and **FileNotFoundException** are located in the **IOException** class. The **EOFException** and **FileNotFoundException** classes inherit these methods, plus those from **Exception**. By organizing the classes this way, there are no redundant methods anywhere in the class hierarchy. We will learn how to build such hierarchies in Chapter 13.

If we can get from one class to a second class by following the arrows in the hierarchy, the second class is called a **superclass** of the first class. For example, **Exception** and **IOException** are both superclasses of **EOFException**, with **IOException** being its **immediate superclass**. Similarly, **Exception** is the immediate superclass of **IOException**.

Going the other direction, **EOFException** is called a **subclass** of **IOException** and **Exception**. A subclass inherits the methods and instance variables of all of its superclasses, so **EOFException** inherits the attributes of **IOException** and **Exception**.

Because a subclass is a more specialized version of its superclass, programmers sometimes describe the relationship between them as an "**is a" relationship**. For example, **RuntimeException** *is a* specialized kind of **Exception**, **NullPointerException** *is a* specialized kind of **RuntimeException**, and so on.

Class **RuntimeException** and its subclasses are called **unchecked exceptions**, because the compiler does not check that they are being handled. However, the rest of the exceptions (**Exception**, **IOException**, and so on) are all **checked exceptions**, meaning the compiler requires you to handle them. If you do not, the compiler will generate a compilation error. For example, the statement on line 13 of Figure 11-2 can generate the **FileNotFoundException** — a checked exception — that our program must handle:

```
Scanner fin = new Scanner(inFile);
```

Java stores its exception classes in different packages, according to the class that generates the exception. Exceptions generated by the classes from the **java.lang** package are stored in **java.lang**, exceptions generated by classes from **java.util** are stored in **java.util**, and so on. The **IOException**, **EOFException**, and **FileNotFoundException** classes are from the **java.io** package. Full descriptions of these classes are available in the Java API.

11.3.1 Throwing Exceptions

In Chapter 10, we saw that one of the uses of the **if** and **switch** statements is to validate parameters. For example, the **PH** class constructor we built in Figure 10-1 uses this approach:

```
public PH(double pH) {
   if (pH < MIN || pH > MAX) {
      System.err.println("PH(): received invalid pH: " + pH);
      System.exit(1);
   } else {
      myValue = pH;
   }
}
```

The problem with this approach is that the method that invoked the constructor has no control over what happens; the decision to terminate the program is made in the `PH` constructor. Suppose the method would prefer to be notified so that it can correct the problem and try again?

A better approach would be to (1) terminate our constructor, (2) alert the invoking method that a bad argument was passed, and (3) leave it up to the invoker to decide what to do next. This is what Java's exception mechanism allows us to do.

To accomplish the first two of these steps (terminate and alert), we can revise the `PH` constructor as shown in Figure 11-10.

```
public PH(double pH) {
   if (pH < MIN || pH > MAX) {
      throw new IllegalArgumentException("*** PH(pH) = "
                                          + pH + "\n");
   } else {
      myValue = pH;
   }
}
```

FIGURE 11-10 Validating arguments with an exception

Our revised constructor now behaves very differently when it detects an invalid argument:

1. It first uses the **`new`** operator to build an instance of an **`IllegalArgumentException`**, passing it an error message.
2. It then "throws" the exception back to the method that invoked the constructor. This terminates the constructor, and alerts the invoker that an exception occurred.

Step 2 is accomplished using Java's **`throw` statement**, which behaves as follows:

Simplified Pattern for Java's `throw` statement:

```
throw ExceptionObject ;
```

where:

`ExceptionObject` is an object from the **`Exception`** class hierarchy.

Purpose:

The method that performs the `throw` statement terminates, returning flow back to the invoker, alerting it that an exception has occurred.

If the invoking method does nothing to *handle* the exception, then that method also terminates and the exception is thrown to whatever method invoked it. This **exception propagation** continues until either the exception is handled, or the exception reaches the **`main()`** method. If the exception reaches the **`main()`** method and no handler is present there, the program will terminate and the error message associated with the exception will be displayed.

Thus, if a program does not handle an exception, then the exception mechanism behaves just like our earlier approach, terminating the program and displaying an error message. However, unlike our earlier approach, the exception mechanism gives the invoker the option of handling the exception, as we shall see next.

11.3.2 Handling Exceptions: `try-catch` Blocks

To handle an exception, a program must "wrap" the potential exception-throwing statement(s) in a statement called a **`try-catch` block**. The program in Figure 11-2 presents an example of one; we can summarize its structure as follows:

```
try {
   // statements of the main() method
} catch (Exception e) {
   // statements to perform in response to an exception
}
```

The `try { ... }` is called a **`try` block**, and the `catch { ... }` is called a **`catch` block**. A `try` block must have at least one `catch` block. The combination is called a `try-catch` block.

If any of the statements in a `try` block throws an exception, and a `catch` block for *that exception or one of its superclasses* is present, the flow immediately jumps from that statement to that `catch` block. Since `Exception` is the superclass of all the other exceptions, every exception subclass "is a" specialized kind of `Exception`. Because of this, an `Exception` `catch` block can be used to catch *any* exception. For example, line 13 of Figure 11-2:

```
Scanner fin = new Scanner(inFile);
```

will throw a `FileNotFoundException` if the file referred to by `inFile` does not exist. However, because `FileNotFoundException` is a subclass of `Exception`, the `catch (Exception)` block will handle a `FileNotFoundException`.

Similarly, `IllegalArgumentException` is a subclass of `Exception`. Figure 11-11 shows the Figure 11-2 program flow if a bad argument is passed to the `PH` constructor.

```
public static void main(String [] args) {
 try {
   ...
     PH ph = new PH(phValue);             public PH(double ph) {
   ...                                      if (ph < MIN || ph > MAX) {
                                              throw new IllegalArgument...
 } catch (Exception e) {
   e.printStackTrace();
 }
}
```

FIGURE 11-11 The flow when an exception occurs

When a bad argument is passed to **PH()** and it throws the **IllegalArgumentException**, the flow immediately jumps to the **catch** block, *bypassing all intervening statements*. The **catch** block then handles the exception by sending it the **printStackTrace()** message, which prints a detailed error message:

```
java.lang.IllegalArgumentException: *** PH(pH): ph = 66.8
  at PH.<init>(PH.java:17)
    at PhLabeler.main(PhLabeler.java:36)
```

The first line displays the exception that occurred, plus its error message. The remaining lines are a **stack trace**, indicating the sequence of messages that produced the exception. From this, we can see that the exception occurred in the **PH** constructor, on line 17 of **PH.java**; which was invoked by the **main()** method of **PhLabeler.java**, on line 36. Learning to read detailed error messages like this is a useful skill, as it can help you track down what triggered an exception.

Never use an empty catch block (that is, **catch (Exception e) {}**) to catch exceptions, since doing so will silently "swallow" exceptions.

Multiple **catch** Blocks

A **try** block can have multiple **catch** blocks. To illustrate, recall that line 13 of Figure 11-2 can throw the **FileNotFoundException**, and line 22 can now throw the **IllegalArgumentException**. If there were a good reason to do so, we could have a separate **catch** block for each of these exceptions, as follows:

```
class PhLabeler {
  public static void main(String [] args) {
   try {
    ...
    Scanner fin = new Scanner(inFile); // throws FileNotFound
    ...
    while ( fin.hasNextDouble() ) {
      phValue = fin.nextDouble();
      Ph ph = new PH(phValue);      // throws IllegalArgument
    ...
   } catch (IllegalArgumentException iae) {
      fout.println( "***" );
      System.err.println( iae.getMessage() );
   } catch (FileNotFoundException fnfe) {
      System.err.println("Failed to open file '" + inFileName
                        + "' or '" + outFileName + "'");
      fnfe.printStackTrace();
   } catch (Exception e) {
      e.printStackTrace();
   }
  ...
```

When multiple **catch** blocks are present and an exception is thrown, Java starts at the first **catch** block and proceeds until it finds one that matches or is a superclass of the exception. Thus, if the **FileNotFoundException** is thrown, Java will skip the first **catch** block, perform the statements in the **FileNotFoundException**'s **catch** block, and then skip the statements in the final **catch** block. If some unanticipated exception (for example, a **NullPointerException**) should occur, Java will skip over the first two **catch** blocks and perform the statements in the **Exception**'s **catch** block.

Arrange multiple catch blocks in order from most specific to most general.

That is, suppose we were to mistakenly place the **Exception**'s **catch** block first:

```
...
} catch (Exception e) {                        // DON'T DO THIS!
   e.printStackTrace();
} catch (IllegalArgumentException iae) {       // Flow will never
   System.err.println( iae.getMessage() ); //  get here
} catch (FileNotFoundException fnfe) {         //  or here
   System.err.println("Failed to open file '" + inFileName
                          + "' or '" + outFileName + "'");
  fnfe.printStackTrace();
}
...
```

Because **Exception** is the superclass of all other exceptions, any exceptions that are thrown by the program will be caught by the first **catch** block. Put differently, the **catch** blocks of the **IllegalArgumentException** and **FileNotFoundException** will never be performed!

11.3.3 Cleaning Up: The `finally` Block

The program in Figure 11-2 wraps the problem-solving part of the program in a **try** block, and then catches any exceptions that get thrown:

```
try {
   // statements to solve the problem
} catch (Exception e) {
   // statements to handle any exception that occurs
}
```

This is a common way to structure exception-handling code, because it keeps the program's exception-handling code separate from its problem-solving code. Such separation can help improve a program's readability.

However, suppose the last value in our input file (**blueLakePhSamples.txt**) is a bad pH value — for example, 66.8 instead of 6.8. (Maybe our data entry person held down the "6" key too long but was too tired to notice.) When the program runs, all of the good values are read from the input file and written to the output file. Then the bad value is read. Passing it to the **PH** constructor triggers the **IllegalArgumentException**, and the flow jumps to the **catch** block at the end of the program, which displays an error message like this:

```
java.lang.IllegalArgumentException: *** PH(pH): pH = 66.8
  at PH.<init>(PH.java:17)
     at PhLabeler.main(PhLabeler.java:36)
```

What is interesting is that when we check the output file, it is empty, even though the exception occurred on the final value!

In Section 11.2.4, we learned that a **PrintWriter** buffers the values written to it until its buffer gets full; then it receives a **flush()** message, or it receives a **close()** message. Although our program contains a statement that sends a **close()** message to **fout**, this statement is bypassed when the **IllegalArgumentException** is thrown, because the flow jumps to the **catch** block, bypassing the **close()** messages.

For situations like this, Java provides the **finally block**, which can be used to perform "cleanup" operations, such as closing any files the program has opened. The statements in a **finally** block are performed after those in a **catch** block. To illustrate, we can shift the statements containing **close()** messages from the **try** block to a **finally** block:

```
Scanner fin = null;
PrintWriter fout = null;
try {
   // statements to solve the problem, may throw exceptions
} catch (Exception e) {
   // statements to handle any exception that is thrown
} finally {
   fin.close();
   fout.close();
}
```

Note that we must also declare **fin** and **fout** prior to the **try** block, or else their scopes will end at the end of the **try** block, making them inaccessible in the **finally** block.

Now, when an exception occurs in the **try** block, flow will jump to the **catch** block. From there it will jump to the **finally** block, which will close the files properly, flushing the **PrintWriter**'s buffer. After making this change, when we check our output file, it contains the output for all input values prior to the one that triggered the exception.

Pattern for Java's **try-catch-finally** blocks:

```
try {
     RiskyStatements
  } catch ( ExceptionClass1 exceptionParam1) {
     HandlerStatements1
  } catch ( ExceptionClass2 exceptionParam2) {
     HandlerStatements2
  ...
  } catch ( ExceptionClassN exceptionParamN) {
     HandlerStatementsN
  } [ finally {
     CleanupStatements
} ]
```

where:

RiskyStatements are statements that may throw an exception

ExceptionClass$_i$ is a class from the **Exception** hierarchy

exceptionParam$_i$ is an identifier

HandlerStatements$_i$ are statements that handle *ExceptionClass*$_i$

CleanupStatements are statements that are (optionally) performed after the exception has been handled

11.4 Example: The Caesar Cipher

When Julius Caesar communicated with his generals, he wrote his messages in a code, so that if his enemies should intercept the messages, they would not be able to read them. In his original code, each letter in the message was shifted forward three positions, as in the following scheme:

```
Original:  ABCDEFGHIJKLMNOPQRSTUVWXYZ
Encoded:   DEFGHIJKLMNOPQRSTUVWXYZABC
```

Thus, to send a message like this:

```
I CAME. I SAW. I CONQUERED.
```

Caesar would have actually sent the encoded message:

```
L FDPH. L VDZ. L FRQTXHUHG.
```

His nephew Augustus Caesar used a similar code, in which each letter was shifted one position. This approach to encrypting messages is accordingly called the *Caesar Cipher*.

In this section, we will write a program that encrypts (and decrypts) the contents of a text file using the Caesar Cipher. For the sake of simplicity, we will restrict our messages to those using uppercase characters.

11.4.1 Defining the Problem

We might start by writing this user story for our program:

> Caesar Cipher Program:
>
> Our program should ask the user for the name of the input file and open that file. It should then ask the user for the number of positions the characters are to be shifted. It should then ask the user for the name of the output file, and open it. It should then read the input file, encrypt what it reads, and write the results to the output file. When finished, it should close both files and display a 'Done' message.

11.4.2 Methods to Open and Close the Files

At this point, we should begin to recognize that most programs that want to read from an input file will need to perform the step of asking the user for the name of the input file and opening that file. Likewise, most programs that want to write to an output file will need to perform the step of asking the user for the name of the output file and opening that file. Since these operations are going to be so commonly needed, it makes sense to build methods for them, and to store them in a class library so that they can be easily reused. We will call this library **`FileOps`**.

The basic logic of each method is the same:

1. Display a *prompt* for the name of the file.
2. Read the name of the file into a **`String`** named *fileName.*
3. Build a **`File`** named *inFile* (or *outFile*) from *fileName.*
4. Build a **`Scanner`** (or **`PrintWriter`**) from *inFile* (or *outFile*).
5. Return that **`Scanner`** (or **`PrintWriter`**).

Different situations may require different prompts, so we will have the user pass the prompt to be displayed as a **`String`** argument to the method.

Since the first three steps are largely the same in each method, we will "factor out" these steps into a third method we will call **`promptForFile()`**, and then invoke that method in each of our other methods.

As described in Section 11.3, Step 4 may throw a **`FileNotFoundException`**, and since this is a checked exception, we must perform it in a **`try-catch`** block. So what should we do in response to this exception? If we embed this **`try-catch`** block in a loop, then we can use the **catch** block to allow the user another chance at entering the name of the file:

1. Set **boolean** *done* to **false**.
2. Do {
3. Try {
   a. Display a *prompt* for the name of the file.
   b. Read the name of the file into a **String** named *fileName*.
   c. Build a **File** named *inFile* (or *outFile*) from *fileName*.
   d. Build a **Scanner** (or **PrintWriter**) from *inFile* (or *outFile*).
   e. Set *done* to **true**.
4. } catch (**FileNotFoundException**) {
   a. Ask the user if he or she wants to try again or quit
   b. Read the user's response into a **char** variable *answer*.
   c. If *answer* indicates quit, terminate the program.
5. } catch (**Exception**) {
   Print a stack trace for the **Exception**.
   }
6. } while (!*done*);
7. Return the **Scanner** (or **PrintWriter**).

Steps a–c in the **catch** block will be almost the same in each method, so we will "factor out" these steps into a fourth method that we will call **quitOrTryAgain()**. Figure 11-12 presents the resulting **FileOps** class.

```
/** FileOps.java provides commonly needed file operations
 */
import java.util.Scanner;
import java.io.*;                    // File, PrintWriter, ...

public class FileOps {
 public static Scanner keyboard = new Scanner(System.in);

 public static File promptForFile(String prompt) {
    System.out.print(prompt);
    String fileName = keyboard.next();  // assumes no spaces
    return new File(fileName);          //   in filenames
 }

 public static Scanner promptForFileIn(String prompt) {
    Scanner result = null;
    boolean done = false;
```

continued

```
      do {
         try {
               File inFile = promptForFile(prompt);
               result = new Scanner(inFile);
               done = true;
         } catch (FileNotFoundException fnfe) {
               quitOrTryAgain("Unable to open input file");
         } catch (Exception e) {
               e.printStackTrace();
         }
      } while (!done);

      return result;
   }

  private static void quitOrTryAgain(String errorMessage) {
     System.out.println(errorMessage);
     System.out.println("Do you want to quit (q) or try again (a)? ");
     char answer = keyboard.next().charAt(0);
     if (answer == 'q' || answer == 'Q') {
        System.exit(1);
     }
  }

   public static PrintWriter promptForFileOut(String prompt) {
      PrintWriter result = null;
      boolean done = false;
      do {
         try {
            File outFile = promptForFile(prompt);
            result = new PrintWriter(outFile);
            done = true;
         } catch (FileNotFoundException fnfe) {
            quitOrTryAgain("Unable to open output file");
         } catch (Exception e) {
            e.printStackTrace();
         }
      } while (!done);

      return result;
   }
}
```

FIGURE 11-12 **FileOps.java**

Using this class, we can now write:

```
PrintWriter pw = promptForFileOut("output file name? ");
```

When invoked, the flow sets **done** to **false**, enters the **do** loop, and then enters the **try** block. The first statement in the **try** block invokes **promptForFile()**, which displays our prompt **"output file name? "**, reads the **String** the user enters, and builds and returns a **File** for that **String**. The next statement tries to build a **PrintWriter** from that **File**. If this succeeds, flow continues to the next statement, which sets **done** to **true**. The flow then skips the two **catch** blocks, and since the **do** loop's condition is **false**, leaves the loop.

However, if the attempt to build a **PrintWriter** from the **File** fails (for example, the user is not permitted to write to the folder where the output file is being created), a **FileNotFoundException** occurs, and flow jumps to the corresponding **catch** block, which invokes **quitOrTryAgain()**. This method displays our error message **"Unable to open output file"**, and then finds out if the user wants to quit. If so, it terminates the program. Otherwise, **quitOrTryAgain()** terminates, returning flow to the **catch** block, from where it jumps to the end of the **do** loop. Since **done** is still **false**, the **do** loop's condition is **true**, and flow returns to the top of the loop, giving the user another chance. This approach will give the user as many chances as necessary to enter a correct file name, without terminating the program.

These methods indicate the real power of Java's exception mechanism. By catching and handling the **FileNotFoundException**, these methods can let the user decide whether he or she wants to quit or try again, rather than the program making that decision.

11.4.3 Reading and Encrypting the File

Now that we have a convenient way to open the input and output files, we can proceed with the next step in our user story, which is to read the input file, encrypt what we read, and write the results to the output file. Wouldn't it be convenient if Java had a class with a method to do this for us? Well, it doesn't, but there is nothing stopping us from building one! We will call the class **CaesarCipherCoder**, and name the method **encodeFile()**.

Thinking about what this method must do, we might write out its behavior as follows:

Method to encode the contents of a file

Given: in, a **Scanner** *to an input file*

shiftAmount, an **int**

out, a **PrintWriter** *to an output file*

Our method should validate shiftAmount, to make sure it is positive, and in and out, to make sure they are not null. Assuming they are okay, our method should read each line from in, encode it by shiftAmount, and write the resulting line to out, followed by a newline.

Since we cannot anticipate in advance how many lines of text might be in the input file, this user story suggests that we use an input loop to (1) read each line from the input file, (2) encode it, and then (3) write it to the output file. Steps 1 and 3 are easy, but Step 2 — encoding a **String** — seems complicated, so let's perform that step by building another method we'll name **encodeString()**. This second method behaves as follows:

> Method to encode a String
>
> Given: *str*, a **String**
>
> *shiftAmount*, an **int**
>
> Return: *codedStr*, a **String**
>
> *Our method should validate shiftAmount, to make sure it is positive. Assuming it is, our method should define codedStr as an empty string, read each character in str, encode it by shiftAmount, and then append it to codedStr. When finished, our method should return codedStr.*

This method encodes the characters in a **String**, which suggests that we need a loop to iterate through the **String**'s characters. Since the number of characters in a **String** can be determined by sending it the **length()** message, we can use a **for** loop for this task. Each iteration of the **for** loop, we must (1) access the ith character, (2) encode that character, and (3) append it to the *codedStr* variable.

Of these steps, we can easily perform Steps 1 and 3, but Step 2 seems complicated. So let's write one final method, named **encodeChar()**, to perform that step.

This third method — **encodeChar(*ch*, *shiftAmount*)** — must compute the character that lies ***shiftAmount*** positions past ***ch***, wrapping around to the beginning if necessary. For example, if ***shiftAmount*** is 5, then we must encode ***ch*** as follows:

```
ch:         A B C D E F G H I J K L M N O P Q R S T U V W X Y Z
chEncoded:  F G H I J K L M N O P Q R S T U V W X Y Z A B C D E
```

Our method must thus distinguish between uppercase letters and other characters, such as spaces and punctuation. We might write out the required behavior as in the following user story:

> Method to encode a char
>
> Given: *ch*, a **char**
>
> *shiftAmount*, an **int**
>
> Return: *chEncoded*, a **char**
>
> *Our method should validate shiftAmount, to make sure it is positive. Assuming it is, if ch is not an uppercase letter, then it should set chEncoded to ch; otherwise, the method should set chEncoded to the character that is shiftAmount positions past it (wrapping around if necessary). The method should then return chEncoded.*

Java's **Character** class provides a number of class methods that are useful in distinguishing between different kinds of characters, including those listed in Figure 11-13.

Method	Returns
`Character.isLetterOrDigit(ch)`	**true**, if *ch* is a letter or digit **false**, otherwise
`Character.isLetter(ch)`	**true**, if *ch* is a letter **false**, otherwise
`Character.isDigit(ch)`	**true**, if *ch* is a digit **false**, otherwise
`Character.isUpperCase(ch)`	**true**, if *ch* is an uppercase letter **false**, otherwise
`Character.isLowerCase(ch)`	**true**, if *ch* is a lowercase letter **false**, otherwise

FIGURE 11-13 A few of the **Character** class methods

Once we have used the **isUpperCase()** method to identify ***ch*** as an uppercase character, we must compute the character that lies ***shiftAmount*** past it, wrapping around from **'Z'** to **'A'** if necessary. Thus, if ***shiftAmount*** is 3, **'A'** should be encoded as **'D'**, **'B'** as **'E'**, **'C'** as **'F'**, ..., **'W'** as **'Z'**, **'X'** as **'A'**, **'Y'** as **'B'**, and **'Z'** as **'C'**.

One way to accomplish this is to recall that **char** values are represented using 16-bit integer numbers. For example, **'A'** is represented as 65, **'B'** is 66, and so on. This means that we can compute the character that lies ***shiftAmount*** past ***ch*** using integer arithmetic. The exact steps are as follows:

1. Subtract 'A' (65) from *ch*, to shift its value into the range 0..25.
2. Add *shiftAmount* to the result, yielding an encoded value in the range *shiftAmount*..25+*shiftAmount*.
3. Find the remainder of the result and 26, the number of alphabet letters, so that encoded values above 25 "wrap around" to 0.
4. Add 'A' (65) to the result, to shift its value back to the range 65..92.
5. Convert the resulting integer back into a **char** value.

The trickiest part is Step 3, in which we find the remainder of the result and 26. We can accomplish that using the modulus (**%**) operator, as we saw in Figure 8.2.2. To illustrate, suppose ***ch*** is **'B'** (66), and ***shiftAmount*** is 3. Then we (1) subtract **'A'** from ***ch***, giving us the value 1; (2) add 3, giving us the value 4; (3) compute 4 % 26 == 4; (4) add **'A'** (65), giving us the value 69; and (5) convert the result to a **char** (**'E'**). We've just encoded **'B'** as **'E'**!

As a second example, suppose **ch** is **'X'** (88), and **shiftAmount** is again 3. Then we (1) subtract **'A'** from **ch**, giving us the value 23; (2) add 3, giving us the value 26; (3) compute 26 % 26 == 0; (4) add **'A'** (65), giving us the value 65; and (5) convert the result to a **char** (**'A'**). We've just encoded **'X'** as **'A'**!

Steps 1 through 4 are straightforward integer operations. Step 5, however, is not. To see why not, suppose **i** is an **int** variable, and we write the following:

```
char ch = i;
```

The Java compiler will generate an error because we are trying to store an **int** value (a 32-bit quantity) in a **char** variable (a 16-bit space). As we saw in Figure 8-4, the largest **int** value is 2,147,483,647; but the largest value a **char** can store is 65,535. If the **int** we are trying to store is greater than 65,535, then information will be lost. By generating this error, the Java compiler is trying to guard against this potential loss of information.

However, in our situation, the **int** value being stored should never be greater than 90 (the integer Unicode uses to represent the letter **'Z'**), so information should never be lost. In such situations, we can temporarily turn off the Java compiler's typing mechanism by writing:

```
char ch = (char) i;
```

The notation **(char)** is called a **cast** or **explicit type conversion**, as it tells the Java compiler to convert **i**'s value's type from **int** to **char**. More generally, an expression of the form:

```
(NewType) Expression
```

tells the Java compiler to convert ***Expression***'s type to ***NewType***.

Because casts turn off Java's type-checking mechanism, they are somewhat dangerous, and should only be used when you are certain no information will be lost. Java's "wrapper" classes (**Character**, **Integer**, **Double**, and so on) contain methods for safely converting between most of the primitive types. These can be used instead of casts in most situations.

Figure 11-14 uses these observations to solve our problem. Lines 7–19 define the **encodeChar()** method. Within this method, lines 13 and 14 perform Steps 1–5, outlined above. Lines 26 to 30 use **encodeChar()** to define **encodeString()**. Lines 38 to 42 use **encodeString()** to define **encodeFile()**.

```
1  /** CaesarCipherCoder.java models the Caesar Cipher.
2   */
3  import java.util.Scanner;
4  import java.io.*;                    // File, PrintWriter, ...
5
6  public class CaesarCipherCoder {
7   public char encodeChar(char ch, int shiftAmount) {
8    if (shiftAmount <= 0) {
9     throw new IllegalArgumentException("encodeChar(): bad argument");
```

continued

```
 }
 char chEncoded;
 if ( Character.isUpperCase(ch) ) {
    int chEncodedAsInt = ((ch - 'A' + shiftAmount) % 26) + 'A';
    chEncoded = (char) chEncodedAsInt;
 } else {
    chEncoded = ch;
 }
 return chEncoded;
}

public String encodeString(String str, int shiftAmount) {
 if (shiftAmount <= 0) {
  throw new IllegalArgumentException(
                                  "encodeString(): bad argument");
 }
 String codedStr = "";
 for (int i = 0; i < str.length(); i++) {
    char ch = str.charAt(i);
    char chEncoded = encodeChar(ch, shiftAmount);
    codedStr += chEncoded;
 }
 return codedStr;
}

public void encodeFile(Scanner fin, int shift, PrintWriter fout) {
 if (fin == null || shift <= 0 || fout == null) {
  throw new IllegalArgumentException("encodeFile(): bad argument");
 }
 while ( fin.hasNextLine() ) {
    String line = fin.nextLine();
    String lineEncoded = encodeString(line, shift);
    fout.println(lineEncoded);
 }
}

public static void main(String[] args) {
  System.out.println("Welcome to the Caesar Cipher file encoder");
  Scanner in = FileOps.promptForFileIn("Input file name? ");
  System.out.print("How many positions are chars to be shifted? ");
  int shiftAmount = FileOps.keyboard.nextInt();
  PrintWriter out = FileOps.promptForFileOut("Output file name? ");
  CaesarCipherCoder ccCoder = new CaesarCipherCoder();
```

continued

```
    ccCoder.encodeFile(in, shiftAmount, out);
    in.close();
    out.close();
    System.out.println("Processing complete.");
  }
}
```

```
Result:
Welcome to the Caesar Cipher file encoder
Input file name? message.txt
How many positions are chars to be shifted? 5
Output file name? codedMessage.txt
Processing complete.
```

FIGURE 11-14 **CaesarCipherCoder.java**

In the sample run shown, if the input file *message.txt* contains the lines:

```
I CAME.
I SAW.
I CONQUERED.
```

then the output file **codedMessage.txt** will contain the lines:

```
N HFRJ.
N XFB.
N HTSVZJWJI.
```

One interesting thing about the Caesar Cipher is that it can also be used to decode its messages. That is, if the original message is encoded using *shiftAmount* == *n*, where *n* is in the range 1..25, then the coded message can be decoded using *shiftAmount* == 26 - *n*. Thus, if we were to receive the encrypted message in **codedMessage.txt**, and we know that it was encoded using *shiftAmount* == 5, we could use our program to decode that message by using a *shiftAmount* == 26 - 5 == 21, as follows:

```
Welcome to the Caesar Cipher file encoder
Input file name? codedMessage.txt
How many positions are chars to be shifted? 21
Output file name? decodedMessage.txt
Processing complete.
```

The file **decodedMessage.txt** will then contain the original message:

```
I CAME.
I SAW.
I CONQUERED.
```

11.5 Example: Tracking Global Warming

Suppose that you have a friend who is an oceanographer, specializing in coral reefs. One of her favorite reefs has been in poor health for some years. To find out if global warming is the cause, she has anchored a buoy near the reef and has attached to it an underwater digital thermometer that continually records the water temperature in the shade beneath the buoy. Once a minute, this thermometer reads and records the temperature in a file on a flash drive. Once a month, your friend takes a boat ride out to the buoy and retrieves the file from the flash drive.

Your friend now has several years worth of monthly data files, and she needs a program to help her analyze the results. What she would like is a program that, given the name of a monthly data file, will display the average of the temperatures in that file, so that she can compare that month's average temperature to the average temperatures of the same month in other years.

There is one complication: in the early years of her research, her digital thermometer recorded the temperatures in the Fahrenheit scale (for example, 70.5° F). However, that thermometer broke and its replacement records the temperatures in the Celsius scale (for example, 21.4° C). Your friend wants the average temperature to be computed in Celsius.

11.5.1 Defining the Problem

We might start by writing this user story for our problem:

Temperature Averaging Program:

Our program should get the name of the input file from the user and open that file. It should then declare variables *sum* and *count*, both set to zero. It should then use an input loop to read each temperature from the input file, find the Celsius equivalent of that temperature, add the magnitude of that Celsius temperature to *sum*, and increment *count*. After all values have been processed, the program should close the file, and display the average (*sum*/*count*) of the temperatures,

Before we can write a program that performs this story, we must decide how we will model the temperature objects mentioned in the story.

11.5.2 Modeling Temperatures

While we often speak of temperatures as mere numbers, a temperature consists of a number and the scale in which that number was measured. For example, we (in the

United States) may speak of it being 90 degrees outside, but 90 degrees Fahrenheit is a very different temperature than 90 degrees Celsius!

Since we cannot model both a temperature's number and its scale with an existing type, we will build a class to do so. Instances of this class will need to "remember" two things:

- The temperature's number, which we will call its *magnitude*
- The temperature's *scale*

To store these attributes, we can declare a minimal class containing instance variables for these:

```
public class Temperature {
  private double myMagnitude;
  private char   myScale;
}
```

A Default Constructor

Since our class has instance variables, we need to be able to initialize them. We might define a default constructor as follows:

```
public Temperature() {
   myMagnitude = 0.0;
   myScale = 'C';
}
```

Given this much, a programmer can now write:

```
Temperature temp = new Temperature();
```

and **temp** will refer to a **Temperature** object modeling 0 Celsius, as shown in Figure 11-15.

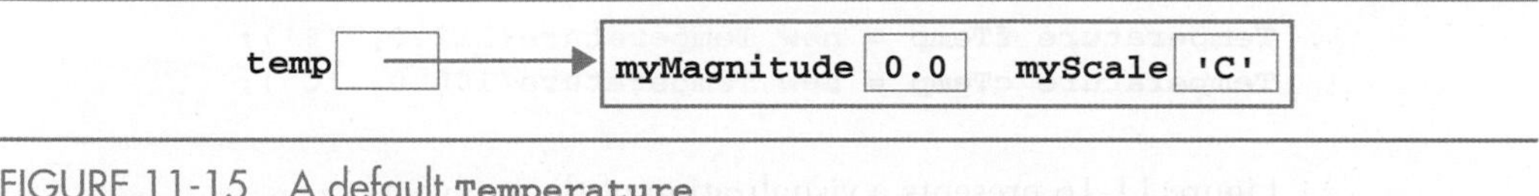

FIGURE 11-15 A default **Temperature**

An Explicit-Value Constructor

It is usually useful to be able to initialize an object to user-supplied arguments, which is the role of the explicit constructor. This constructor generally requires a parameter for each instance variable being initialized.

Explicit-value constructors are trickier than default constructors, because the user may pass invalid arguments. If this is possible, then the explicit-value constructor should validate its parameters. For example, temperatures that are less than *absolute zero* (**-459.67 F**; **-273.15 C**) are invalid, so our explicit value constructor needs to check for this possibility.

We will also need to perform validation when we define an input method, since the user or a file could supply an invalid temperature. Since we will need to validate a temperature in more than one place, we will write a method to do so:

```
public static final double ABS_ZERO_FAHR = -459.67;
public static final double ABS_ZERO_CELS = -273.15;

public static boolean isValid(double magnitude, char scale) {
  switch (scale) {
    case 'f': case 'F':
      return magnitude >= ABS_ZERO_FAHR;
    case 'c': case 'C':
      return magnitude >= ABS_ZERO_CELS;
    default:
      return false;
  }
}
```

With this method available, we can now define the explicit-value constructor as follows:

```
public Temperature(double magnitude, char scale) {
    if ( isValid(magnitude, scale) ) {
       myMagnitude = magnitude;
       myScale = scale;
    } else {
       throw new IllegalArgumentException("bad arguments in "
                                              + "Temperature(m, s)");
    }
}
```

With this constructor, a programmer can now build distinct `Temperature` objects:

```
Temperature fTemp = new Temperature(212.0, 'F');
Temperature cTemp = new Temperature(100.0, 'C');
```

Figure 11-16 presents a visualization of these objects.

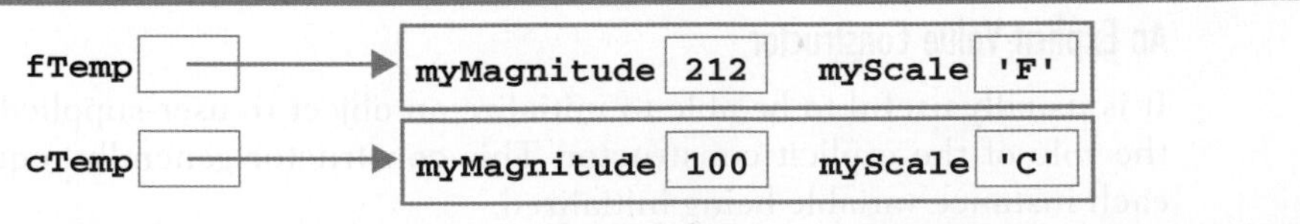

FIGURE 11-16 Explicitly defined `Temperature` objects

Accessors

Writing the accessor methods for our two instance variables is easy:

```
public char   getScale()     { return myScale; }
public double getMagnitude() { return myMagnitude; }
```

With these methods defined, a programmer can now send messages like these:

```
System.out.println( fTemp.getMagnitude()
                     + " " + fTemp.getScale() );
```

to retrieve the two attributes of the first **Temperature** object in Figure 11-16.

Converting to Celsius

In our user story, we need to be able to convert Fahrenheit temperatures into Celsius temperatures. The formula for doing so is as follows:

$$fahrenheitToCelsius(fahrTemp) = \frac{(fahrTemp - 32)}{1.8}$$

To perform this conversion, we will first define a class method named **fahrToCels()** that encodes this formula, providing the numerical part of the conversion:

```
public static double fahrToCels(double fahrTemp) {
   return (fahrTemp - 32.0) / 1.8;
}
```

We can then use that class method to build an instance method named **inCelsius()** that, when sent to a **Temperature** object, will return the Celsius equivalent of that **Temperature**:

```
public Temperature inCelsius() {
  Temperature result = null;
  switch (myScale) {
   case 'F': case 'f':
     result = new Temperature(fahrToCels(myMagnitude), 'C');
     break;
   case 'C': case 'c':
     result = new Temperature(myMagnitude, 'C');
     break;
   default:
     throw new IllegalArgumentException("inCelsius(): bad
           scale");
  }
  return result;
}
```

With this method, a programmer can now write:

```
Temperature fTemp = new Temperature(212.0, 'F');
Temperature cTemp = fTemp.inCelsius();
```

and **cTemp** will refer to the Celsius equivalent of **fTemp**, as shown in Figure 11-16.

Input

Since a **Temperature** object "knows" its own internal structure, it makes sense for it to provide a method that reads values from a **Scanner** into its instance variables. However, to guard against the input of invalid temperature values, we must validate such values:

```
public void readFrom(Scanner scanner) {
    double magnitude = scanner.nextDouble();
    char scale = scanner.next().charAt(0);
    if ( isValid(magnitude, scale) ) {
       myMagnitude = magnitude;
       myScale = scale;
    } else {
       throw new IllegalArgumentException("read(): bad input");
    }
}
```

With this definition and a **Scanner** object named **keyboard**, a programmer can now write:

```
Temperature temp = new Temperature();
temp.readFrom(keyboard);
```

and the **Temperature** object referred to by **temp** will fill itself with values from **keyboard**. Similarly, if **fin** is a **Scanner** object for a file, then the statement:

```
temp.readFrom(fin);
```

will cause that **Temperature** object to fill itself with values from that file.

Output via String Representation

As we have seen previously, it is good practice for a class to provide a **toString()** method that provides an object's **String** representation. This is quite easy for the **Temperature** class:

```
public String toString() { return myMagnitude + " " + myScale; }
```

With this method, a programmer can now write:

```
temp.readFrom(fin);
System.out.println(temp);
```

and the temperature read from **fin** will be displayed on the screen.

The Complete Class

These methods provide sufficient functionality to model the temperatures in our problem. Figure 11-17 presents the class to this point in its development.

```
/** Temperature.java models Fahrenheit and Celsius temperatures.
 */
import java.util.Scanner;

public class Temperature {
  public static final double ABS_ZERO_FAHR = -459.67;
  public static final double ABS_ZERO_CELS = -273.15;

  public Temperature() {
    myMagnitude = ABS_ZERO_CELS;
    myScale = 'C';
  }

  public Temperature(double magnitude, char scale) {
    checkAndSet(magnitude, scale);
  }

  private void checkAndSet(double magnitude, char scale) {
    if ( isValid(magnitude, scale) ) {
      myMagnitude = magnitude;
      myScale = scale;
    } else {
      throw new IllegalArgumentException("checkAndSet(): bad args");
    }
  }

  public static boolean isValid(double magnitude, char scale) {
    switch (scale) {
      case 'f': case 'F':
        return magnitude >= ABS_ZERO_FAHR;
      case 'c': case 'C':
        return magnitude >= ABS_ZERO_CELS;
      default:
```

continued

```
        return false;
      }
    }

    public char getScale() { return myScale; }

    public double getMagnitude() { return myMagnitude; }

    public String toString() { return myMagnitude + " " + myScale; }

    public void read(Scanner scanner) {
      double magnitude = scanner.nextDouble();
      char scale = scanner.next().charAt(0);
      checkAndSet(magnitude, scale);
    }

    public static double fahrToCels(double fahrTemp) {
      return (fahrTemp - 32.0) / 1.8;
    }

    public Temperature inCelsius() {
      Temperature result = null;
      switch (myScale) {
        case 'F': case 'f':
          result = new Temperature(fahrToCels(myMagnitude), 'C');
          break;
        case 'C': case 'c':
          result = new Temperature(myMagnitude, 'C');
          break;
        default:
          throw new IllegalArgumentException(
                                   "inCelsius(): bad scale");
      }
      return result
    }

    private double myMagnitude;
    private char   myScale;
  }
```

FIGURE 11-17 **Temperature.java**

In looking over our class, we saw that the **if** statements in the explicit-value constructor and the **read()** method were almost identical, so in Figure 11-17, we have "factored out" this common code into a separate **checkAndSet()** method, and invoked that method in place of the common code. This is one kind of **refactoring** — reviewing one's code and rewriting it in a way that improves its structure or readability.

11.5.3 Solving the Problem

Now that we have a good model for a temperature, we can use it and the **FileOps** class from Figure 11-12 to solve our friend's problem. We might first create some small input files that we can use to test our program, named **testTemps1.txt**, **testTemps2.txt**, and **testTemps3.txt**, containing different kinds and numbers of valid temperatures. We'll also use **testTemps4.txt**, containing invalid temperatures, as shown in Figure 11-18.

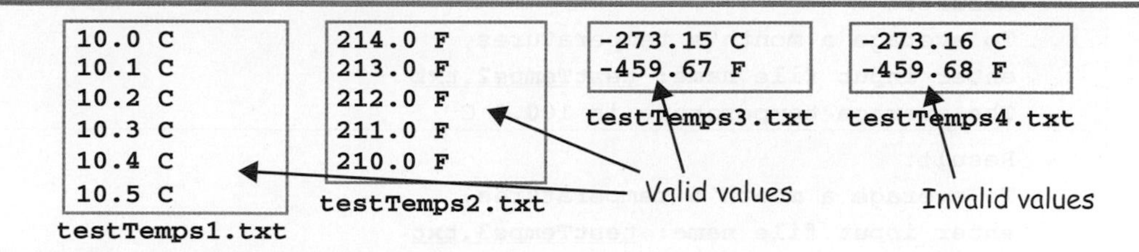

FIGURE 11-18 Test input files

We can then build a program that performs our user story, as shown in Figure 11-19.

```
/** AverageMonthlyTemperatures.java.
 */
import java.util.Scanner;

public class AverageMonthlyTemperatures {
  public static void main(String[] args) {
    System.out.println("To average a month's temperatures,");
    Scanner fin = FileOps.promptForFileIn(
                             "enter input file name: ");
    Temperature temp = new Temperature();
    double sum = 0.0;
    int count = 0;
    while ( fin.hasNext() ) {
      temp.read(fin);
      sum += temp.inCelsius().getMagnitude();
      count++;
    }
    fin.close();
    if (count > 0) {
      System.out.println("The average temperature is "
```

continued

```
20                                  + new Temperature(sum/count, 'C') );
21       } else {
22          System.err.println("No values in input file!");
23       }
24    }
25 }
```

```
Result:
To average a month's temperatures,
enter input file name: testTemps1.txt
The average temperature is 10.25 C
```

```
Result:
To average a month's temperatures,
enter input file name: testTemps2.txt
The average temperature is 100.0 C
```

```
Result:
To average a month's temperatures,
enter input file name: testTemps3.txt
The average temperature is -273.15 C
```

```
Result:
To average a month's temperatures,
enter input file name: testTemps4.txt
Exception in thread "main" java.lang.IllegalArgumentException:
 checkAndSet(): bad arguments (-273.16,C)
... stack trace omitted
```

FIGURE 11-19 **AverageMonthlyTemperatures.java**

When we are confident that our program is behaving correctly, we can give it to our friend, and she can begin using it to process her reef data.

Note that in line 14 of Figure 11-19, we send multiple messages in the same statement. That is, **temp** is a handle for a **Temperature**, so the **inCelsius()** message is performed first:

```
sum += temp.inCelsius().getMagnitude();
```

This returns a **Temperature** object, to which we send the **getMagnitude()** message:

```
sum += temp.inCelsius().getMagnitude();
```

This returns a **double** value, which the **+=** operator adds to **sum**.

Aside from this statement, our program is relatively simple, compared to the **Temperature** class. This is because the class, as a general model of temperatures, is providing all of the temperature-related functionality. This makes it possible for our program to deal with temperatures almost as if they were one of Java's primitive types.

This ability to build software models of things from the real world is one of the things that makes programming with classes so useful in solving real-world problems. Using classes, we can create software representations of just about anything, from abstractions like exceptions and files, to things from the real world like pH values and temperatures.

11.6 Chapter Summary

- The **File** class can be used to model a file in software.
- A **Scanner** can be constructed from a **File**. Once this has been done, values can be read from the file using the familiar **Scanner** input methods: **next()**, **nextDouble()**, **nextInt()**, **nextLine()**, and so on.
- A **PrintWriter** can be constructed from a **File**. Once this has been done, values can be written to the file via the **PrintWriter** using the familiar **print()**, **println()**, and **printf()** methods.
- A class hierarchy organizes classes according to subclass-superclass relationships, where a subclass is a more specialized version of its immediate superclass. A subclass inherits all of the methods and instance variables of its superclass.
- Java uses an **Exception** class hierarchy to model the many things that can go wrong when a program runs.
    - The **RuntimeException** class and its subclasses are *unchecked exceptions.*
    - The other exception classes are *checked exceptions*, so methods that throw such exceptions must be performed in a **try** block, and the exception must be caught and handled in a **catch** block.
- A class "knows" its own structure, so it should provide a **read()** method by which it can fill itself with values from a **Scanner**. Likewise, a class should provide a **toString()** method so that its values can be displayed easily.

11.6.1 Key Terms

buffer, buffering
cast
catch block
checked exception
class hierarchy
exception
exception classes
exception propagation
file system
finally block
flushing
immediate superclass
inherit
input file
"is a" relationship
main memory
opening a file
output file
refactoring
secondary memory
stack trace
subclass
superclass
throw statement
try block
try-catch block
unchecked exception

Programming Projects

11.1 Modify the **CaesarCipherCoder** class from this chapter so that, in addition to encoding uppercase letters, it will also encode lowercase letters and digits. For example, if the *shiftAmount* is 4, then lowercase letters and digits should be encoded as follows:

```
ch:         a b c d e f g ... s t u v w x y z , 0 1 2 3 4 5 6 7 8 9
chEncoded:  e f g h i j k ... w x y z a b c d , 4 5 6 7 8 9 0 1 2 3
```

11.2 Proceed as in Project 11.1, but build a method that, given a **Scanner** and a *shiftAmount*, reads all lines from the **Scanner**, but instead of writing the results to a file, builds and returns a **String** consisting of those lines encoded using *shiftAmount*.

11.3 Words such as *I*, *a*, *and*, and *the* are likely to appear in a message. Proceed as in Project 11.2; then write a program that will decode messages encoded using the Caesar Cipher, using brute force to try all possible *shiftAmount* values. Using the method from Project 11.2, your program should scan the string for commonly used words, to try to automatically identify the *shiftAmount* needed to decode the message. When it finds a potentially correct *shiftAmount* (for example, 21), your program should open a file whose name includes *shiftAmount* (for example, *21.txt*), write the decoded message for that *shiftAmount* in that file, and print the name of the file to the screen for the user.

11.4 A palindrome is a string of characters that reads the same forward or backward, ignoring case and punctuation. For example, the strings **"Madam, I'm Adam"**, **"A man, a plan, a canal, Panama!"**, and **"Sit on a potato pan, Otis!"** are all palindromes. Write a method that, given a **String**, returns **true** if that **String** is a palindrome, and returns **false** otherwise. Then write a program that, for each line in an input file, writes that line to an output file, and indicates whether or not that line was a palindrome.

11.5 In Section 11.5, we wrote a program that will average the temperature values in a given file. Suppose that our researcher friend has given her data files names like **2000-1.txt**, **2000-2.txt**, **2000-3.txt**, ..., **2000-12.txt**, **2001-1.txt**, **2001-2.txt**, ..., **2001-12.txt**, **2002-1.txt**, **2002-2.txt**, ..., **2002-12.txt**, and so on, to the current year, so that each file's name indicates the year and month of its data. Write a program that asks the user for the first year and the last year, and then creates an output file containing a table with a row for each year and a column for each month. The table entry for row *year*, column *month* is the average of the values in the file **year-month.txt**. Use tab characters to separate the columns. To test your program, create a group of sample data files containing easy-to-verify data.

11.6 Write a program that reads an input file named **employees.txt**, and produces an output file named **payroll.txt**. Each line in the input file provides the data for one employee, with the form:

```
firstName    lastName    wage    hours
```

Your program should produce the payroll file containing the same number of lines as the input file, with each line providing one employee's pay:

```
firstName    lastName    pay
```

Be sure to include overtime pay. (For example, employees might be paid 150% of their wage for each hour they work in excess of 40 hours.)

11.7 Modify the **Temperature** class in Figure 11-17, so that it supports the conversion of Celsius temperatures to Fahrenheit temperatures via an **inFahrenheit()** instance method and a **celsToFahr()** class method. The formula is as follows:

$$celsiusToFahr(celsTemp) = celsTemp \times 1.8 + 32$$

Verify that your modifications work by writing a program that reads a series of temperatures from an input file, and then creates an output file containing a 2-column table. For each temperature in the input file, the left column should give that temperature in the Celsius scale, the right column in the Fahrenheit scale. (Extra credit: Modify **Temperature** as necessary to support temperatures in the Kelvin scale, and have your program display a third column of Kelvin temperatures.)

11.8 Using the **Plotter** class discussed in Section 10.3.2, write a program that reads and plots a series of (x, y) point values from an input file. Assume that the first two lines of the input file specify the minimum and maximum (x, y) points (for constructing the **Plotter**), and that every subsequent line in the file contains an (x, y) point to be plotted. Create sample input files to test your program.

11.9 In Section 10.2.2, we built a **PetLicense** class to model pet licenses. Modify this class as necessary to store a pet's name, license number, owner's name, and phone number. Then add a **read()** method that will fill a **PetLicense** with data from a **Scanner**. Use this class to write a "pet owner lookup" program that allows an animal rescue officer to enter a stray pet's license number at the keyboard, and then reads a series of licenses from an input file, displaying the stray pet's name, owner's name, and phone number if a match is found. Create a sample input file for testing.

11.10 In Section 10.2.2, we presented a **`TShirt`** class. Suppose that XS t-shirts cost you $6.00, S t-shirts cost you $7.00, M t-shirts cost you $8.00, L t-shirts cost you $9.00, and XL t-shirts cost you $10.00. Suppose also that one of your senior roommates has created a Web site that allows users to order t-shirts online. The Web site writes all of the t-shirts ordered on a given day to an output file, one shirt per line. Write a program that, using the information in this file at the end of the day, displays on the screen a summary of that day's sales activity, including: (1) the number of t-shirts sold in each size, (2) the total number sold, (3) the total (gross) sales, and (4) the net (gross-cost) profits for that day.

Chapter 12

Arrays and Lists in Java

Modern science has given us a vast array of colors with exciting names like Red! Blue! Orange! Brown! and PINK!

DWAYNE HOOVER (BRUCE WILLIS), IN *BREAKFAST OF CHAMPIONS*

Our gun arrays are now fixed on your ship and will fire the instant you come into range. You will find their power quite impressive... for a few seconds.

SUSAN IVANOVA (CLAUDIA CHRISTIAN) IN *BABYLON 5*

Would someone please wake the person who's sleeping in row 2, seat 3?

V. OREHCK III, DURING A LECTURE ON 2-DIMENSIONAL ARRAYS

This list... is an absolute good. The list is life. All around its margins lies the gulf.

ITZHAK STERN (BEN KINGSLEY), IN *SCHINDLER'S LIST*

Is that what your little note says? It must be hard living your life off a couple of scraps of paper. You mix your laundry list with your grocery list, you'll end up eating your underwear for breakfast.

NATALIE (CARRIE-ANNE MOSS), IN *MEMENTO*

Objectives

Upon completion of this chapter, you should be able to:

- ❑ Understand Java's array data structure
- ❑ Solve problems using Java's **`LinkedList`** data structure
- ❑ Solve problems using Java's **`ArrayList`** data structure

In Chapter 5, we learned about the **array** and **list** data structures. Both let us define variables that store groups of items, and both let us access a given item using a number called an *index*. The differences between these structures include the following:

- The size of an array is fixed while a program runs, but the size of a list can change.
- An array can store a group of items using less memory than a list.
- An array lets us access the item at a given index much faster than does a list.

In this chapter, we will learn more about these data structures and see how to use them in Java.

12.1 Arrays in Java

12.1.1 Introductory Example: Air Pollution Reporting

In Section 10.3.2, we saw how to compute a city's air pollution index from five air pollution level readings collected from the city's center and North-South-East-West compass points. Suppose your supervisor comes to you and, after thanking you for writing the program, asks you to modify it so that it provides more detail. More precisely, she wants it to display the average of the five readings, followed by the five readings used to compute that average. The idea is that someone who just wants the air pollution index can read the first line and get the average, like an executive summary. Those who want more information can continue on to the list of individual readings.

The problem we face is that we must first display the average, and then display the individual readings. If the order of these was reversed, we could solve the problem using the same approach as we did back in Figure 10-14. However, because we must display the average first, before we display the individual readings, we must process each reading *twice*: once to compute the average, and then again to display the readings.

We could solve this problem by writing the values to a file as we read from the keyboard and compute the average. We could then display the average, close the file, reopen it, and read the values from the file, in order to display them. This approach works, but it requires us to read the values twice — once from the keyboard and once from the file. Because reading and writing files are so slow, it should be avoided if there is a better way.

The better way is to read the values into a data structure in the program's memory. Since our problem has a fixed number of values (five), we will use the array data structure. Using an array, we might write the following user story:

Purpose: Report the air pollution index and supporting readings.

1. Build an array named *readings*, capable of storing five numbers
2. Read the air pollution readings into *readings*
3. Compute and display the average of the values in *readings*
4. Display the individual values in *readings*, with appropriate labels

From this user story, we might build the program shown in Figure 12-1.

```
/** AirPollutionReport.java
 */
import java.util.Scanner;

public class AirPollutionReport {
  public static void main(String[] args) {
     final int NUM_READINGS = 5;
     double [] readings = new double[NUM_READINGS];
     readReadingsInto(readings);
     System.out.printf( "\nThe average is %.3f%n",
                              average(readings) );
     print(readings);
  }

  private static void readReadingsInto(double [] array) {
     Scanner keyboard = new Scanner(System.in);
     System.out.println("To compute the air pollution index...");
     for (int i = 0; i < array.length; i++) {
         System.out.print("Enter reading #" + (i+1) + "/" +
                                array.length + ": " );
         array[i] = keyboard.nextDouble();
     }
  }

  public static double average(double [] anArray) {
     if (anArray.length < 1) {
        throw new IllegalArgumentException("average():" +
                                        " array is empty");
     }
     double sum = 0.0;
     for (double item : anArray) {
        sum += item;
     }
     return sum/anArray.length;
  }

  public static void print(double [] arr) {
     for (int i = 0; i < arr.length; i++) {
        System.out.println("Reading #" + (i+1) + ": " +  arr[i]);
     }
  }
}
```

continued

Result:
To compute the air pollution index...
Enter reading #1/5: 14
Enter reading #2/5: 12
Enter reading #3/5: 14
Enter reading #4/5: 12
Enter reading #5/5: 13
The average is 13.000
Reading #1: 14.0
Reading #2: 12.0
Reading #3: 14.0
Reading #4: 12.0
Reading #5: 13.0

FIGURE 12-1 **AirPollutionReport.java**

In the next section, we will use this program to investigate Java's array data structure.

12.1.2 Java Arrays

Defining an Array

Line 8 of Figure 12-1 declares a handle named **readings** for an array of **double** values.

```
double [] readings = new double[NUM_READINGS];
```

The first pair of brackets in the declaration tell the Java compiler that **readings** will be the handle for an array of **double** values, rather than just a normal **double** variable. The rest of line 8 tells the compiler to allocate an array capable of storing 5 **double** values, using the constant **NUM_READINGS** defined on line 7:

```
double [] readings = new double[NUM_READINGS];
```

Since the value of **NUM_READINGS** is 5, this notation tells the compiler to allocate a block of memory big enough to store 5 real numbers, and make **readings** the handle for that block of memory. In general, an **array definition** of the form:

```
Item [] anArray = new Item [ N ];
```

can be used to define an array capable of storing **N** values of type **Item**, which can then be accessed via the handle ***anArray***.

Array Initialization

An array's items are automatically initialized to the "default value" of their type when they are allocated. For numeric types, the default value is **0.0** for **double**s and **0** for **int**s. Thus, after the statement on line 8 is performed, **readings** can be visualized as shown in Figure 12-2.

readings	**[0]**	**[1]**	**[2]**	**[3]**	**[4]**
	0.0	**0.0**	**0.0**	**0.0**	**0.0**

FIGURE 12-2 An array to store five **double** values

The values stored in an array (for example, the **0.0** values in Figure 12-2) are called the array's **items**. The indexed boxes in which the items are stored are called the array's **elements**.

Array Parameters

The program in Figure 12-1 uses three different methods to solve the problem: **readReadingsInto()**, **average()**, and **print()**. Since we pass **readings** as an argument to each of these methods, each of these methods needs to define a parameter capable of storing an array's handle. As can be seen on lines 15, 25, and 37, this can be done by placing a pair of brackets between a parameter's type and its name. For example, the **average()** method calls its parameter **anArray**, which it declares as follows:

```
public static double average(double [] anArray) { ...
```

By placing the brackets within the parameter declaration, we tell the compiler that *any* array of **double** items can be passed to this parameter.

> *An array parameter and its argument are handles to the same array, so any accesses to the parameter will access the argument's array.*

That is, on line 11 of Figure 12-1, we invoke method **average()** and pass it the argument array **readings**. As **average()** is performed, it refers to its parameter, which is named **anArray**. Since **readings** is the argument that corresponds to parameter **anArray**, all accesses to **anArray** within **average()** access elements in its argument array **readings**.

Note that in the **average()** method, the parameter is named **anArray**; in the **readReadingsInto()** method, the parameter is named **array**; and in the **print()** method, the parameter is named **arr**. Any valid identifier can be used, provided it is sufficiently descriptive.

In general, a method can declare a parameter to store an array of **Item** values using the following pattern:

```
public ReturnType methodName( Item [] parameterName ) { ...
```

Accessing Array Elements

Any item in an array can be accessed using the array's handle, the item's index, and the **subscript operator** (**[]**). Since the first element always has index **0**, the first item of **readings** can be accessed using the expression **readings[0]**, the second item can be accessed using **readings[1]**, and the item whose index is ***i*** can be accessed using **readings[*i*]**. Within method **average()**, our handle to the array is named **anArray**, so its first item can be accessed using the expression **anArray[0]**, the second item can be accessed using **anArray[1]**, and the item whose index is ***i*** can be accessed using **anArray[*i*]**. The subscript operation thus behaves much like the **String** method **charAt(*i*)**, which retrieves the character whose index is ***i***.

> The subscript operation ***anArray*[*i*]** accesses the array element at index ***i*** in the array for which ***anArray*** is a handle.

The array subscript operation validates each access to an array. In a subscript operation **anArray[*i*]**, if ***i*** is outside the range of valid index values (for example, negative), then the subscript operation throws an **ArrayIndexOutOfBoundsException**.

The **length** Property

The number of elements in an array can be determined using the **array length property**. For example, after line 8 has been performed, the expression **readings.length** is equal to **5**. An array's **length** is a *property*, not a method, so do not put parentheses after it, or a compiler error will result.

Since the index of the first element of an array is **0**, the index of the last element is always the array's **length-1**.

> The notation ***anArray*[*anArray*.length-1]** can always be used to access the last element of ***anArray***.

Processing Array Elements

A **for** loop provides a convenient way to access each of the elements of an array. The program in Figure 12-1 illustrates this several times. For example, lines 18–22 in the

readReadingsInto() method use the following loop to read the air pollution readings from the keyboard into the array, using the parameter named **array**:

```
for (int i = 0; i < array.length; i++) {
   System.out.print("Enter reading #" + (i+1) + "/" +
                              array.length + ": " );
   array[i] = keyboard.nextDouble();
}
```

As this illustrates, a **for** loop can process the array's items by counting through the array's index values. The loop's condition tests the counting variable against the array's **length** property. Within the **for** loop, we access the item at a given index using the subscript operator.

The **print()** method also uses this approach to display the values in the array:

```
for (int i = 0; i < arr.length; i++) {
     System.out.println("Reading #" + (i+1) + ": " +  arr[i]);
}
```

The **average()** method uses a different approach to sum the values in the array:

```
for (double item : anArray) {
     sum += item;
}
```

Java calls this a **for each loop**, and it behaves just like Alice's **forAllInOrder** loop, repeating the statement **sum += item;** once for each item in the data structure. In the first repetition, **item** refers to **anArray[0]**; in the second repetition, **item** refers to **anArray[1]**; and so on.

As another example, we could have written the **print()** method as follows:

```
public static void print(double [] arr) {
   int i = 1;
   for (double reading : arr) {
      System.out.println("Reading #" + i + ": " +  reading);
      i++;
   }
}
```

The **for each** loop thus provides a convenient, alternative way to process the items in an array, from first to last. Its general pattern is as follows:

> Pattern for Java's **for each** loop:
>
> ```
> for (ItemType it : dataStructure ) {
>     Statements
> }
> ```
>
> where:
>
> ***ItemType*** is the type of value stored in ***dataStructure***
>
> ***it*** is any valid, descriptive identifier
>
> ***dataStructure*** is a handle to an array, list, or other data structure
>
> ***Statements*** are statements to be repeated
>
> Purpose: Statements are repeated once for each item in ***dataStructure***; and ***it*** is varied through those items from first to last.

Note that the **for each** loop accesses an array's *items*, not its *elements*. Because of this:

> The **for each** loop can be used to read an array's items; but it cannot be used write to an array's elements.

For example, the **readReadingsInto()** method reads a number from the keyboard and writes it to an array element, so we cannot use the **for each** loop in defining that method. By contrast, the **average()** and **print()** methods read an array's items, so we can use either the **for each** loop or the **for** loop and the subscript operator to define these methods.

> An array element is a variable whose type is the array's item-type. Any operation (or method) that can be used on a variable of that type can be used on an array element.

12.1.3 Example 2: Month Names From Numbers

In Section 8.1, we wrote a program that converted month numbers (1–12) to their 3-letter abbreviations (*Jan*, *Feb*, *Mar*, ..., *Nov*, *Dec*), to help non-English speaking people recall the full names of the months. We wrote this program to help a friend who was teaching these people.

Suppose that our friend asks us to write another program for her students. This program is to let them practice recalling and spelling the full month names (that is, *January*, *February*, ..., *November*, *December*). Together, we decide that the program should (1) randomly generate a month number; (2) prompt the user to enter the month name for that month number; (3) read the user's response; (4) and either display a positive message if the user's response was correct, or display a message showing what his or her response should have been. The program should let the user keep playing as long as he or she wants.

Using this as a user story, we can organize these steps as follows:

Purpose: Help people learn to spell the names of the months.

1. Display a greeting message that explains how the program works
2. do {
   a. Generate a random *monthNumber* in the range 1...12
   b. Ask the user to enter the name of month # *monthNumber*
   c. Read the user's *response*
   d. Determine the month *m* corresponding to *monthNumber*
   e. If *m*'s name equals *response*, display a positive message
   f. Otherwise, display a message showing *m* (the correct response)
   g. Ask the user if he or she wants to do another (y or n)
   h. Read the user's *answer*

   while (*answer* indicates the user wants to keep going)

The only tricky part is Step 2d, where we must determine the month *m* that corresponds to *monthNumber*. With a bit of thought, it becomes evident that a month has two different aspects to it: its *name* and its *number*. Since we cannot represent both of those aspects in a normal variable, we will build a class to do so. We might start with a minimal class like the following:

```
public class Month {
   private int myNumber;
   private String myName;
}
```

In our algorithm, the program generates a random month number, and then uses that to compute the month's name. Our **Month()** constructor will thus need to be able to construct a **Month** object from a month number. To determine the name of a month from its number, we might store the names of the months in an array, and use the month number to index into this array. Figure 12-3 presents a **Month** class that uses this approach.

```
/** Month.java models a month.
 */
public class Month {
  public Month(int monthNumber) {
    if (monthNumber < 1 || monthNumber > 12) {
      throw new IllegalArgumentException(
                                       "Month(): bad month number");
    }
    myNumber = monthNumber;
    myName = MONTHS[monthNumber-1];
  }

```

continued

```
12    public int    getNumber() { return myNumber; }
13    public String getName()   { return myName; }
14
15    public String toString()  { return myName; }
16
17    private static final String [] MONTHS = {"January", "February",
18                                             "March", "April", "May",
19                                             "June", "July", "August",
20                                             "September", "October",
21                                             "November", "December" };
22    private String myName;
23    private int    myNumber;
24 }
```

FIGURE 12-3 The **Month** class

The thought process in building this class goes as follows: We need a data structure to store the names of the months. Because the number of months (12) does not change, we store them in an array. If we call this array **MONTHS**, we can visualize it as shown in Figure 12-4.

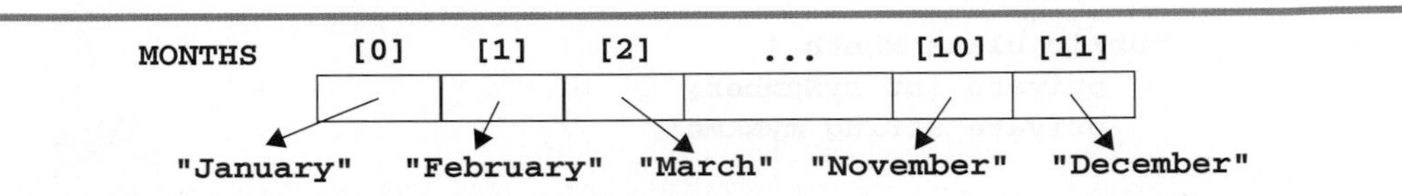

FIGURE 12-4 The **MONTHS** array

Since the names of the months should not change, we declare **MONTHS** as a constant array, using the **final** keyword. To avoid unnecessary duplication of this array in different **Month** instances, we declare it as a class (**static**) variable, so that all instances of **Month** can share the same array.

The declaration of **MONTHS** on lines 17–21 of Figure 12-3 illustrates a new way to define an array. Previously, we used the following pattern to define an array containing ***N*** default items:

```
Item [] anArray = new Item [ N ];
```

However, the declaration in Figure 12-3 uses this alternative pattern:

Item **[]** ***anotherArray*** **= {** $item_0$, $item_1$, $item_2$, **...,** $item_{N-1}$ **};**

When it processes such a statement, the Java compiler will define ***anotherArray*** as the handle of an array containing the **N** listed items. This pattern can be used to separately specify the value of each element of an array, as we do in Figure 12-3.

Our **Month()** constructor uses the array **MONTHS** as a table in which to look up month names. Since the index of the first item in an array is always **0**, the index values in **MONTHS** range from **0** through **11**, whereas the month numbers range from **1** through **12**. That is, if **monthNumber** is **3**, then the month's name (**"March"**) is in **MONTHS[2]**; and if **monthNumber** is **12**, then the month's name (**"December"**) is in **MONTHS[11]**. In general, the name of the month associated with **monthNumber** is in **MONTHS[monthNumber-1]**. On line 9, our **Month** constructor uses this logic to set **myName** to the correct month name for a given **monthNumber**:

```
myName = MONTHS[monthNumber-1];
```

Given a constructor to initialize the instance variables, the remaining methods are (1) accessors for those instance variables, and (2) the **toString()** method, which we can use to output a **Month** value using the **print()** and **println()** methods.

The Program

Given our **Month** class, the program to solve our friend's problem is fairly simple, as shown in Figure 12-5.

```
/** MonthTester.java is a game to help learn month names.
 */
import java.util.*;    // Scanner, Random

public class MonthTester {
   public static void main(String[] args) {
     System.out.println("Welcome to the month name game!");
     System.out.print("\nI will give you a month number;");
     System.out.println(" you should enter its name.");
     Scanner keyboard = new Scanner(System.in);
     Random generator = new Random();
     char answer;
     do {
        int monthNumber = generator.nextInt(12) + 1;
        System.out.print("\nWhat is the name of month #"
                          + monthNumber + "? ");
        String response = keyboard.next();
        Month m = new Month(monthNumber);
        if ( m.getName().equals(response) ) {
           System.out.println("Correct! Very good!");
        } else {
           System.out.println("Sorry. Month #"
                                + monthNumber + " is " + m);
        }
        System.out.print("\nDo you want to do another (y or n)? ");
        answer = keyboard.next().charAt(0);
```

continued

```
    } while ( answer == 'y' || answer == 'Y' );
  }
}
```

```
Result:
Welcome to the month name game!

I will give you a month number; you should enter its name.

What is the name of month #3? March
Correct! Very good!

Do you want to do another (y or n)? y

What is the name of month #8? September
Sorry. Month #8 is August

Do you want to do another (y or n)? y

What is the name of month #9? September
Correct! Very good!

Do you want to do another (y or n)? n
```

FIGURE 12-5 **MonthTester.java**

This program is fairly simple because our **Month** class builds month values from month numbers. A carefully designed class can greatly simplify a problem's solution.

12.1.4 Arrays and Memory

An array's elements reside in adjacent memory locations. The subscript operation uses this adjacency to access any element of an array in the same amount of time. That is, a subscript expression like **anArray[i]** multiplies the index **i** by the size of one item and adds the resulting product to the reference in **anArray**. Figure 12-6 shows this computation for **anArray[4]**.

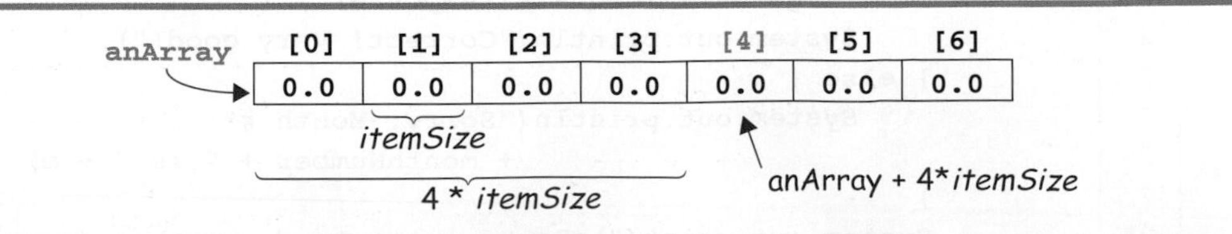

FIGURE 12-6 Computing **anArray[4]**

Because it performs just one multiplication and one addition (**`anArray+i*`*`itemSize`***), the subscript operation **`anArray[i]`** takes the same amount of time regardless of the value of **`i`**. Put differently, a randomly chosen item from an array can be accessed in **constant time**. For this reason, an array is sometimes called a **random access data structure**.

It thus takes the same length of time to access any item in an array, regardless of whether it contains ten items or a million items! This ability to quickly access a random item is one of the array's biggest strengths, and it is only possible because array elements are assigned adjacent memory locations. This adjacency is thus beneficial for the array subscript operation.

However, this adjacency also has its drawbacks. To illustrate, suppose we are using **`friendArray`** to store our friends' names in alphabetical order, as shown in Figure 12-7.

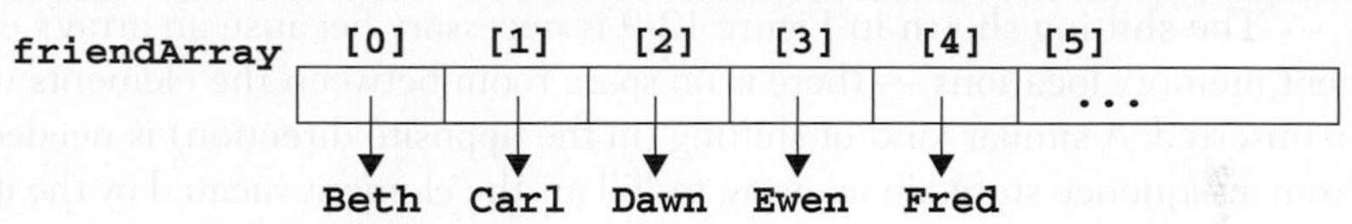

FIGURE 12-7 Storing an ordered sequence of values

Now, suppose we make a new friend named *Alan*, and want to insert his name at the beginning of the sequence to keep it in alphabetical order. If we try to do so by writing:

```
friendArray[0] = "Alan";
```

then the reference to **`"Alan"`** will replace the reference to **`"Beth"`**, as shown in Figure 12-8.

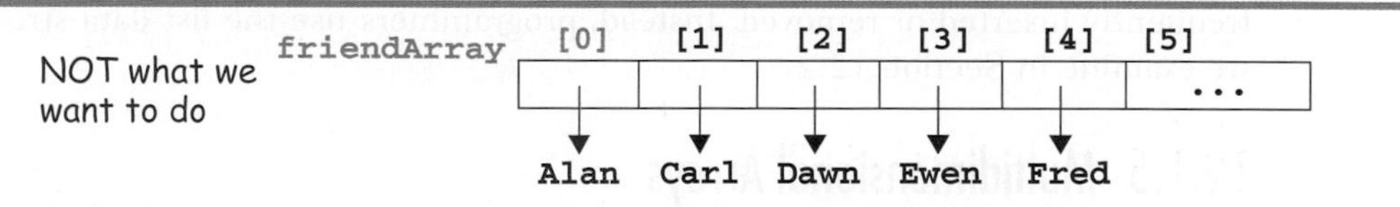

FIGURE 12-8 Mistakenly overwriting an item

To avoid losing Beth from our sequence of friends, we must instead shift each of our other friends out of the way to "clear a space" for Alan, as shown in Figure 12-9.

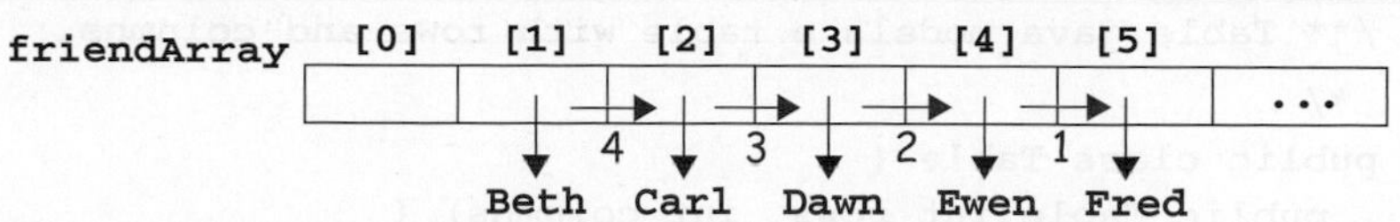

FIGURE 12-9 Making room for a new item

Such shifting can be accomplished using a loop. When we have "made room" for the new item, we can safely insert it into the sequence, as shown in Figure 12-10.

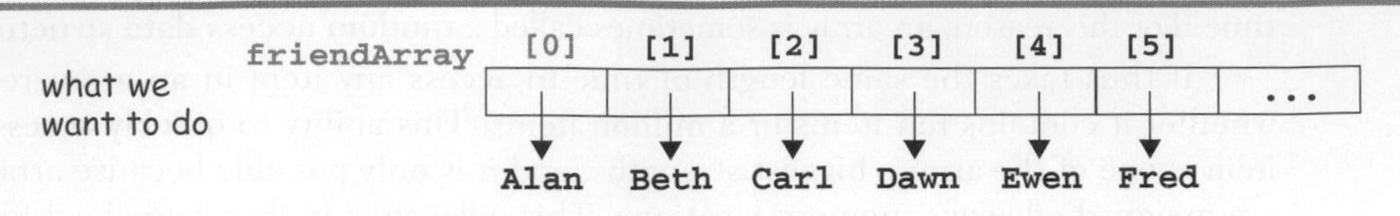

FIGURE 12-10 Making room for a new item

Of course, this assumes that we have unused space available at the end of the array. If we do not, then there is no room to add new items (but if we do, we are wasting some space).

The shifting shown in Figure 12-9 is necessary because an array's elements are in adjacent memory locations — there is no spare room between the elements where an item might be inserted. A similar kind of shifting (in the opposite direction) is needed to remove an item from a sequence stored in an array, to "fill in" the element vacated by the item being removed.

This shifting makes the operations to insert items into and remove items from an array consume time. The more friends we have, the more shifting is required, and the longer it takes. If an array *a1* contains 1,000 items and another array *a2* contains 1,000,000 items, then performing insertion or removal on items in *a2* will take about 1,000 times as long as they will on items in *a1*. The adjacency of elements that made it possible to perform the subscript operation in constant time thus makes it impossible to insert or remove the first item in constant time. The time to perform such shifting increases by a constant amount for each item in the array, so inserting and removing items from an array are called **linear time** operations.

The thing to see is that an array is a very good data structure for storing a sequence whose size does not change, and where random access is needed. However, an array is not a good data structure for storing a sequence whose size changes, or where items are frequently inserted or removed. Instead, programmers use the list data structure, which we examine in Section 12.2.

12.1.5 Multidimensional Arrays

The arrays we have examined to this point have had just one property: **`length`**. Since **`length`** determines the amount of space an array needs, an array's **`length`** is often referred to as its **dimension**, and the arrays we have seen so far have been **one-dimensional arrays**.

Java also allows us to declare arrays with multiple dimensions. For example, many kinds of data can be naturally organized into a *table* that has two dimensions: *rows* and *columns*. To model such tables, we can build a class, as shown in Figure 12-11.

```
/** Table.java models a table with rows and columns.
 */
public class Table {
  public Table(int rows, int columns) {
     if (rows < 1 || columns < 1) {
```

continued

```
            throw new IllegalArgumentException("Table(): bad args");
         }
         myTable = new double[rows][columns];
         myRows = rows;
         myColumns = columns;
      }

      public int getRows()    { return myRows; }
      public int getColumns() { return myColumns; }

      public double get(int row, int col) {
         return myTable[row][col];
      }

      public void set(int row, int col, double item) {
         myTable[row][col] = item;
      }

      public String toString() {
         String result = "";
         for (int r = 0; r < myTable.length; r++) {
            for (int c = 0; c < myTable[r].length; c++) {
               result += (myTable[r][c] + "\t");
            }
            result += "\n";
         }
         return result;
      }

      private int          myRows, myColumns;
      private double [][] myTable = null;
   }
```

FIGURE 12-11 The `Table` class

We can begin testing our class by building a simple test program, as shown in Figure 12-12.

```
/** TableTester.java
 */
public class TableTester {
   public static void main(String[] args) {
      Table table = new Table(4, 7);
      System.out.print(table);
```

continued

```
      testSet(table);
      System.out.println();
      System.out.print(table);
   }

   public static void testSet(Table aTable) {
      for (int i = 0; i < aTable.getRows(); i++) {
         for (int j = 0; j < aTable.getColumns(); j++) {
            aTable.set(i, j, i*aTable.getColumns()+j+1);
         }
      }
   }
}
```

```
Result:
0.0   0.0   0.0   0.0   0.0   0.0   0.0
0.0   0.0   0.0   0.0   0.0   0.0   0.0
0.0   0.0   0.0   0.0   0.0   0.0   0.0
0.0   0.0   0.0   0.0   0.0   0.0   0.0

1.0   2.0   3.0   4.0   5.0   6.0   7.0
8.0   9.0   10.0  11.0  12.0  13.0  14.0
15.0  16.0  17.0  18.0  19.0  20.0  21.0
22.0  23.0  24.0  25.0  26.0  27.0  28.0
```

FIGURE 12-12 **TableTester.java**

Declaring Multidimensional Arrays

To represent the table's data, the class on line 36 declares **myTable** as the handle for a two-dimensional array:

```
private double [][] myTable = null;
```

By using two pairs of brackets instead of one, we are telling the Java compiler that **myTable** is an array of two dimensions. Java does not limit the number of dimensions an array can have, so if we needed to declare **stringTable3D** as the handle for a three-dimensional array of **String** values, we could declare it as follows:

```
String [][][] stringTable3D = null;
```

This approach can be generalized for **N-dimensional arrays** (arrays with *N* dimensions):

> *Use N pairs of brackets to declare an N-dimensional array handle.*

Defining Multidimensional Arrays

One way to define (allocate memory for) a multidimensional array is to use the **new** operator and specify a value for each dimension. Our **Table** class uses this approach on line 8 of Figure 12-11:

```
myTable = new double[rows][columns];
```

Our test program in Figure 12-12 passes the argument 4 to **rows**, and the argument 7 to **columns**, so we can envision the resulting array as shown in Figure 12-13.

myTable

	[0]	[1]	[2]	[3]	[4]	[5]	[6]
[0] →	0.0	0.0	0.0	0.0	0.0	0.0	0.0
[1] →	0.0	0.0	0.0	0.0	0.0	0.0	0.0
[2] →	0.0	0.0	0.0	0.0	0.0	0.0	0.0
[3] →	0.0	0.0	0.0	0.0	0.0	0.0	0.0

FIGURE 12-13 A 4×7 array

Alternatively, if we were to write the following statement:

```
double [][] anArray = { { 0,  1,  2,  3,  4,  5,  6},
                        { 7,  8,  9, 10, 11, 12, 13},
                        {14, 15, 16, 17, 18, 19, 20},
                        {21, 22, 23, 24, 25, 26, 27} };
```

then **anArray** would be the handle for a 2-dimensional array with the same 4×7 structure as the array shown in Figure 12-13, but containing the items **0** through **27**. This form can be used when it is desirable to define an array with non-default values.

Both of these approaches can be generalized to higher-dimensioned arrays. To define a 4×2×3 array using default string values, we can write:

```
String [][][] stringTable3D = new String[4][2][3];
```

and to do so using specified values, we can write:

```
String [][][] stringTable3D = {{{"A", "B", "C"}, {"D", "E", "F"}},
                               {{"G", "H", "I"}, {"J", "K", "L"}},
                               {{"M", "N", "O"}, {"P", "Q", "R"}},
                               {{"S", "T", "U"}, {"V", "W", "X"}}};
```

Accessing a Multidimensional Array Element

To access an element in a one-dimensional array, we used one subscript operator. To access an element in a 2-dimensional array, we must use two subscript operators, as can be seen on line 17 of Figure 12-11:

```
return myTable[row][col];
```

and again on line 21:

```
myTable[row][col] = item;
```

Such an expression accesses the element at row **row**, column **col**, in **myTable**.

Using just one subscript on a two-dimensional array accesses one of its rows. For example, **myTable[0]** is a one-dimensional array of **double** values, as can be seen in Figure 12-13.

The elements of higher-dimensioned arrays can be accessed by generalizing this approach.

> *Use N subscript operators to access the elements of an N-dimensional array.*

Note that in methods **get()** and **set()**, we do not validate these methods' **row** and **col** parameters because the subscript operation validates array accesses, as described previously.

Processing Multidimensional Arrays

Whereas processing a one-dimensional array required one **for** or **for each** loop, processing a two-dimensional array typically requires two nested **for** or **for each** loops. The **toString()** method in Figure 12-11 illustrates this:

```
String result = "";
for (int r = 0; r < myTable.length; r++) {
    for (int c = 0; c < myTable[r].length; c++) {
        result += (myTable[r][c] + "\t");
    }
    result += "\n";
}
```

The inner **for** loop processes the items in one row by appending the item in **myTable[r][c]** and a tab character to **result**. The outer **for** loop uses the inner loop to process each of the rows, and appends a newline character to **result** after a row has been processed.

Since the **toString()** method only reads the items from **myTable**, we could alternatively replace these two **for** loops with two **for each** loops, as follows:

```
String result = "";
for (double [] row: myTable) {
   for (double item: row) {
      result += (item + "\t");
   }
   result += "\n";
}
```

In this version, the outer loop iterates through each **row** in **myTable**, and for a given **row**, the inner loop iterates through each **item** in that **row**, appending the **item** and a tab character to **result**. This version is much simpler, and correspondingly easier to read.

Higher-dimensioned arrays can be processed by generalizing this approach:

> *To process all the elements of an N-dimensional array, use N nested* **for** *loops, with each* **for** *loop processing one dimension.*
>
> *To read the items of an N-dimensional array, use N nested* **for** *loops or N nested* **for each** *loops, with each loop processing one dimension.*

12.2 Lists in Java

The package **java.util** contains a **List**, but it is an *interface*, not a class. A Java **interface** is like a class in that it can be used to declare handles to objects. However, instead of *defining* methods, an interface just *declares* methods. A class can then **implement an interface** by:

1. Stating that it intends to implement the interface; and
2. Defining each of the methods listed in the interface.

To illustrate, the interface **java.lang.CharSequence** declares four methods:

```
public interface CharSequence {
   char         charAt(int index);
   int          length();
   CharSequence subSequence(int start, int end);
   String       toString();
}
```

Java's **String** and other classes implement this interface by (1) stating that they do so:

```
public class String implements CharSequence {
   // ... methods and instance variables of class String,
   //  including charAt(), length(), subSequence(), and
          toString()
}
public class StringBuffer implements CharSequence {
   // ... methods and instance variables of class StringBuffer,
   //  including charAt(), length(), subSequence(), and
          toString()
}
```

and then (2) supplying a definition for each of the four methods listed in **CharSequence**. By stating that it implements an interface, a class promises to provide a definition for each of the methods in the interface. If it neglects to define one or more of the methods in the interface, the Java compiler will not compile the class.

The benefit of this mechanism is this: if we define a **CharSequence** parameter as follows:

```
void print(CharSequence cs) { System.out.println(cs.toString()); }
```

then we can pass to it any object whose class implements the **CharSequence** interface, be it a **String**, a **StringBuffer**, or any other class that implements the interface. Because the class implements the **CharSequence** interface, we know we can send it the **toString()** message, or any of the other methods specified by the interface.

Java's **List** is an interface. The methods it declares include those listed in Figure 12-14.

Java `List` method	Behavior
***aList*.add(*it*)**	appends item ***it*** to the end of ***aList***
***aList*.add(*i*, *it*)**	inserts item ***it*** before the element of ***aList*** whose index is ***i***
***aList*.clear()**	removes all items from ***aList***
***aList*.contains(*it*)**	returns **true** if item ***it*** is present in ***aList***; returns **false** otherwise
***aList*.get(*i*)**	returns the item of ***aList*** whose index is ***i***
***aList*.indexOf(*it*)**	returns the index of item ***it*** within ***aList*** (returns -1 if ***it*** is not present in ***aList***)
***aList*.isEmpty()**	returns **true** if there are no items in ***aList***; returns **false** otherwise
***aList*.remove(*i*)**	removes the item at index ***i*** within ***aList***

continued

Java `List` method	Behavior
***aList*.remove(*it*)**	removes the first occurrence of item ***it*** from ***aList***; returns **false** if ***it*** is not present in ***aList***; returns **true** otherwise
***aList*.set(*i*, *it*)**	stores item ***it*** in the element whose index is ***i*** within ***aList***
***aList*.size()**	returns the number of elements in ***aList***

FIGURE 12-14 Some of the **List** methods

Additional **List** methods and detailed descriptions can be found in the Java API.

There are several Java classes that implement the **List** interface. For now, we will examine just two of them:

- The **LinkedList** class, which is much like Alice's list data structure
- The **ArrayList** class, which combines the fast access time of an array with the ability of a list to grow while a program is running

Because each of these classes implements the **List** interface, we can send any of the **List** messages in Figure 12-14 to either data structure.

Also, either type of data structure can be accessed via a **List** handle or parameter. For example, the **java.util.Collections** class defines a **sort()** method that, given a **List**, arranges its values in ascending order. We can use this one **sort()** method to sort either a **LinkedList** or an **ArrayList** because they implement the **List** interface.

In the next two sections, we will explore how to use these classes.

12.3 The `LinkedList` Class

To illustrate the use of the **LinkedList** class, let's begin with an example.

12.3.1 Example: Managing the Waiting Room

You have been hired by Dr. Suture, M.D., to streamline the patient check-in procedure at his office. The doctor would like a computer program to manage his list of daily appointments and the list of waiting patients so that his office staff can better serve his patients. After talking with the doctor, you begin with this user story:

> *Purpose: Manage the doctor's waiting room*
>
> *The program should read the list of patients with appointments for that day from a file named "today.txt". It should then repeatedly admit patients until all of that day's patients have arrived or been seen.*

To admit a patient, a receptionist asks the patient to sign in on the waiting list, checks that day's appointment list to verify that the patient has an appointment, and then asks the patient to be seated. When the doctor is ready for a new patient, a nurse checks the waiting list, calls the name of the first person on the list, and removes that person's name from it. The doctor wants a program to manage these lists, to free the receptionist and nurse to focus on patients' health needs. Dr. Suture wants the program to manage these lists for the receptionist and nurse:

Purpose: Admit a patient.

The program should greet the patient, and then prompt the patient to enter his or her name. The program should read the patient's name, and check that it is on the appointment list. If not, the program should inform the patient of the mistake; otherwise, the program should remove the patient's name from the appointment list and append it to the waiting list. If the nurse enters a special code (99), the program should remove the first patient on the waiting list. To give patients some idea of how long they'll have to wait, the program should display the current waiting and appointment lists.

We might begin by preparing a test version of the file *today.txt* containing the "patients" shown in Figure 12-15.

```
Ben Dover
Stan Dupp
Neil Down
```

FIGURE 12-15 Test version of *today.txt*

With a test file ready, we can write our program. As described in our user story, we will have to add and remove patients from the appointment and waiting lists. Because these removals are likely to be at or near the front of the list, we will model these lists using Java's **LinkedList** class, as shown in Figure 12-16.

```
/** WaitingRoom.java models a doctor's waiting room
 */
import java.util.*; // LinkedList, Scanner, ...
import java.io.*;   // File, FileNotFoundException, ...

public class WaitingRoom {
   public static void main(String[] args) {
      WaitingRoom self = new WaitingRoom("today.txt");
      self.run();
   }

  public WaitingRoom(String fileName) {
      readAppointmentList(fileName);
```

continued

```
      myWaitList = new LinkedList<String>();
   }

   private void readAppointmentList(String fileName) {
      myApptList = new LinkedList<String>();
      Scanner fin = null;
      try {
         fin = new Scanner(new File(fileName));
         while (fin.hasNextLine()) {
            String patient = fin.nextLine();
            myApptList.add(patient);
         }
      } catch (FileNotFoundException fnfe) {
         fnfe.printStackTrace();
      } finally {
         fin.close();
      }
   }

   public void run() {
      while ( !myApptList.isEmpty() || !myWaitList.isEmpty()) {
         processArrival();
      }
   }

   private void processArrival() {
      System.out.println("\nWelcome to Dr. Suture's office!");
      System.out.print("Enter your name: ");
      String name = keyboard.nextLine();
      if ( name.equals("99") && !myWaitList.isEmpty() ) {
         myWaitList.removeFirst();
      } else if ( myApptList.remove(name) ) {
         myWaitList.add(name);
         System.out.println("Thank you. Please have a seat.");
      } else {
         System.out.println(name + " has no appointment today.");
      }
      System.out.println("Currently waiting: " + myWaitList);
      System.out.println("Today's appointments: " + myApptList);
   }

   private LinkedList<String> myWaitList = null;
   private LinkedList<String> myApptList = null;
   private Scanner keyboard = new Scanner(System.in);
}
```

continued

```
Result:
Welcome to Dr. Suture's office!
Enter your name: Stan Dupp        Stan Dupp arrives and checks in
Thank you. Please have a seat.
Currently waiting: [Stan Dupp]
Today's appointments: [Ben Dover, Neil Down]

Welcome to Dr. Suture's office!
Enter your name: Ben Dover        Ben Dover arrives (late) and checks in
Thank you. Please have a seat.
Currently waiting: [Stan Dupp, Ben Dover]
Today's appointments: [Neil Down]

Welcome to Dr. Suture's office!
Enter your name: 99               Nurse calls "Stan Dupp" and enters code 99
Currently waiting: [Ben Dover]
Today's appointments: [Neil Down]

Welcome to Dr. Suture's office!
Enter your name: Neil Down        Neil Down arrives and checks in
Thank you. Please have a seat.
Currently waiting: [Ben Dover, Neil Down]
Today's appointments: []

Welcome to Dr. Suture's office!
Enter your name: 99               Nurse calls "Ben Dover" and enters code 99
Currently waiting: [Neil Down]
Today's appointments: []

Welcome to Dr. Suture's office!
Enter your name: 99               Nurse calls "Neil Down" and enters code 99
Currently waiting: []
Today's appointments: []
```

FIGURE 12-16 `WaitingRoom.java`

Note that because our program displays the appointment list during each repetition, at the end of the day, any patients who do not show up for their appointments will still be listed in the day's appointment list, letting the doctor's staff easily identify such patients.[1]

1. In a real doctor's office, we would use patient numbers or some other code to guard the patients' privacy.

12.3.2 Using **LinkedLists**

Figure 12-16 illustrates how **LinkedList**s can be used to solve a problem. In the rest of this subsection, we examine the **LinkedList** capabilities in detail.

Declaring a **LinkedList**

To model the appointment and waiting lists, our program declares two **LinkedList** handles, on lines 55 and 56. The types in these declarations are different from those we have seen before, having the following form:

```
private LinkedList<String> myWaitList = null;
private LinkedList<String> myApptList = null;
```

These declarations tell the Java compiler that **myWaitList** and **myApptList** are handles for **LinkedList** objects that will store **String** items.

The type of a **LinkedList**'s items must be a reference type. Trying to write

```
LinkedList<double> listOfNumbers = null;  // ERROR
                                             (primitive type)!
```

will produce a compilation error. However, Java provides a class for each primitive type — **Boolean**, **Byte**, **Character**, **Double**, **Float**, **Integer**, **Long**, and **Short**. Objects of these classes can store a value of the corresponding primitive type. Thus, to store real numbers in a **LinkedList**, we would write:

```
LinkedList<Double> listOfNumbers = null;    // CORRECT!
```

Because these classes "wrap up" a primitive type value, they are known as **wrapper classes**.

In general, to declare a **LinkedList** handle capable of storing items of a reference type named ***ItemType***, we would write:

```
LinkedList<ItemType> handleName = null;
```

Defining a **LinkedList**

Our program defines two **LinkedList** objects on lines 14 and 18. These definitions are also different from those we have seen before:

```
myWaitList = new LinkedList<String>();
myApptList = new LinkedList<String>();
```

These definitions construct empty **LinkedList** objects capable of storing **String** items. We might visualize the resulting lists as shown in Figure 12-17.

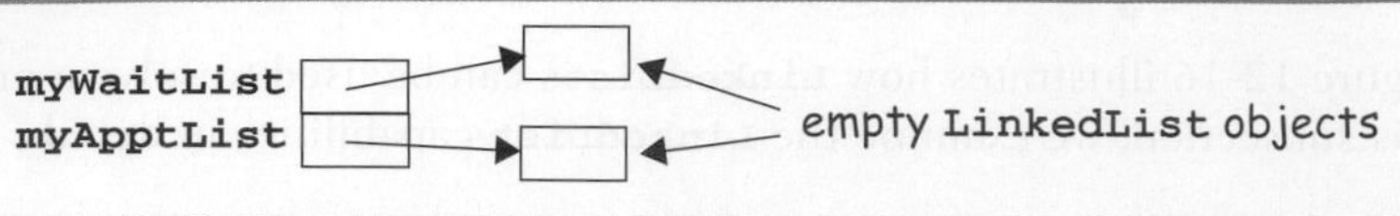

FIGURE 12-17 Declaring empty lists

As with a handle declaration, when we define a **LinkedList** object, we must specify the type of the items we intend to store in it. Generally, this item type should match the item type used to declare its handle. Thus, to define an empty **LinkedList** for the **listOfNumbers** handle we described previously, we would use the **Double** wrapper class and write:

```
listOfNumbers = new LinkedList<Double>();
```

In general, we can use the following pattern to define an empty **LinkedList** object whose items will be of the reference type ***ItemType***:

```
LinkedList<ItemType> handleName = new LinkedList<ItemType>();
```

Filling a LinkedList

Since lists are used to store sequences of values, filling a list with values can be performed by building an input loop that reads an item, either from the keyboard or from a file, and then appends it to the list, using the **add()** operation from Figure 12-14. Our program shows how to do this from a file, on lines 22–25 in Figure 12-16:

```
while (fin.hasNextLine()) {
   String patient = fin.nextLine();
   myApptList.add(patient);
}
```

After this loop terminates, we can visualize the lists in our program as shown in Figure 12-18.

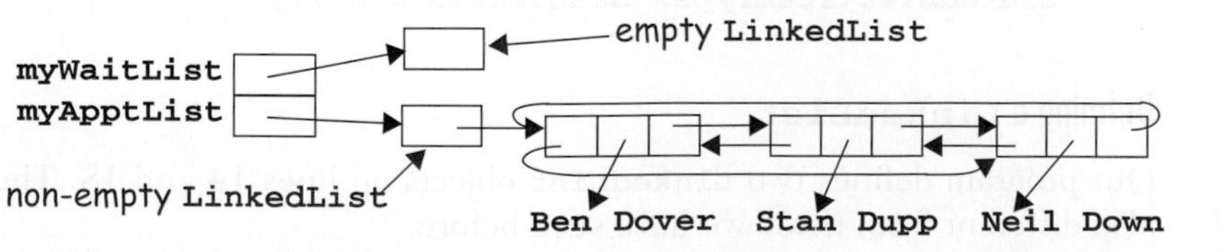

FIGURE 12-18 Non-empty vs. empty lists

As can be seen in Figure 12-18, a linked list creates a chain in which each "link" stores one item. Programmers usually refer to the chain's "links" as nodes. More precisely, a **node** is a data structure that stores an item plus one or more references to other nodes. In the case of Java's **LinkedList** class, each node stores a reference to the next, or successor node, in the chain; and a reference to the previous, or predecessor node, in the chain. Lists like this, in which each node stores the references of its predecessor and successor nodes, are often called **doubly-linked lists**. In a non-empty **circular doubly-linked list**, the first node's predecessor is the last node and the last node's successor is the first node. This arrangement permits the **LinkedList** class to quickly access either end of the list while only storing a reference to the first node.

LinkedList Operations

Because it implements the **List** interface, the **LinkedList** class defines all of the methods in Figure 12-14, so any of those messages can be sent to a **LinkedList**. The program in Figure 12-16 uses several of these methods, including the **add()** message on lines 24 and 46 to add patients to the appointment and waiting lists, respectively:

```
myApptList.add(patient);    // line 24
myWaitList.add(name);       // line 46
```

It also uses the **isEmpty()** method on line 43 to verify that there are waiting patients:

```
if ( name.equals("99") && !myWaitList.isEmpty() ) {
```

It also uses the **remove()** method on line 45 to remove a patient from the appointment list:

```
} else if ( myApptList.remove(name) ) {
```

The **remove()** method returns **true** if the item being removed is present in the list, and returns **false** if it is not present. Our program thus uses this as the condition of an **if** statement to prevent a person without an appointment from being added to the waiting list.

In addition to the **List** methods, the Java **LinkedList** API entry describes several additional methods, including those listed in Figure 12-19.

LinkedList method	Behavior
***linkList*.addFirst(*it*)**	adds item ***it*** to the front of ***linkList***
***linkList*.addLast(*it*)**	appends item ***it*** to the end of ***linkList***
***linkList*.getFirst()**	returns the first item from ***linkList***
***linkList*.getLast()**	returns the last item from ***linkList***
***linkList*.removeFirst()**	removes and returns the first item from ***linkList***
***linkList*.removeLast()**	removes and returns the last item from ***linkList***

FIGURE 12-19 Some of the **LinkedList** methods

On line 44, our program uses the **removeFirst()** method to remove the first waiting patient:

```
myWaitList.removeFirst();
```

When the sample run in Figure 12-16 begins, we can visualize its lists as shown in Figure 12-18. However, when Stan Dupp signs in, the program uses the **remove()** operation on line 45 to verify that he has an appointment and remove him from the appointment list. The program then uses the **add()** message on line 46 to add him to the waiting list, resulting in the lists shown in Figure 12-20.

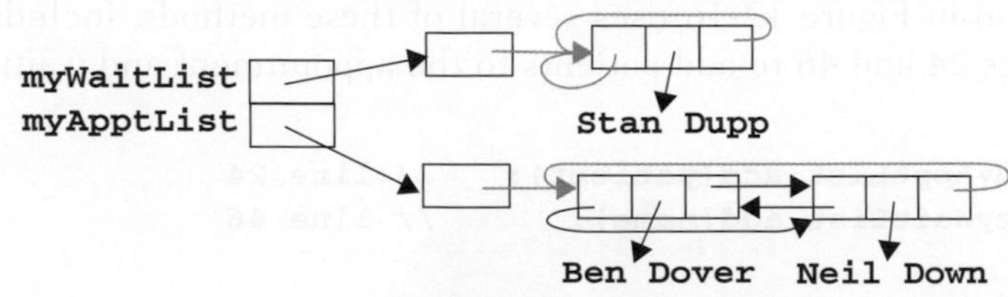

FIGURE 12-20 Admitting Stan Dupp

Next, Ben Dover signs in. Again, the program uses the **remove()** message on line 45 to verify that he has an appointment and remove him from the appointment list. The program then uses the **add()** message on line 46 to add him to the waiting list, resulting in Figure 12-21.

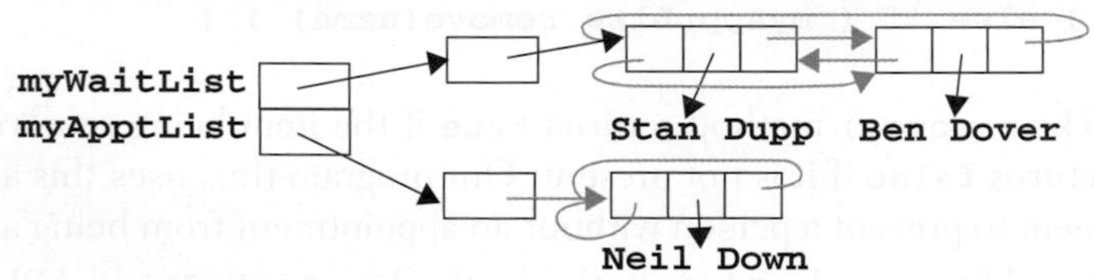

FIGURE 12-21 Admitting Ben Dover

Then, the nurse comes in, checks the waiting list, calls "Stan Dupp," and enters the code causing **removeFirst()** to remove the first item in the waiting list, as shown in Figure 12-22.

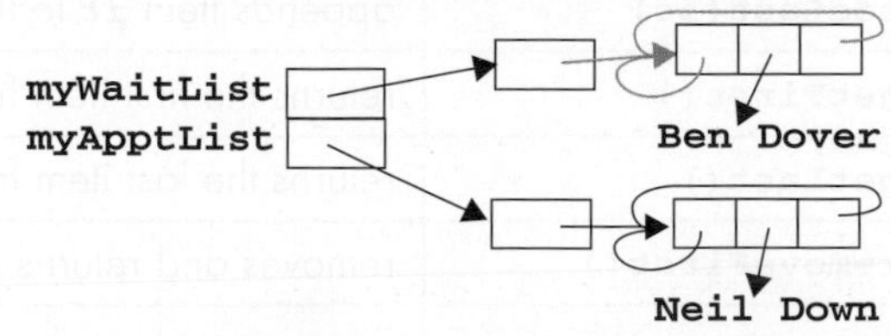

FIGURE 12-22 Removing Stan Dupp from the waiting list

Traversing a **LinkedList**

In Figure 12-16, we used the **LinkedList**'s built-in **toString()** method to display the contents of the appointment and waiting lists. However, what if we need to access each of the items in a **LinkedList**? To make this more concrete, suppose we have a **LinkedList<Double>** containing a sequence of real numbers. How can we compute the average of the numbers that are stored in a **LinkedList**?

To accomplish this, we need to iterate through the list, accessing each of its items in turn. As of Java 1.5, this is very easy to do, using the **for each** loop we discussed in Section 12.1.2. Figure 12-23 presents a definition of an **average()** method that, given a **LinkedList<Double>**, computes and returns the average of the values in that list.

```
1   public static void double average(LinkedList<Double> dList) {
2      if ( dList.isEmpty() ) {
3         throw new IllegalArgumentException("average(): list is empty");
4      }
5      double sum = 0.0;
6      for (double num : dList) {
7         sum += num;
8      }
9      return sum / dList.size();
10  }
```

FIGURE 12-23 Traversing a **LinkedList** (to compute the average)

Note that Java conveniently "unwraps" primitive type values from a wrapper class for us. That is, **dList** is a **LinkedList** of **Double** items; however, in the **for each** loop on line 6, the variable **num** is a **double**. In each repetition of this loop, Java extracts the **double** from a different node's **Double** value, saving us the trouble of doing so.

In general, if we must access and process each item in a **LinkedList<ItemType>** named **aList**, we can do so using the **for each** loop and the following traversal pattern:

```
for (ItemType item : aList) {
   // ... access and process item
}
```

12.3.3 **LinkedLists** and Memory

We saw in Section 12.1.4 that inserting and removing the first item in an array requires linear time. By contrast, removing or inserting the first item in a **LinkedList** can be done in constant time because each operation only requires the changing of a few references.

To illustrate, suppose again that our friends are *Beth*, *Carl*, *Dawn*, *Ewen*, and *Fred*; but this time, we have stored them in a **LinkedList**, as shown in Figure 12-24.

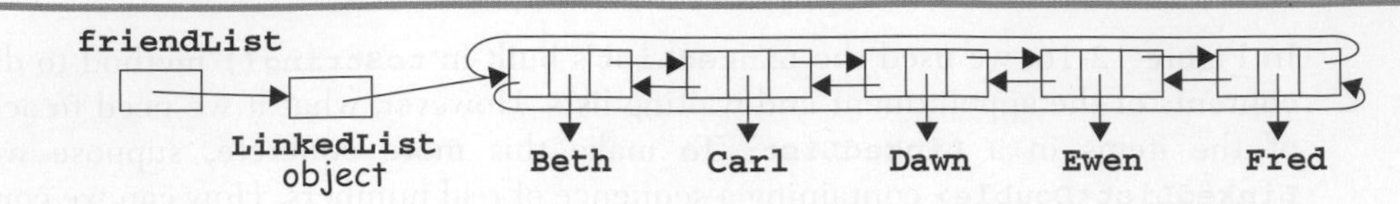

FIGURE 12-24 Storing an ordered sequence of items in a linked list

Now, if we make a new friend *Alan*, and want to insert him at the beginning of our sequence, we just invoke:

```
friendList.addFront("Alan");
```

This inserts "Alan" into our list in constant time by getting a node for *Alan* and changing a few references, as shown in Figure 12-25.

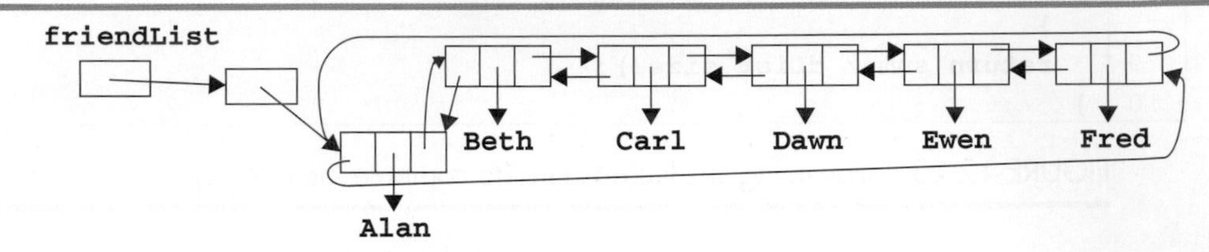

FIGURE 12-25 Inserting an item at the front of a linked list

Note that none of the nodes that were in the list change their physical locations, because the nodes of a **LinkedList** need not be stored in adjacent memory locations. Instead, they can be anywhere in a program's dynamic memory. The order of the items in the list is determined solely by the references or "links" that chain the nodes together.

The **addFront()** and **removeFront()** methods thus perform their tasks by changing a few references. These same references get changed no matter how many items are in the list. No copying or shifting of items is required, so these methods perform their tasks in constant time.

However, because nodes are not stored in adjacent memory locations, a random item in a **LinkedList** cannot be accessed in constant time. That is, where the array subscript operation accesses the item at index *i* in constant time, the **get()** and **set()** operations of a **LinkedList** require linear time to perform such an access. To see why, consider Figure 12-26.

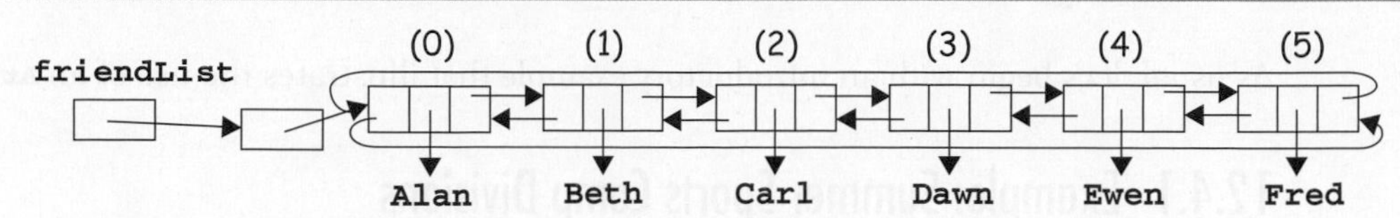

FIGURE 12-26 A linked list with index numbers

The expression **`friendList.get(2)`** will return a reference to **`"Carl"`**. However, to do so, it must count from **`0`** to **`2`**, starting at the first node (**`"Alan"`**) and counting it as **`0`**, moving to its successor node (**`"Beth"`**) and counting it as **`1`**, and moving to its successor node (**`"Carl"`**) and counting it as **`2`**. More generally, each time we **`get()`** or **`set()`** the item at index ***i***, if ***i*** is in the first half of the list, the method starts at the front of the list and counts upward, following successor references until it reaches the ***i***th node. If ***i*** is in the second half of the list, the method starts at the end of the list and counts downward, following predecessor references until it reaches the ***i***th node. Thus, if a list contains 1,000 items, the **`set()`** and **`get()`** methods will require time proportional to 500 accesses to retrieve the middle item; if the list contains 1,000,000 items, these methods will require 1,000 times as long.

Accessing the item at a given index in a **`LinkedList`** is thus a linear time operation, on average. Since accessing an item in a sequence requires that all of its predecessor items (or successor items) be accessed first, a linked list is called a **sequential access data structure.**

Note that if we use a **`for each`** loop to traverse a list, it traverses the list efficiently by accessing the first item in the first iteration, advancing to the second item in the second iteration, and so on. A **`for each`** loop is thus efficient, accessing *all* of a list's items in linear time.

Linked lists are thus very good data structures for sequences that change size and in which items are frequently inserted or removed, especially at the ends of the sequence. They are not good data structures for problems that require frequent accesses to random items, especially items in the middle of the sequence.

In summary, arrays and linked lists are both data structures used for storing sequences of items, but their structural differences produce very different strengths and weaknesses. As a result, they should be seen as complementary structures.

> *Store sequences that have fixed sizes and require random access in arrays.*
>
> *Store sequences that change size, and require no random access in linked lists.*

However, suppose we have a problem where we need to store a sequence that changes size and we need to access arbitrary (random) items from within it? What do we do then?

For these kinds of situations, Java provides the **`ArrayList`** class. Like a linked list, an array list can grow when necessary. Like an array, its items can be accessed in constant time.

12.4 The `ArrayList` Class

As usual, let's begin with an introductory example that illustrates the use of an **`ArrayList`**.

12.4.1 Example: Summer Sports Camp Divisions

Suppose you are working at a summer sports camp for children. Each week, a different group of children arrives at the camp, with the exact number varying from week to week. To let the children compete with others of about the same skill level, the camp divides the children into two divisions: an "A" (less skilled) division, and an "AA" (more skilled) division. To evenly distribute the camp staff, these two divisions need to be the same size.

To assign children to divisions, the children take 10 skills tests the first morning. In each test, a child can score from 0 to 10. These ten scores are then summed to give each child an overall score from 0 to 100. Using these overall scores, the top half of the campers are placed in the "AA" division, and the remaining campers are placed in the "A" division.

The camp staff has a program that takes each student's name and ten scores, and produces a file containing each camper's name and his or her overall score. The camp staff then prints this file and uses it to assign students to divisions. However, as the camp has grown, this process of manually assigning students to divisions is taking too long, currently consuming the entire lunch hour that first day, and threatening to delay the afternoon session.

Knowing how fast computers are, you volunteer to write a program to form the divisions! After consulting with the other camp staff, you develop the following user story:

> The program should ask for the name of the input file containing the campers' names and overall scores, and read it from the keyboard. The program should then print to the screen "Division A" followed by the names and scores of the campers in the A division, and then "Division AA" followed by the names and scores of the campers in the AA division.

For testing purposes, we can create two input files: one with an even number of students, and one with an odd number of students, as shown in Figure 12-27.

```
Dan Doe 35
Max Min 45
Sam Smith 42
Jack Johnson 39
Marky Malarky 40
Mike McGurk 37
```

testData1.txt

```
Dawn Doe 35
Mindy Max 45
Sarah Smith 42
Julie Johnson 39
Mary Malarky 40
Molly McGurk 37
Jane Jones 45
```

testData2.txt

FIGURE 12-27 Two test data files

Using these files, we can construct tests that the program must pass to be working correctly. For example, using **testData1.txt**, the program should produce something like this:

```
Division A:
Dan Doe (35), Jack Johnson (39), Mike McGurk (37)

Division AA:
Max Min (45), Sam Smith (42), Marky Malarky (40)
```

Note that in this problem, the order in which the students are listed within the divisions does not matter, so long as the correct students appear in each division.

Design

Our user story describes what our program must do, but it does not specify how to divide the students into the two divisions. One way to solve this problem is to read the students into a data structure, find the student in the data structure whose score is the middle score, and then traverse the data structure, comparing each student's score against the middle score. If it is higher, we add that student to an "AA division" data structure; otherwise, we add that student to an "A division" data structure. More precisely, we might design this algorithm:

Purpose: Divide students into "A" and "AA" divisions.

Given: *inputFile*, a string

1. Read students from *inputFile* into *myStudents*, an empty data structure
2. Compute *median*, the middle score of the scores in *myStudents*
3. Build *myDivisionA* and *myDivisionAA*, two empty data structures
4. For each student *stu* in *myStudents*:
   a. If *stu*'s score > *median*, add *stu* to *myDivisionAA*
   b. otherwise, add *stu* to *myDivisionA*

This algorithm uses three data structures: *myStudents*, *myDivisionA*, and *myDivisionAA*. When it is finished, the data structures *myDivisionA* and *myDivisionAA* will contain the two divisions, which our program can display.

We have seen how to read items and add them to a data structure (Step 1); we have also seen how to traverse a data structure, processing each of its items in turn (Step 4). However the problem of finding the middle item in a data structure (Step 2) is new to us. Mathematically, this is called *finding the median value* in a sequence of values.

There are a variety of ways to find the median of a sequence of values. One fairly simple approach is to sort the sequence into ascending or descending order. The middle item in the sorted sequence will then be the median value. If there are an even number of items in the sequence, we can use the average of the two middle items' values as the median.

To use this approach, our program must be able to sort the students in *myStudents*. The class **java.util.Collections** provides a **sort()** method for this purpose. In order for this method to be able to sort the items in a data structure, the method must be able to compare those items (for example, to determine if one item is less than another). Since *myStudents* is going to be a data structure of students, this means that we must model a student in such a way as to allow two students to be compared. Thankfully, Java makes this fairly easy.

Modeling a Student

One of the nouns in this problem is "student" and each student has a name and overall score. Since we cannot directly model such a student using any existing type, we will build a class to do so. Figure 12-28 presents such a class.

```
/** Student.java models a camp student and overall score
 */
import java.util.Scanner;

public class Student implements Comparable<Student> {
  public Student() {
    myName = "";
    myScore = 0;
  }

  public String getName()   { return myName; }
  public int getScore() { return myScore; }
  public String toString() { return myName + "(" + myScore + ")"; }

  public int compareTo(Student stu) {
     return myScore - stu.getScore();
  }

  public void read(Scanner in) {
     String name = in.next() + " " + in.next();
     int score = in.nextInt();
     if (score < 0 || score > 100) {
        throw new IllegalArgumentException("read(): bad score");
     }
     myScore = score;
     myName = name;
  }

  private String myName;
  private int myScore;
}
```

FIGURE 12-28 A class to model students and scores

Much of Figure 12-28 is familiar: a default constructor, accessor methods, a `String` conversion method for output, and a `read()` method for input.

The two new things in Figure 12-28 allow the **sort()** method to compare **Student** objects. The first is the declaration of class **Student** on line 5:

```
public class Student implements Comparable<Student> {
```

The second is the definition of the **compareTo()** method on lines 15–17

```
public int compareTo(Student stu) {
   return myScore - stu.getScore();
}
```

In order for the **sort()** method to be able to compare the items in a data structure, those items must implement the **Comparable** interface. Recall from Section 12.2 that a class can implement an interface by defining each of the methods in the interface.

The **Comparable** interface contains just one method, named **compareTo()**. According to the Java API, the message ***obj*.compareTo(*obj2*)** should return an integer that must be:

- 0, if ***obj*** and ***obj2*** are equal
- a positive number, if ***obj*** > ***obj2***
- a negative number, if ***obj*** < ***obj2***

Since our problem requires us to arrange students according to their overall scores, we define the **compareTo()** method in a way that ***stu*.compareTo(*stu2*)** returns 0 if ***stu*** and ***stu2*** have the same score, a positive number if ***stu***'s score is greater than ***stu2***'s score, and a negative number if ***stu***'s score is less than ***stu2***'s score. We can accomplish this by returning the difference of ***stu***'s score and ***stu2***'s score. That is, if ***stu***'s score is 44 and ***stu2***'s score is 33, then ***stu*.compareTo(*stu2*)** will return 11, a positive value indicating ***stu*** is greater than ***stu2***. Alternatively, if ***stu***'s score is 20 and ***stu2***'s score is 25, then ***stu*.compareTo(*stu2*)** will return –5, a negative value, indicating that ***stu*** is less than ***stu2***.

By implementing the **Comparable** interface, we make it possible to send a **Student** object the **compareTo()** message, and determine its relationship to another **Student** object. The **sort()** method uses such **compareTo()** messages to compare and arrange the items in a data structure, so this will allow us to sort a data structure containing **Student** items.

Choosing Data Structures

Given a **Student** class that can be compared, our next task is to choose the data structures for our problem. Since the number of students changes from week to week, we will not use arrays, but will use one of the list data structures. For *myDivisionA* and *myDivisionAA*, we can use linked lists, because the algorithm accesses their items sequentially.

However, for *myStudents*, we need to be able to access the middle item in the data structure, which is a linear time operation for a linked list. By contrast, we can access the middle item of a Java **ArrayList** in constant time, so we will use it for *myStudents*.[2]

Having selected these data structures, we are ready to write our program. Figure 12-29 presents the completed version.

2. Since our algorithm only accesses the middle item in the data structure once, it would not be terrible to define *myStudents* using a **LinkedList**. However, the **ArrayList** is preferable, unless memory is limited.

```java
/** DivisionMaker.java divides students into two divisions.
 */
import java.util.*;          // ArrayList, Scanner, ...
import java.io.*;            // File, ...

public class DivisionMaker {
  public static void main(String[] args) {
     System.out.println("To make the 'A' and 'AA' divisions,");
     System.out.print(" enter the name of the input file: ");
     Scanner keyboard = new Scanner(System.in);
     String inFileName = keyboard.nextLine();
     DivisionMaker dm = new DivisionMaker();
     dm.readStudents(inFileName);
     dm.makeDivisions();
     System.out.println("\nDivisionA:\n" + dm.getDivisionA() );
     System.out.println("\nDivision AA:\n" + dm.getDivisionAA() );
  }

  public void readStudents(String inputFile) {
     myStudents = new ArrayList<Student>();
     Scanner fin = null;
     try {
        fin = new Scanner( new File(inputFile) );
        while ( fin.hasNext() ) {
           Student student = new Student();
           student.read(fin);
           myStudents.add(student);
        }
     } catch (FileNotFoundException fnfe) {
        fnfe.printStackTrace();
     } finally {
        fin.close();
     }
  }

  public void makeDivisions() {
     double median = findMedian();
     myDivisionAA = new LinkedList<Student>();
     myDivisionA = new LinkedList<Student>();
     for (Student stu : myStudents) {
        if (stu.getScore() > median) {
           myDivisionAA.add(stu);
        } else {
```

continued

```
                myDivisionA.add(stu);
            }
        }
    }

    public double findMedian() {
        Collections.sort(myStudents);
        int numStudents = myStudents.size();
        int median, midIndex1, midIndex2;
        midIndex1 = numStudents / 2;
        if ( numStudents % 2 != 0 ) { // size is odd
            median = myStudents.get(midIndex1).getScore();
        } else {
            midIndex2 = midIndex1 - 1;
            median = ( myStudents.get(midIndex1).getScore() +
                       myStudents.get(midIndex2).getScore() ) / 2;
        }
        return median;
    }

    public LinkedList<Student> getDivisionA() {return myDivisionA;}
    public LinkedList<Student> getDivisionAA() {return myDivisionAA;}

    private ArrayList<Student> myStudents = null;
    private LinkedList<Student> myDivisionA = null;
    private LinkedList<Student> myDivisionAA = null;
}
```

```
Result:
To make the 'A' and 'AA' divisions,
 enter the name of the input file: testData1.txt

Division A:
[Dan Doe(35), Mike McGurk(37), Jack Johnson(39)]

Division AA:
[Marky Malarky(40), Sam Smith(42), Max Min(45)]
```

FIGURE 12-29 `DivisionMaker.java`

After verifying that our program passes our tests, we can use it to solve our camp's problem. All the staff are very happy to get their lunch hour back each Monday!

12.4.2 Using **ArrayLists**

The **ArrayList** is a compromise between an array and a **LinkedList**. Like a **LinkedList** (and unlike an array), an **ArrayList** is a reference type data structure that can increase in size as a program runs. Similar to an array subscript operation (and unlike a **LinkedList**), we can access the items in an **ArrayList** in constant time, using the **set()** and **get()** methods. In the rest of this section, we will see how this is accomplished.

Declaring **ArrayList** Handles

As with a **LinkedList**, we must tell Java what kind of item we intend to store in an **ArrayList** handle. Line 67 in Figure 12-29 illustrates this, when it declares the handle **myStudents**:

```
private ArrayList<Student> myStudents = null;
```

Like a **LinkedList**, an **ArrayList** can only store reference types. Thus, if we wanted to declare a handle for an **ArrayList** capable of storing **double** values, we would use the **Double** wrapper class as follows:

```
ArrayList<Double> numbers = null;
```

In general, to declare a handle for an **ArrayList** of items of type ***ItemType***, we would write:

```
ArrayList<ItemType> handle = null;
```

Defining **ArrayList** Objects

We must also specify the type of item we intend to store when we invoke the **ArrayList** constructor. Line 20 in Figure 12-29 illustrates this:

```
myStudents = new ArrayList<Student>();
```

Following the performance of this statement, we can visualize **myStudents** and the new **ArrayList** as shown in Figure 12-30.

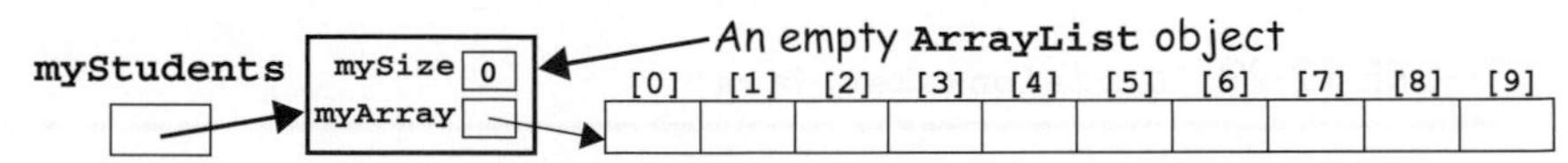

FIGURE 12-30 An empty **ArrayList** and its handle

As can be seen in Figure 12-30, the **ArrayList** default constructor builds an empty **ArrayList** object. According to the current Java API, this empty **ArrayList** has the capacity to store 10 items before it has to grow. This can be accomplished by defining two instance variables: one we will call **myArray** that is a handle for an array of 10 items, and one we will call **mySize** to store the number of items in the **ArrayList**.

Similarly, to define an empty **ArrayList** for storing numbers using the **numbers** handle we declared previously, we could write:

```
numbers = new ArrayList<Double>();
```

In general, an empty **ArrayList** capable of storing items of reference type ***ItemType*** can be defined as follows:

```
ArrayList<ItemType> handle = new ArrayList<ItemType>();
```

If an initial capacity larger than 10 is desired, there is a different **ArrayList** constructor that lets the user specify the array's initial length. For example, to make **numbers** the handle for an **ArrayList** capable of storing 16 numbers without growing, we can write:

```
numbers = new ArrayList<Double>(16);
```

Such an **ArrayList** is empty, but its array contains 16 elements instead of 10.

Adding Items to an ArrayList

Since an **ArrayList** implements the **List** interface, we can use the **add()** method to add items to an **ArrayList**, as shown on line 27 in Figure 12-29.

```
Student student = new Student();
student.read(fin);
myStudents.add(student);
```

The **add()** method stores the item in the next empty element in the **ArrayList**'s array, and increments its size. For example, if **myStudents** is as shown in Figure 12-30, and **student** refers to "Dan Doe," who has an overall score of 35, then Figure 12-31 shows how **myStudents** is changed after these statements are performed.

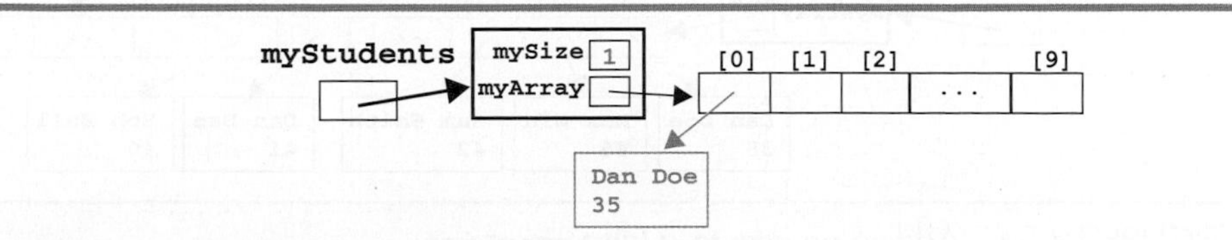

FIGURE 12-31 Adding an item to an **ArrayList**

If we add the student "Max Min" (overall score: 45), our diagram changes to the one shown in Figure 12-32.

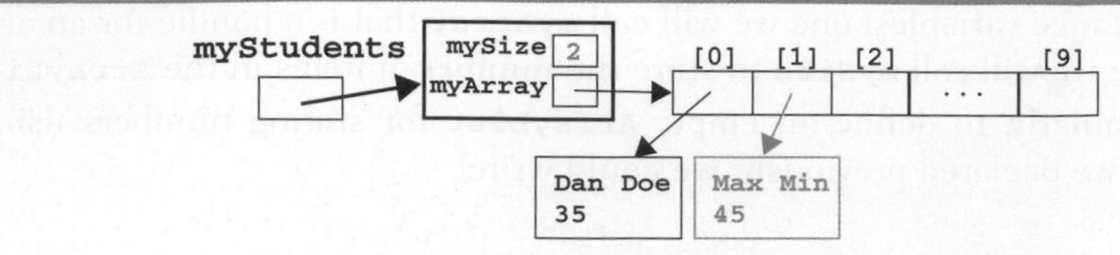

FIGURE 12-32 Adding a second item to an **ArrayList**

If we continue to add items, the array can eventually become full, as shown in Figure 12-33.

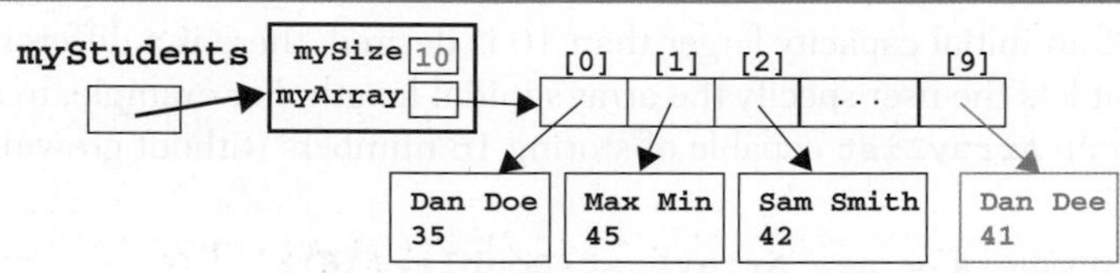

FIGURE 12-33 A full **ArrayList**

Whenever **mySize** is equal to **myArray.length**, the **ArrayList** object is full, so subsequent **add()** messages must somehow make room for the new item. To illustrate, suppose the **ArrayList** is as shown in Figure 12-33 and we add a new student named "Bob Bull" whose overall score is 40. The **add()** method will (1) allocate a new, larger array; (2) copy the **Student** references from the old array into the new array; and (3) make **myArray** refer to the new array. The new student can then be added, as usual.

The Java API does not specify how much bigger the new array will be. However, these three steps can be time-consuming, especially for large arrays. To avoid having to perform these steps too often, a common tradeoff is to sacrifice some space and make the new array twice the size of the current array, as shown in Figure 12-34.

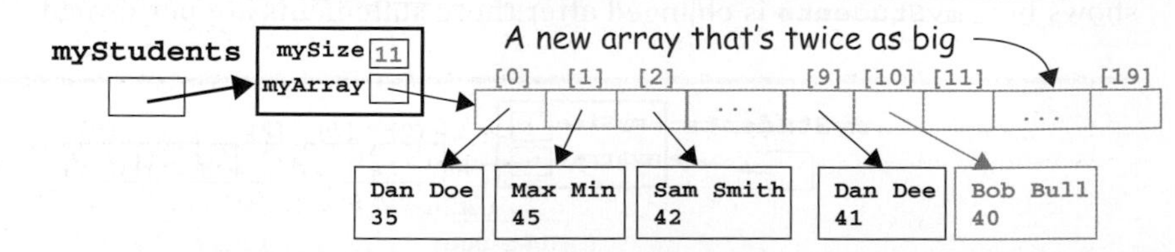

FIGURE 12-34 Adding an item to a full **ArrayList**

Each time we add an item to a full **ArrayList**, these same three steps will be used to make room for the new item. An **ArrayList** thus "grows" whenever it is full and a new item is added. An exception is thrown if there is not enough free memory to allocate the new array.

Finding The Number of Items in an ArrayList

The number of items in an **ArrayList** can be retrieved using the **size()** method, as shown on line 51 of Figure 12-29:

```
int numStudents = myStudents.size();
```

Note that **size()** is different from the length of the array, which cannot be accessed.

Accessing ArrayList Items

To retrieve the item at a given index in an **ArrayList**, the **get()** message can be used. Line 55 of Figure 12-29 illustrates this:

```
median = myStudents.get(midIndex1).getScore();
```

This line sends **myStudents** the **get()** message to retrieve the **Student** at index **midIndex1**, and then sends that **Student** the **getScore()** message to retrieve his or her overall score.

To change the item at a given index in an **ArrayList**, the **set()** message can be used. For example, if **myStudents** is as shown in Figure 12-34, and we perform this statement:

```
myStudents.set(2, new Student("Lou Lug", 31) );
```

then our picture changes as shown in Figure 12-35.

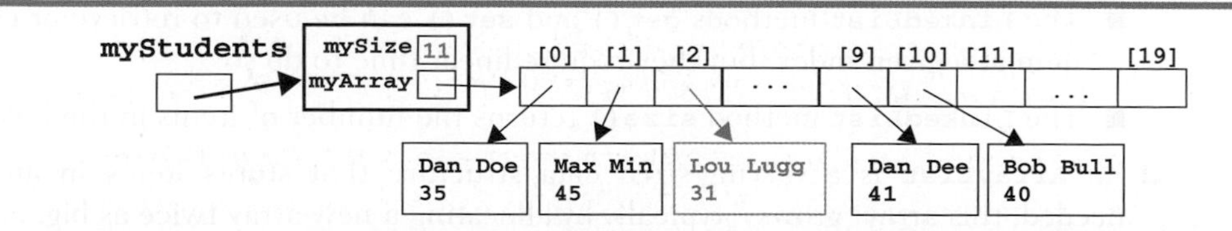

FIGURE 12-35 Changing an item in an **ArrayList**

Since its items are stored in an array, the **ArrayList set()** and **get()** methods let us retrieve or change the item at a given index in constant time, unlike their **LinkedList** counterparts.

> *If the* **get()** *or* **set()** *messages are passed with index values greater than or equal to the* **ArrayList***'s* **size()***, an* **IndexOutOfBoundsException** *is thrown.*

To access and process all of the items in an **ArrayList**, a **for each** loop can be used. Lines 40–46 of Figure 12-29 use this approach to build the two divisions:

```
for (Student stu : myStudents) {
    if (stu.getScore() > median) {
        myDivisionAA.add(stu);
    } else {
        myDivisionA.add(stu);
    }
}
```

As these examples illustrate, we can use any of the **List** methods given in Figure 12-14 to process the items in an **ArrayList**. Additional methods are described in the Java API.

12.5 Chapter Summary

- An array is a fixed-sized data structure that stores items in elements. Adjacent array elements are stored in adjacent memory locations.
    - The array subscript operation can access the item at an arbitrary index in constant time. It throws an **IndexOutOfBoundsException** if the index is invalid.
    - Inserting or removing an item at the front of an array requires linear time to "make room" for the new item, or to "close up the gap" after the removed item.
    - The array **length** property indicates the number of elements in an array.
- A **LinkedList** is a varying-sized data structure that stores items in nodes. Nodes are chained together using references, and may be anywhere in a program's free memory.
    - The **LinkedList** methods **add()**, **addFirst()**, **addLast()**, **getFirst()**, **getLast()**, **removeFirst()**, and **removeLast()** all perform in constant time.
    - The **LinkedList** methods **get()** and **set()** can be used to retrieve or change the item at a given index, but they require linear time to do so.
    - The **LinkedList** method **size()** returns the number of items in the linked list.
- An **ArrayList** is a varying-sized data structure that stores items in an array. As needed, this array "grows," typically by allocating a new array twice as big, copying the items from the old array into the new array, and then replacing the old array with the new array.
    - The **ArrayList** method **add()** appends an item at the end of an **ArrayList**, and performs in constant time, on average.
    - The **ArrayList** methods **add(i)** and **remove(i)** can insert items at or remove items from the beginning or middle of an **ArrayList**. On average, these methods require linear time.
    - The **ArrayList** methods **get()** and **set()** can be used to retrieve or change the item at a given index in constant time.
    - The **ArrayList** method **size()** returns the number of items in the array list.

- ❑ Store sequences:
  - ■ with fixed sizes in arrays
  - ■ without fixed sizes that require no random access in linked lists
  - ■ without fixed sizes that require random access in array lists

12.5.1 Key Terms

array
array definition
array initialization
array **`length`** property
`ArrayList` class
circular doubly-linked list
constant time
dimension
doubly-linked list
element
`for each` loop
implement an interface
interface
item
linear time
`LinkedList` class
`List` interface
N-dimensional arrays
node
one-dimensional arrays
random access data structure
sequential access data structure
subscript operator
wrapper class

Programming Projects

12.1 Modify the **`Month`** class in Figure 12-3 by adding a second constructor that, given a month name, correctly initializes the members **`myName`** and **`myNumber`**. Your constructor should validate the month name. Write a test program that tests the correctness of your modified **`Month`** class.

12.2 Suppose you have the names, phone numbers, and e-mail addresses of all of your friends recorded in a text file. Build a class named **`Friend`** that stores this information about one friend. Then build a class named **`Friends`** that, using your **`Friend`** class and your text file, will store the information about all of your friends. Using your **`Friends`** class, write a program that, given a friend's name, displays the phone number and e-mail address for that friend. The program should handle bad inputs gracefully, and should repeat its task until you enter "quit" as a name.

12.3 Suppose you have a wealthy, absent-minded friend who has so many compact discs (CDs) of music, he has trouble remembering which ones he owns. He has the title, artist, and year for each of his CDs stored in a text file. Help him out by (1) building a **`CD`** class that represents a CD (title, artist, year); (2) building a **`CDCollection`** class that uses his text file and the **`CD`** class to represent his collection of CDs; and (3) writing a program that, given the name of an artist, displays all of the CDs in your friend's collection by that artist. The program should handle bad inputs gracefully, and should continue performing its task until the user enters "quit" as the name of the artist.

12.4 Write a **`read()`** method for the **`Table`** class in Figure 12-11 that, given the name of an input file, builds a table from the numbers in the file. Assume that the first line of the file is two integers specifying the number of rows and the number of columns for the table, and that subsequent lines of the file provide the rows of the table.

Then write a **`write()`** method for the **`Table`** class that, given the name of an output file, creates a file with that name and writes the **`Table`**'s values to that file. Your **`write()`** method should create files that can be read by your **`read()`** method.

Write a test program that tests the correctness of your modified **`Table`** class.

12.5 A *matrix* is a two-dimensional array of numbers whose operations include:

- ❑ **`Matrix()`** — constructs an empty matrix (with zero rows and columns)
- ❑ **`Matrix(`*`r`*`, `*`c`*`)`** — constructs a matrix with ***`r`*** rows and ***`c`*** columns
- ❑ ***`mat`*`.read(`*`fileName`*`)`** — builds a matrix from the values found in ***`fileName`*** (assume that the first line of ***`fileName`*** gives the number of rows and columns)
- ❑ ***`mat`*`.getRows()`** — returns the number of rows in matrix ***`mat`***
- ❑ ***`mat`*`.getColumns()`** — returns the number of columns in matrix ***`mat`***
- ❑ ***`mat`*`.add(`*`mat2`*`)`** — returns a matrix containing the sum of ***`mat`*** and ***`mat2`***; for example:

1	2	3	+	2	4	6	=	3	6	9
4	5	6		8	10	12		12	15	18

- ❑ ***`mat`*`.print()`** — displays a matrix using **`System.out`**

Using the **`Table`** class in Figure 12-11 as a model, build a **`Matrix`** class providing these operations. Test your class using a program that asks the user for the names of two input files containing matrices, and then displays those two matrices and their sum.

12.6 The citizen's action group *Stop Noisy Auto Pollution (SNAP)* has collected the following table of data on the noise levels produced by seven different automobiles at seven different speeds:

Model	MPH 20	30	40	50	60	70	80
1	81	90	92	103	111	121	132
2	78	85	90	99	104	111	118
3	80	86	91	95	100	108	119
4	87	90	95	101	111	121	133
5	66	70	76	86	96	115	125
6	81	83	85	93	102	113	122
7	76	78	80	85	94	104	114

Write a program that displays this table in an easy-to-read format. To the right of each row, display the average noise level for each car model; at the bottom of each column, display the average noise level for that speed; and at the bottom-right corner, display the average noise level overall.

12.7 Using the **`Temperature`** class developed in Section 11.5, write a program that reads an unrestricted number of temperatures from an input file, and displays the maximum, minimum, average, and median temperatures. (Hint: make **`Temperature`** implement the **`Comparable`** interface.)

12.8 A *magic square of order N* is an *N*-by-*N* table in which each of the integers 1, 2, 3, ..., N^2 appear exactly once, and the sum of each row, each column, and each diagonal are equal. For example, the following is a magic square of order 3, in which each row, column, and diagonal sum to 15:

8	1	6
3	5	7
4	9	2

The following is an algorithm for constructing a magic square of order *N*, for any odd integer *N*:

1. Place `1` in the middle of the top row.
2. After integer `i` has been placed, put integer `i+1` one column to the right and one row up, except when one of the following occurs:
   a. If integer `i` is in the top row, place `i+1` one column to the right in the bottom row.
   b. If integer `i` is in the rightmost column, place `i+1` in the leftmost column, one row up.
   c. If `i` is in the top right corner, OR the square where `i+1` should go is already filled, place `i+1` immediately below `i`.

Write a program that, given an odd integer *N*, displays a magic square of order *N*.

12.9 Build a **`SubstitutionCipher`** class that provides the following operations:

- A constructor that builds an **`ArrayList`** containing the characters "A" through "Z," and then uses the **`Collections.shuffle()`** method to randomize that **`ArrayList`.**
- An **`encrypt(`*`inFileName`*`, `*`outFileName`*`)`** method that produces ***`outFileName`*** containing an encrypted version of the contents of ***`inFileName`***. To encrypt the characters in ***`inFileName`***, the method should replace each "A" with $item_0$ from the **`ArrayList`**; replace each "B" with $item_1$ from the **`ArrayList`**; and so on.
- A **`getKey()`** method that returns a two-line **`String`**, the first line of which is the characters "A" through "Z," and the second line of which is the characters $item_0$ through $item_{25}$ from the **`ArrayList`**. For example:

```
A B C D E F G H I J K L M N O P Q R S T U V W X Y Z
N K X H P R Z M C A G F S T D L B Y Q W J U E O V I
```

Write a program that uses your **SubstitutionCipher** class to encrypt a message in a file, and then writes the **String** returned by **getKey()** to a file named **key.txt**. Assume that the message is given in all uppercase letters.

12.10 Proceed as in Project 12.9. Then write a second program that, given a file containing a message encrypted with the Substitution Cipher, and the **key.txt** file used to encrypt that message, produces an output file containing the original message.

Chapter 13
Object-Oriented Programming

Object-oriented programming ... allows software structures to be based on real-world structures, and gives programmers a powerful way to simplify the design and construction of complex programs.

DAVID GELERNTER

Gertrude Stein said, 'A rose is a rose is a rose.' From a different perspective, a rose is a Rosa is a Rosaceae is a Rosales is a Magnoliopsida is a Magnoliophyta is a Plantae is an, um, object.

V. OREHCK III, IN A LECTURE ON CLASS HIERARCHIES

Roberts had grown so rich, he wanted to retire. He took me to his cabin and he told me his secret. 'I am not the Dread Pirate Roberts,' he said. 'My name is Ryan; I inherited the ship from the previous Dread Pirate Roberts, just as you will inherit it from me. The man I inherited it from was not the real Dread Pirate Roberts either... The real Roberts has been retired 15 years and living like a king in Patagonia.'

WESTLEY (CARY ELWES), IN *THE PRINCESS BRIDE*

This attitude [the abstract method in mathematics] can be encapsulated in the following slogan: a mathematical object is what it does.

TIMOTHY GOWERS

Objectives

Upon completion of this chapter, you should be able to:

- ❑ Design and build class hierarchies
- ❑ Understand inheritance and polymorphism
- ❑ Override inherited methods
- ❑ Build abstract classes

In Chapter 11, we introduced the ideas of superclasses and subclasses. We saw that superclasses are more general and subclasses are more specialized, and that subclasses inherit the variables and methods of their superclasses. **Object-oriented programming** is modeling the relationships among a problem's objects using subclass-superclass hierarchies.

To become object-oriented programmers, we must begin to think a bit like biologists, who classify living things by finding where they fit in the *kingdom*, *phylum*, *class*, *order*, *family*, *genus*, and *species* hierarchy, like the one shown in Figure 13-1.

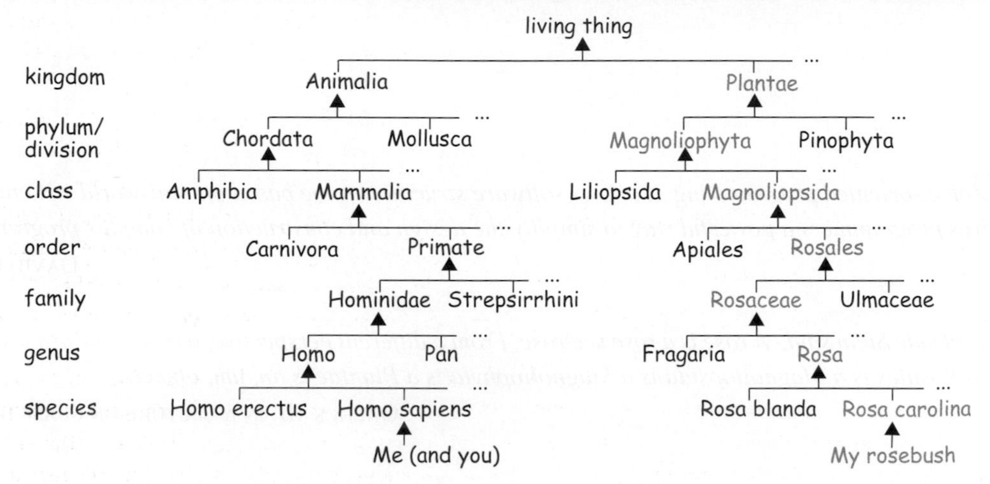

FIGURE 13-1 Biological hierarchical classification

In this chapter, we will learn to design and build class hierarchies. By doing so, we will produce classes that better model objects and their relationships in the real world.

13.1 Introductory Example: Drawing Shapes

Suppose we want a program to draw a logo consisting of a red square containing a green circle containing a blue triangle, like the sketch shown in Figure 13-2.

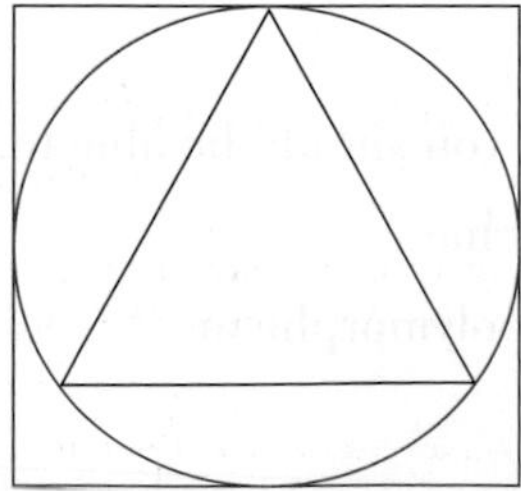

FIGURE 13-2 A logo sketch

13.1.1 Design

The user story for the problem is quite simple:

The program should open a window, and draw within it a red square, containing a green circle, containing a blue triangle.

Looking over the noun phrases in this story, we can use the **Plotter** class from Section 10.3.2 for the window. However, there are no existing types for modeling a red square, a green circle, or a blue triangle, so we will build classes to model these three objects.

Looking over the verb phrases, constructing the **Plotter** will open a window. While the **Plotter** class has **hideAxes()**, **drawPoint()**, **drawLine()**, and **drawOval()** methods, it does not provide methods to draw a square, a circle, or a triangle.

One of the important ideas in object-oriented programming is that an object should be responsible for its own behavior. That is, rather than adding **drawSquare()**, **drawCircle()**, and **drawTriangle()** methods to the **Plotter** class, we can build **Square**, **Circle**, and **Triangle** classes, each containing a **draw()** method, so that our objects "know" how to draw themselves!

If we start to think about what these classes will look like, each has an associated color. We could "hardwire" this color into the different classes (that is, red into the **Square** class, green into the **Circle** class, and blue into the **Triangle** class), but a better approach is to be more general and allow the creator of an object to specify its color. If we start to sketch out these ideas, we might arrive at the group of classes shown in Figure 13-3.

```
class Square {
  public Square(Color, ...) { ... }
  public Color getColor() { ... }
  public void draw() { ... }
  private Color myColor;
}
```

```
class Circle {
  public Circle(Color, ...) { ... }
  public Color getColor() { ... }
  public void draw() { ... }
  private Color myColor;
}
```

```
class Triangle {
  public Triangle(Color, ...) { ... }
  public Color getColor() { ... }
  public void draw() { ... }
  private Color myColor;
}
```

FIGURE 13-3 **Square, Circle**, and **Triangle** class sketches

By thinking carefully about these classes, we can see that each has at least one common attribute: the shape's *color*, and a *getColor*() method to retrieve it. These attributes and methods will be exactly the same in each class. Recall this principle:

If you find yourself doing the same thing more than once, there is probably a better way to do that thing.

In this case, rather than redefine **myColor** and **getColor()** in each class — doing the same thing more than once — the better way is to build a superclass; define **myColor** and **getColor()** once, in the superclass; and then build the **Square**, **Circle**, and **Triangle** classes as subclasses of this superclass. These subclasses will then inherit **myColor** and **getColor()** from the superclass. Since **Square**, **Circle**, and **Triangle** are each a specific kind of shape, we might name this superclass **Shape**.

As long as we are thinking about such relationships, consider this: a square and a triangle are both specializations of a shape that mathematicians call a polygon. That is, a square *is a* polygon, and a triangle *is a* polygon. This suggests that we make **Square** and **Triangle** subclasses of a **Polygon** superclass, which in turn *is a* subclass of **Shape**. The class hierarchy shown in Figure 13-4 summarizes these ideas.

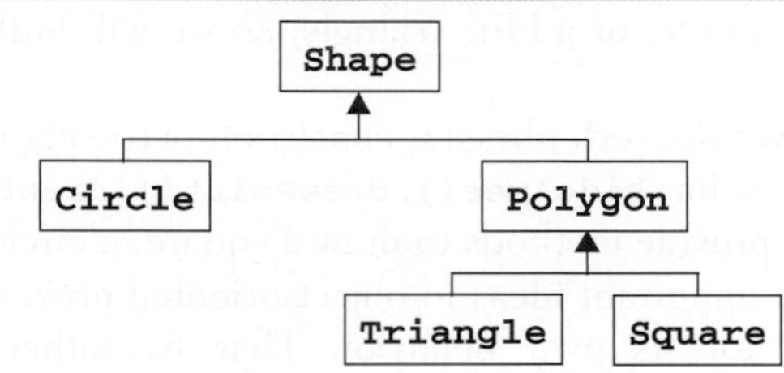

FIGURE 13-4 A hierarchy of shapes

This kind of design, in which we organize a problem's classes into a hierarchy to take advantage of inheritance, is called **object-oriented design**. When people speak of **object-oriented programming**, they refer to the process of turning an object-oriented design into a program.

13.1.2 Implementing the Design

The hierarchy shown in Figure 13-4 can serve as a blueprint for our program. We start with the most general class (**Shape**), and build it, as shown in Figure 13-5.

```
/** Shape.java declares an abstract superclass for shapes...
 */
import java.awt.Color;

abstract public class Shape {
  public Shape(Color aColor) { myColor = aColor; }

  public Color getColor() { return myColor; }

  abstract public void draw(Plotter plot);

  private Color myColor;
}
```

FIGURE 13-5 The **Shape** superclass

As can be seen in Figure 13-5, the **Shape** class has one instance variable to store the shape's color. The **Shape()** constructor merely sets this instance variable to whatever color the user of the class passes when they invoke the constructor.

To see why the **draw()** method is defined as it is on line 10 of Figure 13-5, consider this: Very shortly, we will define the **Circle** and **Polygon** classes as subclasses of **Shape**, and **Square** and **Triangle** as subclasses of **Polygon**. When we have done so, we will be able to store a **Circle**, **Triangle**, or **Square** reference in a **Shape** handle:

```
Shape shape1 = new Square(Color.RED, ...);
Shape shape2 = new Circle(Color.GREEN, ...);
Shape shape3 = new Triangle(Color.BLUE, ...);
```

Figure 13-6 presents a visualization of these handles and objects.

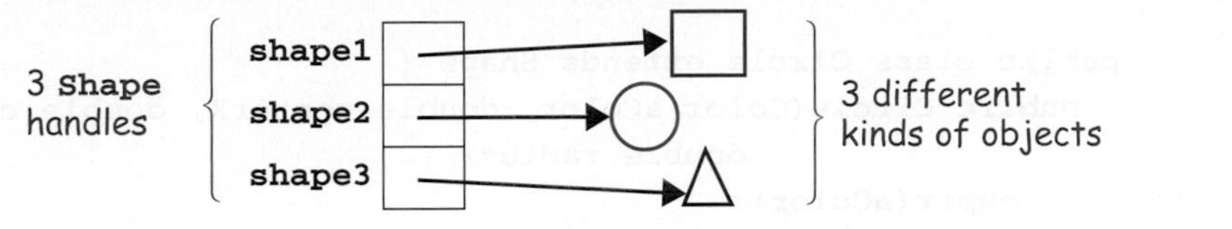

FIGURE 13-6 **Shape** handles for subclass objects

As indicated in Figure 13-3, each subclass of **Shape** will supply its own **draw()** method. However, to send the **draw()** message via a **Shape** handle, the **Shape** class must have a **draw()** method. The difficulty is that **Shape** is such a general class, it does not know what to draw in response to a **draw()** message, although its subclasses will know what to draw.

In this situation, where a superclass needs to declare a method, for which subclasses will supply the definition, the superclass can declare the method as an **abstract method** by placing the keyword **abstract** at the beginning of the method, and putting a semicolon in place of the method's block of statements, as shown on line 10 of Figure 13-5:

```
abstract public void draw(Plotter plot);
```

This declaration tells the Java compiler that **draw()** messages can be sent via a **Shape** handle, but **Shape** subclasses are responsible for providing the definition of the method.

A class that contains an abstract method is called an **abstract class**, and should be defined as such, as shown on line 5 of Figure 13-5:

```
abstract public class Shape {
```

Since an abstract class contains abstract (that is, undefined) methods, Java will not allow a program to create instances of an abstract class. Thus, we may create handles of type **Shape**, but we may not construct an object whose type is **Shape**:

```
Shape aShape = null;                // OK.
aShape = new Shape(Color.BLUE);     // ERROR! Shape is abstract
```

In Java, if a subclass of an abstract class neglects to define all of the superclass's abstract methods, Java treats that subclass as an abstract class, and will prevent a program from creating instances of that subclass. Thus, if one of **Shape**'s subclasses (for example, **Circle**) does not define **draw()**, Java will treat it as an abstract class, and generate a compilation error when we try to construct an object from that class.

The Circle Class

One way to define a circle is to specify its color, the (x,y) coordinates of its center, and its radius. The **Circle** class takes this approach, as shown in Figure 13-7.

```
1  /** Circle.java models a circle using its (x,y) center and radius...
2   */
3  import java.awt.Color;
4
5  public class Circle extends Shape {
6    public Circle(Color aColor, double centerX, double centerY,
7                  double radius) {
8       super(aColor);
9       myX = centerX; myY = centerY;
10      myRadius = radius;
11   }
12
13   public double getRadius() { return myRadius; }
14   public Point  getCenter() { return new Point(myX, myY); }
15
16   public void draw(Plotter plot) {
17      double diameter = myRadius*2;
18      plot.setPenColor( super.getColor() );
19      plot.drawOval(myX, myY, diameter, diameter);
20   }
21
22   private double myRadius, myX, myY;
23 }
```

FIGURE 13-7 **Circle.java**

On line 5 of Figure 13-7, we tell the Java compiler that **Circle** is a subclass of **Shape**:

```
public class Circle extends Shape {
```

In Java, the keyword **extends** tells the Java compiler that the class being declared is a subclass of the class whose name comes next. In general, a declaration of the following form:

```
class SubclassName extends SuperclassName { ... }
```

indicates that ***SubclassName*** is a subclass of ***SuperclassName***.

As can be seen on lines 6 and 7 of Figure 13-7, the **Circle** constructor lets the user define a circle by specifying (1) the color of the circle, (2) the (x,y) coordinates of the center of the circle, and (3) the radius of the circle. Line 22 of Figure 13-7 defines instance variables for storing the radius and the center of the circle, but no instance variable for storing the circle's color. The reason is that class **Shape** already defines such an instance variable, and as a subclass of **Shape**, the **Circle** class inherits that instance variable.

However, as can be seen on line 12 of Figure 13-5, the instance variable **myColor** is declared as **private**, as it should be. This prevents all external classes — including subclasses like **Circle** — from accessing it directly. The **Circle** constructor thus cannot use an assignment statement to initialize **myColor** to the parameter **aColor**:

```
myColor = aColor;     // ERROR! inherited myColor is private
```

Instead, the proper way to initialize an inherited instance variable is to invoke the superclass's constructor. Line 8 of Figure 13-7 shows how this is done in Java:

```
super(aColor);        // Correct way to initialize inherited member
```

To invoke the constructor of its superclass, a subclass can use the notation **super()**, and pass arguments to that constructor's parameters within the parentheses.

> To initialize the values of its inherited instance variables, a subclass should use a constructor of its superclass. In Java, this can be done using **super()**, which *must be the first statement* in the subclass constructor.

Next, we declare two accessor methods, one for the circle's radius (line 13) and one for its center (line 14). In order for the **getCenter()** accessor to return the coordinates of a **Circle**'s center, we have declared a simple **Point** class, which is given in Figure 13-8.

```
/** Point.java models an (x,y) point, where x and y are doubles...
 *  Class java.awt.Point defines x and y as ints; we need doubles.
 */
public class Point {
  public Point(double x, double y) {
    myX = x; myY = y;
  }

  public double getX() { return myX; }
  public double getY() { return myY; }

  private double myX, myY;
}
```

FIGURE 13-8 **Point.java**

Following the accessors, we define the **draw()** method on lines 16-20 of Figure 13-7. This fulfills **Circle**'s responsibility as a subclass of **Shape**, so the Java compiler will permit us to construct **Circle** objects. As we saw in Figure 13-5, the **draw()** method has a **Plotter** parameter. The **Circle** definition of **draw()** computes the circle's diameter, sets the **Plotter**'s pen color to its color, and then sends its **Plotter** the **drawOval()** message, centered at the circle's center coordinates, and with the circle's diameter as the oval's width and height.

A subclass cannot directly access the private instance variables of its superclass. Thus, our **Circle** class cannot directly read the value of its inherited variable **myColor**. Instead, a subclass should read the value of an inherited variable using an accessor method. Line 18 of the program in Figure 13-7 illustrates this, when it sends its superclass the **getColor()** message to set the **Plotter**'s pen color to its (inherited) color:

```
plot.setPenColor( super.getColor() );
```

This is an example of the following important principle:

> **A subclass should use the accessor methods of its superclass to read the values of its inherited instance variables.**

In general, if a subclass wants to send its superclass a message named ***m*()**, it can do so with the notation **super.*m*()**.[1] Java thus uses the keyword **super** in two related ways:

1. A subclass constructor can invoke the constructor of its superclass using the **super();** notation. This statement must be the first statement in the subclass constructor.
2. A subclass can send a message to its superclass by sending it to **super**.

We're finished with the **Circle** class! To test it, we can now write some simple tests like this:

```
Plotter plot = new Plotter(0, 0, 10, 10);  // (0,0) to (10,10)
Shape aShape = new Circle(Color.GREEN,     // color
                          5, 5,            // (x,y) of center
                          5);              // radius
aShape.draw(plot);
```

and verify that a green **Circle** draws itself on the **Plotter**.

---

1. Strictly speaking, the "**super.**" is not needed to invoke an inherited method. For example, on line 18 of Figure 13-7, we could have written **plot.setPenColor(getColor());**. However, we think it is a good practice to include the "**super.**", as doing so makes it clear at a glance that the method being invoked is inherited from the superclass (as opposed to being defined in the current class).

The **Polygon** Class

There are different ways to model a polygon. One way is to store the points that define the polygon's corner. The **draw()** method can then draw lines connecting those points. However, the precise number of corners varies from one polygon to another:

- A triangle has three corners
- A square (and a rectangle, rhombus, or trapezoid) has four corners
- A pentagon has five corners

and so on. One way to manage this is to pass the number of corners in the polygon to the **Polygon** constructor, which can then use this number to allocate an array big enough to store that many points. The class shown in Figure 13-9 takes this approach.

```
/** Polygon.java models a closed polygon...
 */
import java.awt.Color;

public class Polygon extends Shape {
  public Polygon(Color aColor, int numCorners) {
     super(aColor);
      if (numCorners < 3) {
         throw new IllegalArgumentException("Polygon(): "
                                  + "numCorners must be >= 3");
     }
     myPoints = new Point[numCorners];
  }

  protected void setPoint(int i, double x, double y) {
     myPoints[i] = new Point(x,y);
  }

  public Point getPoint(int i) { return myPoints[i]; }

  public void draw(Plotter plot) {
     plot.setPenColor( super.getColor() );
     Point p0 = myPoints[0], p1 = null;
     for (int i = 1; i < myPoints.length; i++) {
         p1 = myPoints[i];
         plot.drawLine( p0.getX(), p0.getY(),
                        p1.getX(), p1.getY() );

         p0 = p1;
     }
     plot.drawLine( p1.getX(), p1.getY(),
                    myPoints[0].getX(), myPoints[0].getY() );
  }

```

continued

```
34     private Point [] myPoints = null;
35 }
```

FIGURE 13-9 `Polygon.java`

Lines 6-13 of Figure 13-9 define the class constructor. After using **super()** to initialize the inherited instance variable **myColor**, and validating parameter **numCorners**, the constructor allocates an array to store the polygon's corners' points. The array's handle is named **myPoints**, which is declared on line 34.

To provide a means of storing a polygon's corners in this array, lines 15-17 define a method named **setPoint()**. A method like this — that lets a user change the class's instance variables — is called a **mutator**, or **setter**.

A mutator is a potentially dangerous operation; once it has been defined, we do not want just anyone to be able to change the corners of a polygon. We therefore define the mutator not as **private** (which would prevent anyone else from using it), nor as **public** (which would allow everyone to use it), but as **protected**:

```
protected void setPoint(int i, double x, double y) {
```

By doing so, we permit this class and its subclasses to send this message, but we prevent casual users of this class from doing so. The **protected** specifier thus provides an intermediate level of access, between **public** and **private**.

> *To let subclasses alter the values of instance variables, define mutator methods. Unless there is a good reason to make them **public**, define mutators as **protected**, to prevent non-subclasses from using them.*

Line 19 defines an accessor named **getPoint(*i*)** that lets us read the ith corner's point.

Lines 21-32 define the **draw()** method. After setting the **Plotter**'s pen color, this method iterates through **myPoints**, drawing a line from corner to corner; first from **myPoints[0]** to **myPoints[1]**, then from **myPoints[1]** to **myPoints[2]**, and so on. The method thus does the equivalent of playing "connect the dots" using the points in the array. Lastly, it closes the polygon by drawing a line between the last and first points in **myPoints**.

Since the **Polygon** class defines **draw()**, it fulfills its responsibility as a subclass of **Shape**, so we may create instances of it. To test it, we might try to draw a "diamond" with corners at (5, 0), (2, 5), (5, 10), and (8, 5):

```
Plotter plotter = new Plotter(0, 0, 10, 10);
Polygon p = new Polygon(Color.CYAN, 4);
p.setPoint(0, 5, 0);      // corner 0 is at (5,0)
p.setPoint(1, 2, 5);      // corner 1 is at (2,5)
p.setPoint(2, 5, 10);     // corner 2 is at (5,10)
p.setPoint(3, 8, 5);      // corner 3 is at (8, 5)
p.draw(plotter);
```

With our **Polygon** class complete, we can continue on to its subclasses.

The Triangle Class

A triangle can be defined by specifying its color and the (x,y) coordinates of its three vertices. The **Triangle** class shown in Figure 13-10 takes this approach.

```
1  /** Triangle.java models a triangle shape,
2   *   using the (x,y) coordinates of its 3 vertices...
3   */
4  import java.awt.Color;
5
6  public class Triangle extends Polygon {
7    public Triangle(Color aColor, double x1, double y1,
8                    double x2, double y2, double x3, double y3) {
9      super(aColor, 3);
10     super.setPoint(0, x1, y1);                  // corner 1
11     super.setPoint(1, x2, y2);                  // corner 2
12     super.setPoint(2, x3, y3);                  // corner 3
13   }
14 }
```

FIGURE 13-10 **Triangle.java**

The **Triangle** class in Figure 13-10 uses the same features we used before, only it is a subclass of **Polygon** instead of **Shape**. For example, on line 6, we tell the Java compiler that **Triangle** is a subclass of **Polygon**, using the **extends** keyword:

```
class Triangle extends Polygon {
```

Similarly, line 9 invokes the **Polygon** constructor using **super()**:

```
super(aColor, 3);
```

and lines 10-12 use **super** to send the inherited **setPoint()** message to **Polygon**, in order to define the triangle's three corners:

```
super.setPoint(0, x1, y1);                  // corner 1
super.setPoint(1, x2, y2);                  // corner 2
super.setPoint(2, x3, y3);                  // corner 3
```

Thanks to inheritance, that is the entire class! To test it, we can write some simple tests:

```
Plotter plot = new Plotter(0, 0, 10, 10);       // (0,0) to (10,10)
Shape aShape = new Triangle(Color.BLUE,         // color
                            0, 0,               // (x,y) of corner1
                            5, 10,              // (x,y) of corner2
                            10, 0);             // (x,y) of corner3
aShape.draw(plot);
```

and verify that the **Triangle** draws itself on the **Plotter**.

The **Triangle** class is this simple, because it inherits everything it needs from its superclasses. More precisely, it inherits **myColor** and **getColor()** from class **Shape**, and it inherits **myPoints**, **getPoint()**, **setPoint()**, and **draw()** from class **Polygon**.

The Square Class

A square can be modeled using its color, the (x,y) coordinates of its center, and the length of one of its sides. If we pass these values to the **Square** constructor, it can then calculate the points of the square's corners, as can be seen in Figure 13-11.

```
1  /** Square.java models a square shape,
2   *  using its (x,y) center and the length of one side...
3   */
4  import java.awt.Color;
5
6  public class Square extends Polygon {
7    public Square(Color aColor, double centerX, double centerY,
8                                double sideLength) {
9       super(aColor, 4);
10      double halfSideLength = sideLength / 2;
11      super.setPoint(0, centerX - halfSideLength,    // x of corner 0
12                        centerY - halfSideLength);   // y of corner 0
13      super.setPoint(1, centerX - halfSideLength,    // x of corner 1
14                        centerY + halfSideLength);   // y of corner 1
15      super.setPoint(2, centerX + halfSideLength,    // x of corner 2
16                        centerY + halfSideLength);   // y of corner 2
17      super.setPoint(3, centerX + halfSideLength,    // x of corner 3
18                        centerY - halfSideLength);   // y of corner 3
19   }
20 }
```

FIGURE 13-11 **Square.java**

As discussed previously, line 6 of Figure 13-11 declares **Square** as a subclass of **Polygon**, not of **Shape**. Lines 7-19 define the class constructor, which takes the square's color, the (x,y) coordinates of its center, and the length of one of its sides.

Since **Square** is a subclass of a **Polygon**, line 9 uses **super()** to invoke the **Polygon** constructor. This initializes the inherited variables **myColor** and **myPoints**. Lines 10-18 of the constructor then compute the coordinates of the four corners, and use the inherited method **setPoint()** to store these coordinates in **myPoints**.

For the problem at hand, this is all that we need! Since a **Square** *is a* **Polygon**, **Square** inherits **Polygon**'s **draw()** method. To verify that the **Square** draws itself correctly, we can test it using simple tests like the following:

```
Plotter plot = new Plotter(0, 0, 10, 10);   // (0,0) to (10,10)
Shape aShape = new Square(Color.RED,         // color
                          5, 5,              // (x,y) of center
                          10);               // side length
aShape.draw(plot);
```

The **Square** and **Triangle** classes are this simple because they need no attributes beyond those they inherit from **Polygon**. By letting us inherit functionality from a superclass, object-oriented programming may seem more complex at the outset, but it can make it a lot easier to build the actual classes in our problem.

Solving the Problem (1)

With our class hierarchy completed, writing a program that solves the problem is now straightforward. Figure 13-12 shows one way to do so.

```
/** Logo1.java draws a logo...
 */
import java.awt.Color;

public class Logo1 {
  public static void main(String[] args) {
     Plotter plotter = new Plotter(0, 0, 10, 10);
     plotter.hideAxes();
     Shape shape = new Square(Color.RED, 5, 5, 10);
     shape.draw(plotter);
     shape = new Circle(Color.GREEN, 5, 5, 5);
     shape.draw(plotter);
     shape = new Triangle(Color.BLUE, 1, 2, 5, 10, 9, 2);
     shape.draw(plotter);
  }
}
```

continued

FIGURE 13-12 **Logo1.java**

The program in Figure 13-12 is pretty simple, because each shape object "knows" how to draw itself. The more an object "knows" how to do, the less a program that uses that object has to do!

Note that we use the same **Shape** handle for each object. Since the objects' classes are subclasses of **Shape**, the same **Shape** handle can refer to a **Square**, a **Triangle**, or a **Circle**. After the statement on line 9 is performed, we can picture our handle as shown in Figure 13-13.

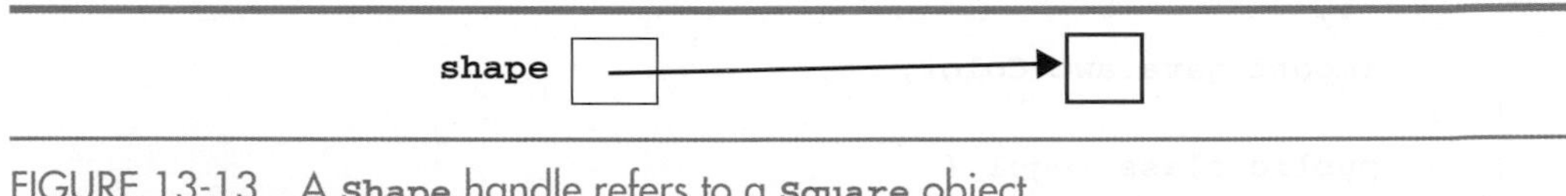

FIGURE 13-13 A **Shape** handle refers to a **Square** object

Another thing to see is that lines 10, 12, and 14 are identical statements:

```
shape.draw(plotter);
```

However, each line invokes a different method, because the object to which **shape** refers keeps changing. That is, the statement on line 10 sends the **draw()** message of the **Square** object, invoking its **draw()** method. The **Square** responds by drawing itself on the **plotter**.

Next, line 11 is performed, and our picture changes to that shown in Figure 13-14.

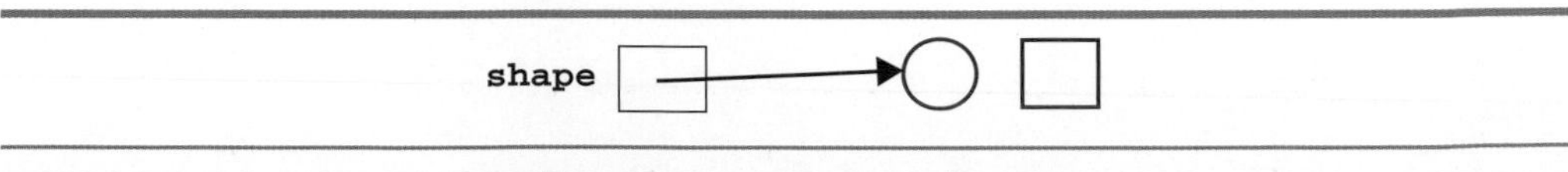

FIGURE 13-14 A **Shape** handle refers to a **Circle** object

Line 12 then sends the **draw()** message to the **Circle** object, which responds by drawing itself on the **plotter**. Since no object refers to the **Square** object, Java's garbage collector will (at some point) reclaim it.

Next, line 13 is performed, and our picture changes to that of Figure 13-15.

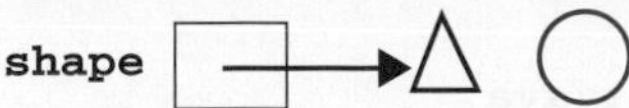

FIGURE 13-15 A **Shape** handle refers to a **Triangle** object

Line 14 then sends the **draw()** message to the **Triangle** object, which responds by drawing itself on the **plotter**. Since the **Circle** object is no longer accessible, Java's garbage collector will eventually reclaim it.

Solving the Problem (2)

An alternative way to draw the logo is to place each of the logo's shapes in a list, and then use a **for each** loop to send the **draw()** message to each item in that list. The program in Figure 13-16 uses this approach, and it builds the logo in a way that can be used by other programs.

```
/** Logo.java draws a logo using a LinkedList...
 */
import java.awt.Color;
import java.util.LinkedList;

public class Logo {
  public Logo() {
     myShapes = new LinkedList<Shape>();
     myShapes.add( new Square(Color.RED, 5, 5, 10) );
     myShapes.add( new Circle(Color.GREEN, 5, 5, 5) );
     myShapes.add( new Triangle(Color.BLUE, 1, 2, 5, 10, 9, 2) );
  }

  public void draw(Plotter plotter) {
     plotter.hideAxes();
     for (Shape shape : myShapes) {
        shape.draw(plotter);
     }
  }

  private LinkedList<Shape> myShapes = null;

  public static void main(String[] args) {
```

continued

```
24        Logo self = new Logo();
25        self.draw( new Plotter(0, 0, 10, 10) );
26    }
27 }
```

FIGURE 13-16 **Logo.java**

Figure 13-16 draws all of the shapes by using a **for each** loop to repeat line 17:

```
shape.draw(plotter);
```

For each repetition of the loop, this solitary **draw()** message may invoke a different method. The first repetition, **shape** refers to the **Square**, so the **draw()** message invokes **Square**'s inherited method **Polygon#draw()**.[2] The second repetition, **shape** refers to the **Circle**, and so the **draw()** message invokes **Circle#draw()**. The third repetition, **shape** refers to the **Triangle**, and so the **draw()** message invokes **Polygon#draw()** again. The same statement can thus invoke different methods at different times, if **shape** refers to different objects.

This phenomenon — in which one statement produces different behaviors as the program runs — is called **polymorphism**, from the Greek word for "many forms." Line 17 of Figure 13-16 literally produces "many forms," as it draws the **Square**, **Circle**, and **Triangle**.

The program in Figure 13-16 has two advantages over that of Figure 13-12. The first is that class **Logo** can be used by other programs to draw the logo on an arbitrary **Plotter**. The code in Figure 13-16 is thus more reuseable than the code in Figure 13-12.

The second advantage is this: to add a new shape to our logo, all we need to do is add the new shape to the program's list. For example, if we build a new **Shape** subclass named **Diamond**, then if we add just one statement after line 11:

```
myShapes.add(new Diamond(Color.BLACK, 0, 5, 5, 10, 10, 5, 5, 0));
```

the new shape will be added to our logo; the rest of our program can remain unchanged.

2. The notation **Polygon#draw()** is shorthand for "the **draw()** method defined in class **Polygon**."

13.2 Class Hierarchies and Object-Oriented Programming

We have seen two class hierarchy diagrams — Figure 11-9 and Figure 13-4 — and learned that:

1. Object-oriented design consists of designing the classes needed to solve a problem, identifying common attributes (methods and/or variables) in those classes, building superclasses to store the common attributes, and using the *is a* relationship to organize the subclasses and superclasses into a class hierarchy.
2. Object-oriented programming consists of building each of the classes in an object-oriented design in some programming language. Needless to say, that language needs to support subclasses, superclasses, inheritance, abstract methods, and so on.

In this section, we will fill in some of the pieces that are still missing.

13.2.1 Java's Class Hierarchy

If you examine the **java.lang** package in the Java API, you will see that Java defines a class named **Object**. This class provides a handful of general-purpose methods (for example, a **toString()** method that returns the name of the class and some additional information).

This **Object** class is the superclass of every standard Java class (for example, **Math**, **Scanner**, **String**, and so on). The **Object** class is also the superclass of every nonstandard Java class, including all of the programs we have written thus far! More precisely, if a class neglects to extend another class, Java makes that class a subclass of **Object** by default. Thus, when we wrote line 6 of Figure 13-16:

```
public class Logo {
```

the Java compiler interpreted it as follows:

```
public class Logo extends Object {
```

Every Java class is thus ultimately a subclass of **Object**. A more complete version of the classes we created in Section 13.1 would thus be as shown in Figure 13-17.

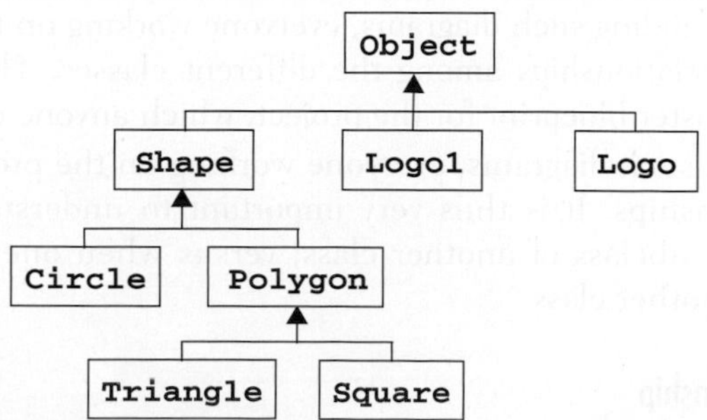

FIGURE 13-17 The class hierarchy for drawing logos

A diagram like Figure 13-17 is called a **class structure diagram**, because it shows how the classes in a project are structured or related to one another.

13.2.2 The *is a* and *has a* Relationships

We have seen that the *is a* relationship relates subclasses to superclasses: a subclass *is a* specialized kind of its superclass. Class structure diagrams use arrows to represent the *is a* relationship.

The *is a* relationship applies from a class to all of its superclasses, not just its immediate superclass. For example, in Figure 13-17, a `Triangle` *is a* `Polygon`, a `Triangle` *is a* `Shape`, and a `Triangle` *is an* `Object`. Put differently, `Polygon` is `Triangle`'s immediate superclass, but `Shape` and `Object` are also its superclasses. A class's superclasses are thus all of the classes that we encounter in following the arrows from itself to the `Object` class.

Another way that classes can be related is the *has a* relationship. If a class A contains an instance variable whose type is class B, we say that A *has a* B. For example, the `Logo` class in Figure 13-16 *has a* `LinkedList<Shape>`, because it has an instance variable of that type. Class structure diagrams use a diamond-headed line ◇— to denote the *has a* relationship. Figure 13-18 uses this to give a more complete class structure diagram for class `Logo`.

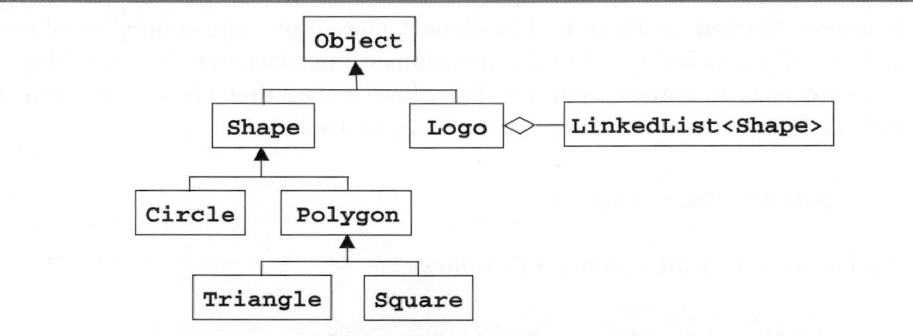

FIGURE 13-18 Class structure diagram for `Logo.java`

Object-oriented software engineers draw class structure diagrams for their software projects. By building such diagrams, everyone working on the project can clearly see the *is a* and *has a* relationships among the different classes. The class structure diagram thus serves as a master blueprint for the project, which anyone can consult if a question arises.

To build such diagrams, everyone working on the project must agree on the *is a* and *has a* relationships. It is thus very important to understand when one class should be defined as a subclass of another class, versus when one class should have an instance variable of another class.

The *is a* Relationship

The first rule of thumb in defining subclasses and superclasses is the ***is a* relationship**. If class X *is a* particular kind of class Y, then X can be defined as a subclass of Y.

To illustrate, suppose we have been hired to model an orchard of apple trees, walnut trees, pear trees, chestnut trees, and peach trees. An apple tree *is a* fruit tree; a peach tree *is a* fruit tree, and a pear tree *is a* fruit tree. Any attributes that such trees have in common can thus be consolidated in a **FruitTree** superclass. Likewise, a chestnut tree *is a* nut tree, and a walnut tree *is a* nut tree. Any attributes that these trees have in common can be consolidated in a **NutTree** superclass. Since a fruit tree *is a* tree, and a nut tree *is a* tree, any attributes that are common to both the **FruitTree** and **NutTree** classes can be consolidated in a **Tree** superclass. From these ideas, we can build the class structure diagram shown in Figure 13-19.

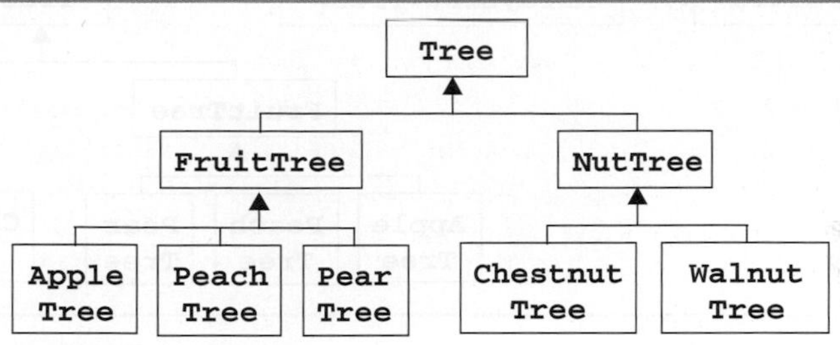

FIGURE 13-19 A **Tree** class structure diagram

The principle governing subclasses, superclasses, and the *is a* relationship is this:

> Superclasses should always be generalizations of their subclasses.
> Subclasses should always be specializations of their superclasses.

Make Sure All Inherited Messages Are Appropriate

The other rule of thumb has to do with the methods a subclass inherits from its superclass. Since a subclass inherits all of the methods of its superclass, any message that can be sent to a superclass object can also be sent to a subclass object. This means that if we are not careful, we can misuse inheritance and define subclasses inappropriately.

To illustrate, let's return to our orchard example again, and think about how we will define the **Orchard** class. To store the orchard's trees, we will need some sort of data structure. Occasionally, new trees will be planted, or trees will die, so we will use a list data structure instead of an array. Supposing that we may frequently need to access specific trees in the orchard, we will give each tree a number and use an **ArrayList** as our data structure, rather than a **LinkedList**.

At this point, we might be tempted to think, "If I can use an **ArrayList** of **Tree** objects to model an orchard, then an **Orchard** *is an* **ArrayList<Tree>**. By doing so, I can send my **Orchard** the **add()**, **get()**, **set()**, and other methods it inherits from **ArrayList**, saving me lots of work!"

```
public class Orchard extends ArrayList<Tree> {   // DON'T DO THIS
```

Saving lots of work sounds great; however, **ArrayList** contains other methods that are not appropriate for an orchard, including **clone()**, **hashCode()**, **listIterator()**, **trimToSize()**, and others. If we make **Orchard** a subclass of **ArrayList<Tree>**, then we will be able to send an **Orchard** these inappropriate messages as well as the appropriate ones.

In situations like this, the ***has a* relationship** should be used instead of the *is a* relationship, as shown in Figure 13-20.

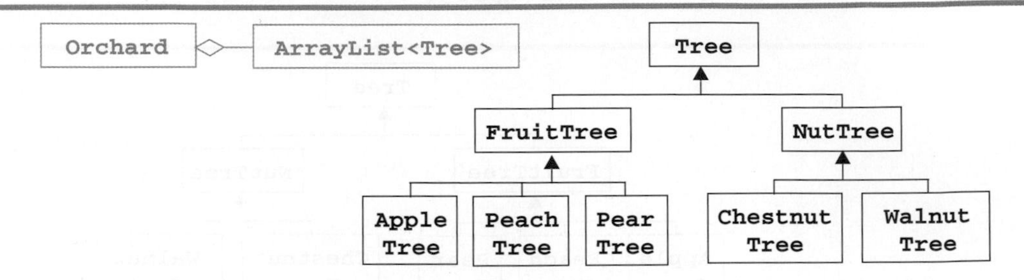

FIGURE 13-20 An **Orchard** class structure diagram

That is, rather than make **Orchard** a subclass of **ArrayList<Tree>**, we instead define an **ArrayList<Tree>** instance variable in class **Orchard**:

```
public class Orchard {                        // THE BETTER WAY
    // Orchard methods omitted...
    private ArrayList<Tree> myTrees = new ArrayList<Tree>;
}
```

By using the *has a* relationship instead of the *is a* relationship, we can ensure that only appropriate messages can be sent to an **Orchard** object. More generally, the rule of thumb is as follows:

If you are considering defining class X as a subclass of class Y, make certain that every message that can be sent to a Y object is appropriate to send to an X object. If this is not the case, Y should not be a subclass of X.

13.2.3 Hierarchy in the Java API

As can be seen in the Java API, Java provides a huge number of standard classes, and all of these classes are a part of the Java class hierarchy. Whenever we look up a class in the Java API, the top-left corner of that class's page traces that class's superclasses all the way back to **Object**. In Figure 13-21, this trace is circled for the **Double** "wrapper" class.

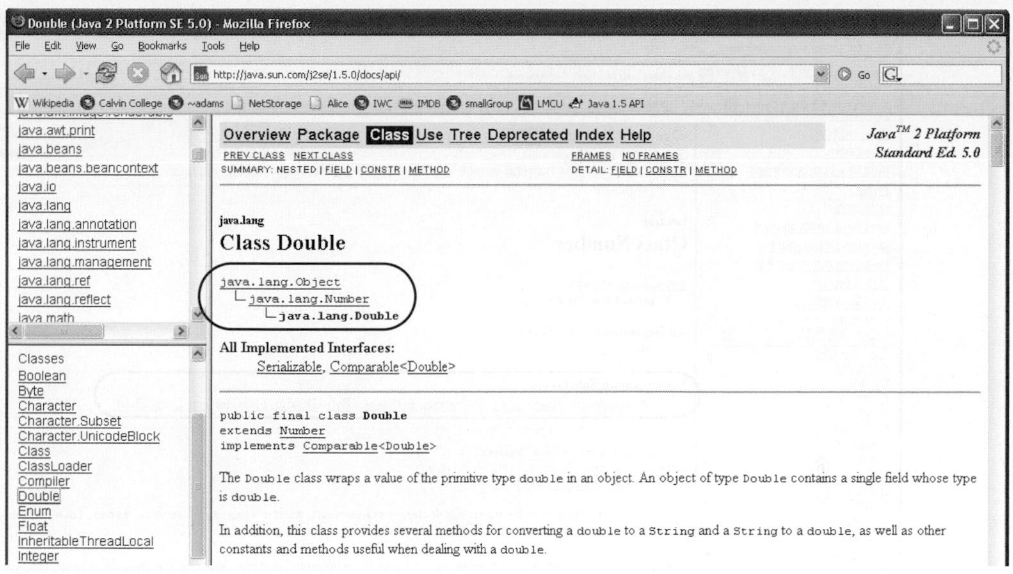

FIGURE 13-21 The superclasses of class **Double**

As shown in Figure 13-21, **Double** is a subclass of **Number**, which is a subclass of **Object**. To view the API for a superclass in this trace, we can click on its name. For example, clicking on **java.lang.Number** brings up the **Number** page, as shown in Figure 13-22. There, we see that the API for a class also lists the subclasses of that class.

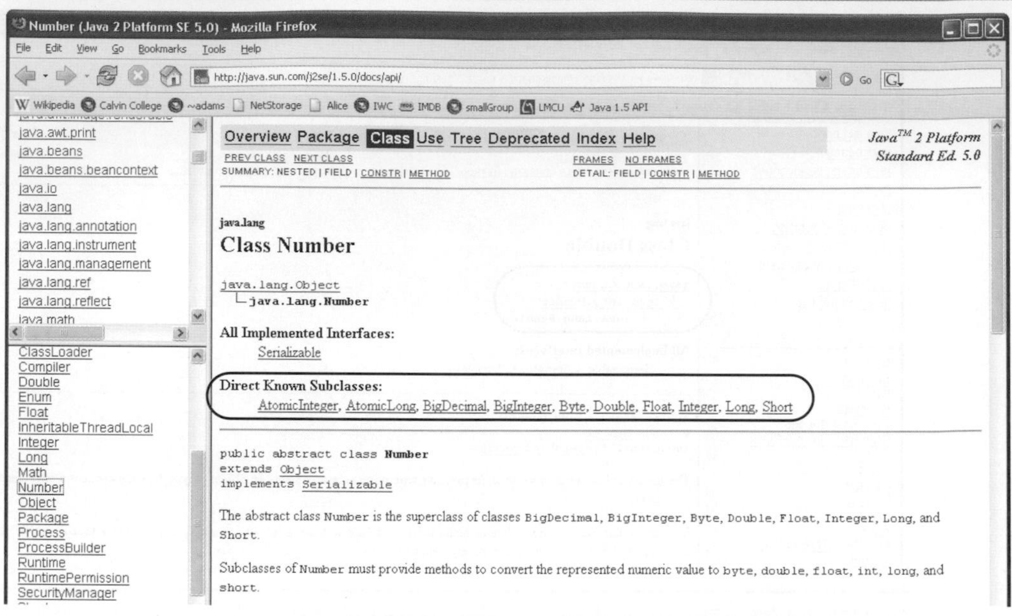

FIGURE 13-22 The subclasses of class **`Number`**

The Java API thus provides a convenient way to navigate Java's class hierarchy.

13.2.4 Bottom-Up Design versus Top-Down Programming

There is one final thing to mention before we return to some examples. In designing the class hierarchies in Figure 13-4 and Figure 13-20, we first identified the objects in our problem, determined what features they had in common, and then designed superclasses to consolidate their common attributes. This was a *bottom-up process*, because we worked our way from the classes named in the user story (shown at the bottom of Figure 13-4) "upward" to their superclasses. Put differently, we design from the most specific classes to the most general, because we begin with our user story, which (hopefully) describes highly specific objects. By identifying common attributes and using the *is a* relationship, we design our way "upward" to increasingly general classes, until every class is included in the hierarchy (even if it's just a subclass of **`Object`**).

By contrast, actually programming the classes in the hierarchy is a *top-down process*. We start by building the topmost superclass. We then test this class before continuing. (If necessary, we can "comment out" any abstract parts of the class.) When we are finished with the topmost superclass in our design, we then build and test each of its subclasses. When they are done, we build and test their subclasses, and so on, until all of the classes are completed. The reason for programming from top to bottom is that a subclass extends a superclass, and if the superclass does not exist, the Java compiler generates an error, making testing impossible. By starting at the topmost superclass and working our way "down," we can avoid this compilation error.

When we are confident that these classes are correct, we write a program that uses them to solve our problem. Writing the program that solves the problem can thus be the last thing we do, after we have built classes to model all of the objects in the problem.

As with most things, it takes practice to learn how to think in an object-oriented manner. So without further ado, let's work through some more examples.

13.3 Example 2: Object-Oriented T-Shirt Sales

In Section 10.2.2, we built a `TShirt` class that we and our friends could use to sell t-shirts. Now that we know more about object-oriented programming, let's write a program that we can use to take an order of t-shirts. Our friends start by giving us this user story:

> The program should take a t-shirt order. At the end, the program should summarize the order, listing the t-shirts in the order, and the total price.

After asking for more details, our friends elaborate as follows:

> To take an order, the program should (1) display a menu: x-small t-shirt: $9.00, small t-shirt: $10.00, medium t-shirt: $10.00, large t-shirt: $10.00, x-large t-shirt: $11.00, and quit; (2) read the user's choice; (3) display that t-shirt and its price; (4) add that t-shirt's price to the total; and (5) repeat steps 1-4 as long as the user is not done.

The noun phrases in the story include:

Noun Phrase	Type of Value	Name
the program	*TShirtOrder*	none
menu	`String`	*MENU*
x-small t-shirt	*XSmallTShirt*	none
small t-shirt	*SmallTShirt*	none
medium t-shirt	*MediumTShirt*	none
large t-shirt	*LargeTShirt*	none
x-large t-shirt	*XLargeTShirt*	none
the user's choice	`int`	*choice*
t-shirt	*TShirt*	*shirt*

continued

Noun Phrase	Type of Value	Name
price	`double`	*shirt.getPrice()*
list of t-shirts	`LinkedList<TShirt>`	*shirts*
total	`double`	*total*

Some of these names may change, depending on whether they end up as local variables or instance variables, but these will suffice to get us started.

Since there are no predefined classes to represent x-small, small, medium, large, or x-large t-shirts, we will design classes to represent such objects. However, these classes will have many attributes in common. We can avoid unnecessary duplication of those attributes (redundant coding) by building a **`TShirt`** superclass to store those attributes, and defining the other t-shirt classes as its subclasses. Figure 13-23 shows the class structure diagram so far.

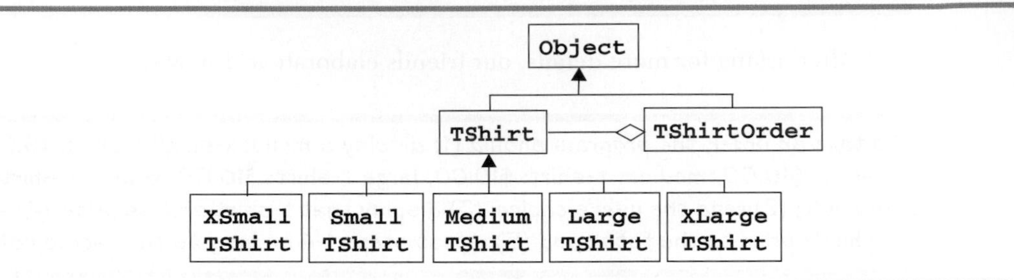

FIGURE 13-23 A `TShirtOrder` class hierarchy

Continuing with our design, we identify the verb phrases in the user story.

Verb Phrase	Method or Operation
display ...	`System.out.print()` or `println()`
read the user's choice	`Scanner#nextInt()`
get a t-shirt's price	`TShirt#getPrice()`
add the t-shirt's price ...	`+=`
repeat steps ...	`do` loop
list order's t-shirts	`TShirtOrder#printShirts()`, `for each` loop
list order's total	`println()`, `TShirtOrder#getTotal()`

The **TShirt** Class

Different t-shirts have different sizes, so a **TShirt** will need to "remember" its size in an instance variable. From the verb phrases, a **TShirt** will also need a **getPrice()** method. However, since three of the t-shirt sizes have the same price, we can have **TShirt#getPrice()** return this price as a default price, and leave it to subclasses to redefine the method if their price is different. The class shown in Figure 13-24 uses this approach.

```
1  /** TShirt.java is the superclass for different sized t-shirts...
2   */
3  public class TShirt {
4    public TShirt(String size) {
5      if ( !(size.equals("XS") || size.equals("S") || size.equals("M")
6          || size.equals("L") || size.equals("XL") ) ) {
7          throw new IllegalArgumentException("TShirt(): bad size: "
8                                              + size);
9      }
10     mySize = size;
11   }
12
13   public String getSize()   { return mySize; }
14   public double getPrice() { return 10.00; }
15   public String toString() { return mySize + " TShirt"; }
16
17   private String mySize;
18 }
```

FIGURE 13-24 **TShirt.java**

The class in Figure 13-24 is mostly straightforward. Its constructor takes the size of the t-shirt, and, after validating it, stores it in the instance variable **mySize** for later use. The accessor on line 13 and the **toString()** method on line 15 are similarly straightforward.

The one thing that needs some explanation is the **getPrice()** method on line 14. Instead of defining an instance variable to store the t-shirt's price, we have defined the **getPrice()** method to return 10.00, the price of the small, medium, and large t-shirts. The thought process in doing so is as follows: Three of the five t-shirt sizes have the same price, so instead of storing the price, or using a multi-branch **if** statement to compute the price based on **mySize**, we define **getPrice()** to return the value that is correct most of the time. When the **SmallTShirt**, **MediumTShirt**, and **LargeTShirt** classes inherit this method, it will provide the correct behavior. The **XSmallTShirt** and **XLargeTShirt** classes will need to redefine this method, so that it returns their correct price. (See Figure 13-25 and Figure 13-27 below.)

Since class **TShirt** contains no abstract methods, it is not an abstract class, and we can test it using simple tests like those below:

```
TShirt shirt = new TShirt("S");
assert shirt.getSize().equals("S");
assert shirt.getPrice() == 10.0;
shirt = new TShirt("M");
assert shirt.getSize().equals("M");
assert shirt.getPrice() == 10.0;
shirt = new TShirt("L");
assert shirt.getSize().equals("L");
assert shirt.getPrice() == 10.0;
```

The **getPrice()** method will return the correct values for small, medium, and large t-shirts, but not for extra small and extra large t-shirts. However, we will add additional tests for those classes after we define them.

If you compare the **TShirt** class in Figure 13-24 against the one in Figure 10-7, you will begin to see a little of the difference between object-*based* programming (Figure 10-7) and object-*oriented* programming (Figure 13-24). Both involve building classes. However, object-based programming does not use inheritance, so the classes tend to be much longer and complex, making errors more likely, and making errors harder to find. By contrast, object-oriented programming tends to produce shorter, simpler classes, in which it is harder to make a mistake, and in which mistakes are easier to find.

How can the **TShirt** class in Figure 13-24 be so much shorter than the one in Figure 10-7? The answer is that the functionality needed to model the different sizes of t-shirts is spread out through the class hierarchy shown in Figure 13-23. Where the class in Figure 10-7 needs a complicated nested **switch** statement[3] to determine the price for a given size of t-shirt, the **TShirt** class in Figure 13-24 only provides a **getPrice()** method that returns the right price for most t-shirts, and leaves it up to the subclasses to change that price if necessary.

The XSmallTShirt Class

In keeping with the class structure diagram shown in Figure 13-23, we next define the **XSmallTShirt** class. This class is quite simple, as shown in Figure 13-25.

```
/** XSmallTShirt.java models an extra-small t-shirt...
 */
public class XSmallTShirt extends TShirt {
  public XSmallTShirt()     { super("XS"); }
  public double getPrice() { return 9.00; }
}
```

FIGURE 13-25 **XSmallTShirt.java**

3. A **switch** statement is the traditional way to select one of several alternatives. Polymorphism is the object-oriented way of doing the same thing. By defining a class hierarchy in which subclasses provide alternative definitions for the same method, most **switch** or other multi-branch selection statements can be eliminated.

As we have seen previously, line 3 of Figure 13-25 uses the **extends** keyword to declare **XSmallTShirt** as a subclass of **TShirt**. Because of this, **XSmallTShirt** inherits the instance variable **mySize**, and the **getSize()**, **getPrice()**, and **toString()** methods.

On line 4, the class constructor initializes the inherited variable **mySize** by using **super()** to invoke the **TShirt** constructor, passing its own size value as an argument.

Because the inherited **getPrice()** method returns the wrong price for an extra-small t-shirt, line 5 redefines **getPrice()** for **XSmallTShirt** objects. This practice — in which a subclass redefines an inherited method because the behavior of the inherited method is inappropriate for the subclass — is called **overriding** a method. By replacing the default behavior with a behavior appropriate for its own objects, **XSmallTShirt#getPrice()** overrides the inherited **TShirt#getPrice()**.

Note that *overriding* is completely different from *overloading*. Overloading is using the same name to define multiple versions of the same operation, each with different parameters, usually in the same class. Overloaded methods differ in the number or types of the parameters they accept; overriding is when a subclass redefines an inherited method using the same number and types of parameters.

> *Overloaded methods have the same name, but differ in the number or types of the parameters.*
>
> *To override an inherited method, a subclass method must have the same name, and the exact same number and type of parameters.*

With **getPrice()** defined properly for extra-small t-shirts, we can test this class by adding this test to the ones we saw previously:

```
shirt = new XSmallTShirt();                  // shirt is a TShirt handle
assert shirt.getSize().equals("XS");
assert shirt.getPrice() == 9.0;
```

The SmallTShirt Class

The next class in the class structure diagram in Figure 13-23 is the **SmallTShirt** class. This class is very simple, as shown in Figure 13-26.

```
/** SmallTShirt.java models a small t-shirt...
 */
public class SmallTShirt extends TShirt {
   public SmallTShirt()    { super("S"); }
}
```

FIGURE 13-26 **SmallTShirt.java**

The **SmallTShirt** class inherits everything it needs from its superclass **TShirt**, including a **getPrice()** method that returns the correct price. The only thing left for this class to do is to supply a constructor, which passes the proper size value to its superclass constructor.

To test this class, we can add these tests to our existing tests:

```
shirt = new SmallTShirt();               // shirt is a TShirt handle
assert shirt.getSize().equals("S");
assert shirt.getPrice() == 10.0;
```

The **MediumTShirt** and **LargeTShirt** classes are very similar to the **SmallTShirt** class shown in Figure 13-26. Building these classes and their tests are left as exercises.

The XLargeTShirt Class

The last subclass of **TShirt** in Figure 13-23 is **XLargeTShirt**. Like the **XSmallTShirt** class, this class is pretty simple, as shown in Figure 13-27.

```
/** XLargeTShirt.java models an extra-large t-shirt...
 */
public class XLargeTShirt extends TShirt {
   public XLargeTShirt()      { super("XL"); }
   public double getPrice() { return 11.00; }
}
```

FIGURE 13-27 **XLargeTShirt.java**

Since the price of an extra-large t-shirt is \$11.00, this class overrides the inherited **getPrice()** method with a definition that returns the correct price for an extra-large t-shirt.

To test the method, we can add the following tests to those we used earlier:

```
shirt = new XLargeTShirt();               // shirt is a TShirt handle
assert shirt.getSize().equals("XL");
assert shirt.getPrice() == 11.0;
```

Solving The Problem

With the **TShirt** hierarchy completed, we are ready to use these classes to write the **TShirtOrder** class that will allow our friends to take t-shirt orders. The program in Figure 13-28 shows one way to do so.

```
/** TShirtOrder.java models a t-shirt order.
 */
import java.util.*;      // Scanner, LinkedList, ...

public class TShirtOrder {
  private double                 myTotal = 0.0;
```

continued

```
    private LinkedList<TShirt> myShirts = new LinkedList<TShirt>();
    private TShirt []        myShirtKinds = { new XSmallTShirt(),
                                              new SmallTShirt(),
                                              new MediumTShirt(),
                                              new LargeTShirt(),
                                              new XLargeTShirt()};

    public double getTotal() { return myTotal; }
    public LinkedList<TShirt> getShirts() { return myShirts; }

    public void takeOrder() {
       final String MENU = "To order a t-shirt, enter:\n"
                         + " 0 - for extra small\n"
                         + " 1 - for small\n"
                         + " 2 - for medium\n"
                         + " 3 - for large\n"
                         + " 4 - for extra large\n"
                         + " 5 - to quit\n"
                         + "--> ";
       final int QUIT = 5;
       int choice = 0;
       Scanner keyboard = new Scanner(System.in);
       do {
          System.out.print(MENU);
          choice = keyboard.nextInt();
          if (choice >= 0 && choice < QUIT) {
             TShirt shirt = myShirtKinds[choice];
             myTotal += shirt.getPrice();
             myShirts.add(shirt);
             System.out.printf("%s: $%.2f%n%n",
                               shirt, shirt.getPrice());
          }
       } while (choice != QUIT);
    }

    private void printSummary() {
       System.out.println();
       for (TShirt shirt : myShirts) {
           System.out.printf("%s: $%.2f\n", shirt, shirt.getPrice());
       }
       System.out.printf("The total price of your order is: $%.2f",
                         this.getTotal());
    }

```

continued

```
   public static void main(String[] args) {
      TShirtOrder self = new TShirtOrder();
      self.takeOrder();
      self.printSummary();
   }
}
```

```
Result:
To order a t-shirt, enter:
0 - for extra small
1 - for small
2 - for medium
3 - for large
4 - for extra large
5 - to quit
--> 4
XL TShirt: $11.00

To order a t-shirt, enter:
0 - for extra small
1 - for small
2 - for medium
3 - for large
4 - for extra large
5 - to quit
--> 3
L TShirt: $10.00

To order a t-shirt, enter:
0 - for extra small
1 - for small
2 - for medium
3 - for large
4 - for extra large
5 - to quit
--> 2
M TShirt: $10.00

To order a t-shirt, enter:
0 - for extra small
1 - for small
2 - for medium
3 - for large
4 - for extra large
5 - to quit
--> 1
S TShirt: $10.00
```

continued

```
To order a t-shirt, enter:
0 - for extra small
1 - for small
2 - for medium
3 - for large
4 - for extra large
5 - to quit
--> 1
S TShirt: $10.00

To order a t-shirt, enter:
0 - for extra small
1 - for small
2 - for medium
3 - for large
4 - for extra large
5 - to quit
--> 0
XS TShirt: $9.00

To order a t-shirt, enter:
0 - for extra small
1 - for small
2 - for medium
3 - for large
4 - for extra large
5 - to quit
--> 5

XL TShirt: $11.00
L TShirt: $10.00
M TShirt: $10.00
S TShirt: $10.00
S TShirt: $10.00
XS TShirt: $9.00
The total price of your order is: $60.00
```

FIGURE 13-28 `TShirtOrder.java`

The only tricky part about this program lies in converting the user's choice (a number) into the corresponding kind of t-shirt. To simplify this, we use an old trick: we make the menu's choices correspond to an array's index values (0-4), and define an array whose items are the corresponding menu choices. We build this array on lines 8-12 of Figure 13-28:

```
private TShirt [] myShirtKinds = { new XSmallTShirt(), // index 0
                                   new SmallTShirt(),    // index 1
                                   new MediumTShirt(),   // index 2
                                   new LargeTShirt(),    // index 3
                                   new XLargeTShirt() }; // index 4
```

With this array in place, we read the user's menu choice on line 31, check that it is not "quit" on line 32, and then convert that choice to the corresponding **TShirt** object on line 33:

```
TShirt shirt = myShirtKinds[choice];
```

That is, if **choice** is **0**, then **shirt** will refer to an **XSmallTShirt** object; if **choice** is **1**, then shirt will refer to a **SmallTShirt** object; if **choice** is **2**, **shirt** will refer to a **MediumTShirt** object, and so on. Once **shirt** refers to the kind of t-shirt object corresponding to the user's menu choice, the rest of the solution is fairly straightforward.

We can summarize what we have learned about abstraction and overriding as follows:

> When all of a superclass's subclasses need a method, but each needs a different behavior from that method, the superclass should declare the method as an abstract method, and leave its definition to the subclasses.
>
> When all of a superclass's subclasses need a method, and many subclasses need the same behavior from that method, define the method with that behavior in the superclass so that those subclasses can inherit it; the remaining subclasses can override it.

13.4 Example 3: Object-Oriented Business Software

Suppose a woman named Ortrera is founder of a company called Amazons.com. When the company was small, she did the weekly payroll by hand, but now the company is growing, and she wants us to write a computer program to compute the payroll.

Ortrera keeps a master file listing the company's employees in the order they were hired. Each employee is listed on a separate line. This line begins with the word **Salaried** or **Hourly**, depending on how the employee is paid. This is followed by the employee's name and ID number. Next comes the employee's salary or hourly rate, depending on how she is paid.

Each pay period, Ortrera uses a program to make a copy of this master file named **payrollData.txt**. This program prompts for and appends the number of hours each **Hourly** employee worked to her line in the payroll data file. Figure 13-29 shows the first twelve lines of this payroll data file.

```
Salaried    Ortrera      001    1000.00
Hourly      Orithyia     002    20.00     42.0
Salaried    Antiope      003    850.00
Hourly      Hippolyte    004    20.00     40.0
Salaried    Penthesilea  005    900.00
Hourly      Clonie       006    20.00     20.0
Hourly      Molpadia     007    20.00     15.0
Salaried    Thalestris   008    750.00
Hourly      Melanippe    009    20.00     30.0
Hourly      Ainia        010    20.00     45.0
Hourly      Antibrote    011    20.00     35.0
Hourly      Helene       012    20.00     10.0
```

FIGURE 13-29 The beginning of an Amazons.com **payrollData.txt** file

Ortrera gives you the following user story:

> The program should use the payrollData.txt file to compute and display how much each employee should be paid.

When you ask her for more information, she adds the following details.

> A salaried employee should be paid her salary. An hourly employee should be paid the product of her hourly rate times the number of hours she worked, unless she worked more than 40 hours, in which case she should be paid an overtime bonus (0.5 times her normal hourly rate) for each hour above 40.

In this user story, we can identify the following noun phrases:

Noun Phrase	Type of Value	Name
the program	*Payroll*	none
the payroll data file	**File**, **Scanner**	*fin*
employee	*Employee*	*employee*
salaried employee	*SalariedEmployee*	none
salary	**double**	*mySalary*
hourly employee	*HourlyEmployee*	none
hourly rate	**double**	*myRate*
number of hours	**double**	*myHours*
overtime bonus	**double**	*OVERTIME_BONUS*

These noun phrases indicate we will need to build four classes. If we consider the relationships among these classes, we can see that a salaried employee *is an* employee, and an hourly employee *is an* employee. We can also see that a payroll *has an* employee (actually, lots of them). We can thus design the class structure diagram shown in Figure 13-30.

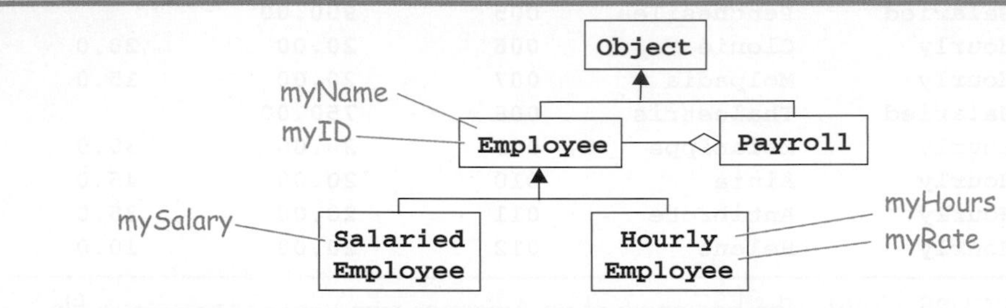

FIGURE 13-30 Class hierarchy for Amazons.com payroll program (1)

We have annotated the diagram in Figure 13-30 to indicate which class is responsible for defining a given attribute. To illustrate, every employee has a name and an ID number, so we make class **Employee** responsible for defining **myName**, **myID**, and their accessors. Anything else that all employees have in common (for example, job titles, phone numbers, addresses, and so on) can also be defined in **Employee**; we are intentionally keeping this example very simple.

By contrast, only salaried employees have a salary, so class **SalariedEmployee** is responsible for defining **mySalary**. Likewise, only hourly employees have a rate and hours, so class **HourlyEmployee** is responsible for defining **myHours** and **myRate**.

In looking over the verb phrases in the user story, most of them have to do with an employee being paid. Every employee gets paid; however, the details of how this is computed depends on whether the person is a salaried employee or an hourly employee. We might thus declare an abstract **getPay()** method in **Employee**, and leave it to **SalariedEmployee** and **HourlyEmployee** to supply appropriate definitions for **getPay()**.

Each class is also responsible for providing accessor methods for the instance variables it defines. Since each employee's information is in a file, **Employee** and its subclasses will also need to define a **read()** method to read information from the payroll data file. If we add annotations to our class structure diagram showing which class is responsible for providing a given method, we get the diagram shown in Figure 13-31.

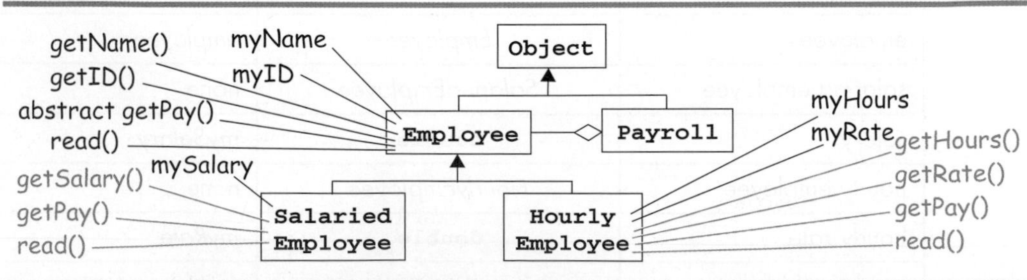

FIGURE 13-31 Class hierarchy for Amazons.com payroll program (2)

The class structure diagram in Figure 13-31 is sufficiently detailed to serve as a blueprint, so let's build the classes! Since the **Payroll** class has an **Employee**, we will start with **Employee**, then build its subclasses, and finally build the **Payroll** class.

The Employee Class

Using Figure 13-31 as our blueprint, building the **Employee** class is straightforward, as shown in Figure 13-32.

```
1  /** Employee.java provides a simple model of an employee...
2   */
3  import java.util.Scanner;
4
5  abstract public class Employee {
6    public Employee() {
7       myName = "";
8       myID = 0;
9    }
10
11   public Employee(String name, int id) {
12      myName = name;
13      myID = id;
14   }
15
16   public String getName() { return myName; }
17   public int    getID()   { return myID;   }
18   public String toString() { return myName + "\t" + myID; }
19
20   abstract double getPay();
21
22   public void read(Scanner in) {
23      myName = in.next();
24      myID = in.nextInt();
25   }
26
27   private String myName = null;
28   private int    myID;
29 }
```

FIGURE 13-32 **Employee.java**

Although not strictly necessary for our problem, we have added a **toString()** method, so that an **Employee**'s information can be easily displayed.

Since **Employee** is an abstract class, we cannot easily test it, unless we "comment out" the word **abstract** on line 5 and the declaration of the abstract **getPay()** method on line 20. We will therefore proceed directly to the **Employee** subclasses.

The `SalariedEmployee` Class

With class **Employee** completed, we turn to class **SalariedEmployee**. This is the simpler of the two subclasses; Figure 13-33 presents its declaration.

```
1  /** SalariedEmployee.java models a salaried employee...
2   */
3  import java.util.Scanner;
4
5  public class SalariedEmployee extends Employee {
6     public SalariedEmployee() {
7        super();
8        mySalary = 0.0;
9     }
10
11    public SalariedEmployee(String name, int id, double salary) {
12       super(name, id);
13       mySalary = salary;
14    }
15
16    public double getSalary() { return mySalary; }
17
18    public String toString() {
19       return super.toString() + "\t" + mySalary;
20    }
21
22    public void read(Scanner in) {
23       super.read(in);
24       mySalary = in.nextDouble();
25    }
26
27    public double getPay() { return mySalary; }
28
29    private double mySalary;
30 }
```

FIGURE 13-33 **SalariedEmployee.java**

Some of the things to note in Figure 13-33 include the following:

- On line 7, the default constructor uses **super();** to initialize the inherited instance variables with default values, before initializing **mySalary** to a default value.
- On line 12, the explicit constructor uses **super(name, id);** to initialize the inherited instance variables with the values passed by the user, before initializing **mySalary** to a value passed by the user.

- As lines 7 and 12 illustrate, a subclass's constructor should always use **`super()`** to initialize inherited instance variables, before initializing its own instance variables.
- On line 18, the **`toString()`** method uses **`super.toString()`** to retrieve the string representation of the inherited instance variables. The method returns the result of concatenating a tab character and **`mySalary`** to that string. Thus, when **`myName`** is *Ortrera*, **`myID`** is *001*, and **`mySalary`** is *1000.00*, this method will return **`"Ortrera\t1\t1000.0"`**.
- On line 23, the **`read()`** method uses **`super.read(in);`** to read values for the inherited instance variables, before reading a number into **`mySalary`**. Thus, if **`in`** contains the characters **`"Ortrera\t1\t1000"`**, then after this method is performed, **`myName`** will be **`"Ortrera"`**, **`myID`** will be **`1`**, and **`mySalary`** will be **`1000.0`**.
- As lines 19 and 23 illustrate, a subclass method that overrides a method can (and often should) invoke the method it is overriding by sending the appropriate message to **`super`**. If the method merely sends the message (for example, **`read(in);`**) without sending it to **`super`**, the result is a recursive method call, and an infinite recursion will likely occur, which is not a good thing. (See Appendix B for more on recursion.)
- On line 27, we define **`getPay()`**, fulfilling the class's obligation as a subclass of **`Employee`**. As a result, **`SalariedEmployee`** is not abstract, and the Java compiler will let us create **`SalariedEmployee`** objects.

Since we can create **`SalariedEmployee`** objects, we can test this class using simple tests like the following:

```
SalariedEmployee salEmp1 = new SalariedEmployee("Ortrera",
                                                 001, 1000.00);
assert salEmp1.getName().equals("Ortrera");
assert salEmp1.getID() == 001;
assert salEmp1.getSalary() == 1000.00;
assert salEmp1.getPay() == 1000.00;
System.out.print(" passed test 1");
```

Note that since **`SalariedEmployee`** is a subclass of **`Employee`**, we can test the **`Employee`** methods (for example, **`getName()`** and **`getID()`**) when we test class **`SalariedEmployee`**.

To test the **`SalariedEmployee`** default constructor, **`read()`** method, and **`toString()`** method, we can add another test:

```
Scanner keyboard = new Scanner(System.in);
System.out.print("Enter a salaried employee: ");
SalariedEmployee salEmp2 = new SalariedEmployee();
salEmp2.read(keyboard);
System.out.print(salEmp2);
```

We can then test these methods interactively, as shown below:

```
Enter a salaried employee: Ortrera 001 1000.00
Ortrera     1          1000.0
```

To automate this test and avoid having to enter test data manually, we can store the data for a few salaried employees in a test data file. The test can then open that file, read salaried employees from it, and assert that the correct values were read. Doing so is left as an exercise.

The `HourlyEmployee` Class

With class **`SalariedEmployee`** written and tested, we turn our attention to the **`HourlyEmployee`** class. Using the class structure diagram from Figure 13-31, we can build the class shown in Figure 13-34.

```
/** HourlyEmployee.java models an hourly employee...
 */
import java.util.Scanner;

public class HourlyEmployee extends Employee {
  public HourlyEmployee() {
     super();
     myHours = myRate = 0.0;
  }

  public HourlyEmployee(String name, int id,
                        double hours, double rate) {
     super(name, id);
     myHours = hours;
     myRate = rate;
  }

  public double getHours() { return myHours; }
  public double getRate()  { return myRate;  }

  public String toString() {
     return super.toString() + "\t" + myRate + "\t" + myHours;
  }

  public void read(Scanner in) {
     super.read(in);
     myRate = in.nextDouble();
     myHours = in.nextDouble();
  }

  public double getPay() {
     final double OVERTIME_BONUS = 0.5;
     double pay = myHours * myRate;
     if (myHours > 40) {
```

continued

```
            double overtimeHours = myHours - 40;
            pay += overtimeHours * myRate * OVERTIME_BONUS;
        }
        return pay;
    }

    private double myHours;
    private double myRate;
}
```

FIGURE 13-34 **HourlyEmployee.java**

Most of the methods in the **HourlyEmployee** class are similar to their **SalariedEmployee** counterparts. The exception is the **getPay()** method, which must provide for overtime pay. This makes it more complicated than its **SalariedEmployee** counterpart.

The **HourlyEmployee** class can be tested using the same techniques as we used to test the **SalariedEmployee** class. We leave the building of such tests as an exercise for the reader.

The **Payroll** Class

With the **Employee** class hierarchy completed, we are ready to solve the problem for which Ortrera hired us. Thanks to the **read()** method in class **Employee** and its subclasses, a **SalariedEmployee** or an **HourlyEmployee** "knows" how to fill itself with data from a **Scanner**, so our program can solve the problem using the following algorithm:

Purpose: Compute payroll for Amazons.com

1. Open a Scanner named *fin* to the input file *payrollData.txt*
2. While *fin.hasNext()*:
   a. Read a string (*Salaried* or *Hourly*) from *fin* into *employeeKind*
   b. Use *employeeKind* to construct a *SalariedEmployee* or *HourlyEmployee* object, as appropriate, with *employee* as its handle
   c. Fill *employee* with data by sending it the message *read(fin)*
   d. Display *employee's* name and pay, by sending it the *getName()* and *getPay()* messages.
3. Close *fin*

The program in Figure 13-35 implements this algorithm.

```java
/** Payroll.java computes the payroll for Amazons.com...
 */
import java.util.Scanner;
import java.io.*;              // File, ...

public class Payroll {
  public void run() {
     Scanner fin = null;
     try {
        fin = new Scanner( new File("payrollData.txt") );
        Employee employee = null;
        while ( fin.hasNext() ) {
           String employeeKind = fin.next() + "Employee";
           employee = Class.forName(employeeKind)
                            .asSubclass(Employee.class)
                              .newInstance();
           employee.read(fin);
           System.out.printf("%20s: $%7.2f%n", employee.getName(),
                                                 employee.getPay() );
        }
     } catch (Exception e) {
        e.printStackTrace();
     } finally {
        fin.close();
     }
  }

  public static void main(String[] args) {
     Payroll self = new Payroll();
     self.run();
  }
}
```

Result:

```
            Ortrera: $1000.00
           Orithyia: $ 840.00
            Antiope: $ 850.00
          Hippolyte: $ 800.00
        Penthesilea: $ 900.00
             Clonie: $ 400.00
           Molpadia: $ 300.00
         Thalestris: $ 750.00
```

continued

Melanippe: $ 600.00
Ainia: $ 900.00
Antibrote: $ 700.00
Helene: $ 200.00
...

FIGURE 13-35 **Payroll.java**

The program in Figure 13-35 uses the same sort of **try-catch** block and input loop we have seen in previous chapters. In each repetition of the input loop, lines 13-16 build an object whose type is one of the **Employee** subclasses; line 17 sends that object the **read()** message, causing it to fill itself with a line of data from the input file; line 18 then sends that object the **getName()** message to retrieve the employee's name; and line 19 sends that object the **getPay()** message to compute her pay.

Line 19 is another example of a polymorphic method. When **employee** refers to a **SalariedEmployee**, line 19 invokes **SalariedEmployee#getPay()**. But when **employee** refers to an **HourlyEmployee**, line 19 invokes **HourlyEmployee#getPay()**.

The Class Class

The trickiest thing in Figure 13-35 is on lines 13-16, where we construct the **SalariedEmployee** or **HourlyEmployee** object. This is very tricky, so we will take it one step at a time.

Line 13 reads the first thing on a line — the kind of employee (either **"Salaried"** or **"Hourly"**) — into a string variable named **employeeKind**, and concatenates the word **"Employee"** to it:

```
employeeKind = fin.next() + "Employee";
```

After doing this, **employeeKind** is a string whose value is the type of object we want to construct: either **"SalariedEmployee"** or **"HourlyEmployee"**.

Our next step is to construct a **SalariedEmployee** object when **employeeKind** is **"SalariedEmployee"**, and construct an **HourlyEmployee** object when **employeeKind** is **"HourlyEmployee"**. We could accomplish this using an **if** statement:

```
if (employeeKind.equals("SalariedEmployee")) {      // This works,
   employee = new SalariedEmployee();                // but there
} else if (employeeKind.equals("HourlyEmployee")){  // is a
   employee = new HourlyEmployee();                  // better way
} else { ...                                         // (see below)
```

The drawback to this approach is that if we someday need to add a new subclass of **Employee** (for example, **PartTimeEmployee**), then we would have to add a new branch to this **if** statement to handle the new kind of employee:

```
if (employeeKind.equals("Salaried")) {
   employee = new SalariedEmployee();
} else if (employeeKind.equals("PartTime")) {
   employee = new PartTimeEmployee();
} else if (employeeKind.equals("Hourly")) {
   employee = new HourlyEmployee();
} else { ...
```

In general, we want to avoid doing things that, in the future, might require us to change working code. It would be better if there were a different way to do this, so that if we do someday add a new class to the **Employee** hierarchy, our program would still work correctly.

The "better" way is to use the name of the class in **employeeKind** to create an instance of that class (that is, a **SalariedEmployee** or **HourlyEmployee** object). To do this, we can use Java's **Class** class. Yes, Java has a class whose name is **Class**! If you look it up in the Java API, you will find that the **Class** class contains various methods that let us model and manipulate classes.

For example, the **Class** class has a **forName()** method that, given a string whose value is the name of a class, returns a **Class** with that name. Since **employeeKind** contains the name of the class we want, the expression:

```
Class.forName(employeeKind)
```

will get a **Class** of that type for us. Line 14 of Figure 13-35 thus produces a **Class** model for a **SalariedEmployee** or **HourlyEmployee**, depending on the value of **employeeKind**.

When the Java compiler compiles this expression, it has no way of knowing what the value of **employeeKind** is going to be, so the next task is to tell it what kind of **Class** we're getting. We can accomplish this by sending that **Class** the **asSubclass()** message, as shown on line 15. The argument that accompanies the **asSubclass()** message must be a **Class** that indicates the superclass of whatever class(es) we are getting; in this case, **Employee**.

> The **Class** model of any class can be retrieved by giving the name of the class followed by **.class**.

In our situation, we thus write:

```
Class.forName(employeeKind).asSubclass(Employee.class)
```

This produces a **Class** that the Java compiler understands will be a subclass of **Employee**.

Once we have the **Class** model for the object we want to construct, we can construct the object by sending that **Class** the **newInstance()** message, as can be seen on line 16:

```
Class.forName(employeeKind).asSubclass(Employee.class)
                  .newInstance()
```

When **employeeKind** is **"SalariedEmployee"**, this expression constructs a **SalariedEmployee** object using its default constructor. Similarly, when **employeeKind** is **"HourlyEmployee"**, this expression constructs an **HourlyEmployee** object using its default constructor. In general, if ***className*** is a string variable containing the name of a class, the statement:

```
HandleType handle = Class.forName(className)
                          .asSubclass(HandleType.class)
                           .newInstance();
```

can be used to construct an object whose type is ***className***.

As we suggested earlier, the advantage to using this approach is that it builds the object directly from the string in the input file. If Ortrera subsequently decides to hire a new kind of employee — for example a **PartTime** employee — and adds her information to the input file, all we have to do is build a subclass of **Employee** named **PartTimeEmployee**, in the same folder as **SalariedEmployee** and **HourlyEmployee**. The program in Figure 13-35 will still work correctly, without our having to make any modifications! By requiring less work to make such modifications, using the **Class** class is less expensive to maintain than using a multi-branch **if** statement.

13.5 Chapter Summary

- Object-oriented design is a bottom-up process in which a problem's objects are identified, classes are designed for those objects, and any common attributes of these classes are consolidated into superclasses, from which the subclasses can inherit those attributes.
- A class structure diagram shows the *is a* and *has a* relationships of a program's classes.
- In Java, **Object** is the superclass of all classes.
- Object-oriented programming is a top-down process, in which the superclass in a class structure diagram is built first, then its subclasses, then their subclasses, and so on.
- A mutator is a method that can be used to change the value of an instance variable.
- A **protected** attribute can be accessed only by a class and its subclasses.
- The **super** keyword can be used to invoke the superclass's constructor (in a subclass constructor) or to send a message to the superclass.
- When a subclass overrides an inherited method, or defines a method that is abstract in its superclass, invocations of that method will be polymorphic.
- Classes that contain abstract methods are abstract classes. Abstract classes cannot be used to construct objects.

13.5.1 Key Terms

abstract class
abstract method
Class class
class structure diagram
extends
has a relationship
inherits
is a relationship
mutator
object-oriented design
object-oriented programming
overriding
polymorphism
setter

Programming Projects

13.1 Build the **Diamond** class described at the end of Section 13.1.2, and use it to add a diamond shape to the logo created by the program in Figure 13-16, centered within the circle.

13.2 The local bank provides checking accounts and savings accounts. Both kinds of accounts have a balance. Checking accounts have no minimum balance, but earn no monthly interest; savings accounts have a minimum balance of $100, but earn 0.25% interest each month. Both kinds of accounts let you make deposits, withdrawals, balance inquiries, and transfer money between accounts. Each kind of account can have its own distinct PIN (personal identification number). Using object-oriented design and programming, design and build **CheckingAccount** and **SavingsAccount** classes, and store any common attributes in a **BankAccount** superclass. Define methods for making deposits, withdrawals, balance inquiries, and transfers. A method should never permit an account balance to go below $0.00.

When you have built and tested your **BankAccount** hierarchy, write a program that behaves like an ATM (automated teller machine). Have your program store **BankAccount** handles in an array or **ArrayList**, and use an account's index as the account number. In lieu of an ATM card, have a customer begin a session by entering his or her account number and PIN; then display menus and let the customer choose what he or she wants to do, just as a real ATM does.

13.3 *2-3 Person Group Project*. A regular polygon is a polygon whose sides all have the same length, and whose corners all have the same angles. For example, an equilateral triangle and a square are both regular polygons. Build a **RegularPolygon** class that is a subclass of the **Polygon** class in Figure 13-9, and revise class **Square** to be a subclass of **RegularPolygon**. Then build the following classes as subclasses of **RegularPolygon**: **EquilateralTriangle**, **RegularPentagon**, and **RegularHexagon**. Using these shapes, write a program that draws your group's unique logo.

13.4 The city pet office wants to upgrade their pet-license software. The city licenses the following pets:

dogs, $10.00	cats, $5.00
birds, $5.00	fish, $1.00

Build a **PetLicense** class hierarchy, with **DogLicense**, **CatLicense**, **BirdLicense**, and **FishLicense** subclasses. The **PetLicense** class should have instance variables **myName** and **myOwner** (both strings), accessors for them, a **toString()** method that produces a string representation of a license (including its kind, name, owner, fee paid, and space for an official signature), and an abstract **getFee()** method that each subclass defines to return the appropriate fee.

When you have built and tested the **PetLicense** hierarchy, write a program that lets users choose a kind of license, and enter their pet's name and their name. The program should then open a text file and print a license for that pet to the file.

13.5 *2-3 Person Group Project*. Temperatures can be measured in the Fahrenheit scale, the Celsius scale, or the Kelvin scale. Build a **Temperature** class hierarchy, with **FahrenheitTemperature**, **CelsiusTemperature**, and **KelvinTemperature** subclasses. In addition to constructors, each kind of temperature should respond to the following messages:

- **getDegrees()** returns this temperature's number of degrees,
- **getScale()** returns this temperature's scale,
- **inFahrenheit()** returns the equivalent of this temperature in the Fahrenheit scale,
- **inCelsius()** returns the equivalent of this temperature in the Celsius scale,
- **inKelvin()** returns the equivalent of this temperature in the Kelvin scale,
- **toString()** returns a string representation of this temperature (for example, **0.0 C**),
- **read(Scanner *in*)** fills this temperature with a value from ***in***,
- **compareTo(Temperature anotherTemp)** returns 0 if this temperature is equal to **anotherTemp**, a negative value if this temperature is less than **anotherTemp**, and a positive value if this temperature is greater than **anotherTemp**. (Hint: 0° C is equal to 32° F.)

Using the **Temperature** hierarchy, write a temperature converter program that lets the user specify the scale he or she wants to convert from, enter a temperature from that scale, and then display that temperature in all three scales.

13.6 Your local pizza shop has hired you to write a program that they can use to take pizza orders. Every pizza comes with sauce and cheese, and customers can add up to twelve extra toppings (pepperoni, sausage, ham, bacon, mushrooms, onion, green peppers, hot peppers, green olives, black olives, pineapple, or anchovies). The shop sells the following kinds of pizzas:

- four-slice personal pizzas for $4, extra toppings are $0.25 each
- eight-slice medium pizzas for $8, extra toppings are $0.50 each
- ten-slice large pizzas for $10, extra toppings are $0.75 each
- twelve-slice extra large pizzas for $12, extra toppings are $1.00 each

Build a **Pizza** class hierarchy, with each kind of pizza as a subclass. Store each pizza's toppings in a linked list, and define a **getToppings()** method to access it. Define an **addTopping()** method to add a topping to a pizza. Declare an abstract method **Pizza#getToppingPrice()**, which each subclass defines appropriately.

Define a **getPrice()** method that returns the total cost of a pizza, including its toppings. The **toString()** method should return a full description of a pizza, including its size, its number of slices, its toppings, and its total cost.

When the **Pizza** hierarchy is built and tested, write a menu-driven program that the shop's customers can use to order one or more pizzas. For each pizza, the program should let the customer select its size, and choose its toppings. The program should display a running total after each choice, and should display a summary of the order when the customer is finished.

13.7 2-3 *Person Group Project*. Among other things, geologists study different kinds of rock, including basalt, chalk, granite, limestone, marble, obsidian, quartzite, sandstone, shale, and slate. Every kind of rock has *hardness* and *density* attributes. Igneous rocks have a *texture* attribute (glassy, fine, medium, or coarse); sedimentary rocks have a *particleKind* attribute (clastic, chemical, or organic); and metamorphic rocks have a *madeFrom* attribute that indicates the kind of rock from which they were made (for example, marble is made from limestone). Design classes for the ten kinds of rock listed above; design **Igneous**, **Sedimentary**, and **Metamorphic** superclasses to consolidate their common attributes, and design a **Rock** superclass that consolidates the attributes that are common to all rocks. Then build these classes, and write a program that repeatedly displays a menu of these ten rocks, reads the user's choice, and then prints the available information for that kind of rock.

13.8 For each of the shapes in the **Shape** class hierarchy given in Figure 13-4, define a **read(Scanner)** method that will fill that shape with data from a **Scanner**. Then write a program that, using the **Class** class, reads and draws a series of shapes from a text file. For example, if the text file contains the following lines:

```
Circle     5        4        3
Square     5        4        6
```

then the program should draw a circle centered at (5,4) whose radius is 3; and draw a square centered at (5,4) whose edges are length 6. Create text files containing several different logos, and use your program to display them.

13.9 2-3 *Person Group Project*. The company Tables-R-Us sells tables, and has hired your group to design and build a **Table** class hierarchy. Visit some local furniture stores, and write down each different kind of table they sell. (For example, *4-legged dining tables*, *pedestal dining tables*, *trestle dining tables*, *coffee tables*, *end tables*, *patio tables*, and so on.) Ask to look at the store's catalog, and note the kinds of characteristics that are recorded for the different kinds of tables. (For example, *height*, *width*, *length*, *material*, *finish*, and so on.) Take special note of what characteristics different tables have in common, as opposed to those that are unique to a particular kind of table. Using this information, design a class for each kind of table. Design superclasses to store common attributes (for example, **DiningTable**, **EndTable**, **PatioTable**), until you reach a **Table** superclass. Then build and thoroughly test your **Table** class hierarchy.

13.10 *All-Class Project*. The Periodic table allows the chemical properties of the elements to be predicted from their position within the table. Each element has a name (for example, Helium), a symbol (He), an atomic number (2), and an atomic weight (4.002602). Within the Periodic table, an element's row or *period* denotes how many electron shells it has, and an element's column or *group* denotes the number of electrons in its outermost shell. An element's group determines the elements with which it will react. There are 18 groups, and 118 elements.

This project is to build an **`Element`** class hierarchy, and use this hierarchy to build a **`PeriodicTable`** class. Each different element should respond to the following messages: **`getName()`**, **`getSymbol()`**, **`getNumber()`**, **`getWeight()`**, **`getGroup()`**, and **`toString()`**. Your instructor will assign you one or more groups to build, to spread the work among your classmates.

Chapter 14
Events and GUIs

At times the world can seem an unfriendly and sinister place. But believe us when we say there is much more good in it than bad. And what might seem to be a series of unfortunate events, may in fact, be the first steps of a journey.

VIOLET BAUDELAIRE (EMILY BROWNING), IN *LEMONY SNICKET'S A SERIES OF UNFORTUNATE EVENTS*

Huge events take place on this earth every day. Earthquakes, hurricanes, even glaciers move. So why couldn't he just look at me?

ANGELA (CLAIRE DANES), IN *MY SO-CALLED LIFE*

I will be a good listener to you if that's what you want... I won't judge you.

JIM KURRING (JOHN C. REILLY), IN *MAGNOLIA*

Go! I'll handle him!

JEAN GREY (FAMKE JANSSEN), IN *X2*

Oh, there's really no need, Mrs. Parr. I can totally handle anything this baby can dish out. Can't I, little baby? Who can handle it? Who can handle it?

KARI THE BABYSITTER (BRET 'BROOK' PARKER) IN *THE INCREDIBLES*

Objectives

Upon completion of this chapter, you should be able to:

- ❑ Use Java's event classes to model user events
- ❑ Design and build listener classes to handle user events
- ❑ Design and build applications that have simple graphical user interfaces (GUIs)

In Chapter 6, we saw that programmers use the term **event** to describe interesting occurrences that happen while a program is running. Such events include mouse clicks, key presses, a variable's value changing, and so on.

We also saw how to write an Alice program that responds to specific events. By writing methods containing the behavior we wanted to occur in response to the event, and then associating that method with the event, we saw how to *handle* events in Alice. Such methods were called **handlers**, and the resulting programs were called **event-driven programs**.

In this chapter, we will learn how to write event-driven programs in Java, how to build graphical user interfaces (GUIs), and how to handle the events they generate.

14.1 Introduction: Miles to Kilometers and Vice Versa

Suppose you have two friends: one who is a U.S. citizen, and one who is from a country where distances are measured in kilometers. Your friends plan to tour each other's countries together. To help them, they ask you to write a program that they can use to convert miles to kilometers and vice versa. After talking it over with them, you arrive at this user story:

> The program should open a window, and display two boxes, one labeled "Miles:" and one labeled "Kilometers:". If the user types a number in the box labeled "Miles:", the program should display the equivalent number of kilometers in the box labeled "Kilometers:". If the user types a number in the box labeled "Kilometers:", the program should display the equivalent number of miles in the box labeled "Miles:". To quit the program, the user should click the Close button in the upper-right corner of the window, like any other window-based application.

To make sure that you and your friends are thinking the same way, you sketch how the program will appear when it starts running, as shown in Figure 14-1.

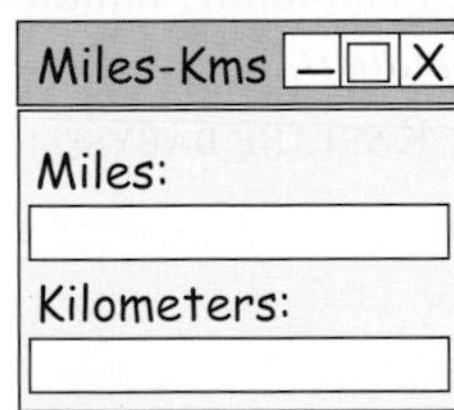

FIGURE 14-1 A storyboard

As indicated by the caption of Figure 14-1, this sketch is a **storyboard** — a drawing that we can show the program's users to ensure that it meets their expectations. Storyboards are a very important design tool in building window-based applications, as they let us get quick feedback from a program's users, before we invest time and effort in programming.

When we draw a storyboard like the one shown in Figure 14-1, we are really sketching the graphical elements (windows, labels, boxes, and so on) through which the program and its user will interact. Programmers say that such a program provides a **graphical user interface (GUI)** through which its users can interact with it.

Once we and our friends agree on the program's GUI, the next step is to sketch out its behavior. Figure 14-2 shows how the GUI will change in response to a user's actions:

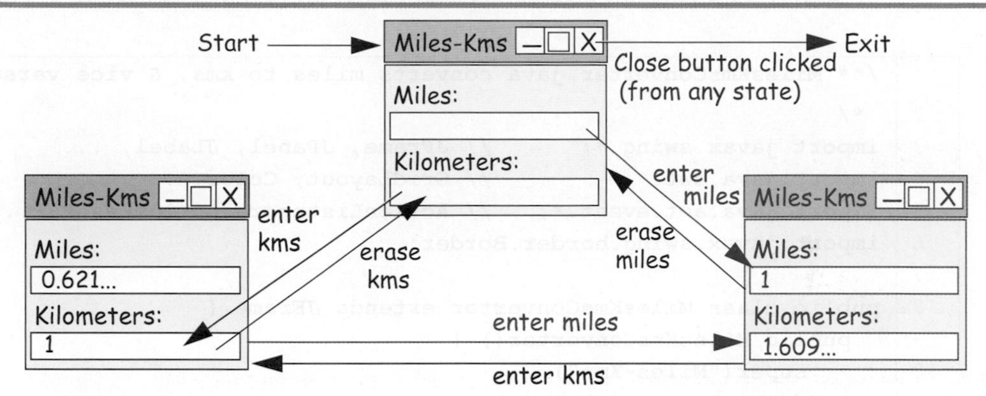

FIGURE 14-2 A transition diagram

We have color-coded the changes in Figure 14-2, to clarify which user actions trigger specific changes. When the program starts, the "Miles:" and "Kilometers:" boxes are both empty. If the user enters a number in the "Miles:" box, the program computes the number of kilometers and displays it in the "Kilometers:" box (shown in green). If the user enters a number in the "Kilometers:" box, the program computes the number of miles and displays it in the "Miles:" box (shown in blue).

Figure 14-2 is called a **transition diagram**, because it shows the transitions or changes that occur in the GUI, in response to the user's actions. Transition diagrams are another important tool in building window-based applications, because the user actions that trigger changes in the GUI correspond to the user events that the program must handle. For example, Figure 14-2 shows us that there are three user events that our program must handle:

- The user clicks the window's Close button
- The user enters a number in the "Miles:" text box
- The user enters a number in the "Kilometers:" text box

As an object-oriented language, Java provides classes for the graphical components that an application can use to build a GUI. For example, the "Miles:" and "Kilometers:" boxes are built using Java's **`JTextField`** class, and the labels for these boxes are built using its **`JLabel`** class. Likewise, Java stores event handlers in classes called **`Listeners`**. To convert miles to kilometers, and vice versa, we can write **`Listeners`** that use these formulas:

$$milesToKms(miles) = miles \times 1.609344$$

$$kmsToMiles(kms) = kms \times 0.621371192$$

Figure 14-3 presents a complete application that solves our friends' problem.

```
/** MilesKmsConverter.java converts miles to kms, & vice versa.
 */
import javax.swing.*;       // JFrame, JPanel, JLabel, ...
import java.awt.*;          // GridLayout, Color, ...
import java.awt.event.*;    // ActionListener, ActionEvent, ...
import javax.swing.border.Border;

public class MilesKmsConverter extends JFrame {
  public MilesKmsConverter() {
     super("Miles-Kms");
     // build control panel
     JPanel controlPanel = new JPanel( new GridLayout(4, 1) );
     Border gap = BorderFactory.createEmptyBorder(5,5,5,5);
     controlPanel.setBorder(gap);
     // add labels and boxes to control panel
     controlPanel.add( new JLabel("Miles:") );
     myMilesBox = new JTextField(16);
     controlPanel.add(myMilesBox);
     controlPanel.add( new JLabel("Kilometers:") );
     myKmsBox = new JTextField(16);
     controlPanel.add(myKmsBox);
     // set content pane; add listeners
     super.setContentPane(controlPanel);
     super.setDefaultCloseOperation(JFrame.EXIT_ON_CLOSE);
     myMilesBox.addActionListener( new MilesListener() );
     myKmsBox.addActionListener( new KmsListener() );
  }

  private class MilesListener implements ActionListener {
     public void actionPerformed(ActionEvent event) {
        final double CONVERSION_FACTOR = 1.609344;
        String milesString = myMilesBox.getText();
        String kmString = null;
        if ( milesString != null && !milesString.equals("") ) {
           double miles = Double.valueOf(milesString);
           double kms = miles * CONVERSION_FACTOR;
```

continued

```
            kmString = new Double(kms).toString();
         } else {
            kmString = "";
         }
         myKmsBox.setText(kmString);
      }
   }

   private class KmsListener implements ActionListener {
      public void actionPerformed(ActionEvent event) {
         final double CONVERSION_FACTOR = 0.621371192;
         String kmString = myKmsBox.getText();
         String milesString = null;
         if ( kmString != null && !kmString.equals("") ) {
            double kms = Double.valueOf(kmString);
            double miles = kms * CONVERSION_FACTOR;
            milesString = new Double(miles).toString();
         } else {
            milesString = "";
         }
         myMilesBox.setText(milesString);
      }
   }

   private JTextField myMilesBox = null;
   private JTextField myKmsBox = null;
   private static final long serialVersionUID = 1L;

   public static void main(String[] args) {
      MilesKmsConverter self = new MilesKmsConverter();
      self.pack();
      self.setVisible(true);
   }
}
```

Result:

Miles-Kms | Miles: | Kilometers: → type a number → Miles-Kms | Miles: 1.0 | Kilometers: → press Enter → Miles-Kms | Miles: 1.0 | Kilometers: 1.609344

continued

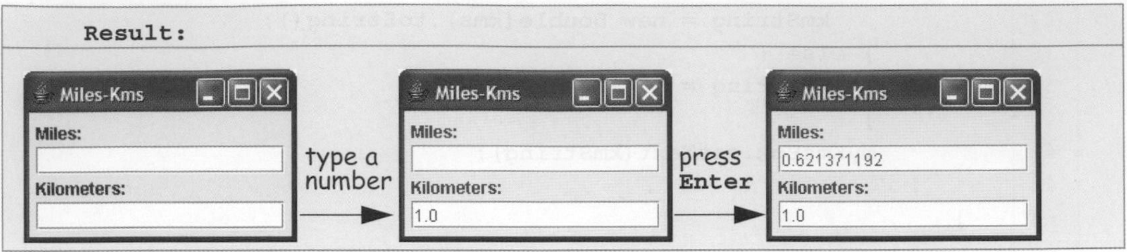

FIGURE 14-3 `MilesKmsConverter.java`

In the next section, we examine **`MilesKmsConverter`** piece by piece.

14.2 Java GUI Components, Events, and Listeners

The program in Figure 14-3 consists of four distinct pieces:

- The **`MilesKmsConverter`** constructor (lines 9-27), which constructs the GUI
- The **`MilesListener`** class (lines 29-43), which handles user events in the "Miles:" box
- The **`KmsListener`** class (lines 45-59), which handles user events in the "Kilometers:" box
- The **`main()`** method (lines 65-69), where flow begins when the program is run

In the rest of this section, we examine each of these pieces in detail.

14.2.1 The `main()` Method

The application's **`main()`** method is quite short, as can be seen on lines 65-69 of Figure 14-3:

```
public static void main(String[] args) {
    MilesKmsConverter self = new MilesKmsConverter();
    self.pack();
    self.setVisible(true);
}
```

This method may be confusing, as it seemingly just builds an object, sends that object **`pack()`** and **`setVisible()`** messages, and then terminates. Or does it?

Thanks to Java and event-driven programming, the answer is "no." That is, the first statement does indeed use the class constructor to create a **`MilesKmsConverter`** object, and store a reference to it in a handle named **`self`**. As we shall see shortly, this constructor builds the application's GUI, which resides in a window called a **`JFrame`**.

The second statement — the **`pack()`** message — tells the GUI's window to resize itself to the minimum size needed to display the graphical components it contains.

Similar to an Alice object, a Java graphical object has a **`boolean`** property we will call *isVisible*, that determines whether or not that object can be seen. By default, a **`JFrame`** is not visible, so our **`main()`** method then sends **`self`** the message

setVisible(true). By changing *isVisible* from **false** to **true**, the final statement makes the application's GUI appear.

Thanks to the Java Runtime Environment (JRE), this is all our **main()** method has to do! Once the statements in the **main()** method have constructed the GUI, the JRE takes over. Very simplistically, we can visualize the JRE as behaving something like this:

```
while (true) {
    Event event = getNextEvent();
    if ( event == QUIT ) { System.exit(0); }
    else { event.getSource().getListener().runHandler(); }
}
```

That is, the JRE waits for the user to generate an event. When he or she does, the JRE checks to see if it was a **QUIT** event. If so, it terminates the program; otherwise, it runs the handler in the listener associated with that event. Because it does all of these things inside an infinite loop, JRE keeps maintaining the GUI, getting the events it generates, and running the application's event handlers, until the user generates a **QUIT** event.

14.2.2 GUI Components

Java provides a variety of components for building GUIs. Figure 14-4 shows some of the components provided in the package **javax.swing**.

GUI Component	Description	Event/Listener
JFrame	A window	various
JPanel	A window pane	**Mouse**
JLabel	A character string	
JTextField	A single-line box for text	**Action**
JTextArea	A multi-line box for text	
JButton	A clickable button	**Action**
JCheckBox	A clickable box; many can be checked at once	**Item**
JRadioButton	A clickable button; only one can be checked	**Action**
JComboBox	A box containing a drop-down menu	**Action**
JSlider	A clickable sliding scale	**Change**
JSpinner	A box for displaying a value from a range, with increment/decrement buttons	**Change**
JTabbedPane	A pane with clickable "notebook" tabs	

continued

GUI Component	Description	Event/Listener
JMenuBar, **JMenu**, **JMenuItem**	A menu bar	**Action**
JOptionPane	Alert & message dialog boxes	
JFileChooser	Dialog boxes to open or save files	

FIGURE 14-4 Some of the **javax.swing** components

The program in Figure 14-3 uses some of these components, as illustrated in Figure 14-5.

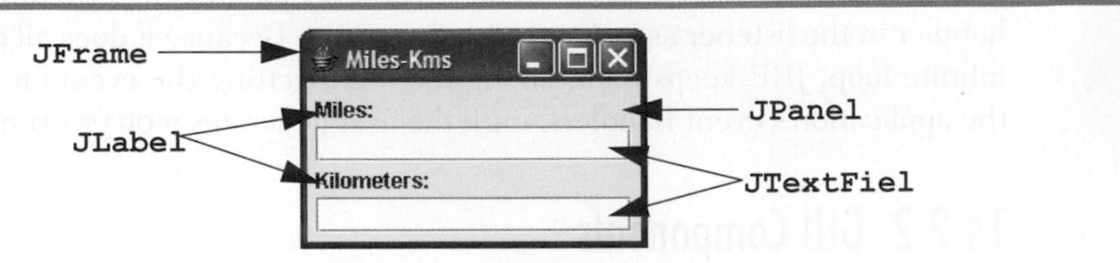

FIGURE 14-5 Some **swing** components in **MilesKmsConverter.java**

The **JFrame** Class

The first step in building a GUI like the one shown in Figure 14-3 is to declare its class to be a subclass of **JFrame**, as can be seen on line 8:

```
public class MilesKmsConverter extends JFrame {
```

By default, a **JFrame** is a window that includes a title bar and a border, plus any other standard window features, such as buttons to minimize, maximize, and close the window. Figure 14-5 shows a **JFrame** as it appears in the Microsoft Windows XP operating system; when run on computers running MacOS or Linux, the same **JFrame** will appear as a normal window on those systems (quite different from the one in Figure 14-5).[1]

As a subclass of **JFrame**, a **MilesKmsConverter** *is a* **JFrame**, inheriting all of its characteristics. Thus, when the program builds a **MilesKmsConverter** object on line 66:

```
MilesKmsConverter self = new MilesKmsConverter();
```

the effect is to create a new, specialized kind of **JFrame**, the details of which are specified by the **MilesKmsConverter** constructor.

1. To give an application an identical appearance on different operating systems, use Java's **UIManager** class: **UIManager.setLookAndFeel(UIManager.getCrossPlatformLookAndFeelClassName());**

Build a program's GUI in the constructor of a subclass of `JFrame`.

Lines 9-27 of Figure 14-3 define the **`MilesKmsConverter`** constructor. On line 10, this constructor begins by invoking the superclass constructor to initialize the attributes that **`MilesKmsConverter`** inherits from **`JFrame`**:

```
super("Miles-Kms");
```

As detailed in the Java API, there are several **`JFrame`** constructors. Line 10 uses one that accepts the frame's title-string as an argument. This is what causes the title **`Miles-Kms`** to appear in the title bar in Figure 14-5. Without it, no title would be displayed.

The constructor of a subclass of `JFrame` should always use `super()` to invoke one of the `JFrame` constructors, to initialize the inherited attributes.

A GUI application's constructor is responsible for building the GUI, so after the superclass constructor has been invoked, the rest of the constructor decorates the new window with the graphical components needed to solve the problem.

The `JPanel` Class

If a **`JFrame`** corresponds to a window, a **`JPanel`** corresponds to a window pane. The GUI shown in Figure 14-5 has just one pane, which is defined in lines 12-14 of Figure 14-3. Line 12 begins by building a **`JPanel`** object, with a handle named **`controlPanel`**:

```
JPanel controlPanel = new JPanel( new GridLayout(4, 1) );
```

There are several different **`JPanel`** constructors listed in the Java API. In line 12, we are using one that takes as an argument a **layout manager** — an object that determines how graphical components will subsequently be "laid out" on the pane. The **`JLabel`**s and **`JTextField`**s shown in Figure 14-5 form a grid consisting of 4 rows and 1 column, so we use a layout manager called **`GridLayout`**, and pass to it the number of rows and columns we need.

Layout Managers

Java provides a variety of different layout managers, including those listed in Figure 14-6.

Layout Manager	Lay Out Components In ...
`GridLayout(r,c)`	a grid of *`r`* rows and *`c`* columns
`FlowLayout()`	a single, flowing row (the default for a `JPanel`)

continued

Layout Manager	Lay Out Components In ...
`BorderLayout()`	any of five areas: **`TOP`**, **`BOTTOM`**, **`LEFT`**, **`RIGHT`**, or **`CENTER`**
`BoxLayout(pane, axis)`	a row (`axis == X_AXIS`) or a column (`axis == Y_AXIS`)
`CardLayout()`	a panel that can display different things at different times
`SpringLayout()`	a flexible arrangement of edge-relationships to one another
`GridBagLayout()`	a flexible grid of cells that can vary in width and height

FIGURE 14-6 Some of Java's layout managers

After a **`JPanel`** has been constructed, a graphical component can be added to it by sending it the message **`add(component)`**. A layout manager determines exactly what happens when the **`JPanel`** receives such a message, since it determines how the graphical components are positioned within the pane.

To illustrate, a **`GridLayout`** places graphical components in the grid's cells from left-to-right and top-to-bottom, starting at the top-left cell. We are using a 4-row, 1-column **`GridLayout`**, so the first component we add will be placed at the top row, the second component we add will appear underneath it, the next component will appear beneath the second, and so on, as indicated in Figure 14-7.

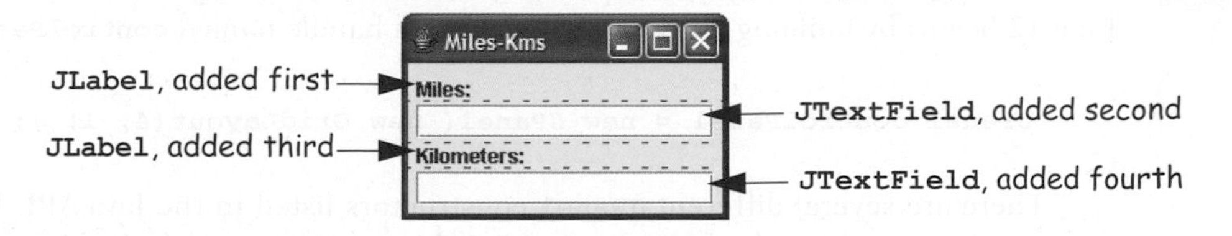

FIGURE 14-7 Adding components to a **`JPanel`** using a **`GridLayout`**

Borders

By default, graphical components that are added to a **`JPanel`** are placed at the edge of the pane. For example, if we just start adding graphical components to the **`JPanel`**, it will appear as shown in Figure 14-8.

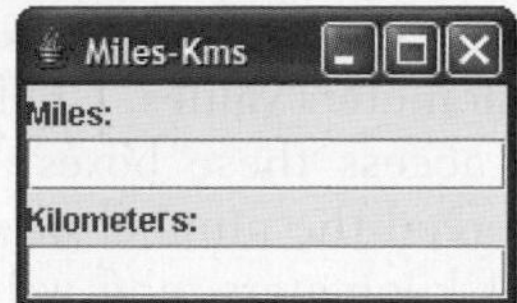

FIGURE 14-8 Our GUI with no border

The GUI in Figure 14-8 isn't awful, but the extra space at the edge of the one in Figure 14-7 makes it more aesthetically pleasing. To add such space at the edges of a **JPanel**, we can build a **Border** object, and then tell our **JPanel** to use that object as its border.

Line 13 of Figure 14-3 shows how to build an empty **Border** object:

```
Border gap = BorderFactory.createEmptyBorder(5,5,5,5);
```

This statement creates an empty border of **5** pixels (picture elements — the tiny dots that make up the picture on your computer's screen) on each side. Java's **BorderFactory** class also provides methods to build borders with lines, beveled edges, titles, and so on.

Line 14 of Figure 14-3 then tells our **JPanel** to use this object as its border:

```
controlPanel.setBorder(gap);
```

Now that our **JPanel** is ready, we can begin adding graphical components to it.

The JLabel Component

The topmost graphical component in Figure 14-1 is a **JLabel**. Since this **JLabel** never changes, our program does not need a handle to it. As a result, we can create and add it to the GUI in the same statement, as shown on line 16 of Figure 14-3.

```
controlPanel.add( new JLabel("Miles:") );
```

This statement invokes a **JLabel** constructor, passing it the string **"Miles:"**. The resulting label is then passed as an argument to the **add()** message, which adds this label to the pane. Since our pane has a 4-row, 1-column grid layout, and this label is the first thing we've added, this label appears in the top row of the pane.

Line 19 of Figure 14-3 uses this same approach to add the **"Kilometers:"** label as the third graphical component in our pane.

If, after creating a **JLabel**, an application needs to change the label's text (for example, in response to an event), this can be done using the **setText()** message. To do so, the program should define an instance variable that is a handle to that **JLabel**, as we will demonstrate in Section 14.3. The various **JLabel** methods are described in the Java API.

The `JTextField` Component

As described previously, we can use Java's **`JTextField`** class to build the boxes where the user will enter miles or kilometers values. Unlike our GUI's labels, the event handlers we write later will need to access these boxes. For example, the event handler for the "Miles:" box will need to read the number of miles from the "Miles:" box, calculate the corresponding number of kilometers, and write that number to the "Kilometers:" box. Since both the constructor and the event handler will need to access these boxes, we declare **`JTextField`** instance variables on lines 61 and 62 of Figure 14-3:

```
private JTextField myMilesBox = null;
private JTextField myKmsBox = null;
```

We initialize these handles using a **`JTextField`** constructor on lines 17 and 20:

```
myMilesBox = new JTextField(16);
...
myKmsBox = new JTextField(16);
```

This particular constructor lets us specify the number of columns or spaces in the **`JTextField`**. Since we are converting potentially large real numbers, we choose a number that will let us display large numbers and many decimal places.

Once we have built a **`JTextField`**, it can be added to the pane using the **`add()`** message, as can be seen on lines 18 and 21:

```
controlPanel.add(myMilesBox);
...
controlPanel.add(myKmsBox);
```

We have now decorated a **`JPanel`** with all the graphical components needed to build our GUI. The next step is to make that **`JPanel`** a part of the **`JFrame`** that is our GUI's window.

Setting the Content Pane

A **`JFrame`** has a number of different panes, most of which we can safely ignore. However, the pane on which graphical components appear is called the **content pane**, so the next step in building our GUI's appearance is to make the **`JPanel`** containing our graphical components the **`JFrame`**'s content pane. This can be accomplished using the **`JFrame#setContentPane()`** method, as shown on line 23:

```
super.setContentPane(controlPanel);
```

Note that by sending the **`setContentPane()`** message to **`super`**, our application sends the message to **`JFrame`**, its superclass. Strictly speaking, the "**`super.`**" notation can be omitted. However, we prefer to include it so as to clearly indicate that this is an inherited method.

There is another way to build GUIs that you will see in examples on the Internet. Instead of decorating a **JPanel** with graphical components and then using **setContentPane()** to make that **JPanel** the **JFrame**'s content pane, the other way is to use the **getContentPane()** message to retrieve the **JFrame**'s original content pane:

```
Container contentPane = super.getContentPane();
```

Graphical components can then be added to **contentPane** using **add()** messages, just as one would add them to a **JPanel**. This approach works, but it has some limitations. For example, it is possible to draw lines, ovals, rectangles, and other things on a **JPanel** subclass, which can then be used as the content pane; but we cannot draw on the **Container** returned by the **getContentPane()** message. To avoid such limitations, we prefer to decorate a **JPanel**, and then use the **setContentPane()** method to make it our **JFrame**'s content pane.

The QUIT Event

If, having written this much, we run our program, it will build and display our program's GUI. However, by default, the Close button on a **JFrame** *hides* the window, as opposed to terminating the application. That is, clicking the window's Close button will make the window disappear, but the program will continue to run, leaving no obvious way to terminate it.[2] Line 24 of Figure 14-3 addresses this problem:

```
super.setDefaultCloseOperation(JFrame.EXIT_ON_CLOSE);
```

The **setDefaultCloseOperation()** method lets us specify what happens when the window's Close button is clicked. Besides **EXIT_ON_CLOSE**, the **JFrame** class also defines the constants **HIDE_ON_CLOSE**, **DO_NOTHING_ON_CLOSE**, and **DISPOSE_ON_CLOSE**.

With this statement in place, we can run our program and terminate it by clicking its Close button. This allows us to show it to our friends who will be using it, get their feedback, and make any corrections or modifications they suggest, before proceeding further.

Registering Event Handlers

Once our users are satisfied with the GUI's appearance, our last step is to register event handlers with our **JTextFrame**s. When the user presses the **Enter** key in a **JTextField**, the JRE generates an event called an **ActionEvent**, as shown in Figure 14-4. An **ActionEvent** must be handled by an object called an **ActionListener**. To inform a **JTextField** what **ActionListener** will be handling its events, we send it the **addActionListener()** message, as can be seen on lines 25 and 26 of Figure 14-3:

```
myMilesBox.addActionListener( new MilesListener() );
myKmsBox.addActionListener( new KmsListener() );
```

2. To terminate such a program from Eclipse, click the red "Terminate" button on the title bar of the *problems and output area*. To terminate a program from Windows, right-click the taskbar, choose **Task Manager**, click the **Applications** tab, select your application in the list, and click the **End Task** button. To terminate a program in MacOS X, choose **Force Quit** from the Apple menu, select your application, and click the **Force Quit** button. In Linux, enter **ps** on the command line; find your process's ***idNumber***; and enter **kill -9 *idNumber***.

The first statement constructs a **MilesListener** object (see Section 14.2.3, below), and passes it to **myMilesBox**, which will register it as the listener for events it generates. In essence, this statement creates an object and then tells the "Miles:" **JTextField** that any events it generates will be handled by that object.

The second statement is similar, constructing a **KmsListener** object (see below), and registering it as the listener for any events generated by the "Kilometers:" box. We are thus telling the "Kilometers:" **JTextField** that this **KmsListener** object will handle any events it generates.

The **addActionListener()** message can be sent to any of the graphical components listed in Figure 14-4 that generate **ActionEvent**s.

Miscellaneous

Before we see how to build the listener classes that will handle the events generated by our two **JTextField**s, let's take just a moment to see what would happen if we had done things differently in building our GUI.

Suppose that, on line 12 of Figure 14-3, we had used a 2-row, 2-column grid layout:

```
JPanel controlPanel = new JPanel( new GridLayout(2, 2) );
```

Then our graphical components would be laid out in a 2-by-2 grid, as shown in Figure 14-9.

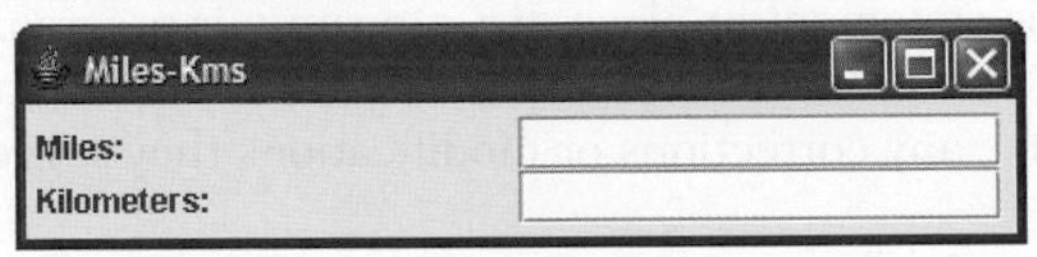

FIGURE 14-9 Our GUI using a 2-by-2 grid layout

As can be seen in Figure 14-9, a **GridLayout** gives each cell the same amount of space, and a **JLabel** by default left-justifies its label within that space. To right-justify the label within its space, we can use a different **JLabel** constructor on line 16:

```
controlPanel.add( new JLabel("Miles:", SwingConstants.RIGHT) );
```

This constructor lets us specify how a label will be justified. Java's **SwingConstants** class declares a variety of constants, including **LEFT**, **RIGHT**, **CENTERED**, **LEADING**, or **TRAILING**, that can be used to control a label's justification. If we construct both of the labels this way, the GUI changes as shown in Figure 14-10.

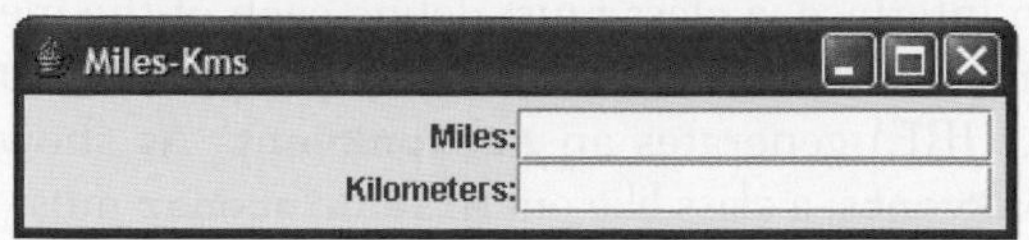

FIGURE 14-10 Labels right-justified within a 2-by-2 grid layout

The extra space to the left of each label seems awkward; this is due to our using a **GridLayout**, which makes each cell the same size; plus the 16-column size of our **JTextFields**. However, if we reduce the size of the **JTextFields** too much, they will have insufficient room to display large numbers with many decimal places. This is the reason we used the 4-by-1 grid instead of a 2-by-2 grid.

14.2.3 Events

As indicated in Figure 14-4, some GUI components can generate events. For example, an **ActionEvent** is generated when the **Enter** key is pressed in a **JTextField**, when the mouse is clicked on a **JButton** or **JRadioButton**, or when a **JMenuItem** is selected with the mouse. By contrast, an **ItemEvent** is generated when the mouse is clicked on a **JCheckBox**, and a **ChangeEvent** is generated when the mouse is clicked on a **JSlider** or **JSpinner**.

Each different kind of event is handled by a different kind of listener. Figure 14-11 lists the various listeners and event handlers for each kind of event.

Event	Listener	Handler Method
ActionEvent	ActionListener	actionPerformed()
ItemEvent	ItemListener	itemStateChanged()
ChangeEvent	ChangeListener	stateChanged()
KeyEvent	KeyListener	keyPressed() keyReleased() keyTyped()
MouseListener	MouseEvent	mouseClicked() mouseEntered() mouseExited() mousePressed() mouseReleased()
MouseMotionListener	MouseEvent	mouseDragged() mouseMoved()

FIGURE 14-11 Listeners and their handler methods

Java's listeners are *interfaces* that a class must *implement* in order to handle events. To implement an interface, a class must define each of the methods the interface declares.

For example, when the **Enter** key is pressed in a **JTextField**, the Java Runtime Environment (JRE) generates an **ActionEvent**. As shown in Figure 14-11, in order to handle **ActionEvent**s, a class like our **MilesListener** must implement the **ActionListener** interface. To do so, it must define the **actionPerformed()** method, as given on lines 29-43 of Figure 14-3:

```
private class MilesListener implements ActionListener {
   public void actionPerformed(ActionEvent event) {
      // ... statements to handle event go here...
   }
}
```

This **actionPerformed()** method will then be used as the handler for **ActionEvent**s generated by the **JTextField**. More precisely, when the **Enter** key is pressed in the **JTextField**, the JRE will generate an **ActionEvent** describing that event, and send the **actionPerformed()** message to the **ActionListener** registered for that **JTextField**, with the **ActionEvent** as an argument. Figure 14-12 presents a visualization of these steps.

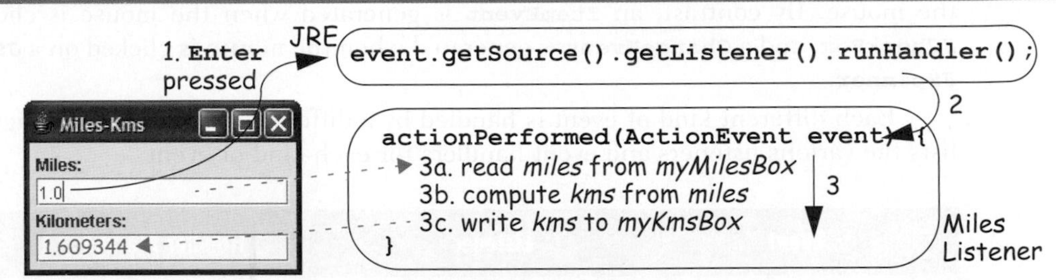

FIGURE 14-12 Handling an event from **myMilesBox**

Since **actionPerformed()** will be invoked when the user presses the **Enter** key, the statements in **actionPerformed()** must perform the work of converting the miles value to the corresponding kilometers value. To do so, the method must retrieve the contents of the "Miles:" box, convert that string to a number, compute the number of kilometers corresponding to that number, convert the number of kilometers into a string, and write that string to the "Kilometers:" box:

```
private class MilesListener implements ActionListener {
  public void actionPerformed(ActionEvent event) {
       final double CONVERSION_FACTOR = 1.609344;
       String milesString = myMilesBox.getText();
       String kmString = null;
       if ( milesString != null && !milesString.equals("") ) {
          double miles = Double.valueOf(milesString);
          double kms = miles * CONVERSION_FACTOR;
          kmString = new Double(kms).toString();
       } else {
          kmString = "";
       }
       myKmsBox.setText(kmString);
  }
}
```

To retrieve the contents of the "Miles:" box, the handler sends **myMilesBox** the **getText()** message, which returns the **JTextField**'s contents as a string. If this retrieves a non-**null** and non-empty string, the handler uses the **Double** class to convert that string to a **double** value, computes the equivalent number of kilometers, and then uses the **Double** class again to convert the number of kilometers into a string we call **kmString**. It then sends **myKmsBox** the **setText()** message to change its contents to **kmString**.

The user could press **Enter** in the "Miles:" box without typing a number, or could erase a number in the box and then press **Enter**. In either case, nothing should be displayed in the "Kilometers:" box. To accomplish this, line 34 of Figure 14-3 sets **kmString** to the empty string if **myMilesBox.getText()** returns **null** or the empty string. Line 41 then sets **myKmsBox** to this empty string.

The **KmsListener** class that handles events from the "Kilometers:" box is complementary to the **MilesListener** class, as can be seen on lines 45-59 of Figure 14-3:

```
private class KmsListener implements ActionListener {
   public void actionPerformed(ActionEvent ae) {
       final double CONVERSION_FACTOR = 0.621371192;
       String kmString = myKmsBox.getText();
       String milesString = null;
       if ( kmString != null && !kmString.equals("") ) {
          double kms = Double.valueOf(kmString);
          double miles = kms * CONVERSION_FACTOR;
          milesString = new Double(miles).toString();
       } else {
          milesString = "";
       }
       myMilesBox.setText(milesString);
   }
}
```

Since the **MilesKmsConverter** constructor registers an instance of this class as the **ActionListener** for the "Kilometers:" box, its **actionPerformed()** method will be invoked whenever **Enter** is pressed in that **JTextField**. Figure 14-13 provides a visualization of what occurs.

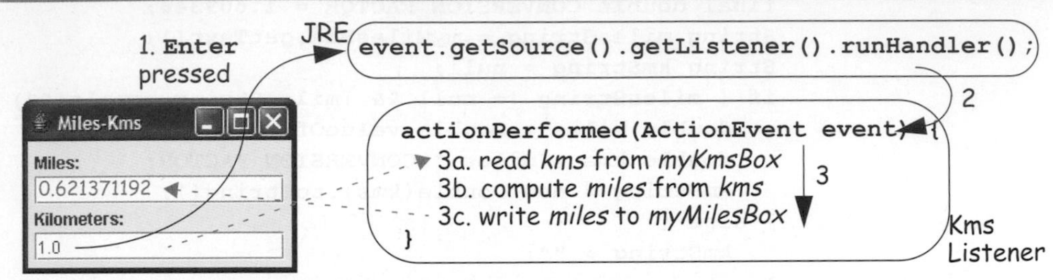

FIGURE 14-13 Handling an event from **myKmsBox**

In summary, handling the events generated by a graphical component involves three steps:

1. Identify what kinds of events that graphical component generates, and what kind of listener is used to handle them
2. Define a class that implements the listener's interface to handle the component's events
3. Create an instance of that class, and register it as the listener for the graphical component

Using the ActionEvent Parameter

In Figure 14-3, we define a separate **ActionListener** for each graphical component, to handle the events generated by that component. This approach works very well, as it clearly indicates which class is the listener for which component.

Many of the example programs on the Internet define just one **ActionListener** for all of a program's graphical components. In this approach, the **actionPerformed()** method sends its **ActionEvent** parameter the **getSource()** message to identify the graphical component that triggered the event, and then uses an **if** statement to select the appropriate response:

```
public void actionPerformed(ActionEvent event) {
   if ( event.getSource().equals(myMilesBox) ) {
      // ... statements to convert miles to kms
   } else if ( event.getSource().equals(myKmsBox) ) {
      // ... statements to convert kms to miles
   } else {
      // ... error: throw an exception
   }
}
```

This approach works. However, unlike the approach shown in Figure 14-3, this approach tends to produce **actionPerformed()** methods that are long, complex, and harder to debug.

By instead writing a "short and sweet" listener class for each component, each **actionPerformed()** method can focus on providing the correct behavior for its own component. This reduces the length and complexity of the handler, making errors less likely, and making such errors easier to find and correct when they do occur. Any behavior that is common to different listeners can be "factored out" and placed in a separate method, which the listeners can then invoke to elicit that behavior. We will see an example of this in the next section.

14.2.4 The serialVersionUID Attribute

You may be wondering about line 63 in Figure 14-3:

```
private static final long serialVersionUID = 1L;
```

As of Java 1.5, most of Java's graphical components — including **JFrame** — implement an interface named **Serializable**, which permits objects to be transmitted across a network, written to or read from a file, and so on. The Java API strongly recommends that classes implementing this interface define a **long** instance variable named **serialVersionUID**, and set it to a unique number. When such an object is, say, transmitted across a network, the JRE will use this value to identify the kind of object that needs to be rebuilt.

We have no intention of transmitting our **MilesKmsConverter** across a network. However, it is a subclass of **JFrame**. Any time we build a subclass of **JFrame** (or any other class that implements **Serializable**) but neglect to define this variable, then many Java compilers — including Eclipse's compiler — will generate a warning:

```
The serializable class MilesKmsConverter does not declare a
static final serialVersionUID field of type long
```

By declaring the recommended instance variable, line 63 follows the Java API's recommendations and eliminates the warning. So long as we do not intend to make use of it, it can be given any value; line 63 sets it to **1L** (the literal for **1** as a **long** value).

14.3 Example 2: Using Sliders and Buttons

Suppose we have a graphic artist friend, who often deals with RGB colors. An RGB color is formed by combining different amounts of red, green, and blue, with the amount of each color being an integer from the range 0-255. An RGB color is thus a triplet giving the amounts of Red, Green, and Blue in the RGB color. Figure 14-14 lists a few RGB colors and their triplets:

RGB Color	(Red, Green, Blue) Triplet
BLACK	(0, 0, 0)
RED	(255, 0, 0)
GREEN	(0, 255, 0)
BLUE	(0, 0, 255)
YELLOW	(255, 255, 0)
MAGENTA	(255, 0, 255)
CYAN	(0, 255, 255)
WHITE	(255, 255, 255)

FIGURE 14-14 Some RGB colors

Our friend asks us to help her by writing a "ColorPicker" program that will let her view the color that results from varying the amounts of red, green, and blue in an RGB color. Her idea is to have three sliders — one for red, one for green, and one for blue — that she can slide back and forth to increase or decrease that part of the RGB color, plus numbers showing the sliders' current values. As they are changed, the sliders should set the color of a pane to the specified RGB color. Below that pane she would like to have three "quickset" buttons to quickly reset the pane's color to red, green, or blue. She sketches the GUI shown in Figure 14-15.

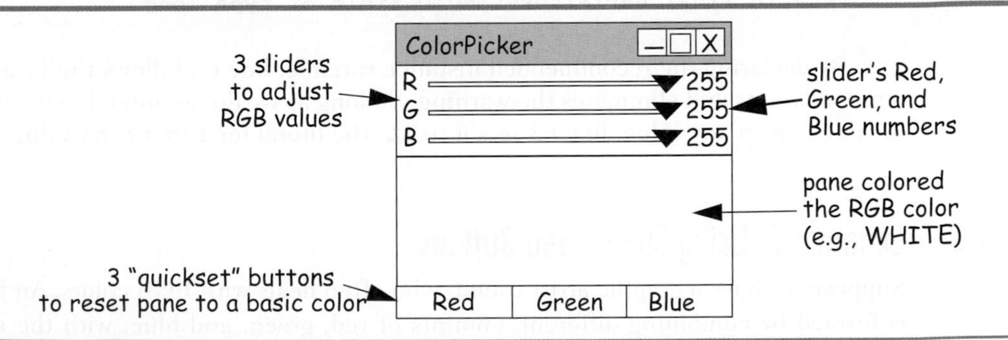

FIGURE 14-15 Storyboard for ColorPicker program

We take our friend's sketch and annotate it with the graphical components needed to build it. If we number these components from the outside-to-inside, left-to-right, and top-to-bottom, we get the diagram shown in Figure 14-16.

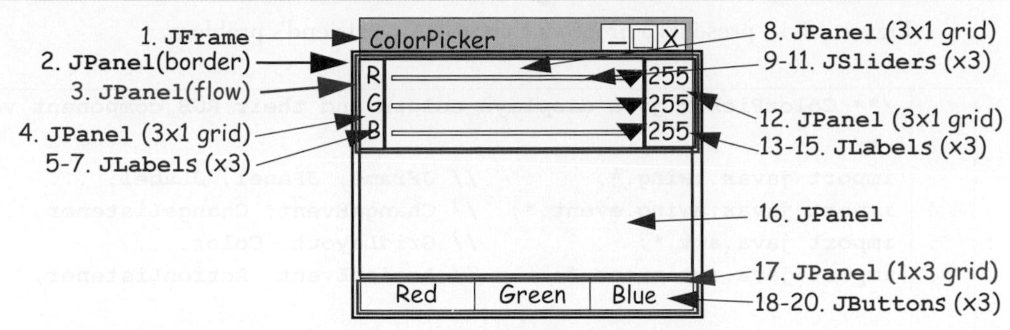

FIGURE 14-16 Annotated storyboard for ColorPicker program

We can also build a transition diagram to indicate what should happen when our friend interacts with the program. Since each of the three sliders has 256 different settings, it is impractical to develop a diagram showing all possible combinations. However, a small diagram like the one shown in Figure 14-17 suffices to illustrate what graphical components change in response to specific events.

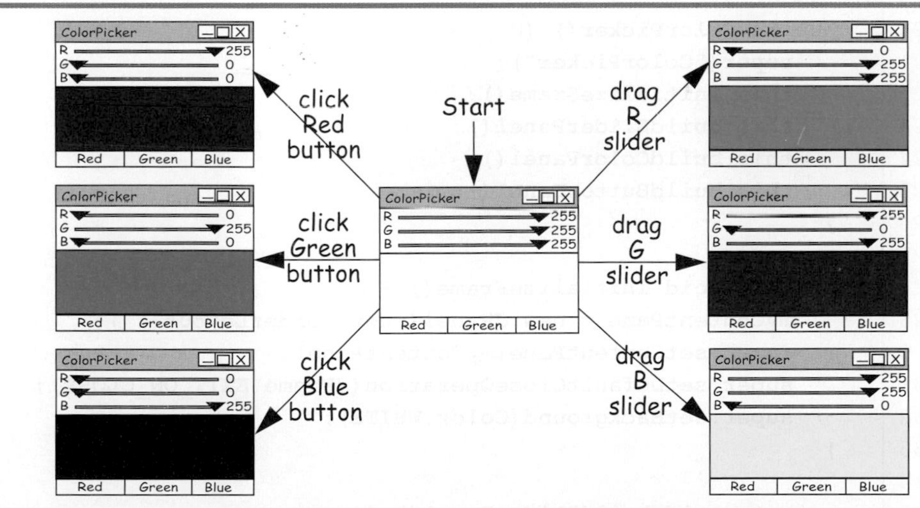

FIGURE 14-17 Partial transition diagram for ColorPicker program

For example, when a button is clicked, the central pane must be colored, up to three sliders must be changed, and up to three of the sliders' number labels must be changed. However, when a slider is dragged, the central pane must be colored and only that slider's number pane must be updated to indicate its new value.

14.3.1 The ColorPicker Program

Figure 14-18 presents a program that solves our friend's problem.

```
/** ColorPicker.java displays colors and their RGB component values
 */
import javax.swing.*;          // JFrame, JPanel, JLabel, ...
import javax.swing.event.*;  // ChangeEvent, ChangeListener, ...
import java.awt.*;             // GridLayout, Color, ...
import java.awt.event.*;       // ActionEvent, ActionListener, ...

public class ColorPicker extends JFrame {
  private JPanel  myContentPane = null;
  private JSlider myRedSlider = null;
  private JSlider myGreenSlider = null;
  private JSlider myBlueSlider = null;
  private JLabel  myRedLabel = null;
  private JLabel  myGreenLabel = null;
  private JLabel  myBlueLabel = null;
  private JPanel  myColorPanel = null;
  private int     myRed, myGreen, myBlue;
  private static final long serialVersionUID = 0;

  public ColorPicker() {
     super("ColorPicker");
     this.initializeFrame();
     this.buildSliderPanel();
     this.buildColorPanel();
     this.buildButtonPanel();
  }

  private void initializeFrame() {
     myContentPane = new JPanel( new BorderLayout() );
     super.setContentPane(myContentPane);
     super.setDefaultCloseOperation(JFrame.EXIT_ON_CLOSE);
     super.setBackground(Color.WHITE);
  }

  private void buildSliderPanel() {
     JPanel sliderPanel = new JPanel( new FlowLayout() );
     this.addRGBLabelsTo(sliderPanel);
     this.addSlidersTo(sliderPanel);
     this.addNumberLabelsTo(sliderPanel);
     myContentPane.add(sliderPanel, BorderLayout.NORTH);
     myRed = myGreen = myBlue = 255;
  }
```

continued

```

   private void addRGBLabelsTo(JPanel containingPanel) {
      JPanel labelSubPane = new JPanel( new GridLayout(3,1) );
      labelSubPane.add( new JLabel("R") );
      labelSubPane.add( new JLabel("G") );
      labelSubPane.add( new JLabel("B") );
      containingPanel.add(labelSubPane);
   }

   private void addSlidersTo(JPanel containingPanel) {
      JPanel sliderSubPane = new JPanel( new GridLayout(3,1) );
      myRedSlider = new JSlider(0, 255);
      myRedSlider.setValue(255);
      myRedSlider.addChangeListener( new RedSliderListener() );
      sliderSubPane.add(myRedSlider);
      myGreenSlider = new JSlider(0, 255);
      myGreenSlider.setValue(255);
      myGreenSlider.addChangeListener( new GreenSliderListener() );
      sliderSubPane.add(myGreenSlider);
      myBlueSlider = new JSlider(0, 255);
      myBlueSlider.setValue(255);
      myBlueSlider.addChangeListener( new BlueSliderListener() );
      sliderSubPane.add(myBlueSlider);
      containingPanel.add(sliderSubPane);
   }

   private void addNumberLabelsTo(JPanel containingPanel) {
      JPanel numberSubPane = new JPanel( new GridLayout(3,1) );
      myRedLabel = new JLabel("255");
      numberSubPane.add(myRedLabel);
      myGreenLabel = new JLabel("255");
      numberSubPane.add(myGreenLabel);
      myBlueLabel = new JLabel("255");
      numberSubPane.add(myBlueLabel);
      containingPanel.add(numberSubPane);
   }

   private void buildColorPanel() {
      myColorPanel = new JPanel();
      myColorPanel.setBorder( BorderFactory.createEtchedBorder() );
      myColorPanel.setPreferredSize( new Dimension(300, 100) );
      myColorPanel.setBackground(Color.WHITE);
      myContentPane.add(myColorPanel, BorderLayout.CENTER);
   }
```

continued

```

   private void buildButtonPanel() {
      JPanel buttonPanel = new JPanel( new GridLayout(1, 3) );
      buttonPanel.setBackground(Color.WHITE);
      buttonPanel.setBorder(
                       BorderFactory.createEmptyBorder(4,4,4,4) );
      JButton redButton = new JButton("Red");
      redButton.setBackground(Color.RED);
      redButton.setForeground(Color.WHITE);
      redButton.addActionListener( new RedButtonListener() );
      buttonPanel.add(redButton);
      JButton greenButton = new JButton("Green");
      greenButton.setBackground(Color.GREEN);
      greenButton.setForeground(Color.WHITE);
      greenButton.addActionListener( new GreenButtonListener() );
      buttonPanel.add(greenButton);
      JButton blueButton = new JButton("Blue");
      blueButton.setBackground(Color.BLUE);
      blueButton.setForeground(Color.WHITE);
      blueButton.addActionListener( new BlueButtonListener() );
      buttonPanel.add(blueButton);
      myContentPane.add(buttonPanel, BorderLayout.SOUTH);
   }

   // Handler classes for RGB sliders
   private class RedSliderListener implements ChangeListener {
      public void stateChanged(ChangeEvent event) {
         myRed = myRedSlider.getValue();
         myRedLabel.setText( Integer.toString(myRed) );
         myColorPanel.setBackground(new Color(myRed, myGreen,
                                                          myBlue));
      }
   }

   private class GreenSliderListener implements ChangeListener {
      public void stateChanged(ChangeEvent event) {
         myGreen = myGreenSlider.getValue();
         myGreenLabel.setText( Integer.toString(myGreen) );
         myColorPanel.setBackground(new Color(myRed, myGreen,
                                                          myBlue));
      }
   }

   private class BlueSliderListener implements ChangeListener {
```

continued

```
      public void stateChanged(ChangeEvent event) {
         myBlue = myBlueSlider.getValue();
         myBlueLabel.setText( Integer.toString(myBlue) );
         myColorPanel.setBackground(new Color(myRed, myGreen,
                                                        myBlue));
      }
   }

   // Handler classes for buttons
   private class RedButtonListener implements ActionListener {
      public void actionPerformed(ActionEvent event) {
         setColor(255, 0, 0);
      }
   }

   private class GreenButtonListener implements ActionListener {
      public void actionPerformed(ActionEvent event) {
         setColor(0, 255, 0);
      }
   }

   private class BlueButtonListener implements ActionListener {
      public void actionPerformed(ActionEvent event) {
         setColor(0, 0, 255);
      }
   }

   private void setColor(int red, int green, int blue) {
      myRedSlider.setValue(red);
      myRedLabel.setText( Integer.toString(red) );
      myGreenSlider.setValue(green);
      myGreenLabel.setText( Integer.toString(green) );
      myBlueSlider.setValue(blue);
      myBlueLabel.setText( Integer.toString(blue) );
      myColorPanel.setBackground(new Color(red, green, blue) );
      myRed = red; myGreen = green; myBlue = blue;
   }

   // utility method to center the JFrame
   private void centerFrame() {
      Dimension screen = Toolkit.getDefaultToolkit().getScreenSize();
      int drawAtX = screen.width / 2 - super.getWidth() / 2;
      int drawAtY = screen.height / 2 - super.getHeight() / 2;
      super.setLocation(drawAtX, drawAtY);
   }
```

continued

```
173
174     public static void main(String[] args) {
175         ColorPicker self = new ColorPicker();
176         self.pack();
177         self.centerFrame();
178         self.setVisible(true);
179     }
180 }
```

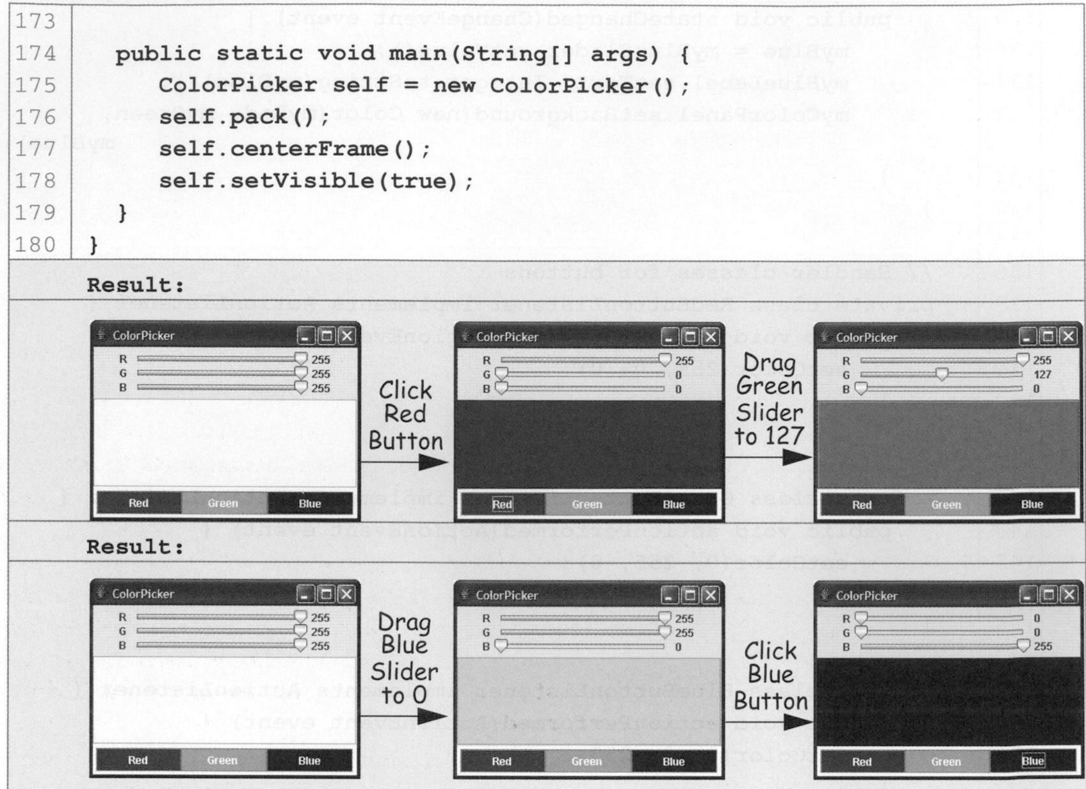

FIGURE 14-18 **ColorPicker.java**

As can be seen in Figure 14-18, this program is longer than others we have written. Most of that length stems from the complexity of building the program's GUI. In the rest of this section, we highlight the new features this program introduces.

14.3.2 Building the ColorPicker GUI

On line 8, we declare a class named **ColorPicker**. Since our class is to provide a graphical user interface, we declare it as a subclass of **JFrame**:

```
public class ColorPicker extends JFrame {
}
```

Instance Variables

On line 9-18, we declare the class's instance variables.

```
public class ColorPicker extends JFrame {
  private JPanel  myContentPane = null;
  private JSlider myRedSlider = null;
  private JSlider myGreenSlider = null;
  private JSlider myBlueSlider = null;
  private JLabel  myRedLabel = null;
  private JLabel  myGreenLabel = null;
  private JLabel  myBlueLabel = null;
  private JPanel  myColorPanel = null;
  private int     myRed, myGreen, myBlue;
  private static final long serialVersionUID = 0;
  ...
```

Because the program has many graphical components, its constructor will have many components to initialize. To keep the constructor from becoming too long, we will break it down into several methods, each of which will add components to the content pane. To make it easy for these methods to access the content pane, we declare a **JPanel** instance variable for it on line 9.

A slider must be accessed by the constructor. Our transition diagram indicates that its own event handler and the event handler for a button will need to access the sliders. To facilitate this, we declare **JSlider** instance variables for the sliders on lines 10-12. Similarly, a slider's number label must be accessed by the constructor and the event handlers for that slider and the buttons, so we declare a **JLabel** instance variable for each number label on lines 13-15.

Our transition diagram also indicates that each slider's event handler and each button's event handler will need to change the color of the central pane, so we declare a **JPanel** instance variable for it on line 16.

On line 17, we declare three **int** instance variables to store the red, green, and blue components of the current color. While not strictly necessary, when one slider is changed, these will let us update the central pane's color without having to reread all three sliders' values.

The Constructor

Lines 20-26 of Figure 14-18 define the constructor, which initializes each instance variable, builds the GUI, and registers listeners for the components that need them. If we were to do all of this within the constructor, it would be more than 60 lines long — much longer than our "half a page" guideline. To keep the constructor "short and sweet," we have broken it up into submethods, organized around the major pieces of the GUI.

The first of these submethods is **initializeFrame()**, defined on lines 28-33. As its name implies, this method initializes the **JFrame**. The only new feature here is on line 29, where we define the content pane **JPanel** to use the **BorderLayout** layout manager.

```
myContentPane = new JPanel( new BorderLayout() );
```

We use a **BorderLayout** because the panel of sliders is to appear at the *top* of the GUI, the panel we will color is to appear at the *center* of the GUI, and the panel of buttons is to appear at the *bottom* of the GUI. If we were to use a 3-row, 1-column grid layout, each cell in the grid would be the same size. This would make the panel of sliders, the color panel, and the button panel all equal in size, which is not the way they appear in Figure 14-15.

A **BorderLayout** divides a panel into five regions, as shown in Figure 14-19.

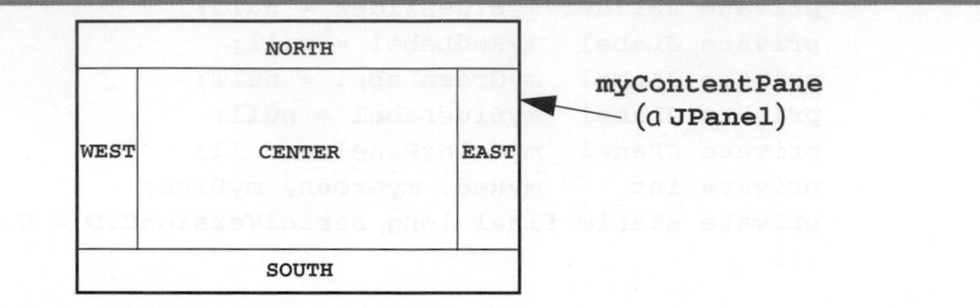

FIGURE 14-19 The regions within a **JPanel** using **BorderLayout**

By defining the content pane to use the **BorderLayout**, we can build a panel of sliders and add it to the **NORTH** region of the content pane, build the color panel and add it to the **CENTER** region of the content pane, and build a panel of buttons and add it to the **SOUTH** region of the content pane. The **BorderLayout** class defines constants for each of the five regions shown in Figure 14-19. If an application does not use a region, the **BorderLayout** shrinks that region to a minimal size when it draws the **JPanel**.

Building the Slider Panel

The next submethod in our constructor is **buildSliderPanel()**. The first line of this method builds the **JPanel** to store the RGB labels, the sliders, and their numeric labels. These components have different widths, but occupy one row, so we use a **FlowLayout** layout manager for this **JPanel**:

```
JPanel sliderPanel = new JPanel( new FlowLayout() );
```

If we had instead used a 1-row, 3-column **GridLayout**, the cells containing the labels, sliders, and number labels would have equal widths, which would not look like Figure 14-15.

Initializing the RGB labels, sliders, and number labels requires about 30 lines of statements. To keep this method "short and sweet," we have broken it down by defining a separate method for each of the three **JPanel**s that make up the slider panel. If we think of **buildSliderPanel()** as being like a "scene" method, these three methods are like "shot" methods.

The first of these "shot" methods is **addRGBLabelsTo()**, defined on lines 44-50. Since each label has the same width and height, this method defines a **JPanel** subpane using a 3-row, 1-column **GridLayout**, adds the labels to that subpane, and then adds the resulting subpane to the slider panel. However, there is no instance variable that refers to the slider panel. We can either define one, or we can pass the slider panel as a parameter to this method. We have chosen the latter approach, to illustrate it, and to avoid defining extraneous instance variables.

The next "shot" method is **addSlidersTo()**, defined on lines 52-67, which is responsible for initializing the three sliders. Since each slider has the same width and height, we use a 3-row, 1-column **GridLayout** to define a **JPanel** subpane for them. We then define and add the three sliders to this subpane, and finally add the subpane to the slider panel. To define the sliders, we use the **JSlider** class. For example, the following statements define the Red slider:

```
myRedSlider = new JSlider(0, 255);
myRedSlider.setValue(255);
myRedSlider.addChangeListener( new RedSliderListener() );
sliderSubPane.add(myRedSlider);
```

As indicated in the Java API, the first line uses a **JSlider()** constructor that lets us specify the slider's low and high values. The second line sends the resulting **JSlider** the **setValue()** message, to give it its initial value of **255**. Using the information from Figure 14-4, the third line registers the listener for this slider — an instance of **RedSliderListener** — which is defined below. With our slider defined and its listener registered, the fourth line adds it to the **sliderSubPane**. The method uses this same approach to initialize the other two sliders.

The final "shot" method is **addNumberLabelsTo()**, defined on lines 69-78. Everything in this method should be familiar.

Once these three "shot" methods have been performed, the slider panel is complete! Line 40 then adds the slider panel at the **NORTH** position on the content pane, using a version of the **add()** method that allows us to specify the location at which a component should be added:

```
myContentPane.add(sliderPanel, BorderLayout.NORTH);
```

With this accomplished, the top portion of our GUI is now complete!

Building the Color Panel

Our next task is to build the color panel. This is accomplished by **buildColorPanel()**, which is defined on lines 80-86.

```
private void buildColorPanel() {
   myColorPanel = new JPanel();
   myColorPanel.setBorder( BorderFactory.createEtchedBorder() );
   myColorPanel.setPreferredSize( new Dimension(300, 100) );
   myColorPanel.setBackground(Color.WHITE);
   myContentPane.add(myColorPanel, BorderLayout.CENTER);
}
```

The first line of the method initializes instance variable **myColorPanel** as a new **JPanel**. Since we will not add any components to it, we create it using the **JPanel** default constructor.

The second line then gives **myColorPanel** a border, so as to separate this panel from the panels above and below it. After trying out several different borders from the **BorderFactory** class, we chose a simple etched border.

The third line is very important. It sends **myColorPanel** the **setPreferredSize()** message to tell it how big it should be. If we do not specify a size, Java will build a tiny **JPanel** that is much smaller than the one shown in Figure 14-15. The Java API indicates that the **setPreferredSize()** has a **Dimension** parameter. Since the width of the color panel in Figure 14-15 is about three times its height, we build a 300-pixel-by-100-pixel **Dimension** object and pass it to set the size of **myColorPanel**.

> When you need to set a graphics object's width and height, send it the **setPreferredSize()** message with an appropriate **Dimension** value.

The fourth line sets the color panel to its initial color, and the final line adds the resulting color panel to **myContentPane**. Since **myContentPane** is using the **BorderLayout**, this last line uses the version of **add()** that lets us specify where we add it:

```
myContentPane.add(myColorPanel, BorderLayout.CENTER);
```

Building the Button Panel

Our next task is to build the panel at the bottom of the GUI, housing the Red, Green, and Blue buttons. This is performed by the **buildButtonPanel()** method, defined on lines 88-109. Because each button has the same height and the same width, the method defines this panel using a 1-row, 3-column **GridLayout**:

```
JPanel buttonPanel = new JPanel( new GridLayout(1, 3) );
```

To create the three buttons, this method uses the **JButton** class. For example, the following lines build the Red button, and add it to the button panel:

```
JButton redButton = new JButton("Red");
redButton.setBackground(Color.RED);
redButton.setForeground(Color.WHITE);
redButton.addActionListener( new RedButtonListener() );
buttonPanel.add(redButton);
```

The first line uses a **JButton** constructor that takes a string to be used as the button's label. The second line sets the button's background color to be red. Since a black label is hard to read on a red background, the third line sets the button's foreground color (that is, the color of the text on the button's label) to white. Since a **JButton** generates **ActionEvents**, the fourth line registers a listener to handle its events. The final statement adds the button to the button panel.

After the Green and Blue buttons have been built and added to the button panel, the final statement adds the finished button panel at the bottom of the content pane:

```
myContentPane.add(buttonPanel, BorderLayout.SOUTH);
```

14.3.3 Testing the GUI

With that, the **ColorPicker** GUI is complete! Before proceeding further, it is a good idea to test the GUI. To do so, we can "comment out" the statements in which we register listeners for the sliders and buttons, and then define a **main()** method, as shown in lines 174-179 of Figure 14-18. We can then run the program for our friend, to make certain that its appearance matches her wishes. When we run it, we get the GUI shown in Figure 14-20, which is a pretty good match for Figure 14-15.

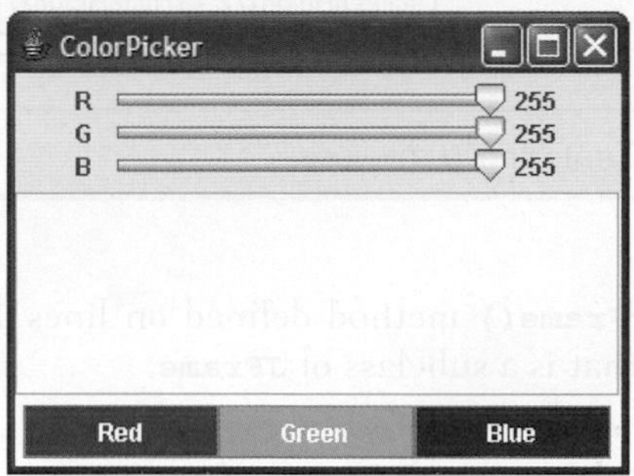

FIGURE 14-20 The ColorPicker GUI

With no listeners registered to handle events, none of the sliders or buttons do anything yet, but this is still sufficient to get our friend's approval for what we have done so far.

Centering a JFrame

By default, Java builds **JFrame** objects at the upper-left corner of the computer's screen. When our friend runs the program, we notice that she drags the **JFrame** from that position to the center of the screen, and says, "It would be nicer if the program would center the window automatically." In response to this user feedback, we can define a **centerFrame()** method that will center the GUI on the screen.

To center a **JFrame** on the screen, we need to know the dimensions of both the screen and the **JFrame**. (See Figure 14-21.) While a given computer screen's dimensions are fixed, a **JFrame**'s dimensions are not known until all of its graphical components have been added to it. Because of this, *a* **JFrame** *can only be centered after its GUI has been constructed*.

The basic idea in centering the frame is to find the screen center's x value by dividing its width by 2, and the center's y value by dividing its height by 2. Java draws a **JFrame** starting at its upper-left corner, so to find where to begin drawing the frame, we need to subtract half of the frame's width from the screen center's x value, and subtract half the GUI's height from the screen center's y value, as shown in Figure 14-21.

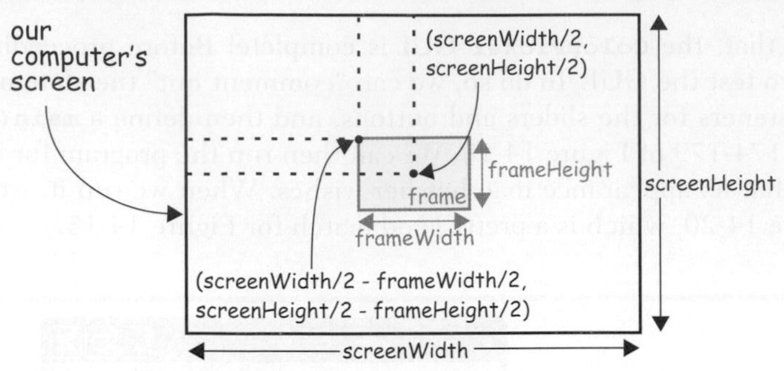

FIGURE 14-21 Centering a **JFrame**

The **centerFrame()** method defined on lines 167-172 uses these calculations to center an object that is a subclass of **JFrame**:

```
private void centerFrame() {
   Dimension screen = Toolkit.getDefaultToolkit()
                             .getScreenSize();
   int drawAtX = screen.width / 2 - super.getWidth() / 2;
   int drawAtY = screen.height / 2 - super.getHeight() / 2;
   super.setLocation(drawAtX, drawAtY);
}
```

To compute the screen's dimensions, this method uses the **Toolkit** class from package **java.awt**. If we send the **ToolKit** class the **getDefaultToolKit()**, it produces a **Toolkit** object describing various attributes of the computer, including the screen's dimensions. If we then send the resulting **ToolKit** the **getScreenSize()** message, it returns a **Dimension** object whose **width** attribute is the computer screen's width, and whose **height** attribute is the screen's height. The second and third lines use these components to calculate the (x,y) values of the computer screen's center point.

A subclass of **JFrame** inherits **getWidth()** and **getHeight()** methods. Our **centerFrame()** method uses these methods in the second and third lines to compute the (x,y) values of the point where we must begin drawing in order for our GUI to be centered. It also inherits a **setLocation()** method, which we use in the final line to draw our GUI at that (x,y) point.

Recall that the **pack()** message in our **main()** method is what "packs" the frame around the graphical components within it. Because of this, our GUI's width and height will not be set until after we have sent it the **pack()** message. As a result, we send our GUI the **centerFrame()** message in the **main()** method, after sending it the **pack()** message.[3]

3. Alternatively, we can place **super.pack();** and **this.centerFrame();** at the end of the **ColorPicker** constructor.

```
public static void main(String[] args) {
   ColorPicker self = new ColorPicker();
   self.pack();
   self.centerFrame();
   self.setVisible(true);
}
```

By centering the frame before making it visible, it is centered on our screen when it first appears.

14.3.4 Building the ColorPicker Listeners

To complete the class, we must build the listener classes to handle the events generated by the sliders and buttons.

The Slider Listeners

Whenever the user drags the knob of a **JSlider**, a **ChangeEvent** is generated. In order to be registered as a handler for that event, the handler's class must implement the **ChangeListener** interface. As indicated in Figure 14-11, the **ChangeListener** interface declares one method: **stateChanged()**. Once a handler is registered, each time the user drags the slider's knob, JRE will invoke the **stateChanged()** method in the slider's handler. This handler must thus (1) get the value of the slider, (2) update the slider's number label to reflect its changed value, and (3) update the color panel to reflect the new color. To illustrate these steps, here is the handler for our Red slider (lines 112-118 of Figure 14-18):

```
private class RedSliderListener implements ChangeListener {
  public void stateChanged(ChangeEvent event) {
     myRed = myRedSlider.getValue();
     myRedLabel.setText( Integer.toString(myRed) );
     myColorPanel.setBackground(
                        new Color(myRed, myGreen, myBlue) );
  }
}
```

The method is fairly simple, because it only has to handle events generated by the Red slider. The first line sends the Red slider the **getValue()** message to retrieve its numeric value, storing that value in the instance variable **myRed**. The second line updates the slider's number label by using **Integer.toString()** to compute the string equivalent of **myRed**. It then updates the Red numeric label by sending **myRedLabel** the **setText()** message, with that string as an argument. The third and final line uses a **Color** constructor to build a new **Color** object from the updated **myRed** number and the unchanged **myGreen** and **myBlue** numbers. It then sends **myColorPanel** the **setBackground()** message with the new **Color** as an argument.

As can be seen on lines 120-134, the handlers for the Green and Blue sliders are similar to that of the Red slider. Each is "short and sweet" because it only needs to handle events from one slider.

To test our program, we can "uncomment" the lines that register the handlers for the sliders. When we do so, all three of the sliders should behave correctly.

The Button Listeners

Whenever a **JButton** is clicked, it generates an **ActionEvent**. To handle this event, an object's class must implement the **ActionListener** interface and define the **actionPerformed()** method.

The handlers for each of the buttons perform the same actions, using different values. To avoid redundant coding, we "factored out" the common steps into a separate **setColor()** method, with parameters for the different values, as can be seen on lines 155-164.

```
private void setColor(int red, int green, int blue) {
   myRedSlider.setValue(red);
   myRedLabel.setText( Integer.toString(red) );
   myGreenSlider.setValue(green);
   myGreenLabel.setText( Integer.toString(green) );
   myBlueSlider.setValue(blue);
   myBlueLabel.setText( Integer.toString(blue) );
   myColorPanel.setBackground(new Color(red, green, blue) );
   myRed = red; myGreen = green; myBlue = blue;
}
```

With this "utility" method defined, the handler for a button becomes almost trival, because all it needs to do is invoke **setColor()** with the proper RGB values, as can be seen on lines 137-153. For example, to handle clicks on the Red button, all we need to do is this:

```
private class RedButtonListener implements ActionListener {
  public void actionPerformed(ActionEvent event) {
     setColor(255, 0, 0);
  }
}
```

The handlers for the other buttons are similar, as can be seen in Figure 14-18.

To finish the program, all we need to do is "uncomment" the lines that register listeners for these buttons. With that, our program is complete and ready for our friend to use.

14.4 Applets and the World Wide Web

Our final example is to build a simple game we'll call Click-Clack-Cloe. The game is played on a 3-by-3 grid. There are two players, who take turns clicking on cells in the grid. When the first player clicks on an empty cell, it turns red. When the second player clicks on a cell, it turns blue. The goal is to be the first player to get three adjacent cells of the same color in a line, which can be horizontal, vertical, or diagonal. Above the grid, we will place a panel in which we can display feedback for the users, such as whose turn it is, the winner of a game, and so on. Figure 14-22 presents a rough sketch of how the game will appear.

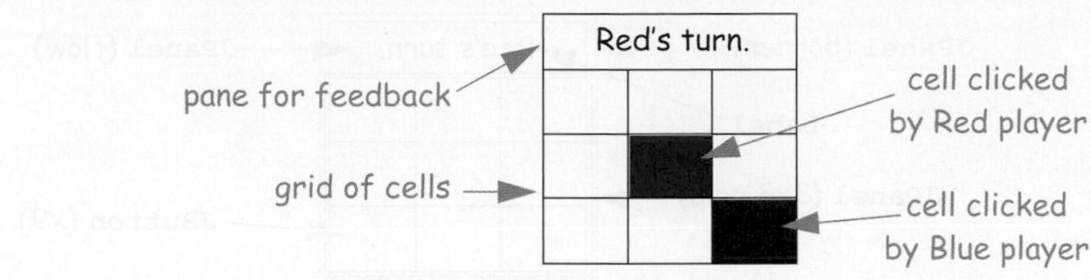

FIGURE 14-22 Click-Clack-Cloe storyboard

One way to do this is to make each cell a button, so that when a user clicks on it, we can handle that event by changing the button's color from white to the appropriate color, and then see whether or not that click won the game. To determine the appropriate color, the game must keep track of whose turn it is (among other things). To see whether a click wins the game, the handler can check each row, each column, and each diagonal for three cells of the same color.

14.4.1 Applets vs. Applications

We could build a *ClickClackCloe* application by defining it as a subclass of **`JFrame`**. For variety, we are instead going to build it as an **applet** — a Java program that can be downloaded from a Web site as part of a Web page, that runs in a Web browser. This makes it possible to build Web pages that are dynamic and interactive, rather than static and passive.

There are several important differences between applets and applications, including:

- An applet is defined as a subclass of Java's **`JApplet`** class, from the package **`javax.swing`**.
- Most applets define GUIs, and perform their tasks by handling events.
- An applet has no constructor or **`main()`** method. Instead, it has an **`init()`** method that builds the applet's GUI and registers listeners for any events it generates.
- To prevent security problems, applets may only read files from their own Web site, not from a user's computer.
- An applet must be embedded in a Web page and run in a Web browser, or run using the **`appletviewer`** application that comes with Java.

14.4.2 Designing the Applet

We can design an applet the same way we have designed previous programs. For example, we might start by annotating the storyboard in Figure 14-22 with the graphical components it requires, as shown in Figure 14-23.

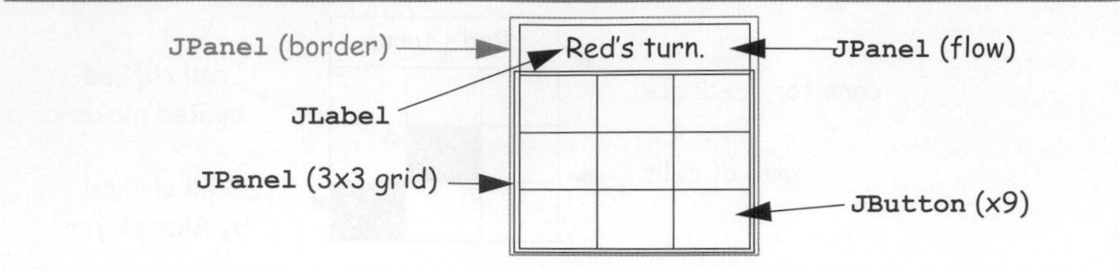

FIGURE 14-23 Annotated Click-Clack-Cloe storyboard

We can also build a transition diagram showing how the GUI changes in response to user events. Figure 14-24 shows the beginning of such a diagram.

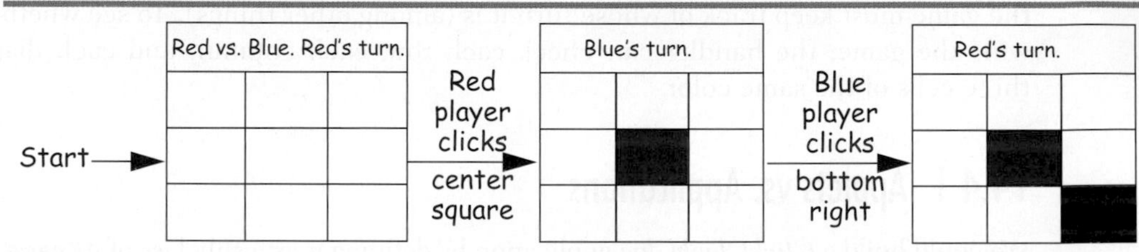

FIGURE 14-24 Click-Clack-Cloe transition diagram

From Figure 14-24, we can see that when the user clicks a cell, the handler for that event must change the color of that cell, and update the feedback label to indicate it is the other player's turn. We will therefore need instance variables to act as handles for the feedback label and the nine cells. We will also need to register a listener for each of these nine cells.

Since our game must "remember" whose turn it is, we will also define an instance variable to store this information.

Finally, when the game is over, the program should ignore subsequent clicks on cells. To help do this, we will also define an instance variable to "remember" when a player has won.

14.4.3 Building the Applet

As described previously, an applet has no constructor or **main()** method. Instead, it uses a method named **init()** to build the GUI and register listeners for the components that generate events. A simple applet thus consists of instance variables, an **init()** method, and the listeners it requires. The program in Figure 14-25 follows this structure.

```
/** ClickClackCloe.java is a simple "connect 3 in a row" game...
*/
import javax.swing.*;          // JApplet, JButton, ...
```

continued

```
import java.awt.*;          // BorderLayout, Color, ...
import java.awt.event.*;  // ActionEvent, ActionListener, ...

public class ClickClackCloe extends JApplet {
  private final int           MY_ROWS = 3,
                              MY_COLUMNS = 3;

  private JLabel              myFeedbackLabel = null;
  private JButton [][]        myGrid = null;
  private boolean             itsRedsTurn = true,
                              gameIsDone = false;
  private static final long serialVersionUID = 1L;

  public void init() {
     JPanel contentPane = new JPanel( new BorderLayout() );
     contentPane.setBorder( BorderFactory.createEtchedBorder() );
     JPanel topPane = new JPanel( new FlowLayout() );
     topPane.setBorder( BorderFactory.createEmptyBorder(5,5,5,5) );
     myFeedbackLabel = new JLabel("Red vs. Blue. Red's turn");
     topPane.add(myFeedbackLabel);
     contentPane.add(topPane, BorderLayout.NORTH);
     JPanel gridPane = new JPanel( new GridLayout(MY_ROWS,
                                                   MY_COLUMNS) );
     gridPane.setBorder( BorderFactory.createEtchedBorder() );
     myGrid = new JButton[MY_ROWS][MY_COLUMNS];
     ButtonListener buttonListener = new ButtonListener();
     for (int r = 0; r < MY_ROWS; r++) {
        for (int c = 0; c < MY_COLUMNS; c++) {
           myGrid[r][c] = new JButton();
           myGrid[r][c].setBackground(Color.WHITE);
           myGrid[r][c].addActionListener(buttonListener);
           gridPane.add(myGrid[r][c]);
        }
     }
     contentPane.add(gridPane);
     this.setContentPane(contentPane);
  }

  // One handler for all nine buttons
  private class ButtonListener implements ActionListener {
     public void actionPerformed(ActionEvent event) {
        if ( !gameIsDone ) {
           Object eventSource = event.getSource();
           if (eventSource instanceof JButton) {
```

continued

```
         JButton buttonClicked = (JButton) eventSource;
         if (itsRedsTurn) {
            handleClick(buttonClicked, Color.RED,
                            "Red", "Blue");
         } else {
            handleClick(buttonClicked, Color.BLUE,
                            "Blue", "Red");
         }
       }
     }
   }

   private void handleClick(JButton button, Color playerColor,
                           String thisPlayer, String nextPlayer) {
     if (button.getBackground() == Color.WHITE) {
       button.setBackground(playerColor);
       if ( this.gameOver() ) {
         myFeedbackLabel.setText(thisPlayer + " WINS!");
         gameIsDone = true;
       } else {
         myFeedbackLabel.setText(nextPlayer + "'s turn.");
       }
       itsRedsTurn = !itsRedsTurn;
      }
   }

   private boolean gameOver() {
     if ( checkDiagonals() ) return true;
     else if ( checkRows() ) return true;
     else if ( checkColumns() ) return true;
     else { return false; }
   }

   private boolean checkDiagonals() {
     Color middleColor = myGrid[1][1].getBackground();
     if (middleColor != Color.WHITE) {
       return middleColor == myGrid[0][0].getBackground()
          && middleColor == myGrid[2][2].getBackground() ||
            middleColor == myGrid[0][2].getBackground()
          && middleColor == myGrid[2][0].getBackground();
     }
     return false;
   }
```

continued

```
 91
 92     private boolean checkRows() {
 93         for (int r = 0; r < MY_ROWS; r++) {
 94             Color cellColor = myGrid[r][0].getBackground();
 95             if ( cellColor != Color.WHITE
 96                 && cellColor == myGrid[r][1].getBackground()
 97                 && cellColor == myGrid[r][2].getBackground()) {
 98                 return true;
 99             }
100         }
101         return false;
102     }
103
104     private boolean checkColumns() {
105         for (int c = 0; c < MY_COLUMNS; c++) {
106             Color cellColor = myGrid[0][c].getBackground();
107             if ( cellColor != Color.WHITE
108                 && cellColor == myGrid[1][c].getBackground()
109                 && cellColor == myGrid[2][c].getBackground()) {
110                 return true;
111             }
112         }
113         return false;
114     }
115   } // ButtonListener
116 } // ClickClackCloe
```

FIGURE 14-25 `ClickClackCloe.java`

Line 7 of Figure 14-25 declares **`ClickClackCloe`** as a subclass of **`JApplet`**:

```
public class ClickClackCloe extends JApplet {
```

Since **`ClickClackCloe`** *is an* applet, it inherits much of its functionality from **`JApplet`**.

Instance Variables

Lines 8-15 declare the instance variables and constants. For example, to declare an instance variable for the feedback label, we use the **`JLabel`** class on line 11.

To declare a cell, line 12 uses the **`JButton`** class. However, instead of declaring nine separate **`JButton`** instance variables, line 12 declares one instance variable in which we will model the grid using a 3-by-3 array of **`JButton`**s. This array provides a data structure in which the relationships between the array's elements correspond to the relationships between the grid's cells. This will prove useful in determining when a user has won the game, since getting "three cells in a diagonal, horizontal, or vertical line" is only meaningful using the grid's relationships.

The game must "remember" whose turn it is, and we have just two players, so line 13 accomplishes this using a **boolean** variable named **itsRedsTurn**. When its value is **true**, it will be the Red player's turn; when its value is **false**, it will be the Blue player's turn.

To remember when a player has won, line 14 declares a second **boolean** variable named **gameIsDone**, which a handler can set to **true** when a player gets three cells in a line.

The **init()** Method

As described previously, the **init()** method is responsible for building the applet's GUI and registering any listeners it needs. The **init()** method is not too long, so we place all of its statements in one method, on lines 17-40 in Figure 14-25.

Line 18 initializes the **JPanel** we will use as the applet's content pane, using a **BorderLayout** as its layout manager. Since an applet may have no frame around it, line 19 gives this content pane a border, to provide a minimal frame.

Lines 20-24 then build the feedback panel and add it to the content pane. Everything in these lines should be familiar by now.

Lines 25-38 then build the grid panel and add it to the content pane. Lines 25 and 26 begin by creating the **JPanel**, using a 3-by-3 **GridLayout** as its layout manager. After giving it a border, line 28 initializes the array instance variable **myGrid** as a 3-by-3 array of **JButton** handles:

```
myGrid = new JButton[MY_ROWS][MY_COLUMNS];
```

The next lines initialize this array. Since each button will need to respond to mouse clicks the same way, line 29 builds one **ButtonListener** that we will register as the listener for each button. Lines 30-37 then use two nested for loops to initialize the array. For a given row **r** and column **c** in the grid, line 32 initializes **myGrid[r][c]**:

```
myGrid[r][c] = new JButton();
```

Line 33 then sets the button's background color to White:

```
myGrid[r][c].setBackground(Color.WHITE);
```

Line 34 registers the button's listener:

```
myGrid[r][c].addActionListener(buttonListener);
```

Finally, line 35 adds the initialized button to the grid panel:

```
gridPane.add( myGrid[r][c] );
```

When these two nested loops finish, the grid panel has been built, so lines 38 and 39 add the grid panel to the content pane, and then tell the applet to utilize the content pane.

The ButtonListener

Since a **JButton** generates **ActionEvents**, the **ButtonListener** class must implement the **ActionListener** interface and define the **actionPerformed()** method, as can be seen on lines 43 and 44 of Figure 14-25.

The first statement in **actionPerformed()** (line 45) is an **if** statement that prevents the rest of the statements from being performed if the game is over, using the **gameIsDone** instance variable. Thus, once **gameIsDone** is set to **true** (see below), the statements that respond to mouse clicks in cells will be effectively disabled.

Any of the nine buttons could have been clicked, so our handler's next task is to determine which button was clicked, so that it can change its color. In this program, every **ActionEvent** will be generated by a **JButton**; however, in a more complicated program, there might also be non-**JButton** components generating **ActionEvents**. Lines 46 and 47 show how to deal with such situations. Line 46 defines **eventSource** as a handle for the source of the event by sending the event the **getSource()** message, which returns an **Object**:

```
Object eventSource = event.getSource();
```

Line 47 is an **if** statement that determines whether the source was a **JButton**:

```
if (eventSource instanceof JButton) {
```

The **instanceof** operation used in line 47 returns **true** if the source of the event was a **JButton**, and returns **false** if it was anything else. A program with a more complicated GUI could use an **if-else-if** statement to determine which kind of component generated an **ActionEvent**:

```
if (eventSource instanceof JButton) { ... }
else if (eventSource instanceof JTextField) { ... }
else if (eventSource instanceof JComboBox) { ... }
else if (eventSource instanceof JRadioButton) { ... }
else ...
```

The **instanceof** operation thus permits an event handler to determine the kind of component that generated an event, and then take a different action for each kind of component.

Once we have determined that the event was generated by a **JButton**, line 48 uses a cast to define **buttonClicked** as a **JButton** handle for the particular button the user clicked, so that we can send **JButton** messages to it:

```
JButton buttonClicked = (JButton) eventSource;
```

The remainder of the handler is an **if** statement whose branches handle the click differently, based on whose turn it was. In each case, the handler must change the button's color and update the feedback label, so we have written a **handleClick()** method to perform these actions:

```
if (itsRedsTurn) {
   handleClick(buttonClicked, Color.RED, "Red", "Blue");
} else {
   handleClick(buttonClicked, Color.BLUE, "Blue", "Red");
}
```

As can be seen on lines 60-72, the **handleClick()** method first checks that the button's background color is White, to prevent a player from changing a button the other player already clicked. If the button is White, it sets the button's background color to the correct color, and then updates the feedback label.

To update the feedback label appropriately, **handleClick()** checks to see if this click has won the game:

```
if ( this.gameOver() ) {
   myFeedbackLabel.setText(thisPlayer + " WINS!");
   gameIsDone = true;
} else {
   myFeedbackLabel.setText(nextPlayer + "'s turn.");
}
```

If so, it sets the feedback label to indicate that the player who clicked this button won the game and sets the **gameIsDone** instance variable to **true**. Otherwise, it just changes the feedback label to indicate that it is the next player's turn. Once the feedback label has been updated, line 70 updates instance variable **itsRedsTurn** to indicate that it is the other player's turn.

The **gameOver()** method on lines 74-79 returns **true** if it finds a line of three buttons that are the same color, and returns **false** otherwise. The **gameOver()** method breaks this problem down using three sub-methods:

- **checkDiagonals()** on lines 81-90, which returns **true** if and only if the buttons across either of the two diagonals have the same color
- **checkRows()** on lines 92-102, which returns **true** if and only if the buttons across any of the three rows have the same color
- **checkColumns()** on lines 104-114, which returns **true** if and only if the buttons across any of the three columns have the same color

Each of these methods uses the instance variable **myGrid**. As a 3-by-3 array of buttons, **myGrid** preserves the diagonal, row, and column relationships of the cells in the program's GUI. For example, **myGrid[0][0]**, **myGrid[1][1]**, and **myGrid[2][2]** together make up the diagonal line running from the grid's top-left corner to its bottom-right corner, so **checkDiagonals()** compares the background colors of these three buttons. Similarly, **myGrid[0][0]**, **myGrid[0][1]**, and **myGrid[0][2]** together make up the grid's top row, so **checkRows()** compares the background colors of these three buttons.

Note that **gameOver()** does not check for stalemates — games in which all of the squares have been clicked, but no one has won. Fixing this deficiency is not difficult, and is left as an exercise at the end of the chapter.

Once we have defined the **init()** method that builds the applet's GUI, and defined the listener classes that handle its events, the applet is complete!

14.4.4 Running the Applet

As indicated earlier, there are two ways to run an applet: using the **appletviewer** application that is distributed with Java, or viewing the applet with a Web browser. In either case, the applet must be embedded in a Web page before it can be viewed. Software engineers often use the **appletviewer** approach while they are developing an applet, and then once it has been thoroughly tested and debugged, use the Web browser approach to deploy the applet for the world to use. In the remainder of this section, we examine both of these approaches.

The appletviewer Approach

As its name implies, Java's **appletviewer** lets you run and view applets without having to run a Web browser. The **appletviewer** application should accompany a Java distribution, so if you have Java installed on your computer, the **appletviewer** should also be installed.

The simplest way to use the **appletviewer** is using an IDE like Eclipse, which will run the **appletviewer** for you. To run your applet in Eclipse, simply right-click anywhere in the applet's editing area, and choose **Run as -> Java Applet** from the menu that appears, as shown in Figure 14-26.

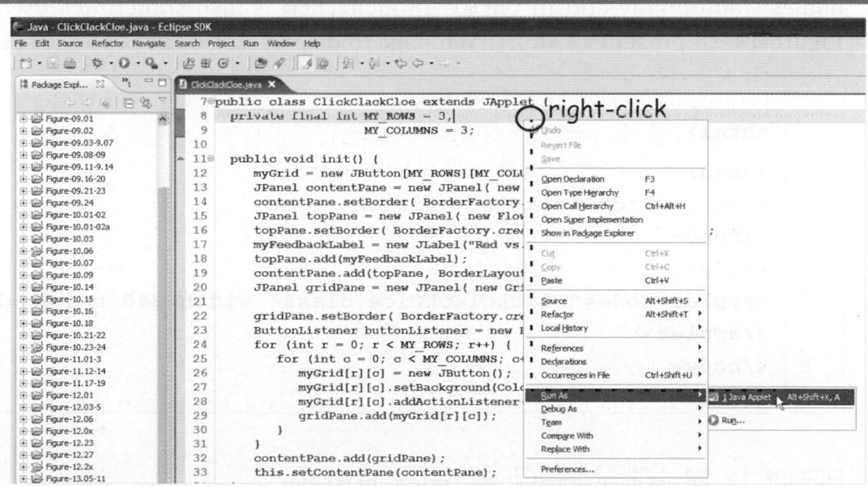

FIGURE 14-26 Running an applet from within Eclipse

Eclipse will then launch the **appletviewer** application, displaying your applet as shown in Figure 14-27.

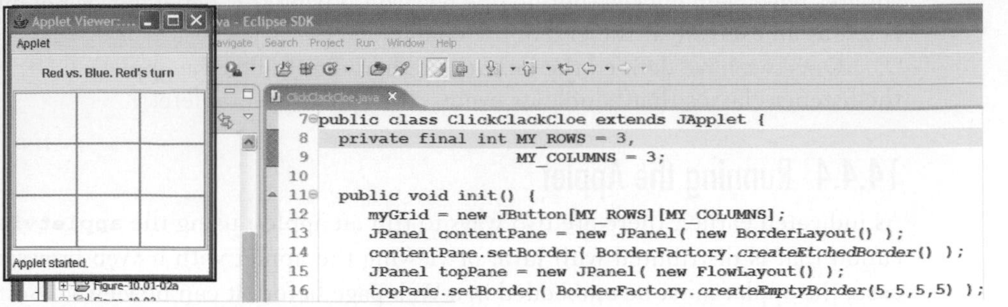

FIGURE 14-27 An applet running in Eclipse

If you do not have an IDE like Eclipse that will run applets for you, then you need to first build a Web page containing a reference to your compiled applet (see below), and then run the **appletviewer** application.[4]

Building a Simple Web Page

Web pages are text files containing hypertext markup language (HTML) directives and textual information. They can be created with a text editor, or with a specialized program like Dreamweaver or FrontPage. To distinguish them from other text files, Web page file names traditionally end in **.html**, though **.htm** is also sometimes used. To illustrate, Figure 14-28 presents a short Web page to display our **ClickClackCloe** applet.

```
<html>
<head>
<title>ClickClackCloe</title>
</head>
<body>
<applet code="ClickClackCloe.class" width=240 height=260>
</applet>
</body>
</html>
```

FIGURE 14-28 ClickClackCloe's **index.html** file

4. To run the **appletviewer** from the command line, launch a command shell or terminal window on your computer, use **cd** commands to navigate to the folder containing your applet and its **index.html** file, and then enter the command **appletviewer index.html**. Avoiding this hassle is one more reason to use a good IDE like Eclipse!

A Web page can be given any name, but **index.html** is most commonly used. The reason is this: if a user types a Web address into his or her browser, that address ends in a folder, and that folder contains a file named **index.html**, the browser will display that **index.html** file. For example, if you enter this Web address into your browser:

```
http://alice.calvin.edu/books/alice+java/examples/14/29/
```

your browser will display the page named **index.html** from the folder named **29** in the folder named **14** in the folder named **examples** in the folder named **alice+java** in the folder named **books** on the server named **alice.calvin.edu**!

As can be seen in Figure 14-28, a Web page consists of pairs of directives like **<html>** and **</html>**, **<head>** and **</head>**, **<title>** and **</title>**, and so on. These directives are called **tags**, and they act much like the curly braces in a Java block. For example, the **<html>** and **</html>** tags mark the beginning and end of the sequence of tags that define the Web page. The **<title>** and **</title>** tags define the title that the Web browser displays for a page, and these tags must appear within the **<head>** and **</head>** tags.

The **<body>** and **</body>** tags define the content of the Web page, and they must follow the **<head>** and **</head>** tags. To embed our applet in the page, we place **<applet>** and **</applet>** tags between the **<body>** and **</body>** tags.

The **<applet>** tag includes a number of parameters. The first is **code**, whose value is a string indicating the name of the file containing the *compiled* applet (in this case, **ClickClackCloe.class**). The other two parameters are **width** and **height**, whose values we can adjust to change the applet's dimensions within the Web page, as desired.

> To avoid problems, store a compiled applet and the HTML file that references it in the same folder, so that the HTML file can find the applet.

The Browser Approach

Given a compiled applet and a Web page that references that applet using **<applet>** and **</applet>** tags, you can run the applet in a Web browser by opening its Web page from within the browser. The exact procedure to do this varies from browser to browser, but tends to be similar. For example:

- In Firefox or Safari, choose **File->Open File...** and then use the dialog box that appears to navigate to the Web page on your computer
- In Internet Explorer, choose **File->Open...**, click the **Browse...** button, and then use the dialog box that appears to navigate to the Web page on your computer

When you open the file using the dialog box, your browser will load the page. Since the page refers to the applet, the browser will fetch and display the applet, as shown in Figure 14-29.

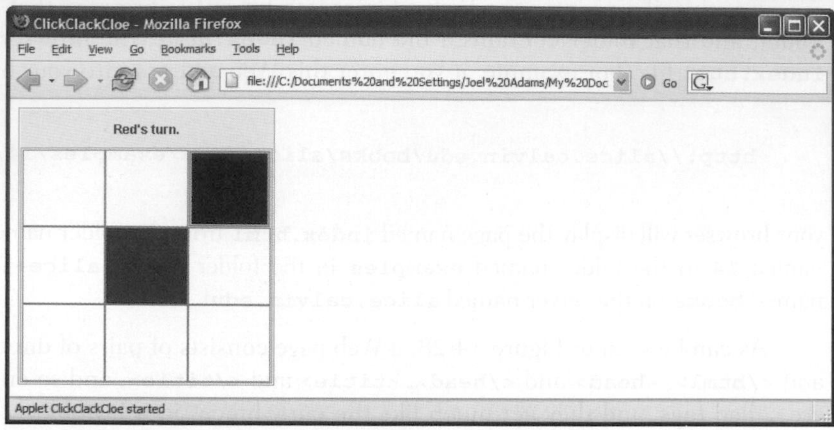

FIGURE 14-29 The ClickClackCloe applet running in Firefox

The World Wide Web

The World Wide Web is a system of programs called **Web servers** (for example, the most popular Web server is a program named *apache*) running on computers connected to the Internet. To specify the location of a file within the Web, the system uses a special kind of address called a **uniform resource locator** (**URL**). A URL has the form:

```
http://HostName/pathToFileOrFolder
```

where ***HostName*** is the name of the computer running the Web server, and ***pathToFileOrFolder*** is the location of the file or folder on that computer. Thus, in the URL we saw earlier:

```
http://alice.calvin.edu/books/alice+java/examples/14/29
```

the computer is named **alice.calvin.edu**, and the path to the folder containing the **ClickClackCloe** applet is **books/alice+java/examples/14/29**.

Given a URL, a **Web browser** like Firefox, Internet Explorer, or Safari contacts the server named in the URL, and requests a file by sending it the path part of the URL. If the path specifies a file, the Web server retrieves that file and transmits it to the browser, which displays its contents according to the HTML directives it contains. If the URL's path ends in a folder, the server retrieves the **index.html** file from that folder, if one is present. If no **index.html** file is present in the folder, the server may send a directory listing of the contents of that folder, or generate an error page, depending on how the server is configured.

Publishing an Applet

If we want people to be able to access an applet via the World Wide Web, the folder containing the applet and its Web page must be stored on a computer running a Web server, and that folder must be accessible by the Web server. In short:

> To publish an applet on the Web, you need access to a Web server.

Many colleges and universities serve their students by providing computers where their students can publish personal Web pages. The exact procedure varies from one institution to another, but if your college or university provides this service, you can use it to publish an applet. The basic steps are as follows:

1. On your computer, prepare a folder containing your compiled applet (the **.class** file) and the **index.html** Web page that refers to it. Give the folder a descriptive name.

2. Transfer the folder to your folder on the computer at your institution where people may publish personal Web pages. At some schools, this may be as simple as dragging the folder from one window to another; others may want you to use a program like Dreamweaver or FrontPage; others may have you use a file transfer utility like the SSH Secure Shell Client; others may require you to use a file transfer program like **ftp**, **sftp**, or **scp** from the command line. Ask your instructor how this is done at your institution.

3. Make certain that the access permissions are set so that everyone can *read* the folder and its files. On some systems, it may also be necessary to set the permissions so that everyone can *execute* the folder containing the applet. Ask your instructor how to do this at your institution.

4. Test your work, by trying to access the Web page via your browser. If it works, send the URL to your friends and family, so that they can see what you've been up to! If it doesn't, ask your instructor if there are special circumstances at your institution that are not covered in these steps.

Building GUI applets and applications can be a lot of fun, and we have just scratched the surface of what Java can do. (For example, Eclipse is written entirely in Java!) To learn more about GUI and event-driven programming in Java, a good place to start is Sun's *Swing Tutorial*, which is online at **java.sun.com/docs/books/tutorial/ui/**. This will teach you more about the components and events we have seen in this chapter, plus many others. Have fun!

Let's close this book with one final, relevant quote:

Now this is not the end. It is not even the beginning of the end. But it is, perhaps, the end of the beginning.

WINSTON CHURCHILL

14.5 Chapter Summary

- In an event-driven GUI application, the `main()` method builds, sizes, positions, and makes visible the GUI; then the Java Runtime Environment (JRE) takes over, delivering events to the program until it receives a `QUIT` event
- Some GUI components generate events when the user interacts with them:
  - Pressing the `Enter` key in a `JTextField`, clicking a `JButton`, or `JRadioButton`, or choosing an item from a `JComboBox` or `JMenuItem` generates an `ActionEvent`
  - Clicking a `JCheckBox` generates an `ItemEvent`
  - Dragging a `JSlider` generates a `ChangeEvent`
- To handle an event, an object must be registered as a listener for the graphical component that generates those events, and it must implement the appropriate listener interface:
  - `ActionListener` for `ActionEvent`
  - `ChangeListener` for `ChangeEvent`
  - `ItemListener` for `ItemEvent`
  - and so on
- Java applets are a means of building event-driven GUI programs that can be downloaded from the World Wide Web and run in a user's Web browser

14.5.1 Key Terms

ActionEvent
ActionListener
applet
BorderLayout
ChangeEvent
ChangeListener
event
event-driven program
FlowLayout
graphical user interface (GUI)
GridLayout
handler
JApplet
layout manager
listener
JButton
JFrame
JLabel
JPanel
JSlider
JTextField
storyboard
transition diagram
uniform resource locator (URL)
Web browser
Web server

Programming Projects

14.1 Alter the `ColorPicker` example in Figure 14-18 by adding Black, Gray, and White buttons, in a row below the existing Red, Green, and Blue buttons. When clicked, these buttons should update the color panel, sliders, and number labels appropriately with their respective colors.

14.2 Design and build a GUI application or applet that converts dollars to euros, and vice versa. (Feel free to substitute or add different currencies — for example, yen, rupees, francs, pesos, dinars, etc.) The program should provide three labeled boxes: one for the conversion rate, one for dollars, and one for euros. If the user enters a number in either the dollars box or the euros box and the conversion rate box is not empty, the program should compute and display the corresponding amount of money in the other currency box. If the conversion rate box is empty, the program should inform the user that he or she needs to supply a conversion rate.

14.3 Design and build an application or applet that performs temperature conversions. The program should provide three labeled boxes — one for Fahrenheit, one for Celsius, and one for Kelvin temperatures. If the user enters a valid numeric temperature in any of the three boxes, the program should compute and display the equivalent numeric temperatures of the other two scales in the other two boxes. If the user enters an invalid numeric temperature in a box, the program should display a red error message in the other two boxes.

14.4 In Section 10.3.3, we built a program that plays the "Guess My Number" game. Design and build a GUI application or applet that plays this game. The program should begin by displaying instructions on how to play the game, and a `Start` button that begins the game. The program should provide a box in which the user can enter his or her guess, an area in which the program provides feedback — for example, "higher", "lower", and so on — and anything else needed to play the game.

14.5 In Section 10.3.2, we built an application that let the user enter five air pollution readings, and which computed and displayed the average of the five readings. Design and build a GUI application or applet that provides boxes in which the user can enter air pollution readings, plus a button labeled `Average`. When the user clicks the `Average` button, the program should compute and display the average of the values in the boxes. If fewer than five readings are entered, the program should only average the entered readings. If no readings are entered, the program should display a red error message. (Hint: Build an array of handles to the boxes, so that you can process them conveniently.)

14.6 Using the `Plotter` class from Section 10.3.2, design and build a GUI application or applet that lets the user play the game *Hangman*. (If you have not played *Hangman* before, you can play online at a site like `www.hangman.no`.) The program should read a list of words from a file into a data structure and select one at random for the user to guess. Its GUI should display an underscore or asterisk (_ or `*`) for each letter in the word, and provide a means for the user to guess letters. When the user guesses a letter in the word, the program should replace the appropriate underscore(s) with that letter. When the user guesses a letter that is not in the word, the program should draw a new piece of scaffolding or body part of the man being hanged on the `Plotter`. If the player guesses all of the letters before the picture is completed, the program should display a congratulatory message; otherwise, it should display a consolation message.

14.7 Using the `Plotter` class from Section 10.3.2, design and build a GUI application that provides four boxes in which the user can supply the minimum and maximum (x,y) values for a `Plotter`, plus a means of specifying a function to be plotted. The program should then display a **Plotter** showing a plot of the function. (Hint: Locate and work through Sun's **JComboBox** tutorial on the Web; then use a **JComboBox** to let the user select the function he or she wants to display.)

14.8 The **ClickClackCloe** applet in Figure 14-25 does not account for a *stalemate*: if all cells have been clicked but no one has won, its feedback label indicates it is still the "Blue" player's turn. Modify the applet to fix this problem.

14.9 Proceed as in Project 14.8. Then add a **Reset** button to the right side of the feedback label that a user can press to reset the game to its initial state.

14.10 Proceed as in Project 14.9. Then design and build a **ClickClackCloePlayer** class, that plays the game as the "Blue" player, so that a person can play the game against the computer.

14.11 2-3 *Person Group Project*. Proceed as in Project 14.9. Then design and build two **ClickClackCloePlayer** classes, one for the "Red" player who goes first, and one for the "Blue" player who goes second. Then alter the GUI so that at the beginning of a game, a person can specify whether the computer goes first or second. (Hint: Locate and work through Sun's **JRadioButton** tutorial on the Web; then use a pair of radio buttons to let the person specify whether the computer goes first or second.)

14.12 2-3 *Person Group Project*. Choose a fun game you have enjoyed playing, or design your own original game. Build an application or applet that lets the user play the game against the computer.

Appendix A Alice Standard Methods and Functions

A.1 Alice Standard Methods

Alice *methods* are messages that we can send to an object, commanding it to do something. The object then responds with a behavior (hopefully the one we intended). The table below provides a complete list of Alice's standard methods — the commands to which all Alice objects will respond.

Method	Behavior Produced
***obj*.move(*dir*,*dist*);**	***obj*** moves ***dist*** meters in direction ***dir*** = **UP**, **DOWN**, **LEFT**, **RIGHT**, **FORWARD**, or **BACKWARD**
***obj*.turn(*dir*,*revs*);**	***obj*** turns ***revs*** revolutions in direction **LEFT**, **RIGHT**, **FORWARD**, or **BACKWARD** (that is, about its UD- or LR-axis)
***obj*.roll(*dir*,*revs*);**	***obj*** rotates ***revs*** revolutions in direction **LEFT** or **RIGHT** (that is, about its FB-axis)
***obj*.resize(*howMuch*);**	***obj***'s size changes by a factor of ***howMuch***
***obj*.say(*message*);**	***obj*** says ***message*** (via a cartoon balloon)
***obj*.think(*thought*);**	***obj*** thinks ***thought*** (via a cartoon balloon)
***obj*.playSound(*soundFile*);**	***obj*** plays the audio file ***soundFile***
***obj*.moveTo(*obj2*);**	***obj***'s *position* becomes that of ***obj2*** (***obj***'s *orientation* remains unchanged)
***obj*.moveToward(*obj2*,*dist*);**	***obj*** moves ***dist*** meters towards the position of ***obj2***

continued

Method	Behavior Produced
***obj*.moveAwayFrom(*obj2*,*dist*);**	***obj*** moves away from ***obj2***, ***dist*** meters from its current position
***obj*.orientTo(*obj2*);**	***obj***'s *orientation* becomes that of ***obj2*** (***obj***'s *position* remains unchanged)
***obj*.turnToFace(*obj2*);**	***obj*** rotates about its UD-axis until it is facing ***obj2***
***obj*.pointAt(*obj2*);**	***obj*** rotates so that its FB-axis points at ***obj2***'s center
***obj*.setPointOfView(*obj2*);**	***obj***'s *position* and *orientation* change to that of ***obj2***
***obj*.setPose(*pose*);**	***obj*** assumes the pose specified by ***pose***
***obj*.standUp();**	***obj*** rotates so that its UD-axis is vertical
***obj*.moveAtSpeed(*dir*,*mps*);**	***obj*** moves direction **UP**, **DOWN**, **LEFT**, **RIGHT**, **FORWARD**, or **BACKWARD** at ***mps*** meters/sec (for **duration** secs)[a]
***obj*.turnAtSpeed(*dir*,*rps*);**	***obj*** turns direction **LEFT**, **RIGHT**, **FORWARD**, or **BACKWARD** at ***rps*** revolutions/sec (for **duration** secs)
***obj*.rollAtSpeed(*dir*,*rps*);**	***obj*** rolls direction **LEFT** or **RIGHT** at ***rps*** revolutions/sec (for **duration** secs)
***obj*.constrainToPointAt(*obj2*);**	***obj*** points at ***obj2*** for the duration of this message

a. To make ***obj*** accelerate: use ***obj*.moveAtSpeed(*dir*, *speed*);** make ***speed*** a variable;and use a **doTogether** block to simultaneously perform the **moveAtSpeed()** method while changing the value of ***speed***.

A.2 Alice Standard Object Functions

Alice *functions* are messages we can send to an object to ask it a question. The object responds by producing a *result* — the answer to our question. The table below provides a complete list of Alice's standard functions — the questions that all Alice objects will answer:

Function	Result Produced
***obj*.isCloseTo(*dist*,*obj2*)**	**true**, if ***obj*** is within ***dist*** meters of ***obj2***; **false**, otherwise
***obj*.isFarFrom(*dist*,*obj2*)**	**true**, if ***obj*** is at least ***dist*** meters away from ***obj2***; **false**, otherwise
***obj*.distanceTo(*obj2*)**	the distance between ***obj*** and ***obj2***'s centers
***obj*.distanceToTheLeftOf(*obj2*)**	the distance from the left side of ***obj2***'s bounding box to ***obj***'s bounding box (negative if ***obj*** is not left of ***obj2***)
***obj*.distanceToTheRightOf(*obj2*)**	the distance from the right side of ***obj2***'s bounding box to ***obj***'s bounding box (negative if ***obj*** is not right of ***obj2***)
***obj*.distanceAbove(*obj2*)**	the distance from the top of ***obj2***'s bounding box to ***obj***'s bounding box (negative if ***obj*** is not above ***obj2***)
***obj*.distanceBelow(*obj2*)**	the distance from the bottom of ***obj2***'s bounding box to ***obj***'s bounding box (negative if ***obj*** is not below ***obj2***)
***obj*.distanceInFrontOf(*obj2*)**	the distance from the front of ***obj2***'s bounding box to ***obj***'s bounding box (negative if ***obj*** is not in front of ***obj2***)
***obj*.distanceBehind(*obj2*)**	the distance from the back of ***obj2***'s bounding box to ***obj***'s bounding box (negative if ***obj*** is not in back of ***obj2***)
***obj*.getWidth()**	the width (LR-axis length) of ***obj***'s bounding box
***obj*.getHeight()**	the height (UD-axis length) of ***obj***'s bounding box
***obj*.getDepth()**	the depth (FB-axis length) of ***obj***'s bounding box
***obj*.isSmallerThan(*obj2*)**	**true**, if ***obj2***'s volume exceeds that of ***obj***; **false**, otherwise

continued

Function	Result Produced
`obj.isLargerThan(obj2)`	**true**, if ***obj***'s volume exceeds that of ***obj2***; **false**, otherwise
`obj.isNarrowerThan(obj2)`	**true**, if ***obj2***'s width exceeds that of ***obj***; **false**, otherwise
`obj.isWiderThan(obj2)`	**true**, if ***obj***'s width exceeds that of ***obj2***; **false**, otherwise
`obj.isShorterThan(obj2)`	**true**, if ***obj2***'s height exceeds that of ***obj***; **false**, otherwise
`obj.isTallerThan(obj2)`	**true**, if ***obj***'s height exceeds that of ***obj2***; **false**, otherwise
`obj.isToTheLeftOf(obj2)`	**true**, if ***obj***'s position is left of ***obj2***'s left edge; **false**, otherwise
`obj.isToTheRightOf(obj2)`	**true**, if ***obj***'s position is right of ***obj2***'s right edge; **false**, otherwise
`obj.isAbove(obj2)`	**true**, if ***obj***'s position is above ***obj2***'s top edge; **false**, otherwise
`obj.isBelow(obj2)`	**true**, if ***obj***'s position is below ***obj2***'s bottom edge; **false**, otherwise
`obj.isInFrontOf(obj2)`	**true**, if ***obj***'s position is before ***obj2***'s front edge; **false**, otherwise
`obj.isBehind(obj2)`	**true**, if ***obj***'s position is in back of ***obj2***'s rear edge; **false**, otherwise
`obj.getPointOfView()`	the point of view (*position+orientation*) of ***obj***
`obj.getPosition()`	the *position* (with respect to the world's axes) of ***obj***
`obj.getQuaternion()`	the *orientation* (with respect to the world's axes) of ***obj***
`obj.getCurrentPose()`	the current ***Pose*** (*position+orientation* of subparts) of ***obj***
`obj.partNamed(piece)`	the subpart of ***obj*** named ***piece***

A.3 Alice World Functions

Alice *world functions* are implementations of commonly needed computations. The table below provides a complete list of Alice's world functions.

Function	Result Produced
`!a`	`true`, if ***a*** is `false`; `false`, otherwise
`(a && b)`	`true`, if ***a*** and ***b*** are both `true`; `false`, if ***a*** or ***b*** is `false`
`(a || b)`	`true`, if either ***a*** or ***b*** are `true`; `false`, if neither ***a*** nor ***b*** is `true`
`a == b`	`true`, if ***a*** and ***b*** have the same value; `false`, otherwise
`a != b`	`true`, if ***a*** and ***b*** have different values; `false`, otherwise
`a < b`	`true`, if ***a***'s value is less than ***b***'s value; `false`, otherwise
`a > b`	`true`, if ***a***'s value is greater than ***b***'s value; `false`, otherwise
`a <= b`	`true`, if ***a***'s value is less than or equal to ***b***'s value; `false`, otherwise
`a >= b`	`true`, if ***a***'s value is greater than or equal to ***b***'s value; `false`, otherwise
`Random.nextBoolean()`	a pseudo-randomly chosen `true` or `false` value
`Random.nextDouble()`	a pseudo-randomly chosen number
`a + b`	the string consisting of ***a*** followed by ***b*** (concatenation)
`what.toString()`	the string representation of ***`what`*** (string conversion)
`NumberDialog(question)`	a number entered by the user in response to ***`question`***

continued

Function	Result Produced
`BooleanDialog(`***`question`***`)`	**`true`**, if the user responds to ***`question`*** by clicking the dialog box's **`Yes`** button; **`false`**, otherwise
`StringDialog(`***`question`***`)`	a string entered by the user in response to ***`question`***
`mouse.getDistanceFromLeftEdge()`	the number of pixels the mouse is from the left edge of the window (corresponds to x of an [x,y] coordinate)
`mouse.getDistanceFromTopEdge()`	the number of pixels the mouse is from the top edge of the window (corresponds to y of an [x,y] coordinate)
`getTimeElapsedSinceWorldStart()`	the number of "ticks" since the world began running
`getYear()`	a number representing the current year
`getMonthOfYear()`	a number representing the current month (Jan-0, Feb-1, etc.)
`getDayOfYear()`	a number representing the current day of the year
`getDayOfMonth()`	a number representing the current day of the month
`getDayOfWeek()`	a number representing the current day of the week (Sun-1, etc.)
`getDayOfWeekInMonth()`	a number for how many times the current day of the week has occurred in the current month
`isAM()`	**`true`**, if the current time is between midnight and noon; **`false`**, otherwise
`isPM()`	**`true`**, if the current time is between noon and midnight; **`false`**, otherwise
`getHourOfAMOrPM()`	the hour value of the current time, 12-hour format
`getHourOfDay()`	the hour value of the current time, 24-hour format
`getMinuteOfHour()`	the minute value of the current time

continued

Function	Result Produced
`getSecondOfMinute()`	the second value of the current time
`Math.min(a, b)`	the minimum of **a** and **b**
`Math.max(a, b)`	the maximum of **a** and **b**
`Math.abs(a)`	the absolute value of **a**
`Math.sqrt(a)`	the square root of **a**
`Math.floor(a)`	the largest integer smaller than **a**
`Math.ceiling(a)`	the smallest integer larger than **a**
`Math.sin(a)`	the sine of **a**
`Math.cos(a)`	the cosine of **a**
`Math.tan(a)`	the tangent of **a**
`Math.asin(a)`	the angle whose sine is **a**
`Math.acos(a)`	the angle whose cosine is **a**
`Math.atan(a)`	the angle whose tangent is **a**
`Math.atan2(x, y)`	the polar coordinate angle associated with Cartesian coordinate (**x, y**)
`Math.pow(a, b)`	**a** raised to the power **b** (a^b)
`Math.natural log of(a)`	the number **x** such that e^x == **a**; **e** being Euler's number
`Math.exp(a)`	Euler's number **e** raised to the power **a** (e^a)
`Math.IEEERemainder(a, b)`	the remainder of **a/b** using integer division
`Math.round(a)`	the integer whose value is closest to **a**
`Math.toDegrees(r)`	the angle in degrees corresponding to radians **r**
`Math.toRadians(d)`	the angle in radians corresponding to degrees **d**
`superSquareRoot(a, b)`	the bth root of **a**
`getVector(right, up, forward)`	an x-y-z vector [x==**right**, y== **up**, z==**forward**]

Appendix B Recursion

Hundreds of years before there were computers, programming languages, or loop statements, mathematicians were defining functions, many of which required repetitive behavior. One way to provide such behavior without using a loop is to have a function or method *invoke itself*, causing its statements to repeat. Such a method (or function) is called **recursive**. To illustrate, suppose we were to define a method for Alice's **camera** named **repeatRoll()** as follows:

```
void camera.repeatRoll() {
   camera.roll(LEFT, 1);
   camera.repeatRoll();
}
```

When invoked, this method will make the **camera** roll left 1 revolution, and then invoke itself. That second invocation will make the **camera** roll left 1 revolution, and then call itself. That third invocation will make the **camera** roll left 1 revolution, and then call itself; and so on. The result is thus an "infinite" repetition, or **infinite recursion**.[1]

To avoid infinite repetition, recursive methods and functions typically have (1) a **Number** parameter, (2) an **if** statement that only performs the recursion if the parameter's value exceeds some lower bound, and (3) a recursive call within the **if** statement that passes a value smaller than the parameter as an argument. The net effect is that the function or method counts downward toward the lower bound, typically 0 or 1. To illustrate, we might revise the preceding **repeatRoll()** method as follows:

```
void camera.repeatRoll(Number count) {  // the parameter count
   if (count > 0) {                      // if statement guards
      camera.roll(LEFT, 1);
      camera.repeatRoll(count - 1);     // ... the recursive call
   }
}
```

1. Since each recursive call consumes additional memory, the looping behavior will eventually end — when the program runs out of memory. However, we will become tired of the **camera** rolling long before that occurs!

When invoked with a numeric argument ***n***, this version of the function will roll the camera ***n*** times and then stop. For example, if we send the message **camera.repeatRoll(3);**

1. This starts **repeatRoll(3)**, in which parameter **count** == **3**.
2. The method checks the condition **count > 0**.
3. Since the condition is true, the method (a) rolls the **camera** left 1 revolution, and (b) sends the message **camera.repeatRoll(2);**.
4. This starts **repeatRoll(2)**, a new version in which parameter **count** == **2**.
5. The method checks the condition **count > 0**.
6. Since the condition is true, the method (a) rolls the **camera** left 1 revolution, and (b) sends the message **camera.repeatRoll(1);**.
7. This starts **repeatRoll(1)**, a new version in which parameter **count** == **1**.
8. The method checks the condition **count > 0**.
9. Since the condition is true, the method (a) rolls the **camera** left 1 revolution, and (b) sends the message **camera.repeatRoll(0);**.
10. This starts **repeatRoll(0)**, a new version in which parameter **count** == **0**.
11. The method checks the condition **count > 0**.
12. Since the condition is false, the method terminates; flow returns to the sender of **repeatRoll(0)** — **repeatRoll(1)** — the version where **count** == **1**.
13. The version in which **count** == **1** terminates; flow returns to the sender of **repeatRoll(1)** — **repeatRoll(2)** — the version in which **count** == **2**.
14. The version in which **count** == **2** terminates; flow returns to the sender of **repeatRoll(2)** — **repeatRoll(3)** — the version in which **count** == **3**.
15. The version in which **count** == **3** terminates; flow returns to the sender of **repeatRoll(3)**.

Steps 1–11, in which the repeated messages are counting downward toward the lower bound, are sometimes called the **winding phase** of the recursion. Steps 13–15, in which the chain of recursive messages terminates, are sometimes called the **unwinding phase** of the recursion.

Recursion thus provides an alternative way to achieve repetitive behavior. When the recursive message is the last behavior-producing statement in the method, as follows:

```
void camera.repeatRoll(Number count) {
    if (count > 0) {
        camera.roll(LEFT, 1);
        camera.repeatRoll(count - 1);   // the last statement
    }
}
```

it is called **tail recursion**, because the recursive message occurs at the end or "tail" of the method. Any function defined using tail recursion can be defined using a loop, and vice versa. But in Section B.2, we will see that one recursion method can produce behavior that would require multiple loops.

B.1 Tail Recursion

Suppose that at the end of Scene 1 of a story, the main character goes to sleep at 11 p.m., and the **camera** zooms in to a closeup of the clock in his or her bedroom. Shot 1 of Scene 2 begins with that same clock, showing the time to be 11 p.m. Suppose that our story calls for the clock's hands to spin, indicating that time is "flying ahead." When the hands reach 3 am, a fairy appears and works some sort of mischief on the sleeping main character exactly what mischief is left up to you).

To build the scene, we can go to the Alice Gallery, add a **bedroom** from the **Environments** folder, add a **Dresser** from the **Furniture** folder, add a **mantleClock** from the **Objects** folder, and add **OliveWaterblossom** from the **People** folder as our fairy. To set the scene, we can manually advance the clock's hands to 11 p.m. (using right-click**->methods->mantleClock.roll()** messages), make **OliveWaterblossom** smaller, position her next to the clock, set her **opacity** to zero, and then position the **camera** appropriately. Our scene thus starts as shown in Figure B-1.

FIGURE B-1 Beginning Scene 2

To follow the story, we need a way to make the clock's hands spin forward to 3 a.m. Since this is a counting problem, we could do so using a **for** loop; but for variety, let's instead use tail recursion. The basic algorithm is as follows:

Algorithm: advance-the-clock's-hands *hours* hours

Given: *hours*, the number of hours to spin the clock's hands forward

1. If *hours* > 0:
   a. Spin the hour and minute hands forward one hour
   b. advance-the-clock's-hands *hours*-1

Building a **mantleClock.advanceHands()** method this way is straightforward. However, when we perform the recursion by drag-and-dropping the **mantleClock.advanceHands()** method into the same method, Alice warns us that we're sending a recursive message, as shown in Figure B-2.

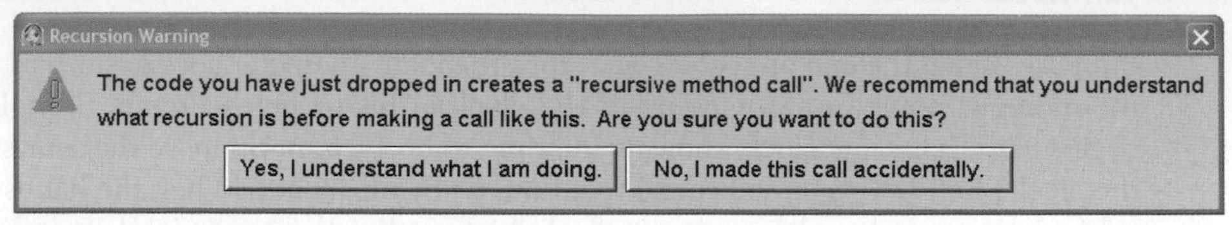

FIGURE B-2 Alice's recursion warning dialog box

Since we think we know what we are doing, we click the **Yes, I understand what I am doing** button. The resulting method is shown in Figure B-3.

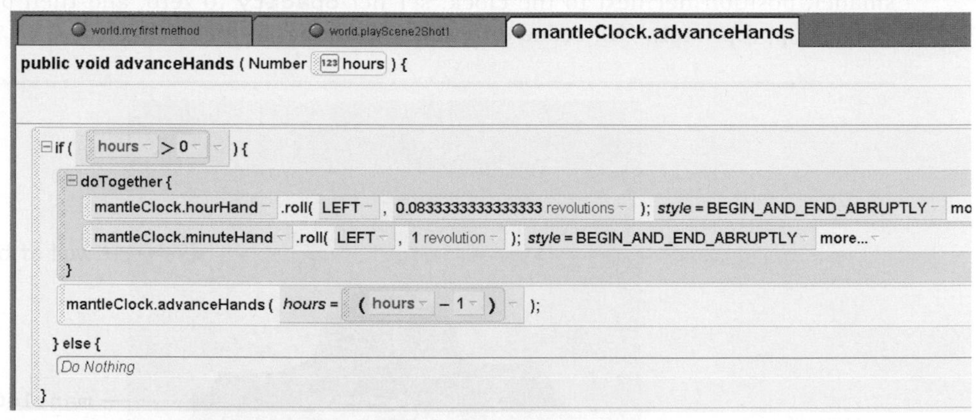

FIGURE B-3 An **advanceHands()** method

When invoked with a positive **hours** value, this method spins the clock's hands forward one hour, and then invokes itself recursively with **hours-1** as an argument. The method thus "counts down" recursively from whatever **hours** value it receives initially, until it is invoked with an **hours** value of 0, at which point the recursion terminates.

We can use this method to build the **playScene2Shot1()** method, as shown in Figure B-4.

world.my first method | world.playScene2Shot1 | mantleClock.advanceHands

```
public void playScene2Shot1 () {

  doInOrder {
    mantleClock.advanceHands( hours = 4 );
    OliveWaterblossom .set( opacity , 1 (100%) ); more...
    OliveWaterblossom .say( I'm feeling mischievous... ); duration = 2 seconds fontSize = 30 more...
    // The fairy does something magical...
  }
```

FIGURE B-4 The **`playScene2Shot1()`** method

When performed, the scene begins with the setup shown in Figure B-1. The **`advanceHands(4)`** message then spins the clock's hands forward four hours, after which **`OliveWaterblossom`** appears and says she's feeling mischievous, as shown in Figure B-5.

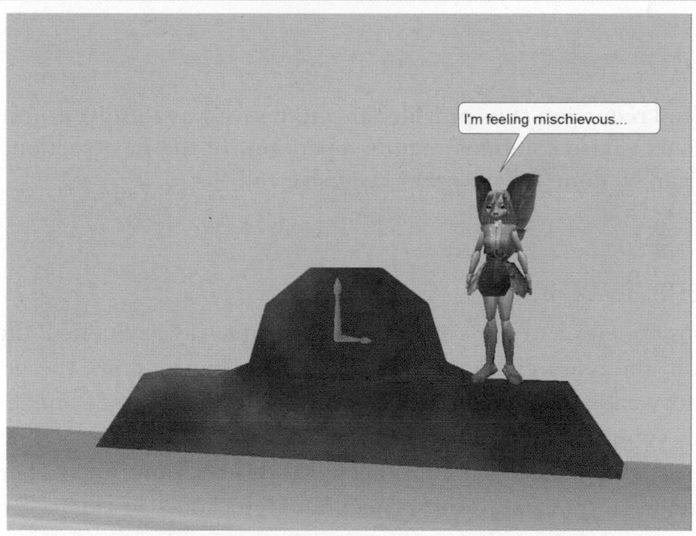

FIGURE B-5 The end of Shot 1 of Scene 2

If you compare the definition of the **advanceHands()** method with the **repeatRoll()** method we described earlier, you'll see that both follow the same basic pattern:

Simplified Pattern for Tail Recursion:

```
void tailRecursiveMethod ( Number count ) {
    if ( count > LOWER_BOUND ) {
        produceBehaviorOnce();
        tailRecursiveMethod( count-1 );
    }
}
```

where:

produceBehaviorOnce() produces the behavior to be repeated.

A method that follows this pattern will produce results equivalent to those produced by the following nonrecursive pattern:

```
void nonRecursiveMethod( Number count ) {
    for ( int i = count; i > 0; count-- ) {
        produceBehaviorOnce();
    }
}
```

Tail recursion thus provides an alternative way to solve counting problems and other problems whose solutions require repetition. In the next section, we will see that useful work can be done *following* the recursive call.

B.2 General Recursion

Suppose Scene 3 of our story begins the same way as Scene 2 did: with a closeup of the clock in the main character's bedroom, showing 11 p.m., the next night. In this scene, our story calls for time to fly ahead eight hours to 7 a.m., once again indicated by the clock's spinning hands, Then **OliveWaterblossom** appears, once again intent on mischief. In this scene, her mischief is to reverse time everywhere except for the main character, so that upon waking up after eight hours of sleep — fully rested — it will be 11 p.m. again! To indicate that time is flowing in reverse, we must spin the clock's hands backward eight hours.

We could accomplish this by using our **advanceHands()** method to spin the clock's hands forward eight hours, and then writing a **reverseHands()** method to make the hands spin backward eight hours, using either tail recursion or a **for** loop. Instead, let's see how recursion lets us perform both of these steps in one method.

The key idea is to use recursion's winding phase to spin the hands forward (as before), and then use the unwinding phase to make the hands spin backward. In between the two phases — when we have reached our lower bound — **OliveWaterblossom** can work her magic.

Algorithm: wind-and-unwind-the-clock's-hands *hours* hours

Given: *hours*, the number of hours to spin the clock's hands forward

1. If *hours* > 0:
   a. Spin the hour and minute hands forward one hour
   b. wind-and-unwind-the-clock's-hands *hours-1*
   c. Spin the hour and minute hands backward one hour
2. Else:
   a. OliveWaterblossom appears
   b. OliveWaterblossom works her magic

Understanding how this works can be difficult the first time you see it. One way to understand it is to see that Step 1c does the exact opposite of Step 1a. That is, during the winding phase, Step 1a spins the clock's hands forward one hour; then Step 1b sends the recursive message, preventing flow from reaching Step 1c (for the time being). When the lower bound is reached, the **if** statement's condition is false, so **OliveWaterblossom** works her magic; and since no recursive message is sent, the repetition halts. The recursion then starts to unwind, with flow returning to Step 1c in each message, which "undoes" the effects of Step 1a. Figure B-6 gives a numbered visualization of what happens when *hours* has the value 8. The steps that are performed within each message at a given point are highlighted.

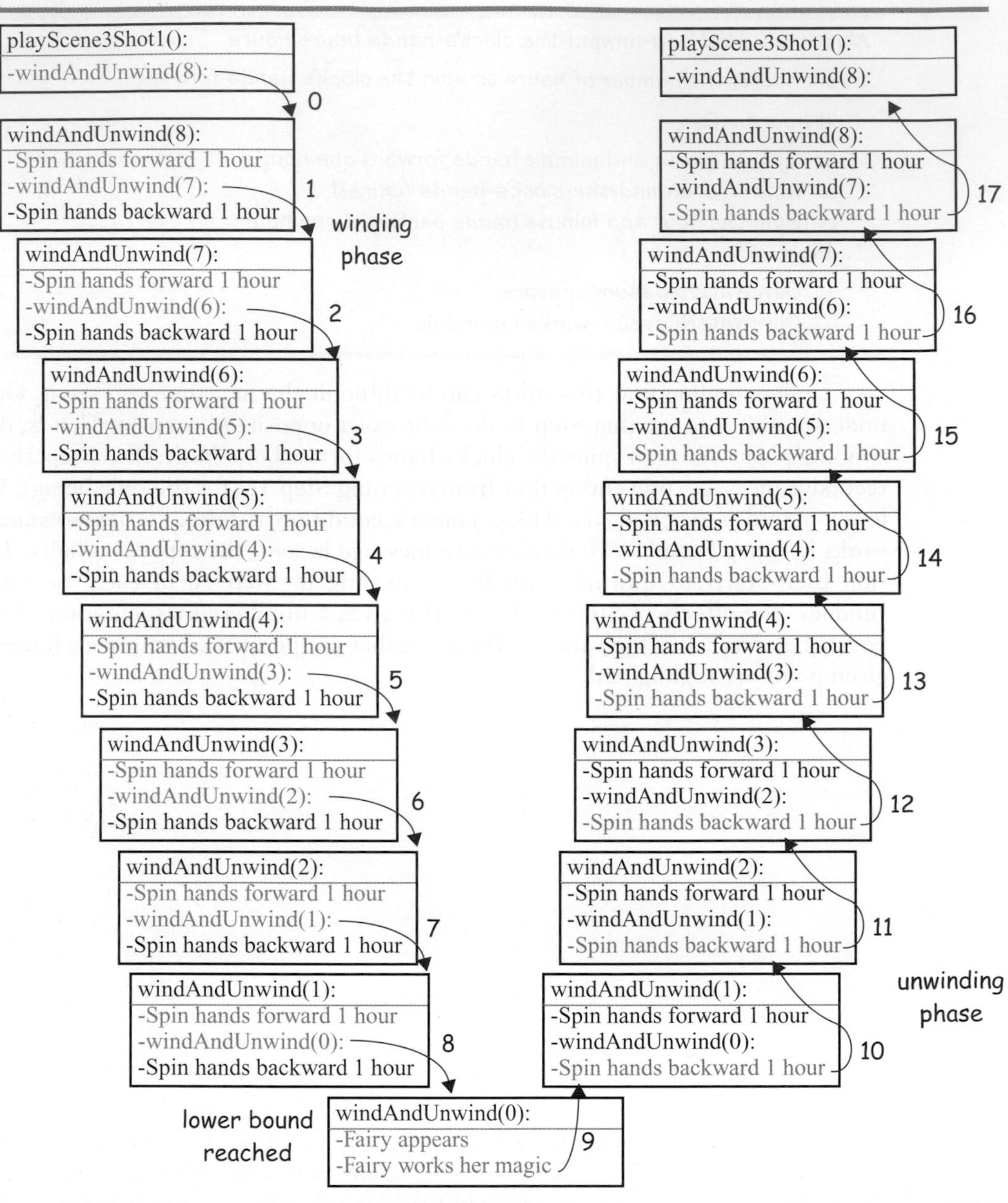

FIGURE B-6 Recursive winding and unwinding

We can define this method in Alice, as shown in Figure B-7.

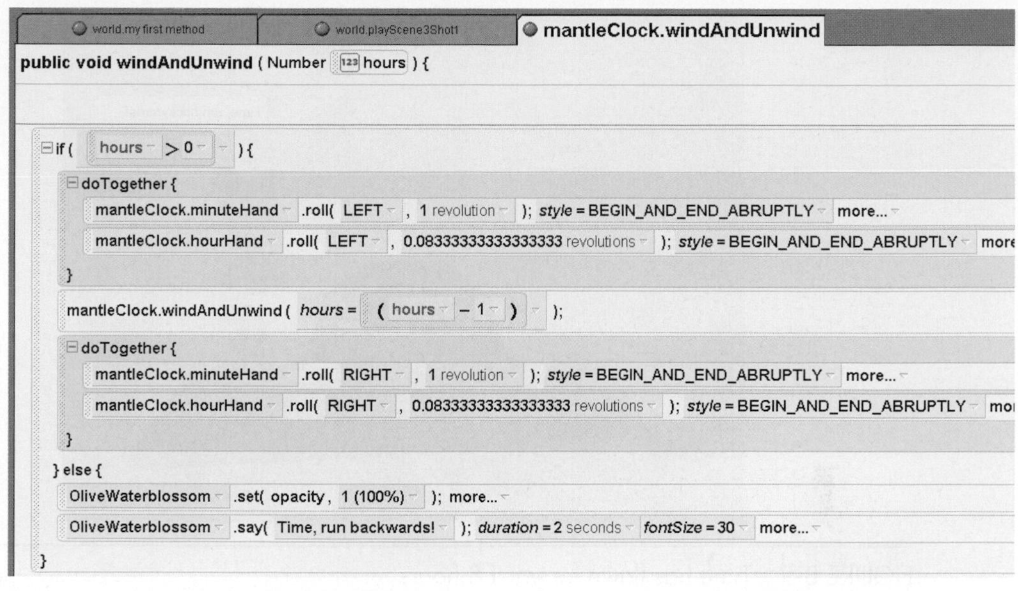

FIGURE B-7 The **windAndUnwind()** method

Given such a method, **playScene3Shot1()** is quite simple, as shown in Figure B-8.

```
world.my first method | world.playScene3Shot1 | mantleClock.windAndUnwind
public void playScene3Shot1 ( ) {

mantleClock.windAndUnwind ( hours = 8 );
// Now do the rest of Shot 1 of Scene 3
```

FIGURE B-8 The **windAndUnwind()** method

When performed, the method starts out with the scene shown in Figure B-1. Once again, we see "time fly" as the hands wind forward, but this time they advance eight hours. Our fairy then appears and says her line, as shown in Figure B-9.

FIGURE B-9 Time has flown forward 8 hours

The hands then spin backward, returning to their original positions, as shown in Figure B-10.

FIGURE B-10 Time has flown backward 8 hours

It is thus possible to do work during both the winding and the unwinding phases of a chain of recursive messages. Any statements that we want to be performed during the winding phase must be positioned before the recursive call, and any statements that we want to be performed during the unwinding phase must be positioned after the recursive call.

The pattern below can be used to design many recursive methods:

```
Simplified Pattern for Recursion:
void recursiveMethod ( Number count ) {
    if ( count > LOWER_BOUND ) {
        windingPhaseBehavior();
        recursiveMethod( count-1 );
        unwindingPhaseBehavior();
    } else {
        betweenPhasesBehavior();
    }
}
```

B.3 Recursion and Design

Now that we have seen some examples of recursive methods, how does one go about designing such methods?

Recall that recursive methods usually have a **Number** parameter. Designing a recursive method generally involves two steps: (1) identifying the **trivial case** — how to solve the problem when the value of this parameter makes the problem trivial to solve; and (2) identifying the **nontrivial case** — how to use recursion to solve the problem for all of the other (nontrivial) cases. Once we have done so, we can plug these cases into this template:

```
someType recursiveMethod(Number count) {
   if (count indicates that this is a nontrivial case) {
      solve the problem recursively, reducing count
   } else { // it's the trivial case
      solve the trivial version of the problem
   }
}
```

To illustrate, let's apply this approach to one of the functions mathematicians defined recursively long before there were computers.

Pretend for a moment that you are an elementary school student, whose teacher just caught you misbehaving during math class. As a "punishment," your teacher makes you stay in at each recess until you have calculated 10! (10 factorial), 20! (20 factorial), and 30! (30 factorial). Even with a calculator, this will take us a long time, because the factorial function *n!* is defined as follows:

$$n! = 1 \times 2 \times \ldots \times (n-1) \times n$$

FIGURE B-11 n!, in open form notation

That is, 1! == 1, 2! == 2, 3! == 6, 4! == 24, 5! == 120, and so on. 0! is also defined to equal 1, and the function is not defined for negative values of *n*.

While we could solve this problem by hand, doing so would be long and tedious, and we would lose lots of recess time. So let's instead write an Alice program to solve it!

To do so, we can start out like we did in Section 3.5.2, and build a scene containing a character (**`Roommate`**, in this case) who can do factorials "in her head," positioned within an Alice **`School`** environment, as shown in Figure B-12.

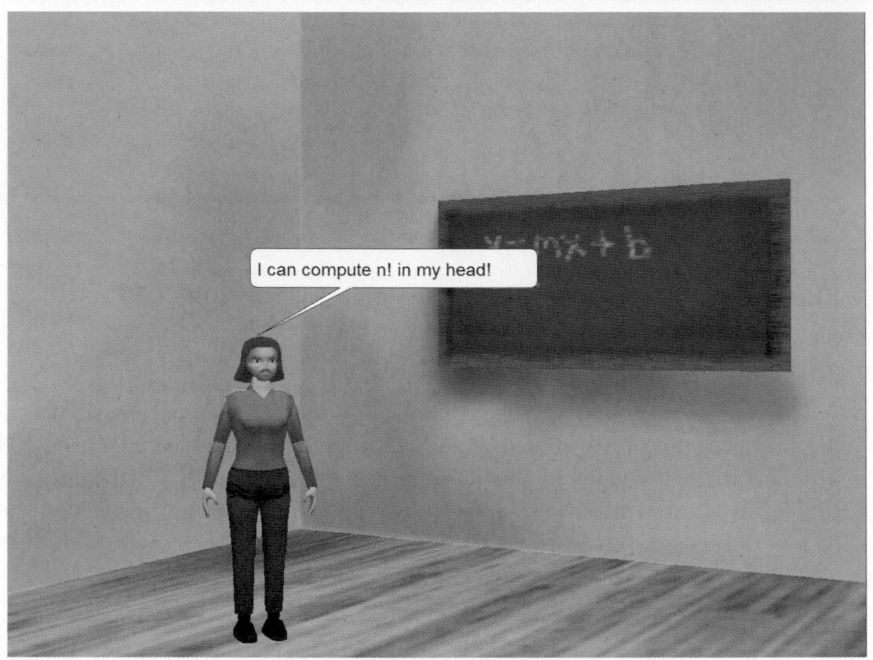

FIGURE B-12 Setting the scene to compute n!

With such a scene in place, we just have to (1) write a **`factorial()`** function, (2) get ***`n`*** from the user, (3) invoke and save the answer of **`factorial(`*`n`*`)`**, and (4) display the answer.

Let's begin by writing the **`factorial()`** function. If we examine the description given in Figure B-11, it should be evident that this is a counting problem, and so we could solve it using a **`for`** loop. However, let's instead see how the mathematicians would have solved it back in the days before there were **`for`** loops.

B.3.1 The Trivial Case

We start by identifying the trivial case. What is a version of the problem that is trivial to solve? Since 0! == 1 and 1! == 1, we actually have two trivial cases: when n == 0, and when n == 1. In either case, our function needs to return the value 1.

B.3.2 The Nontrivial Cases

To solve the nontrivial cases, we look for a way to solve the general **n!** problem, assuming that we can solve a smaller but similar problem (for example, **(n-1)!**). If we compare the two:

$$n! = 1 \times 2 \times \ldots \times (n-1) \times n$$

$$(n-1)! = 1 \times 2 \times \ldots \times (n-1)$$

it should be evident that we can rewrite the equation in Figure B-11 by performing a substitution, as shown in Figure B-13.

$$n! = (n-1)! \times n$$

FIGURE B-13 n!, in recursive, closed form notation

B.3.3 Solving the Problem

The trivial and nontrivial cases can be combined into a complete solution to the problem, as shown in Figure B-14.

$$n! = \begin{cases} (n-1)! \times n, \text{ if } n > 1 \\ 1, \text{ if } n == 0 \text{ OR } n == 1 \\ \text{undefined, otherwise} \end{cases}$$

FIGURE B-14 Recursive algorithm for n!

The equation given in Figure B-14 can serve as an algorithm for us to define our **factorial()** function in Alice, as shown in Figure B-15.

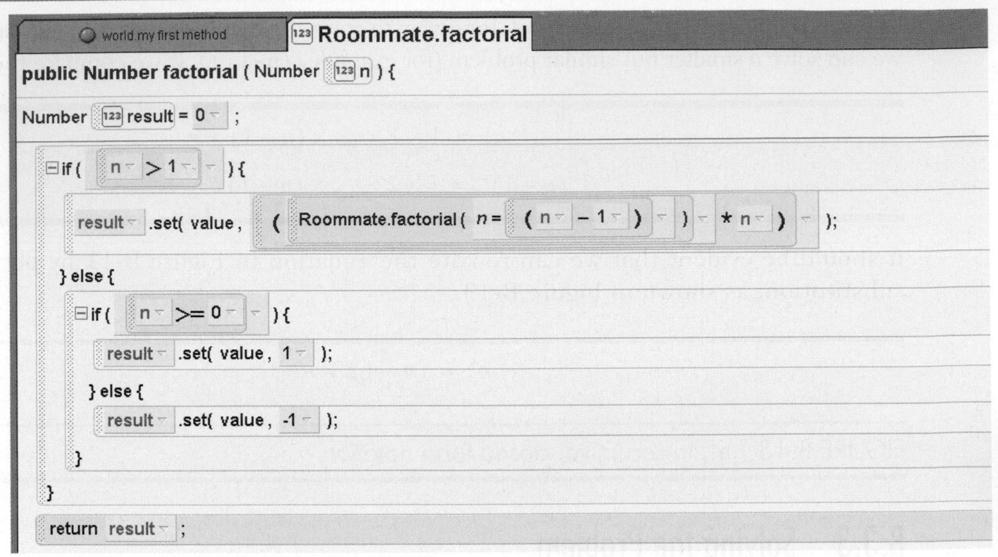

FIGURE B-15 The `factorial()` function in Alice

Note that because **n!** is undefined when **n** is negative, and **n!** never returns **-1** under normal circumstances, we have our function return **-1** when **n** is negative.

With this function defined, we can now finish our program, as shown in Figure B-16.

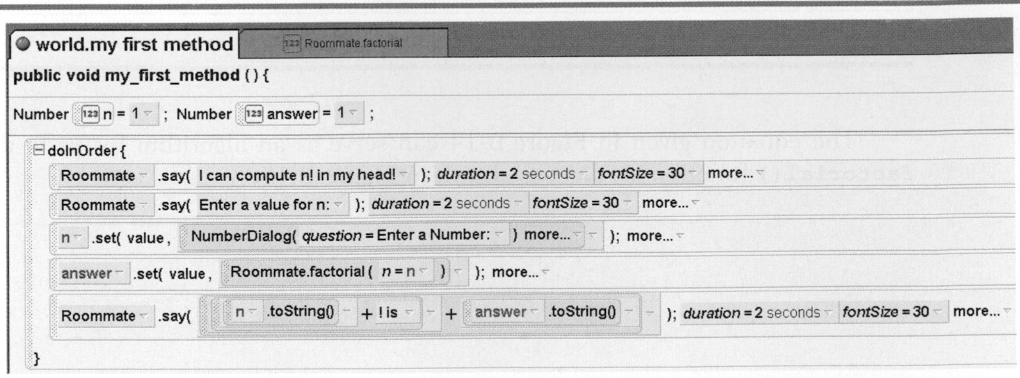

FIGURE B-16 The `factorial()` program in Alice

When run, the program has us enter a value for ***n***, and then displays ***n!***. After testing our function on easily verified values (such as 0, 1, 2, 3, 4, and 5), we can solve the problems our teacher assigned. Figure B-17 shows the result when we use the program to compute 10!.

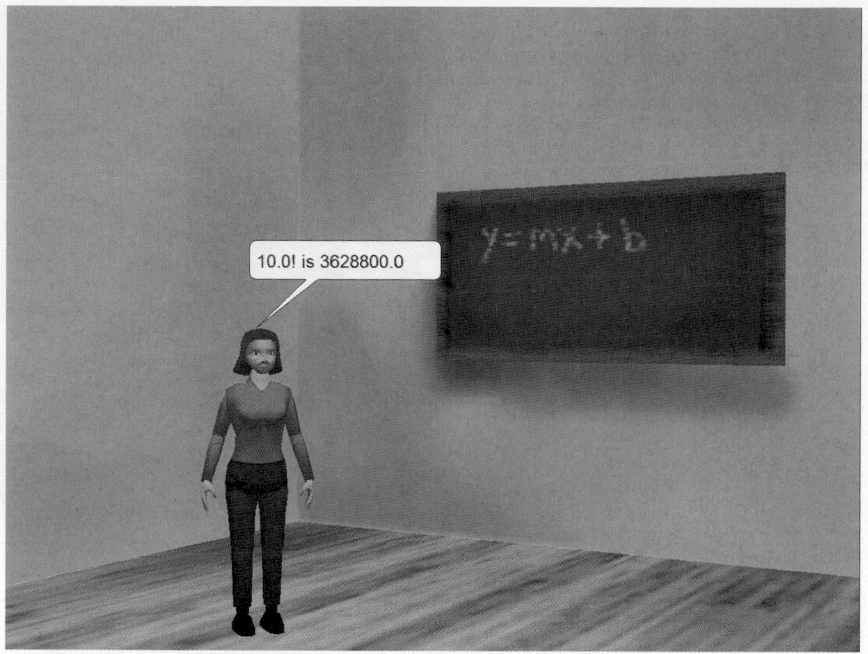

FIGURE B-17 The `factorial()` program in Alice

It's recess time!

B.4 Another Recursive Method

Consider the following user story.

> Scene 1, Shot 1: zeus, socrates, aliceLiddell, plato, euripides, and the white Rabbit are all waiting to practice basketball. The coach says, "Ok, everyone line up by height!" The players line up, tallest to shortest.
> Scene 1, Shot 2: The coach says, "No, line up the other way -- shortest to tallest!" The players reverse their order.

Scene 1, Shot 1 is mainly to get things set up, so we will leave it as an exercise. What we want to do is to build Scene 1, Shot 2, especially that part in which the players reverse their order.

It is fairly easy to get our scene to the point shown in Figure B-18.

FIGURE B-18 Scene 1, Shot 2 (beginning)

But how can we make our players reverse their order?

Since we have a group of players, and their number is fixed, one idea is to store them in an array, tallest to smallest, as shown in Figure B-19.

```
world.my first method    world.playScene1Shot2
public void my_first_method () {
Object[] anArray = zeus, socrates, plato, euripides, aliceLiddell, whiteRabbit ;
world.playScene1Shot2 ( );
```

FIGURE B-19 Scene 1, Shot 2 (beginning)

The first array element is the tallest player, the second array element is the second tallest player, and so on. We can visualize **anArray** as shown in Figure B-20.

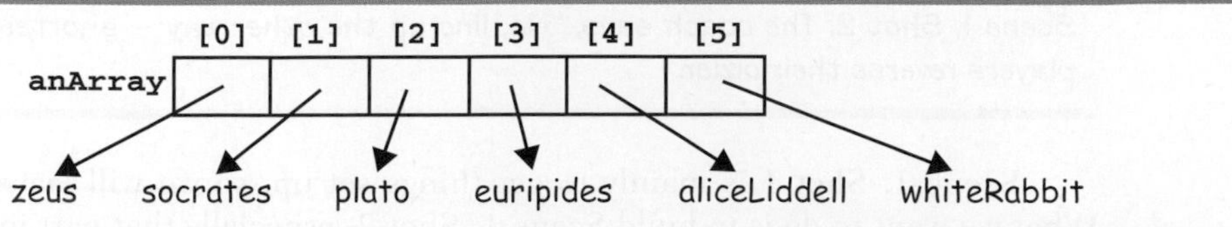

FIGURE B-20 Visualizing **anArray**

With the players in order within the data structure, we can transform our problem into this one:

Reverse the positions of the players in anArray.

One way to accomplish this is to (1) make the first and last players in the array swap positions within our world, as shown in Figure B-21, and then (2) reverse the remaining players in the array (that is, ignoring the **whiteRabbit** and **zeus**) the same way — a recursive solution!

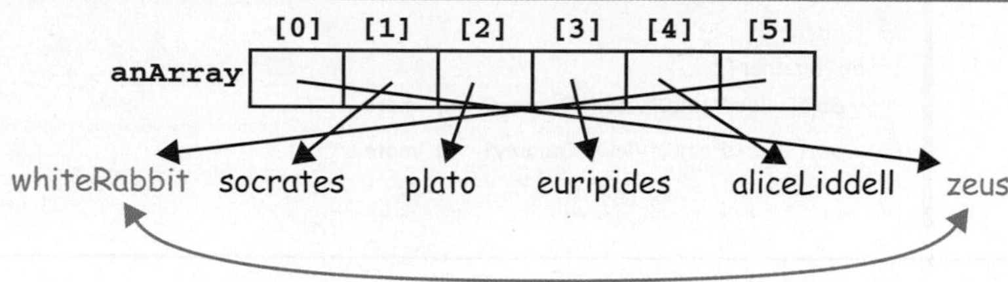

FIGURE B-21 The tallest and smallest players swap positions

To do so, we would need a method named **reverse()**, to which we can pass the array containing our players, plus the indices of the players that are to swap positions:

```
reverse(anArray, 0, 5);
```

Our method thus requires three parameters: an **Object** array, a **Number** to store the first index, and a **Number** to store the second index:

```
void reverse(Object [] arr, Number index1, Number index2) {
}
```

To get two objects to swap positions, we can write a method named **swapPositions()**, and pass to it the two objects whose positions we want to swap. Figure B-22 shows one way to do so, by adding two dummies to our world, and then using them within our method to mark the original positions of the two objects we wish to move.

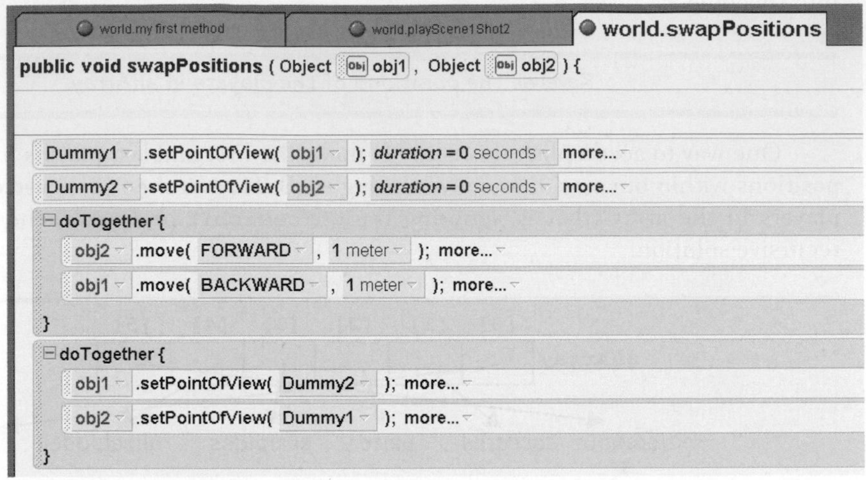

FIGURE B-22 Exchanging two objects' positions

In this definition, the two objects move simultaneously, one moving in front of the line of players, and the other moving behind the line of players, to avoid colliding with one another.

With method **swapPositions()** in hand, we are ready to define the recursive **reverse()** method.

B.4.1 The Trivial Case

As we have seen, the first step in defining a recursive method is to find a case where the problem is trivial to solve. Since our **reverse()** method has this form:

```
void reverse(Object [] arr, Number index1, Number index2) {
}
```

any trivial cases must be identified using the **Number** parameters, **index1** and **index2**.

At this point, it is helpful to generalize our thinking from the specific problem at hand to the more general problem of reversing the positions of objects stored in an arbitrary array **arr**, where **index1** contains the index of the array's first element, and **index2** contains the index of the array's last element. Thinking this way, there are two cases in which the problem of reversing the positions of the items in **arr** is trivial to solve:

1. If there is just one object in **arr**, then the object is already in its final position, so we should do nothing. There is one object in the array when **index1 == index2**.
2. If there are zero objects in **arr**, then there are no objects to move, so we should do nothing. There are zero items in the array when **index1 > index2**.

Since we do the same thing (nothing) in each of our trivial cases, the condition **`index1 >= index2`** will identify both of our trivial cases. Conversely, the condition **`index1 < index2`** can be used to identify our nontrivial cases.

B.4.2 The Nontrivial Cases

We have hinted at how the nontrivial cases can be solved. Since **`index1`** is the index of the first (tallest) object in the array, and **`index2`** is the index of the smallest object in the array, we:

1. Swap the positions of the objects in **`arr[index1]`** and **`arr[index2]`**
2. Reverse the rest of the objects (ignoring the ones we just swapped) recursively.

The trick is to figure out how to do Step 2. Drawing a diagram is often helpful, as shown in Figure B-23:

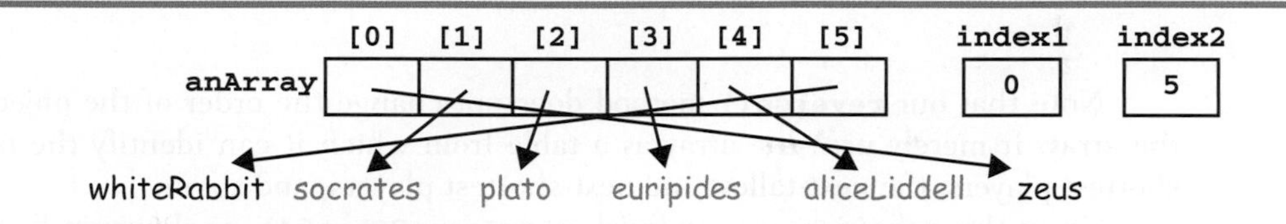

FIGURE B-23 Visualizing the recursive step

This allows us to clearly see the sub-array of objects that Step 2 must reverse; it begins at index 1 and ends at 4. However, to correctly solve the problem, we must express the arguments in Step 2 in terms of changes to our method's parameters, **`index1`** and **`index2`**. Expressed this way, the sub-array to be processed by Step 2 begins at index **`index1+1`**, and ends at **`index2-1`**. That is, we can solve the nontrivial cases of the problem as follows:

1. Swap the positions of the objects in **`arr[index1]`** and **`arr[index2]`**.
2. Recursively invoke **`reverse(arr, index1+1, index2-1)`**.

That's it! Figure B-24 presents a definition of **`reverse()`** that uses this approach.

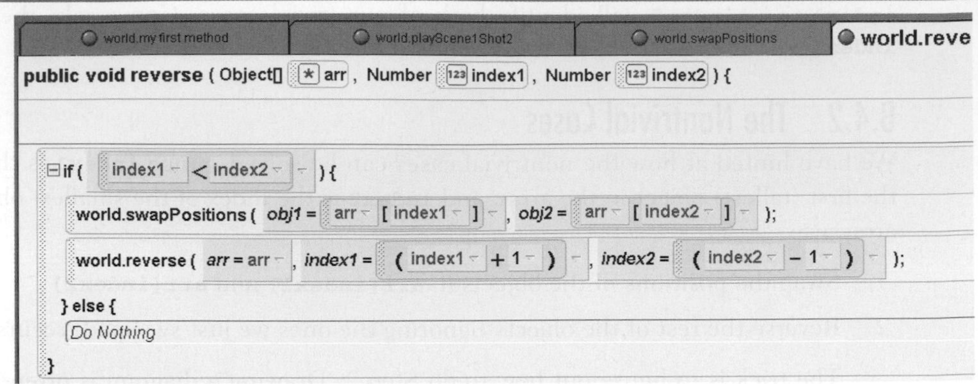

FIGURE B-24 The recursive `reverse()` method

Note that our **`reverse()`** method does not change the order of the objects within the array. It merely uses the array as a table from which it can identify the tallest and shortest players, the next-tallest and next-shortest players, and so on.

Given this definition, we can finish **`playScene2Shot2()`**, as shown in Figure B-25.

```
world.my first method | world.playScene1Shot2 | world.swapPositions | world.reverse
public void playScene1Shot2 () {
coach .say( No, line up the other way -- shortest to tallest! ); duration = 3 seconds fontSize = 30 more...
world.reverse ( arr = anArray , index1 = 0 , index2 = 5 );
```

FIGURE B-25 Completed `playScene1Shot2()` method

Figure B-26 presents some screen captures taken as **`playScene1Shot2()`** runs. Compare them to the initial setting shown in Figure B-18 to see the progression of changes.

FIGURE B-26 Screen captures of Scene 1, Shot 2

Figure B-27 provides a conceptual view of what happens as **`reverse()`** runs.

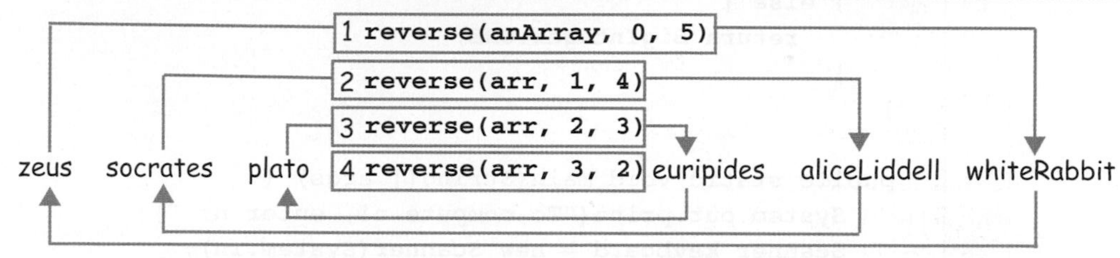

FIGURE B-27 Conceptualizing **`reverse()`**

The fourth message, **`reverse(arr, 3, 2)`**, invokes the trivial case, halting the recursion.

Recursion is a powerful programming technique that can be used to solve any problem that can be decomposed into one or more "smaller" problems that are solved in the same way.

B.5 Recursive Factorials in Java

Java also supports recursion. For example, the same recursive algorithm we designed in Section B.3 to solve the factorial problem can be programmed in Java. Figure B-28 presents the same algorithm encoded twice. The method **`factorial1()`** uses the type **`long`** as its return type, while the method **`factorial2()`** uses Java's **`BigInteger`** class as its return type. The **`BigInteger`** class is specifically designed to handle very large integers like those generated by the factorial function.

```
/** FactorialFinder.java performs the factorial function...
 */
import java.util.Scanner;
```

continued

```java

public class FactorialFinder {
  public static long factorial1(int n) {
     if (n > 1) {
        return factorial(n-1) * n;
     } else {
        return 1;
     }
  }

  public static BigInteger factorial2(int n) {
     if (n > 1) {
        String nAsString = Integer.toString(n);
        BigInteger bigN = new BigInteger(nAsString);
        return factorial2(n-1).multiply(bigN);
     } else {
        return BigInteger.ONE;
     }
  }

  public static void main(String[] args) {
     System.out.print("To compute n!, enter n: ");
     Scanner keyboard = new Scanner(System.in);
     int n = keyboard.nextInt();
     System.out.printf("%d! == %d%n", n, factorial1(n) );
     System.out.printf("%d! == %s%n", n, factorial2(n) );
  }
}
```

```
Result:
To compute n!, enter n: 5
5! == 120
5! == 120
Result:
To compute n!, enter n: 20
20! == 2432902008176640000
20! == 2432902008176640000
Result:
To compute n!, enter n: 30
30! == -8764578968847253504
30! == 265252859812191058636308480000000
```

FIGURE B-28 Two recursive factorial methods in Java

The **factorial1()** method returns a **long** instead of an **int** because the factorial function's rapid growth will cause a 32-bit **int** to overflow when computing **13!**. Using **long** as the return type is better, but still overflows when computing **21!** We could use the type **double**, but that only helps a little, as **22!** produces inaccurate results. The numbers just become too big for Java's primitive types to handle, since each uses a limited amount of memory.

For these kinds of situations, Java provides the **BigInteger** class used in **factorial2()**. The **add()**, **subtract()**, **multiply()**, and **divide()** methods produce completely accurate results for "arbitrary precision" integer numbers (see the Java API). To get such precision, the **BigInteger** class allocates as much memory as is required to store a large integer's digits. Because of this, the **BigInteger** methods are much slower than the corresponding **int** or **double** operations. **BigInteger** (and **BigDouble**) is thus very useful when accuracy beyond that provided by **double** is required, and when such accuracy is more important than speed.

B.6 Reversing a List in Java

In Section B.4, we designed a recursive method to reverse the items in an array. This method relies on the direct access provided by the array's subscript operator. As discussed in Chapter 12, a **LinkedList** doesn't provide direct access to its items, because one has to start at the end of the list and follow links to get to an item in the middle of the list. So how do we reverse the items in a **LinkedList**, if we only have fast access to its ends?

B.6.1 The Trivial Case

There are two instances of the problem that are trivial to solve, which are like those we saw before:

1. If there is just one item in the list, then we need do nothing to reverse it.
2. If there are zero items in the list, then we need do nothing to reverse it.

So in either of the trivial cases, there is nothing we need to do.

B.6.2 The Nontrivial Cases

We just saw that we need to do nothing if there is one item in the list. Suppose it contains two items? We could reverse a list containing two items by:

1. Removing the first item, and storing it in *firstItem*
2. Appending *firstItem* to the end of the list

So far so good. Suppose the list contains three items? We could reverse such a list by:

1. Removing the first item, and storing it in *firstItem*
2. Recursively reversing the resulting list of two items
3. Appending *firstItem* to the end of the (newly reversed) list of two items

We can generalize these steps into the following algorithm:

Reverse a list: Given aList, a **LinkedList**

1. *If the list's length is greater than 1*
   a. *Remove the first item from aList, storing it in firstItem*
   b. *Reverse(aList)*
   c. *Add firstItem to the end of aList*

Using this algorithm, we can define the `reverse()` method shown in Figure B-29, where we use it to reverse a `LinkedList` of `int` items.

```
/** LinkedListReverser.java reverses a linked list recursively...
 */
import java.util.LinkedList;

public class LinkedListReverser {
  public static void reverse(LinkedList<Integer> aList) {
     if ( aList.size() > 1 ) {
        int firstItem = aList.removeFirst();
        reverse(aList);
        aList.add( firstItem );
     }
  }

  public static void main(String[] args) {
     LinkedList<Integer> theList = new LinkedList<Integer>();
     theList.add(11);
     theList.add(22);
     theList.add(33);
     theList.add(44);
     theList.add(55);
     System.out.println("Before: " + theList);
     reverse(theList);
     System.out.println("After: " + theList);
  }
}
```

```
Result:
Before: [11, 22, 33, 44, 55]
After: [55, 44, 33, 22, 11]
```

FIGURE B-29 Reversing a `LinkedList` in Java

Note that unlike the version defined in Figure B-24, the **`reverse()`** method in Figure B-29 uses no index values, so the only argument we pass to it is the list we want to reverse.

This approach removes the first item during the recursion's winding phase, and appends that item during the unwinding phase, as shown in Figure B-30.

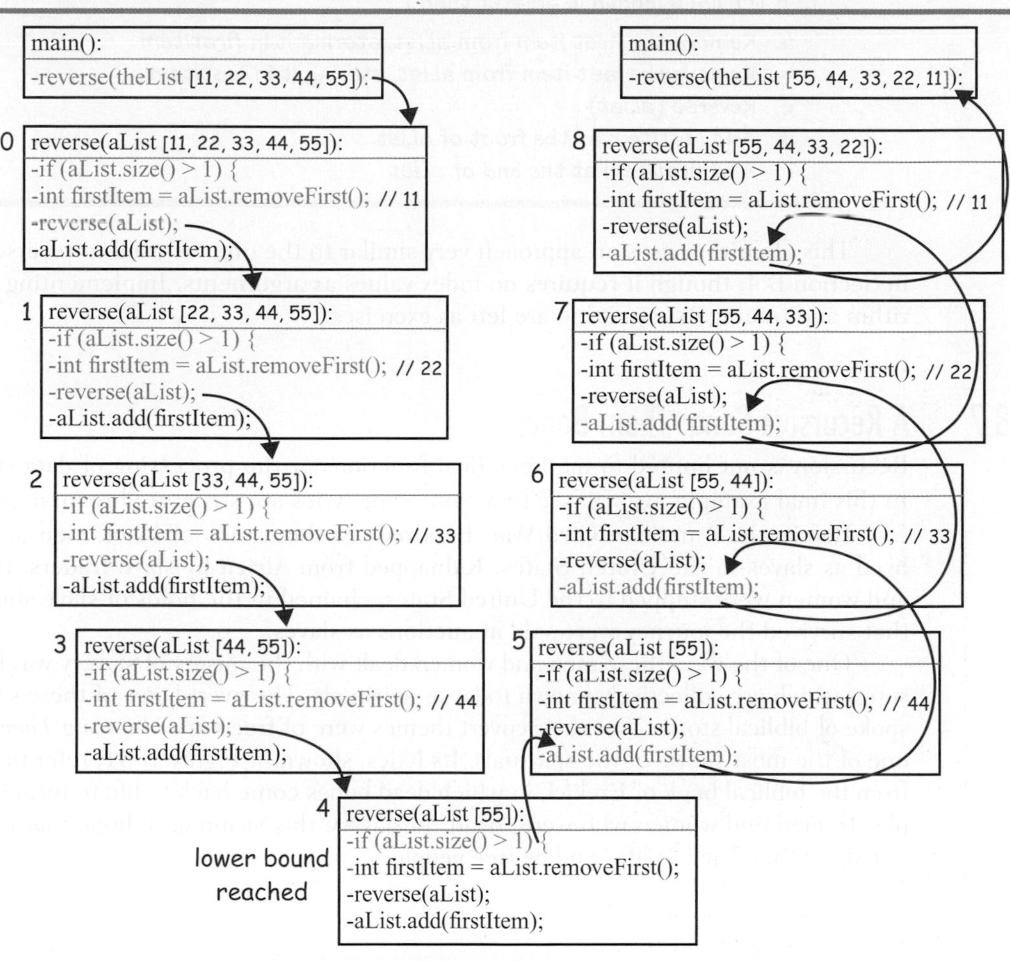

FIGURE B-30 Trace of **`LinkedListReverser.java`**

The approach used in Figure B-24 works well for any list that allows us to efficiently remove the first item and add an item at the end, whether it be singly-linked or doubly-linked. A doubly-linked list like Java's **`LinkedList`** class also allows us to remove the last item efficiently, so for these kind of lists, we could also use the following recursive algorithm:

Reverse a list 2: *Given aList, a* `LinkedList`

1. If the list's length is greater than 1
   a. Remove the first item from *aList*, storing it in *firstItem*
   b. Remove the last item from *aList*, storing it in *lastItem*;
   c. Reverse (*aList*)
   d. Add *lastItem* at the front of *aList*
   e. Add *firstItem* at the end of *aList*

This algorithm uses an approach very similar to the one we used to reverse an array in Section B.4, though it requires no index values as arguments. Implementing this algorithm and tracing its execution are left as exercises.

B.7 A Recursive Song: Them Bones

Recursion is not limited to mathematical functions or the processing of data structures. In this final example, we will see that some song lyrics are structured recursively, too.

Before the American Civil War, hundreds of thousands of black men and women lived as slaves in the United States. Kidnapped from Africa by slave traders, these men and women were shipped to the United States, chained in the holds of slave ships. Those that survived the journey were sold at auctions as slaves.

One of the ways these men and women dealt with the misery of slavery was by singing songs which are collectively known today as spirituals. The overt lyrics of these songs often spoke of biblical stories, but their covert themes were of freedom. The song *Them Bones* is one of the most subtle of the spirituals. Its lyrics, shown in Figure B-31, refer to a passage from the biblical book of Ezekiel, in which dead bones come back to life to form living people. To men and women who were "dead" in slavery, this vision gave hope that they would one day "come back to life" and be free people.

Ezekiel cried, "Them dry bones!"
Ezekiel cried, "Them dry bones!"
Ezekiel cried, "Them dry bones!"
Now hear the word of the Lord!

The toe-bone connected to the foot-bone
The foot-bone connected to the ankle-bone
The ankle-bone connected to the leg-bone
The leg-bone connected to the knee-bone
The knee-bone connected to the thigh-bone
The thigh-bone connected to the hip-bone
The hip-bone connected to the back-bone
The back-bone connected to the shoulder-bone
The shoulder-bone connected to the neck-bone
The neck-bone connected to the head-bone
Now hear the word of the Lord!

Them bones them bones gonna walk around
Them bones them bones gonna walk around
Them bones them bones gonna walk around
Now hear the word of the Lord!

The head-bone connected to the neck-bone
The neck-bone connected to the shoulder-bone
The shoulder-bone connected to the back-bone
The back-bone conected to the hip-bone
The hip-bone connected to the thigh-bone
The thigh-bone connected to the knee-bone
The knee-bone connected to the leg-bone
The leg-bone connected to the ankle-bone
The ankle-bone connected to the foot-bone
The foot-bone connected to the toe-bone
Now hear the word of the Lord!

Them bones them bones gonna walk around
Them bones them bones gonna walk around
Them bones them bones gonna walk around
Now hear the word of the Lord!

FIGURE B-31 Lyrics to *Them Bones*

Suppose we wanted to build a class to display the lyrics to this song. The first part of the song is different from the others, so we can easily write a method to build it:

```
private String firstPart() {
   return "Ezekiel cried, \"Them dry bones!\"\n"
        + "Ezekiel cried, \"Them dry bones!\"\n"
        + "Ezekiel cried, \"Them dry bones!\"\n"
        + "Now hear the word of the Lord!\n\n";
}
```

It is similarly easy to write a method that builds the last part of the song, as can be seen below. But what about the middle part? What is interesting about the middle is that it exhibits the same kind of "winding" and "unwinding" behavior as recursion. That is, the second group of lyrics "winds" from the "toe-bone" to the "head-bone," and the fourth group of lyrics "unwinds" from the "head-bone" back to the "toe-bone," with the third group of lyrics acting as an anchor case in between the winding and unwinding. This suggests that this middle part can be built using a recursive method. The program in Figure B-32 shows one way this can be done.

```
/** ThemBonesSong.java computes the lyrics of "Them Bones"...
 */
public class ThemBonesSong {
  private String myLyrics = null;
  private String [] myBones = { "head", "neck", "shoulder",
                                "back", "hip", "thigh", "knee",
                                "leg", "ankle", "foot", "toe" };

  public ThemBonesSong() {
     myLyrics = firstPart();
     myLyrics += middlePart(myBones.length - 1);
     myLyrics += lastPart();
  }

  private String firstPart() {
     return "Ezekiel cried, \"Them dry bones!\"\n"
          + "Ezekiel cried, \"Them dry bones!\"\n"
          + "Ezekiel cried, \"Them dry bones!\"\n"
          + "Now hear the word of the Lord!\n\n";
  }

  private String middlePart(int i) {
     if (i > 0) {
        String winding = "The " + myBones[i]
                         + "-bone connected to the "
                         + myBones[i-1] + "-bone\n";
```

continued

```
        String middle = middlePart(i-1);
        String unwinding = "The " + myBones[i-1]
                        + "-bone connected to the "
                        + myBones[i] + "-bone\n";
        return winding + middle + unwinding;
     } else {
        return lastPart() + "\n";
     }
  }

  private String lastPart() {
     return "Now hear the word of the Lord!\n"
            + "\nThem bones them bones gonna walk around.\n"
            + "Them bones them bones gonna walk around.\n"
            + "Them bones them bones gonna walk around.\n"
            + "Now hear the word of the Lord!\n";
  }

  public String toString() {
     return myLyrics;
  }

  public static void main(String[] args) {
     System.out.println( new ThemBonesSong() );
  }
}
```

```
Result:
Ezekiel cried, "Them dry bones!"
Ezekiel cried, "Them dry bones!"
Ezekiel cried, "Them dry bones!"
Now hear the word of the Lord!

The toe-bone connected to the foot-bone
The foot-bone connected to the ankle-bone
The ankle-bone connected to the leg-bone
The leg-bone connected to the knee-bone
The knee-bone connected to the thigh-bone
The thigh-bone connected to the hip-bone
The hip-bone connected to the back-bone
The back-bone connected to the shoulder-bone
The shoulder-bone connected to the neck-bone
The neck-bone connected to the head-bone
Now hear the word of the Lord!
```

continued

```
Them bones them bones gonna walk around.
Them bones them bones gonna walk around.
Them bones them bones gonna walk around.
Now hear the word of the Lord!

The head-bone connected to the neck-bone
The neck-bone connected to the shoulder-bone
The shoulder-bone connected to the back-bone
The back-bone connected to the hip-bone
The hip-bone connected to the thigh-bone
The thigh-bone connected to the knee-bone
The knee-bone connected to the leg-bone
The leg-bone connected to the ankle-bone
The ankle-bone connected to the foot-bone
The foot-bone connected to the toe-bone
Now hear the word of the Lord!

Them bones them bones gonna walk around.
Them bones them bones gonna walk around.
Them bones them bones gonna walk around.
Now hear the word of the Lord!
```

FIGURE B-32 **ThemBonesSong.java**

On line 50 of Figure B-32, the **main()** method simply displays an instance of **ThemBonesSong**. To do so, it invokes the **ThemBonesSong()** constructor, which initializes the instance variable **myLyrics** by concatenating the values returned by the methods **firstPart()**, **middlePart()**, and **lastPart()**. The **middlePart()** method recursively processes **myBones**, an array containing the names of the bones, arranged in order from **head** to **toe**:

```
private String [] myBones = { "head", "neck", "shoulder",
                              "back", "hip", "thigh", "knee",
                              "leg", "ankle", "foot", "toe" };
```

We might visualize **myBones** as follows:

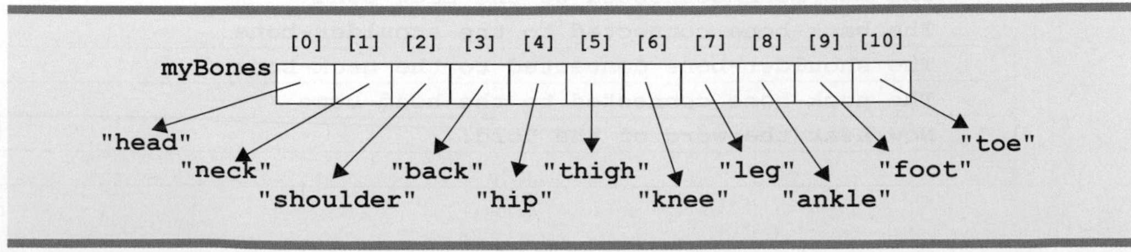

On line 11, the class constructor uses this array to invoke **middlePart()**:

```
myLyrics += middlePart(myBones.length - 1);
```

This statement builds the middle part of the song by invoking **middlePart()** and passing it **myBones.length - 1**, the index of the last item in **myBones**, so that when **middlePart()** begins running, its **int** parameter **i** has the value **10**. The statement on lines 24–26 that computes **winding** is then performed:

```
String winding = "The " + myBones[i]
               + "-bone connected to the "
               + myBones[i-1] + "-bone\n";
```

The expression **myBones[i]** thus refers to **"toe"** and **myBones[i-1]** refers to **"foot"**, so winding is computed as **"The toe-bone connected to the foot-bone"**.

The next thing that happens is the recursive call on line 27:

```
String middle = middlePart(i-1);
```

This starts a new version of **middlePart()**, in which parameter **i** has the value **9**. When this version of the method computes its value for **winding**, the expression **myBones[i]** refers to **"foot"** and **myBones[i-1]** refers to **"ankle"**, so **winding** equals **"The foot-bone connected to the ankle-bone"**.

This pattern continues as shown in Figure B-33, with each recursive invocation of **middlePart()** computing a different string for **winding**, and then computing **middle** by invoking itself with the argument **i-1**, until the argument **i-1** is **0**.

```
middlePart(i: 10):
return winding: "The toe-bone connected to the foot-bone"
+ middle:
  middlePart(i: 9):
  return winding: "The foot-bone connected to the ankle-bone"
  + middle:
    middlePart(i: 8):
    return winding: "The ankle-bone connected to the leg-bone"
    + middle:
      middlePart(i: 7):
      return winding: "The leg-bone connected to the knee-bone"
      + middle:
        middlePart(i: 6):
        return winding: "The knee-bone connected to the thigh-bone"
        + middle:
          middlePart(i: 5):
          return winding: "The thigh-bone connected to the hip-bone"
          + middle:
            middlePart(i: 4):
            return winding: "The hip-bone connected to the back-bone"
            + middle:
              middlePart(i: 3):
              return winding: "The back-bone connected to the shoulder-bone"
              + middle:
                middlePart(i: 2):
                return winding: "The shoulder-bone connected to the neck-bone"
                + middle:
                  middlePart(i: 1):
                  return winding: "The neck-bone connected to the head-bone"
                  + middle:
                    middlePart(i: 0):
                    return: "Now hear the word of the Lord!"
                        + "Them bones them bones gonna walk around.
                        + "Them bones them bones gonna walk around.
                        + "Them bones them bones gonna walk around.
                        +  "Now hear the word of the Lord!"
                  + unwinding: "The head-bone connected to the neck-bone"
                + unwinding: "The neck-bone connected to the shoulder-bone"
              + unwinding: "The shoulder-bone connected to the back-bone"
            + unwinding: "The back-bone connected to the hip-bone"
          + unwinding: "The hip-bone connected to the thigh-bone"
        + unwinding: "The thigh-bone connected to the knee-bone"
      + unwinding: "The knee-bone connected to the leg-bone"
    + unwinding: "The leg-bone connected to the ankle-bone"
  + unwinding: "The ankle-bone connected to the foot-bone"
+ unwinding: "The foot-bone connected to the toe-bone"
```

FIGURE B-33 Tracing the flow of `middlePart(10)`

When `i` reaches `0`, the statement on line 33 is performed as an anchor case, returning the middle group of lyrics, and halting the recursion.

The recursion then begins to unwind. As shown by the red arrow in Figure B-33, the flow returns through each version of **`middlePart()`**, which uses **`myBones[i-1]`** and **`myBones[i]`** to compute its own distinct string for the **`unwinding`** variable. For example, when flow returns from the anchor case to the version of **`middlePart()`** in which **`i`** is **`1`**, **`myBones[i-1]`** is **`"head"`** and **`myBones[i]`** is **`"toe"`**, so that version computes **`unwinding`** as **`"The head-bone connected to the neck-bone"`**. When flow returns from that version to the version in which **`i`** is **`2`**, **`myBones[i-1]`** is **`"neck"`** and **`myBones[i]`** is **`"shoulder"`**, so that version computes **`unwinding`** as **`"The neck-bone connected to the shoulder-bone"`**.

Each version of **`middlePart()`** thus computes its own values for **`winding`**, **`middle`**, and **`unwinding`** variables and returns the concatenation of these values. The string returned by **`middlePart(10)`** is thus the song's second, third, and fourth groups of lyrics.

It is, of course, possible to compute the second group of lyrics using a **`for`** loop that counts down from **`10`** to **`1`**, and to compute the fourth group of lyrics using a second **`for`** loop that counts back up from **`1`** to **`10`**. However, one recursive method can accomplish the same thing as one **`for`** loop, and in cases like this, two **`for`** loops.

I hope that this appendix has helped you see that recursion can be useful in lots of different places, including mathematical functions that require repetition, processing arrays and lists, and in stories and songs that exhibit "winding" and "unwinding" behaviors.

Appendix C
Java Keywords

Keywords are words that have a predefined meaning in the language. As such, keywords cannot be used as identifiers; any attempt to do so will produce a compilation error. Figure C-1 provides a complete list of all of Java's keywords, as of Java 6.0.

`abstract`	**`final`**	**`public`**
`assert`	**`finally`**	**`return`**
`boolean`	**`float`**	**`short`**
`break`	**`for`**	**`static`**
`byte`	`goto`	`strictfp`
`case`	**`if`**	**`super`**
`catch`	**`implements`**	**`switch`**
`char`	**`import`**	`synchronized`
`class`	**`instanceof`**	**`this`**
`const`	**`int`**	**`throw`**
`continue`	**`interface`**	**`throws`**
`default`	**`long`**	`transient`
`do`	`native`	**`try`**
`double`	**`new`**	**`void`**
`else`	`package`	`volatile`
`enum`	**`private`**	**`while`**
`extends`	**`protected`**	

FIGURE C-1 Java 5.0 keywords

The keywords in black are those that we have covered in this introductory book. Those that are a different color are either not yet used in Java (**`const`**, **`goto`**), are not essential (**`enum`**, **`package`**), or are beyond the scope of an introductory text (**`continue`**, **`native`**, **`strictfp`**, **`synchronized`**, **`transient`**, **`volatile`**). For the reader interested in learning more, we recommend Java's excellent online tutorial, at **`java.sun.com/docs/books/tutorial/java/`**.

Appendix D
Unicode Basic Latin Character Set

Symbol	Decimal Code	Hexadecimal Code
control characters	0–31	0000-001F
SPACE	32	0020
!	33	0021
"	34	0022
#	35	0023
$	36	0024
%	37	0025
&	38	0026
'	39	0027
(	40	0028
)	41	0029
*	42	002A
+	43	002B
,	44	002C
-	45	002D
.	46	002E
/	47	002F

Symbol	Decimal Code	Hexadecimal Code
0	48	0030
1	49	0031
2	50	0032
3	51	0033
4	52	0034
5	53	0035
6	54	0036
7	55	0037
8	56	0038
9	57	0039
:	58	003A
;	59	003B
<	60	003C
=	61	003D
>	62	003E
?	63	003F
@	64	0040

continued

Symbol	Decimal Code	Hexadecimal Code
A	65	0041
B	66	0042
C	67	0043
D	68	0044
E	69	0045
F	70	0046
G	71	0047
H	72	0048
I	73	0049
J	74	004A
K	75	004B
L	76	004C
M	77	004D
N	78	004E
O	79	004F
P	80	0050
Q	81	0051
R	82	0052
S	83	0053
T	84	0054
U	85	0055
V	86	0056
W	87	0057
X	88	0058
Y	89	0059
Z	90	005A
[	91	005B

Symbol	Decimal Code	Hexadecimal Code
\	92	005C
]	93	005D
^	94	005E
_	95	005F
`	96	0060
a	97	0061
b	98	0062
c	99	0063
d	100	0064
e	101	0065
f	102	0066
g	103	0067
h	104	0068
i	105	0069
j	106	006A
k	107	006B
l	108	006C
m	109	006D
n	110	006E
o	111	006F
p	112	0070
q	113	0071
r	114	0072
s	115	0073
t	116	0074
u	117	0075
v	118	0076

continued

Symbol	Decimal Code	Hexadecimal Code
w	119	0077
x	120	0078
y	121	0079
z	122	007A
{	123	007B
|	124	007C
}	125	007D
~	126	007E
DEL	127	007F

For more information and other Unicode character sets, please visit **`www.unicode.org`**.

Index

Symbols

Numerics

A

B

C

D

E

F

M

N